ALSO BY DAVID MILNE

America's Rasputin:
Walt Rostow and the Vietnam War

WORLDMAKING

WORLDMAKING

★ ★ ★

THE ART AND SCIENCE OF
AMERICAN DIPLOMACY

DAVID MILNE

FARRAR, STRAUS AND GIROUX

NEW YORK

Farrar, Straus and Giroux
18 West 18th Street, New York 10011

Grateful acknowledgment is made for permission to reprint an excerpt
from *Nixon in China*, by John Adams/Alice Goodman, reprinted by
permission of Boosey and Hawkes Music Publishers Ltd.

Library of Congress Cataloging-in-Publication Data
Milne, David, 1976–
    Worldmaking : the art and science of American diplomacy / David Milne. —
First edition.
        p.   cm.
    Includes bibliographical references and index.
    ISBN 978-0-374-29256-0 (hardcover) — ISBN 978-0-374-71423-9 (e-book)
    1. United States—Foreign relations—1897–1901.   2. United States—
Foreign relations—20th century.   3. United States—Foreign relations—
21st century.   4. United States—Foreign relations—Philosophy.   5. Statesmen—
United States.   6. Intellectuals—United States.   I. Title.

E744. M566 2015
327.73—dc23

                                                                                    2015003943

Designed by Abby Kagan

Farrar, Straus and Giroux books may be purchased for educational, business, or
promotional use. For information on bulk purchases, please contact the
Macmillan Corporate and Premium Sales Department
at 1-800-221-7945, extension 5442, or write to
specialmarkets@macmillan.com.

www.fsgbooks.com
www.twitter.com/fsgbooks • www.facebook.com/fsgbooks

1   3   5   7   9   10   8   6   4   2

For Emma, Benedict, and Anna

There is a spirit that rules us . . . that we are chosen and prominently chosen to show the way to the nations of the world how they shall walk in the paths of liberty.

—WOODROW WILSON

All plans of government, which suppose great reformation in the manners of mankind, are plainly imaginary.

—DAVID HUME

Politics is an art and not a science, and what is required for its mastery is not the rationality of an engineer but the wisdom and the moral strength of a statesman.

—HANS J. MORGENTHAU

History is just littered with problems that were solved that were supposed to be impossible.

—PAUL WOLFOWITZ

CONTENTS

WORLDMAKING

———————— ★ ————————

INTRODUCTION

In September 1949, a WB-29 took off from Okinawa, Japan, and flew north toward the Kamchatka peninsula, which hangs from northeastern Russia like a mastiff's tail. The bomber had been refitted to conduct surveillance and carried filters to detect anomalies in the atmosphere. As the plane flirted with Soviet airspace, radiation was detected at unnaturally high levels. Navy scientists at sea level confirmed that radioactive sludge was also present in the rainwater. There was only one plausible explanation: the Soviet Union had detonated its first atomic bomb.

It fell to David Lilienthal, the chairman of the U.S. Atomic Energy Commission, to inform the president. Truman found the news so surprising—surely it was too soon for Moscow to have tested an atomic device—that he scarcely lent it credence. He asked Lilienthal if he was sure that the radiation stemmed from a nuclear weapon and not a reactor malfunction. When Truman finally accepted Lilienthal's word that the atomic source was weaponized, the president was confronted with a major decision: whether to respond by ordering the development of the hydrogen bomb, a fusion rather than a fission device with a destructive potential that was theoretically boundless.

Winston Churchill captured the H-bomb's epochal nature in observing that the device was as far from the A-bomb as the "atomic bomb itself from the bow and arrow."[1] Whether to proceed was not simply a military decision; it was a philosophical one too. To facilitate a robust decision-making process, Truman established a three-man committee to present him with a majority recommendation, composed of Lilienthal, Secretary of Defense Louis Johnson, and Secretary of State Dean Acheson. Johnson was certain to recommend its development and Lilienthal was opposed. So Acheson would likely have the deciding vote. The secretary asked his two best strategic thinkers, George Kennan, the director of the Policy Planning Staff (PPS), and his deputy, Paul Nitze, to advise on whether America's military future should be thermonuclear.

Reclusive and deliberative, Kennan set about his task in the usual way. He retreated to his office with books on history, philosophy, and literature and settled down to think and to write. Addressing a question of vast moral and strategic dimensions, confronting hypothetical worst-case scenarios that included the end of human life on earth, Kennan soon found himself physically and emotionally exhausted. His wife, Annelise, had recently given birth to their third child, and after completing his first draft Kennan joked to Acheson that he "was tempted, day before yesterday, to go into the baby's room and say: 'Go on, get up. You're going to work today. I'll get in the crib.'"[2] He crafted a seventy-nine-page paper, rich in history and philosophy, which counseled against building this fearsome weapon. A fusion device was morally repugnant and the whole idea of honing an "atomic strategy" was diabolical—leading as it could to a war in which everyone loses—so an international organization, in this unique instance, offered the best way forward. Kennan sought to display this through the elegance of his prose and breadth of literary allusion, including a quotation from Shakespeare's *Troilus and Cressida*:

> And appetite, an universal wolf,
> So doubly seconded with will and power,
> Must make perforce an universal prey,
> And last eat up himself.[3]

Where a war with conventional weapons offered the possibility of conventional outcomes—"the possibility of surrender and submission"—Kennan believed that "weapons of mass destruction do not have this quality. They reach backward beyond the frontiers of western civilization, to the concepts of warfare which were once familiar to the Asiatic hordes . . . They imply the admission that man not only can be but is his own worst and most terrible enemy." Summing up, Kennan quoted St. Paul, "We know in part and we prophesy in part," before appealing to American values to guide the decision-making process: "In such a time there is only one thing a nation can do which can have any really solid and dependable value: and that is to see that the initial lines of its policy are as close as possible to the principles dictated by its traditions and its nature."[4]

Paul Nitze's operating style was very different. He was a former Wall Street banker adept in mathematics and deductive logic, a bureaucratic infighter who knew when to reach for the jugular, a Harvard postgraduate with a sophisticated understanding of international economic affairs. These qualities—his facility with quantitative analysis in particular—led Kennan to ask permission from Acheson in 1947 to add Nitze to his Policy Planning Staff. Acheson declined, observing that Kennan should be looking to hire a "deep thinker," not a "Wall Street operator"—a typically pointed Achesonian put-down.[5] But Acheson formed a more positive view of Nitze in the intervening years. In mid-1949, Kennan decided to take a leave of absence from State, asking Acheson if he could appoint Nitze as his deputy with a view to his succeeding him after his departure. This time the secretary of state said yes, and with real enthusiasm. Nitze was implacably anti-Soviet and did not share Kennan's view that agreement might be reached with Moscow over German reunification. Nitze was also a firm believer in maintaining the strongest possible military, that peace was primarily secured through strength. Nitze's approach was data driven and scientifically oriented. Kennan and Nitze's responses to the H-bomb dilemma revealed different worldviews and priorities.

Nitze first sought to comprehend the science of nuclear fusion. On consecutive days he met with J. Robert Oppenheimer (later a friend to Kennan) and Edward Teller, the first a skeptic of the wisdom of developing thermonuclear weapons, the second a strong proponent. Having played a key role in fathering the atomic bomb—a role that he viewed as justifiable in those wartime circumstances—Oppenheimer wanted to play no part in siring a more terrible progeny. His personal view was that the United States should refuse to develop the weapon on moral grounds and hope that the Soviet Union would follow its example. But he understood that Nitze was unlikely to be swayed by wishful thinking and instead sought to convince him that the science of the hydrogen bomb was actually science fiction. While it was technically possible to construct and detonate a hydrogen bomb, Oppenheimer observed, moving such a necessarily massive device was another thing entirely. He told Nitze that a plane could not carry the cumbersome weapon—rather, it would require an oxcart. This meant the fusion bomb was tactically impotent. "All in all," Nitze recalled, "[Oppenheimer] concluded the world would be much better off if no one had such weapons."[6] Nitze found his performance unconvincing, writing later that "we had no scruple . . . in ignoring those of his recommendations which seemed to be based on political rather than scientific considerations."[7] Oppenheimer misrepresented the science as he feared the unleashing of a great evil.

Edward Teller was more successful with his sales pitch, mainly because he believed in the necessity of the product. Nitze said, "Teller had a clear and powerful mind and could make his ideas understandable even to one who was not a professional physicist. He went to the blackboard and showed me two different approaches to solving the problem."[8] Warming to the subject, and to his interlocutor, Nitze ended up talking physics with Teller for more than two hours. By the end of their conversation, Nitze was convinced that the fusion bomb was feasible and that Oppenheimer's warnings about its immobility were unfounded. Nitze surmised, correctly, that Oppenheimer's politics had clouded his advice. Teller was focused and compelling in argument, and he had no moral qualms about the enterprise at hand. A Jewish Hungarian émigré, Teller despised the Soviet Union and the pernicious ideology that sustained it. There should be no question of America restraining itself in competition with such a regime. Of course, politics had also shaped Teller's advice, and he continued moving rightward through the remainder of his career. In 1954, for example, Teller testified before Congress that Oppenheimer's pacific leanings made him a "security risk."[9]

While Kennan remained isolated in his office, identifying the appropriate Shakespeare quotation to support his cause, Nitze joined the Atomic Working Group within the State Department. To skeptics of the hydrogen bomb, concerned that money spent on its development would be siphoned from the service budgets, Nitze suggested ways to sweeten the pill, such as connecting the development of thermonuclear weapons with a larger strategic review, designed to redress and fund conventional military deficiencies. When Nitze received a draft of Kennan's paper, he scribbled dissenting notes on the margin: "no!," "Misreading of what we are *about*," "prohibition." In his formal response to Kennan, Nitze observed that declining to develop a fusion weapon, and thus allowing the Soviets to gain a tactical advantage, would be foolish and reckless.[10] Nitze advised that the United States develop the hydrogen bomb with all due haste. Moral qualms were otiose if the antagonist did not share them. Stalin's Soviet Union was no place to vest an act of faith.

Acheson admired the professional manner in which Nitze set about his task and was convinced by his recommendations. Nitze had figured the science, taken soundings, prepared the bureaucracy, placated critics, and decisively rebutted Kennan. Acheson, conversely, had nothing but scorn for Kennan's methods and advice. His approach—which did not extend beyond deployment of his principal weapon: his prose—had fallen flat. The secretary of state remembered Kennan telling him that it was preferable for Americans to "perish rather than be party to a course so evil as producing that weapon." Acheson snapped in response, "If that is your view you ought to resign from the foreign service and go out and preach your Quaker gospel, but don't do it within the department."[11] President Truman's decision was now a formality.

But this did not even come down to a majority vote. In a meeting on January 31, 1950, Truman asked Acheson, Lilienthal, and Johnson just one question: "Can the Russians do it?" When the trio came back with a unanimous yes, the president replied, "In that case we have no choice. We'll go ahead." According to one despondent opponent of the fusion bomb, it was "like saying no to a steamroller."[12] But subsequent events appeared to vindicate Nitze and Truman's belief that the decision could not have been otherwise. The day after the president's announcement was cheered on the floor of the House of Representatives, Truman was informed that Klaus Fuchs, a German émigré scientist who had worked on the Manhattan Project, was in fact a Soviet spy. The director of the FBI, J. Edgar Hoover, noted that the revelations "would very much reinforce the hands of the president on the strength of [his H-bomb] decision [and] it will make a good many men who are in the same profession as Fuchs very careful of what they say publicly." After learning of Fuchs's espionage, Lilienthal wrote in his diary: "The roof fell in today . . . It is a world catastrophe, and a sad day for the human race."[13]

Nitze and Kennan's disagreement over the so-called Super bomb is fascinating on multiple levels. For one thing, Kennan's case against the H-bomb did not stem from a cold appraisal of Soviet capabilities and intentions; rather, it was moral, instinctive, and emotional. In an obvious way, Kennan—usually identified as a foreign policy "realist," someone who believes that all states seek to maximize power and advantage in an anarchic world system— was dispensing unrealistic advice.[14] No nation in modern history had ever declined to develop a more lethal weapons system. When technology and resources permitted, the English developed the longbow in the twelfth century; the Swedish developed the howitzer in the seventeenth; the Germans developed the V1 and V2 rocket-propelled missiles—thankfully, at a late stage in the Second World War. For a man so steeped in history, Kennan's opposition to the hydrogen bomb was curiously unhistorical. It was based on the Wilsonesque hypothesis that declining to develop a fusion bomb and vesting faith in an international organization would persuade the Soviet Union to do the same, principally by the moral quality of American restraint. It was an original proposition, to be sure, and the laws of history would have been altered had the experiment succeeded, for genies like these are not easily returned to lamps.

But Kennan's recommendation was highly risky, as we now know. Three months before Truman's January decision, Stalin had ordered the development of a Soviet H-bomb. The United States tested its first fusion device in 1952, and the Soviet Union did so just a year later—which again was far ahead of American expectations. Had Kennan's voice carried, Moscow alone might have possessed thermonuclear weapons—a very real "missile gap" with potentially dire consequences. The physicist (and later dissident) Andrei Sakharov, who led the development of the Soviet Union's H-bomb, later suggested that his political masters would not have been impressed by American restraint: "Any American steps to suspend or permanently cancel the development of a thermonuclear weapon would have been judged as either a sly, deceptive move, or the manifestation of stupidity and weakness. In both cases the reaction would have been unambiguous—not to get caught in the trap and to take immediate advantage of the stupidity of the enemy."[15]

Kennan's advice was well-intentioned but dangerous; Nitze's, less clouded by emotion, counseling what could be construed, counterintuitively, as a "safer" course of action. Kennan viewed a thermonuclear world as intolerable; the United States should play no part in its creation. His advice was shaped by adherence to an absolute moral principle, a perspective with which one can easily sympathize given the nature of the weapon. But Nitze confronted a hard reality and was more attentive than Kennan—in this rare instance—to the lessons of history.

Yet there is more to it than that. The debate over the hydrogen bomb also suggests that U.S. foreign policy is often best understood as intellectual history.[16] Divergent philosophies, disciplinary preferences, religious sensibilities, and life experiences indelibly shape the structure and quality of the advice that foreign policymakers dispense. Kennan's civilizational pessimism, religiosity, and wide reading in moral philosophy; the horror evoked by visiting his beloved Hamburg in 1949—"The immensity of its ruin overwhelmed me"—and his conviction that the hydrogen bomb posed an existential threat—all these sources combined to shape a policy recommendation that departed from his usual skepticism about the ability of Wilsonian supranational institutions to achieve meaningful results.[17] It was an artful and emotional response.

Nitze was not as well-read or as contemplative as Kennan. But he understood that September 1949—the month that Mao Zedong secured victory in the Chinese Civil War and just a few months after the Soviet Union ended its blockade of Berlin—was no time to attempt a bold play conditioned by notions of pure morality. Nitze excised emotion from his thought process because he believed the circumstances demanded it. Kennan and Nitze both intellectualized the dilemma—Kennan pondered ethics; Nitze, science and the strategic balance—and arrived at opposite conclusions. Each believed his recommendation stood the better chance of saving the world.

The stakes are not always so high, nor the personalities so colorful and dramatically intertwined, but a basic principle holds true throughout American history: its foreign policy is difficult to understand without an ideational frame. There are multiple divides that can shape decision making: realism versus idealism; ethics versus technics; emotionality versus instrumental rationality; theory versus intuition; pragmatism versus monism.[18] The debate between Kennan and Nitze involved all these categories to varying degrees. Binaries like these can be helpful because they capture elemental forces that sometimes prove irresistible within policymaking. But I am mindful that they can also sometimes mislead, for to paraphrase Walt Whitman in *Leaves of Grass*, people are "large" and "contain multitudes."

This book is an intellectual history of U.S. foreign policy. It focuses on ideas, their authors, and the context in which ideas were formed and examines their traction and consequences. My purpose is to identify, explain, and critique the disputatious ideas that have informed the making of U.S. foreign policy since the end of the nineteenth century—the moment when America truly announced itself as a great power with its resounding military victory against Spain. I do so through an interlinked narrative history of nine intellectuals—Alfred Thayer Mahan, Woodrow Wilson, Charles Beard, Walter Lippmann, George Kennan, Paul Nitze, Henry Kissinger, Paul Wolfowitz, and Barack Obama—whose ideas and disagreements about America's role in the world take the story of U.S. foreign relations from the Civil War (in which Mahan served) to the present. While each chapter focuses primarily on an individual, the broad approach is dialogic rather than biographical. Each figure was consciously engaged in a process of world-making, formulating strategies that sought to deploy the nation's vast military and economic power—or indeed its retraction through a domestic reorientation—to "make" a world in which America is best positioned to thrive.[19]

In writing a book with a biographical frame, I am conscious that choices can appear arbitrary. Individuals such as Woodrow Wilson, George Kennan, Henry Kissinger, Paul Wolfowitz, and Barack Obama are well known as shapers of American foreign policy. Presidents and high-level policy advisers, after all, are less likely to raise hackles about the criteria for their inclusion. The Nobel Prize–winning psychologist Daniel Kahneman and his collaborator Amos Tversky described this phenomenon as the "availability heuristic," which applied to this book suggests that if a name is easily recognizable, that person must be important.[20] But Alfred Mahan, Charles Beard, and Walter Lippmann are not so prominent, did not assume direct policymaking roles, and require more by way of explanation.

Alfred Thayer Mahan's ideas are alive today, possessed of a timeless quality also evident in Thucydides, Sun Tzu, Machiavelli, and Clausewitz. Author of the seminal *The Influence of Sea Power upon History*, Mahan was prescient on the big issues of war, trade, and the central importance of sea power, making his inclusion a straightforward decision. As the subject of my first chapter, I might have discussed Theodore Roosevelt, Henry Cabot Lodge, or Secretary of State John Hay, who all presented powerful and influential diplomatic visions at the end of the nineteenth century. But none of their foreign-policy contributions rivaled Mahan's in sweep and originality. Inspired by Pax Britannica, Mahan anticipated a Pax Americana that was historically unprecedented: an economic and cultural empire that did not require the formal annexation of vast swaths of territory. His books and essays propelled the debate about American expansion through the 1890s and beyond.

Until, that is, Woodrow Wilson rejected the materialism and amorality of Mahan's worldview—the president believed that narrowly emulating British practice betrayed America's promise—and set U.S. foreign policy on a very different course. When he became president in 1913, Wilson's foreign-policy philosophy was inchoate. But when he concluded in 1917 that there was no choice but to declare war on Germany, he proposed nothing less than a revolution in world affairs. On how to reincorporate Germany into the international system after its likely defeat, Wilson sought a "peace without victory" that would disavow retribution and secure postwar stability through its broad-based legitimacy. More broadly, however, Wilson believed that the establishment of a League of Nations was the only sure way to prevent cataclysmic wars from occurring again. At the Paris Peace Conference, the president hoped to craft a "scientific peace."[21]

Wilson's hopes for the League of Nations wilted on home soil as the nation reverted to its long-standing tradition of eyeing Europe's major powers warily and haughtily from a comfortable distance. It is essential for any study of U.S. foreign policy to understand why this happened, to engage with the real historical rather than the epithet version of isolationism.[22] And so the book turns next to discuss the historian and political scientist Charles Beard, who believed Mahan and Wilson were reckless interventionists, similarly driven by the illusory benefits to America of free trade—although the amoral Mahan was the guiltier party. Beard became the most articulate and intellectually coherent advocate of "continental Americanism," an autarkic version of isolationism, in the interwar years.

The 1920s and 1930s are vitally important decades in the history of American foreign relations, and many other individuals—such as Senator Gerald Nye of North Dakota; Senator William Borah of Idaho; the aviator and chairman of the America First Committee, Charles Lindbergh; and the radio priest and demagogue, Charles Coughlin—also argued that the United States should abjure involvement in the looming European crisis. But none presented a sustained and coherent exploration of how America's isolation from global conflict and trading patterns might plausibly be achieved. (Plus Lindbergh and Coughlin were shallow thinkers motivated by a crude chauvinism and anti-Semitism.) With a series of books and articles published during the 1930s and 1940s Charles Beard made the strongest case that retrenchment would make the United States a fairer and more successful nation—at all societal strata—and that this would allow it to serve as a beacon for other nations.

Of course, Beard's "continental Americanism," and the less edifying visions of other isolationists, did not carry the day. Instead, Franklin Delano Roosevelt led the United States toward activist global leadership—which leads directly to the nation's pivotal world role today. Yet while Roosevelt's presidency is of vast significance in the history of U.S. foreign relations, it is difficult to identify a grand strategy or strategist that defined his presidency. The president himself was not a deep thinker. George Kennan later described FDR as an "intellectually superficial but courageous and charming man," which is fair in one sense, although it scarcely does justice to his qualities of political judgment, which were superior to Kennan's.[23] Roosevelt was adept at improvisation and placed great store in the importance of personal diplomacy; he danced around fixed principles, blurring lines where he believed it served the greater good.[24] "You know, I am a juggler," FDR observed in 1942, "and I never let my right hand know what my left hand does . . . I may have one policy for Europe and one diametrically opposite for North and South America. I may be entirely inconsistent, and furthermore I am perfectly willing to mislead and tell untruths if it will help me win the war."[25]

Roosevelt juggled and used whatever ideas best served his goals at a particular time. And from 1939 to 1945, the most original foreign-policy ideas came from outside his administration, which is why I devote a chapter to the journalist Walter Lippmann. The most read, revered, and trusted print journalist in America from Calvin Coolidge to Lyndon Johnson, Lippmann performed multiple roles during the Second World War. Lippmann helped FDR formulate a persuasive rationale for providing Great Britain with material support—so much so that a journalist from the *St. Louis Post Dispatch* threatened to investigate Lippmann's role in "this plot to get America into the war."[26] From 1939, he identified through his syndicated "Today & Tomorrow" columns a compelling strategic rationale for facing down Germany and Japan. Then in 1943 Lippmann published *U.S. Foreign Policy: Shield of the Republic*, a book that sold close to half a million copies and was syndicated in *Reader's Digest*. Lippmann drew inspiration from Mahan, repudiated Wilson's idealism, and shot down Beard's isolationism with élan. Roosevelt needed a shaper of public opinion more than he needed a grand strategist. While there was no overt collaboration between the two men, Lippmann and Roosevelt's goals happily overlapped.

Kennan and Lippmann shared many views, but it was a bitter dispute that first brought them together. Lippmann believed that the continuation of a strong U.S.-Soviet alliance was essential to maintain postwar stability. In 1946, George Kennan made a strong case that such views were naïve. From his post at the U.S. embassy in Moscow, Kennan cabled Washington his view that Stalin was determined to expand his nation's power at the expense of American interests; thus it was essential to resist Soviet adventurism that was fueled by nationalism, deep-rooted fears of vulnerability, and a messianic Marxist-Leninist ideology. This nearly six-thousand-word "Long Telegram" is the most famous communication in the history of the State Department, and its impact in Washington was profound. A year later, writing anonymously under the letter "X," Kennan published an essay in *Foreign Affairs* titled "The Sources of Soviet Conduct" that elaborated on this "containment" strategy, comparing the Soviet Union to a wind-up toy that would move relentlessly in a particular direction unless a barrier was placed in its way. His authorship was soon revealed, and Kennan was met with acclaim from most and scorn from some.

In a series of articles that were subsequently published as a book titled *The Cold War*—a phrase that caught on—Lippmann attacked Kennan's "containment" as a "strategic monstrosity" that would imperil the United States through the accumulation of unsustainable obligations in areas of low importance. Kennan was stung by Lippmann's assault, but he subsequently came to agree with most of what he wrote. Kennan believed a sagacious foreign policy requires flexibility and intuition, but somehow or other he bequeathed an ambiguous document—it looked a lot like a blueprint—ripe for misinterpretation. Kennan was a principal author of the central strategy America pursued through the Cold War—containment—and one of the most powerful dissenters from the decisions made in its name.

Kennan's successor as chair of the Policy Planning Staff, Paul Nitze, figured that he was simply fleshing out his predecessor's ideas when he chaired a committee that authored the top secret NSC-68 (its official title: "United States Objectives and Programs for National Security"), a seminal policy document signed by President Truman in 1950, which Kennan disliked intensely. Throughout his career, Nitze believed that a combination of psychology and systems analysis could be used to accurately assess Soviet capabilities (and hence intentions) and this could be weighed against America's military ability to discourage any Soviet attack. He described this calculation as the "correlation of forces," and Nitze usually believed that this tilted more in Moscow's favor than was generally recognized. NSC-68 identified the Soviet Union's principal goal as "the complete subversion or forcible destruction of the machinery of government and structure of society in the countries of the non-Soviet world" and recommended a huge military buildup combined with a greater willingness to combat communism in the "Third World" as the appropriate American response.[27] When North Korea invaded South Korea two months after NSC-68 was completed, Nitze appeared vindicated.

A central figure in the final years of the Truman administration, Nitze was also a significant presence throughout the 1950s, when he lambasted the Eisenhower administration for allowing the Soviets to develop a lead in nuclear and nonnuclear military capabilities. John F. Kennedy used Nitze's identification of a "missile gap" to devastating effect against Nixon, and the logic of NSC-68 helped propel Kennedy's and Johnson's foreign-policy

activism. JFK's inaugural promise to "pay any price . . . to assure the survival and the success of liberty" was a fair précis of NSC-68. These significantly expanded foreign-policy parameters gave individuals like Walt
Rostow (an influential adviser to Kennedy and Johnson, and the subject of
my first book) the space to thrive—he operated in the Age of Nitze. Though he
was deeply ambivalent about Johnson's decision to Americanize the Vietnam
War, a perspective shared by Lippmann and Kennan, Nitze's foreign legacy
cannot be disentangled from the calamitous war in Southeast Asia.

Henry Kissinger believed that America had to step sharply back from
the unsustainable commitments that Nitze's NSC-68 had encouraged.
Throughout his tenure as national security adviser and later secretary of state,
Kissinger encouraged a policy of détente (a relaxation of tensions) with the
Soviet Union, a reduction in America's overseas commitments by delegating
roles to regional powers, and formally recognizing the People's Republic of
China. Kissinger was a polarizing figure: George Kennan applauded his
efforts and advised him to ignore his detractors; Paul Nitze abhorred his
worldview and questioned his patriotism.

Yet the foreign-policy value that Kissinger revered above all others was
"credibility." He recognized that the United States had to withdraw from
Vietnam, but in a way that communicated to enemies and allies alike that
the nation remained a force to be reckoned with. This was achieved through
bombing and launching an "incursion" into Cambodia as well as bombing
North Vietnam (with fewer qualms about civilian casualties than the Johnson administration), while at the same time withdrawing American troops
and reallocating primary defensive responsibilities to the Army of the
Republic of (South) Vietnam. Elsewhere, Kissinger launched a destabilization
campaign against the democratically elected government of Salvador Allende
in Chile, supported a Pakistani government perpetrating terrible crimes
against Bengalis in the 1971 Indo-Pakistani War, and invested American
credibility in a tangential though bloody conflict against communist proxies
in mineral-rich Angola. Kissinger's legacy is highly controversial, combining
genuine insight with reckless bellicosity, seminal diplomatic achievements,
and vivid illustrations of how an amoral worldview can lead to immoral
outcomes.

Like Kissinger, Paul Wolfowitz is a Jewish intellectual with a political
science Ph.D. from an Ivy League college—but the similarities end there.
Wolfowitz believed that Kissinger's service to the Nixon and Ford presidencies was tactically and morally deficient. Wolfowitz drew from Woodrow
Wilson the exceptionalist notion that the United States was a uniquely moral,

democratizing force in world affairs, and that to believe otherwise was to betray its ideals. Through his service to Presidents Carter, Reagan, and both Bushes, Wolfowitz was consistent in his view that his nation had a duty to lead the world in the direction of democracy and liberal capitalism, and that merely serving as a beacon was not enough.

During George H. W. Bush's presidency, Wolfowitz argued strongly against reducing defense spending following the collapse of the Soviet Union, and made the case, unheeded, that regime change in Iraq should have followed the ejection of Saddam Hussein's forces from Kuwait. In the immediate aftermath of the 9/11 attacks, Wolfowitz forcefully remade the case that removing Saddam Hussein from power was imperative. But this was simply a first step. Mimicking Woodrow Wilson's vaulting ambitions in 1918—and showing a similar lack of respect for Mahanian historical precedent— Wolfowitz called for a wholesale transformation of the Middle East. He observed that the United States had successfully occupied Japan and Germany after the Second World War and transformed these societies into high-performing democracies. Without reference to the historical context of those nation-building campaigns, he provocatively extended his analysis to ask: What was stopping the United States from doing the same in Iraq? Though costly in human and financial terms, such a move could ultimately pacify not just Iraq but also a restive and dangerous region. With Saddam gone and Iraq thriving, its neighbors would inevitably tilt in the direction of representation, accountability, and economic competence. A democratic wave would redound to the advantage of all.

Wolfowitz's campaign did not end well. On December 18, 2007, Barack Obama, then a candidate for the Democratic presidential nomination, observed, "I am running to do more than end a war in Iraq. I am running to change the mindset that got us into war."[28] He had identified that mind-set in his most significant speech on foreign policy prior to his winning the presidency, delivered at an "antiwar rally" in Chicago in 2002. Obama lambasted the move to war against Saddam Hussein's Iraq as a "dumb war. A rash war. A war based not on reason but on passion, not on principle but on politics . . ." "What I am opposed to," said Obama, "is the cynical attempt by Richard Perle and Paul Wolfowitz and other armchair, weekend warriors in this administration to shove their own ideological agendas down our throats, irrespective of the costs in lives lost and in hardships borne."[29]

President Obama's foreign policies have been shaded by this aversion to ideology. The president is opposed to declaring allegiance to a fixed foreign-policy principle, and it seems highly unlikely that he will bequeath a presidential foreign-policy "doctrine"—unless the absence of one counts as one. He declined to consult Congress over the intervention in Libya in 2011, but did so in regard to Syria in 2013. He ordered a troop surge in Afghanistan in 2009—which he now seems to view as his gravest foreign-policy error—and then retreated from further commitments with alacrity. Obama drew a red line on Syria regarding the use of chemical weapons, invited Congress to decide what to do when Assad crossed it, and then ceded a starring role in finding a solution to Vladimir Putin. "Folks here in Washington like to grade on style," Obama told ABC News. "I'm much more concerned about getting the policy right."[30] More than any other individual surveyed in this book, Obama believes that foreign policy is an imperfect art, that consistency is not a virtue in and of itself. The president appears to concur with Ralph Waldo Emerson (and FDR) that "a foolish consistency is the hobgoblin of little minds, adored by little statesmen and philosophers and divines."

These nine individuals are difficult to pigeonhole using the conventional terminology favored by scholars of international relations. This book challenges the oft-cited distinction between realism and idealism as an imperfect expression of the principal divide in U.S. foreign policy. There is insight to be gleaned in interrogating diplomacy through this prism, clearly. But it has also become a little tired. Instead, I suggest that another binary reveals something different about America's interactions with the world: art versus science.

Each of the individuals in this book approached foreign policymaking with contrasting manners of thought and expression—their education and subsequent disciplinary preferences were quite different. Some—like Mahan, Kennan, and Kissinger—were drawn primarily to history, philosophy, and literature, which tended to impart a sense of tragedy and caution, and a reluctance (unless the fate of the world was deemed to be at stake as per Kennan and the H-bomb) to depart from observed historical precedent. But others, including Wilson, Nitze, and Wolfowitz, were trained in the social sciences—political science, economics, psychology, and later the fledgling discipline of international relations—and were more inclined to view the world as "makable" following the identification and application of the appropriate patterns and theories. Individuals possessed of such ideas often seek to transcend history rather than operate within its observed confines— to do things that have never been tried.

This was certainly the case with Wilson at the Paris Peace Conference and Wolfowitz in the aftermath of the 9/11 attacks. Both believed that the world (or significant parts of it) had to be remade to suit American interests—which in the long run was best for everyone—not that America should regard the world's complexities with clearer eyes and work with what could be seen. Or as George W. Bush asserted in his second inaugural address, "The survival of liberty in our land increasingly depends on the success of liberty in other lands. The best hope for peace in our world is the expansion of freedom in all the world."[31] Shapers of such sentiments often have a strong sense that history is heading in a particular direction, which brings firmness and consistency in the application of policy. But those who claim to have discerned the world's final destination often possess undue certainty about the quality of their counsel and are unwilling to accept errors in conception, only in implementation.

Those who view foreign policy as an art, conversely, believe that the world cannot be treated as a laboratory, that the course of history is unknowable, that policymakers must rely upon intuition and creativity alone. Their recommendations address the world that actually rather than potentially exists. Precedent is essential, and policymaking based on abstract theorizing is dismissed as reckless. Foreign-policy artists view their job as to cope as best they can with a world that cannot be bent to the will of a single nation—no matter how powerful. They do not seek to produce new systemic knowledge; their artistry is applied to advancing American interests, protecting its borders, and preventing the world from blowing up in a million possible ways. To attempt more invites Nemesis.

To varying degrees, the art of foreign policy has been practiced by both George Kennan and Barack Obama. "International relations are not a science," Kennan once cautioned.[32] Deeply reluctant to outline a sweeping grand strategic doctrine, Barack Obama has stated that his preference is for approaching foreign-policy challenges on a case-by-case basis—that he is "comfortable with complexity."[33] Critics tend to characterize individuals such as these as passive, reactive, and inattentive to the promise of American power. This is a nation, so the "exceptionalist" narrative runs, that broke free from history, plowed a singular path, and is uniquely positioned to help the rest of the world. Or as Woodrow Wilson phrased it in 1912, "We are chosen and prominently chosen to show the way to the nations of the world how they shall walk in the paths of liberty."[34] Those who believe foreign policy is an art diverge from this vaulting, Universalist logic.

The individuals who populate this book exhibit these disciplinary tendencies to varying degrees; their modes of thought are wired in different ways. But this is no clear-cut binary. Any individual's foreign-policy views are forged by more than mere disciplinary contact, and some are partial to both artistry and scientism. Individuals trained in the social sciences are not all destined to grand-strategize to realize ambitious goals; those trained in the arts and humanities do not all intuit and improvise in the face of timeless, oppressive uncertainty. A political science major at Columbia University, Barack Obama has been particularist, nonideological, and attentive to history's cautionary lessons. Then again, the individuals who criticize Obama most vehemently for failing to enunciate a doctrine are usually think-tank-based political scientists—such as Paul Wolfowitz, Vali Nasr, and Anne-Marie Slaughter—who each view the world through a neo-Wilsonian ideological prism.[35] If Obama had completed a doctorate in international relations rather than a law degree at Harvard, might he now favor the systemic application of a core diplomatic principle, like his Ph.D.-wielding critics? Obama's suppleness makes this difficult to imagine. What we do know is that Obama's courses in international relations at Columbia were insufficient to unleash his inner grand strategist.

Regardless of their precise disciplinary lineage—and the art-science binary is intended as an illuminating background theme, not as a reductive master narrative—the ideas surveyed in this book often entered the stream of foreign policymaking, leading to multiple outcomes: farsighted diplomacy, necessary wars, adroit alliance building, Pyrrhic economic and political victories, the maladroit use of the CIA, reckless foreign-policy misadventures, and numerous others. The intellectual paths to these and other outcomes will be delineated and critiqued.

Which does not mean that I dismiss or minimize other causal and contextual factors that shape America's foreign relations. There is too much insular debate in the historical profession about the relative virtues of the various subfields. But the writing of history is clearly not a zero-sum game. Social, cultural, intellectual, political, military, economic, and diplomatic historians contribute in different and equally legitimate ways to collective knowledge. One need not practice one to slight the other. In this respect, I like the observation made by the novelist Jean Rhys: "I don't believe in the individual Writer so much as in Writing. All of writing is a huge lake . . . All that matters is feeding the lake. I don't matter. The lake matters."[36]

While this book at its best—to follow Rhys's metaphor—is a modest stream that feeds into a lake, there are aspects that I wish were otherwise. Although I discuss the important foreign-policy interventions made by Jeane Kirkpatrick, Madeleine Albright, Condoleezza Rice, Anne-Marie Slaughter, Samantha Power, and Susan Rice, no chapter focuses on a woman. This can mainly be explained by the gender discrimination present in foreign policy-making, academia, and journalism throughout the twentieth century, and which persists—more subtly—to this day. "Grand strategy" is a masculine discourse (one of its many problems), and this has discouraged female participation, or worked against women who have entered the realm. To give just one example—and there are many—Henry Kissinger lauded Nixon's bellicosity during the 1971 Indo-Pakistani War because it illustrated to Moscow that "we are coming off like men."[37] As Jeane Kirkpatrick, U.S. ambassador to the United Nations during the Reagan administration, remarked, "I can't think of any advantages to being a woman in U.S. politics, frankly."[38]

But other factors have also shaped my decisions. Most of the chapters (those that don't cover Kennan and Kissinger) cover significant time periods, and I do not think, yet, that the contributions made by Kirkpatrick, Albright, and Rice compare, in terms of traction and longevity, to those made by Mahan, Kissinger, and Wolfowitz. For example, Condoleezza Rice was national security adviser and secretary of state from 2001 to 2009, and presided over significant accomplishments in the second term—primarily through counseling a course of restraint and the avoidance of any more calamitous wars. But Rice was also something of a weather vane during Bush's first term—tilting in the direction of the strongest gusts. She was a manager-bureaucrat, in the mold of McGeorge Bundy, not a philosopher-king like Walt Rostow.[39] In fact, Bundy and Rice share much in common: both had leadership roles at elite universities and both were ineffective national security advisers when America launched its two most disastrous foreign-policy interventions.

A similar regret is present in regard to race and religion. *Worldmaking* examines six Christians and three Jews; eight whites and one African American; no nonbelievers or adherents of other faiths or, indeed, any other ethnic minority. In a book that focuses on the nexus between knowledge and power—a privileged milieu that self-perpetuates and excludes—I have found it difficult to proceed differently without skewing reality. But there exists some cause for optimism, at least. The composition of the George W. Bush and Obama administrations, in particular, give hope that the nation's foreign-policymaking and policy-debating elite might more closely resemble the nation at large.

These nine individuals, placed in conversation with one another in the chapters that follow, form what I hope is a fresh perspective on America's foreign relations—one that purposefully downplays the significance of compartmentalized epochs like the "Cold War" or the "Reagan administration" and instead focuses on the ideas that predate and outlive these discrete events and presidencies. Conventional periodization tends to obscure foreign-policy trends that are more appropriately viewed in the *longue durée*. Woodrow Wilson's ideational legacy—Wilsonianism—is more significant than his presidency, which, after all, ended ingloriously. George Kennan left government for Princeton in 1950, convinced that the PPS "has simply been a failure," that he had been unable to bring "order and foresight into the designing of foreign policy."[40] Yet many scholars would identify Kennan's "containment" as the Cold War strategy par excellence. Few things in history are as important as the life of an idea.

1

★

THE PHILOSOPHER OF SEA POWER

ALFRED THAYER MAHAN

The ideas contained in Alfred Thayer Mahan's *The Influence of Sea Power upon History* have certainly resonated through the ages. Published in 1890, the book's principal argument was that the United States must abandon the small satisfactions of regional hegemony and any hope of attaining economic self-sufficiency. Instead the nation should consciously emulate Great Britain in building a dominant navy to enhance its security, project power globally, and hence expand economically through free trade—where the nation's advantages in natural resources and ingenuity could best be brought to bear. Mahan's biographer, Robert Seager II, described the volume as "perhaps the most powerful and influential book written by an American in America in the nineteenth century."[1]

This provocative claim invites us to reflect on what is meant by power and influence when comparing literature to history. Yet if we stick to nonfiction, Seager's judgment appears broadly sound. As Arthur Schlesinger Jr. wrote in 2005, "No American since the Founding Fathers had worked out so systematic an analysis of the Republic's geopolitical position in the world. To a people accustomed to thinking of foreign policy in terms of legal right or moral purpose, Mahan now offered hard talk about national interest, naval bases, firepower, lines of communication."[2] *The Influence of Sea Power upon History* was read and admired by Theodore Roosevelt, Henry Cabot Lodge, Admiral John Fisher of Britain's Royal Navy, and Kaiser Wilhelm II. In the decades after publication, the book was translated and used as a textbook for sailors in the German and Japanese navies. Charles Beard detected the book's insidious influence on multiple levels: "Besides setting politicians aflame in the United States, Mahan set their rivals on fire in Europe and Asia and prepared the way for a world conflagration which began in 1914 in full force."[3] Whether Mahan's theory of sea power helped cause the First World War is an exotic open question. What we do know is that *The Influence* figures prominently on naval training syllabi in the United States and across the world today—in China, most notably and, from a U.S. perspective, perhaps most worryingly.[4] When China's president Xi Jinping observed in July 2013 that the "oceans and seas have an increasingly important strategic status concerning global competition in the spheres of politics, economic development, military, and technology," he was speaking Mahan's language.[5]

Mahan's body of work, which ultimately ran to 20 books and 137 articles, was an inescapable point of reference for many of the individuals discussed herein. Woodrow Wilson drew little instruction from Mahan's Anglophilia, hardheaded realism, and incessant lobbying for greater naval "preparedness." In 1914, the Wilson administration forbade all former naval officers from writing on the European war, silencing Mahan's agitation for a more explicitly pro-entente stance. Wilson and Mahan disagreed sharply over the leadership America owed the world. Mahan viewed international arbitration as an unnecessary constraint to action that powerful nations like the United States should avoid—for this Achilles should have no unprotected heel. Wilson, conversely, believed that history's cycle of devastating wars—destined to become more and more lethal due to technological advances—could be broken only if every nation ceded sovereignty and committed seriously to the success of a supranational entity vested with genuine power.

Wilson had a low opinion of Mahan's worldview, but his hostility was a mere trifling compared to the contempt Charles Beard felt toward a man he considered one of the great villains in American history. Beard described Mahan as "the most successful propagandist ever produced in the United States." He observed that Theodore Roosevelt "made Mahan's work his bible of politics for the United States," and decried the expansionary, imperialistic policies—culminating in the Spanish-American War—that his works had encouraged. He charged that Mahan had helped transform the United States from a nation that tilled its own land—a Jeffersonian idyll—into one that emulated Britain in exploiting other nations for the fiduciary advantage of a narrow elite. In attacking Mahan, Beard rounded on his compromised, politically motivated scholarship (a charge, ironically, that was often leveled at Beard):

> What Mahan did in his propaganda was to "historicize" his creed for popular consumption, that is, to use history to "prove" that it was true, inevitable, and desirable. He had no training whatever in historical research, the scrutiny and authentication of documents, or the philosophy of historical composition. In all this he was a veritable ignoramus. He took such old works as suited his preconceived purposes, tore passages and fragments out of their context, and pieced his notes together in such a fashion as to represent his own image of life, economy, sea power, greed, and war.[6]

Beard believed that Mahan had played a pivotal role in transforming the United States into a more violent and materialistic nation—shredding its virtuous, exceptional nature in the process. Thanks to Mahan and his policymaking acolytes, America left Arcadia and became as flawed and self-interested as every other nation.

It was during Franklin Roosevelt's presidency and in the early Cold War that Mahan appeared less like a siren and more like a prophet. In the late 1930s, as Adolf Hitler's Germany dismantled the Treaty of Versailles with ever-increasing confidence, the journalist Walter Lippmann led the way in calling for a stronger appreciation for Mahanian principles: chief among them that no hostile power, such as Nazi Germany, be permitted to assume control of the Atlantic. George Kennan similarly viewed Mahan in positive terms, as a man who rejected isolationism as a comforting unhistorical dream, and who anticipated the importance of naval expansion and free trade: he charted "new paths at that time in the analysis of international realities—paths which led in the direction of a more profound appraisal of the sources of American security." Kennan identified in Mahan and the historian Brooks Adams (brother of Henry) "an isolated spurt of intellectual activity against a background of general torpor and smugness in American thinking about foreign affairs."[7] For Kennan, it was Woodrow Wilson's idealistic illusions that caused American foreign policy to become disastrously unmoored from reality.

Mahan's antagonists have raised some strong objections to his writings through the ages. A common theme is that Mahan's worldview does not resonate with American values—a charge later leveled at Henry Kissinger. One can follow Charles Beard in criticizing Mahan's worldview for being "based on the pure materialism of biological greed."[8] Or one can follow Woodrow Wilson in rejecting Mahan's pessimistic view that war is interwoven into the fabric of the international system, that the United States should shun arbitration proposals and prepare for the worst. But it is impossible to deny Mahan's prescience on so much of what would unfold. The world in which we live resembles the one he said would come to pass in the late nineteenth and early twentieth centuries. The Washington-led world economic system is dominated by free trade facilitated by open shipping lanes; the U.S. Navy has no peer competitor in its global reach; significant world crises are rarely resolved through the good offices of the United Nations; and the United States reserves the right to act unilaterally if its interests are threatened. In all of these matters, for good and for worse, Mahan anticipated the shape of the modern world. And so the story begins here.

On an early autumn day in 1871, an agitated elderly gentleman paced the decks of a Hudson River steamboat, mulling the indignities of government service. Adorned in quality fabrics, with piercing eyes and a neatly trimmed beard, Dennis Hart Mahan's distinguished appearance did not deceive. Through his long career as a professor of engineering at West Point, Mahan dined with the Marquis de Lafayette in Paris, taught military science to virtually every senior officer who fought in the Civil War, and wrote seminal texts that revolutionized battlefield tactics.[9] West Point made the man, and Mahan in turn had indelibly shaped its graduates: William Tecumseh Sherman, Ulysses S. Grant, Robert E. Lee, and Thomas "Stonewall" Jackson all benefited from his instruction. Yet despite compiling a towering record of achievement, Mahan was not reconciled to retirement. Although President Grant had previously assured Mahan that he could remain in his post for as long as he desired, West Point's Board of Visitors had insisted on placing the sixty-nine-year-old professor on the retired list. As the steamboat approached Stony Point, Mahan decided with finality that the wrench of leaving his beloved West Point was too much to take—that life without purposeful labor was not worth living. He climbed the railings of the boat and cast himself onto the paddle wheel rotating below.

Obituaries attributed Dennis Mahan's suicide to a momentary "fit of insanity," the exculpation deployed in that era when distinguished gentlemen committed suicide. But the actual cause of Mahan's death was the prospect of enforced indolence—compelling testimony to his unbalanced work ethic. The dangers of this trait were deftly avoided by his eldest son, Alfred Thayer, who bequeathed a legacy even more substantial than that of his father, but who managed his work-life balance with greater care. Alfred found his father impressive in certain aspects: upstanding, diligent, and possessed of a virtuous value system. Yet he could scarcely bring himself to acknowledge the shameful manner in which his father had abandoned his family.[10] His only recorded reflections speak privately to his "seasons of great apprehension" that he might have inherited his father's tendency toward melancholy and, potentially, self-destruction.[11]

Beyond these words, Alfred spoke little of his father's suicide, either in his memoir or in his voluminous correspondence to friends and family. His reticence was indicative of the Victorian age in which he lived, but it also dovetailed with Mahan's yearning for privacy and an aversion to making a spectacle of himself. While Alfred followed his father in educating the military's brightest prospects, he never lost his dread of having to stand at a lectern and hold court for an hour or more. "I have . . . an abhorrence of public speaking," Mahan confessed, "and a desire to slip unobserved into a backseat wherever I am, which amount to a mania."[12] It was the timeliness and logic of Mahan's ideas—not an attention-seeking disposition—that brought him renown.

Born in West Point on September 27, 1840, Alfred was the first of six children raised in a solvent, stable family that set great store in the value of education. His father was raised in Virginia to Irish parents, although his Anglophilia—he shed his Irish affectations with breezy abandon—was untypical of second-generation emigrants from the old country. Alfred's mother, Mary Okill, was a devout Christian who prayed daily that her eldest son would pursue a career as a clergyman. Mary was a northerner, and this was the only flaw that her husband could discern in his wife, informing Alfred that "your mother is Northern and very few can approach her but still, in the general, none compare for me with the Southern woman."[13] That Mahan was a child of the South is reflected in his father's reaction to discovering him reading a copy of Harriet Beecher Stowe's *Uncle Tom's Cabin*: "My father took it out of my hands," Alfred recalled, "and I came to regard it much as I would a bottle labeled Poison."[14] Living in remote West Point—accessible only by steamboats in its prerailroad years and isolated by a frozen Hudson through the winter—ensured that Alfred's early years were closeted but conducive to scholarly endeavor. Surrounded by his father's books on military history, and compelled daily to display his mastery of Scripture by his loving but demanding mother, Alfred's intellectual development was impressive, even if his parents' stern pedagogical instruction left his social skills, hampered by a narrow circle of playmates, lagging behind the swiftness of his reading and the fluency of his writing.

Dennis Mahan's desire to immerse his children in the societal norms of the genteel, slaveholding South informed his decision to send Alfred to Saint James School in Maryland, an Episcopalian boarding school attended overwhelmingly by the well-heeled offspring of conservative southerners desirous of an education that ignored *Uncle Tom's Cabin* and treated chattel slavery as part of the natural order of things. Yet Alfred's father was also pragmatic, so when Saint James failed to provide Alfred with what he took to be adequate instruction in mathematics, he had few qualms about sending him northward to the racier, cosmopolitan setting of Columbia College in New York City. Alfred entered the college as a freshman in 1854 and remained in New York for two years—the time it took for him to identify his calling. Keen to expand his horizons beyond the northeastern seaboard, Mahan decided that a career in the Navy offered an unparalleled combination of discipline, travel opportunities, and the moral and spiritual well-being that comes with pursuing a selfless life in the service of one's nation.

Dennis Mahan's reaction to his son's plans for a career at sea was distinctly cool. Looking back in later years, Alfred could not help but applaud his father's prescience: "My entrance into the navy was greatly against my father's wish. I do not remember all his arguments, but he told me he thought me much less fit for a military than for a civilian profession, having watched me carefully. I think myself now that he was right; for, though I have no cause to complain of unsuccess, I believe I should have done better elsewhere."[15]

So why did his father judge Alfred so unsuitable for naval life? The answer lies largely in the fact that the earnest and bookish young Mahan lacked the spirit of camaraderie that lured so many young men to the Navy. Reveling in the company of his fellow men was simply not Mahan's thing. He was upstanding to the point of sanctimony, and his introspective nature and unbending interpretation of the rules made him a lonely student through his college years. "It takes at least twenty gentlemen to remove the bad impression made by one rowdy," he complained to his father after observing uncouth behavior on a New York ferryboat.[16] His sense of right and wrong was wound to an unsustainably high level, and this trait tended to antagonize all but the most prissy.

Placing his reservations to one side, Dennis Mahan went to great lengths to secure his son's acceptance to the Naval Academy. He arranged an audience with Secretary of War Jefferson Davis, who had trailed Dennis by just three classes at West Point. Davis advised the aspiring sailor to meet with Congressman Ambrose S. Murray from New York, who in turn agreed to support Alfred's admission to Annapolis. As Mahan acknowledged, "It has pleased me to believe, as I do, that I owed my entrance to the United States Navy to the interposition of the first and only President of the Southern Confederacy, whose influence with Mr. [President] Pierce is a matter of history."[17] Mahan had Jefferson Davis to partly thank for his success, but his route to Annapolis would have been much less certain with a different surname. His father offered unequivocal support, in the form of his personal prestige, when the stakes were highest for his cerebral, straitlaced son.

Mahan was struck down by "melancholia" upon arriving in Annapolis—a pretty but provincial town of approximately eight thousand residents—in September 1856. The immediate onset of this affliction did not augur well for his career as a sailor, but he soon shook off his blues and in a warm letter to Elizabeth Lewis, the stepdaughter of his uncle, the Reverend Milo Mahan, professed himself wholly satisfied with both his classmates and his early experiences of sailing: "You can form no idea what a nice class we have . . . Our mutual attachment renders us I fear rather disloyal to the fair sex . . . Life at sea, so far as I have experienced it, is the most happy careless and entrancing life that there is. In a stiff breeze when the ship is heeling well over there is a wild sort of delight that I never experienced before."[18]

These words are joyful and without guile. Yet this would be the first and last time that Mahan would wax lyrical about his fellow classmates and being at sea. Mahan concluded that Annapolis was "a miserable little town" and that he was destined for greater things than carousing with his philistine cohort of midshipmen. Mahan also soon discovered that he wasn't really much of a sailor. In fact, he actively disliked the sea—the tedium of sailing broken only by sudden storms that he failed to endure stoically.

Instead, Mahan cruised through the academy's unchallenging syllabus and devoted his spare time to reading the French medieval historian Jean Froissart, the diarist and diplomat Henry Lytton Bulwer, and the Scottish Romantic novelist Sir Walter Scott. His close friend, Samuel Ashe, was duly impressed by his friend's range of learning, describing him as "the most intellectual man I have ever known. He had not only a remarkable memory but also a capacity to comprehend and a clarity of perception."[19] At Annapolis,

Mahan managed to graduate second in his class without exerting himself beyond some last-minute cramming.

Alfred graduated in 1859 on the eve of the Civil War, and the loyalties of his graduating class were split by the conflict that ensued. His views on the looming crisis were understandably mixed, combining as he did staunch Unionism with an implacably southern upbringing and no real hostility to slavery. His view of America's black population was entirely typical of someone of his age and background, and he habitually deployed terms such as "nigger" and "darkie" to refer to free and enslaved African Americans. While never relenting in his opinion that America's black population was inherently inferior to those of European stock, Mahan did amend his views on the "peculiar institution" upon encountering field slaves for the first time in South Carolina. As he remarked in his memoir, "It was my first meeting with slavery, except in the house servants of Maryland . . . and as I looked into the cowed, imbruted faces of the field hands, my early training fell away like a cloak. The process was not logical; I was generalizing from a few instances, but I was convinced." Even his father, a proud Virginian who supported slavery and oozed contempt for the abolitionist cause, backed Abraham Lincoln instinctively in his struggle to restore the Union: "My son, I did not think I could ever again be happy should our country fall into her present state; but now I am so absorbed in seeing those fellows beaten that I lose sight of the rest."[20]

Mahan's Civil War was uneventful. The Confederacy's naval assets were relatively inconsequential, so the Union enjoyed a mastery that was rarely challenged, allowing Lincoln to impose a strangulating blockade of the South's main ports. Serving on the Union blockade, Mahan heard a shot fired in anger just once—at Port Royal, South Carolina, on November 7, 1861—and his references to the conflict invariably speak to the essential tedium of serving through the defining conflict of American history. The Civil War did not make Mahan in the way that later diplomatic thinkers were shaped by their experience of the First and Second World Wars. Mahan made one serious attempt to join the action, requesting a transfer to the *Monongahela*, which was then engaged in the "sociable" (and more perilous) blockade of Mobile, Alabama. His transfer was declined and his classmate Roderick Prentiss was ordered to the ship instead. It was a fortunate rejection for Mahan, for Prentiss was killed aboard the *Monongahela* during the Battle of Mobile Bay of August 1864. The main highlight of Mahan's war was an encounter with a victorious General William Sherman, whom he had approached in Savannah with a message from his father. When Mahan introduced himself, Sherman "broke into a smile—all over as they say—shook my hand forcibly, and exclaimed 'What, the son of old Dennis?' reverting instinctively to the familiar epithet of school days." Sherman confessed to feeling a great glow of pride whenever Professor Mahan "dismissed him from the blackboard with the commendation, 'Very well done Mr. Sherman.'"[21] Victorious in Georgia with the Union's most celebrated general, Mahan found that his father still cast quite a shadow.

Through his mother's instruction, and the high regard that he felt for his uncle Milo, an Episcopalian minister who published to acclaim on various theological issues, Mahan was a devout Christian. Indeed, understanding the depth and sincerity of Mahan's faith is essential to understanding his subsequent foreign-policy views. He tithed his income to the church throughout his lifetime—including the substantial royalties he would accumulate from 1890—and was near faultless in his church attendance. When he visited England, he was discomfited by the secular direction in which this otherwise exemplary country appeared to be headed. This was reflected in the haphazard fashion that its aristocracy and upper middle class regarded devotion to their maker—skipping Sunday service when frivolities like hunting got in the way. Tied to his religiosity were prudish tendencies that did not sit well with a naval career. When he rose to positions of command, for example, Mahan believed that talk of sex was improper and so he refused to discuss "sanitary precautions against syphilis" with fellow officers, declaring that the "morals of factory girls" and those of "Charlestown Navy Yard girls" were also "unclean subjects and to be avoided."[22]

Yet while Mahan's Christianity was traditional in its approach to Scripture, it was also fairly progressive by the standards of the day. Mahan was a staunch Republican and throughout his life was a vocal opponent of radical progressivism, socialism, and indeed anything that smacked of excessive government interference in one's private sphere. But he recognized that he owed a duty to God to invest some time in ameliorating the conditions of others less blessed. In later years he decried the growing epidemic of homelessness in America's major cities: "There is no condition of life that should appeal more strongly to the sympathy of the fortunate than that of the homeless."[23] He was sympathetic to many progressive causes. Sharing Theodore Roosevelt's distaste for the excesses of the Gilded Age, he opposed trusts, monopolies, and the "malefactors of great wealth," as TR famously described them. This is not to say that Mahan was at the vanguard of the Progressive movement. He opposed the imposition of the eight-hour day, was relaxed about child labor, and was shaken at the prospect of women being granted the vote—"the proposition to give women the vote breaks down the constant practice of the past ages by which to men is assigned the outdoor rough action of life and to women that indoor sphere which we call the family."[24] An orthodox conservative in many respects, Mahan nonetheless possessed the capacity to surprise.

At the close of the Civil War, Mahan embarked on a series of voyages that took him across the world, affording him a wonderful opportunity to observe America's global competitors firsthand. In the winter of 1867–1868, Mahan traveled to Japan on board the *Iroquois*, a "beautiful sea boat," as the young sailor described it to his mother, although his dread of storms also led him to observe that "despite what romancers have written, a gale of wind is uncomfortable and anxious to everyone responsible . . . who can say when an accident may happen or what chastening God may intend for us."[25] Having been spared God's wrath across the Pacific, Mahan arrived in Japan at a propitious time, as Western-inclined modernizers were in the midst of casting aside the feudal Tokugawa shogunate in the Meiji Restoration of 1868. The declared aim of Japan's new oligarchs was now to "enrich the country, strengthen the military," a program that Mahan supported for all right-thinking nations. While his first impressions were xenophobic, "I find the people uninteresting and don't care for their peculiarities, nor for their customs," he soon decided that "I think I shall like Japan; all agree in representing the people as amiable and goodnatured to the utmost. The two sworded fellows are the only ones who give trouble and they only rarely and when drunk."[26] Mahan was impressed by Japan's efforts to emulate Western models of development, and he remained well disposed toward Japanese tenacity and ingenuity, even while in later years insisting that restrictions be placed on the ability of Japanese emigrants to settle permanently in the United States. Even then, his justification was reasonably complimentary:

> Personally, I entirely reject any assumption or belief that my race is superior to the Chinese, or to the Japanese. My own suits me better, probably because I am used to it; but I wholly disclaim, as unworthy of myself and of them, any thought of superiority . . . Now while recognizing what I clearly see to be the great superiority of the Japanese, as of the white over the Negro . . . America doubts her power to digest and assimilate the strong national and racial characteristics which distinguish the Japanese, which are the secrets of much of their success.[27]

While Japan was forward thinking in its emphasis on Western-modeled modernization, Mahan believed that its people—"a very small race and nearly beardless, which tends to make them appear like boys playing at soldiers"— lacked the martial qualities to truly become a power of the first rank. The nation that he admired above all was Great Britain, which combined political stability, cultural achievement, the rule of law, economic ingenuity, hirsuteness, and a judicious emphasis on the vitality of naval preeminence. Throughout the 1870s and 1880s, as Mahan was attached to ships destined for East Asia, Europe, and Latin America, his greatest comfort came not in the company of his fellow Americans but on British ships, where he could congregate with men of superior taste and sensibilities—and where his Anglophilia guaranteed a warm welcome. Reflecting on the historical necessity of the British seizure of the Yemeni port of Aden in 1839, Mahan would remark, "Are a pack of savages to stand in the way of the commerce of the world?"[28] This sentiment neatly crystallizes his worldview. The British were doing the world a favor in their colonial expansion during the nineteenth century. They were opening backward nations up to trade, cleansing the arteries of global commerce, and thus doing all exporting nations a great service. As Great Britain inevitably lost strength, Mahan believed that the United States had to follow its path in building a similarly dominant navy.

This instinctive preference for British models and values, which his father imparted from an early age, was the bedrock upon which Mahan's philosophy of sea power was built. Bolted up in his room, poring over volumes of those two giants of French and German historiography— François Pierre Guillaume Guizot and Leopold von Ranke—Mahan developed a sophisticated understanding of world history. But it was through traveling and observing the world that Mahan could see firsthand the Royal Navy's unrivaled reach and influence, which in turn allowed Britain to enjoy high levels of economic growth and a constantly improving quality of life (even if it was becoming increasingly godless). Meanwhile, the United States was the rising power of the world. A combination of America's abundant natural resources, high fertility rates, and a declaration of fidelity to British models of economic and military development would make it virtually unstoppable. But the America of 1880 was still far from reaching that Promised Land.

In 1880 the sultan of Turkey, concerned at the parlous state of his nation's finances, made some cuts to its diplomatic service. He closed his missions and embassies in Sweden, Belgium, the Netherlands, and the United States. His rationale was straightforward: all were medium-size powers that played a minimal role in world diplomacy.[29] In retrospect it is easy to characterize the sultan's decision as myopic, but in 1880 few world leaders would have been surprised by the news. In the two decades after the Civil War, successive U.S. presidents failed to chart a distinct, activist path either at home or abroad, and all have relatively undistinguished reputations today. From 1865 to 1885, Andrew Johnson, Ulysses S. Grant, Rutherford B. Hayes, and Chester Arthur scarcely approached Abraham Lincoln's leadership and sense of purpose. Drift at the top meant that America was commensurately weakened as its prestige and position on the world stage waned. Particularly distasteful to Mahan was the pervasive corruption of that era.

With Congress ascendant in this same period, there was little appetite for authorizing the expenditure that might have made the United States into a top-rank military and diplomatic power. In 1869, Congress allocated a paltry thirty-one clerks to serve the far-reaching requirements of the entire State Department. Only with the greatest reluctance was this number nudged upward to fifty in 1881.[30] Throughout the 1870s, the American Navy ranked twelfth in the world behind the sultan's Turkey and a sullen and passive China.[31] A punitive naval expedition against Chile was called off in 1881 when Washington planners noticed that the Chilean navy was superior in number to the U.S. Navy.[32] In economic terms, the United States was moving through the process of displacing the United Kingdom as the world's preeminent nation. But this bulky economic stature cast a faint military shadow.[33]

Throughout the 1880s, steps were taken to ensure that the United States packed a military punch that better matched its financial buoyancy. In 1882, the Republican Chester Arthur administration persuaded Congress to fund the production of seventeen steel-hulled cruisers to replace the wooden ships on which Mahan had learned his basic seamanship. None of these ships possessed armor or maneuverability to compare with the great navies of Great Britain or France. But adding metal to the fleet was clearly a step in the right direction for those individuals—overwhelmingly Republicans— who wanted America to play a greater role in world affairs. There was a clear partisan divide on the issue of what kind of global stance the United States should adopt. The Democrats favored states' rights and local control, and were instinctively skeptical of increasing the size of the federal government. In light of the devastating Confederate defeat in the Civil War, it was hardly surprising that most Democrats subscribed to the view that, as one southern politician phrased it, "no man has the right or duty to impose his own convictions upon others."[34] Such moderation was anathema to most Republicans, who backed an active federal government in a dangerous world. And many, like Mahan, viewed Great Britain as the finest expression of what might be achieved when an activist foreign policy is allied with the moral and temperamental advantages of the Anglo-Saxon race. Imposing one's convictions on others was simply indicative of well-placed self-belief and a fair reading of the future. If southern Democrats disliked this forceful logic, it owed everything to their shattered self-confidence, and nothing to a dispassionate reading of international affairs.

Even though Mahan agreed with his Republican friends and colleagues that the government should increase the size of the U.S. Navy, he did not embrace conventional imperial acquisition as a path to American greatness. In private correspondence in the 1870s and early 1880s, Mahan made clear that he expected the United States to develop a dominant presence in the Gulf of Mexico and the Caribbean basin, specifically at the Isthmus of Panama, where he, along with many others, believed it imperative that America link the Atlantic to the Pacific through the building of a trans-isthmian canal. But to Samuel Ashe in 1884, Mahan had written, "I don't know how you feel, but to me the very suspicion of an imperial policy is hateful; the mixing our politics with those of Latin republics especially. Though identified, unluckily, with a military profession, I dread outlying colonies or interests, to maintain which large military establishments are necessary."[35] He was an expansionist but not an imperialist—an important distinction at that time. Mahan soon realized that the United States did not need colonies; it simply needed guaranteed access to adequate harbors to refuel its ships. This was a powerful insight.

In 1883, Mahan published his first book, *The Gulf and Inland Waters*. For the previous three years he had been navigation officer at the Brooklyn Navy Yard, a position with little responsibility, leaving him ample time to write.[36] The publisher Scribner's had offered Mahan $600 to write the book, and as he sheepishly recalled to Samuel Ashe, "As I wanted the money I consented with great misgivings as to whether I could do justice to the subject, but believing I would probably do as well as another."[37] The book was a well-researched account of naval tactics during the Civil War, and Mahan's main contention was that Union control of the Gulf, Mobile Bay, and the Mississippi and Red Rivers had been critical to the defeat of the Confederacy. The process of researching and writing the book—allied to its positive critical reception—recalibrated Mahan's ambitions away from achieving promotion through active duty and toward seeking self-realization, and winning influential adherents to his thesis on the primacy of sea power, through the pen.

Soon afterward, Mahan's scholarly ambitions received a significant boost. It had long been the ambition of Admiral Stephen B. Luce, a decorated sailor who admired *The Gulf and Inland Waters*, to establish a federally funded Naval War College in Rhode Island. Luce believed this new institution should offer an advanced, historically informed syllabus, far removed from the nuts-and-bolts training offered by the Naval Academy in Annapolis. In July 1884, Luce wrote to Mahan inviting him to join the faculty of the new institution, which he surmised had gained unstoppable momentum within the Arthur administration. Mahan leapt at the opportunity. He was keen to take any job that served the dual purpose of reuniting his family and realizing his passion for naval history. On September 4, 1884, his eagerness to return home was strikingly expressed in the acceptance letter he wrote to Luce:

> I should like the position, like it probably very much. I believe I have the capacity and perhaps some inherited aptitude for the particular study; but I do not, on questioning myself, find that I now have the special accurate knowledge that *I* should think necessary . . . I ought to go home at once and be given till at least next summer to get up the work; I can only promise hard work . . . If you say come—I should wish to go home at once and be put on special duty.[38]

Mahan was evidently not worried about coming on too strong. A month later, on October 6, Luce's inkling that the government was coming around to his way of thinking was proved correct when Secretary of the Navy William E. Chandler authorized the creation of the college in Newport, Rhode Island, under the supervision of the Bureau of Navigation. But it was not possible for Luce to spirit Mahan home quite as rapidly as he desired.

In November, the *Wachusett*, a sloop of war captained by Mahan, was anchored off the Peruvian capital city of Lima. Desperately bored and frustrated in his wait for good news, Mahan decided to take leave from the ship to catch up on some reading. He wandered through the city until he found the English Club of Lima, which was home to a small library housing some classics of literature and history. It was there that he read Theodor Mommsen's *The History of Rome*, which told the story of the Roman Republic's rise and fall. Mahan found Mommsen's account of Hannibal's heroic passage through the Alps—in which he lost a quarter of his army of approximately forty-five thousand—particularly insightful. Hannibal's achievement in moving his army, including thirty-seven elephants, through arduous, snow-peaked Alpine terrain, is rightly considered one of the great logistical operations in military history. But think of what damage Hannibal might have wreaked against the Romans, Mommsen proposed, had he assumed control of the Mediterranean and circumvented the need for that perilous passage.

Mahan reflected on this insight for some time and had his eureka moment. In a letter to Admiral Luce in May 1885, he outlined his inaugural lecture course, which would focus on the vital strategic benefits that accompanied mastery of the sea. As he recounted to Luce, "Hannibal for instance had to make that frightful passage of the Alps in which he lost the quarter part of his remaining army because he did not control the sea . . . I read 2½ volumes of Mommsen in this one view."[39] Mahan wanted to update Mommsen's thesis with specific reference to the Anglo-French strategic rivalry that had dominated the previous two hundred years. Britain's victories, achieved primarily by the Royal Navy's superiority, would serve as a virtuous example for his students to ponder and emulate.

It was not until October 16, 1885, that Mahan finally reported to Luce for teaching duty in Newport. A month previously, Mahan had warned Luce not to "expect anything in the way of lecture or instruction from me this year."[40] A forbearing Luce himself taught the nine student officers who turned up for instruction. But from this slow start, the Naval War College would establish itself as a vital pedagogical cog in the American military machine, educating such Navy luminaries as Ernest J. King, Chester W. Nimitz, Thomas H. Moorer, and William J. Fallon. Its future was uncertain through the late 1880s, however, dependent as it was on the vagaries of party politics. Republicans generally viewed the enterprise in a more favorable light than did Democrats.

In a letter to Samuel Ashe dated February 2, 1886, Mahan explained what his new job entailed:

> The object is to impart, or at any rate, afford, courses of teaching in advance of what is taught at the Naval Academy, in many branches, but most especially on the more purely professional subjects—military subjects. Among these I have had assigned to me the subject of Naval Strategy and Tactics involving of course to a considerable extent Naval History . . . How to view the lessons of the past so as to mould them into lessons for the future, under such differing conditions, is the nut I have to crack.[41]

It was a broad remit that allowed him space and time to pursue his own academic interests. But a potential impediment appeared in Mahan's path in the summer of 1886, when Admiral Luce was called up to assume command of the North Atlantic Station. With few credible successors readily apparent, Mahan stepped into the breach to assume the presidency of the college—a time-consuming job that curtailed the amount of time he was able to spend in the library. But Mahan still made rapid progress on the book that would eventually be fashioned from his lecture series.

Mahan worked long hours at the college, reading through the secondary literature on the naval history of the past two centuries. Having been able, due to the rigors of active duty, to read only infrequently and furtively for much of the past thirty years, Mahan was now being paid to read, to reflect, and to write—academic life lived up to all his expectations. And his presidency of the college also allowed him to invite guest speakers to Newport whose research interests and strategic predilections corresponded with his own. One such individual was Theodore Roosevelt, an effervescent, politically ambitious Harvard graduate—then dividing his time between ranching in North Dakota and politicking in New York City—who himself had published an influential naval history, *The Naval War of 1812*, at the tender age of twenty-three.[42] *The New York Times* described Roosevelt's debut as "an excellent one in every respect, and shows in so young an author the best promise for a good historian—fearlessness of statement, caution, endeavor to be impartial, and a brisk and interesting way of telling events."[43] *The Naval War of 1812* established Roosevelt's reputation for strategic thinking predicated on a judicious combination of deft diplomacy and the maintenance of a powerful military. Roosevelt appropriated the West African proverb that summarized this approach: "Speak softly and carry a big stick."

Theodore Roosevelt and Alfred Mahan were very different in background, appearance, and personality. Roosevelt was garrulous, barrel-chested, and formidable in argument, a force of nature with a hardwired proclivity to lead. Mahan was tense, slender, and reclusive, more inclined to retreat to his study than lead a debate in a crowded, politically charged room. But Mahan and Roosevelt held strikingly similar views on the ideal composition of the Navy and the correct parameters for U.S. foreign policy.[44] Both believed that the United States had learned the wrong lessons from the War of 1812—in which Britain and America had fought to a painful stalemate over the course of three years and America's plan to annex Canada had been foiled—and this had retarded its naval development. The conventional view held that the United States had scored some notable victories against its more power-ful opponent through the deployment of small, maneuverable single cruis-ers that targeted British merchant shipping and bled resolve through small-scale but painful engagements. Roosevelt believed that this strategy was unduly defensive—that, as Mahan phrased it, "we wanted a navy for coast defense only, no aggressive action in our pious souls."[45] Rather than being satisfied with a modest navy of small vessels with small ambitions, limited to the protection of America's coastal waters, Mahan and Roosevelt believed that America needed to build a navy that better anticipated the global pre-eminence for which the nation was destined: large ships devoted to substan-tial causes in all four corners of the globe.

Following Roosevelt's lecture to Mahan's students in the fall of 1887, the two men talked at length on how this aim would be achieved. While it was not evident then, as Roosevelt's vast potential had yet to be translated into tangible political influence, the division of responsibility would become ap-parent in subsequent years. Mahan would provide the ideas—the imprima-tur of the respected intellectual—and Roosevelt would deploy his formidable powers of political persuasion. But to assume his share in this unspoken division of responsibility, Mahan had to first publish his magnum opus.

Throughout 1888 and 1889, Mahan devoted a great deal of time to se-curing a publisher for a book-length version of his lecture series at Newport, which he titled "The Influence of Sea Power upon History, 1660–1783." He first approached Charles Scribner's Sons, the house that had published *The Gulf and Inland Waters*:

> While lecturing at this institution during the past two years I have accumulated the text for a work, whose general scope is the bearing of naval power upon the general course of History in Western Europe and America between the years 1660 and 1783, the end of the American Revolution. It carries along a general thread of the history of the times, with a view to eliciting the effect of naval and commercial power events . . . and so afford an opportunity for pointing a lesson.[46]

Oblivious of the potential carried in Mahan's final nine words, Scrib-ner's turned him down on the basis that his study was too narrow. Mahan sent his proposal to countless other publishers, but to no avail. As Mahan despaired to Luce on September 21, 1889, "I am naturally a teacher and would like to increase my audience . . . But I am not willing . . . to go on begging publishers. It both distracts, vexes and hinders me in my other work."[47]

While Mahan did not go so far as to beg, he was impressively dogged in his attempts to track down a suitable outlet for his big idea. Later that month, John Murray Brown, the head of Little, Brown and Company, agreed to publish Mahan's book, subject to revisions and additions. The publisher informed Mahan that the book would be priced at $4 a copy ($95 in today's prices), suggesting that it viewed the book as a specialized scholarly title with an appeal limited to college libraries and wealthy individuals. A relieved Mahan was in no position to dispute the wisdom of its selling price.

Mahan's manuscript—as he sent it to Brown—constituted an 185,000-word narrative study of the Anglo-French naval rivalry that raged through the late seventeenth and eighteenth centuries. Impressive as this was, it lacked a sense of immediate relevance, which was why so many publishers had taken a pass. What lessons could the United States glean from Britain's successful campaign to forestall French dominance and expand its empire and, in turn, its commercial interests? How could a study of naval conflict in Europe speak to contemporary American concerns? To boost its appeal, Little, Brown asked Mahan to write a provocative introduction to the book, making clear what lessons his study should offer the United States. Mahan set about his task quickly and produced a memorable, punchy encomium to the vitality of the naval supremacy in an increasingly interconnected world.

Mahan's hastily conceived introduction, titled "Elements of Sea Power," ran to more than one hundred pages and overshadowed—in succinctness, originality, and impact—the original manuscript that had fared so poorly with publishers. His introduction stressed the vital importance of securing naval mastery and connected the links between sea power and commercial expansion, which, Mahan explained, assured the fundamental well-being of the nation. Mahan first praised Holland, a path-breaking maritime nation that overcame limitations in size and natural resources to grow wealthy off the trade secured by its magnificent navy. He next turned to Great Britain, a small island nation that wisely emulated the policy of naval primacy pursued by the Dutch in its successful bid to accrue wealth through expanded trade assisted by the acquisition of overseas territory. Although impressed by the British achievement, Mahan cautioned that the primary purpose of a strong navy is to secure the safe passage of trade—allowing a nation of America's natural advantages to achieve economic preeminence—not necessarily to allow a government to annex land and gratuitously pick fights with its competitors:

The necessity of a navy, in the restricted sense of the word, springs . . . from the existence of a peaceful shipping, and disappears with it, except in the case of a nation which has aggressive tendencies, and keeps up a navy merely as a branch of the military establishment. As the United States has at present no aggressive purposes, and as its merchant service has disappeared, the dwindling of the armed fleet and general lack of interest in it are strictly logical consequences.[48]

But Mahan also recognized the necessity of progressive nations waging war periodically against those with less enlightened views on the efficacy of free trade, whose governments repress their citizens and seek overseas expansion to exploit and pillage, not to construct enduring commercial relationships. To ensure that the United States was not disadvantaged against such an enemy, Mahan suggested that it should establish a global presence in the form of overseas bases and coaling stations, to assure the continuance of trade in wartime and to allow the Navy's military arm to strike decisive blows against its enemies. While Great Britain had built a formal empire to further this goal, Mahan believed that securing access to strategic ports, not annexing the nations to which they are connected, was a perfectly respectable route to wealth and power. His insight was borne out by the available evidence. Between 1870 and 1900, as Europe gorged on the territorial pickings available in sub-Saharan Africa, Great Britain added 4.7 million square miles to its empire and France expanded by 3.5 million square miles. The United States added a relatively meager 125,000 square miles to its territory in this same period but still leapt ahead of both nations in every important economic indicator.[49]

One of the most penetrating parts of Mahan's introduction is his discussion of the "principal conditions affecting the sea power of nations," which he divides into six categories—Geographical Position, Physical Conformation, Extent of Territory, Number of Population, Character of the People, and Character of the Government—which predict whether a nation is destined for naval greatness or not. The first of these, an unfortunate geographical position, might detract significantly from a nation's naval potential. This occurs specifically when a nation shares a land border with dangerous enemies, increasing a nation's susceptibility to land invasion and mitigating the potency of its navy. This factor strongly disadvantaged France— bordering Germany, Italy, and Spain—against Great Britain, protected by the Atlantic, North Sea, and English Channel. The United States shared

some of Britain's advantages in the sense that Canada and Mexico were unlikely aggressors, and the Atlantic and Pacific constituted vast barriers against
the real threat posed by Europe and Japan. If a canal were successfully carved
out of arduous terrain in Central America, however, this connection between the two great oceans would present both opportunities and threats to
the United States. The trading benefits of a transisthmian canal were vast:
"The position of the United States with reference to this route will resemble
that of England to the Channel, and of the Mediterranean countries to the
Suez route."[50] But American dominance of Central America and the Caribbean should not be taken as a given, particularly in light of America's own
naval weaknesses vis-à-vis her Old World competitors. To assure strategic
dominance in this vital part of the world, "the United States will have to
obtain in the Caribbean stations fit for contingent, or secondary, bases of
operations; which by their natural advantages, susceptibility of defence, and
nearness to the central strategic issue, will enable her fleet to remain as near
the scene as any opponent."[51]

Physical conformation is Mahan's second prerequisite for achieving
naval greatness. Deep harbors, connecting with long, navigable rivers, were
essential to the accumulation of substantial wealth derived from trade.
Although the United States was blessed with an abundance of deep-water
ports and trade arteries such as the Mississippi, Mahan cautioned against
complacency:

> Except Alaska, the United States has no outlying possession—no foot of
> ground inaccessible by land. Its contour is such as to present few points
> specially weak from their saliency, and all important parts of the fron-
> tiers can be readily attained—cheaply by water, rapidly by rail. The
> weakest frontier, the Pacific, is far removed from the most dangerous
> of possible enemies. The internal resources are boundless as compared
> with present needs; we can live off ourselves indefinitely in "our little
> corner," to use the expression of a French officer to the author. Yet
> should that little corner be invaded by a new commercial route through
> the Isthmus, the United States in her turn may have the rude awakening
> of those who have abandoned their share in the common birthright of
> all people, the sea.[52]

Again, Mahan reinforces a central message. More financial resources and
political capital must be spent to maintain America's dominant position in

the western hemisphere, for the creation of a Panama Canal will both create opportunities and invite numerous challenges.

Extent of territory, Mahan's third category, refers not to "the total number of square miles which a country contains, but the length of its coast-line and the character of its harbors." The critical issue in this respect is whether a country's population is adequate to protect the length of its coast. Great Britain, a small nation with a crowded population, clearly had sufficient bodies to patrol its waters and pack a significant naval punch. The Confederacy during the Civil War, conversely, had a long seaboard to defend with insufficient population to man the coastal defenses. The North's blockade of the southern ports was highly effective and a critical component in its success. But the outcome of the Civil War might have been very different if the South's population had been sufficient to defend its many ports: "Had the South had a people as numerous as it was warlike, and a navy commensurate to its other resources as a sea power, the great extent of its sea coast and its numerous inlets would have been elements of great strength . . . [The blockade] was a great feat, a very great feat; but it would have been an impossible feat had the Southerners been more numerous, and a nation of seamen."[53]

Size of population was not as important a factor to Mahan as one might imagine. In the period following the French Revolution, "the population of France was much greater than that of England," Mahan writes, "but in respect of sea power in general, peaceful commerce as well as military efficiency, France was much inferior to England." Mahan understood that a large population meant a large domestic market and this sometimes meant that foreign trade, and the naval expansion to facilitate it, was not prioritized. And while having adequate numbers to man an effective navy was one thing, the quality of seamen themselves was the more important consideration. In 1793, the British Navy made a concerted effort to employ Cornish miners, "reasoning from the conditions and dangers of their calling . . . that they would quickly fit into the demands of sea life."[54] In other words, the lot of the average Cornish tin miners was so dank and perilous that the relative respite offered by naval life ensured that their work rate and hardiness greatly surpassed that of their soft French counterparts. Of course, the ideal naval power would be blessed with a high numerical population infused with a Calvinist work ethic—like Britain or the Netherlands on a much larger scale.

In Mahan's opinion, national character was a vital condition affecting the sea power of a nation. Nations that aspire to strength, wealth, and global respect should have "aptitude for commercial pursuits." In this regard, Mahan compares successful trading empires such as the British and Dutch with plundering nations like Spain and Portugal, which sought gain through "avarice" alone. While the Iberian peoples were "bold, enterprising, temperate, patient of suffering, enthusiastic, and gifted with intense national feeling," they became blinded by gold-lust, failing to build the rudiments of a sound, diversified national economy: a functioning infrastructure, heavy industry, export-led manufactures, a sophisticated banking sector, and an entrepreneurial spirit that matched their spirit of adventure. On this matter, Mahan approvingly quotes a contemporary:

> The mines of Brazil were the ruin of Portugal, as those of Mexico and Peru had been of Spain; all manufactures fell into insane contempt; ere long the English supplied the Portuguese not only with clothes, but with all merchandise, all commodities, even to salt-fish and grain. After their gold, the Portuguese abandoned their very soil; the vineyards of Oporto were finally bought by the English with Brazilian gold, which had only passed through Portugal to be spread throughout England.

Whereas Napoleon Bonaparte had mockingly dubbed Britain a "nation of shopkeepers," Mahan made clear that this label was something to embrace: "The jeer, in so far as it is just, is to the credit of their wisdom and uprightness. [The British] were no less bold, no less enterprising, no less patient." By character and temperament, Mahan asserted, the British "were by nature business-men, traders, producers, negotiators . . . The tendency to trade, involving of necessity the production of something to trade with, is the national characteristic most important to the development of sea power."[55] The French were superior in temperament and industry to the Spanish and the Portuguese—"France has a fine country, an industrious people, an admirable position"—but common among Frenchmen was a self-defeating tendency to save, practice thrift, and live a cloistered existence in their beautiful nation. "Who was it said there are two kinds of nature," Mahan wondered, "human nature and French nature?"[56] There was timidity inherent in the French DNA, which contrasted unfavorably with the British sense of adventure, reflected in their greater propensity to travel and spend hard-earned resources on riskier investments overseas. Britons sagely regarded the hoarding of money as a route to adequate but second-class status. It was fine for a self-satisfied nation such as France, but the British Empire aspired toward a grander ideal, namely, global supremacy founded on the unrelenting accumulation of wealth:

It is said to be harder to keep than to make a fortune. Possibly; but the adventurous temper, which risks what it has to gain more, has much in common with the adventurous spirit that conquers worlds for commerce. The tendency to save and put aside, to venture timidly and on a like small scale, may lead to a general diffusion of wealth on a small scale, but not to the risks and development of external trade and shipping interests.[57]

Britain's acquisition of vast colonial territory—the "planting [of] healthy colonies," as Mahan phrased it—and the pecuniary benefits this brought to the mother country, was another realm where national traits played a decisive role. Britain's success, in Mahan's opinion, owed much to the fact that "colonies grow best when they grow of themselves, naturally," and that Britons did not feel compelled to remake their adopted homes into replicas of the mother country, as the French invariably did, or simply take what was valuable and send it back homeward, as was the case with Spain and Portugal.[58]

The English colonist naturally and readily settles down in his new country, identifies his interest with it, and though keeping an affectionate remembrance of the home from which he came, has no restless eagerness to return. In the second place, the Englishman at once and instinctively seeks to develop the resources of the new country in the broadest sense. In the former particular he differs from the French, who were ever longingly looking back to the delights of their pleasant land; in the latter, from the Spaniards, whose range of interest and ambition was too narrow for the full evolution of the possibilities of a new country.[59]

That Britons were better suited to the task of empire building owed much to the fact that the nations they colonized were invariably more inviting than the gray, wet, windswept country from which they came. The French had sunshine, an indigenous cuisine that was the envy of the world, and a cultural attachment to leisure that offended northern Europeans. How could the French compare with the British as a colonizing force? Leaving Blackburn for Burma was no great wrench for a Briton. But giving up Marseille for Martinique was likely to give a Frenchman far greater pause.

How did the character of Americans match up with their Old World competitors? Mahan viewed his countrymen favorably in that the U.S. population had an "instinct for commerce, bold enterprise in the pursuit of gain, and a keen scent for the trails that lead to it . . . It cannot be doubted that Americans will carry to them all their inherited aptitude for self-government and independent growth."[60] "Inherited" is the operative word. Mahan believed that Anglo-Saxon virtues had been passed down from Britain to its white settler progeny: Canada, Australia, New Zealand, and most important, the United States. But unleashing the nation's latent capacity for expansion required bold leadership. A population possessed of an enterprising spirit was not sufficient. Channeling these potentialities into a coherent strategy required strong guidance from an American president cognizant of the manner in which maritime commercial success determined a nation's place in the global pecking order.

Mahan's final condition affecting a nation's sea power was character of government, in which the book's contemporary resonance was made most explicit. While Mahan instinctively preferred democracy, he was sharply aware that less representative governments often made the better choices on behalf of their people:

> In the matter of sea power, the most brilliant successes have followed where there has been intelligent direction by a government fully imbued with the spirit of the people and conscious of its true general bent . . . but such free governments have sometimes fallen short, while on the other hand despotic power, wielded with judgment and consistency, has created at times a great sea commerce and a brilliant navy with greater directness than can be reached by the slower processes of a free people.[61]

Oliver Cromwell's England was a good example of what farsighted despotism might achieve. Cromwell's Navigation Act held that all imports into England or its colonies must be carried in English ships or in ships registered to the country where the goods originated. This decree was greatly resented by the Dutch, whose navy had carved out a niche as the preferred carrier service of that era—the FedEx of its day—but Cromwell's actions greatly benefited English commerce.

Sound leadership was thus essential in the building of naval greatness. In peacetime, "the government by its policy can favor the natural growth of a people's industries and its tendencies to seek adventure and gain by way of the sea." In wartime, "the influence of the government will be felt in its most legitimate manner in maintaining an armed navy, of a size commensurate with the growth of its shipping and the importance of the interests connected with it."[62] The parameters of U.S. foreign policy had to expand radically to allow the nation to thrive—and to survive. America lacked the capacity to project power, and this was a critical limitation in a world that was shrinking in the face of rapid technological advances. Worse than this, the U.S. Navy lacked the ability to adequately protect its major cities from blockade, a blind spot that could be ruthlessly exploited by any nation determined to challenge the status quo. In its war against France, Britain had successfully blockaded Brest, the Bay of Biscay, Toulon, and Cádiz. What if a hostile nation attempted to do the same to Boston, New York, Delaware, the Chesapeake, and the Mississippi? Mahan was determined that throughout the twentieth century the United States would emulate the forceful, prescient Great Britain, not the wasteful, defensive France.

Mahan's vision for America corresponded fairly closely with the reality that unfolded throughout the twentieth century. Historians are divided on whether the United States is an "Empire," an "Empire in Denial," or an explicitly anti-imperial power.[63] Irrespective of which term best encapsulates America's capabilities and intentions, the nation's route to achieving unrivaled global interventionist capability was the acquisition of geographically dispersed military installations—such as Okinawa, Japan; Holy Loch, Scotland; Diego Garcia; Guantánamo Bay, Cuba; and more than *seven hundred* other bases across the world—in precisely the manner favored by Mahan.[64] Mahan recognized that America, blessed with abundant natural resources, need not acquire colonies in the fashion of Britain, Spain, and France. Indeed, the military expert John E. Pike observed in 2009 that "even if the entire Eastern Hemisphere has drop-kicked" the United States from every base on its territory, the American military should still be able to "run the planet from Guam and Diego Garcia by 2015."[65]

This is what differentiates the American empire from its predecessors. Charles V, Philip II, Louis XIV, Napoleon Bonaparte, Lord Palmerston, and Benjamin Disraeli had expanded their nations' power primarily through the sword. All that America required was a peaceful world in which free trade was practiced. In this benign environment, America's inherent advantages—a people protected by two vast oceans, self-sufficient in vital natural resources, and able to sustain a growing population through large-scale immigration—made its ascendancy virtually ordained. Mahan's achievement was to make this so lucid.

Mahan's foreign-policy vision was driven by an instinctive "realism"—the notion that a nation's actions in international affairs must be driven by self-interest. He agreed with the British philosopher Thomas Hobbes that international politics was driven by a struggle for power. Conflict in the international system was inevitable—indeed, it was ennobling and virtuous in certain circumstances—and such circumstances precluded most countries from practicing anything that resembled altruism in world affairs. Unlike his friend Theodore Roosevelt, he was not stirred by Rudyard Kipling's call to take up the "White Man's Burden" and improve the lot of less fortunate nations through selfless but stern colonial instruction. He admired Great Britain's willingness to rule multiple territories and believed these subjugated people benefited from their acceptance of British values, laws, and models of governance. But America possessed sufficient power and natural resources to eschew such activities as an unnecessary encumbrance. Mahan drew the lessons from history he deemed pertinent to the United States at the end of the nineteenth century; he did not believe that the nation should follow the historical experience of any other nation to the letter. He was a nuanced, contextual thinker.

In addition to this geopolitical particularism, Mahan concurred with the Scottish political economist Adam Smith that self-reliance and the pursuit of individual advantage would create a virtuous cycle of wealth creation that might benefit all socioeconomic strata. If the people of all nations worked hard and looked after their own, some kind of global equilibrium might be attainable, in the sense that wealthy nations were satisfied nations and that conflict, while unavoidable, might be curtailed in time through this diffusion of wealth. He was less convinced by another Enlightenment thinker, Immanuel Kant, who believed that "Perpetual Peace" might be achieved if nations had the bravery and foresight to subsume their national interest in the name of a larger good guided by a supranational entity—a league of nations. This notion was fanciful and potentially dangerous, in Mahan's opinion. A more peaceful world would be achieved by individual nation-states practicing the Mahanian virtues of free trade, export-led commerce, and the creation of advanced financial institutions, to enable a nation to invest adventurously and profitably across the world. This would ensure that all nations had a vital economic stake in the maintenance of global stability. "Peace" would be achieved from the bottom up, not downward from abstract Kantian heights.

Mahan's magnum opus was received rapturously upon its publication in 1890. Theodore Roosevelt holed himself up in his library over the weekend of May 10–11 and read the book from cover to cover. Delighted by what he had read, he wrote a warm note to Mahan singing its praises: "During the last two days I have spent half my time, busy as I am, in reading your book. That I found it interesting is shown by the fact that having taken it up, I have gone straight through and finished it . . . It is a *very* good book—admirable; and I am greatly in error if it does not become a naval classic."[66]

According to Edmund Morris, Roosevelt's most eloquent biographer, America's future president "flipped the book shut a changed man."[67] In a review in *The Atlantic Monthly*, Roosevelt praised Mahan's skill in "subordinating detail to mass-effects" and extolled his mastery of French sources. But the main purpose of Roosevelt's review was to set out his store as Mahan's foremost champion, to make clear what lessons his book held for the United States. What America needed more than anything else, Roosevelt asserted, was a "large navy, composed not merely of cruisers, but containing also a full proportion of powerful battleships able to meet those of any other nation. It is not economy, it is niggardly and foolish short-sightedness, to cramp our naval expenditures while squandering money right and left on everything else, from pensions to public buildings." The *Chicago Times* admitted that it was "startling" to discover that "control of the sea has throughout history been the prime factor in deciding the leadership, the prosperity, and often the existence of nations, and . . . by throwing away her commercial marine and the occupations related to it [America] has deprived herself of the very means of creating a navy."[68]

But the book's warm reception in America was nothing compared to the enthusiasm its publication engendered in Britain and Germany. *The Times* of London decreed that Mahan's achievement was of an order that British historians had yet to emulate, that the United States now stood "first in order of merit in the production of naval historical works which are truly philosophical."[69] An appreciative reviewer for *Blackwood's Magazine* touched upon the prime reason for the book's appeal in Britain, noting that it "might almost be said to be a scientific inquiry into the causes which have made England great."[70] In 1893, Mahan visited England and was hosted for dinner by Captain William H. Henderson of HMS *Edgar*. In an effusive toast to his distinguished guest, Henderson joked that the Royal Navy owed to Mahan's instructive book the "£3,000,000 just voted for the increase of the navy." Later that summer, Mahan dined with Queen Victoria and Kaiser Wilhelm of Germany. The kaiser sent a telegram to Mahan declaring that he was "devouring" his book and later ordered that a copy be placed on every ship in the German fleet. Theodore Roosevelt wrote to the German ambassador, Hermann Speck von Sternburg, that "I am glad Mahan is having such influence with your people, but I wish he had more influence with his own. It is very difficult to make this nation wake up."[71] Mahan was awarded honorary degrees from Oxford and Cambridge Universities. During a private dinner at 10 Downing Street, Prime Minister Lord Rosebery told Mahan that "no literary work in his time had caused such enthusiasm as *Sea Power*."[72] In 1894, *The Times* declared Mahan to be the "new Copernicus"— that Mahan had revolutionized naval history in the same way as the great Polish thinker had remade astronomy.[73]

This adulation transformed Mahan into one of the most prominent writers of the late nineteenth century. But he still found time to grouse that Britain's swoon had not been replicated at home. "Recognition is pleasant, particularly after the almost entire absence of it at home," Mahan complained to his wife. "Except Roosevelt, I don't think my work gained me an entrée into a single American social circle."[74] With rather more grace, Mahan wrote to his one and only big-hitting American fan that he had "derived great satisfaction from the lavish expressions of appreciations given to me personally—that is, to my work."[75] Appreciative words aside, Mahan was disappointed that his name carried greater luster in Britain than in the United States. While he had dined with Queen Victoria and Prime Minister Rosebery, invites to President Benjamin Harrison's White House were noticeable in their absence. But given the choice to gain entrée into just one American's social circle in 1890, Theodore Roosevelt would be at the top of most people's lists. Mahan's enduring legacy as an architect of American naval expansion owed more to Roosevelt's good opinion than all the bouquets that England could offer.

From 1888 to 1895, Theodore Roosevelt worked for the New York Civil Service Commission, before serving a two-year stint as president of the board of the New York City Police Commissioners. These relatively low-key roles belied Roosevelt's vast potential for national leadership, evident to most seasoned political observers at the time. Intellectually inquisitive and historically literate, as evidenced by *The Naval War of 1812*, Roosevelt made a strong impression on whomever he came into contact with. As John Hay, a future secretary of state, memorably recounted: "I have heard Mr. Rudyard Kipling tell how he used to drop in at the Cosmos Club at half-past ten or so in the evening, and then young Roosevelt would come and pour out projects, discussions of men and politics, criticisms of books . . . 'I sat in the chair opposite,' said Kipling, 'and listened and wondered, until the universe seemed to be spinning round and Theodore was the spinner.' "[76]

Roosevelt was nonetheless skeptical of those individuals who espoused big ideas based on cold, abstract reasoning, who lacked practical experience in a cognate field and a well-defined moral compass. He remarked, "Character is far more important than intellect to the race as to the individual." As his career progressed to high office, he complained, "Oh, how I wish I could warn all my countrymen . . . against that most degrading of processes, the deification of mere intellectual acuteness, wholly unaccompanied by moral responsibility."[77]

These cautionary words partly explain why Roosevelt viewed Mahan so favorably. He respected his naval experience and his duty in the Civil War, even if he was an unskilled and reluctant sailor and lacked the masculine virtues—an ability to hunt, fight, climb mountains, chase down robbers, and subsist in North Dakota's Badlands—that made Roosevelt such a colorful character. Mahan adhered to a deeply felt value system in the form of his devout Christianity and possessed a strong sense of right and wrong. He knew where he stood on all the great matters of diplomacy and morality that were posed to him throughout his career. Mahan's self-assurance, life experience, and depth of historical insight represented a potent combination that enthralled Roosevelt and led to him fervently championing his virtues. According to Warren Zimmermann, "Roosevelt acted as a self-appointed press agent for the *Influence of Sea Power upon History*."[78] The success of Mahan's book came as a distinct relief to John Hay, "as Theodore would now no longer feel obliged to make [us] all go . . . to hear his lectures."[79]

Although Roosevelt lacked a "bully pulpit" through the 1890s, his friend Henry Cabot Lodge, who represented Massachusetts in the U.S. Senate from 1893 to 1924, certainly had a forum for his ideas.[80] His career spanned two seminal wars for the United States, and his influence on both was profound. Austere and haughty, Lodge possessed a fine mind—he completed a doctoral dissertation in history at Harvard under the supervision of Henry Adams—and agreed with Mahan and Roosevelt that the United States had to exert itself much more forcefully on the international stage. Throughout the 1890s, the United States was a regional power, whose only unassisted victory over another nation had been its defeat of institutionally weak, revolution-prone Mexico in 1848. Lodge recognized that American territory, and the virtual limits of American power, was restricted to the North American continent and that this had to change. Like Japan up until recently, the United States possessed the second-largest economy in the world. And like Japan, America was a bit-part geostrategic player, content enough to pursue a singular path in its quiet corner of the world. But even America's fast-rising economic strength was looking a little shaky in the 1890s. In the midst of a depression that commenced in 1893, the acquisition of foreign markets appeared increasingly attractive to the leaders of American industry, and to ambitious politicians like Lodge and Roosevelt. Providing further impetus to overseas expansion, the U.S. Census Bureau had declared the continental frontier closed in 1890—Americans would have to look beyond their continent for acquiring additional territory. Across the ocean, the great European powers were carving up Africa in their scramble for colonial possessions. Many argued that the United States should be pursuing a similar path in the western hemisphere and the Pacific.

Lodge lacked the warmth and charisma to establish a national reputation—he was the archetypal Boston Brahmin in his wealth, seriousness, and lack of empathy for the "common man"—but with his keen mind and powerful oratory he became a major figure in the Senate. In 1895, Lodge made a speech on the Senate floor that owed a clear debt to Alfred Mahan:

> It was the sea power in history which enabled Rome to crush Hannibal, perhaps the greatest military genius of all time; it was the sea power which enabled England to bring Napoleon's empire to ruins . . . It is the sea power which is essential to the greatness of every splendid people. We are a great people; we control this continent; we are dominant in this hemisphere; we have too great an inheritance to be trifled with or parted with. It is ours to guard and to extend.[81]

Lodge's tribute to Mahan's theory of sea power tied the latter even tighter to the Republican Party. He wrote to his wife on his growing displeasure with the Democratic Cleveland presidency: "A year of this administration has convinced me, I think finally, that the future is with the Republican party—the outward necessary aspirations of the U.S. will only be fulfilled by the Republicans. With rare exceptions the Democrats know nothing of Sea Power—neither by knowledge nor by instinct."[82] Which side to back in the election of 1896—pitting the populist Democrat William Jennings Bryan against the pro-business Republican William McKinley—provoked no agonizing on Mahan's part. As he wrote to Samuel Ashe, "I have not found in the *speeches* of Mr. Bryan the proof that he is both intelligent and honest. He may be the one or the other, I can't find it in his speeches that he is both."[83]

He believed that a Bryan presidency would embolden and radicalize the labor movement and that his shortsighted preference for silver over gold would create rapid inflation and a slump in the value of the dollar—in short, that a Democratic victory would be a "terrible catastrophe" for the nation.[84] What Bryan might do to Mahan's beloved navy was disturbing. It thus came as a considerable relief to Mahan—and like-minded friends such as Roosevelt and Lodge—that McKinley defeated Bryan handily on November 3, 1896. The United States had elected a president whose views on an expansive economic and military strategy corresponded closely with Mahan's. President-elect McKinley wasted little time in proving this point by appointing Theodore Roosevelt to serve as his assistant secretary of the Navy. While Roosevelt doubted the sincerity of McKinley's dedication to a more muscular foreign policy—he remarked that he had all the backbone of a "chocolate éclair"—he was confident in his own ability to add ballast to the administration.[85]

Mahan and Roosevelt had maintained regular correspondence since the publication of *The Influence of Sea Power upon History,* and the latter's elevation to government hastened this flow—although Mahan's pen was the busier. In a candid letter to Roosevelt in May 1897, Mahan explained the purpose of his correspondence: "You will believe that when I write to you it is only to suggest thoughts, or give information, not with any wish to influence action, or to ask information. I have known myself too long not to know that I am the man of thought, not the man of action . . . The comparison may seem vain but it may be questioned whether Adam Smith could have realized upon his own ideas as Pitt did."[86]

Mahan was being a little coy in this instance for, as subsequent letters make clear, there is little to distinguish the desire to "suggest thoughts" and the "wish to influence action." The issue that Mahan pushed with the greatest energy was the necessity that the United States move swiftly to annex Hawaii. Japan had launched a highly ambitious program of naval building—taking a direct cue from Mahan's writings—that threatened to tilt the balance of power in the Pacific toward Japan. To assert American interests in the Pacific, and forestall Japan's potential advance, it was vital that McKinley take the Hawaiian Islands "under our wing," as Mahan suggestively put it to Roosevelt.[87] Mahan further pressed Roosevelt to lobby President McKinley for substantial increases to the naval budget, noting that "it is lamentable to have to insist on such commonplaces . . . but at times I despair of our country arousing until too late to avert prolonged and disastrous conflict."[88] Roosevelt replied that "all I can do towards pressing your ideas into effect will be done," affirming Mahan's efforts and inviting additional correspondence. He further confided that in an ideal world the United States would construct a canal through Nicaragua "at once," build a dozen battleships, annex Hawaii, and expel Spain from Cuba "tomorrow." Aware that these sentiments were incendiary, Roosevelt advised Mahan to be discreet on the issues raised in their correspondence: "I speak to you with the greatest freedom, for I sympathize with your views, and I have precisely the same idea of patriotism and of belief in and love for our country. But to no one else, excepting Lodge, do I talk like this."[89]

In August 1897, Roosevelt wrote to Mahan that "I wish I could get a chance to see you. There are a number of things about which I want to get your advice, and a number of things I would like to talk over with you."[90] The foreign-policy issue that Roosevelt wanted to discuss with Mahan above all was Spain's war against nationalist rebels in Cuba, and the myriad opportunities that the insurrection offered to the United States.

A Castilian proverb offers insight into Spain's shortcomings as a colonial power. In a bout of generosity, the story goes, God granted Spain a wonderful climate, fine grapes, and beautiful women. But when angels requested that he also give the nation effective political leadership, he refused, stating that granting this wish would make Spain heaven on earth—disincentivizing virtuous living in pursuit of the afterlife.[91] Spain's record of governing Cuba offered confirmation. Its colonial government was distant, repressive, and polarizing; the island's economy was hamstrung by Madrid's imposition of shortsighted restrictions on trade with other nations; and huge disparities in wealth, evident soon after Christopher Columbus's arrival in 1492, created tight-wound social tensions. In 1895, José Martí, the great Cuban nationalist and poet, sailed from the Dominican Republic to lead a popular revolt against Spanish rule. Just one month after his arrival, Martí was killed by the Spanish during the Battle of Dos Ríos. Cuban nationalists quickly overcame this setback and the insurrection gained force as the months progressed. The brutality of Spain's response increased proportionally with the threat posed to its imperial prestige. Its troops murdered, raped, and pillaged in an effort to terrorize its opponents into submission. The war was a humanitarian catastrophe for Cuba, and belligerent sections of the United States press attacked Spain for the massacres it perpetrated. For American expansionists, the Cuban Revolution represented a gilt-edged opportunity to fight a beatable European power in the name of a conveniently altruistic goal. The spoils of any victory against overstretched, territorially bloated, imperial Spain were likely to be significant. And with the dissolution of Spain's restrictive trade practices, U.S. business interests could penetrate Cuba's economy and make substantial profits. Sensing an economic opportunity, Henry Cabot Lodge declared in a speech to the Senate that "free Cuba would mean a great market to the United States; it would mean an opportunity for American capital."[92] Political momentum for a war against Spain had been gathering pace during the final years of the Cleveland administration. With a new Republican president in place, the clamor intensified.

William McKinley remains one of America's most enigmatic presidents, a legacy that he purposefully bequeathed. America's twenty-fifth president refused to commit himself to paper, so historians and biographers have no personal correspondence from which to fashion a portrait. His friends' papers are disappointingly guarded on the subject of McKinley's character. So we have in our possession just tidbits of evidence from which to draw our conclusions: McKinley was commended for gallantry several times during the Civil War, he was a devout Christian who refused to work on the Sabbath, and he was utterly devoted to his invalid wife, Ida Saxton, whose life was blighted by epileptic seizures. He was high-minded, virtuous and, like Mahan, something of a prude—chastising friends and colleagues for bad language or inappropriate anecdotes.[93] At the time of his inauguration, McKinley was an unknown quantity on foreign policy. In Congress he had avoided service on committees that attended to foreign or military affairs. Throughout the presidential campaign, he made no reference to Cuba, and he assured those who asked that there would be "no jingo nonsense" in his administration.[94] Having fought on Virginia's bloodstained battlefields during the Civil War, he evinced little interest in military adventure of the type that Theodore Roosevelt—who was too young to have fought in the conflict—believed was natural and ennobling. William McKinley was not, in other words, the obvious man to launch America's first war of imperial acquisition against a major European nation.

For Mahan, as for many other "jingos," Cuba was extremely important in geostrategic terms. Located 90 miles from Key West and measuring 760 miles in length, Mahan observed that its "positional value" was incalculable, and that a hostile navy in Santiago Bay "could very seriously incommode all access of the United States to the Caribbean mainland, and especially to the Isthmus." As Mahan described it, Florida, Cuba, Haiti, and Puerto Rico formed a long peninsular line interrupted by narrow passages to the sea. If this line was interrupted by an avowedly hostile power, then the Gulf of Mexico might be blocked, causing untold damage to American commerce.

This dismal potential outcome made Cuba as important—and potentially dangerous—to the United States as Ireland was to Great Britain.[95]

On February 15, 1898, the USS *Maine*, docked in Havana harbor, was destroyed by an explosion that claimed the lives of 260 of its 347 crew. Fitzhugh Lee, the U.S. consul general in Havana, witnessed the devastation. He noticed flames rising above the harbor walls, hurried down to establish the cause, and returned promptly to his office to inform Washington that the *Maine* had been sunk with the loss of many lives and that Spanish officers had been helpful and courageous in rescuing wounded Americans from the harbor as ammunition exploded around them. Lee was in no position to speculate on the cause of the explosion, but he noted, "I am inclined to think it was accidental."[96] The majority of Navy Department officials agreed with Lee's assessment, although some suspected a more malevolent cause.

The cause of the explosion eludes us even today, although foul play appears highly unlikely. For the past century, official investigators and amateur sleuths have attributed the destruction of the *Maine* to either an accidental coal bunker fire or a collision with a Spanish mine. There was less equivocation in 1898 when prominent American newspapers, and politicians such as Roosevelt and Lodge, instinctively attributed the "attack" on the *Maine* to Spanish skullduggery and demanded an appropriately fierce response from President McKinley. In the week following the explosion, William Randolph Hearst's New York *Journal* devoted eight pages daily to the sinking of the *Maine*. Lurid allegations stated as fact, such as "The *Maine* was destroyed by treachery" and "The *Maine* was split in two by an enemy's secret infernal machine," increased the *Journal*'s circulation from 416,885 copies on January 9 to 1,036,140 on February 18.[97] It even printed implausible diagrams showing how Spanish saboteurs had attached underwater mines to the hull and detonated them from the beach. When the illustrator Frederic Remington arrived in Cuba to find much ado about nothing, as the oft-recited story goes, he cabled Hearst: "There is no war. Request to be recalled." Hearst was said to have replied, "Please remain. You furnish the pictures, I'll furnish the war."[98] Joseph Pulitzer's *World* was more restrained, but its editors were similarly convinced that this was no accident. Taking their cue from New York's "yellow press," jingo editors from across the nation joined the action, although some believed that fighting Spaniards in Cuba was beneath the nation's dignity. As William A. White, a Kansas editor, wrote: "As between Cuba and Spain there is little choice. Both crowds are yellow-legged, garlic-eating, dagger-sticking, treacherous crowds—a mixture of Guinea, Indian and Dago. One crowd is as bad as the other. It is folly to spill good Saxon blood for that kind of vermin . . . Cuba is like a woman who lets her husband beat her a second time—she should have no sympathy."[99]

As the French ambassador to the United States observed, "A sort of bellicose fury has seized the American nation."[100] On March 14, Roosevelt, who was similarly spoiling for a fight, complained to Mahan, "I fear the President does not intend that we shall have war if we can possibly avoid it."[101] The beating of the war drum was deeply unsettling to the level-headed Mahan, who was genuinely appalled by the irresponsibility of the Hearst press and its chauvinistic aspirants across the nation. In a speech to the New Jersey chapter of the Society of the Cincinnati, he pleaded for restraint: "We should be very cautious in forming hasty conclusions in reference to such things as this disaster. People are liable to jump at conclusions at a great national crisis like this which might involve them seriously."[102] Mahan, still focused intently on the Pacific and on the transisthmian canal, was not convinced that an American war against Spain was a strategic priority.

President McKinley shared Mahan's caution, but the saber-rattling mood across the nation made it difficult for him to pursue a moderate course.[103] Seven weeks after the *Maine* tragedy, with no declaration of war against Spain in sight, McKinley was hung in effigy in Colorado. The Hearst press reported with satisfaction that the president's picture was commonly booed and hissed in New York theaters. As Ernest May writes,

> To maintain a business-like "hands-off" policy toward Cuba could easily infuriate veteran, Negro, church, or other groups in the party . . . In no circumstances could McKinley, either as a Republican or as a conservative, ignore his responsibility to maintain a united party . . .
>
> McKinley found himself faced with a terrible choice. He could embark on a war he did not want or defy public opinion, make himself unpopular, and risk at least the unseating of the Republican party if not the overthrow of what he conceived to be sound constitutional government.[104]

On March 28, a Naval Court of Inquiry issued a report that claimed presumptuously that the *Maine* had been destroyed "by the explosion of a submarine mine which caused the partial explosion of two or more of the forward magazines."[105] The logic of the battle cry "Remember the Maine! To hell with Spain!" had become impossible for McKinley to ignore.

On April 11, 1898, President McKinley's request for authorization to stop the fighting in Cuba was read out in the House of Representatives. The president's primary justification for U.S. intervention was startling in its humanitarian emphasis. He requested Congress

> to authorize and empower the President to take measures to secure a full and final termination of hostilities between the Government of Spain and the people of Cuba, and to secure in the island the establishment of a stable government, capable of maintaining order and observing its international obligations, insuring peace and tranquility and security of its citizens as well as our own, and to use the military and naval forces of the United States as may be necessary for these purposes.[106]

Thus McKinley sought war to protect Cubans, and Americans, from the deprivations of a particularly unpleasant conflict. In emotive terms he evoked the suffering of Cubans, "a dependent people striving to be free," who were being killed and maimed by "cruel, barbarous, and uncivilized practices of warfare." McKinley justified the conflict not in terms of America's national interest but "in the cause of humanity and to put an end to the barbarities, bloodshed, starvation, and horrible miseries now existing there, and which the parties to the conflict are either unable or unwilling to stop or mitigate."[107] His humanitarian casus belli allowed him to justify the conflict with some measure of sincerity. But as Ernest May astutely observes, McKinley led "his country unwillingly toward a war that he did not want for a cause in which he did not believe."[108] McKinley appeared to be a prisoner of events—dragged to war by a popular swelling of pugnacity.[109]

When the president's war message was announced, impromptu street parties sprang up across American towns and cities, the Stars and Stripes were unfurled in the hundreds of thousands, and young men patiently stood in line to volunteer, appreciatively accepting free drinks from men and kisses from the ladies.[110] The United States, not McKinley's administration, stood up, puffed out its chest, and picked a fight with Spain, mainly because it could—it was cathartic. War also served the useful purpose of tying the North and South together in a patriotic embrace just thirty-three years after the end of the Civil War. When Congress authorized McKinley's message and declared war on Spain on April 19, it disavowed the notion of imperial expansion. It fell to Albert J. Beveridge—a fast-rising political star who would serve as U.S. senator for Indiana from 1899 to 1911—to grasp the significance of the moment in a blissfully unvarnished speech justifying expansionary war. His words closely echo Mahan's view that the military's purpose is to protect and project commercial interests:

American factories are making more than the American people can use; American soil is producing more than they can consume. Fate has written our policy for us; the trade of the world must and shall be ours . . . And American law, American order, American civilization, and the American flag will plant themselves on shores hitherto bloody and benighted, but by those agencies of God henceforth to be made beautiful and bright.[111]

Mahan was enjoying a family vacation in Europe when he was summoned to advise his wartime government. In mid-March, Mahan had sent Roosevelt contingency plans for a "strict blockade" of Havana and the western half of Cuba in the event of war against Spain. While Mahan had doubts about the wisdom of prioritizing Cuban independence above what he viewed as more substantive strategic goals, he remained keen to prove his intellectual worth to Roosevelt and McKinley in this moment of crisis. Delighted with the strategic merits displayed in Mahan's blockade proposal, Roosevelt informed his mentor that "there is no question that you stand head and shoulders above the rest of us! You have given us just the suggestions we want, and I am going to show your letter to the Secretary."[112] Mahan's blockade of Cuba was incorporated into U.S. naval strategy when Secretary of the Navy John Davis Long instructed Rear Admiral William T. Sampson, commander of the North Atlantic Station, to follow the plan. Impressed by the blockade recommendation, President McKinley appointed Mahan to serve on a three-man Naval War Board—alongside Rear Admiral Montgomery Sicard and Rear Admiral Arent Schuyler Crowninshield—charged with coordinating U.S. strategy.

The newly constituted board's strategizing was aided by the fact that the enemy was hopelessly outgunned—a decrepit Spanish fleet faced a modern steel-hulled American navy consisting of four ten-thousand-ton first-class battleships, one six-thousand-ton second-class battleship, two armored cruisers, eleven protected cruisers, and a vast array of auxiliary cruisers, gunboats, and torpedo vessels. It was a war between the twentieth century and the nineteenth, and the victor was never in doubt. As Rear Admiral Pascual Cervera confided to his diary as war loomed in 1898, "We may and must expect a disaster. But as it is necessary to go to the bitter end, and as it would be a crime to say that publicly today, I hold my tongue and go forth resignedly to face the trials which God may be pleased to send me."[113] The trials that materialized were likely worse even than Cervera could imagine.

As Mahan voyaged back across the Atlantic from April 30 to May 7,

Admiral of the Navy George Dewey scored a remarkable victory against the Spanish fleet far from Cuba in the Pacific theater. In previous years, Mahan's Naval War College had carried out contingency planning for war against Spain, extolling the merits of an attack on the Philippines, its sprawling colony in the Pacific. On May 1, Dewey's Asiatic Squadron had followed this logic and destroyed the Spanish fleet led by Admiral Patricio Montojo y Pasarón. The battle was so one-sided that Dewey was able to place the American fusillade on hold so his men could eat breakfast. In the space of a few hours, at the cost of just one American life (induced by a heart attack), Spain's position in the Pacific was destroyed.

Mahan was delighted with Dewey's comprehensive victory but less enamored of the planning authority on which he served. He was quite happy to be put out of a job. On May 10, Mahan advised Secretary Long to disband the board and allocate all planning authority to a single naval officer on active duty. He believed that the unwieldy Naval War Board impeded effective decision making: "Individual responsibility . . . alone achieves results in war." Mahan's response to finding himself in a position of genuine power and influence was admirable. If the apocryphal quote attributed to Henry Kissinger is correct and "power is the ultimate aphrodisiac," it certainly didn't excite Alfred Mahan. Nevertheless, Long was not impressed by Mahan's selflessness, and the board continued in its existing form with Mahan, in Warren Zimmermann's words, "the dominant figure."[114]

On May 19, 1898, Rear Admiral Cervera made a fateful decision to dock his fleet in Cuba's Santiago Bay. Hemmed in by Mahan's blockade, Cervera was unable to dodge the heavily armed American ships—the *Indiana, New York, Oregon, Iowa, Texas*, and *Brooklyn*—that loomed ominously in the distance. After six weeks of inaction, Cervera concluded that he had little choice but to face his destiny with as much vim as possible. On July 3, in full daylight, Cervera sailed his flagship, *Infanta Maria Teresa*, directly into the path of the American battleships in the hope that the distraction might allow the rest of his ships to break for the open sea. The Battle of Santiago Bay lasted just four hours. It is estimated that 160 Spaniards were killed, 240 were wounded, and 1,800 were captured, including Cervera himself. One American was killed during the battle and no U.S. warship suffered any damage. As Mahan wrote after the conflict, "We cannot expect ever again to have an enemy so entirely inept as Spain showed herself to be."[115] Steeped in the history of the great Anglo-French naval battles, Mahan could muster little enthusiasm for writing about the Spanish-American War. His *Lessons of the War with Spain*, published in 1899, was an underwhelming affair.

The main lesson he conveyed was that the United States should never allow itself to become as unprepared and technologically deficient as Spain was in 1898.

Spain had been trounced at sea—its fleet incapacitated—and it took heavy punishment from the U.S. Army in Cuba itself. Theodore Roosevelt had been disappointed to miss the Civil War—and by the fact that his father did not serve—and he viewed the Spanish-American War as an opportunity to hone this martial aspect of his character. He resigned as assistant secretary of the Navy when hostilities commenced and set about raising a volunteer force, the First United States Volunteer Cavalry ("Rough Riders," as they were colloquially known), to do battle against Spain in Cuba. The force mirrored Theodore Roosevelt's myriad interests, background, and personality traits, comprising Dakota ranch hands, Ivy League scholars, East Coast polo players, cowboys, and policemen. The Rough Riders scored a much-storied victory against entrenched Spanish forces at San Juan Hill, and Colonel Theodore Roosevelt emerged from the war a popular hero. But it was the two crushing naval victories that paved the way for America's ultimate success. The decapitation of Spain's Caribbean fleet, allied with Mahan's suffocating blockade, detached their vulnerable forces from the Spanish mainland some four thousand miles away. Hostilities ceased on August 12, 1898, and a formal peace treaty between the United States and Spain was signed in Paris on December 10. Cuban nationalists played no substantive role in the peace negotiations—they would learn their fate from afar. An important precedent was established that would hold true through the twentieth century: the destiny of newly liberated colonial peoples would be dictated by great powers at "international conferences" with less than pure motives.

America's victory against Spain was one-sided, predictable perhaps, but it sent shock waves across the nations of the Old World—France, Britain, Russia, and Germany—long accustomed to viewing the United States as economically powerful, territorially sated, and avowedly isolationist: a second-tier power in world affairs. The United States was no longer a suitable target for embassy belt-tightening. As America celebrated and Spain lay supine, *The Times* of London offered a prescient editorial: "This war must in any event effect a profound change in the whole attitude and policy of the United States. In future America will play a part in the general affairs of the world such as she has never played before. When the American people realize this, and they realize novel situations with remarkable promptitude, they will not do things by halves."[116]

It was with "remarkable promptitude" that President McKinley recognized the strategic and economic possibilities opened up by his famous victory. Although he initially harbored doubts about the wisdom of an imperial landgrab, informing Secretary of State John Hay soon after Dewey's victory that he would be happy enough with "a port and necessary appurtenances," he had been pushed toward bold actions yet again by the popular clamor to realize the spoils of war.[117] At the war's end, American forces occupied Cuba, the Philippines, Guam, and Puerto Rico. More than ten million people—Hispanics, Indians, Polynesians, Chinese, and Japanese—were now in Washington's care. Dominating the North American continent in the name of Manifest Destiny was one thing. But the United States now had in its grasp the power to transform itself into a bona fide imperial nation—a possibility that some Americans found seductive.

Ostensible independence was granted to Cuba—in keeping with the original declaration of war—but the Platt Amendment, passed enthusiastically by Congress and reluctantly by a helpless Cuban Assembly in 1899, transferred Guantánamo Bay to the American military on a perpetual lease and gave the U.S. government virtual carte blanche to intervene in Cuba's affairs when its commercial and strategic interests were threatened. This was "independence" of the most compromised type. Puerto Rico, Guam, and the Philippines were simply annexed in their entirety. President McKinley later told a group of fellow Methodists that he had prayed to God to seek guidance on what to do with the Philippines. The Almighty, an apparent devotee of realpolitik, answered that independence might leave the islands open to French or German imperialism—an unconscionable threat to American-led stability in the Pacific—and that the Filipinos were regardless "unfit for self-government." God advised McKinley "that there was nothing left for us to do but to take them, and by God's grace do the very best we could by them, as our fellow men for whom Christ also died."[118] Filipinos were not pleased to lose one colonial master only to have another take its place so quickly. A popular insurrection against U.S. rule commenced in 1899. In embracing imperialism with such equanimity, the pragmatic philosopher William James wondered how America could "puke up its ancient soul . . . in five minutes without a wink of squeamishness."[119]

Mahan believed that annexing the Philippine archipelago in its entirety was likely to create significant problems for the United States. As he confided to a considerably more gung-ho Henry Cabot Lodge, "I myself, though rather an expansionist, have not fully adjusted myself to the idea of taking them, from our own standpoint of advantage."[120] His preferred option was to keep the island of Luzon, with Manila and Subic Bay—an ideally situated Pacific base for the United States—and leave the remaining islands to Spain. Mahan's skepticism about the wisdom of annexing the Philippines looks insightful in retrospect. The United States would spend the next fifty years there, quelling one popular revolt after another, resorting to brutal tactics that sullied its name in the court of world opinion and revealed an obvious disconnect between virtuous words and unpleasant deeds. Direct imperial rule was a wholly unpleasant experience for America. The informal commercial empire that Mahan favored better allowed the United States to cling to claims of higher virtue vis-à-vis its European competitors. The reality of empire jarred with America's lily-white self-image.

While Mahan had doubts about swallowing the Philippines whole, he was nevertheless delighted that America had strengthened its position in the Pacific and Caribbean at scant material cost. He wrote to Henry Cabot Lodge congratulating him on his skill in smoothing the ratification of the Treaty of Paris through the Senate, declaring that "the country is now fairly embarked on a career which will be beneficent to the world and honorable to ourselves in the community of nations. I try to respect, but cannot, the men who utter the shibboleth of self-government, and cloud therewith their own intelligence, by applying it to people in the childhood stage of race development."[121] Mahan's racist paternalism, entirely unremarkable of a man of that era cocooned in a privileged milieu, explains why he thought giving much of the Philippines back to Spain was a good idea—the indigenous population simply lacked the sophistication to establish stability and a measure of prosperity in the nation. Even inept Spanish rule was preferable to self-rule. The notion of national self-determination was ludicrous to Mahan; it was a well-intentioned but dangerous chimera.

Another fashionable theory to which Mahan objected vehemently was that international collaboration designed to limit armaments and mediate conflict was a potential route to world peace. Nothing in history suggested to him that such a course was plausible. An opportunity to vent his spleen on this issue was presented when Secretary of State John Hay appointed Mahan as a delegate to the First Hague Conference of 1899. Created at the behest of Tsar Nicholas II, the conference was designed to seek constructive agreement on ways to limit the production of armaments, outlaw certain weapons systems that were currently in development (submarines and poison gas were the two most prominent targets), create diplomatic machinery to arbitrate on future conflicts, and extend the protections afforded by the Geneva Convention of 1863 to naval warfare. Twenty-six nations attended this hugely ambitious conference, which was predictably mocked in the American press as the "Czar's Peace Picnic."[122]

The skepticism was understandable in many respects. Russia had fallen behind its great power competitors in the development of advanced weaponry, and the notion that the conference was a ruse to have the world crouch to Moscow's modest level was hardly fanciful. Mahan's "own persuasion" was that "the immediate cause of Russia calling for the Conference was the shock of our late war, resulting in the rapprochement of the U.S. and Great Britain and our sudden appearance in Asia, as the result of a successful war."[123] Consequently, Mahan did not take the conference seriously, using his ten weeks at The Hague to finish some articles, correspond with his publishers, and advise the Russians on their plans to establish their own Naval War College. In lambasting the conference, Mahan formulated a powerful critique of pseudoscientific, multilateral institution-building that Henry Cabot Lodge deployed against Woodrow Wilson in 1919.

Mahan had no patience with the idea—predicated on universal restraint based on trust—of binding restrictions being placed on naval building. As he explained to the eminent British admiral Lord Fisher of Kilverstone, "The conditions which constitute the necessity for a navy, and control its development, have within the past year changed for the United States so markedly that it is impossible yet to foresee, with certainty, what degree of naval strength may be needed to meet them."[124] He also opposed the extension of the 1863 Geneva Convention to protect those involved in naval warfare. During the Civil War, Mahan had been appalled that the British had rescued Confederate sailors from vessels sunk by Union ships—these men would invariably find a way back home to rejoin the battle to uphold secession. Humanity had no place in naval conflict, and that is exactly what the extension of the Geneva Convention promised. Third parties should steer well clear of the belligerents. Defeated sailors should either die in the water or be taken as prisoners of war—it was only fair that naval victories should be recognized by imposing the harshest penalties on the defeated enemy. Finally, Mahan made a strong case "not to sign away [the] right to maintain justice by war by entering into a pledge beforehand to arbitrate, <u>except</u> on questions most strictly limited and defined."[125] As the United States assumed Brobdingnagian dimensions, it should resist attempts by Lilliputians to constrict its freedom of action. The notion that the world's nations would agree to collaborate in this unprecedented fashion was a philosophical thought-experiment, not a serious proposal.

Underlying Mahan's critique of the Hague Conference's utopianism was the belief that war was a necessary, beneficial stage in the development of nations. As he explained to the reformer-philanthropist Grace Hoadley Dodge, "The shocking evils of war have so impressed [advocates of 'international arbitration'] that they fail to recognize its moral character. Yet worse things can happen to a man—far worse—than to be mangled by a shell, or to a nation than to be scourged by war." He concluded that if the United States avoided necessary wars against abhorrent enemies, under the cover of international arbitration, "it will have been better for the nation that it had never been born."[126] These remarks seem callous, and they did not convince Dodge. But Mahan was not blindly valorizing all wars and cruelly downplaying their human cost. He simply believed that some wars had to be fought to the end, no matter the blood sacrifice involved. In an article titled "The Peace Conference and the Moral Aspect of War," Mahan argued convincingly that international arbitration during America's war of independence, or during the Civil War, would have damaged America's development and self-respect. Do-gooders can get in the way of natural justice. Compromise peaces are extremely damaging in wars against enemies that pose an existential threat. Unconditional surrender was Mahan's mantra in such circumstances—just as it was Franklin Delano Roosevelt's forty years hence.

In the 1900 general election, William McKinley scored another decisive victory against William Jennings Bryan, winning 292 electoral votes to Bryan's 176. McKinley's victory had been aided by his popularly acclaimed choice of Theodore Roosevelt as his running mate. But as is often the case, Roosevelt was worried that the assumption of largely ceremonial duties might rob him of his vitality and bore him half to death. His concerned friend Mahan quickly identified a silver lining, advising Roosevelt to view the vice presidency as a benign form of imprisonment:

> I do, however, rejoice in one thing; and that is that you are withdrawn perforce, and not by your own volition, for a prolonged rest from the responsibilities and cares of office . . . A very sagacious clergyman once remarked to me on the providential ordering in the life of St. Paul—whose career, I think, you will agree was at least strenuous, by which in midcourse he was arrested, and spent two years of enforced inactivity under Felix in Judaea, followed by two more in the Roman captivity. The total, four, as you will observe, is just a Vice Presidential term; and I trust this period may be to you, as it was to him, a period of professional rest coupled with great intellectual advance and ripening.[127]

Roosevelt's contemplative incarceration was cut abruptly short when a young anarchist named Leon Czolgosz shot President McKinley in Buffalo on September 6, 1901. A telegram was dispatched to Roosevelt, hiking in the Adirondacks at the time, to inform him of the situation: "The president is critically ill. His condition is grave. Oxygen is being given. Absolutely no hope." A second telegram arrived soon after, stating: "The president appears to be dying and members of the Cabinet in Buffalo think you should lose no time coming."[128] As Roosevelt received these telegrams on September 14, McKinley died from gangrene caused by his wounds. Roosevelt hurried to Buffalo to meet the exalted fate he had long expected. At just forty-two years of age, he was set to become the youngest president in American history. One of his daughters allegedly remarked that "Father always wanted to be the bride at every wedding and the corpse at every funeral." He had certainly assumed the limelight now, and not everyone relished the prospect.[129] McKinley's chief political strategist, Mark Hanna, crystallized the fears of many Republicans concerned by Roosevelt's domestic progressivism and muscular foreign-policy instincts when he despaired, "Now look! That damned cowboy is president of the United States."[130]

Roosevelt's presidency witnessed eight years of assertive diplomatic activity designed to realize many of the goals that Mahan had been urging for the past decade. In 1903, President Roosevelt encouraged a powerful minority of wealthy Panamanian landholders to demand independence from Colombia. He amply displayed his sincerity by dispatching U.S. ships to the region to exert pressure on Colombia's political leadership which, fearing the devastation that would accompany war, caved quickly. On November 3, 1903, Panama declared its independence and published a constitution drafted well in advance by Washington. The path was now clear for the United States to carve a "Panama Canal" through harsh terrain in a tropical, malarial climate, one of the most challenging engineering feats in history. The task was completed with consummate efficiency and singular brute determination—some fifty-five hundred workers died in the process. The canal was formally opened ten years later, in the summer of 1914.[131] At a cabinet meeting called soon after the declaration of Panama's independence, Roosevelt tested a defense of the amoral means he had deployed to separate Panama from Colombia, asking Secretary of War Elihu Root if he had answered his critics. Root replied, "You certainly have, Mr. President. You have shown that you were accused of seduction and you have conclusively proved that you were guilty of rape."[132] Mahan was predictably delighted with the outcome and cared little whether it was achieved by fair means or foul. American ships traveling from New York to San Francisco no longer had to navigate the Cape of Good Hope, slashing the distance from fourteen thousand to six thousand miles. The United States could now move its fleet swiftly between the Pacific and the Atlantic, depending on the threats posed on either flank.[133] The creation of the Panama Canal was an essential prerequisite in making the twentieth-century America's.

Roosevelt further reinforced U.S. supremacy in the western hemisphere through asserting its unilateral right to intervene militarily in the Caribbean or Central America if economic and political instability threatened its interests. The so-called Roosevelt Corollary to the Monroe Doctrine stated that "chronic wrongdoing . . . may in America, as elsewhere, ultimately require intervention by some civilized nation, and in the Western Hemisphere the adherence of the United States to the Monroe Doctrine may force the United States, however reluctantly, in flagrant cases of such wrongdoing or impotence, to the exercise of an international police power." Mahan had long worried that the Monroe Doctrine of 1823—warning European nations to refrain from further interference in Latin America—was not accorded sufficient respect by the major European powers. He was delighted that Roosevelt had acted so strongly in asserting America's police role in the region. Europe should now have little doubt that encroachment in America's backyard would be met with a swift response. In a similar fashion, Caribbean and Central American leaders knew that they had to act in accordance with America's interests lest they be punished. Subsequent presidents, including Woodrow Wilson, would follow the logic of the Roosevelt Corollary in ordering U.S. military action in Cuba, Nicaragua, Haiti, and the Dominican Republic.

As a president wholly in accord with Mahan on the preeminence of naval power, Roosevelt transformed the U.S. Navy into one of the top three in the world. By 1907, the Atlantic Fleet comprised sixteen state-of-the-art battleships. According to Secretary of the Navy Victor H. Metcalf, this force constituted "in weight and numbers combined, the most powerful fleet of battle ships under one command in any navy."[134] In 1908, the United States was ranked second among naval powers in the index of capital ships. In a remarkable show of force, President Roosevelt ordered four battleship squadrons, with attendant escorts, to circumnavigate the globe—a vast fleet manned by 12,793 sailors.[135] Upending the conventional wisdom that secrecy should surround the movement of battleships, the so-called Great White Fleet advertised its movements well in advance to attract the maximum media exposure. Indeed, a press center was established on one of the ships, the USS *Connecticut*, to feed information to the large pool of reporters invited to hitch a ride, who, it was hoped, would file patriotic copy with their editors back home. Only Britain's navy bettered America's in size and technological prowess. The Great White Fleet was powerful testimony to Mahan's influence as a strategist; Roosevelt's presidency surpassed his wildest dreams. During his final months in office, Roosevelt compiled a list of his greatest presidential achievements, placing his success in doubling the size of the U.S. Navy at the top of the list, ahead of the construction of the Panama Canal and his successful mediation of the Russo-Japanese War.[136]

As Europe edged toward the primordial bloodletting of World War I, the United States stood on the cusp of greatness. Between 1860 and 1910, America's population had tripled, from thirty-one million to more than ninety-two million—a demographic revolution made possible by mass migration from southern and eastern Europe.[137] This massive influx of human capital, allied with the vast boundaries of America's fertile landmass, allowed it to overtake Great Britain as the preeminent economic power by the turn of the twentieth century. In contrast to Britain, however, American industry mostly responded to domestic demand—just 5 percent of U.S. output was sent abroad compared to the equivalent British figure of 25 percent. As the historian John Darwin observes of fin de siècle Washington, "The economic colonies of American business lay in the west and south of the United States, not overseas. There was no consensus for adopting the aggressive style or military preparedness of the other world states. But what turned out to be critical in shaping American views was the astonishing growth of the U.S. industrial economy, setting off fears of exclusion from other world markets."[138] Mahan's Anglo-American-dominated global trading system—facilitated by the sagacious acquisition of strategically located military bases in 1898—had not yet come to pass. But the domestic market appeared to be reaching a point of saturation. As America's economic health became increasingly connected with a stable international environment conducive to free trade, so its days of detachment from European affairs became numbered.

Theodore Roosevelt left the White House in March 1909 and was succeeded by his secretary of war, William Howard Taft.[139] A man not remembered for his charisma, or indeed for many of the skills usually deemed useful when winning elections, Taft still had sufficient savvy to consign William Jennings Bryan to his third defeat at the polls—a victory that was aided by Roosevelt's strong endorsement of Taft's merits as a principled Progressive, emphasizing a sense of continuity in leadership. Yet Taft's presidency was markedly different from Roosevelt's in the sense that his leadership was purposefully low-key—Taft disliked the way Roosevelt stretched executive power to the constitutional breaking point—and that Taft was less confrontational in his approach to big business. While he issued eighty antitrust lawsuits while president, he refused to criticize specific companies or business practices directly. Progressives of many hues, including Theodore Roosevelt himself, were disappointed with what they took to be Taft's timorous leadership, conveying the erroneous impression that he was kowtowing to wealthy interests. In a speech in April 1912, Roosevelt declared that "the Republican party is now facing a grave crisis. It is to decide whether it will be as in the days of Lincoln, the party of the plain people . . . or whether it will be the party of privilege and of special interest, the heir to those who were Lincoln's most bitter opponents."[140]

When Roosevelt failed to wrest the nomination from Taft at the Republican National Convention on June 22, 1912, he left the GOP and formed the Progressive Party to contest the presidency in the forthcoming election. Running on a platform that called for woman suffrage, new inheritance and income taxes, social welfare legislation for women and infants, and wholesale improvements to America's transport infrastructure, the Bull Moose Party (as it became known following Roosevelt's response that he was "as strong as a bull moose" to a journalist's question regarding his health) attracted many supporters impressed by its Progressive agenda and the breakaway candidate's stature as a forceful former president with a formidable record of achievement.

Mahan was on the conservative wing of the Republican Party and so was dismayed by Roosevelt's steeply Progressive policy agenda. He was consequently torn by the Republican split of 1912, as he confided to his friend Henry White:

Personally, my views are nearer those of Taft than those of Roosevelt, but I have lost faith in the former as able to guide the ship, because he has not commanded the confidence of his people, as I think Roosevelt has . . . If I see reason to believe that Roosevelt can be carried in by a third party, I shall vote for him and use any influence I can in the same direction. But if I conclude that the only effect of the third party will be to defeat the Republicans and put in the Democrats, I shall vote for Taft.[141]

The only thing Mahan knew for certain was that the Democrats were unfit for office, and their leader, Woodrow Wilson, whom he had met for lunch in New York City earlier in the year, was worryingly dogmatic in his approach to domestic and foreign affairs:

> We are threatened, and I fear the accession to power of a doctrinaire party—the Democratic—which is dominated by a number of theories which can by no means be made to fit present facts; like the wrong key to a lock. Among others [is] that of keeping the navy well below strength, and ignoring all the dangerous contingencies of the present by the simple process of shutting their eyes, and taking a sleeping potion of the doctrines of a man who died nearly a century ago. Perhaps you know the name Jefferson. He made a hideous mess in his own day, and yet has a progeny of backwoodsmen and planters who think what he taught a great success.[142]

Mahan identified in Wilson's Jeffersonian disposition an abstract and theoretical quality—one that might ultimately lead to policies "which can by no means be made to fit present facts." On Election Day, Mahan cast his vote for Roosevelt, surmising that he was better placed than Taft to stop Wilson in his tracks and to pursue a purposeful yet carefully calibrated policy toward the fast-escalating military tensions in Europe. Mahan believed that much rested on the election of 1912.

2

★

KANT'S BEST HOPE

WOODROW WILSON

Not in universal harmony, nor in fond dreams of unbroken peace, rest now the best hopes of the world . . . Rather in the competition of interests . . . in these jarring sounds which betoken that there is no immediate danger of the leading peoples turning their swords into ploughshares—are to be heard the assurance that decay has not touched yet the majestic fabric erected by so many centuries of courageous battling. —ALFRED THAYER MAHAN

The election of 1912 was one of the most ill-tempered and intellectually charged in American history.[1] Republican loyalties had been split by Theodore Roosevelt's bolt for the convention exit, the Democrats had nominated a southern-born Ivy League professor as their candidate, and support for Eugene V. Debs's Socialist Party was approaching a historic high. It was one of those rare years when voters could not complain about lack of choice. To make the campaign even more compelling, the three main candidates attacked each other with ill-concealed rancor. The Republican antagonists, Taft and Roosevelt, clashed in print and on the campaign trail. On foreign affairs, Roosevelt alleged that Taft was blindly focused on securing international cooperation at the expense of America's national sovereignty. In an article for *Outlook* magazine, for example, Roosevelt dismissed the arbitration treaty that Taft had secured with Great Britain as "a sham" that was dangerous to American security. President Taft had failed to put "righteousness first," in Roosevelt's harsh estimation. This intervention, combined with Henry Cabot Lodge's blocking maneuver in the Senate, killed the treaty before it reached the Oval Office. A furious Taft observed of Roosevelt (with more than a hint of veracity), "The truth is he believes in war and wishes to be a

Napoleon and to die on the battlefield. He has the spirit of the old berserk-ers."[2] Unsurprisingly, relations degenerated further. By May, Roosevelt was describing Taft as a "puzzlewit" and "fathead" while Taft returned fire, de-scribing Roosevelt as a "dangerous egotist" and a "demagogue."[3]

Under normal circumstances, a battle royale between a sitting president and a colorful former president would have dominated media accounts of the election and defined its historical significance for generations to come. Yet most seasoned observers recognized that Taft's chances were slim; the election was a two-horse race between Roosevelt and Woodrow Wilson, with the latter holding a marked advantage due to the split in the Republican vote. Roosevelt was fully aware of Wilson's strengths, and his own under-dog status, dismissing "Professor Wilson's" impractical "academic theories" with revealing contempt.[4] To be verbally assaulted by the former president was a mark of recognition, if not necessarily respect, and Roosevelt conceded privately that Wilson was likely to win a plurality in the electoral college. The election was Wilson's to lose, although he refused to get carried away. In a letter to his friend and confidante Mary Peck, Wilson cautioned her not to be "too confident of the result. I feel that Roosevelt's strength is altogether incalculable . . . He appeals to . . . [people's] imaginations; I do not. He is a real, vivid person whom they have seen and shouted themselves hoarse over and voted for, millions strong; I am a vague, conjectural personality made up more of opinions and academic prepossessions than of human traits and red corpuscles. We shall see what will happen!"[5] That Wilson refers here to "red corpuscles" rather than "red blood cells" illustrates his intellectualism rather well. But he wasn't wholly "conjectural," having been battle hardened in the bruising world of New Jersey politics. Wilson could certainly hold his own in a war of words, summoning the animus to describe Roosevelt as "a very, very erratic comet on the horizon."[6]

This election was also the first in which primaries played a decisive part, enlivening the contest and necessitating a much closer connection between the politicians and the citizens they sought to persuade. Primaries usually rewarded the best communicators and helped Wilson, who had honed his oratory as president of Princeton University and governor of New Jersey, to secure the Democratic nomination. His appeal to Democrats and the country at large was based on multiple strengths. Leading one of America's most prestigious colleges had allowed Wilson to establish a na-tional reputation, for those were the days when a professorship launched rather than bookended a political career. A minor snag relating to Wilson's academic background did occur when the Boot and Shoe Workers' Union refused to endorse him because he was, in their damning assessment, an "intellectual."[7] But Wilson's chosen profession was not a critical disadvantage. Like Thomas Jefferson before him, Wilson spoke strongly in favor of the superior wisdom of the common man, as this campaign address illustrates:

> What I fear is a government of experts. God forbid that in a democratic country we should resign the task and give the government over to experts. What are we for if we are to be scientifically taken care of by a small number of gentlemen who are the only men who understand the job? Because if we don't understand the job, then we are not a free people . . . I want to say I have never heard more penetrating debate of public questions than I have sometimes been privileged to hear in clubs of workingmen; because the man who is down against the daily problem of life doesn't talk about it in rhetoric; he talks about it in facts. And the only thing I am interested in is facts.[8]

Wilson's strengths went well beyond his erudition and ability to wear it lightly. Like Alfred Mahan, Wilson was a southerner in upbringing, but not southern enough to allow Republicans to attack him as a potential catalyst for disunity. Wilson had made his unionism clear as a twenty-three-year-old at the University of Virginia, when he had declared, "because I love the South I rejoice in the failure of the Confederacy."[9] Wilson was also a political Progressive—indeed, Roosevelt pushed him farther to the "left"—which allowed him to woo floating voters who admired Roosevelt's domestic proposals but found his foreign-policy bellicosity off-putting: a significant demographic. Indeed, there was little to substantively distinguish the Progressivism of Wilson's New Freedom from Roosevelt's New Nationalism—TR once gleefully observed to a group of friends: "Wilson is merely a less virile me."[10] Taft and Debs were the more conventional right-left candidates in 1912. Looking to end the run of three William Jennings Bryan–led defeats, Democratic Party strategists had identified the eloquent and authoritative Wilson as a potential winner, even against a political giant such as Roosevelt. It was a remarkable contest between two towering figures in American history whose varied gifts brought to mind the dramatis personae who dominated the first half century of the republic. As a recent Wilson biographer has observed, the 1912 election "pitted the most colorful presidential politician since Andrew Jackson against the most articulate presidential politician since Thomas Jefferson."[11]

Thomas Woodrow Wilson was born on December 28, 1856, in Staunton, Virginia, where his father, Joseph, was the town's Presbyterian minister. He was literally a child of the manse. Wilson was a plump and preternaturally quiet infant, and his father joked "that baby is dignified enough to be Moderator of the General Assembly."[12] Growing up in the South during the Civil War, Wilson was affected directly and viscerally by the conflict. Wilson's father's church served as a Confederate hospital for a time, where the inflow of bloodied and mutilated soldiers would have been deeply disturbing for any child, while the graveyard doubled as a holding area for Union prisoners. In May 1865, a nine-year-old Wilson looked on as the captured Confederate president, Jefferson Davis, was paraded through Augusta, Georgia (where the Wilsons had moved subsequently), in chains. Davis's humbling was a harrowing sight for Confederates to behold.

The South had been crushed by force of Union arms, facilitated by the vast superiority of the northern economy, and its humiliation only worsened throughout Reconstruction. But while many well-to-do southerners suffered significant losses in wealth and status during and after the Civil War, the Wilsons, secure within the warproof Presbyterian Church, were largely unaffected. Woodrow—or Tommy, as friends and family knew him—had a stable childhood. In familial circumstances, Wilson shared a great deal in common with Alfred Mahan. But whereas the philosopher of sea power had served in the Civil War on the Union side, convinced of the necessity of waging righteous war, Wilson drew a different lesson. It is to his traumatic Civil War childhood that some scholars attribute Wilson's aversion to armed conflict and his sincere attempts as president to avoid it except as a very last resort.[13]

Tommy stood out at school for the wrong reasons. He did not learn to read with any facility until he was eleven years old, a cognitive delay that twentieth-century pediatricians would have diagnosed as dyslexia. Lacking awareness of such extenuating circumstances, Wilson's teachers, grandfather, and uncle, if not his admirably defensive parents, simply dismissed young Tommy as not too sharp. The method Wilson used to conquer his affliction was remarkable, constituting a model in self-possession and drive. With close tutelage from his father, he immersed himself in repetitive rote learning. He reread books to master them, rather than dipping widely into a range of literature, reciting long passages aloud from memory. This dull, exacting work gave Wilson a narrow knowledge base, but it was vital in the development of his written and spoken English.

Since writing longhand posed problems, Tommy learned shorthand by the time he was sixteen. He also bought a typewriter as soon as they were available. The key factor that allowed Wilson to realize his potential, however, was his doting parents and their boundless encouragement. In a family less devoted to words, and the word of God in particular, Wilson might have withered on the vine scholastically. But his father's intellect and rhetorical facility were inspirational, and his confidence in his son was unwavering. He devoted all his spare time to tutoring Tommy and instilled in him a strong work ethic and appreciation for fluent, compelling rhetoric. Wilson's teenage years were more formative than most, and his drive was more firmly entrenched than it was in his peers. At sixteen, Wilson enrolled at Davidson College in North Carolina, where he discovered a passion for history, improved his writing skills, and identified heroic historical figures to consciously emulate—orators all, such as Cicero, Edmund Burke, the British free-trade advocates Richard Cobden and John Bright, and William Gladstone (a portrait of whom hung on his dormitory wall). Nonetheless, Wilson found Davidson's narrow curriculum unchallenging; he expended most of his energies on the debating society and left before his freshman year was out. In 1875, Wilson enrolled at the College of New Jersey, the institution now known as Princeton University.

In many ways, Wilson found Princeton as uninspiring as Davidson. His teachers failed to rouse his enthusiasm, although he read voraciously in private and threw himself into the abundant opportunities for extracurricular activity. He joined the American Whig Society, founded a debating club, became editor of the student newspaper, *The Princetonian*, and secured admission into one of the less socially exclusive eating clubs, the Alligators. As editor of *The Princetonian*, Wilson made his own priorities as a student clear: dispensing advice on how to improve the underperforming football team and campaigning for debate to be introduced into the university's formal curriculum. But beyond these pet passions, Wilson's narrow reading as a teenager had limited his intellectual horizons, leading him to flounder when he was forced outside his comfort zone. In his shorthand diary on June 15, 1876, he complained that he was compelled to study "Xenophon's Memorabilia for examinations all the afternoon and evening. Very stupid work." A couple of days later, he took exception to another scholarly discipline in similarly banal terms: "Studied geometry from 8 to 10—very stupid work indeed."[14]

In appearance, Wilson was tall, slightly ungainly in the manner of Abraham Lincoln, and stern in countenance, conforming in later years with his father's description of him as a baby. Raymond B. Fosdick, who came to know Wilson well as an adviser at the Paris Peace Conference, penned a marvelous physical description that captures Wilson as well at age sixteen as sixty; photographs of Wilson at both ages show a remarkable physical constancy:

> Wilson on first appearance was not what would be called a handsome man. Indeed he was curiously homely. He had what he himself described as a "horse face"—a long, thin and generally unsmiling visage with strong jaws. He had also an extraordinarily keen gaze, which could sometimes be disconcerting. But his eyes were nonetheless his best feature; they could light up with humor and kindliness, and his whole face would soften as it reflected his thoughts.[15]

Wilson lamented the fact that he resembled his angular mother rather than his conventionally handsome father. His high cheekbones, slightly hooked nose, firm jaw, and impassive blue eyes conveyed a forbidding aspect. Yet the private Wilson ran counter to appearances. Fosdick recalls Wilson as "a superb raconteur, with an amazing fund of anecdotes and stories. Indeed his dialect stories, told in Scotch, Irish, or Negro accents, were often side-splitting . . ."[16] With friends and family, Wilson was gregarious, enjoying emotional and physical intimacy with those he loved. At work, Wilson's drive and focus allowed him to be hugely productive and led some who observed his working persona to suspect him of being one-track and ascetic. What many missed was how deftly Wilson disentangled his private and working lives, allowing him to thrive in both spheres. This self-discipline enabled him to achieve as much as he did with few complaints of neglect from those closest to him.

At Princeton, Wilson's intellect was shaped through reading philosophers such as John Locke and Edmund Burke, who elevated the sanctity of private property and held that judicious, enduring political reform was necessarily incremental. He was also greatly influenced by the British journalist Walter Bagehot (later venerated as a constitutional scholar) and located in the British unitary government an ideal polity, which he compared favorably to America's purposefully unwieldy system. Wilson found Burke's *Reflections on the Revolution in France* compelling in its denunciation of revolution based on well-meaning abstractions. Yet he admired the Parliament in which Burke was active for the speed and efficiency with which legislation could be debated and enacted—Britain represented an orderly, well-governed middle ground between French mercurialness and American inertia. Like Mahan, the Founding Father whom Wilson revered above others was Alexander Hamilton, another Anglophile who believed the federal government, not the states, must possess preponderant political power, and that government works best when unified.

Shortly after his graduation in 1879, Wilson's article "Cabinet Government in the United States" appeared in the Boston-based journal *International Review*. It called for a stronger connection between the cabinet and Congress, as was the case in Britain, to improve cabinet performance by subjecting its members to greater oversight. Wilson believed the cabinet should be members of Congress, not appointed from outside. He dismissed the separation of powers as "not in accord with the true spirit" of Anglo-American institutions and argued that his proposals would streamline government decision making to America's enduring advantage. The editor of the journal who accepted this piece was Henry Cabot Lodge, then an instructor at Harvard (and a fellow worshiper of Alexander Hamilton), who would later find Wilson's views less congenial. But Wilson said or wrote very little on foreign policy, save for his belief that the president's power should be unconstrained in those fast-moving matters of war and diplomacy.

It is of course impossible to distill the essence of Wilson's intellect and worldview without considering his religion. As the son, grandson, and nephew of Presbyterian ministers, Wilson could scarcely avoid inheriting his family's religiosity, which he did completely, deriving his belief system from three sources: the Shorter Catechism, the Presbyterian scholastics, and his father's learned sermons. As Wilson's most distinguished biographer, Arthur S. Link, puts it:

> The foundations of all of Wilson's political thinking were the religious and ethical beliefs and values that he inherited from the Christian tradition and from his own Presbyterian theology. In matters of basic Christian faith, Wilson was like a little child, never doubting, always believing, and drawing spiritual sustenance from Bible reading, church attendance, and prayer . . . He believed in a sovereign God, just and stern as well as loving; in a moral universe, the rules of which ruled nations as well as men.[17]

Wilson was a predestinarian, believing that God controlled history and used men and nations to serve a grand purpose. Indeed, throughout his career Wilson exhibited a marked tendency to conflate his favored causes with the will of God, leading Sigmund Freud to diagnose him with a messiah complex—without ever meeting him—in a polemical study coauthored with the diplomat William Bullitt.[18] Yet Wilson's views were in the mainstream of Protestantism and unexceptional for a man of his era. The Presbyterianism in which Wilson was steeped was progressive and worldly, with lifelong educational self-improvement as a central component. His greatly respected paternal uncle, James Woodrow, had taught Darwin's theory of evolution at the Columbia Theological Seminary. Although he lost his job in the process, Uncle James's willingness to be led by his intellect—disentangling faith from science—was a trait Wilson admired. On the challenges that Charles Darwin's theory posed to believers, Wilson confided to his diary, "I *saw* the intellectual difficulties, but I was not *troubled* by them: they seemed to have no connection with my faith in the essentials of the religion I had been taught . . . I am capable, it would seem, of being satisfied spiritually without being satisfied intellectually."[19] Wilson's contentment in leaving hanging threads was certainly preferable to the common response from believers of theological absolutism. There was an openness and complexity to Wilson's thought that his detractors, Freud most notably, fail to credit.

Wilson's religion and political value system directly informed his early views on foreign policy. Whereas Mahan had written little on the merits of democracy, and viewed the Anglophone world as politically and economically unique, Wilson's reading of the Enlightenment philosophes at Princeton led him to view elected government as the ideal polity and to further believe that all nations could benefit from the economic, political, social, and cultural advantages that accompanied democracy's embrace. His inclusive Universalist Presbyterianism, furthermore, led him to believe that all people held the potential to assume the attributes that Wilson conceded, at that stage, Anglo-Saxons possessed in greater quantity than other ethnicities. Time and patience were essential if political transformations were to endure.

Wilson was similar to Mahan in that he reviled slavery but was steeped in the casual racism prevalent in that era. Those of African descent faced the longest journey to cognitive and political maturity, Wilson believed, although he criticized those who deployed flawed scientific measures such as cranial measurements to rationalize a racial pecking order. He was opposed to woman suffrage, believing that the vitality of the family would be undermined if women were granted the right to vote. By today's standards Wilson appears reactionary. But in late-nineteenth-century America, his Universalism—his belief expressed later that "when properly directed, there is no people not fitted for self-government"—placed him near the vanguard of liberal, progressive thought.[20] Wilson's taciturnity made him a difficult man to read, but the value system that informed his life work was infused with positivity. Where Mahan was largely pessimistic on the future course of international relations, Wilson was more optimistic—a Kant to Mahan's Hobbes—and he believed that all people, given time and encouragement, were heading toward the same prosperous and peaceable destination.

Wilson's geopolitical Universalism was one of the factors that led him to break with fellow Democrats and offer wholehearted support for war with Spain in 1898. Wilson believed that defeating Spain and assuming control of the Philippines, Guam, and Hawaii was the surest way to prevent Germany and Russia from projecting their power into the Pacific—an identifiably Mahanian rationale. He also followed Mahan and Senator Albert J. Beveridge in identifying a clear economic justification for expanding American power abroad: trade follows colonial acquisition and would be greatly facilitated by the acquisition of geographically dispersed coaling stations and deep-water harbors.

But Wilson differed with Mahan in offering a grander reason for holding on to the Philippines in the medium term, believing that America possessed a special duty to lead hitherto blighted nations toward democracy and prosperity; catalyzing this dynamic was an end in itself. While Britain was a political exemplar and beacon of stability, the people of the United States, as Wilson described them, were something more: "custodians of the spirit of righteousness, of the spirit of equal-handed justice, of the spirit of hope which believes in the perfectibility of the law with the perfectibility of human life itself."[21] Fulfilling America's potential required more than perfecting the nation itself and persuading by example. The United States alone could spearhead the diffusion of freedom, prosperity, and democracy that in time would render armed conflict anachronistic. Wilson joked that the "beauty about a Scotch-Irishman is that he not only thinks he is right, but knows he is right. And I have not departed from the faith of my ancestors."[22] On the imperative that America owed the world its leadership, his belief was absolute.

Wilson graduated from Princeton with no clear sense of how to fulfill the political ambitions he had acquired in college. Prodded in the direction of law by his father, Wilson enrolled at the University of Virginia, but he quickly came to view law as uncongenial. While Wilson had necessarily engaged himself in rote learning to overcome his early learning difficulties, Princeton had broadened his intellectual horizons, leading him to revel in the creative impulse, particularly in the fields of literature and history. "I wish now to record the confession that I am most terribly bored by the noble study of law sometimes," Wilson wrote to a friend in 1879. "I think that it is the want of variety that disgusts me . . . When one has nothing but Law, served in all its dryness, set before him from one week's end to another, for month after month and for quarter after quarter, he tires of this uniformity of diet."[23] Wilson dropped out of law school after eighteen months but, in that less professionalized era, still managed to establish himself as one half of an Atlanta law firm, Renick and Wilson, where the practicalities of being a lawyer bored him just as much as the process of mastering the subject. A concerned Joseph Wilson warned his increasingly disenchanted son to "stick to the law and its prospects be they ever so depressing or disgusting." He worried that Woodrow, as he now preferred to be called, would give up a lucrative profession to pursue a "mere literary career."[24] But his entreaties were to no avail; Wilson had no desire to persist in a job he disliked for pecuniary advantage alone. He abandoned the security of law and decided instead to pursue an academic career, concluding that "a professorship was the only feasible place for me."[25]

Wilson commenced his doctoral studies in political science in 1883 at Johns Hopkins, the first university in the United States to cite research as its founding purpose, and an institution widely regarded as possessing the finest Ph.D. program in the nation. It was the process of thinking and writing, not the teaching element, that propelled Wilson toward this path. In this respect he conformed to the German research ideal that privileged the production of fresh knowledge over the education of undergraduates—a task in which anyone with enthusiasm and a relevant bachelor's degree could engage. But in other respects he diverged from the Teutonic veneration of narrow professionalization. Like Mahan, Wilson was determined to reach a general audience, not just write scholarly monographs with small print runs and paltry royalties. He was similarly unenthusiastic about the rigors of archival research. To his wife, Ellen, Wilson confided in 1884 that "I want to write books which will be read by the great host who don't wear spectacles— whose eyes are young and unlearned!"[26] He believed his scholarship could serve a pedagogical function and secure him a national reputation as a compelling and relevant thinker, while his lectures would allow him to further hone his rhetorical skills. Wilson viewed an academic career as the best available path open to him, but it was always pursued with a view to becoming a politician—to make history, not to write it, as the cliché goes.

With remarkable speed and purpose, Wilson began researching and writing his Ph.D. as a book, turning the conventional way of establishing a scholarly reputation on its head. He began writing in January 1884, finished the manuscript in September, and the book was accepted quickly and published by Houghton Mifflin in January 1885. That just one year elapsed between Wilson first putting pen to paper and the book appearing might suggest a facile, error-strewn effort. But *Congressional Government: A Study in American Politics* was a substantial piece of scholarship for a writer of any age, let alone a second-year graduate student with a history of dyslexia. The book was reviewed to acclaim and retains its status today as a seminal work of American political analysis, although its lack of primary sources remains a major shortcoming in a research culture still dominated by the Germanic ideal. One reviewer gushed that the book represented "the best critical writing on the American constitution which has appeared since the 'Federalist' papers."[27] It propelled Wilson toward a successful academic career.

With analytical verve, *Congressional Government* developed many of the core assumptions that informed his earlier article on the merits of cabinet government. The crux of Wilson's argument, as described by the historian John A. Thompson, is that "American government suffered in many ways from a lack of a clear and responsible center of authority like the British cabinet."[28] To remedy deficiencies in the Constitution, Wilson believed that aspects of the British system had to be imported, although his argument was not as prescriptive as that presented in his earlier article. "I have abandoned the evangelical for the exegetical—so to speak," Wilson informed a friend.[29] Through his survey of the U.S. political system, Wilson identified the Founding Fathers' sectional compromise that created the pivotal system of "checks and balances" as the greatest impediment to effective government. He compared the three branches of American government unfavorably with the British parliamentary system, which privileged action and accountability over the requirement that executive energy be dampened through countervailing power bases. The world had become too complex for America's unwieldy political system to navigate—it had to be rationalized and rendered more efficient. To achieve this goal, as the historian John G. Gunnell writes, Wilson believed that "the social scientist, like the statesman, was to play a crucial role."[30]

While Wilson spends comparatively little time discussing foreign policy in the book, he elaborated on this critical executive function in a follow-up work, *Constitutional Government in the United States*, in a revealing passage that portended later political setbacks:

> The initiative in foreign affairs, which the President possesses without any restriction whatever, is virtually the power to control them absolutely. The President cannot control a treaty with a foreign power

without the consent of the Senate, but he may guide every step of diplomacy, and to guide diplomacy is to determine what treaties must be made, if the faith and prestige of the government are to be maintained. He need disclose no step of negotiation until it is complete, and when in any critical matter it is completed the government is virtually committed. Whatever its disinclination, the Senate may feel itself committed also.[31]

Streamlining and expediting the process of government was the political reform close to Wilson's heart, and *Congressional Government* accomplished his central aim in reaching out to the general reader and establishing a national reputation. Yet with that goal achieved, Wilson never again wrote a book or article that might be deemed intellectually pathbreaking. He wanted to look after his wife and three daughters in some style and recognized that he possessed the literary gifts to do so. He followed up his scholarly debut with the five-volume *A History of the American People*, which Wilson described frankly as a "high-class pot boiler."[32] Other minor works followed, which sank without academic trace but attracted a loyal following beyond the university. Wilson, like Mahan, drew a substantial amount of his income from frequent royalty checks, happily oblivious of the opprobrium of Humboldtian research scholars.

Congressional Government set Wilson on a swift rise through the ranks of American universities. He took a job at Bryn Mawr College in 1885, moved to Wesleyan College in 1888, and returned to his alma mater two years later to assume a professorship in jurisprudence and political economy. Wilson was a popular figure on the Princeton campus, with colleagues and students alike, and his reputation as a scholar—strong but fading—and as a deft and forceful administrator, led the universities of Illinois and Virginia to offer him the presidencies of their institutions. Wilson remained loyal to Princeton, however, and was in turn rewarded by significant salary increases that eventually made him its highest-paid professor. In 1902, Wilson's gifts as a leader landed him the academic job he valued the most: the presidency of Princeton.

Wilson's second stint at Princeton was the happiest time of his life.[33] Assuming the head of one of America's most venerable institutions provided a platform for him to convey larger messages on education, politics, and society to a wide audience. But Wilson also made multiple enemies during his tenure. He was determined to raise academic standards, to challenge the centrality of the eating clubs and the tradition of the gentleman's C, to hire fresh talent to inject scholarly rigor into a parochial faculty, and to

make Princeton equal to Harvard and Yale in respect to academic reputation and endowment.[34] He was only partly successful in embedding meritocratic principles—in respect to staff recruitment and student attainment—in
a university that had traded for too long on past glories. His campaign for
reform provoked the ire of entrenched elites who liked things the way they
were and did not care for the sanctimonious manner in which this Virginian
upstart went about his task.

Wilson also established himself as something of a public intellectual (a
term that had not yet entered the lexicon), a major educational figure whose
writings and speeches entered the national consciousness. He made his ultimate ambitions clear on the eve of his Princeton inaugural address when he
remarked to his wife, "I feel like a new prime minister getting ready to address his constituents."[35] The subjects Wilson discussed publicly ranged widely,
focusing primarily on domestic reform—both elite political and grassroots
social. Yet foreign affairs also came to interest him more than previously. In
1906, for example, Wilson delivered a high-profile speech in which he observed that America's vast latent energy would propel its strength and ideals
outward: "Soon . . . the shores of Europe and then Autocratic Europe shall
hear us knocking at their back door, demanding admittance for American
ideas, customs and arts."[36] Significantly, Wilson also recognized that "the
President can never again be the mere domestic figure he has been throughout so large a part of our history. The nation has risen to the first rank in
power and resources . . . Our President must always, henceforth, be one of
the great powers of the world, whether he act greatly and wisely or not."[37]

Crucially, Wilson believed that his discipline of political science could
play a central role in improving the nation's domestic and foreign policies.
In 1909–1910, Wilson served as president of the American Political Science
Association. During his presidential address, he expressed hope that the political scientist, "out of his full store of truth, discovered by patient inquiry,
dispassionate exposition, fearless analysis and frank inference [would] enrich the thinking and clarify the vision of the statesman of action."[38] Wilson's
demonstrated talent as a political scientist and vast potential as a "statesman
of action" was not lost on him. He embodied the nexus between the social
sciences and politics, meaning he was peculiarly well positioned to practice
a new kind of leadership.

Wilson's wider political ambitions were made clear in a sharply progressive speech he delivered in Pittsburgh in February 1910. Turning to the problems that beset the institution he led, and that were common to many other
universities besides, Wilson said that the "colleges are in the same dangerous

position as the churches . . . They serve the classes not the masses." In his rousing peroration he said he had "dedicated every power that there is within me to bring to the colleges that I have anything to do with to an absolutely democratic regeneration in spirit."[39]

It was rhetorical flourishes like these that led Democratic strategists in New Jersey to identify the potential that would take Wilson first to the governor's mansion in Trenton and then to the White House. Two prominent individuals in the party—Colonel George Harvey, editor of *Harper's Weekly*, and former New Jersey senator James Smith—urged Wilson to run for the governorship of New Jersey in 1910 as a preliminary to running for the presidency two years later. Wilson's interest was piqued immediately. He wrote to Mary Peck that "this is what I was meant for, this rough and tumble of the political arena. My instinct all turns that way."[40] The Democrats' carefully laid plans were realized when Wilson prevailed in New Jersey and then nationally in 1912 against Roosevelt and Taft. It was a meteoric rise—a two-year governorship and then straight to the White House—that has not been repeated. It was testament to his ambition as much as to his capabilities.

On Election Day, 6.3 million Americans cast their vote for Wilson, 4.1 million for Roosevelt, 3.5 million for Taft, and 900,000 for Debs. The electoral college, which is unkind to third-party candidates, translated these results into 435 votes for Wilson, 88 for Roosevelt, 8 for the unfortunate Taft, and none for Debs. Wilson had secured a comprehensive victory with just 43 percent of the popular vote. A united Republican Party would have certainly secured Taft's reelection, but Roosevelt was not to be denied denying Taft, who in turn was consoled by denying Roosevelt. It was a peculiar election all around. Taft and Roosevelt had foreseen their fate well in advance and both were gracious in defeat. As Roosevelt observed of Wilson, "I think him a very adroit man; I do not think he has any fixity of conviction."[41] Roosevelt's assessment was informed by good manners, but it was also shaped by recognition that he and Wilson shared a common Progressivism on domestic politics. As the early Wilson biographer William Allen White observed, "Between the New Nationalism and the New Freedom was that fantastic imaginary gulf that always has existed between tweedle-dum and tweedle-dee."[42] Foreign policy was a different matter entirely, however, and it took little time for Roosevelt to retract his generous assessment, viewing Wilson as being driven by a misguided "fixity of conviction" in the transformative power of good intentions.

At that stage, Wilson could scarcely have visualized what his foreign-policy agenda might look like—he was necessarily reactive. Up to 1912, his most important recorded statement on foreign affairs related to his belief that the president possessed absolute power in respect to diplomacy. This lack of sustained interest is comprehensible in light of the fact that the outside world scarcely registered among the electorate and the candidates during the campaign. The only international issue of note covered comprehensively by the media related to the revolution in neighboring Mexico, and Wilson said very little on that subject or, indeed, on the increasing tensions in Europe. Wilson would craft his foreign policies on the job, although certain traits established through his academic career would become apparent. With a sense of foreboding, perhaps, a few days after the election Wilson remarked to a former colleague at Princeton, the biologist Edwin Grant Conklin, that "it would be an irony of fate if my administration had to deal chiefly with foreign problems, for all my preparation has been in domestic matters."[43]

As the transitional period between Election Day and the inauguration had yet to be shortened, Woodrow Wilson was sworn in as the twenty-eighth president of the United States on March 4, 1913. It was an overcast but uncommonly mild day, with the first floral signs of spring making their appearance. A jovial President Taft welcomed the Wilson family to the White House graciously and with good humor—relieved perhaps not to have to vacate the premises to Roosevelt's tender care—before he accompanied Wilson to the inaugural dais on Capitol Hill in a grand horse-drawn carriage. As the president and president-elect surveyed the crowds from the stand, Wilson beckoned the audience, positioned some distance away, closer. "Let the people come forward," he declared, before taking his oath of office and delivering his inaugural address:

> This is not a day of triumph; it is a day of dedication. Here muster, not the forces of party, but the forces of humanity. Men's hearts wait upon us; men's lives hang in the balance; men's hopes call upon us to say what we will do. Who shall live up to the great trust? Who dares fail to try? I summon all honest men, all patriotic, all forward-looking men, to my side. God helping me, I will not fail them, if they will but counsel and sustain me![44]

The address was pitch-perfect for an incoming president who lacked a plurality of the popular vote. Wilson's focus was entirely domestic, covering issues such as tariff reduction, banking reform, and antitrust legislation, which the new president planned to move quickly through a

Democratic-controlled Congress. Foreign policy was a lacuna in the speech, just as it was throughout the campaign.

In many respects Wilson remained true to his academic background in viewing the office of the presidency as possessing a vital "didactic function," in respect to both domestic politics and international affairs.[45] The aspects of Theodore Roosevelt's career he admired most related to his persuasive gifts, rendered more potent by utilizing the majesty afforded to the office of the presidency—that unique vantage point he described memorably as the "bully pulpit." Wilson was similarly inclined to Roosevelt, and his speech-making style was more elegant if less insistent. One of his first actions as president was to reinstitute the practice of delivering the State of the Union address in person, rejecting Thomas Jefferson's rationale for ceasing the speeches in 1800 that they echoed British political hierarchies. He was the second-to-last American president (Herbert Hoover being the last) to write all his own speeches. No American president before or after Wilson has spoken more to Congress. No president held more press conferences, then or since, or spoke to the media in such an unvarnished fashion. Few presidents come close to Wilson in the frequency and urgency with which he traveled the nation and appealed directly to the people. His presidency was the most rhetorical (literally) in history, and this emphasis helps us to better understand his successes and failures. President Wilson believed that just about anything was possible by appealing directly to his people.

The first foreign-policy crisis the new president confronted could not have been closer to home. Just three weeks before Wilson's inauguration, a coup occurred in Mexico—memorialized in that nation as the Ten Tragic Days— in which a ruthless army general, Victoriano Huerta, ordered the overthrow and assassination of the moderate, reform-inclined incumbent president, Francisco Madero. The official U.S. reaction was one of studied indifference. President Taft's ambassador to Mexico, Henry Lane Wilson, was relaxed about the coup as Madero's progressive agenda had threatened American business interests—particularly those organizations with significant land-holdings. Indeed, he was indirectly complicit in the whole affair. With only a brief time left in the Oval Office, Taft left to his successor the decision of whether to support Henry Wilson's pro-business advice. Oblivious of the pleas by representatives of big business for swift recognition, Wilson stood strong on principle, upending the conventional wisdom, again established by Jefferson, that held that any government able to uphold existing treaty commitments was worthy of recognition, regardless of whether its founding was violent. On March 12, Wilson issued a policy statement affirming that his sincere feelings of friendship toward the "sister republics of Central and South America" was predicated on the "orderly processes of just government based upon law, not upon arbitrary and irregular force." Without identifying Huerta by name, Wilson made clear that his government would "have no sympathy with those who seek the power of the government to advance their own personal interests or ambitions."[46] When quizzed on his broad approach by a British diplomat, Wilson remarked, "I am going to teach the South American republics to elect good men."[47]

Wilson's condescending tone toward feckless Latinos reminded some observers of the paternalistic approach set out in Theodore Roosevelt's Corollary to the Monroe Doctrine. But the most interesting aspects of Wilson's statement were his insistence on commitment to representative democracy and his unwillingness to recognize a brutal regime that would have boosted the profits of big business. Both of these motivations ran directly counter to Mahan's writings, which were deeply skeptical on the utility of spreading democracy and driven primarily by economic self-interest—pursuit of commercial advantage should be the principal focus of any nation's foreign policy. A potent strain of idealism was emerging in Wilson's foreign-policy approach, which sought to make a clean break with past practice by dismissing the diplomatic foundations of the McKinley, Roosevelt, and Taft administrations. The new president was testing out some new ideas on *raison d'état*.

This shift in emphasis was driven by Wilson's view of a president's foreign-policy power as "very absolute," and he had been unimpressed by the passive, nepotistic State Department, whose entrenched practices he distrusted and whose garbled diplomatic dispatches offended his literary sensibilities.[48] But while Wilson viewed the State Department warily, and was intent on directing foreign policy from the White House, he did respect the man he nominated as his secretary of state, William Jennings Bryan, with whom he shared many characteristics.

Just like Wilson's, Bryan's worldview was shaped by his Christianity—even more so, in fact. And, like Wilson, Bryan was an idealist who believed diplomacy served a higher function than pleasing big business; U.S. behavior should be exemplary, to persuade other nations to follow its example. Yet Bryan was pacific in temperament, regarding peace, pursued at virtually all costs, as the ultimate goal of diplomacy. He was sanctimonious, dogmatic, and ascetic to a degree that made Wilson—who at least savored single-malt whiskey in small measures—appear bacchanalian in comparison. (Bryan banned alcohol at State Department functions, a practice that was duly mocked by Republicans as "grape juice diplomacy."[49]) Bryan's views were anathema to the diplomatic verities that Mahan and Roosevelt considered sacrosanct: that war was sometimes necessary and always ennobling, and that power projection, through territorial acquisition, was vital to facilitate commercial expansion. Roosevelt made no effort to hide his scorn for Bryan, describing him to Henry Cabot Lodge as "the most contemptible figure we have ever had as Secretary of State, and of course Wilson must accept full responsibility."[50]

Although Wilson had private misgivings about Bryan's moral fervor, he shared his hostility toward the way corporate interests had been privileged previously in foreign policymaking. Bryan was contemptuous of the "dollar diplomacy" practiced by previous Republican administrations and sought to undermine the role played by Wall Street banks in promoting investment in Latin America and the Far East. With his president's blessing, Bryan pulled the plug on the American contribution to an international syndicate of bankers that had been established to fund railroad construction in China and that was certain to make vast profits. In announcing the pullout, Wilson criticized the loan for appearing to "touch very nearly the administrative independence of China itself; and this administration does not feel that it ought, even by implication, to be a party to those conditions."[51] This decision ran directly counter to Mahanian precepts. Critics later alleged that Wilson's high-mindedness opened the door for Japan to further expand its influence in China, with dismal consequences for the balance of power in East Asia.

The secretary of state was as determined as Wilson to guide Latinos— "our political children," as Bryan described them—toward liberty and democracy, and was aware that Washington's success in effecting such change depended upon reputational rehabilitation.[52] To assist Pan-American relations, Wilson and Bryan negotiated a treaty with Colombia that offered a formal apology and financial compensation to the tune of $25 million, for the brutish manner in which President Roosevelt had detached Panama from Bogotá's control. This well-intentioned maneuver infuriated Roosevelt, who described it as "a crime against the United States," and it led to an almighty battle in the Senate, in which Henry Cabot Lodge worked successfully to deny ratification.[53] In a speech in Mobile, Alabama, in October 1913, an undeterred Wilson repudiated economic imperialism, connecting the battle against "degrading" business practices overseas with his own Progressive political agenda at home.[54] He added that the "United States will never again seek one additional foot of territory by conquest."[55] Wilson's aversion to anything that smacked of imperialism was shaping his geopolitical agenda. In his idealism and ambition, the president was opening a new chapter in the history of America's foreign relations.

While a strong measure of altruism informed Wilson's hostility toward the Huerta regime in Mexico, there was a clear divergence between his views and those of his secretary of state on the best means forward. The president had applied a series of diplomatic pressures to Huerta, including the threat of sanctions, to facilitate free and open elections to anoint a leader with a clear mandate. These efforts had failed, however, and Huerta—clinging to power with an obstinacy that Wilson could not help but respect—further tightened his control by arresting opposition members of what was already a neutered Congress. Actions that went beyond diplomatic censure and economic sanctions were clearly required.

Wilson was presented with an opportunity to force the matter when in April 1914 Mexican officials in Tampico mistakenly arrested a group of American sailors who had ventured from their ship to secure provisions. This damaging error was quickly remedied, the sailors were released, and expressions of regret were extended for hurt feelings. But unsatisfied by this more or less reasonable Mexican response, the admiral of the ship, with Wilson's backing, demanded a formal apology and a twenty-one-gun salute, which he contended were necessary to fully restore American dignity. Huerta balked at this request before proposing simultaneous salutes to allow both sides to emerge with self-esteem intact. Wilson rejected the compromise and secured congressional authorization to deploy U.S. troops to Mexico to right this wrong and, more important, get rid of Huerta. Regime change was Wilson's primary purpose. The president believed that deploying American troops would encourage Huerta's opponents to take up arms against their oppressor. It was a pugnacious ploy that caused a great deal of discomfort for his conflict-averse secretary of state. But this incursion into Mexican territory failed to satisfy Henry Cabot Lodge, who expressed a clear preference for all-out war and military occupation, and whose ambitions were ultimately frustrated by the commander in chief, who kept the military on a tight leash. As it turned out, Lodge was more realistic than Wilson about the number of troops required.

At the time of the military incursion into Vera Cruz, "Colonel" Edward House (the title was an honorific, not an actual rank), who had established himself as Wilson's most trusted confidant and adviser, observed that if "Mexico understood that our motives were unselfish she should not object to our helping adjust her unruly household."[56] This "unselfish" invasion was met with strong objections, however, in the form of fierce nationalist resistance. Two hundred Mexicans and nineteen Americans were killed in the initial stages of the fighting. In several of Mexico's cities, American consular offices were attacked by mobs. Rather than welcoming Americans as liberators, the leader of the main opposition group to Huerta, Venustiano Carranza, demanded a prompt withdrawal to restore Mexico's sovereignty. The rationale for the deployment of troops had disintegrated as quickly as it had been cobbled together.

When Argentina, Brazil, and Chile offered to mediate the conflict, Wilson gratefully embraced this prospective exit strategy. Matters improved in the months that followed. As negotiations stalled inconclusively, and the civil war worsened, Carranza regrouped and was eventually able to force Huerta to concede defeat in the summer of 1914. Wilson's policy now appeared vindicated. A brutal leader had been dispatched and a better one had taken his place. Speaking at a press conference on November 14, he outlined his rationale for the initial incursion in refreshingly candid terms: "A situation arose that made it necessary for the dignity of the United States that we should take some decisive step; and the main thing to accomplish was a vital thing. We got Huerta. That was the end of Huerta. That was what I had in mind. It could not be done without taking Vera Cruz."[57]

Yet Huerta's demise and Carranza's ascension were far from the end of the story. Two populist leaders, Emiliano Zapata and Francisco "Pancho" Villa picked up and dusted off Huerta's nationalist mantle and began the fight against Carranza's unstable government, whose founding had been so tainted by association with the gringo invaders. With great success, Villa was able to impugn Carranza's patriotism in permitting "the sale of our country" to the Americans. President Wilson was another easy target, whom Villa dismissed as an "evangelizing professor" determined to reduce Mexico to "vassal" status. Soon these harsh words were joined by bullets, and the situation grew bloodier. Villa's foot soldiers began to target American business interests in Mexico, confiscating William Randolph Hearst's well-appointed ranch in a particularly daring move. In January 1916, seventeen American engineers were killed on a train traveling through northern Mexico. As Villa informed his ally Zapata, his primary intention was to communicate to Wilson that his homeland was a "tomb for thrones, crowns and traitors."[58] Growing bolder by the month, five hundred Villa supporters crossed the border to attack Columbus, New Mexico, resulting in seventeen more American deaths.[59] Such was the chaos that followed a well-intentioned move to depose a despot to whom Wilson took exception.

An attack on American territory demanded a strong response, and Wilson duly obliged. The president assembled a force of fifty-eight hundred men, which subsequently rose to ten thousand, under the command of General John J. Pershing. Its purpose was described ominously as a "punitive expedition." The force pushed some 350 miles into Mexico, encountering hit-and-run guerrilla-type resistance from Villa's army, which again successfully attacked U.S. territory at Glen Springs, Texas. The prospect of full-scale war with Mexico was fast materializing. Yet Wilson pulled back from the brink, reassuring Jane Addams—the Progressive reformer and peace activist—that "my heart is for peace."[60] The expedition withdrew in January 1917, and Mexico was more or less left alone to resolve the myriad political and socio-economic problems that had been exacerbated by conflict with the United States.

Wilson's Mexican intervention inaugurated a tradition in U.S. foreign policy—a militarized approach to "bad" or "evil" regimes in the name of democracy promotion—that endures to this day. It is difficult to view Wilson's policies toward the Mexican Revolution, and subsequent civil war, as anything but maladroit, leaving a legacy of distrust and animosity in U.S.-Mexican relations that still lingers. While Wilson resisted calls made by Lodge, Root, Roosevelt, and the Hearst press for all-out war, his Mexican intervention was a case study in how fine-sounding intentions can go badly awry. It was ironic that Wilson drew from the military engagement in Mexico a skepticism about the ability of the United States to effect regime change and produce a stable aftermath. This experience colored his later desire to avoid a large-scale intervention in the Russian Civil War. Wilson's caution in this instance is often lost on his modern-day devotees on both sides of the political divide.

Foreseeing problems at the end of 1913, Mahan had dismissed Wilson's democracy-promoting rationale for toppling Huerta as "amateurish diplomacy," which failed to "recognize that self-government is not practicable for all peoples, merely because the English-speaking peoples have made it work."[61] This was precisely the type of adventure that the United States should shun, Mahan's geopolitical philosophy held, as it depleted resources, undercut business, and constituted something of a blow to America's global reputation—for the conflict ended not in victory but in stalemate. Mahan feared the negative, unpredictable repercussions that accompanied leaps into the unknown. He felt that Wilson had departed from historical precedent with these ambitious plans to democratize and improve other nations. The president was leading with theory rather than framing policy on the basis of observed reality and an appropriately sober view of what constituted America's core interests.

In an address in Cincinnati on October 26, 1916, President Wilson offered a succinct account of the origins of the First World War: "Nothing in particular started it, but everything in general." Later in the campaign speech, he distilled the essence of the disastrous alliance system that led to a conflict that few of the great powers really wanted but that none believed they could escape without losing critical diplomatic face: "There had been growing up in Europe a mutual suspicion, an interchange of conjectures about what this government and that government was going to do, an interlacing of alliances and understandings, a complex web of intrigue and spying, that presently was sure to entangle the whole of the family of mankind on that side of the water in its meshes."[62] War came to Europe because its powers were fixed in an alliance system that precluded flexibility and thus portended disaster.[63] Yet there were more specific grievances that caused the balance-of-power system—devised by Charles-Maurice de Talleyrand-Périgord, Viscount Castlereagh, and Prince Metternich at the Congress of Vienna in 1814—to tumble down after a century of relative stability. First, France and Germany were still engaged in a dispute over the status of Alsace-Lorraine, the border region wrested from Paris following the Franco-Prussian War of 1870–1871 (an action that the German chancellor Otto von Bismarck opposed in anticipation of inspiring French antipathy). Second, there was the continuing crisis in the Balkans provoked by the efforts of various ethnic groups to secure independence from either the Habsburg (Austro-Hungarian) or Ottoman (Turkish) Empire. Third, there existed a long-standing dispute among the major European powers over competing colonial aspirations in the Third World, particularly in Africa, the only continent with much land still available to grab. Finally, Germany and Great Britain were engaged in a hotly contested naval race to outdo each other in the provision of dreadnought-class battleships. Here it is possible to identify the influence of Mahan's theories on the centrality of naval dominance, even though he was personally slow to appreciate the revolution in military affairs catalyzed by these technological advances. For the influence exerted by his belief in vigilant military preparedness, the British diplomat and historian Sir Charles Webster opined that "Mahan was one of the causes of the First World War," which does seem unduly harsh.[64]

Europe was divided into two camps at the start of 1914: the Entente

Powers, principally composed of Great Britain, France, and Russia, and the Central Powers, composed of Germany, Austria-Hungary, and Italy. All parties were bound to their allies by treaty commitments. While there were various points of friction that made a European-wide war a distinct possibility, the trigger point was an assassin's bullet. On June 28, 1914, Archduke Franz Ferdinand, heir apparent to the throne of the Habsburg Empire, was shot dead in Sarajevo by a nineteen-year-old Serbian nationalist named Gavrilo Princip. Austria-Hungary interpreted this as an act of war, secured a "blank check" from Berlin on July 6 that promised unconditional German support, and then made ten demands of Serbia that were purposefully unacceptable. When Serbia refused to sign two of the demands, on July 28 Austria-Hungary declared war. Rising indignantly in support of its Slavic cousins, the next day Russia offered its support when Tsar Nicholas II ordered a partial mobilization, an act designed to deter German involvement. The warning shot did not work, however; Berlin mobilized in response, which then led France, Russia's ally, to do the same on August 1. Germany declared war on Russia that very same day, leaving just one major power unaccounted for. Playing its usual historic role as a counterweight in European disputes, Great Britain entered the fray on August 4, when it declared war on Germany for refusing to honor Belgium's neutrality. With such speed and asininity began the cataclysm that was the First World War. During the next five years, more than fifteen million people would die. The war marked the beginning of the end of European primacy in global affairs.

Alfred Mahan was surprised by the speed in which war engulfed Europe, but he had few doubts about which side bore principal responsibility. On August 3, 1914, Mahan gave an interview to the *New York Evening Post* in which he argued that Vienna had used the assassination as a pretext for Austria and Germany to attack Russia, to which the essential corollary was the invasion of France to prevent a two-front war. In those circumstances Mahan believed that Britain had no choice but to "declare war at once," which it did a day later. Anticipating the inevitability of war from the events of August 1–3, Mahan had been working on an article for *Leslie's Weekly* in which he argued that Britain could defeat Germany by imposing a naval blockade, choking the nation into submission—just as the Union navy had done against the Confederacy during the Civil War.

Sensing an opportunity to rally Americans behind a pro-British stance, Mahan began working on another piece, provisionally titled "About What Is the War?" which dismissed the notion that effective international arbitration would have prevented this war and might do so in the future—a clear attack on the proclivities of the sitting president. Mahan's hardheaded analyses were in huge demand. The Wood Newspaper Syndicate, Pulitzer Publishing Company, Paul R. Reynolds literary agency, Charles Scribner's Sons, *The Independent*, and *Leslie's* all enticed Mahan to write for them with significant financial inducements—the latter two publications offered him $100 a week for the duration of the conflict for short dispatches on military developments as they happened.[65] But this promise of rapt nationwide attention and a significant payday was ended abruptly by Woodrow Wilson. Concerned that Mahan's august reputation, pro-British sympathies, and gifts of literary persuasion would whip up support for the Entente, and constrain his freedom of action, the president silenced Mahan. He sent the following letter to his secretary of war, Lindley Miller Garrison:

> I write to suggest that you request and advise all officers of the service, whether active or retired, to refrain from public comment of any kind upon the military or political situation on the other side of the water . . . It seems to me highly unwise and improper that officers of the Army and the Navy of the United States should make any public utterances to which any color of political or military criticism can be given where other nations are involved.[66]

There is no doubt that Mahan was Wilson's primary target, and he was furious. He was compelled to return a $100 fee from *The Independent*. Worse, Wilson had suppressed a message that was vital to America's national security. Mahan was convinced that German control of the European continent would allow Kaiser Wilhelm to project power into the Caribbean, thus threatening U.S. interests and making a mockery of the Monroe Doctrine. He composed two letters to Secretary of the Navy Josephus Daniels, both dated August 15, urging him to ask Wilson to reconsider:

> Public opinion being in the last analysis the determining force in our national polity, the effect of the Order is to disable a class of men best qualified by their past occupation, and present position, to put before the public considerations which would tend to base public opinion in matters of current public interest, upon sound professional grounds . . . At the age of seventy-four, I find myself silenced at a moment when the

particular pursuits of nearly thirty-five years . . . might be utilized for the public. I admit a strong feeling of personal disappointment . . . When I was in France eighteen months ago, a leading French statesman, a member of the present cabinet, told me that Germans had said to him that if they got France down again they would bleed her white. If a nation of that temper gets full control on the continent, which is what she is trying for, do you suppose it will long respect the Monroe Doctrine? At this moment Germany suffers from a lack of coaling stations here. If she downs France, why not take Martinique? Or if Great Britain, some Canadian port?[67]

Having been encouraged by McKinley to write on the Spanish-American War and by Roosevelt on the Russo-Japanese War and Second Hague Conference, Mahan was being silenced by a Democratic president determined to keep America out of what he viewed as Europe's descent into senseless conflict—in which all sides shared culpability—and who opposed Mahan's rationale for assisting Britain, France, and Russia. Daniels replied tersely, noting that Mahan's well-established pro-British affinities would "trench upon the line of American neutrality."[68] The president's muzzling order would stand and there was to be no future debate on the matter.

With no choice but to cease writing on the war, Mahan continued to attack those who argued that greater military preparedness, in the form of high defense spending, increased the prospects of future conflict, a misguided view to which Democrats were particularly susceptible. In a letter to *The New York Times* on August 31, Mahan wrote, "The hackneyed phrase, 'Vital interests or national honor,' really sums up the motives that lead nations to war. Armament is simply the instrument of which such motives avail themselves. If there be no armament, there is war all the same."[69] Unfortunately, this was one of Mahan's final public pronouncements on foreign policy. He passed away on December 1, 1914, after suffering a heart attack. He was eulogized by Theodore Roosevelt, in a reference to the halcyon era in which he and like-minded Republicans had been ascendant, as "one of the greatest and most useful influences in American life."[70] He died during a presidency that was utterly hostile to his views.

Wilson's reaction to the onset of war in Europe was complex. Just two days after the British declaration of war on Germany, Ellen Axson Wilson, the president's beloved wife, died suddenly. Wilson was consumed by grief, leading him to reduce meetings and speaking engagements to the barest minimum required. His statements during this critical time in world affairs were thus spare, somber, and typically eloquent. Wilson affirmed that the United States' position was one of scrupulous neutrality and called on his fellow Americans to display "the fine poise of undisturbed judgment, the dignity of self-control." The president believed that "the United States must be neutral in fact as well as in name during these days that are to try men's souls."[71] That this was a difficult task to achieve in a multiethnic, hyphenated America was not lost on Wilson. A third of America's citizens in 1914 had been born overseas. The majority, including the elite northeastern establishment, favored Britain and France (forgiving their alliance of convenience with tsarist Russia) due to a shared ethnic and cultural heritage, and a belief that Prussian militarism was at the root of Europe's problems. German Americans naturally supported the Central Powers, as did Irish Americans, through their enmity toward Britain, and some Jewish and Scandinavian Americans, who despised tsarist Russia for its institutionalized anti-Semitism and territorial ambitions to its western borders. In such a volatile national environment, Wilson sincerely believed that "we have to be neutral since otherwise our mixed populations would wage war on each other."[72]

Accompanying Wilson's strongly declared neutrality was an aversion to ordering any significant increases in the defense budget, the course urged by Mahan up to his death, and by Roosevelt and Lodge thereafter. In his State of the Union address of December 8, 1914, Wilson rebuffed those advocates of military preparedness, whose expensive contingency plans would "mean merely that we had lost our self-possession, that we had been thrown off our balance by a war with which we have nothing to do, whose causes can not touch us, whose very existence affords us opportunities of friendship and disinterested service which should make us ashamed of any thought of hostility or fearful preparation for trouble."[73] The opportunity to which Wilson referred was the possibility that the war would be stalemated, allowing the United States to serve as arbiter, affording Wilson increased leverage to preside over peace negotiations that would refashion international relations on more collaborative grounds. With prescience, Wilson remarked to the journalist Herbert B. Brougham that the best opportunity for "a just and equitable peace, and of the only possible peace that will be lasting, will be happiest if no nation gets the decision by arms; and the danger of an unjust peace, one that will be sure to invite further calamities, will be if some one nation or group of nations succeeds in enforcing its will upon the others."[74]

Wilson's assessment combined unimpeachable reasoning with a corresponding reluctance to consider how nations' hearts can be hardened in time
of war.

At the beginning, there was a remarkable unanimity of approach toward
the war across the Wilson administration. As Assistant Secretary of the Navy
Franklin Delano Roosevelt observed, "To my astonishment on reaching
the Dept., nobody seemed the least bit excited about the European crisis—
Mr. Daniels feeling chiefly very sad that his faith in human nature and
civilization and similar idealistic nonsense was receiving such a rude shock.
So I started in alone to get things ready and prepare plans for what ought to be
done by the Navy end of things."[75] One Democrat, at least, was displaying
an appreciation for Alfred Thayer Mahan's teachings.

FDR's second cousin was even less impressed by what he viewed as Wilson's self-righteous detachment. Theodore Roosevelt observed to his friend
Rudyard Kipling that Wilson's cowardliness was regrettable but explicable
considering that none of his family "fought on either side in the Civil War."
Roosevelt believed that Germany was the aggressor, that the Entente deserved
full American support, and that the course of the war threw into sharp
relief "the utter folly of the present administration and its pacifist supporters"
in promoting Pollyannaish arbitration schemes at the expense of military
preparedness. He concluded that Wilson was "a college president with an
astute and shifty mind, a hypocritical ability to deceive plain people."[76]

Yet Wilson's neutrality policy favored the Entente (or Allied) Powers more
than it did Germany, Austria-Hungary, and Italy. To pursue a true neutrality policy would have required the United States to cease all its exports to
Europe, which amounted to $900 million annually. The purest application
of neutrality was thus entirely unacceptable for the United States, as it would
have led to a sharp economic recession. During the period when Wilson
curtailed his official duties to grieve, Secretary of State Bryan, in an attempt
to define neutrality's "true spirit," imposed a blanket ban on American
loans to all belligerents. This action led the Allied Powers, more dependent
than the Central Powers on overseas finance, to swiftly run out of money to
purchase American goods, a situation as injurious to American business as
it was to Anglo-French military prospects. In October 1914, recognizing the
extent of the damage wreaked by this policy, Wilson ordered an amendment that permitted credits—but not public loans financed by the American
taxpayer—to be extended to Paris, London, and Moscow. Some $80 million
in credits were granted in the six months that followed, and the remaining
restrictions on loans were removed a year later. In the spring of 1915,

Colonel House, whose pro-British sentiments were firmer than those of his president, conceded that the American national interest was "bound up more or less" in Allied victory.[77]

Wilson also assisted the Allied cause in tolerating the British naval blockade of Germany, the strategy advocated by Mahan. The blockade prevented all neutral shipping from passing into Northern European ports and significantly curtailed the American export market. Recognizing that American trade with Germany was worth sacrificing for the sake of Anglo-American amity, however, Wilson rejected the confrontational precedent bequeathed by Thomas Jefferson and James Madison and declined to challenge the Royal Navy's dominance of the North Atlantic. American acquiescence to a British policy viewed by many as inhumane—starving Germans into submission was the aim, after all—earned Wilson enemies at home, abroad, and even within his own cabinet. William Jennings Bryan, for one, believed that Wilson had shown too much favoritism toward Britain.

The German government realized that an unchallenged blockade presaged its eventual defeat and launched a U-boat campaign around the British Isles on February 15, 1915, to target merchant shipping and hopefully sap London's morale as well as its finances. Germany justified this policy as retaliation against the blockade. Prior to 1915, the submarine had played a minor part in armed conflict; this German deployment opened a new, more ignoble, era in naval warfare. While traditional naval engagements sought to avoid civilian casualties, submarine-launched torpedoes killed innocents without warning. Realizing the threats posed by these developments, the president declared that Germany would be held to "strict accountability" for any attacks that hurt American interests.[78] Wilson's response was not stern enough to satisfy Roosevelt (or, indeed, House) but was confrontational enough to worry Bryan. Plotting a middle course between the pugnacity and pacifism of these two men would become increasingly difficult.

In fact, these early Bryan-Wilson disagreements were ossifying to produce two very different visions of how the United States should comport itself in world affairs. As the fighting grew bloodier in Europe, with no apparent end in sight, Wilson began to take a far greater interest in military preparedness, repudiating the Bryanite tradition in Democratic foreign policy that a large standing military threatened the virtue of the republic. Rather than recoiling from the European war with haughty disgust, as Bryan assuredly did, Wilson sensed an opportunity to intervene so as to better serve the interests of the United States and indeed the world. His preference was that his intervention be diplomatic, that he should preside over negotiations to end the war evenhandedly at the conference table. But if American intervention became unavoidable, Wilson realized that defense spending had to rise sharply in anticipation. Step by laborious step, urged on by the Anglophile Colonel House, Wilson was beginning to display a clear preference, expressed discreetly at this stage, for Allied victory. When Theodore Roosevelt impugned the "Wilson-Bryan attitude of trusting to fantastic peace treaties . . . A milk and water righteousness unbacked by force," he failed to perceive the way the president and his secretary of state were diverging in outlook.[79]

The Bryan-Wilson dispute came out into the open on May 7, 1915, when a German U-Boat torpedoed the British cruiser *Lusitania*. This vast luxury liner sank to the bottom of the ocean in eighteen minutes, and twelve hundred civilians perished. The harrowing casualty list included 94 children and, most significantly from Wilson's perspective, 128 Americans. The brutality of the assault was scarcely mitigated by the fact that the *Lusitania* was carrying Allied munitions, as the U-boat captain suspected. Such details lost saliency as the bodies of children washed up on the Irish coast weeks after the sinking. Theodore Roosevelt railed against German "piracy," demanded an immediate declaration of war, and observed that "as a nation, we have thought very little about foreign affairs; we don't realize that the murder of the thousand men, women, and children on the *Lusitania* is due, solely, to Wilson's abject cowardice and weakness in failing to take energetic action when the *Gulflight* [an American oil tanker] was sunk a few days previously."[80] Roosevelt and other Republicans were sensing an opportunity to land some significant blows on Wilson one year ahead of the general election.

While shocked by the loss of life, Wilson still retained hope that his services as an honest broker might yet be deployed in the event of military stalemate in Europe, a prospect that would sink with the *Lusitania* if the United States declared war. And so he dispatched a note to Berlin criticizing submarine warfare as an assault on "sacred principles of justice and humanity" and making clear that further attacks on civilian ships would be perceived by him as "deliberately unfriendly."[81] It is difficult to see how Wilson could have avoided dispatching such a note in the circumstances—and the language deployed was critical but restrained. But William Jennings Bryan decided that his president had been unduly provocative and that his actions would drag the nation inevitably into this infernal war. The secretary of state believed that American citizens should simply desist from traveling on belligerent ships, and that the British naval embargo, though nonlethal to Americans, was a comparable affront to the nation's neutral rights. When Wilson declined to accept this reasoning, Bryan tendered his resignation, removing himself as the primary antiwar voice from the administration. A path to war was becoming discernible.

At the moment when the German torpedoes struck the *Lusitania*, the land war in Europe was stalemated. During the early skirmishes, the German army had driven to within thirty miles of Paris, at which point they were held and then repulsed by a French and British counteroffensive. At France's eastern boundary, each side began digging trenches—in conformance with Dennis Hart Mahan's teachings—two narrow lines 475 miles in length and just a few hundred yards apart, from the North Sea to the mountainous borders of neutral Switzerland. At the beginning of 1915, Germany controlled 19,500 square miles of French and Belgian territory. Twelve months later, after ferocious fighting, the Allies had recaptured just eight.[82] It was from these fixed and filthy trenches—primarily efficient in their incubation of disease and vermin—that many of the men who fought on the western front lived and died.

There was little movement in the trench lines from November 1914 to March 1917, just wave after wave of inconclusive assaults that followed a broadly similar pattern. The attacking side was stalled by barbed wire, craters, and bodies, and then mowed down by defending machine gun fire. Then the roles were reversed to the same effect—the former defenders well able to visualize their fate—and battlefield deaths increased in multiples of thousands, then tens of thousands, and then hundreds of thousands. German and French casualties at the Battle of Verdun exceeded those of all Americans during the Civil War. Great Britain suffered four hundred thousand casualties during the inconclusive Somme offensive—some sixty thousand men died or were seriously wounded over the course of one day. The deployment of poison gas by both sides was an additional layer of horror. Wilson captured the nature of this war well when he described it as a "vast, gruesome contest of systematized destruction."[83]

The bestiality of the First World War was harrowing, and it is in this context—a cataclysmic human tragedy at the heart of the supposedly most advanced and "civilized" continent on earth—that we must appraise Wilson's authoring of a grand strategy that was similarly unprecedented. Through 1915 and 1916, Wilson devoted more and more of his time to considering how he might deploy American power, which would be embraced for the purity of its intentions, to end the war and prevent the outbreak of future conflicts on a comparable scale. What was required was nothing less than a rewriting of the rules of international engagement. His ultimate aspiration was to fashion a new world system in which geopolitical rivalry was solely commercial (and peaceable) in nature, and in which spheres of influence, alliances of convenience, and rapacious colonial acquisition were consigned to history. The entire balance-of-power system was to be jettisoned in favor of binding international collaboration, policed ultimately by the world's preeminent economic power, which was biased in no particular direction.

His vision was also informed by his belief that democratization was the key to creating a more peaceable world, because democracies are far less likely to resort to war, a belief that was later developed by adherents of Democratic Peace theory.[84] As Wilson would later put it: "A steadfast concert for peace can never be maintained except by a partnership of democratic nations . . . Only free peoples can hold their purpose and their honour steady to a common end and prefer the interests of mankind to any narrow interest of their own."[85] This insight was conditioned by his political science background, which encouraged the unveiling of new behavioral norms. Wilson did not want to simply defeat Germany and its allies. He wanted to reveal new truths about the world and humanity's essentially collaborative nature. Mahan was correct that he had departed from precedent. The president was practicing foreign policy as a science; the world at that time was his laboratory.

Of course, Wilson's Presbyterian Universalism also played a role in shaping his idealistic solution to a conflict straight from the pages of the Old Testament. The president was propagating a radically new foreign-policy doctrine: America's security was intertwined with the maintenance of a peaceable world, and its duty was to confront aggression wherever it threatened the global equilibrium. Observing humanity's best effort yet at creating Armageddon, his visionary response, as expressed in fledgling form in his December 7, 1915, State of the Union address, appears both explicable and justifiable:

> Because we demand unmolested development and the undisturbed government of our own lives upon our own principles of right and liberty, we resent, from whatever quarter it may come, the aggression we ourselves will not practice. We insist upon security in prosecuting our self-chosen lines of national development. We do more than that. We demand it also for others. We do not confine our enthusiasm for individual liberty and free national development to the incidents and movements of affairs which affect only ourselves. We feel it wherever there is a people that tries to walk in these difficult paths of independence and right.[86]

Throughout 1916 Wilson continued to craft his foreign-policy vision and prepare his nation for the worst. At the end of January, the president took a nine-day tour of the Northeast and Midwest in which he delivered eleven speeches emphasizing the importance of military preparedness. At one point Wilson even channeled Mahan, calling for the creation of "incomparably the greatest navy in the world."[87] Pacifists, Jeffersonian idealists, social reformers, and some Progressives were appalled. They suspected that his speeches portended greater profits for big business and the permanent militarization of American society. Wilson's speaking tour, and the preparedness stance he adopted, more or less killed the Bryanite Democratic Party that Mahan had known and reviled. He paved the way for the passage of preparedness legislation through Congress, opposed by Bryanites in both chambers. But the overall balance of votes cast represented a powerful vindication of Wilson's persuasive talents—only two Democrats in the Senate and a quarter of House Democrats voted against their president.

The Democratic Party had been changed irrevocably; never again would it propose pseudo-isolationism from European affairs as a position. The National Defense Act of June 1916 increased the regular army to 223,000 men over five years and increased the number of active members of the National Guard to 450,000. A Naval Expansion Act launched a flurry of construction activity at Virginia's shipyards, in which four dreadnoughts and eight cruisers were built in just one year. To pay for this military expansion, Wilson raised America's first income tax, which he had introduced in 1913. This action appeased some fellow Democrats by ensuring that the wealthy bore the preponderant financial burden of assuring America's safety from harm. Theodore Roosevelt's description of Wilson's program as "flintlock legislation" rang hollow in such remarkable circumstances.[88]

Wilson's decisive move toward military preparedness solidified a division in American politics between internationalists—who believed that greater U.S. engagement with the world at the socioeconomic-diplomatic level should be celebrated, not feared—and isolationists, who held that maintaining an arm's-length relationship with Europe (though not necessarily the rest of the world) was the best way to preserve American liberties and ensure its citizenry would spill no blood for the chicaneries of the Old World. These labels are approximate and can often obscure historical understanding, particularly when one considers that many individuals subscribed to elements of both. But the terms have a broad utility in capturing the tenor of those times.[89] The isolationist strain in geopolitical thought was exemplified in the person of William Jennings Bryan, whose popularity in the South meant that his resignation badly hurt Wilson in Congress. The president's foreign-policy allies were increasingly to be found in a subdivision of the Grand Old Party, where the conservative internationalist William Howard Taft, who had raised Roosevelt's hackles in advocating arbitration in 1911, and other (mainly Ivy League, patrician) Atlanticists were beginning to view German victory as a scenario that the United States could not tolerate.

In June 1915, Taft announced the formation of the League to Enforce Peace with the grand aspiration of spurring on the creation of a world parliament that would arbitrate disputes and, in time, realize Immanuel Kant's ambition of securing perpetual peace. In foreign-policy matters, Republicans were divided between those, like Roosevelt and Mahan, who extolled war as ennobling and viewed arbitration as a dangerous illusion, and others, like Taft and Elihu Root, who were as shocked as Wilson by the human tragedy in Europe and consequently were intent on devising a comprehensive cure for the centuries-old malady of great power conflict. These three strains of foreign-policy ideology—isolationism, internationalism, and Mahanian realism—emerged with clarity in 1916.

Wilson had been thinking along similar lines to Taft, and a speech he delivered in June 1916 stated that the United States should "become a partner in any feasible association of nations" dedicated to preserving peace.[90] As Election Day approached, Democratic strategists employed the sound bite "He kept us out of war" to persuasive effect across the nation, a gambit that immediately aroused Wilson's concern. In a revealing letter to Josephus Daniels, the president complained that "I can't keep the country out of the war. They talk of me as though I were a god. Any little German lieutenant can put us into war at any time by some calculated outrage."[91]

Unsurprisingly, foreign policy was a more significant issue on the campaign trail in 1916 than it had been four years earlier. During a Roosevelt-less election, and up against the moderately pro-Allied and relatively characterless Republican candidate Charles Evans Hughes, Wilson was consistent in advocating the creation of a league of nations to ensure peace, and he accused his opponent, whom Theodore Roosevelt supported enthusiastically, of dangerous belligerency. To a popular backdrop that remained hostile to U.S. involvement in the European war, and one that was broadly impressed by the president's domestic accomplishments, Wilson secured a narrow victory: winning 277 electoral college votes to Hughes's 254. The most satisfying element of the election from Wilson's perspective was that he had prevailed against unified Republican opposition and had increased his share of the vote from 41 to 49 percent—not an outright majority but not far off either. It is difficult to claim that election was a ringing endorsement of Wilson, yet it still made him the first Democrat since Andrew Jackson to win two consecutive terms. In many ways it was a remarkable achievement that hinted at future electoral dominance for his party. But his margin of victory was narrow considering he was a national leader at a time of war.

Wilson had little time to savor his victory. Anticipating a moment when neutrality would be impossible to maintain, the president invited the Old World belligerents to state their final war aims and commence negotiations that he would broker evenhandedly in the New World. All sides rebuffed Wilson's offer with alacrity. British prime minister David Lloyd George formulated a list of demands patently unacceptable to Germany, while Berlin replied haughtily that if the belligerents did move to the conference table, it would insist on excluding Wilson's grandstanding participation. Germany believed it was gaining the upper hand on the western front, while Britain was confident that the blockade was close to forcing surrender through starvation—at this stage the average German was subsisting on just one thousand calories a day, insufficient for a small child, let alone a full-grown adult.[92] Nobody was much interested in Wilson's peaceable platitudes. Britain wanted American participation to tilt the balance in its favor and crush the Hun. Germany was concerned that Wilson's urge to play peacemaker might deny them a victory that could be won quickly if it threw off the shackles and deployed the full force of its U-boat fleet.

On January 22, 1917, Wilson delivered a speech in the Senate that took aim at such false hopes and proposed a radical new approach to international affairs. The president declared that the war must conclude with "peace without victory," the only course available that was guaranteed to prevent the onset of future hostilities based on unfinished business. It was one of Wilson's most memorable phrases, for it contained a fundamental diplomatic truism that none of the belligerents were willing to accept. The speech did not end there. Wilson further contended that for peace to be enduring, a "community of power" must replace the nineteenth-century concept of the "balance of power," which was no longer fit for purpose. All nations must be accorded equal standing and protection under international law, Wilson believed. He again called for the creation of an international organization whose central purpose was to ensure "no such catastrophe shall ever overwhelm us again." In a concluding salvo against isolationism, Wilson warned that without engaged American leadership, "no covenant of cooperative peace [could] keep the future safe against war."[93]

Wilson also tried to connect his broader ambitions regarding the establishment of "international concert of peace" to long-standing traditions on American foreign policy:

> I am proposing, as it were, that the nations should with one accord adopt the doctrine of President Monroe as the doctrine of the world: that no nation should seek to extend its polity over any other nation or people, but that every people should be left free to determine its own polity; its own way of development—unhindered, unthreatened, unafraid, the little along with the great and powerful.
>
> I am proposing that all nations henceforth avoid entangling alliances which would draw them into competitions of power, catch them in a net of intrigue and selfish rivalry, and disturb their own affairs with influences intruded from without. There is no entangling alliance in a concert of power. When all unite to act in the same sense and with the same purpose, all act in the common interest and are free to live their own lives under a common protection.[94]

It was smart politics for Wilson to cite precedent for his ambitions in the Monroe Doctrine and George Washington's farewell warning against "entangling alliances." He was likely correct in surmising that summoning these totemic foreign-policy pronouncements would reassure.

But of course Wilson was proposing not simply the logical broadening of an established principle. He was taking two distinctly American foreign policy axioms and universalizing them to the point where their original purpose was unrecognizable. The 1823 Monroe Doctrine—warning European nations against interference in any part of the western hemisphere—served the U.S. national interest above all, pacifying the hemisphere in which it resided. And it was sustained, first and foremost, by the Royal Navy's dominance in the Atlantic, not by American military power or moral legitimacy per se. The Monroe Doctrine claimed U.S. dominance over Latin America, riling the citizens of those nations the doctrine claimed to protect. It is doubtful that many Mexicans, for example, felt themselves "free to determine" their own polity. The idea that there was "no entangling alliance in a concert of power" would not have instilled much confidence in the "little" nations. And it was optimistic of Wilson to suppose that the "great and powerful" nations might take risks with their national sovereignty. There was no precedent for the world system Wilson had in mind.

It did not take long for Theodore Roosevelt to register his disapproval:

"Peace without victory is the natural ideal of the man who is too proud to fight."[95] And for all its eloquence, Wilson's "peace without victory" speech did not produce the desired mellowing of the protagonists when confronted with a more palatable future. Suffering grave depredations under the British blockade, Germany removed all restrictions on U-boat warfare on February 1, 1917, a policy that treated as fair game any vessel detected in the North Atlantic. Fully aware that an unrestricted U-boat campaign was likely to provoke American belligerency, Germany's goal was to destroy British resolve before the United States had time to marshal its vast resources and bring them to bear on the western front. It was a calculated gamble that did not come off.

Wilson immediately broke diplomatic relations with Germany and assembled his cabinet to discuss the American response. All were at one in their advice that American participation in the war was now inevitable. Yet even at this stage, Wilson strove to avoid an American declaration of war. The president's equivocation led Theodore Roosevelt to complain to California governor Hiram Johnson that the United States was being led by "a very cold and selfish man, a very timid man when it comes to dealing with physical danger . . . As for shame, he has none, and if anyone kicks him, he brushes his clothes, and utters some lofty sentence."[96] The president's options were finally exhausted when he received news on February 19 that Germany was attempting to formalize a military alliance with Mexico against the United States.

On January 16, 1917, the German foreign secretary, Arthur Zimmermann, had cabled the German embassy in Mexico instructing the ambassador to explore the possibility of a German-Mexican military alliance with President Venustiano Carranza. If Mexico assisted Germany in the event of war with the United States, Zimmermann proposed that Carranza should be amply rewarded with the Mexican recovery of Texas, New Mexico, and Arizona. The proposal was fanciful in the extreme but held incendiary potential if the details were made public. This worst-case scenario materialized when the Zimmermann Telegram was decoded by British cryptographers, who gleefully forwarded it to the U.S. embassy in London on February 19. It took awhile for American intelligence analysts and members of the Wilson administration to accept that the intercept was genuine and not just British propaganda (a dark art at which London was adept). Convincing Wilson of the cable's provenance was further complicated by the British requirement that it would not reveal the full extent of its highly sophisticated intelligence-gathering operations, which mopped up American as well as

German telegraphic traffic. When the cable's authenticity was proved beyond doubt, Wilson reluctantly accepted the mantle of war that events had thrust upon him. On April 2, 1917, he delivered a thirty-six-minute speech to Congress requesting a declaration of war against Germany:

> It is a fearful thing to lead this great peaceful people into war . . . But the right is more precious than peace, and we shall fight for the things which we have always carried nearest our hearts, for democracy, for the right of those who submit to authority to have a voice in their own governments, for the rights and liberties of small nations, for a universal dominion of right by such a concert of free peoples as shall bring peace and safety to all nations and make the world itself at last free.[97]

The manner in which Wilson declared war—for congressional approval was all but guaranteed—was remarkable. While Wilson took aim at Germany's "cruel and unmanly" U-boat attacks on neutral shipping, the broad casus belli he offered to justify American participation in the deadliest conflict in human history was purposefully grandiose, and some might say unattainable. The United States had to defeat Germany because "a steadfast concert for peace can never be maintained except by a partnership of democratic nations . . . The world must be made safe for democracy," a phrase that echoed through the twentieth century and into the twenty-first.[98] As Wilson spoke those visionary words, Senator John Sharp of Mississippi stood up and clapped alone. The rest of the chamber followed, creating a stirring cacophony that instead struck Wilson as dissonant. "Think what it was they were applauding," he later observed. "My message today was a message of death for our young men. How strange it seems to applaud that."[99]

Wilson's idealistic rationale for war was born of sincere conviction that a revolution in world affairs was necessary in the midst of an appalling conflict, one that held the potential to eradicate an entire generation of working-age European men. His ambition was conditioned by his intellectual background and his disciplinary proclivities that tended toward the social scientific, and by his desire to depart from precedent and attempt something never attempted before. It should also be borne in mind, however, that convincing Wilson's fellow Americans of the efficacy of participation in Europe's war was a formidable challenge, which required poetry in presentation as well as ambition in detail. The progressive journalist Walter Lippmann captured this requirement well when he wrote that "men will not die and starve and freeze for the things which orthodox diplomacy holds most precious."[100] The speech carried off this trick and was as well received in the press as it was on Capitol Hill, where war was authorized by a margin of 82–6 in the Senate and 373–50 in the House. Bryanites were again in the vanguard of this small but spirited congressional opposition, although some Republicans joined in and were duly stigmatized for their lack of patriotism. When the Progressive Nebraskan Republican George Norris stood up in the House and warned that "we are going into war upon the command of gold . . . I feel that we are about to put the dollar sign on the American flag," his colleagues shouted him down with the most incendiary word in politics: "Treason! Treason!"[101]

The American military contribution to Allied victory in the First World War was more decisive than its actions to defeat Hitler twenty-five years hence—a statement that appears odd at first sight. The U.S. Army was dwarfed in size by those of the Old World belligerents in 1917, although its latent potential—sustained as it was by the world's largest economy—was vast. America fought for a little under a year on the western front in 1918, while its participation in the Second World War lasted four years and carried a far greater blood price. How are the two conflicts even comparable? The answer lies not in the numbers of U.S. troops deployed, nor the facility with which they fought, but in the fact that the military balance in 1917 was finely poised between the Allied and Central Powers, making the full weight of American participation, when fully mobilized, almost impossible for Germany and its allies to resist. The European component of the Second World War was decided primarily on the eastern front, by the gargantuan efforts of Stalin's Soviet Union and the twenty-six million Soviet citizens who died resisting the existential threat posed by Hitler. The European component of the First World War was decided by America's timely and decisive intervention. Nearly ten million French, German, British, Russian, Ottoman, Italian, Austrian, Hungarian, Belgian, Greek, Serbian, Romanian, Montenegrin, Indian, Australian, Canadian, South African, and New Zealand troops died on the battlefields to deny victory to the other side, producing a stalemate that offered just enough hope to maintain the momentum of death. With the combatants locked in lethal balance, Wilson's declaration of war saved countless lives. The United States was the only irresistible force in the First World War.

The main problem from the Allied perspective was that it took a full year for American troops to make their way to Europe in decisive numbers.

And in the meantime, emboldened by American support but lacking its tangible benefits, Britain and France launched offensives throughout the summer of 1917 that ended badly. Low morale, which led to widespread desertions and mutiny, enervated the French army, which to that point had suffered nearly a million battlefield deaths. Then in October 1917, the Bolsheviks under Vladimir Lenin seized power in Russia and announced their intention to seek peace with Germany so as to better protect the revolution at home. In signing the Treaty of Brest-Litovsk on March 3, 1918, Lenin and Trotsky ceded one-third of the Russian Empire to Germany and gave it a free hand to devote all its attention to the western front.

Realizing that they now possessed the best and last chance to secure outright victory, Germany and its allies launched a series of furious offensives in the spring of 1918, just as the slow-turning cogs of U.S. mobilization propelled its army onto the battlefield. This infusion of fresh manpower, well-fed, spoiling for a fight, and oblivious of the horrors of the previous years, allowed the Allies to repulse Germany and strike back with a counteroffensive throughout the summer. By the late summer and autumn of 1918, a million American troops were launching themselves into battle—while three million were preparing to join the fray soon. The failure of its spring offensive, and the arrival of the American "doughboys," hurt German morale. The Central and Allied Powers had fought to something approaching exhaustion by that summer, with the latter wilting badly. The U.S. Army reinvigorated the spirits of one side and rained down a deathblow on the other.

Wilson had joined the conflict on the Allied side as an "associate power," meaning that the army, led by General Pershing, operated outside the Allied command structure, and the president retained more freedom of action than he would as a formal ally. Some might detect an irony here in that Wilson's veneration of international collaboration appeared not to extend to winning the war. Yet Wilson's rationale is explicable and admirably pragmatic: the American public was not prepared for a full-scale alliance with Britain and France, and the president retained hope that Germany might come to view American participation as the best way to concede surrender on more or less equitable terms—a possibility that would be extinguished if he hugged Paris and London too close. Wilson viewed his war aims as quite different from those of Britain and France. An important corollary to this stance of evenhandedness was making clear to the American public that the United States was fighting against the militaristic German government, not the people who suffered under its rule.

As the war continued, however, it became impossible for Wilson to lead the fight against Kaiser Wilhelm while restraining anti-German sentiment at home. At the highbrow end of the spectrum, concert halls refused to host performances of Beethoven and Bach. At a more workaday level, dachshunds were renamed "liberty hounds," sauerkraut became "liberty cabbage," and phrases such as "liberty measles" even became common parlance.[102] Anti-German feeling increased in intensity, turning violent at times, just as Wilson had predicted it would to the editor of the New York *World*. "To fight you must be brutal and ruthless," Wilson lamented to Frank Cobb, "and the spirit of ruthless brutality will enter into the very fiber of our national life, infecting Congress, the courts, the policemen on the beat, the man in the street."[103]

Wilson might have included "the president in the White House," for the Espionage Act of 1917 and the Sedition Act of 1918 were both informed by a ruthless aim: to silence internal dissent. In October 1917, the historian Charles Beard resigned from Columbia University's history department to protest the firing of two colleagues who had publicly criticized the war. Beard had earlier observed that "if we have to suppress everything we don't like to hear, this country is resting on a pretty wobbly basis. This country was founded on disrespect and the denial of authority, and this is no time to stop free discussion."[104] The socialist leader Eugene Debs was jailed for uttering the factually accurate remark "The master class has always declared the wars: the subject class has always fought the battles." In April 1918, a mob in St. Louis lynched Robert Prager, a German-born American with suspected socialist leanings. The orchestrators of the lynching were acquitted by a jury after twenty minutes of "deliberation."[105] Wartime America was becoming increasingly febrile, as Wilson had feared. But his Espionage and Sedition Acts made the situation yet more volatile by fueling the actions of hate-filled "patriots."

As the federal government mobilized its military capabilities, and Americans learned to dislike Germans, the president applied the finishing touches to his strategy to win the peace. In the fall of 1917, Wilson requested Colonel House, his closest adviser, to assemble a group of scholars to identify the most salient postwar problems and offer advice on the best way to secure an enduring peace. The "Inquiry," consisting of over 150 staff members, produced more than three thousand papers and reports and displaced the State Department, in the president's mind, as the principal repository of usable foreign-policy expertise.[106] In October 1917, Wilson's intellectuals convened for the first time, at the New York Public Library. After passing through its Beaux Arts portico, each scholar would inform either the head librarian or his associate—the only staff aware of their purpose—that they were members of the "Inquiry," at which point they were ushered away to a private room to commence deliberations.[107] James T. Shotwell, a historian from Columbia University, came up with the group's title, later remarking that it constituted a useful "blind to the general public; but would serve to identify it among the initiated."[108] Increasingly concerned by the need to preserve anonymity, House moved the Inquiry in November from the bustle of 42nd Street and Fifth Avenue to the headquarters of the American Geographical Society, on West 155th Street and Broadway. The director of the society, and soon to be president of the Inquiry, Isaiah Bowman, declined to inform his board of the purpose of his new tenants. For the Inquiry's intellectuals, these cloak-and-dagger thrills were quite a change from the normal routine of students, seminars, and archives.

Walter Lippmann served as the first secretary of the Inquiry. As an undergraduate at Harvard, he had worked with the philosopher George Santayana and "took tea" with the father of pragmatism, William James. Lippmann's intellectual gifts were such that Theodore Roosevelt described the twenty-eight-year-old as "the most brilliant young man of his age in all the United States."[109] Three years later, Wilson instructed Edward House to hire Lippmann—who was serving at that point as an assistant to Secretary of War Newton D. Baker—and allow him significant latitude in forming the Inquiry's membership and its recommendations. It was a task he performed with his customary verve. "We are skimming the cream of the younger and more imaginative scholars," Lippmann remarked. "What we are on the lookout for is genius—sheer, startling genius, and nothing else will do."[110]

On December 23, 1917, the three primary participants in the Inquiry, Sidney Edward Mezes, David Hunter Miller, and Walter Lippmann, presented a long memorandum to the president titled "The Present Situation: The War Aims and Peace Terms It Suggests."[111] After the Christmas holidays, on January 15, 1918, Wilson and House got together to draft a definitive statement of foreign-policy aspirations, culled from the Inquiry's memorandum. As House noted in his diary, "We actually got down to work at half past ten and finished remaking the map of the world, as we would have it, at half past twelve o'clock."[112] The British diplomat and intellectual Harold Nicolson later observed: "Had the Treaty of Peace been drafted solely by the American experts it would have been one of the wisest as well as the most scientific documents ever devised."[113]

Wilson and House condensed the most important of the Inquiry's recommendations and divided them into "Fourteen Points," identified by scribbling on the margins of the original document. In a speech delivered to a joint session of Congress on January 8, Wilson presented what he described as "the only possible programme" to safeguard the world's peace.

    I. Open covenants of peace, openly arrived at, after which there shall be no private international understandings of any kind, but diplomacy shall proceed always frankly and in the public view.

    II. Absolute freedom of navigation upon the seas, outside territorial waters, alike in peace and in war, except as the seas may be closed in whole or in part by international action for the enforcement of international covenants.

    III. The removal, so far as possible, of all economic barriers and the establishment of an equality of trade conditions among all the nations consenting to the peace and associating themselves for its maintenance.

    IV. Adequate guarantees given and taken that national armaments will be reduced to the lowest point consistent with domestic safety.

    V. A free, open-minded, and absolutely impartial adjustment of all colonial claims, based upon a strict observance of the principle that in determining all such questions of sovereignty the interests of the populations concerned must have equal weight with the equitable claims of the Government whose title is to be determined.

    VI. The evacuation of all Russian territory and such a settlement of all questions affecting Russia as will secure the best and freest co-operation of the other nations of the world in obtaining for her an unhampered and unembarrassed opportunity for the independent determination of her own political development and national policy, and assure her of a sincere welcome into the society of free nations under institutions of her own choosing; and, more than a welcome, assistance also of every kind that she may need and may herself desire.

    VII. Belgium, the whole world will agree, must be evacuated and restored, without any attempt to limit the sovereignty which she enjoys in common with all other free nations.

    VIII. All French territory should be freed and the invaded portions restored, and the wrong done to France by Prussia in 1871 in the matter of Alsace-Lorraine, which has unsettled the peace of the

world for nearly fifty years, should be righted, in order that
peace may once more be made secure in the interest of all.

IX. A readjustment of the frontiers of Italy should be effected along
clearly recognizable lines of nationality.

X. The peoples of Austria-Hungary, whose place among the nations
we wish to see safeguarded and assured, should be accorded the
freest opportunity of autonomous development.

XI. Rumania, Serbia, and Montenegro should be evacuated; occupied
territories restored; Serbia accorded free and secure access to the
sea; and the relations of the several Balkan States to one another
determined by friendly counsel along historically established
lines of allegiance and nationality; and international guarantees
of the political and economic independence and territorial integrity of the several Balkan States should be entered into.

XII. The Turkish portions of the present Ottoman Empire should be
assured a secure sovereignty, but the other nationalities which are
now under Turkish rule should be assured an undoubted security
of life and an absolutely unmolested opportunity of autonomous
development, and the Dardanelles should be permanently opened
as a free passage to the ships and commerce of all nations under
international guarantees.

XIII. An independent Polish State should be erected which would include the territories inhabited by indisputably Polish populations,
which would be assured a free and secure access to the sea, and
whose political and economic independence and territorial integrity should be guaranteed by international covenant.

XIV. A general association of nations must be formed under specific
covenants for the purpose of affording mutual guarantees of political independence and territorial integrity to great and small
states alike.[114]

Wilson's Fourteen Points promised a new system of international relations that jettisoned the logic of alliance formation based on national self-
interest—the diplomatic verity to which all nation-states had subscribed
since the 1648 Treaty of Westphalia—and replaced it with point fourteen: "a
general association of nations." As Henry Kissinger observes in *Diplomacy*,
"Woodrow Wilson told the Europeans that, henceforth, the international
system should be based not on the balance of power but on ethnic self-
determination, that their security should depend not on military alliances

but on collective security, and that their diplomacy should no longer be conducted secretly by experts but on the basis of 'open agreements, openly arrived at.' "[115] The Fourteen Points distilled the essence of a geopolitical philosophy that remains vital today: Wilsonianism. Whether Wilson could convince France and Britain of the points' merits remained moot, although the auguries were not promising. Upon reading the transcript of Wilson's speech, the French prime minister Georges Clemenceau remarked, "The good lord himself required only ten points."[116] He later dismissed Wilson's Fourteen Points as constituting "the most empty theory," a dig at Wilson's scientistic pretensions. "He believed you could do everything by formulas."[117]

The usual domestic suspects were similarly concerned by the grandiosity of Wilson's ambition. Appalled by the diminution of U.S. national sovereignty promised by the Fourteen Points, Theodore Roosevelt thundered in Chicago that "we are not internationalists. We are American nationalists."[118] Sensing the inevitability of German defeat, and Wilson's ardent focus on realizing his Fourteen Points, Roosevelt urged the American people at the forthcoming midterm elections to "emphatically repudiate the so-called Fourteen Points and the various similar utterances of the president."[119] He thought the elevation of ethnic self-determination (implied, rather than explicitly stated) muddle-headed and dangerous, just as Wilson's emphasis on democracy promotion failed to accord to the reality that confronted him: a fallen world of flawed, self-interested nations. Roosevelt similarly viewed the Fourteen Points' promotion of "open diplomacy" as unrealistic and its approach to colonial claims as likely to hurt America's closest ally, Great Britain. He suspected that Germany, much more than Britain and France, might come to embrace Wilson's vision for reasons of self-interest, the very notion that the Fourteen Points were designed to transcend.

And so it came to pass. As the year progressed, bearing the full brunt of an American-assisted Allied assault, and aware that the deployment of three million more Americans spelled certain defeat, Germany approached Wilson directly in October 1918 to request the drafting of an armistice based on his Fourteen Points. A new parliamentary government in Germany had decided to swallow its pride (and earlier barbs concerning Wilson's suitability as a mediator) and embrace Wilson's peace without victory, or peace without defeat, as Germany might have hoped. The president responded cautiously but interestedly to this advance and did not inform Britain and France, a discourtesy that Edward House, for one, deplored. Roosevelt reentered the fray on October 24, when he wrote an open letter to Henry Cabot

Lodge—who would become chair of the Foreign Relations Committee after Republicans won control of the House and the Senate—affirming that the United States "must obtain peace by the hammerings of the guns and not chat about peace to the accompaniment of the clicking of typewriters."[120]

Lodge's sympathy toward Roosevelt's views was clear. He had earlier confessed to Roosevelt that he had "never expected to hate anyone in politics with the hatred I feel towards Wilson."[121] Roosevelt's final pronouncement on foreign policy, which he dictated on January 3, 1919, declared it unconscionable that Washington might be compelled by a multilateral institution to send "our gallant young men to die in obscure fights in the Balkans or in Central Europe." The only matters that should concern Americans were those that pertained directly to the national interest; the United States, Roosevelt added, must never assume "a position of international Meddlesome Matty."[122] Three days later, a heart attack killed Roosevelt as he slept. Wilson's vice president, Thomas R. Marshall, offered an apt eulogy: "Death had to take Roosevelt sleeping, for if he had been awake, there would have been a fight."[123] Mahan and Roosevelt both died offering stern criticisms of Woodrow Wilson. But Henry Cabot Lodge remained.

Having been tempted to coerce Paris and London into accepting peace on his own terms—threatening to withdraw America's military, a bargaining tool of considerable weight—Wilson agreed to work with his allies and signed off on terms "laid down in the president's address to Congress of 8 January 1918, and the principles of settlement enunciated in his subsequent address."[124] While at first sight these terms of German surrender represented a victory for Wilson, Clemenceau and Lloyd George insisted that two caveats be added to this message. First, Britain and France reserved the right to decide how "freedom of the seas" should be interpreted. Second, and much more significant, Germany should be made liable for the substantial damage caused to Allied civilians and property over the course of the conflict. How these addenda might color the complexion of the peace treaty remained to be seen. One thing was sure: when the belligerents laid down their weapons at 11:00 a.m. on November 11, 1918, Wilson lost the main tool he possessed to craft a peace based on his Fourteen Points. The trump card that was the U.S. Army had been played to devastating effect—Wilson later remarked that his nation "had the infinite privilege of fulfilling her destiny and saving the world"—but higher-stakes diplomatic games remained.[125] Hereafter, Wilson would have to rely on his wits and his advisers at the negotiating table to craft an evenhanded and durable peace. Thereafter, any peace treaty would require ratification from a Republican-controlled

Senate. These were the biggest tests of Wilson's career and, regrettably, they were ones that he failed.

As a global hegemon, Europe had been mortally wounded by World War I. Three empires—the German, Austro-Hungarian, and Ottoman—lay in ruins, while subsequent Anglo-French expansion at their expense mainly revealed an inability to finance such commitments. After scoring a notable success in Russia, the threat of Bolshevik revolution hung ominously over Germany and much of Central Europe. The Czech leader Tomáš Masaryk captured the scene perceptively when he described Europe on the eve of peace negotiations as "a laboratory resting on a vast cemetery."[126] It is in this context that we may appreciate the cathartic enthusiasm that greeted Woodrow Wilson upon his arrival in France, a mood that is captured evocatively by the Austrian Jewish writer Stefan Zweig:

> We believed—and the whole world believed with us—that this had been the war to end all wars, that the beast which had been laying our world waste was tamed or even slaughtered. We believed in President Wilson's grand program, which was ours too . . . We were foolish, I know. But we were not alone. Anyone who lived through that time will remember how the streets of all the great cities echoed to cries of jubilation, hailing President Wilson as the savior of the world . . . There was never such trusting credulity in Europe as in those first few days of peace . . . Hell lay behind us, what could make us fear now?[127]

America's intervention had shortened the war, and Wilson's new vision for international affairs proffered perpetual peace as its seductive primary goal. Raymond Fosdick recalled that "Wilson's welcome in Paris was accompanied by the most remarkable demonstration of enthusiasm and affection on the part of the Parisians that I have ever heard of, let alone seen." In his diary he wrote that "an American can be anything he wants to be today; he owns the city."[128] In *The Shape of Things to Come*, a work of science fiction that anticipated the development of world government, H. G. Wells wrote that for "a brief interval, Wilson stood alone for mankind . . . He ceased to be a common statesman; he became a Messiah."[129] The British economist John Maynard Keynes observed that "when Wilson left Washington he enjoyed a prestige and moral influence throughout the world unequalled in history . . . Never had a philosopher held such weapons wherewith to bind the princes of this world."[130]

While Wilson enjoyed the support of a spellbound public audience, the princes, David Lloyd George and Georges Clemenceau, would prove less susceptible to his charms. In a conversation with Edward House, Clemenceau had remarked that "I can get on with you, you are practical. I understand you but talking to Wilson is something like talking to Jesus Christ." Responding to Wilson's oft-repeated declaration of faith in the League of Nations, Clemenceau reassured the French Chamber of Deputies, to hearty applause, that "there is an old system of alliances called the Balance of Power—this system of alliances, which I do not renounce, will be my guiding thought at the Peace Conference." He then made a reference to Wilson's charming *candeur*, which in translation can mean either candor or naïveté. His hostility becomes explicable when one considers the scale of French losses. A quarter of the male population between eighteen and thirty had died in the war, and he had serious doubts about Wilson's ability to prevent comparable future bloodshed by appealing to humanity's "better angels," as Abraham Lincoln had phrased it. It was said that Clemenceau, nicknamed Le Tigre, had requested that he be buried upright facing Germany when he died.[131] He was a formidable negotiator: proud, Machiavellian, and utterly committed to the pursuit of France's national self-interest. He was determined that Germany be made to pay dearly for its culpability—which he deemed total—in causing the war.

The British prime minister, David Lloyd George, was less driven by revenge than was the Tiger, but he would prove an equally forceful negotiator. Sensitive to British public opinion, which appeared as desirous of retribution as Clemenceau, Lloyd George liked many aspects of Wilson's new vision, but he realized that supporting his plans for a balanced peace treaty would be electorally poisonous in light of his 1916 commitment to fight Germany to a "knock-out."[132] The aristocratic John Maynard Keynes was no fan of the humble Welshman Lloyd George, describing him memorably and viciously as "this goat-footed bard, this half-human visitor to our age from the hagridden magic and enchanted woods of Celtic antiquity."[133] Yet he still recognized that Lloyd George possessed the Old World skills to run rings around the naïve arriviste from the United States. Keynes served on the British delegation to the conference and observed that Wilson "had no plan, no scheme, no constructive ideas whatever for clothing with the flesh of life the commandments which he had thundered from the White House." Given the apparent rigidity of Wilson's mind—which Keynes attributed to his "theological temperament"—and the fact that the president's advisers were ill prepared to counter the experience and the ingenuity of their French and British counterparts, he was outmaneuvered on virtually every point.

Keynes was hardly an impartial chronicler of events. His 1920 book, *The Economic Consequences of the Peace*, was a scathing critique of the Treaty of Versailles, informed by his belief that Wilson's initial vision of a "peace without victory" was appropriate—indeed, essential—and that his failure to convince Clemenceau and Lloyd George of its merits was calamitous. Yet he captures the essence of what transpired at the Paris peace negotiations with his usual literary facility:

> The President's slowness amongst the Europeans was noteworthy. He could not, all in a minute, take in what the rest were saying, size up the situation with a glance, frame a reply, and meet the case by a slight change of ground; and he was liable, therefore, to defeat by the mere swiftness, apprehension, and agility of a Lloyd George . . .
>
> At the crisis of his fortunes the President was a lonely man. Caught up in the toils of the Old World, he stood in great need of sympathy, of moral support, of the enthusiasm of masses. But buried in the Conference, stifled in the hot and poisoned atmosphere of Paris, no echo reached him from the outer world, and no throb of passion, sympathy, or encouragement from his silent constituents in all countries.[134]

Wilson reluctantly acceded to the French and British insistence that all war guilt be placed on Germany's shoulders and that the nation pay massive reparations for Allied losses. The Treaty of Versailles redrew the maps of Europe on broadly ethnic lines (although a large population of ethnic Germans in the Sudetenland became citizens of Czechoslovakia), sliced Germany in two with the creation of the so-called Polish corridor to permit Warsaw access to the sea at the newly created free city of Danzig, provided for the permanent demilitarization of the Rhineland, and added significant heft to the French and British Empires in the transfer of "mandates." On the cavalier way national boundaries were redrawn, and former Central Power colonies parceled out, Harold Nicolson wrote to his wife, Vita Sackville-West, "But darling, it is appalling, those three ignorant and irresponsible men cutting Asia Minor to bits as if they were dividing a cake . . . Isn't it terrible— the happiness of millions being decided in that way."[135] Finally, Germany was compelled to pay $33 billion in war reparations—equivalent to more than $400 billion in today's terms.

On the Treaty of Versailles, George Kennan later wrote: "Truly, this was a peace which had the tragedies of the future written into it as by the devil's own hand."[136] Soon after it was signed, John Maynard Keynes described the peace as Carthaginian, redolent of the brutal peace that Rome imposed on the Phoenician city of Carthage in 146 B.C. following the Punic Wars. This description takes things a little too far—Clemenceau for one was disappointed that the treaty did not treat Germany more harshly—although there is little doubt that Versailles bore scant relation to the treaty Wilson envisioned when he declared war on Germany in 1917. The president made a series of vitally important concessions to his fellow negotiators, seemingly resigned to the fact that Britain and France's huge losses accorded them the right to play a larger role in punishing their tormentor. Unsurprisingly, Progressive support for Wilson at home evaporated. The cover of *The New Republic* blared: THIS IS NOT PEACE.[137] Resigned to strong Republican opposition, Wilson had now provoked the ire of Progressives, who had played such a strong supporting role in the election of 1916 and who backed his subsequent rationale for war. The president's political and diplomatic options were narrowing to a needle's eye.

The president instead vested all hope on a single thread: the creation of an all-powerful League of Nations. On this matter he received strong support from the British diplomat Lord Robert Cecil and General Jan Christian Smuts, who would soon become prime minister of the Union of South Africa. The drafting of the League of Nations Covenant, which was presented to the conference on February 14, 1919, was a remarkable achievement for which Wilson may claim preponderant credit. In theory, the League of Nations was vested with sufficient potency to eradicate "balance-of-power" diplomacy from international affairs. Article X guaranteed the independence and territorial integrity of all established nations. Article XI held that the league possessed the right to intervene in the event of "war or threat of war" anywhere in the world. Articles XII to XV laid out procedures for arbitration, which would be channeled through a Permanent Court of International Justice. Article XVI asserted the league's authority to impose economic boycotts, and resort to the use of military force, to dissuade nations with warlike intentions.

If all the world's leaders had possessed Wilson's faith in the League of Nations, then the harshness of the Treaty of Versailles might have been softened over a period of sustained peace; the world might well have transcended its hardwired tendency toward conflict. General Smuts credited Wilson with drafting "one of the great creative documents in human history."[138] Yet the success or otherwise of the covenant's bold creativity was predicated on unanimity of international support and a common understanding of what membership in the league entailed. And each leader understood the League of Nations in different ways, stretching its meaning to justify individual goals and proclivities. In September 1918, Lloyd George had announced, "I am for a League of Nations," which must have appeared encouraging from Wilson's perspective. But the British prime minister continued: "In fact the League of Nations has begun. The British Empire is a League of Nations."[139]

The response to these words is immediate: How could it ever have succeeded? Many intellectuals and nationalist leaders in Asia had been impressed by Wilson's references to "self-determination" and the "equality of nations." The historian Erez Manela identifies a "Wilsonian Moment" of high expectations that coursed through those nations colonized by the Old World, a point at which freedom from European rule appeared tantalizingly close and Wilson appeared their best hope. A major Shanghai newspaper printed the text of the Fourteen Points, describing Wilson's ideas as "a beacon of light for the world's peoples." A little after the armistice, a nationalist publisher in India, Ganesh, printed a collection of Wilson's speeches under the adulatory and hopeful title *President Wilson: The Modern Apostle of Freedom*.[140] Ultimately those hopes were dashed, as the victorious European nations retained their empires and carved up those of their adversaries for good measure under the so-called mandate system. The ephemerality of the Wilsonian moment caused profound disillusionment in Asia and elsewhere. One young Vietnamese nationalist, who would later take the name Ho Chi Minh, was deeply affected by America's failure to live up to its Universalist rhetoric.

While it was embraced by much of the colonized world, the covenant of the League of Nations met a more hostile response in the United States. William Borah, the isolationist senator from Idaho, observed, "If the Savior of mankind should revisit the earth and declare for a League of Nations, I would be opposed to it."[141] Henry Cabot Lodge criticized the covenant for undermining the Monroe Doctrine, constraining America's freedom of action, and opening the door for partisan attacks on the United States—afforded the imprimatur of "international law." *The New Republic* observed that "the League is not powerful enough to redeem the treaty. But the treaty is vicious enough to incriminate the League."[142] A degree of disillusionment was setting in at home of which Wilson, sequestered in Paris, was largely oblivious. For their part, Lloyd George and Clemenceau were happy to sign on to Wilson's cherished project, satisfied to varying degrees that Anglo-French objectives had been met in respect to the president's earlier concessions. Neither man believed as truly as Wilson in the league's epoch-redefining potential, but failing its full effectiveness, French and British interests would hardly be impeded by working through a League of Nations in which they would exert significant clout. Wilson was generally pleased with what had been achieved in Paris, even though the Treaty of Versailles bore little relation to his Fourteen Points. All that remained was to secure ratification of the peace treaty in its original form, the difficulty of which scarcely seemed to occur to the president. The day before he set sail, Wilson told the French president, Raymond Poincaré, that while a fierce battle awaited, it would be over in just one day.[143]

On July 8, 1919, Wilson returned to the United States, where a ticker-tape parade in New York City carried the president to Carnegie Hall for a brief speech. He then traveled to Washington, D.C., where one hundred thousand well-wishers met his train at midnight. When asked at a press conference in Washington on July 10 if the Senate would ratify the treaty on acceptable terms, Wilson tartly replied, "I do not think hypothetical questions are concerned. *The Senate is going to ratify the treaty.*"[144] Later that same day, Wilson presented the treaty to a packed chamber in the Senate. Declining to dwell on the minutiae of the Treaty of Versailles, Wilson emphasized the League of Nations' vast potential. The president presented the negotiation of the treaty as a zero-sum game by asking, "Dare we reject it and break the heart of the world?" As Wilson continued his speech, religious invocations began to inhabit the space where substance would have better resided: "The stage is set, the destiny disclosed. It has come about by no plan of our conceiving, but by the hand of God who led us into this way. We cannot turn back. We can only go forward, with lifted eyes and freshened spirit, to follow the vision. It was of this that we dreamed at our birth. America shall in truth show the way. The light streams upon the path ahead, and nowhere else."[145]

While Wilson's speech was greeted with rousing applause in the chamber, astute observers noticed that only one Republican—the iconoclastic League of Nations enthusiast Porter McCumber from North Dakota—applauded. Even Democrats were worried by the hollowness of Wilson's words. Henry Ashurst of Arizona likened Wilson's effort to a businessman explaining his primary functions to a board of directors by reciting "Longfellow's Psalm of Life . . . His audience wanted red meat, he fed them cold turnips."[146] To leave so many people disappointed was hugely damaging, but one significant extenuating circumstance partly explains his stuttering performance. In the weeks prior to the speech, Wilson had been suffering from headaches and tight neck muscles that we now know were early signs of a stroke that would hit him three months later. A combination of combative-ness, ill-advised appropriation of higher powers, and debilitating health all served to undermine Wilson's formidable communicative skills at a critical juncture.

Wilson had refused to invite two groups of individuals to accompany him to the negotiations in Paris: senators and Republicans. That both groups possessed absolute power over the fate of the Treaty of Versailles in the United States—and would indeed "break the heart of the world" in the due course of time—illustrates the magnitude of Wilson's error. The president had reasoned that accommodating Republicans within his negotiating team would circumscribe his freedom of action, precluding the conjuring of rad-ical initiatives to realize his ambitions. Propelled forward by absolute belief in the righteousness and logic of his ideas, Wilson at Paris was intent on realizing his thesis: the creation of a collaborative world system. Yet he was dangerously insulated from the reality of a domestic political calculus that was stacked against him, particularly after Democrat losses in the midterm elections. Surrounded by friends, Wilson failed to see that a world governed by a League of Nations was an abstraction, not an actionable reality. The flight of Wilson's intellectualism—his scientism—took him away from what was politically possible. That this astute student of American politics failed to finesse the limitations of his approach is testament to two things: the seductiveness of crafting grand strategy and the fiendish nature of the war that had just visited the world.

Wilson compounded his initial errors regarding the composition of the delegation with an adamant refusal to negotiate with those Senate Republi-cans who were amenable to a watered-down version of the treaty, in which American sovereignty was better protected. For perhaps understandable reasons, Wilson despised Henry Cabot Lodge and his cohort of Senate allies and press admirers. The president's press secretary, Ray Stannard Baker, observed that Wilson was "a good hater," an attribute that doesn't help when the political chips are down.[147] Edward House was well aware of the strengths and limitations of his president's style of decision making: "Whenever a question is presented he keeps an absolutely open mind and welcomes all suggestion or advice which will lead to a correct decision. But he is receptive only during the period that he is weighing the question and preparing to make his decision. Once the suggestion is made it is final and there is an absolute end to all advice and suggestion. There is no moving him after that."[148] That this approach was antithetical to steering a revolutionary treaty through a recalcitrant Senate scarcely needs emphasizing.

The Senate's opposition to the treaty was divided into "irreconcilables," cross-party isolationists who opposed all aspects of the treaty; "strong reservationists," who might vote for the treaty in a much reduced form; and "mild reservationists," composed mainly of Republican internationalists who supported the crux of the treaty but wanted some changes before their vote could be assured. As is well known, Wilson's stance toward those who opposed the treaty, to whatever degree of reservation, was uncompromising. In a barb directed at the "strong reservationist" Lodge—in a speech provocatively delivered in Worcester, Massachusetts, the senator's home state—Wilson warned that "any man who resists the present tides that run in the world will find himself thrown upon a shore so high and barren that it will seem as if he had been separated from his human kind forever," which more or less captures Wilson's views on political compromise circa 1919.[149]

Which is not to say that Wilson did not try to talk down his opposition. The president held a series of face-to-face meetings with his opponents in the Senate but was unable to convince them to back down. Steadfast in his aversion to negotiation, and warming to a very different tack, Wilson at the end of August decided to embark upon a nationwide speaking tour, designed to build public support for the treaty, which in turn would convince hold-out senators that ratification was in their political interests. Wilson's new wife and doctor expressed deep concerns about how a tour of this nature might impact his health. From a different perspective, members of his administration struggled to imagine how a public-speaking tour at this stage might translate into Senate votes. But detecting a specious parallel to his previous nationwide speaking tour, which had drummed up critical support for his preparedness agenda, Wilson rejected these reservations and took his message above the heads of the senators whom he most needed to convince.

Wilson set out on his tour at the beginning of September 1919, delivering forty-two speeches in twenty-one days without the assistance of a microphone. It was a magnificent effort, in which he displayed all the rhetorical skills that his father had encouraged from a young age. Wilson described the League of Nations as "the only possible guarantee against war," and sought to allay fears that Article X of the treaty would result in American boys being dispatched to Central Europe to settle atavistic, irresolvable disputes. While he struggled to compromise with senators, the president was infinitely better at respecting and meeting the doubts expressed by the general public. And it is at this point that the story turns Shakespearean.

Drained by his cumulative efforts, on September 25 Wilson collapsed onstage in Pueblo, Colorado. Ushered away onto another train, Wilson confided to an aide, "I just feel as if I am going to pieces," before looking away to shield tears that were welling in his eyes. One week later, in Washington, Wilson suffered a massive stroke. Death toyed with Wilson for a week before releasing him partly blind and paralyzed down the left side of his body. If the president had died, one might imagine the Senate passing the treaty with minor amendments: an apt eulogy to a major presidency. As it happened, the wounded Wilson proved even less prone to compromise than before, instructing fellow Democrats to vote down any version of the treaty that was sullied by Republican reservations.[150] On March 19, 1920, twenty-one Democrats—ignoring their president's pleas for purity in defeat—and twenty-eight Republicans voted for Lodge's version of the treaty, which greatly reduced the potency of the League of Nations but left much of the original intact. Yet this cross-party tally fell seven short of the two-thirds majority required for ratification.

During the 1920 Democratic Convention, Wilson reluctantly declined to stand for reelection, and the nomination was secured by a rank outsider aided mainly by his lack of connection to the president: Governor James M. Cox of Ohio. Wilson and his followers scored a partial success when Franklin Delano Roosevelt—a Wilson devotee and League of Nations enthusiast—secured the vice presidential nomination. FDR performed well during the campaign and set an important marker in defeat that served him well during later nomination tussles within his party. A few months later, Republicans swept to power, electing Warren Harding to the presidency in a landslide—Harding won more than 60 percent of the vote compared to Cox's sub-Bryan showing of 34 percent. The American public had delivered a damning indictment of Wilson's diplomatic vision, which hurt the president a great deal in the four years that remained of his life. It fell to Elihu Root to register an apt appraisal of the Wilson presidency, observing that Americans "had learned more about international relations within the past eight years than they had learned in the preceding eighty years," and they were "only at the beginning of the task."[151]

3

★

AMERICANS FIRST

CHARLES BEARD

The historian and political scientist Charles Beard was unimpressed by Woodrow Wilson's efforts to avoid involvement in the European conflict from 1914 to 1916. He supported early American entry into the First World War, a stance that appears improbable at first sight. Beard hailed from Quaker origins, opposed the expansionist thrust of the McKinley-Roosevelt years, and the main cause of his celebrity was a book reviled by millions of patriotic Americans. His *An Economic Interpretation of the Constitution of the United States* was a provocative reinterpretation of America's founding, which sold in large numbers and made him famous.

Published in 1913, the book observed that while most political actors are driven to some degree by economic self-interest, the Founding Fathers had elevated this imperative to a fine art. Fearful of the chaos created by the Articles of Confederation, in which states' rights trumped those of the federal government, Beard argued, the Founding Fathers had an overarching goal during their deliberations in Philadelphia: to protect men of means from the threat posed by broad-based political activity. The American Constitution was for Beard "essentially an economic document based upon the concept that the fundamental private rights of property are anterior to government and morally beyond the reach of popular majorities."[1]

It was a radical piece of revisionism that created an almighty stir. President Wilson denounced the book, as did *The New York Times* in an editorial.[2] *The Ohio Star* presented an evocative (and provocative) banner headline, "Scavengers, Hyena-like, Descecrate the Graves of the Dead Patriots We Revere," then added that the book was "libelous, vicious, and damnable" and that true Americans "should rise to condemn [Beard] and the purveyors of his filthy lies and rotten aspersions."[3] With admirably dry humor, William Howard Taft wondered why Beard had to depress people by telling the truth.[4]

In 1912, Beard refused to vote for either Theodore Roosevelt or Woodrow Wilson, viewing their Progressivism as timid affairs driven by the same economic self-interest—albeit cloaked in ameliorative rhetoric—that motivated the Founders. Away from domestic policy, Beard criticized Wilson's attempts to export democracy to Mexico, dismissing the president's "loose talk . . . about restoring order by bayonets," and observing that if worldwide democratization is inevitable, "it is better to let it alone or to aid in its culmination."[5] Yet there was something about the First World War—and German motives in particular—that roused Beard's pugnacity. On a trivial level, Charles and his wife, Mary Ritter, a distinguished scholar in her own right, had honeymooned on the European continent in 1900, where Beard was "amused at the pretensions of German professors and fuming at Prussian soldiers who forced him into the gutter rather than share the sidewalk," according to his later friend and colleague, the historian Eric F. Goldman.[6] More substantively, Beard had delivered a speech at the City College of New York in the autumn of 1914 that condemned German militarism so forcefully that the college president banned future talks by Beard on that subject.[7] As German U-boat attacks increased, Beard criticized President Wilson for his weak responses, observing "that this country should definitely align itself with the Allies and help eliminate Prussianism from the earth."[8]

Beard detected something rotten in Germany's heart, and his fierce egalitarianism led him to view the nation as a dangerous adversary to be defeated if Progressive causes were to survive at home and abroad. In a speech at Amherst College in 1917, he warned that the "present plight of the world seems to show that mankind is in the grip of inexorable forces which may destroy civilization if not subdued to humane purposes."[9] Like Walter Lippmann, Beard viewed American participation in the war as an opportunity to effect lasting social reform in the United States and beyond. Even the robber barons would be compelled to serve a larger good. Dispensing praise that would likely have stirred disquiet among its recipients, Beard lauded the Rockefellers, Morgans, Vanderbilts, and Harrimans as "creative pioneers," anticipating a time when their "magnificent economic structures" would be used for "public purposes."[10]

Irritated by the irresponsibility of the Wilson campaign's slogan in 1916—"He kept us out of war"—Beard held his nose and voted for Charles Evans Hughes, until recently an associate justice of the Supreme Court, primarily due to his support for military preparedness (it also helped that the Republican candidate offered clear support for national woman suffrage). Deploying Mahanian reasoning, Beard observed that "war has been one of the most tremendous factors in the origin of the State and the progress of mankind," and that ducking a necessary fight was an abdication of responsibility.[11]

During the election year, Beard mischievously claimed to understand the tenor of public opinion better than Wilson's campaign advisers: "Millions of Americans would give their life blood to prevent the establishment of [a Prussian state] on these shores. In this I mean no breach of neutrality. With due scientific calm and without expressing any preference in the matter I think I am stating accurately the opinions of most of my countrymen."[12] Sarcasm aside, Beard's words revealed his sense of urgency. As Wilson edged slowly toward intervention, Beard condemned the president's cant. He complained to *The New York Times* that the "Peace Without Victory" speech was "not much of a basis for negotiation," and unless Wilson was operating from a script written with the other belligerents, "he was just preaching a sermon." Wilson's support for ethnic self-determination, meanwhile, brought to mind Pandora opening her box. "Does it mean an independent Ireland?" Beard wondered. "What about Alsace-Lorraine? What about Bohemia? What about Croatia and the scores of little nations in the Balkans? What about India? What about Haiti and Santo Domingo, where the United States is ruling according to President Wilson's orders."[13] Beard was relieved when Wilson finally requested a declaration of war. Distancing himself from the president's grander ambitions, however, he called for "poise, cold-bloodedness, and a Machiavellian disposition to see things as they are . . . whether we like them or not."[14]

The First World War witnessed a remarkable mobilization on the part of America's universities and intellectuals. When America's war began, its research universities—inspired by early efforts, such as Robert La Follette Sr.'s "Wisconsin Idea," to have universities serve a wider political purpose— willingly donated their resources to help realize Wilson's plans. Hopeful that national planning would elevate the significance of the social sciences, Beard wrote in an article for *The New Republic* on November 17, 1917, that "political science, economics, social economy, and sociology are now in the crucible of circumstance."[15] Yet it was the natural and physical sciences, not the social sciences, that found it easier to embrace their elevation to circumstance. In February 1918, for example, Columbia University's mechanical and electrical engineering departments offered all the assistance to the Navy Department that it deemed useful—a windfall for the government. Science and engineering departments followed suit across the nation.

Concerned lest they be left behind, humanities and social science scholars also began to offer their services to wartime America. Alongside distinguished fellow historians such as Carl Becker, Albert Bushnell Hart, and J. Franklin Jameson, Beard propagandized for President Wilson under the aegis of the Committee on Public Information. His scholarly efforts primarily consisted in placing Wilhelmine Germany in its proper historical context: as a ruthless expansionary power that posed a direct threat to the United States.[16] In an appeal to support President Wilson's fourth Liberty Bond Drive, Beard wrote in *Harper's Magazine* that America "and her allies are now pitted against the most merciless despotism the world has ever seen . . . A German victory means the utter destruction of those ideals of peace and international goodwill which have been America's great reliance."[17] Beard was aware that presenting despotism versus democracy in Manichaean terms obscured as much as it revealed. But he willingly set aside complexity to serve a larger good.

Ultimately, though, regimentation of purpose made Beard queasy. In the spring of 1916, when American participation still seemed a distant prospect, Columbia's Board of Trustees had warned Beard against any teaching that was "likely to inculcate disrespect for American institutions"—an admonition that Beard cheerfully ignored, as it would have required disavowal of his *Economic Interpretation of the Constitution.* The president of Columbia University, the effervescent and strong-willed Nicholas Murray Butler, then warned the faculty at the onset of hostilities that any professor who failed to support the war would jeopardize his position at the university.[18] In March 1917, the university rescinded a speaking invitation that had been issued to the Russian pacifist intellectual Count Ilya Tolstoy (son of Leo). This infuriated Beard, who viewed freedom of speech as inviolable. In a speech on June 6, 1917, President Butler observed that "what had been tolerated before becomes intolerable now . . . What had been folly was now treason," before delivering "the last and only warning to any among us . . .

who are not with whole heart and mind and strength committed to fight with us to make the world safe for democracy."[19] A few months later, Columbia's Board of Trustees dismissed two professors, Henry W. L. Dana (active in the Anti-Militarism League) and James McKeen Cattell (a pacifist), for expressing unpatriotic sentiments. Butler intervened to stall the promotion of a professor who had failed to accord sufficient respect to the Supreme Court.

On October 9, 1917, Beard concluded a lecture to a class of seventy students with the announcement that this would be his last. The university's efforts to "humiliate or terrorize every man who held progressive, liberal, or controversial views" compelled him to sever his association with the institution.[20] The students rose to their feet and applauded for twenty-five minutes, an affirmation that left Beard in tears.[21] President Butler was blindsided and dismayed, remarking that Beard's "resignation was completely unnecessary; I did my best to get him to stay; he had no excuse for going."[22]

In a firm letter of resignation, Beard reminded Butler that "I have, from the beginning, believed that a victory for the German Imperial Government would plunge all of us into the black night of military barbarism. I was among the first to urge a declaration of war by the United States, and I believe that we should now press forward with all our might to a just conclusion." In spite of this prowar stance, however, Beard found something unsettling about the silencing of dissent compelled by the Board of Trustees, whose members he described as "reactionary and visionless in politics, and narrow and mediaeval in religion." Beard's letter of resignation was reprinted in *The New York Times*, as was part of an earlier speech that distilled his position succinctly. "This country was founded on disrespect and the denial of authority," Beard observed, "and it is no time to stop free discussion."[23] Indeed, Beard's resignation was newsworthy enough to make the front page of the nation's paper of record. Its wider significance was further emphasized when *The Times* printed a mean-spirited editorial titled "Columbia's Deliverance," which celebrated Beard's departure, aimed a few kicks at *An Economic Interpretation of the Constitution*, and offered a philistine précis on the appropriate responsibilities of the intellectual:

> Columbia University is better for Beard's resignation ... If [Beard's] sort of teaching were allowed to go on unchecked by public sentiment and the strong hands of university Trustees, we should presently find educated American youth applying the doctrine of economic determinism to everything from the Lord's Prayer to the binomial theorem ... Trustees

may be visionless in politics and mediaeval in religion, but they have
the hard, common sense to know . . . that infallible wisdom does not
perch upon the back of every chair occupied by a professor bearing the
degree of Doctor of Philosophy, and they know that if colleges and
universities are not to become breeding grounds of radicalism and socialism, it must be recognized that academic freedom has two sides, that
freedom to teach is correlative to the freedom to dispense with poisonous
teaching.[24]

Such abuse was grist to Beard's mill. Entirely comfortable in the persona
of enfant terrible—and dismayed to find himself in such a cowed public
sphere—he joined the educationalist philosopher John Dewey and Leo-
nara O'Reilly of the Women's Trade Union League in protesting the firing of
three teachers at DeWitt Clinton High School in New York City who allegedly held "views subversive of good discipline and of undermining good
citizenship." One year later, two of Beard's coauthored textbooks were banned
from Army training camps. In January 1919, Beard castigated President
Wilson for failing to release political prisoners, such as Eugene V. Debs, "whose
offense was to retain Mr. Wilson's pacifist views after he abandoned them."[25]
Turning his attention to geopolitics, Beard wondered with faux innocence
whether Wilson's promotion of "liberty, self-government, and the undictated
development of all peoples" also applied to the British Empire.[26] His baiting
of the president soon got him in trouble. The following week Beard was cited
in the record of a Senate committee charged with investigating German propaganda as one of sixty-two people whose actions had undermined the
battle against the Central Powers. Infuriated by this allegation, Beard wrote
a strong letter to *The New York Times* that recounted his support for an early
declaration of war against Germany, frustration at President Wilson's dith-
ering, and the service he provided to the U.S. government in publicizing
bond issues and the malevolence of German intentions. Pointedly, he observed that, unlike the president, he had never been "too proud to fight."[27]
Beard's experience of the First World War shaped his strong aversion
toward U.S. participation in future conflicts. If independent thinking could
not survive war, then it was clear that the conflict was not worth fighting.
The suppression of civil liberties in wartime America was not the only
issue that vexed Beard. Following the Bolshevik Revolution, Vladimir Lenin
released details of secret diplomatic cables that showed all the Allied Powers
in a duplicitous and self-serving light. Their effect on Beard was salutary.
Angered that this correspondence revealed Great Britain's intentions to

assume control of Germany's colonies after the war, and dismayed that Wilson's moderate peace was being mauled by the French and the British in Paris, Beard lost all hope in the president's ability to serve a useful diplomatic purpose. He attributed many of the president's failings to his languid professorial temperament, which explained his refusal to place "before Lloyd George and Clemenceau the vital questions of an independent mind, which he could have done forcefully . . . [Wilson had] remained *just a professor* after all." Equally culpable were the "American professors of his expert loyal guard," the Inquiry, who had collectively failed to remind the president of his core "mission" to think independently and artfully. In the United States, and indeed in France and Britain, Beard observed that too many intellectuals had been "full of wonder and admiration for W.W.—'one of our boys made it,'" and had failed to subject his diffidence at the negotiating table to a bracing critique.[28]

The only intellectual to stand up for "*the* university" in its truest sense was John Maynard Keynes, who had identified how the reparation and war-guilt provisions critically undermined the Treaty of Versailles. Keynes had remained true to his intellect and had not been swayed by wishful thinking, a trait that Beard came to deplore in himself when revisiting his own response to the war. Beard's World War I commenced with pugnacity and closed with profound disillusionment. Writing in later years, the radical journalist Max Lerner suggested that Beard must have felt that "after all he had been had. The sense of humiliation [in supporting war] became a rankling resolve to be revenged on his own folly."[29]

Much of the remainder of Beard's life was devoted to ensuring that Americans were never again duped into supporting speciously rationalized foreign-policy crusades. Throughout the 1930s, Beard railed against the notion that the United States had any obligation—moral, economic, or strategic—to the rest of the world. Instead, Beard urged President Franklin Roosevelt to follow a policy of "continental Americanism": the reallocation of America's vast resources and energies from resolving the quarrels of others to self-improvement and self-reliance. The formation of a more perfect union could set a powerful example, and that was the sum total of America's obligation to the world. Beard believed in worldmaking through example.

In essence, Beard wanted to turn the clock back to before Mahan's *The Influence of Sea Power upon History* had been published and the nation lost its way. Where Mahan believed that the world was becoming smaller, rendering American detachment from European affairs anachronistic, Beard believed that the United States was more or less invulnerable to serious threats—that it benefited from what the historian C. Vann Woodward described as "free security."[30] Right up to the Japanese attack on Pearl Harbor, Beard argued that fortunate geography and abundant natural resources permitted the United States to ignore whatever convulsions were affecting the Old World at any given time. The United States *was* a "city upon a hill," and Beard believed that nothing launched from the foot of the hill could reach the top. He mocked credulous Americans for "imagining German planes from Bolivia dropping bombs on peaceful people in Keokuk or Kankakee."[31]

In *The Idea of the National Interest*, published in 1934, Beard rounded on Mahan's assertion that greater American participation in global trade ultimately benefited the nation. Through close statistical analysis, Beard proved, to his satisfaction, at least, that the costs of the Spanish-American War far outweighed the economic benefits of acquiring overseas territory and opening up markets for American exports. Beard charged that Mahan's theory of sea power and American expansion rested on a dangerous fallacy. The nation was more than capable of pursuing a singular path and needed to draw no lessons from any other nation—particularly one as sullied through empire as Great Britain. Beard deployed mild sarcasm in chiding Woodrow Wilson's naïve internationalism: "In fine, historic wrongs are to be righted, nations put on a permanent footing, and the peace of all guaranteed by all. Never had the dream of universal and final peace seemed so near to realization."[32] But it was Mahan he truly despised for counseling an insidious and unnecessary course of expansion that debased America.

From today's perspective it is easy to dismiss Beard's views as the last hurrah of an antediluvian generation that could not perceive that the Mahanian flood of economic interdependence and military expansion had already happened. Yet one must be careful to avoid hindsight, which makes gods of us all. After the disappointments of Wilson's presidency, and in the midst of the Great Depression, the appeal of Beard's continentalism—harking back to a simpler and more isolated era—is not difficult to comprehend. As the historian Brooke Blower has noted, antifascist foreign correspondents for American newspapers, such as Dorothy Thompson and Vincent Sheehan, found it hugely challenging to rouse the interest of their fellow Americans in wars and crises afflicting Spain, Poland, and Czechoslovakia—let alone Manchuria and Abyssinia. One journalist observed that as the world edged toward chaos, Americans conceived of themselves as "collectively a nation of Robinson Crusoes."[33] The comfort offered by such a mind-set is easily forgiven, as is the appeal of an individual who characterized America as a bounteous and self-sufficient island. To better understand America's perspective on world affairs during the 1920s and 1930s, one must attempt to enter a world as yet untouched by the horrors that ensued. Following Charles Beard's journey through this era provides an erudite perspective on a nation seriously at odds over its world role, its capabilities, its purpose, and what to do about looming threats.

Charles Austin Beard was born on his father's sixty-acre farm near Knightstown, Indiana, on November 27, 1874. As F. Scott Fitzgerald, a fellow midwesterner, put it in *The Great Gatsby*, Beard was raised in "that vast obscurity beyond the city, where the dark fields of the republic rolled on under the night." His family was wealthy, stable, and English and Scotch-Irish in lineage. Indeed, it was a source of family pride that the Beards could trace ancestry to two pilgrims. While the Beards had begun their American incarnation in New England and Virginia, financial opportunities had lured the more intrepid of them westward. East-central Indiana was fecund, and Charles's father, William, had tilled its mineral-rich soil with great success, ensuring that all his family's needs were met. In 1880, the Beards relocated to a thirty-five-acre farm in Spiceland, to allow their two sons, Charles and Clarence, to attend Spiceland Academy, a Quaker school with a fine academic pedigree. As well as receiving an excellent education, Charles lived an active life that embraced agrarian Jeffersonian virtues, recalling, "By the time I was fifteen I had had enough exercise to last me a lifetime. My muscles and body were hard as steel. I could ride wild horses bare back, and split an oak log with a maul and a wedge."[34]

His parents' farmhouse was lined with books, important local dignitaries were frequent dinner guests, and the Grand Old Party was the Beards' natural political home. It was a childhood of great material privilege and social entitlement, which continued into Beard's early adulthood. Following Charles's graduation from high school in 1891, his father purchased a local paper in Knightstown, *The Sun*, for his sons to manage. They reveled in their task, offering steady editorial support for the Republican Party, until their joint venture ended in 1894 when Clarence resigned to establish a new organ, *The Henry County Republican*. This thrilling experience left quite an impression on Charles, who edited the *DePauw Palladium* during his undergraduate studies and later wrote frequently for the national press. Beard came to believe that truly important ideas should reach the widest possible audience and that journalistic and academic writings were necessarily complementary.

When in 1895 Beard commenced his studies at DePauw University, Indiana's most prestigious liberal arts college, his political views were conventionally Republican. Asked in later years why his historical scholarship was colored by economic determinism, Beard replied, "People ask me why I emphasize economic questions so much. They should have been present in the family parlor, when my father and his friends gathered to discuss public affairs."[35] It was not until he made his first trip to Chicago, in 1896—an industrial behemoth scarred by slums and sharp ethnic tensions—that he located and embraced the social conscience that would define his subsequent activism and scholarship. In Chicago he joined the vocal and learned discussions held at Hull House, the West Side settlement house founded by Jane Addams and Ellen Gates Starr that became an influential center for social reform. Discovering his voice in such an august and multiethnic setting—so different in composition from the political parlors of Indiana—instilled in Beard confidence and sophistication.

Having moved steadily leftward during his time at DePauw, his political awakening was fully realized when he departed the United States for Oxford University in 1898, on the good advice of one of his tutors. Oxford was not renowned for awakening social consciences—its libraries and academics were the main attraction. And indeed Beard made good intellectual use of the four years he spent at England's oldest university, impressing its dons with his acuity and graciousness. The Regius Professor of Modern History, Frederick York Powell, declared him "the nicest American I've ever met."[36] But Beard also used Oxford as a base to tour the industrial heartland, meeting giants of the British trade union movement such as James Keir Hardie, Ben Tillett, and James Sexton. Keir Hardie, in particular, was inspirational. He started his working life at age seven, overcame a crushing educational disadvantage, and founded the Independent Labour Party thirty years later, transforming British politics in the process.

Inspired by the commendable pedagogical function served by Hull House—and by the lessons of self-improvement contained in Keir Hardie's remarkable life story—Beard set himself the task of improving educational opportunities for the "working classes" (to deploy the British idiom) upon his arrival at Oxford. By the start of his second term, Beard had accumulated endorsements from unions representing some three hundred thousand workers, as well as the imprimatur of Keir Hardie's Independent Labour Party, to establish an educational institution that met the needs of those who had been previously marginalized. A swell of Britain's laboring poor had offered their support for this young idealistic American to establish a workingman's college in Oxford—a remarkable story in itself. Ruskin Hall, named by Beard in honor of the Victorian critic and moralist John Ruskin, was established in 1899 largely thanks to the efforts of Beard and two other visiting American students, the Kansan socialists Walter and Amne L. Vrooman.[37] Ruskin College remains an important provider of education to this day, educating, among other politicians, scholars, and unionists, a former deputy prime minister of the United Kingdom, John Prescott.

Driven by what the historian Richard Hofstadter described as a "demonic intensity," Beard put his Oxford sojourn to good academic use by completing all of the archival work—in English county record offices—on what would become his Columbia University Ph.D. thesis: *The Office of the Justice of the Peace in England: Its Origins and Development.*[38] Rarely has the aridity of a doctoral dissertation stood in more marked contrast to the color and variety of a subsequent body of work. Yet there was clearly much more to Beard's Oxford experience than doctoral research. Besides establishing a new college and completing the fieldwork for a Ph.D., Beard wrote extensively on topics of wide resonance. His first book, *The Industrial Revolution*, was written and published while Beard was in Oxford, and it is still in print after more than a century. The book presents a fast-paced account of industrialization through the eighteenth and nineteenth centuries with preponderant focus on those who lost out during Britain's remarkable rise to economic preeminence. *The Industrial Revolution* was designed to serve a pedagogical function in emphasizing the indignities visited on workers to enrich elites.

These were also tumultuous years in the United States, and Beard took a close interest in the foreign-policy developments anticipated and shaped by Mahan's books and articles on the primacy of sea power. Beard initially supported President McKinley's declaration of war on Spain—indeed, he volunteered and was turned down, on grounds of health, for active service—but soon felt great unease over the popular exuberance that accompanied the course of the conflict and at the acquisitive evolution of America's war aims.[39] According to his wife, Beard wondered aloud "how an intelligent rational man can be anxious for war, with all its dire consequences . . . It is a gory path to glory."[40] Mary Beard added that it was during the Spanish-American War that "[William Jennings] Bryan's anti-imperialism took roots in Beard's soul." In 1948, Beard told the historian Arthur M. Schlesinger Sr. that he "left the GOP in imperialism in 1900 and . . . found no home anywhere since."[41]

If the Spanish-American War had driven Beard toward Bryanite anti-imperialism, it didn't particularly show in an article he wrote for an Oxford student magazine, *New Oxford*, in November 1901. The essay considered whether imperialism, on the whole, was a good or bad thing. In the case of the United States, Beard believed British imperial endeavor had been vindicated because "the Americans, as bad and half-civilized as they are, are better than the howling, scalping Comanches whose places they have taken." The British colonial legacy in America, Canada, Australia, and New Zealand was beneficial enough to inspire pride, not shame. Yet in surveying America's recent imperial efforts, Beard recorded some strong words about America's forlorn adventure in the Philippines. Sending hundreds of "expensively equipped teachers to the Philippines to instruct naked natives while thousands of white children in American cities" were "under-fed and under-educated" suggested that the likes of McKinley and Roosevelt were not "brute imperialists but self-destructive lunatics."[42] Only when the United States and the nations of Europe had attended to their own problems should they attempt to improve the lot of the poorer nations.

Only at this juncture did Beard believe that development could be encouraged under the auspices of an "international bureau" charged with directing irrigation, swamp drainage, land reclamation, and large-scale infrastructure projects. In words that would have repelled Jane Addams and Keir Hardie, Beard suggested that the work would be completed by "mongol and negro" workers "always under white foremen," suggesting that the hierarchical notions learned through his privileged childhood were still present. And while one should be careful not to set great store in anyone's scribblings in a student magazine, Beard is more culpable than most, having already published his first book and, thanks to his editorship of a newspaper, being far from naïve when it came to the permanence of the printed word. Beyond the racism contained in some of the language, however, the article's primary significance lies in Beard's mixed views on well-meaning global activism. This was the first time that Beard privileged national self-improvement over overseas missionary work, a prioritization that defined his later views on foreign policy.[43]

After politely rebuffing the attempts of Ramsay MacDonald (who became Labour's first prime minister in 1924) to convince him to stay in Britain to assist the fledgling Labour Party, Beard returned home to commence his postgraduate study at Columbia University in 1902, gaining his master's degree a year later, and submitting his Ph.D. dissertation the year after that—

all testament to the scholarly benefit derived from his four years traversing England's many local archives.

It is important to note that Beard's Ph.D. was in political science, not history. At Oxford, as the historian Mark C. Smith writes, Beard learned from Frederick York Powell that "history's purpose was not to praise institutions or theories but to understand them; history was a science, rather than theology or ethics."[44] The political science emphasis in Beard's early years is notable, although it remained present throughout the entirety of his career, particularly as he turned his attention toward foreign policy. Indeed, the political scientist Clyde Barrow categorizes twenty-eight of Beard's forty-nine books as falling within the field of political science, with topics including political theory, comparative politics, municipal reform, and public administration.[45] Columbia appointed Beard as a lecturer in history in 1904, later moving him to an adjunct position in politics and government.

At Columbia—then at the height of its powers as an institution that challenged disciplinary boundaries—Beard was greatly influenced by Professors James Harvey Robinson and E.R.A. Seligman, two giants in the historical field. Robinson was at the vanguard of the so-called New History movement, which expanded beyond narrow political history to emphasize the social, cultural, scientific, and intellectual roots of society formation. The New History was something of an amalgam of history and political science, which explains why it roused Beard's admiration. Seligman's major work, *The Economic Interpretation of History*, was published in 1902 and it came to exert a profound influence on Beard's scholarship. Seligman taught Beard to follow the money when tracing the taproots of political motivation, an emphasis he pursued subsequently. Columbia was thus a good intellectual home for the young, idealistic advocate of social reform, and he stayed happily there until his resignation fifteen years later. He also embraced New York City and assumed a stake in maintaining its upkeep and development. A true believer in the science of politics, Beard pursued his interest in urban planning by working for the New York Bureau of Municipal Research; his interests were myriad, as were his talents. He was much like certain of the Founding Fathers, who lived and extolled the merits of the generalist intellect. Beard was an engaged public citizen, a much-loved teacher, and a highly regarded scholar.

Beard's politics were a fascinating amalgam of Jeffersonian idealism, midwestern self-reliance, and urban cosmopolitanism. He was a man of the left, but his journey to that position was atypical. The historian Arthur M.

Schlesinger Sr., Beard's contemporary at graduate school, remembered him as "in no sense a Marxist or single track economic determinist," but someone who "endowed everything he said with a bracing air of realism" and whose "recurrent theme" was "the role of material self-interest in America's political and constitutional development."[46] Yet even this recurrent theme conceals complexity in the manner of its formation. When Beard began work on *An Economic Interpretation of the Constitution*, his admiration for the Founders soared, in spite of the fact that the book served mainly to identify and skewer the self-interested way the Constitution was framed and the disingenuous manner of its public presentation. In 1935, Beard declared that Jefferson was the greatest of the Founders because he "combined in his person the best of both the Old World and the New." Yet he also praised the two main authors of *The Federalist*, Alexander Hamilton and James Madison, and compared that book favorably to anything written in Europe during the Enlightenment.[47]

Beard is the most left-wing, but also the most conventionally patriotic, of all the individuals this book surveys. He reveled in his nation's unique virtues. Every chapter of Charles Beard's career can be explained, to varying degrees, in reference to his love for the United States. In 1927, Beard wrote that "among the many historic assemblies which have wrought revolutions in the affairs, it seems safe to say that there has never been one that commanded more political talent, practical experience, and sound substance than the Philadelphia Convention of 1787."[48] This was a proudly conventional and patriotic description of the founding generation. Indeed, Beard had something of a proprietary interest in the United States, which is not surprising given his family's long history in the colonies and the nation. William Appleman Williams, the University of Wisconsin scholar who embraced New History revisionism with fewer interpretive qualms, did not deny that Beard had offered "radical insights into the malfunctioning of the existing system." Nonetheless, Williams distilled his mixed feelings in describing Beard as a "Tory-Radical," a man "torn between concern for his fellow men and a personal and philosophic commitment to private property."[49]

Beard's character and raison d'être are similarly complex in origin and evolution. His friend the writer Matthew Josephson wrote that he had "never met anywhere a man who so thoroughly enjoyed his own sense of freedom or who was so jealous of his intellectual and moral independence."[50] This singularity is reflected in his decision to leave Columbia, as well as in the thrust of his scholarship, which is almost willful in its hostility to bland ingratiation. Another constant throughout his career was his belief that "objectivity" in historical scholarship is unattainable—although he did not believe that this should discourage anyone from trying. Beard contested the Germanic ideal of scholarship, as famously expressed by Leopold von Ranke, that the historian's task was "to describe the past as it actually was," not to judge it through the lens of preconceived ideology.[51] A skeptical Beard believed that this imperative was a "noble dream."[52] "Every historian's work, that is, his selection of facts, his emphasis, his omissions, his organization, and his methods of presentation—bears a relation to his own personality and the age and circumstances in which he lives."[53] For Beard, history was necessarily a relativist, political activity.

Accompanying Beard's critique of the self-deluding sanctimony that accompanied the Rankean search for "truth" was his belief that historians must make their work accessible to a general audience and address, so far as possible, the most pressing problems of the contemporary world. Convinced that "specialization in particular, cut off from wider relations, leads to mere thoughtless scholasticism," Beard's ambitions as a historian became increasingly divorced from his profession as a whole—and indeed from the discipline of political science, the field in which he earned his doctorate.[54] His ability to speak persuasively to two audiences garnered him the unique distinction of being elevated by his peers to the presidency of both the American Historical Association and the American Political Science Association.

Yet Beard believed that political science was as blameworthy as history in its embrace of the margins. In 1918, he complained that too much political science was "concerned with minutiae, not great causes and ideas . . . The only way we can know the state is through concrete manifestation of power . . . The only way to find the manifestation is to discover its historical circumstance."[55] Scholars should serve their public not by seeking ever-narrower "truths," but by engaging accessibly with the wider forces that govern political affairs. In his presidential address to the American Political Science Association in 1926, titled "Time, Technology, and the Creative Spirit in Political Science," Beard observed that relying solely on mathematical modeling to address narrow phenomena was "myopic" and "barren"—denying the rightful role of creativity and intuition. He called on his fellow political scientists to dare "to be wrong in something important rather than right in some meticulous banality."[56] He chided historians and political scientists alike for parochialism and obscurantism. History needed to draw more from political science and political science needed to attend more to history. Beard believed that the United States was improvable if scholars from both disciplines set their goals higher—if they communicated with the general public rather than with themselves.

Achieving this goal, of course, assumed confidence in the ability of ordinary Americans to react constructively to compelling testimony, and in this respect Beard was unashamedly optimistic. Unlike Walter Lippmann, who viewed the American people as a "phantom public" lacking the ability to distinguish between sophistry and substance—an artless mass that responded more to sound bites and crude stereotypes than to measured analyses—Beard believed that political progress had been driven by "the activities of millions of men and women, most of them unknown to the pages of written history." The general public yearned for knowledge and possessed an irresistible latent power. It might take only "a word, an article, a pamphlet, a speech, or a book [to] set in train forces of incalculable moment."[57]

The reverse was also true: where ignorance reigned, susceptibility to extremism was heightened. Beard held German historical scholarship partly responsible for that nation's failure to lay strong pluralist foundations, thus permitting strong-willed despots to run amok. Although historians were vested with a grave duty to illuminate the past as widely as possible, German historians had failed to write an accessible, panoptic history of the nation for its people. Brilliant as certain of them were, German research historians sought their "truth" by narrowing horizons and developing jargon: an abdication of responsibility. Beard came to assume his role as a public intellectual with high seriousness, for the stakes were high in interwar America.

The United States emerged from the First World War as the world's largest economic power by a considerable margin.[58] The conflict had hollowed out the European belligerents, whose populations had been devastated and whose debts—owed to the United States primarily—had assumed gargantuan dimensions. The United States' gold reserves were vast, and the nation's economic output was equivalent to its next six competitors combined. As battlefield deaths and disease took a wrecking ball to European demography, America's population increased by 30 percent between 1900 and 1920, constituting 106 million in total—compared to 44 million in Great Britain, 37 million in France, and 64 million in Germany.[59] Major economic shifts were also occurring in the complexion of America's overseas trade, as the historian Odd Arne Westad has observed. During the 1920s and 1930s, the United States became the hub of the global economy, yet more and more of its trade spokes were connected to the Third World. In Latin America, for example, the United States displaced Britain as the primary provider of capital investment. America's exports to South Asia tripled between 1920 and 1940. And this increased influence and visibility went beyond the reach of cold cash. As Westad writes, "This influence was far more profound than just American models for production and management. In urban popular culture, in Europe and in the Third World, America established itself as the epitome of modernity, conveying ideas that undermined existing concepts of status, class and identity."[60] The global economy throughout the 1920s was coming to resemble the interconnected trading entity that Alfred Mahan prophesized would benefit the fluid, innovative American economy more than its competitors. For these reasons, the term "isolationism" must be treated with great caution when considering U.S foreign policy between the wars.

The League of Nations was a toxic entity in American political debate in 1920. President Warren Harding's inaugural address of 1921 had lambasted global multilateralism: "A world super-government is contrary to everything we cherish and can have no sanction by our republic."[61] For a time Harding forbade the State Department from responding to official correspondence from the league's headquarters in Geneva, an action that in the genteel world of international diplomacy was truly obnoxious, not to say self-defeating. Attacking the nascent league was a bipartisan project, however. Wilson's Democratic Party was cool toward the league in the 1924 general election, not that it did them much good. The Democratic candidate, John W. Davis, was trounced by Calvin "Silent Cal" Coolidge, a Vermonter of remarkable stillness and self-possession who was reelected to the presidency—which he had assumed following Harding's death in 1923—in a landslide. Upon Coolidge's death in 1933, Dorothy Parker had famously quipped, "How could they tell?" In losing to such an uncharismatic politician, the Democratic Party's weaknesses were revealed.

While the 1920s were owned by the anti-Wilsonian Republican Party, its internationalist wing was active and influential. Conservative internationalists like Elihu Root, William Howard Taft, and Secretary of State Charles Evans Hughes, all major figures in the GOP, fiercely defended the activist legacy bequeathed by McKinley and Roosevelt, steering Harding's and Coolidge's foreign policies away from narrow isolationism. In the early 1920s, American diplomats began to meet unofficially with league representatives and sit in on its meetings. In 1925, the United States sent official observers to the league. Of course, the League of Nations sans America was a low-key affair driven by two exhausted nations, Britain and France, with economic and colonial interests to protect and limited means to do so. Some minor territorial disputes were resolved, but important absences in membership prevented the league from enforcing anything close to "collective security," Wilson's original aim.[62]

Nonetheless, the United States came in time to interact freely with this flawed entity. Secretary of State Hughes wielded genuine foreign-policy influence during the Harding and Coolidge presidencies, carefully weaning America off an instinctive distrust of European involvement that had spiked in 1920 and 1921. Aware of the problems created by President Wilson's overreach, Hughes's approach was incremental and low-key, allowing him to present seventy-one treaties sufficiently modest to secure Senate approval. The maxim by which Hughes lived was "a maximum of security with a minimum of commitment," which offers a neat summary of the tenor of U.S. foreign policy in the first half of the 1920s.[63]

Beard's thinking on world affairs throughout the 1920s oscillated between a grudging recognition of the need for international engagement and a growing fear that the nation must avoid the type of economic entanglements, and grandiose diplomatic ambitions, that brought it into the First World War. During a trip to Paris in 1922, Charles and Mary hungrily purchased a "trunk load" of books on the banks of the Seine that documented the secret tsarist diplomatic activity that had been made gleefully public by Vladimir Lenin.[64] Making good use of this material, Beard delivered a series of lectures at Dartmouth College, later published as *Cross-Currents in Europe Today*, which cast preponderant blame on France and Russia—in scheming to destroy the Austro-Hungarian Empire in 1908—for causing the First World War. Beard was moving away from viewing Prussian militarism as some kind of insatiable geopolitical evil. Further lamenting that the "world is an economic unit and the United States is being woven into the very fabric of that unity," Beard urged the United States to resist this trend by refusing to facilitate or protect the "foreign trade or investments of American citizens," granting the Philippines independence so that U.S. interests did not extend beyond Hawaii, and focusing much more on internal development. Such a stance, Beard wrote, would "bend all national genius upon the creation of a civilization which, in power and glory and noble living, would rise above all the achievements of the past."[65] He continued to delineate this theme in *The Rise of American Civilization*, a two-volume history of the United States, coauthored with his wife, considered among his and their finest works. The Beards observed that America's vast material abundance— not its ideology, government, or westward-facing development—was its most important defining characteristic. It was thus the duty of government both to spread this natural bounty more equitably and to avoid any overseas adventures that might challenge the primacy of internal development.[66] Beard described his prioritization of the domestic sphere as "continental-ism" and decried those who sought to characterize his advocacy of selective retrenchment as "little Americanism." Replying to an appreciative review of *The Rise* by the historian and philosopher Lewis Mumford, Beard echoed Thomas Paine's revolutionary intentions: "We have to create the new world, not dig it from the past."[67]

Beard was also concerned by the increase in defense spending through-out the 1920s—which harmed domestic progress by failing to correspond with the absence of genuine military threats at this time. (Beard's concerns here were exaggerated.) At the close of the war, America's demobilization was rapid, but numbers crept up gradually so that a regular army of fourteen thousand was supplemented by a much more significant reserve of citizen-soldiers. The U.S. Navy had displaced Great Britain's as the world's stron-gest at the time of the armistice, but Harding and Coolidge were content to concede parity with Britain in capital ships. In hindsight, giving up such a military lead appears reckless. But the world was a different place in the 1920s: somber rather than combustible in its international relations. The historian George Herring has observed that "it was quite appropriate for the United States during these years to be economically powerful, and only moderately strong militarily."[68] Beard, however, felt that U.S. defense cuts should be much deeper so that the more pressing domestic problems of inner-city deprivation, inadequate health care, and nationwide poverty could be fully addressed. In August 1928, the signatories of the Kellogg-Briand Pact—a long list that included all the major world powers—renounced war as "an instrument of national policy," except in clear cases of self-defense. Referencing the fact that world military spending was higher in 1928 than in 1912, Beard noted the irony that "at the very moment when war as an instrument of national policy (with reservations) is solemnly renounced, the civilized world, comparatively speaking, has ready for death and destruction bigger and better armaments than ever in its history."[69]

Beard had not given up on assisting the rest of the world in the 1920s, however, and often went out of his way to make clear that his preference for diplomatic modesty was not influenced by a pacific ideology shaped by his family's Quakerism. On April 4, 1925, for example, Beard wrote to Senator Albert J. Beveridge, informing him that "I am no pacifist." Nonetheless, Beard wrote, "I hold it to be a crime to waste any of our blood on empire not to be peopled by our stock but by alien races." The U.S. government had to be much more selective about where it allocated finite resources. "Let us not fight over a whim," Beard continued, "or a bit of pique or a few dollars worth of trade to enrich more idle plutocrats. Land that has two or three hundred people to the square mile is worthless to *us*, no matter if a handful of capitalists get ten percent of it."[70] Here Beard was alluding to a growing American concern with China, which was looking increasingly vulnerable to its formidable neighbor Japan. Every nation was of differing importance to the United States, and China was somewhere near the middle. In classic realist fashion, Beard was distinguishing between diplomatic interests in order of their importance to the United States—not suggesting that America raise the drawbridge and disband the State Department. Indeed, as late as 1930, Beard would criticize pure isolationists for sticking blindly to a "dogma" rendered dangerous by lack of understanding of the technological developments that undermined the supposed protection offered by the Atlantic and the Pacific Oceans. In a book written with his son, William, Beard warned that "the creed of isolationism, which once seemed convincing . . . may be employed to defeat its own purposes, namely, the maintenance of national security."[71] It took a near-perfect economic storm to convince Beard that his variant on isolationism was the best way to assure America's safety and prosperity.

A speculative boom in the 1920s had persuaded increasing numbers of Americans to invest their savings in stocks and shares. In fact, three decades of economic growth, beginning with the boom precipitated by the Spanish-American War, seemed to suggest that cyclical economic slumps had been eradicated. This was an illusion. Economic contractions in 1907–1908, 1914–1915, and 1919–1922 should have cautioned against exuberance. But the broad trend toward growth seemed inexorable. To cash in on such benign circumstances, many Americans borrowed money to invest in the stock market, which in turn created an investment bubble driven by overconfidence and overexposure. As individual portfolios became less diverse, the risks to the wider economy were heightened: more and more of the country's wealth was tied to the vagaries of Wall Street.

On Tuesday, October 23, 1929, the New York Stock Exchange's ticker tape—which records fluctuations in share prices—kept running for 104 minutes after the day had officially ended. Relentless "sell" instructions were causing a marked depreciation in stocks on the tape. The next day nearly thirteen million shares were traded, the most ever recorded in a single day. On October 25, President Herbert Hoover sought to calm market sentiment by announcing that "the fundamental business of the country, that is, production and distribution of commodities, is on a sound and prosperous basis."[72] Investors, however, were not mollified by the president's reassurance. On October 28 and 29, the market went into free fall. In America, over the course of the crash, $85 billion in share value was wiped out, affecting approximately three million American shareholders, proliferating bankruptcies, which later increased unemployment, repossessions, and homelessness.[73] Share ownership was not as widespread as some have contended: the NYSE, inflating its own centrality to the nation, had overestimated in 1929 that twenty-five million Americans owned stocks.[74] But the numbers were high enough to cause more than a ripple effect. This was a seismic event that portended yet more tectonic activity.

The Wall Street crash did not directly cause the Great Depression. This also required a clumsy government response, which was not long in coming. The Fordney-McCumber Tariff of 1922 had imposed significant levies on imports. This was a politically popular course of action, as the purpose of tariffs—if not the outcome—is to protect jobs at home, a lesson heeded by Republicans and Democrats in 1928 when both parties promised support for even higher tariffs. The Hawley-Smoot Tariff of 1930 followed the logic of its 1922 predecessor in extremis: tariffs were increased to 40 percent, their highest level in American history. It was, in the words of the historian David Kennedy, "an economic and a political catastrophe." One thousand economists signed a petition urging Hoover to veto this narrow and self-defeating bill, which invited the rest of the world to engage in similarly protectionist practice. The influential J. P. Morgan partner Thomas Lamont, a close adviser to the president, recalled, "I almost went down on my knees to beg Herbert Hoover to veto the asinine Hawley-Smoot Tariff. That Act intensified nationalism all over the world."[75] Indeed, the French believed the tariff was akin to a declaration of war and vowed to retaliate in kind. But Hoover signed the bill in June 1930, leading Walter Lippmann, previously a Hoover supporter, to lambast the president for accepting "a wretched and mischievous product of stupidity and greed."[76] Hopeful that America, a land of plenty, was better placed than anywhere else to subsist through its own efforts and resources, Hawley-Smoot's supporters consigned the rest of the world economy to a dismal fate and scarcely served their homeland any better. The United States was not nearly as self-sufficient as protectionists believed its resources suggested. Over the course of 1930, the gross national product fell by 24 percent and unemployment increased from 8.9 to 11.9 percent. This rate more than doubled over the next two years.

In the final two months of 1930, six hundred banks were forced to close, leaving their depositors empty-handed. Thanks partly to President Andrew Jackson's assault on Alexander Hamilton's system of centralized, federally regulated banking, many of America's banks, according to Carter Glass, the cofounder of the Federal Reserve, were "pawn shops" managed by "little grocery corner-men calling themselves bankers—and all they know is how to shave a note."[77] And while a liquidity crisis afflicting the small banks of the provincial hinterland was one thing, the contagion soon spread to bigger, more esteemed enterprises. New York City's Bank of United States collapsed on December 11, 1930—the largest commercial bank failure in American history. Panic spread across the nation's banks and their depositors, clogging the arteries of credit. Viable banks recalled loans as quickly as depositors could close their accounts. As loans became harder to acquire, small and medium-size businesses went to the wall and millions of workers were made redundant. As export markets collapsed, U.S. unemployment rose to 25 percent by the beginning of 1933, the Depression's trough. Perhaps for the first time, an atmosphere of despondency descended upon a nation known for its optimism. At a micro level, this theme was captured in the suicide note written by a mechanic in Houston: "The depression has got me licked. There is no work to be had. I can't accept charity and I am too proud to appeal to my kin or friends, and I am too honest to steal. So I see no other course. A land flowing with milk and honey and a first-class mechanic can't make an honest living. I would rather take my chances with a just God than with unjust humanity."[78]

As the historian Anthony J. Badger writes, "So many people in Memphis jumped off the Hanrahan Bridge into the Mississippi that the telephone numbers of local clergymen willing to counsel would-be suicides were listed in the press. The efficacy of this assistance was substantially lessened by the newspaper headline 'Memphis Preacher Jumps Off.' "[79] The Depression was a low point in American self-esteem, memorialized in works of affecting social realism such as John Steinbeck's *The Grapes of Wrath*.

President Herbert Hoover continues to receive a hard rap for his mishandling of the Great Depression's early years—some of which is warranted and some of which is not. His critics often forget that Hoover was remarkably talented, a victim of circumstance as well as of his orthodox belief that small government worked best, even during a crisis of that magnitude. The Stanford University scholar Thomas Sowell is surely correct to observe, "Had he never become president, Herbert Hoover could have gone down in history as one of the greatest humanitarians of the century."[80] In the after-

math of the First World War, Hoover formed a philanthropic organization, seeded in the first instance by his own personal fortune, to alleviate
starvation on the European continent. He was successful—not to say uncommonly proactive and brave—in spearheading this endeavor. John Maynard
Keynes observed that Hoover was "the only man who emerged from the or-
deal of Paris with an enhanced reputation."[81] This led some Democrats to
approach Hoover about standing for president in 1920, with Franklin Roosevelt as his running mate. Hoover demurred, feeling more at home in the
Republican Party, and instead performed distinguished service, during
an admittedly economically buoyant decade, as secretary of commerce to
Harding and Coolidge.

Hoover's belief in the superiority of well-meaning voluntarism to
government-provided safety nets—and his aversion to running budget
deficits—shaped his passivity in the face of irresistible economic forces that
served to destroy his reputation. His name remains something of an epithet
today. Throughout the 1980s, whenever the Democratic Speaker of the House
Tip O'Neill wanted to dismiss President Reagan as a doctrinaire conservative of deceptive affability, he would describe him as "Hoover with a smile."[82]
Hoover consistently appears on the periodic attempts to rank the presidents
as faring better only than Andrew Johnson, James Buchanan, and Franklin
Pierce. This does a disservice to Hoover. Beard certainly didn't view Hoover's
response to this grave economic crisis as especially misdirected in the context of the times. Indeed, in 1931 he applauded not just his tariff policy but
also the manner in which the president refused to bow to the Navy League's
demands to increase defense spending in what was claimed as a more dangerous world—support that earned Beard an appreciative phone call at home
from the president.[83]

Much as the cataclysmic events of the First World War guided Woodrow
Wilson's attempt to begin the practice of international relations anew, so the
Great Depression—shattering in different ways—informed Charles Beard's
efforts to formulate a similarly bold vision for America's foreign policy. Wilson and Beard were both political science Ph.D.s responding to calamity
with a radical theory, although each had a starkly different point of departure. Whereas Wilson believed the United States had to assume a leadership
role to change the world, Beard believed that the nation had to retreat from
the world and change itself.

So Beard supported Hawley-Smoot because a 40 percent import tariff
was almost guaranteed to compel self-reliance. Beard further envisioned

the creation of a barter system in which nations would trade only in essential items not provided by domestic enterprise, removing wasteful competition that leads to needless conflict. He urged tighter controls governing the extension of loans so as to prevent "irresponsible governments" from securing American credit, and sought a substantial contraction in diplomatic activity. Beard believed it was high time the government rejected the rationale that the U.S. military should be strong enough "to protect any American citizen who wants to make ten per cent on the bonds of Weissnichtwo or sell cornflakes, shoehorns and collar buttons to the . . . world willy nilly."[84]

To manage this statist edifice, predicated on much wishful thinking, Beard called for Congress to establish what he named a "National Economic Council," charged with coordinating all the nation's economic requirements in the realms of finance, production, and distribution.[85] The name he gave to this strategy of foreign-policy retrenchment and domestic statism was "continental Americanism," elaborating more fully on themes developed in the 1920s. The only problem was that President Hoover steadfastly refused to heed Beard's advice, or anything even approaching the activism he counseled. It took the election of Franklin Delano Roosevelt in 1932 to raise Beard's hopes that his views might find a more receptive audience. Indeed, Beard hoped that he would serve as a freelance tutor of sorts to the new president.

Franklin Roosevelt's public persona is indelibly carved in historical memory: his broad, optimistic smile, half-glasses, finely tailored suits, ever-present cigarette holder, and projection of utter confidence in his and his nation's destiny. Yet for a man on first-name terms with virtually everyone he encountered, his inner self was safely guarded—FDR was a Fabergé egg in his dazzling, unpenetrable exterior. Born in 1882 in upstate New York to a wealthy patrician family, Roosevelt was educated at Groton and Harvard before embarking on a political career: an occupation often deemed beneath a man of his class. Unlike Wilson, FDR was not an intellectual—he assimilated rather than created useful knowledge. After meeting Roosevelt in 1934, John Maynard Keynes recorded surprise that the president was not more "literate, economically speaking."[86]

While Roosevelt brought to domestic and foreign policy no original insights of his own devising, he was adept at delegating the task of policy and strategy innovation to others, and he had a wonderful knack—with some notable exceptions, like the Supreme Court–packing plan—of identifying the ideas and policies that would effect positive, enduring change *and* pass muster in Congress and the nation at large. His political skills were abundant. He drew important cautionary lessons from his service as assistant secretary of the Navy in the Wilson administration, recognizing that the White House and public opinion had to be closely aligned for major policy innovations to take root. And it was a fortunate and marvelous thing that Roosevelt was so amply gifted in political matters. For his presidency coincided with the worst economic downturn, and most dangerous war, in American history. His unflappability and charisma—as displayed in his masterly radio Fireside Chats—were indispensable in those perilous circumstances.

FDR was clear in his admiration for Alfred Thayer Mahan, remarking that "as a young man I had the pleasure of knowing Admiral Mahan and I have an almost complete collection of his books and articles."[87] His mother observed that her son "loved history in any form and used to pore over Admiral Mahan's 'History of Sea Power' until he had practically memorized the whole book."[88] Roosevelt believed in the indispensability of a powerful navy, and during the first year of his presidency, in the most challenging economic circumstances, he catalyzed a naval renaissance, allocating a massive $238 billion in June 1933 to improve the fleet and prioritize the development of high-pressure and high-temperature steam propulsion—a farsighted funding decision that allowed the U.S. Navy to launch ships that were up to 25 percent more efficient than those of its peers.[89] But FDR's views on Woodrow Wilson were more qualified in their admiration. In 1928, Roosevelt chided Republicans in *Foreign Affairs* for positively aiding "the charge that in a time when great constructive aid was needed in the task of solving the grave problems facing the whole earth, we have contributed little or nothing."[90] Throughout the 1920s, Roosevelt recorded strong opposition to America's continued reluctance to become a full member of the League of Nations.

Political expediency trumped fidelity to Wilson's league during the nomination tussle in 1932, however, when FDR disavowed his previous support for league membership and the Democratic Party later dropped references to Wilson's cherished project, eradicating nearly all mention of this pathbreaking two-term president. Repudiating Woodrow Wilson was cruel but perhaps vindicated in the nature of the campaign and its outcome: Roosevelt crushed Hoover on Election Day. FDR took 57.4 percent of the popular vote and left the incumbent president with just 59 electoral college votes from the states of the Northeast, whose long-standing affinity for the GOP would not survive the coming age of Roosevelt. Of course, the overwhelming manner of the Democratic Party's victory might also suggest that dismissing Wilson's legacy was unneccesary.

Charles Beard welcomed Roosevelt's election for the president's keen attention to the Depression. Both men shared a common optimism about America's future and its capacity for evolution and improvability. Throughout his thirteen years as president, FDR led a step change in the purpose and reach of the federal government, implementing some of the statist policies Beard had advocated and whose implementation he celebrated. What was not to like in a presidency devoted to job creation, social security, large-scale public works programs, the promotion of labor union rights, and federal subsidy of the arts? Of course, the president rejected Beard's counsel in refusing to centralize economic planning in a single source that would have brought the nation closer in affinity to the corporatism of fascist Italy than the ameliorative, paternalist state capitalism in, say, France or even Great Britain. But Beard forgave him that, recognizing that a change of that magnitude was out of reach for the present time—even for so gifted a politician as Roosevelt.

What worried Beard was the president's affinity for the Navy. In this regard, and in this alone, he much preferred Hoover, who shared his aversion to Mahanian naval theory. FDR's support for naval expansion seemed to portend an outward-facing foreign policy. And Beard worried that this foolish emphasis might result in the president proving susceptible to "a grand diversion—a diversion that might not be unwelcome, should the domestic recovery program fall far short of its aims"—a remarkably farsighted observation for Beard to have registered in 1933.[91] At this juncture, Beard blamed some of Roosevelt's hawkish advisers rather than the man himself. He identified a split in the administration between Jeffersonians who favored political and economic self-sufficiency, such as the president and Secretary of Agriculture Henry Wallace, and dangerous Wilsonian internationalists like Secretary of State Cordell Hull, who believed that the United States must promote order, spread democratic values, and continue to facilitate greater economic interdependence. Hoping to tilt the administration in a continentalist direction, Beard embarked on the task of convincing Roosevelt of his indispensability as an adviser.

In October 1933, Beard dined with Roosevelt at the White House. Like countless others, Beard had been thoroughly charmed by his presidential host and returned home in an optimistic frame of mind, hopeful that FDR might again prove receptive to his views on how to deal with the economic crisis and assure America a more modest place in world affairs.[92] In 1932, the Social Science Research Council had awarded Beard a $25,000 grant to formulate a precise definition of that vexing term, "the national interest." The result of this research program was two books published in 1934, "with the collaboration of" the lawyer and Yale academic George H. E. Smith. Put together, *The Idea of the National Interest* and *The Open Door at Home* represent Beard's only attempts to emulate Alfred Mahan in formulating a foreign-policy vision that stood a realistic chance of being actioned. Realizing that time was not on his side, Beard was more forward than Mahan in identifying his intended audience. The core chapter in *The Open Door at Home*, titled "The Ethical Roots of Policy," was addressed directly to President Roosevelt: "the statesman . . . the socially-minded, public personality engrossed in the public interest." Beard described himself as a "scholar conscious of his role . . . a statesman, without portfolio, to be sure, but with a kindred sense of public responsibility."[93] In 1934, the stars were never better aligned for Beard to assume a position of policy influence.

Though published simultaneously, the two books are quite different in style and purpose. *The Idea of the National Interest: An Analytical Study in American Foreign Policy* is the most ostensibly Rankean book Beard ever wrote. His intention was to be "coldly factual throughout," and the result is a dry reading experience so challenging to the reader's forbearance as to make it positively un-Beardian.[94] The yin and yang of the book are Thomas Jefferson and Alexander Hamilton, whose conceptions of the national interest were starkly different. For Jefferson, the national interest was primarily agrarian in economic form. The United States should pursue a policy of expansion, but only within the continent, to create a self-sufficient population truly independent from the Old World. For Hamilton, America's national interest was primarily urban and commercial. As the U.S. economy grew, through exploitation of its vast natural resources and technological innovation, a point would come when its political leaders would have to unshackle the nation from the continental sphere.

To Beard's mind, the logical outcome of Hamilton's elevation of overseas trade as the central driver of progress was reckless adventurism in the Caribbean and the Pacific, culminating in the Spanish-American War and its land-grabbing outcome. While Jeffersonianism was not without its flaws, Beard believed fidelity to Hamiltonianism was a greater danger for the United States, since implict in its rationale is a perpetual expansion of international commitments and a massive navy to protect them. It was in the nature of big business to urge a restless, expansive foreign policy, which was anathema to America's true national interest. Where commerce went, so the military would be compelled to follow. This resulted in "outward thrusts of power" that damaged the United States, in neglecting its domestic sphere, nearly as much as the nation on the receiving end of the thrust.[95]

The Open Door at Home was more philosophically wide-reaching and friendlier to the reader. Beard argued that the Great Depression was the logical outcome of the type of economic interdependence extolled by the likes of Hamilton and Mahan. Following the analytical thread developed in *The Rise of American Civilization*, Beard celebrated America's natural abundance, which permitted the nation to avoid the cataclysmic class struggles predicted by Karl Marx and Friedrich Engels. He recommended that the federal government assume absolute control of imports and exports, that peripheral territorial possessions be handed back to their rightful owners, that U.S. diplomatic contact be limited to the minimum necessary to avoid counterproductive rudeness, and that a radical "standard of life" budget be created so as to redistribute the nation's vast wealth more equitably and to eliminate the cancer of unemployment that blighted the American body politic. Beard promised that this program would produce marvelous outcomes for the United States, and conceivably for the rest of the world too:

> By domestic control over all foreign trade, by the relaxation of the capitalistic pressure of the United States on world markets in standardized manufactures and commercial investments, by concentrating national energies on the development of national resources and the efficient distribution of wealth at home, by deliberately withdrawing from the rivalries of imperialistic nations, the United States would take its official nose out of a thousand affairs of no vital concern to the people of the United States, would draw back its defense lines upon zones that can be defended with the greatest probability of victory in case of war, and would thus have a minimum dependence on the "strategic products" indispensable to war. And by multiplying many fold its outlays for scientific research in analytic and synthetic chemistry, it could steadily decrease its dependence on world markets for the essentials indispensable to our material civilization in time of peace . . .
>
> In short, by cultivating its own garden, by setting an example of national self-restraint (which is certainly easier than restraining fifty other nations in an international conference, or beating them in war), by making no commitments that cannot be readily enforced by arms, by adopting toward other nations a policy of fair and open commodity exchange, by refraining from giving them any moral advice on any sub-

ject, and by providing a military and naval machine as adequate as possible to the defense of this policy, the United States may realize maximum security, attain minimum dependence upon governments and conditions beyond its control, and develop its own resources to the utmost.[96]

This was a vision every bit as radical as Woodrow Wilson's. Yet its premise was antithetical to nearly everything presented in the Fourteen Points. It was also unremittingly hostile to Mahan's vision of the United States as a maritime trading empire ennobled and hardened, from time to time, by participation in necessary wars. Where Wilson and Mahan wanted America to make peace with the interlinked nature of world affairs, Beard instead believed that the nation should retreat and "cultivate its own garden." Where Wilson believed America owed the world its leadership, Beard believed it owed it nothing—although other nations were welcome to test America's developmental path if they so wished. In Darwinian terms, Beard believed that the United States was similar to places like Australia and the Galápagos Islands, remote enough from outside predators to support a unique and remarkable ecosystem. "Enthroned between two oceans," Beard wrote, "with no historic enemies on the north or south, the Republic can be defended against any foes which such a policy may raise up against it."[97]

Certain signs had suggested to Beard that the president might be sympathetic to this radical reimagning of America's future. In July 1933, Roosevelt had withdrawn from the London Economic Conference, designed to hammer out a common global response to the economic depression—which by now affected every nation. To protect the trading benefits that accompanied a weak dollar, however, Roosevelt had refused to join a shared policy of currency stabilization. Beard applauded FDR's actions, which he believed followed the Jeffersonian tradition, for imparting the lesson that foreign trade was not necessary for domestic recovery.[98] In January 1934, the journalist Ernest K. Lindley, known to be close to FDR, reported that Beard was "one of the intellectual parents of the New Deal," a welcome validation. In a generally warm review of *The Open Door at Home* in *The American Historical Review*, the historian Samuel Flagg Bemis observed that the book held the potential to become "a classic of American political thought" and that well-placed sources had informed him that President Roosevelt had read the book and jotted comments in the margins.[99]

Bemis was right about Roosevelt scribbling in his book, and indeed that the president "kept it in his desk for callers to see for three weeks!" But Beard also learned in time that one of FDR's handwritten comments described the book as "a bad dish." His feeling of disappointment was compounded when Secretary of Agriculture Henry Wallace penned an evenhanded but critical review of *The Open Door at Home* in *The New Republic*. Wallace observed that Beard "dreams a great dream of a beautiful and peaceful future of our great land," to which "the heart thrills . . . [but] even Beard has not seen the whole problem. He is not so good an economic technician as he is a historian." Rather than securing the United States a blissful future, Wallace believed it was impossible, and potentially very damaging, for the United States to abandon world trade in favor of domestic development alone. In another review, the historian Herbert Feis, then working as an economic adviser to the State Department, detected chauvinism in Beard's recommendations and worried his model might invite the kind of reciprocal belligerency he deplored. If France viewed Hawley-Smoot as a declaration of war, what might Paris make of America's move to autarky? Feis further worried that technological innovation would soon rob the United States of the protection offered by two great oceans.[100] The United States might just about achieve self-sufficiency, but nations with formidable militaries and vast potential for further growth—Germany and Japan in particular—lacked the natural resources to follow a similar path. What would stop them from seeking redress from the bountiful United States when military technology permitted? Wallace and Feis detected significant shortcomings in Beard's thesis. Put together, alongside FDR's "bad dish" comment, their critiques might be described as the official administration response to Beard's continentalist vision for his beloved United States. His hopes for policy relevance were crushed in 1934. Beard's views on Roosevelt continued their trajectory from hope to concern to strident opposition.

Like Germany and Italy, Japan felt it had been given a raw deal at the Paris Peace Conference. For fighting valiantly on the side of the Entente, winning important battles against the German fleet in the Pacific, Tokyo believed that the acquisition of the League of Nations' South Sea Mandate—constituting what we know today as Palau, the Northern Mariana Islands, the Federated States of Micronesia, and the Marshall Islands—was inadequate recompense, particularly when compared to the mandate booty engineered and acquired by France and Great Britain. A nation for which Beardian autarky was a hopeless dream, lacking vital natural resources such as rubber and oil, Japan was a first-rank power implacably opposed to the territorially restrictive interwar status quo. And so Japan fell under the spell of militarists during the 1920s and 1930s, ambitious and ruthless men who believed the only way to secure Japan a more glorious future was to annex the rich northern regions of China and as much of Southeast Asia and the Dutch East Indies as its formidable military could conquer. This plan for expanding the Japanese empire at its neighbors' expense was given an Orwellian title in 1940: "The Greater East-Asia Co-Prosperity Sphere."

The first stage in creating this arc of prosperity was the Japanese annexation of Manchuria, in northern China. This was achieved in 1931 when the territory was invaded, declared independent from China, and renamed Manchukuo. Half a million Japanese men and women subsequently emigrated to settle and till the resource-rich land, with a view to alleviating some of the economic woes afflicting the homeland. In response, the Hoover administration promulgated what became known as the Stimson Doctrine—named after Secretary of State Henry Stimson—which held that the United States would not recognize Manchukuo as an independent nation, or indeed any other Chinese territory that Japan decided to hack off and subsume in its pursuit of self-sufficiency. The Stimson Doctrine was directly challenged in 1937 with Japan's full-scale invasion of China, unleashing a brutal conflict in which Japanese war crimes were legion. Following the Japanese capture of Nanjing (Nanking), for example, its troops murdered some two hundred thousand Chinese civilians and soldiers, and raped tens of thousands of women.[101] The "Rape of Nanjing" was a dark episode in Japan's quest for regional dominance, and more were to come. Roosevelt's response was critical but muted, influenced to some degree by the coldly realist advice he received from his adviser William C. Bullitt: "We have large emotional interests in China, small economic interests, and no vital interests."[102]

Berlin and Rome were plotting a similarly destructive and expansionist path. Italy was the lesser of those irredentist powers—though a pioneer in embracing fascism first—and it invaded Abyssinia (Ethiopia) in 1935 with ambitions of rekindling the glories of the Roman Empire. More plausibly, it hoped to exact revenge for the humiliating defeat that the Abyssinians had dealt the Italian army during the Battle of Adowa in 1896. This time the Italian military prevailed against the hopelessly outgunned Abyssinians—who nonetheless managed to deal some embarrassing blows to Benito Mussolini's invading forces. In a shameful diplomatic episode, Britain and France combined in an attempt to placate Mussolini in the hope that he might ally Italy against Adolf Hitler's Germany. The two nations refused to close the Suez Canal, which would have stranded the Italian army in the Horn of Africa, and proposed a plan devised by their foreign secretaries, Sir Samuel Hoare and Pierre Laval, which ceded much of Abyssinia to Italy. When the details of this supine plan were made public, Hoare-Laval was torpedoed and the two men were forced to resign. A halfhearted League of Nations embargo was imposed in its place, which, fatally, did not include oil. But the damage to the reputations of both Britain and France was profound. Observing diplomatic adversaries that were irresolute at their core, an emboldened Hitler recognized that the time was opportune to attack the reviled Versailles Treaty.

Hitler's challenge to the European status quo proceeded cautiously. First the führer ordered the remilitarization of the Rhineland—which the victors at Versailles had shorn of military capabilities—in March 1936. Britain and France did nothing in response. During the summer, Hitler dispatched German troops, and state-of-the-art military hardware, to assist the efforts of fellow fascist General Francisco Franco to overthrow the democratically elected Popular Front government in Spain. Direct participation in the Spanish Civil War allowed Hitler to test new battlefield strategems, the blitzkrieg and indiscriminate aerial bombardment, which were deployed to devastating effect in all theaters during the Second World War. German support was also decisive in allowing Franco to prevail, leading to the establishment of another fascist nation on the European continent. A German "Axis" with Mussolini's Italy was declared later that year—displaying the futility of Anglo-French efforts to lure Il Duce to their side. In February 1938, Germany gave up its hopes of reacquiring its Pacific territories and agreed to a formal alliance with Japan. In that same month, German troops entered Austria and a pan-German Anschluss was declared, later ratified by a plebiscite that registered Austrian approval at a suspiciously high level of 99 percent.

Confident that continued Anglo-French acquiescence to his assault on Versailles proved that those nations were irredeemably effete, Hitler turned next to Czechoslovakia, whose Sudetenland was peopled by a large proportion of ethnic Germans. While caving to German aggression had not worked well to that point, British prime minister Neville Chamberlain gave it one final go at the Munich conference in late September 1938. With Chamberlain as master of ceremonies, he, French prime minister Édouard Daladier, and Hitler hashed out an agreeement, signed on September 30, which gifted the Sudetenland—the industrial heart of Czechoslovakia—to Germany. With dubious grounds for self-congratulation, and infused with a large dose of Polyannaish optimism, Chamberlain hailed the Munich agreement for assuring "peace in our time." This peace lasted until March 1939, when

Slovakia seceded from Czechoslovakia and became a pro-Nazi satellite, and the remainder of the now impotent nation was incorporated into the Third Reich at the point of the German bayonet.

On March 31, France and Britain, finally conceding the failure of their appeasement of Hitler, pledged their full support for an independent Poland, which by now was hemmed in by Nazi Germany to the west and Stalin's Soviet Union to the east. Britain further solidified its commitments when it signed an Anglo-Polish military alliance in August, which Chamberlain promised to honor. A few years too late, a line had finally been drawn in the sand, not that its permanence much convinced Hitler, who had reason to doubt that Britain would risk war over Poland. A million and a half battle-ready German troops flooded across the Polish border on September 1, exactly one week after the signing of the Molotov-Ribbentrop Pact. This pact of convenience between two of the twentieth century's worst mass murderers promised nonaggression between Germany and the Soviet Union as their armies feasted on Polish territory, visiting hellish destruction as they went. Holding true to their word this time, Britain and France declared war on Germany two days later. Conditioned to Anglo-French pliability, Hitler was genuinely surprised when he received the news.

With such audacity and brutality did Adolf Hitler destroy almost all that had been drawn up by Wilson, Lloyd George, and Clemenceau in Paris. In fact, Hitler could even claim to be following the logic of ethnic self-determination—he was gathering all German peoples under the benign control of the Third Reich. Totalitarian governments in Japan, Germany, and Italy were taking what they believed was rightfully theirs, and the rest of the world—with Britain and France sharing most of the blame—seemed to lack the will and ability to stop them. A strong, unified Anglo-French response to these Versailles transgressions might have halted his momentum, shattering the cult of personality he and his propagandists so capably developed, and encouraging his opponents to launch a coup of the type that Hitler had tried in Munich in 1923 and Berlin in 1933.

The parameters of President Roosevelt's response to these harrowing geopolitical events were circumscribed by the isolationist tenor of the times, which Beard, through his voluminous writings in national newspapers and magazines, helped in small part to create. In 1934, however, it was H. C. Engelbrecht and F. C. Hanighen's sensational *Merchants of Death: A Study of the International Armaments Industry* that truly captured the public's imagination. A national bestseller, widely circulated by the influential Book-of-the-Month Club, *Merchants of Death* argued that the armaments industry played a major role in bringing the world to war in 1914 and provoking American participation three years later. Responding to the apparent plausibility of some of the claims, and the furor they created, Senator Gerald Nye of North Dakota led a congressional investigation charged with establishing the true origins of the First World War. Nye offered dramatic and incendiary conclusions, laying blame at the feet of reckless, internationalist American banks—whose interests were dangerously intertwined with those of the arms industry—that extended credits to Britain and France that could be redeemed only if Germany and its allies were defeated. The Nye Committee's findings were published at the beginning of 1935 and soon began to exert significant influence on congressional and public opinion. A 1936 straw poll revealed that 95 percent of Americans opposed participation in any future war with Hitler's Germany. Roosevelt understood that he confronted "a public psychology of long standing—a psychology which comes very close to saying 'peace at any price.' "[103]

Congress passed three major neutrality acts with sweeping majorities. The first, passed in 1935—as Mussolini prepared to attack Abyssinia—required that during a state of war the U.S. should impose an arms embargo on *all* belligerents and warned Americans against traveling on belligerent-owned ships. The second neutrality act was passed in February 1936. Taking its direct cue from the Nye Committee, it prohibited war loans and credits for belligerents. The third act, passed in May 1937, renewed the earlier restrictions and made American travel on belligerent ships unlawful, rather than simply cautioning Americans against it. The rationale behind all these acts was clear: an isolationist congressional majority wanted to foreclose to Roosevelt all the maneuvers that Wilson allegedly deployed in bringing the United States into war in 1917. On a visit to the United States, the sister of British prime minister Neville Chamberlain described her host nation as "hardly a people to go tiger shooting with."[104]

It was Japan's invasion of China in 1937, and fear that a resurgent Congress, if not contained, could derail Roosevelt's broad political agenda, that convinced the president to reassert authority and lead public opinion with a major speech on international affairs. As the New Deal faltered in the face of renewed recession, and FDR's efforts to pack the Supreme Court with sympathetic justices ran into an almighty political/judicial roadblock, Secretary of State Cordell Hull recalled that in this context of political crisis he "was becoming increasingly worried over the growth of isolationist senti-ment in the United States." He urged the president to challenge his tormen-tors in Congress and in the media by delivering a major speech on the efficacy of "international cooperation in the course of his journey." Roo-sevelt agreed to Hull's request and delivered an address in Chicago on Octo-ber 5, 1937—the famous "Quarantine Speech."[105]

Hundreds of thousands of people thronged the sidewalks, framing the president's leisurely route through Chicago, desperate to catch a glimpse of a leader still viewed as a potential savior. In a powerful speech, FDR referred directly to the wars raging in China and Spain, observing that world civili-zation was threatened by the terror that authoritarian regimes were visiting upon the earth. He attacked those well-intentioned but dangerous idealists who argued that America's comfortable perch in the western hemisphere was distant enough from the world's travails to avoid involvement and attack. It was a remarkable speech that exerted a profound influence on the future course of world affairs:

> The peace-loving nations must make a concerted effort in opposition to those violations of treaties and those ignorings of humane instincts which today are creating a state of international anarchy, instability from which there is no escape through mere isolation or neutrality . . . When an epidemic of physical disease starts to spread, the community approves and joins in a quarantine of the patients in order to protect the health of the community against the spread of the disease . . . We are adopting such measures as will minimize our risk of involvement, but we cannot have complete protection in a world of disorder in which confidence and security have broken down.[106]

The crowd's response was ecstatic. On the train back to Washington, the president, seeking further affirmation, asked his secretary, "How did it go, Grace?" When she nodded appreciatively, Roosevelt mused, "Well, it's done now. It was something that needed saying."[107] While it might have needed saying, it also provoked a backlash. As news of Roosevelt's speech reached Washington, D.C., Congressmen Hamilton Fish and George Tinkham called for the president's impeachment. Cordell Hull recalled that the "reac-tion against the quarantine idea was quick and violent. As I saw it, this had the effect of setting back for at least six months our constant educa-tional campaign intended to create and strengthen public opinion toward international cooperation."[108] FDR's line in the sand had been drawn as quickly as his political survival permitted.

In January 1938, Congressman Louis A. Ludlow sponsored a constitutional amendment that would have required a national referendum on the declaration of war, except in the event of a direct military attack on American territory. This proposal was defeated in the House by 209 votes to 188. Sensing that momentum was now on his side, Roosevelt requested a substantial increase in military preparedness expenditure, which was duly authorized. Through 1939, FDR grew bold enough to challenge the neutrality laws. After Germany's invasion of Poland, a fourth neutrality act was passed, which repealed the blunt-instrument nature of the three that preceded it. Passed in November 1939, the fourth act allowed belligerent nations (meaning all those that opposed Hitler) to purchase American arms on a cash-and-carry basis—a lifeline that Britain and France grasped as long as financial reserves permitted. On May 10—a day that was auspicious only in the sense that Winston Churchill replaced Neville Chamberlain as prime minister—Germany invaded Belgium, the Netherlands, and France. The defensive Maginot Line, in which French hopes were mainly vested, was outflanked, and one by one, in rapid succession, each nation fell to the German blitzkrieg within five weeks. Paris fell to the Germans on June 14. The British Empire was the only force that remained to thwart Hitler's ambitions, and it desperately needed American supplies. But how could America supply a nation that couldn't afford its wares?

Beard was relaxed about Japan's acquisitive ambitions in its Pacific backyard. In a speech delivered at the University of Southern California, one week after the establishment of Manchukuo in 1931, Beard observed that Japanese expansionism was the natural outgrowth of a system in which the navy and army operate outside the reach of civilian authority and are accorded too much institutional respect. He further cautioned that what Japan did to China was of no real concern to the United States, occupied as it was with defending its "continental heritage" in arduous economic circumstances.[109] He despaired of the internationalist rationale presented by Walter Lippmann in 1933, who argued that "this damnable crisis is international whether we like it or not . . . It is international in spite of all prejudices, preferences, and wishes to the contrary, and the man who tries to act as if it weren't is trying to put out a great fire with one bucket of water."[110] Beard believed that Lippmann was wrong, and the public opinion he so disparaged would present the strongest bulwark against internationalist-led expansionism: "With much twisting and turning the American people are renewing the [George] Washington tradition and repudiating both the Kiplingesque imperialism of Theodore Roosevelt and the universal philanthropy of Woodrow Wilson."[111] But the public still had to be on their guard. Beard strongly suspected that President Roosevelt was seeking participation in a foreign war to deflect attention from continued depression at home. "The Jeffersonian party gave the nation the War of 1812, the Mexican War, and its participation in the World War," Beard wrote in February 1935. "The Pacific War awaits."[112]

Following Italy's invasion of Abyssinia, Beard turned fire on those observers sanctimonious enough to pin the label of "good" or "bad" on Italian actions, and who recklessly "employ the risk of war to prevent war" in fidelity to such distinctions.[113] In an asymmetric war that pitted the narcissistic, bellicose Benito Mussolini against the noble, diminutive Haile Selassie, Beard's denigration of the good-bad dichotomy seems difficult to fathom, let alone agree with. But his broad motivation—to avoid American entanglement in a larger war precipitated by Italy's interest in a godforsaken part of a godforsaken continent—is clear enough. Following this line of reasoning, in September 1937 Beard observed that Roosevelt, ill-advisedly emulating Woodrow Wilson, was still following "the creed that the United States must do good all around the world."[114]

Beard nonetheless was plotting a difficult path between his obvious distaste for Japan, Italy, and Germany, and his desire to undermine America's stake in forestalling their advance. His sense of comradeship with progressives and socialists elsewhere was still clearly present. Beard supported, for example, supplying the "Loyalist" Popular Front in Spain with American weaponry and munitions—it was clearly a moral good that Franco's insurrection be defeated. Following Japan's invasion of China in 1937, Beard penned a perceptive, morally informed critique of what Japan, Italy, and Germany had wrought, and what this portended:

> By their faith in force . . . Hitler and Mussolini are more or less beyond the reach of the old-fashioned calculations. Japanese militarists belong in the same emotional category. Having a philosophy of history in which "anything may happen," the directors of these three groups may fling prudence to the winds and make the experiment [of aggressive war], or without any deliberate intention or open declarations, the great powers may find themselves at war in the midst of a dissolving civilization.[115]

But then in February 1938, fearing that the brutality of Japanese actions in China might permit FDR to convince Americans of a phantom stake in East Asia, Beard presented a stark choice between privileging the fates of exotic peoples thousands of miles away and privileging American development itself:

> It is easy to get into a great moral passion over the distant Chinese. It costs nothing much now, though it may cost the blood of countless American boys. It involves no conflict with greedy interests in our own midst. It sounds well on Sunday . . . [But] anybody who feels hot with morals and is affected with delicate sensibilities can find enough to do at home, considering the misery of the 10,000,000 unemployed, the tramps, the beggars, the sharecroppers, tenants and field hands right here at our door.[116]

While it was difficult for Beard to reconcile his contempt for Berlin, Rome, and Tokyo with his belief that America was best advised to tend to its own Edenic garden, the latter strain in his thinking became dominant with FDR's Quarantine Speech, which he believed portended disaster. Responding to the self-serving support extended to the president by Earl Browder, general secretary of the American Communist Party, Beard wondered of the speech: "How can we have the effrontery to assume that we can solve the problems of Asia and Europe, encrusted in the blood-rust of fifty centuries? Really, little boys and girls, how can we?"[117] Called to testify before the House of Representatives on February 9, 1938, Beard decried FDR's "policy of quarantine" as necessarily requiring "big battleships to be used in aggressive warfare in the Far Pacific or the Far Atlantic." He also cast scorn on those sensationalists who entertained the possibility of the "fascist goblins of Europe . . . marching across the Atlantic to Brazil . . . [This was] the kind of nightmare which a holder of shipbuilding stocks had when ordinary business is bad . . . the new racket created to herd the American people into Roosevelt's quarantine camp."[118]

A convenient way to dance around any residual discomfort about Japanese, German, and Italian transgressions was to blame Britain and France for inviting this mess with their irresolution—which Beard did relentlessly. Having seen the nation close-up during his time at Oxford, Beard had mixed feelings toward Britain. He admired its orderly society and myriad political and cultural achievements, but he despised its class system and its empire. Reviewing an anti-British polemic penned by Quincy Howe, titled

England Expects Every American to Do His Duty, Beard agreed wholeheart-
edly with the author's central contention that America should let its elderly
colonial parent fight its own battles, which were invariably waged in defense
of its own interests. But clear commonalities in language, economics, and
cultural traditions assured "that even blind isolationists must recognize
this fact in all their thought about practice."[119] For all that, Beard believed
that Britain should face down Hitler and Mussolini alone—or with any
help that France could muster. In early 1939, Beard advised that Paris and
London should "call [Hitler's] bluff and stop the peril within forty-eight
hours. They can establish solidarity, if that is their real and secret wish.
They have the men, the materials, the money, and the power."[120] Here, Beard
was overestimating Anglo-French capabilities and underestimating those of
the German Wehrmacht. But he was far from alone in misdiagnosing the
European military balance in the late 1930s.

Where Beard was prescient was in comprehending the horrific threat
posed by Hitler's warped sensibilities. In *Foreign Affairs* in 1936, he wrote that
Mein Kampf should be taken at face value, that "no other book approaches
in authority this sacred text." He also formed some general sense of what
Hitler's accession meant for Germany's Jewish population—"Jews are condemned in language unprintable. They are to be driven to the Ghetto or out
of Germany"—and nailed with unerring accuracy Hitler's expansionist design: "Turned in upon themselves, nourishing deep resentments, and lashed
to fury by a militant system of education, the German people are conditioned for that day when Hitler, his technicians and his army, are ready and
are reasonably sure of the prospects of success in a sudden and devastating
attack, East or West."[121]

One thing that Beard could not be accused of was underestimating
Hitler. Yet in 1939, in contrast to his earlier advocacy of Britain stiffening its
resolve, he weclomed continued equivocation. On May 20, the radical journalist H. L. Mencken wrote to Beard that "if the danger of war passes it certainly won't be Roosevelt's fault. He had done his best to encourage an
unyielding spirit in England." Beard replied, "I fear that you are right as to
our being served up for the next crusade . . . Let us hope that the wild men
in Europe manage to bluff one another cold . . . and thus grant us a little respite." To Beard's credit, a year later—as Britain's fate as an independent
nation was contested in the skies above—he chastised Mencken for suggesting in an article that "there is not the slightest evidence that the Totalitarian
Powers . . . have been planning any attack on this country." Beard responded
that "the statement is right—there is not the slightest evidence—in the sense

that we do not know what they are doing in this respect, if anything. But there are grounds for suspicion . . . I am for staying out of this mess in Europe, but experience and prudence, coupled with the pains of an oft-singed tail, suggest to me that we keep our powder dry and our neck well in." Backing down only slightly, Mencken wrote unvaliantly that "the blame for whatever happens rests with Roosevelt, it seems to me, far more than on Hitler."[122]

Beard made some questionable and contradictory calls on the darkening situation in Europe. But as this exchange suggests, his intellect remained supple enough to recoil from unsubstantiated assertions such as Mencken's. Throughout the late 1930s, however, Beard's continentalism placed him in unpleasant company. The isolationist camp was a broad church, but many of its members were regrettably on the side of the devil. The priest and radio demagogue Charles Coughlin was virulently anti-Semitic and didn't expend much effort shielding his fascist sympathies. The chief spokesman of the isolationist America First Committee, the aviator Charles Lindbergh, held ugly views on eugenics and the influence exerted by Jews. Lindbergh's admiration for the Third Reich—and what he viewed as its irresistible Luftwaffe—led him to advise FDR to accommodate Hitler in America's best interests. Isolationists drew their strength from a smorgasbord of sectional interests: draft resisters, anti-Semites, Irish Americans, pro-fascist German and Italian Americans, William Randolph Hearst and his credulous readers, midwestern xenophobes, pacifists, Quakers, and Bryanite Democrats. The sociologist Talcott Parsons observed that isolationists were consumed by something akin to social pathology, a variant on what Émile Durkheim labeled anomie: "the unbearable loss of normative regulation that signaled the breakdown of social structure and the disorientation of isolated individuals."[123] Beard operated in the midst of that cacophony of strident, chauvinistic, disoriented voices.

Compared to these unpleasant rationales for American noninvolvement, Beard's continentalism was a paragon of humanity, driven by benign social-reformist statism. There is something laudable about his injunction to perfect the United States before attempting to export an unrealized model elsewhere. He wasn't the only isolationist from the academic community. John Bassett Moore (Columbia), Edwin M. Borchard (Yale), Philips Bradley (Dartmouth), Harry Elmer Barnes (Smith), Robert M. Hutchins (Chicago), and Henry Noble MacCracken (Vassar) were all firmly opposed to American participation in a second world war. But Beard provided the most humane and intellectually compelling rationale for global noninvolvement. Although he defended Lindbergh against his detractors in 1940—refusing to attribute base, racist motives to such a hero—Beard also declined to offer public support for America First, writing to Matthew Josephson that "I wanted to speak out for peace. But I found that the wrong kind of people were in that camp, while those I like seem to be on the other side."[124]

Beard's final plea for geopolitical sanity was published as France fell to the force of German arms. In *A Foreign Policy for America*, Beard identifies two villains who combined to create a momentum for wrongheaded overseas entanglement that might eventually destroy the republic: Alfred Thayer Mahan and Woodrow Wilson—and the success of one led inexorably to the overstretch of the other. Beard describes Mahan as "the most successful propagandist ever produced in the United States," lamenting that Theodore Roosevelt "made Mahan's work his bible of politics for the United States." In condemning Mahan with a full repertoire of vitriol, Beard displays almost virtuosic ability:

> Perhaps in the whole history of the country there had never been a more cold-blooded resolve to "put over on the people" such a "grand" policy, in spite of their recalcitrance, "ignorance," and "provincialism" . . . [Mahan] was a veritable ignoramus. He took such old works as suited his preconceived purposes, tore passages and fragments out of their context . . . In sum and substance, Mahan's foreign policy for the United States was based on the pure materialism of biological greed, although it was more or less clouded by rhetorical confusion, religious sentiments, and a clumsy style . . . Much which passed for argument in the Mahan system was little more than the rationalized war passion of a frustrated swivel-chair officer who had no stomach for the hard work of navigation and fighting.[125]

Having put Mahan and Roosevelt to the sword, Beard turned to Wilson. For Beard, the segue was seamless: "From their participation in collective world politics, from the imperialistic theory of 'doing good to backwards people,' it was but a step to President Wilson's scheme for permanent and open participation in European and Asiatic affairs in the alleged interest of universal peace and general welfare."[126] Beard clearly despised Mahan, but he had more sympathy for Wilson and his Fourteen Points:

> It went beyond the fondest dreams of many pacificators. It raised some dubious issues. But it was a program for *world* peace, put forward by the highest authority in the country . . . In fine, historic wrongs are to be

righted, nations put on a permanent footing, and the peace of all guaranteed by all. Never had the dream of universal and final peace seemed so near to realization . . . By President Wilson's program the old foreign policies of the United States—continentalism and imperialism—were to be resolutely discarded and a new policy of internationalism was to be substituted. Active and continuous participation in the affairs of Europe was to take the place of non-intervention.[127]

Yet this fine-sounding plan was critically undermined by its insidious economic foundations. Wilson's internationalism "placed its main reliance on laissez faire in international commerce as the chief economic support of the new order. Thus in every respect it was in flat and irreconcilable contradiction to continentalism for the United States, the program of peace for America in this hemisphere, and pacific relations elsewhere."[128] Mahan was driven by brute materialism, Wilson by self-deluding altruism, and both were operating against the Jeffersonian spirit of American continentalism:

Twice in American history the governing elite had turned the American nation away from its continental center of gravity into world adventures, ostensibly in a search for relations with the other countries or regions that would yield prosperity for American industry and a flowering of American prestige. First in 1898; second in 1917. But each time the main body of the people had resisted the propulsion, had found delusions in the false promises, and had returned to the continental orbit.[129]

It was in the American people that Beard found his greatest cause for optimism. He still hoped that a swell of public opinion would embrace his vision, making it impossible for FDR to realize the war plans that Beard believed he clearly now possessed.

On the inside cover of his personal copy of Beard's *A Foreign Policy for America*, President Roosevelt wrote: "40 years' hard and continuous study has brought forth an inbred mouse."[130] The book's critical reception was scarcely more restrained. The Protestant theologian and noted foreign-policy realist Reinhold Niebuhr wrote that Beard did not hide his "moral indifferentism."[131] At a time in which Nazi Germany had overrun the European continent and was setting itself for an invasion attempt against Great Britain, Niebuhr found Beard's neglect of these events unconscionable. Allan Nevins echoed Niebuhr in decrying Beard's "frigid indifference to moral considerations . . . The democratic world is slipping into dissolution and despair. Men are dying under bombs and machine guns to save part of it. They speak the language we speak, they hold our faith. But Mr. Beard turns away."[132] Once a firm admirer of Beard, Lewis Mumford believed that a serious threat to Western civilization rendered the author of continentalism "like a sundial [that] cannot tell the time on a stormy day." "The isolationism of a Charles Beard," Mumford wrote with utter comtempt, "is indeed almost as much a sign of barbarism as the doctrines of a[n Alfred] Rosenberg or a Gottfried Feder."[133] Attacked from all sides, with American public opinion falling in line with the administration, Beard was cutting an increasingly beleaguered figure. A July 1940 poll in *Fortune* magazine had found that two-thirds of respondents supported the president furnishing aid to any nation that opposed Germany and Japan.[134]

It was in such inauspicious circumstances that Beard testified, on February 4, 1941, before the Senate Foreign Relations Committee against President Roosevelt's main strategy to defend Britain short of a formal military alliance: Lend-Lease. David Lilienthal, a director of the Tennessee Valley Authority, one of the New Deal's crowning achievements, wrote admiringly of the distinguished figure that Beard cut in Congress. He was "a grand-looking man with a mobile face that at times is gentle even to the point of seeming 'harmless,' an impression that is heightened by his deafness and age. His eyes will darken and sharpen, his brows tighten, and a lowering hawklike expression takes over, and then he can lay on the whip in a way that is a joy to see."[135]

Beard made good use of the whip in his testimony. Under the provisions of the Lend-Lease Bill, the United States promised to lend Britain significant military matériel without any need for up-front payment. The bill stipulated that after the war, the matériel would be returned to the United States or else "bought" at a 90 percent discount. FDR explained the rationale by observing that in the event of a fire at a neighbor's house, the appropriate response was not to say, "Neighbor, my garden hose cost me $15; you have to pay me $15 for it," but to say, "I don't want $15—I want my fire hose back after the fire is over."[136] Beard disputed the wisdom of the president's logic and contended that the program would bring America inexorably into the conflict; it would take more than a well-aimed garden hose to prevent the fire from spreading.

Before criticizing Lend-Lease, Beard extended an apology for previously overestimating the ability of France and Britain to repulse Hitler's Germany unaided, adding by way of self-exculpation that he was not alone in making this mistake. "Who among us in September 1939," Beard asked the committee, "could foresee that the French nation, which had stood like a wall for four cruel years, would collapse like a house of cards in four cruel months?"[137] His basic position was that Lend-Lease was unconstitutional. Given his views on the economic foundations of the Constitution, lending matériel without obvious recompense did indeed jar with the Founders' intentions. Beard urged Congress to vote against the bill "with such force that no president of the United States will ever dare, in all our history, to ask it to suspend the Constitution and the laws of this land and to confer upon him limitless dictatorial powers over life and death." For Beard, Lend-Lease was "a bill for waging undeclared war. We should entertain no delusions on this point."[138] Looking forward to the possible defeat of Germany, Japan, and Italy, Beard wondered what America would do next: "After Europe has been turned into flaming shambles, with revolutions exploding left and right, will this Congress be able to supply the men, money, and talents necessary to reestablish and maintain order and security there?"[139] It fell to later politicians and thinkers to mull the practical implications of Beard's final point. Roosevelt secured the bill and Beard lost the argument, further sullying his name in the process. His Senate testimony was the last time that Beard recorded a significant observation on U.S. foreign policy prior to the Japanese attack on Pearl Harbor, Hawaii.

It was Beard's unfortunate fate to deploy relativism in opposing one of the few Manichaean conflicts in world history. Japan attacked the American Pacific Fleet at Pearl Harbor on December 7, 1941—sinking 4 battleships and 2 destroyers, destroying 188 aircraft, and killing 2,400 service personnel— and Germany and Italy declared war on the United States four days later. Pearl Harbor dealt the rationale for isolationism a mortal blow. Gardening was no longer an option. Privately, Beard felt vindicated that his mid-1930s prophesy about FDR inciting Japan to precipitate war had been borne out. In imposing an embargo on oil exports to Japan in July 1941, Roosevelt had more or less forced Tokyo's hand. Due to a paucity of oil reserves, Japan was immediately confronted with two options: either step back from the brink, or secure its own independent supply of oil through territorial acquisition. Tokyo opted for the latter option, deduced that the U.S. Navy was the only force that could frustrate its ambitions, and acted accordingly in attacking Pearl Harbor. Indeed, Japan could claim to be following a Beardian path to development. America had colonized a continent in creating conditions for self-sufficiency. Japan would attempt to colonize Southeast Asia and some of the Pacific islands to realize that very same aim. In awakening the United States, a slumbering giant, Imperial Japan had signed its own death warrant. As Admiral Hara Tadaichi observed in 1945, "We won a great tactical victory at Pearl Harbor and thereby lost the war."[140]

Advances in military technology rendered the world a much smaller place in the years that followed. During a war in which huge mobile fleets—including aircraft carriers, the dimensions of which Mahan could scarcely have conceived—operated with crushing lethality far from home shores, Beard's call for insularity was shown up as a failure of imagination. Instead of adjusting to a new reality, recanting some of the ideas that patently hadn't stood the test of time, Beard chose to revisit the history of the Roosevelt administration, identifying deception and executive skullduggery at every turn. Beard followed the logic contained in Dylan Thomas's villanelle that "old age should burn and rave at close of day," although he directed his fury at Franklin Roosevelt, not his own mortality. From 1941 to his death in 1948, Beard raged at FDR's duplicity—and the dying of the isolationist light—shredding friendships as he strode proudly toward pariah status, hopeful, like Wilson, that vindication might come later. It was a sad end to the career of a pathbreaking scholar who possessed admirable traits in personality and who offered a well-intentioned rationale for geopolitical retrenchment as self-improvement. Yet these priorities have not entirely disappeared from view. From President Barack Obama's dedication to "nation building here at home" to Senator Rand Paul's valorization of geopolitical "modesty," aspects of Beard's "continental Americanism" are returning to view.

4

★

THE SYNDICATED ORACLE

WALTER LIPPMANN

Lippmann is a man of agile mind and great natural gifts . . . He thumps his tub as if he were God. He is handicapped only by his inability to emit fire and brimstone through the printer's ink of his column.
—CHARLES BEARD

The early summer of 1940 was harrowing for Great Britain. German victories in the Low Countries and France made certain that the nation—and the battle-ready components of its empire—would face the Axis alone. In six weeks in May and June, some 112,000 French soldiers were killed attempting to repulse the German advance—a rate of attrition that was too high for a nation still traumatized by the First World War.[1] The advancing Nazi troops toyed with Paris, pondering when to strike. No decision was required, as it turned out, because the defending French chose to abandon Haussmann's elegant boulevards rather than see them mutilated by German bombers, artillery fire, and panzer divisions. At the French port of Dunkirk, the entire British expeditionary force of 200,000 men, plus 140,000 French soldiers, were trapped by the advancing Wehrmacht. Through a hastily improvised evacuation, in which private vessels sailed alongside the Royal Navy's destroyers, this vast defeated army was ferried safely back to England. Against all odds, the British soldiers would regroup, rearm, and resume battle at a later stage (the French troops, conversely, returned swiftly and bravely to the mainland and to defeat). But this miraculous deliverance could not hide the shame and humiliation. In an address to the House of Commons on June 4, Prime Minister Winston Churchill described Dunkirk as a "miracle," but cautioned that "we must be very careful not to assign to this deliverance the attributes of a victory. Wars are not won by evacuations."[2]

Churchill recognized that the United States offered his nation the brightest prospect of salvation, and that securing American public support for the British cause was essential. As part of a no-stone-unturned diplomatic strategy, London turned to America's most powerful print journalist for help. Walter Lippmann's thrice-weekly column "Today & Tomorrow" was read by millions across the United States, and by millions more in syndication around the world. Successive presidents craved his approval, domestic and foreign politicians sought his counsel, and the American people relied on Lippmann to explain the world's complexities. He was immortalized by a *New Yorker* cartoon of the 1920s showing two elderly women dining in a railroad car, one saying to the other: "Of course, I only take a cup of coffee in the morning. A cup of coffee and Walter Lippmann is all I need."[3] A "Talk of the Town" column on the reputed formation of a Monarchist Party reported that "many Americans would be glad to settle for Walter Lippmann" as their philosopher-king.[4]

As France confirmed abject surrender terms with Germany, the British ambassador to the United States, Lord Lothian, a keen admirer of Lippmann, asked him to visit the embassy on a matter of highest significance. Upon his arrival, Lothian warned Lippmann that if defeatist politicians ousted Churchill to sue for "peace" with Hitler, an Atlantic without the Royal Navy would become a Nazi lake. Britain's survival as an independent maritime power thus depended on the United States providing material assistance to shore up Churchill's position and keep the ocean in virtuous hands. Lippmann needed little by way of persuasion, asking, "What would make a difference?" "The difference will be arms and destroyers," Lothian replied, "because the Royal Navy is woefully weak in destroyers, and we cannot defend the sea lanes to Britain without them."[5] Lippmann agreed with this logic but cautioned that American largesse on this scale would require Britain to give up something substantial in return. After considering this dilemma, the two men devised a plan through which Washington would provide destroyers in exchange for leases to British bases in the western hemisphere. On such clandestine ground was the "destroyers-for-bases" deal sewn. Yet Lippmann still had to convince the American people of its merits.[6]

Lippmann commenced his campaign in the *New York Herald Tribune*, warning readers of his celebrated column that Nazi domination of Europe would threaten America's own survival. If Germany assumed possession of the French and British fleets, Lippmann bleakly intoned, Hitler's military reach would henceforth extend to the northeast seaboard. All Americans had to come together to aid Britain in a cause that transcended partisan politics.[7] For his part, Lothian took his plan to President Roosevelt, deploying a crack legal team to explain how a destroyers-for-bases deal could circumvent the Neutrality Acts through claiming a solely defensive purpose. FDR found the rationale and loophole compelling and convenient. Lippmann later wrote that Lothian "showed Roosevelt—and showed the country—the basis on which we would gradually intervene to save England."[8]

To bring the American public decisively around to viewing Britain's defense as a top priority, Lippmann identified the ideal persuasive medium in General John Pershing, the heroic leader of American troops during the First World War. Over drinks at New York's Carlton hotel, Lippmann asked Pershing if he might be willing to deliver a radio address firmly connecting British survival with congressional passage of the destroyers-for-bases deal. Moved by the force of Lippmann's request, Pershing agreed, delivering a widely reported pro-intervention address—drafted in its entirety by Lippmann—which closed with an urgent plea: "Today may be the last time when by measures short of war we can still prevent war." A living embodiment of bipartisan patriotism, Pershing's intervention had a significant effect on the voting public's willingness to assist Great Britain.[9] The speech also made it difficult for Wendell Willkie, the Republican Party's presumptive presidential nominee, to resist the passage of destroyers-for-bases. Opposing a man of Pershing's standing was either brave or foolhardy in a general election year. Willkie decided that it was not worth the risk.

Lippmann's maneuvering did not remain clandestine for long. After doing "his part" to fashion the deal, Lippmann traveled to Maine to take a vacation with his wife. His solitude was disturbed when a reporter from the staunchly isolationist *St. Louis Post-Dispatch* called to ask about what had transpired in recent weeks. He asked, "Is it true that you had a hand in Pershing's speech?" to which Lippmann replied, "I won't say anything for quotation. If you want to know off the record, I'll say 'Yes, I did.'" The reporter replied, "We're trying to start a Congressional investigation of this plot to get America into the war, and you're in it. You're in the plot warmongering." Panicked at the prospect of such a high-profile investigation, Lippmann turned to his extensive list of contacts to halt the reporter's momentum. He called Joseph Pulitzer, the publisher of the *Dispatch*, exclaiming, "For God's sake, Joe! Have you gone stark raving mad? Why don't you call off your lunatics down there!" Pulitzer did as requested, to Lippmann's considerable relief. "Nothing came of it," he was pleased to report. "They did write a violent editorial, but they didn't start an investigation."[10]

Lippmann successfully led a great cause close to his Atlanticist heart, though he had flown perilously close to the sun in doing so. That Pulitzer pulled the plug on the *Dispatch* suggested, in a small way, that the mood was changing, that isolationism was entering its endgame as a meaningful political force. From being friendly in the 1920s, for example, Charles Beard had grown to dislike Lippmann through the 1930s and beyond. Lippmann's political moderation, closeness to elite business interests, and advocacy of military preparedness all suggested to Beard that Lippmann was a saber-rattling stooge of the propertied classes. For his part, Lippmann viewed Beard and his isolationist brethren as operating on nonsensical assumptions regarding American self-sufficiency that applied—if indeed they ever did—only to the early years of the republic. In later years Beard poked fun at Lippmann for accusing isolationists of "cherishing ancestral prejudices." He observed bitingly, in reference to Lippmann's nominal Judaism, that such remarks show "his lack of humor as a member of the 'chosen people'—devoid presumably of ancestral prejudices."[11]

But the Second World War was Lippmann's time, not Beard's—as the latter's bitterness suggests. The stage was ideally set for a thinker of Lippmann's intellectual caliber. His journalistic prose was lucid and forceful, and he commanded significant bipartisan admiration, appearing to inhabit a plane far above the quotidian political fray. Throughout his long career, Lippmann endorsed Democratic and Republican presidential candidates in almost equal number. He was incredibly well connected, his friends and acquaintances spanning the worlds of politics, journalism, academia, and literature. When in London, he met with Churchill, Keynes, and George Bernard Shaw. He developed a close friendship with Charles de Gaulle. He maintained regular correspondence with Franklin Roosevelt's cabinet. The president, for his part, understood that retaining Lippmann's support for his war policy was important. Most significantly, Lippmann shaped public opinion in a manner that is difficult to trace but impossible to deny. His support for responsible American internationalism—his call for a balanced and realistic foreign policy—relieved many Americans of their geopolitical naïveté. Lippmann's writings on diplomacy speak to the dilemmas of U.S. foreign policy as we know them today. He shared a podium with Bob Dylan and Coretta Scott King when Princeton awarded him an honorary degree in 1970.[12] Born to Victorian gaslight, Walter Lippmann is a bridge to the modern.

Lippmann was born on September 23, 1889, in a grand town house on Lexington Avenue, in New York City, to wealthy parents of German-Jewish descent. Walter's grandfather had fled Germany after the failed liberal uprisings of 1848, and he and his children never looked back, accumulating substantial wealth over two generations—first through garment manufacturing, a popular route to a stable income for émigré Jews, and then with a substantial inherited real estate portfolio.[13] Walter's parents, Jacob and Daisy, made sure that their son did not want for anything. From the tender age of six, Walter was taken on annual trips to Europe, traveling to London, Paris, Florence, and Berlin, where he was introduced to the Old World's cultural jewels. Walter attended Sachs's School for Boys, an elite German-Jewish establishment notable for its intense curriculum, which subjected its young charges to sixteen hours of Latin and Greek a week.[14] A combination of inspiring teaching, Sachs's well-stocked library, and a fierce work ethic fashioned an intellectual prodigy. A fellow student at Sachs, Carl Binger, recalled, "I don't suppose that [Walter] . . . ever got less than an A on any examination in his life."[15] His brilliance was confirmed when Lippmann joined Harvard University's class of 1910, which counted T. S. Eliot and John Reed among its illustrious cohort.

Reveling in the laissez-faire elective system introduced by Harvard's reformist president, Charles William Eliot, Lippmann was drawn to the study of philosophy, swept away by the rhetorical gifts of the two towering figures on campus: George Santayana and William James. Santayana was an inspiring teacher and wonderfully gifted writer and philosopher, with a particular knack for aphorism. "Those who cannot remember the past," Santayana wrote famously in his Life of Reason, "are condemned to repeat it." In that same work, forming a critique to which Lippmann became increasingly amenable during the Cold War, Santayana wrote, "Fanaticism consists in redoubling your effort when you have forgotten your aim." Yet while Lippmann admired Santayana's Platonism, his detailed reading of history, and his contempt for Germanic idealism (for Kant and Hegel in particular), he found his value system and personality troubling in other aspects, particularly when compared to the greater optimism, and likability, of William James: "The two men I admired were James and Santayana. James was the one I loved . . . The truth of the matter is that Santayana was a fearful snob. He was awfully nice to me, but he really disliked the human race as few people I ever met dislike it. I remember the shock he gave me when I first heard him say something rather mean about William James, which didn't seem a nice thing to do . . . James was too American to suit him."[16]

William James was a legendary figure at Harvard, best known for developing pragmatism as a coherent—and distinctly American—philosophical tradition, which abhorred dogma and valorized practical rather than abstract reasoning. Impressed by his range of intellect and sharpening social conscience, James grew close to Lippmann, meeting him every week for tea and conversation. James had become increasingly preoccupied by issues of social reform, and Lippmann, inspired partly by reading Charles Beard, was similarly inclined.

According to Ronald Steel, James's influence on Lippmann can be detected in three areas. First, James taught him that meliorism—the belief system that holds that incremental progress is achievable but perfection is unattainable—was the only plausible way to view the political world. Second, James stressed that men must make decisions, often quickly and decisively, without recourse to a pool of vast, objective knowledge. Lippmann posed this dilemma succinctly in observing, "We must choose whether we will it or not, and where all is doubt."[17] Finally, James instilled in Lippmann a work ethic grounded in strict observation of a recurring daily regimen. Every writer, said James, should draft one thousand words a day, irrespective of whether he has something important to say. Lippmann digested these lessons, which informed his work habits, intellect, and wider ambitions at every level. James and Lippmann wanted to improve the parlous lot of America's poor, but both were modest about the speed of progress that could be attained in a nation in which social reform had historically moved glacially.

A formative moment arrived for Lippmann in the spring of 1908, when a fire razed approximately half of the nearby town of Chelsea. Lippmann volunteered to assist in the relief process and was shocked by the deprivation he encountered in this overwhelmingly working-class town. Lippmann recalled, "That was the first time I realized the amount of poverty there was. In fact, it was the first time I realized the outer world in the sense that I'd been so immersed in philosophy and literature—Goethe, Dante, and Lucretius— and fine arts that I hadn't seen it."[18] Lippmann's social awakening recalled Charles Beard's in the slums of Chicago. And it moved him in a similarly leftward direction. He founded Harvard University's Socialist Club and formed a strong attachment to the visiting British professor Graham Wallas, an eminent social psychologist who had cofounded the London School of Economics and Political Science in 1895.

Lippmann was something of a phenomenon at Harvard. At a meeting of Harvard's Western Club, John Reed, who would find enduring fame as a chronicler of the Russian Revolution, introduced Lippmann with the words "Gentleman, the future President of the United States!" There followed laughter and cheers of a knowing sort. Reed even composed a poem about Lippmann:

> Lippmann,—calm, inscrutable,
> Thinking and writing clearly, soundly, well;
> All snarls of falseness swiftly piercing through,
> His keen mind leaps like lightning to the True;
> His face is almost placid—but his eye—
> There is a vision born to prophecy!
> He sits in silence, as one who has said:
> "I waste not living words among the dead!"
> Our all-unchallenged Chief![19]

Harvard's faculty was as impressed by Lippmann's talent and potential as were his fellow students. George Santayana was determined to keep his protégé close and asked him to serve as an instructor for his course on introductory philosophy—to which Lippmann readily assented. Santayana was enigmatic and unlovable, but his wit and brilliance kept his teaching assistant enthralled. What could be more disarming and seductive than his description of the intellectual: "There are always a few men whose main interest is to note the aspect of things in an artistic or philosophical way. They are rather useless individuals, but as I happen to belong to that class, I think them much superior to the rest of mankind."[20] Yet Lippmann held no desire to embrace philosophical inconsequence, even when presented facetiously. In May 1910, he crossed the Charles River to start work as a journalist for the *Boston Common*.

Lippmann did not get along at the *Common*, a progressive weekly funded by the department store owner Edward A. Filene. Its editor insisted on draining oxygen from his journalists' prose, creating a chokingly dry effect that Lippmann found uncongenial. He complained to Lincoln Steffens, the famous muckraking journalist whom he had come to know in 1908, that "any attempt to find the meaning, or the tragedy, or the humor of the story is rigorously edited out as an expression of opinion which belongs only in the editorial column . . . The work is so mechanical that I am learning nothing.

I might as well be attached to a clipping bureau."²¹ Lippmann desperately wanted to work for Steffens, whose crusading journalism and muscular prose he greatly admired. His wish was granted when Steffens hired Lippmann to serve as his assistant for a series of investigative articles commissioned by *Everybody's* magazine. He spent a year investigating the corrupt symbiotic relationship that existed between Wall Street financiers and Tammany Hall political hacks. Lippmann honed his craft under Steffens's guidance, learning that the best journalism was mined from empirical graft and written for the ages: "If I wrote a paragraph about a fire down the street, I must write it with as much care as if that paragraph were going down in one of the anthologies."²² The series of "money power" articles was a great success, and an acquaintance named Alfred A. Knopf—a twenty-year-old Columbia graduate setting out on what would be a glittering publishing career—encouraged Lippmann to write a brief book on politics.

Lippmann's *A Preface to Politics* was published in 1913, when its author was just twenty-three years old. A work of daring self-confidence, owing something of an iconoclastic debt to Charles Beard's *An Economic Interpretation of the Constitution*, the book took aim at the naïve excesses of certain Progressives, dwelled on the ingrained flaws of human nature that invited political corruption, and cast early doubt on the common man's ability to act in his own or his country's best interests. Powerful political machines, for example, came into being to serve this inchoate mass, not necessarily to exploit it—which Lippmann characterized as a damning indictment of democracy in itself. "Tammany," Lippmann wrote provocatively, "is not a satanic instrument of deception, cleverly devised to thwart 'the will of the people.' It is a crude and largely unconscious answer to certain immediate needs, and without those needs its power would crumble." The book marked Lippmann's departure from socialism—"socialism has within it the germs of that great bureaucratic tyranny which Chesterton and Belloc have named the Servile State"—and delivered a strong endorsement of Theodore Roosevelt's Bull Moose Progressivism, combining strong leadership, big (though not overbearing) government, and monopoly reform to ideal effect.

But Lippmann did worry about Roosevelt's tendency to operate on assumptions formed in the last century: "It has been necessary to retire Theodore Roosevelt from public life every now and again . . . Every statesman like every professor should have a sabbatical year." Lippmann found Woodrow Wilson a more interesting political prospect in the medium term, writing that "Wilson, less complete than Roosevelt, is worthy of our deepest interest because his judgment is subtle where Roosevelt's is crude. He is a foretaste of a more advanced statesmanship."[23] A definitive endorsement of the president, however, was still a while away. Lippmann cast his vote for Theodore Roosevelt in the election of 1912 and made his preference for him clear in *A Preface to Politics*. But he was keeping an open mind about the cerebral presidential incumbent, whose *Congressional Government* he had read and admired at Harvard.

Roosevelt declared himself an admirer of *A Preface to Politics*, just as he had with *The Influence of Sea Power upon History*.[24] Where Mahan had provided robust and original views on foreign policy, Roosevelt believed that Lippmann could deliver the same in the domestic sphere. Roosevelt had read the book while spending a winter and autumn in Brazil's tropical climes, shooting crocodiles, contracting jungle fever and, consequently, finding a lot of time with a book, rather than a rifle, in his hands. Lippmann recalled of his evidently selective reading that "he was very pleased with my criticisms of Wilson and very pleased with my eulogies of him . . . He told me that he approved of the book and wanted to see me as soon as we got back."[25] The two men met at the Harvard Club in New York in 1914, joined by a mutual friend, the Harvard law professor and future Supreme Court justice Felix Frankfurter. Roosevelt informed Lippmann that he was planning another run at the presidency in 1916 and asked him to assist in drafting his labor platform. Lippmann, who in his own words was "an unqualified hero worshiper" of Roosevelt, eagerly assented, and the two men shook hands on what Roosevelt described as a "common cause."[26] Yet while Lippmann helped Roosevelt with this specific request, he gradually shifted his affections from the old warrior to the philosopher-king in the Oval Office.

In October 1913, a high-profile intellectual and political commentator named Herbert Croly invited Lippmann to dine with him at Players, one of New York's private clubs. Croly had published *The Promise of American Life* to glowing reviews in 1909. In this influential Progressive tract, Croly argued that the United States' affirming story of societal progress, and vast latent potential, might combine to perfect not just America but also other nations, like Panama, where "order and good government" could be established with the right kind of tutelage.[27] In respect to improving America, Croly believed that the government must play a larger role in managing the economy and redistributing wealth, so as to ensure the nation's continued vitality: "The Promise of American life is to be fulfilled—not merely by a maximum amount of economic freedom, but by a certain measure of discipline; not merely by the abundant satisfaction of individual desires, but by a large measure of individual subordination and self-denial."[28] Lippmann admired Croly's ambition to approach good governance and politics in a scientific fashion.

When Croly invited him to join the editorial staff of the new Progressive weekly, *The New Republic*, funded by Willard and Dorothy Straight, he a Morgan banker and she a Standard Oil heiress, Lippmann accepted on the spot. He now possessed a job that better matched his ambitions. The magazine was generously funded, strongly associated with Bull Moose Progressivism, and afforded Lippmann a gilt-edged opportunity to interact with the most powerful figures in New York City. Theodore Roosevelt was delighted at the prospect of a weekly magazine championing the political causes he held dear. Lippmann recalled, "During that period we were often in consultation with Theodore Roosevelt, who gave us his blessing and was very much interested in it."[29] Thrilled by his new job, Lippmann wrote to his friend Van Wyck Brooks, a prominent literary critic, to explain the magazine's purpose:

> We're starting a weekly here next fall—a weekly of ideas—with a paid up capital—God save us—of 200,000. The age of miracles, sir, has just begun . . . If there is any word to cover our ideal, I suppose it is humanistic, somewhat sharply distinguished (but not by Irving Babbitt) from humanitarianism. Humanism, I believe, means this real sense of the relation between the abstract and the concrete, between the noble dream and the actual limitations of life.[30]

Croly captured the magazine's essence more succinctly when he remarked, "We shall be radical without being socialistic and our general tendency will be pragmatic rather than doctrinaire."[31] This disavowal of socialism was perhaps a good thing in light of the magazine's unproletarian office on West 21st Street, lavishly equipped with resources that modern journalists would find inconceivable. The Straights' philanthropy funded a wonderfully stocked library, a wood-paneled dining room, and the services of an excellent French chef, who prepared lunches of uncommon quality for *The New Republic*'s lucky scribes.

It is doubtful that Lippmann saw anything exceptional in this. He rarely questioned the justness of his elevated station. With his impeccably tailored suits, elegant gray fedora, and air of high intellectual seriousness, Lippmann tended to impress—and maybe even unnerve—those he met. He was a solidly built man, five foot ten, 190 pounds, although the chubbiness of his

early years earned him the affectionate nickname "Buddha." A happy im-
biber of Greenwich Village bohemia, in spite of his buttoned-up appearance,
Lippmann formed a friendship with Mabel Dodge—a bisexual patron of
the arts and friend of Picasso, Gertrude Stein, and John Reed—who convened a high-culture bacchanalian salon at her apartment. Dodge described
Lippmann as "big and rather fat, but he had . . . intellectualized his fat so
that it shone a little."[32] The quality of his mind was a wondrous thing for his
friends and colleagues to behold. He moved from one success to another,
remaining true to his Stakhanovite work habits and unerring self-belief. He
knew exactly who he was, liked what he saw, and did not adjust his personality depending on his audience. The variety of his intellectual interests
made him stand out as an individual capable of discerning connections that
others missed and offering large-canvas analyses of which few others were
capable. He shone brightly in the early stages of his journalistic career, although foreign policy did not yet figure highly in his range of interests. This
would change when total war visited the European continent in 1914.

Lippmann was in England, meeting with H. G. Wells, Sidney and Beatrice
Webb, and George Bernard Shaw, when the chain reaction of ultimatums
and mobilizations commenced. Progressives and British Fabians were intellectually blindsided by the conflict and struggled to finesse a position in its
wake. Beatrice Webb told Lippmann that "we don't form opinions on foreign
affairs. We don't know the technique."[33] Neither did Lippmann. He wrote to
Felix Frankfurter that "nothing can stop the awful disintegration now. Nor
is there any way of looking beyond it: ideas, books, seem too utterly trivial,
and all the public opinion, democratic hope and what not, where is it today?
Like a flower in the path of a plough."[34] The first issue of *The New Republic*
hit the newsstands on November 7, 1914. A magazine created to proselytize
for Progressive domestic reform was now compelled to fix its attention on
alliance-driven bloodletting in Europe. Lippmann's debut editorial continued the lamenting tone of his letter to Frankfurter: "Who cares to paint
a picture now, or to write any poetry now but war poetry, or to search the
meaning of language, or speculate about the constitution of matter?" After
dwelling on the humanities' limitations, Lippmann turned to their centrality
as a means to achieve a more peaceable world: "The final argument against
cannon is ideas . . . For while it takes as much skill to make a sword as a
ploughshare, it takes a critical understanding of human values to prefer
the ploughshare."[35] These were hopeful words, naïve, even, but Lippmann
would soon form a much stronger sense of what was required of America.

Lippmann's views on the First World War were largely conditioned by his appreciation of the works of Alfred Thayer Mahan. On August 5, 1915, he wrote to Graham Wallas that "British sea power is the decisive factor in the future arrangement of the globe but I personally prefer its semi-benevolent autocracy to the anarchy of 'equal.' And I am prepared to have the U.S. join with Britain in the control of the seas, rather than see a race of 'sovereign states' oscillating in insecure 'balance.'"[36] The sinking of the *Lusitania* mainly suggested to Lippmann that the United States had ill-advisedly neglected its navy under Wilson and Taft, rendering the nation dangerously dependent upon Great Britain's merchant marine to ferry passengers and trade across the Atlantic. The unspoken dependency logic of the Monroe Doctrine had to be abandoned in favor of rapid naval expansion to allow Britain and the United States to operate as equals. Nothing less than America's sovereignty was at stake. German U-boats had shown beyond doubt that the Royal Navy was an unreliable instrument around which to build a nation's commerce and wealth.

To further develop his knowledge on foreign policy, Lippmann decided to write a book on the subject. Published in 1915, *The Stakes of Diplomacy* observed that conflict arose from an emotional nationalism hardwired into human nature: "It is the primitive stuff of which we are made, our first loyalties, our first aggressions, the type and image of our souls . . . They are our nationality, that essence of our being which defines us against the background of the world." Lippmann believed Mahan had been correct in identifying the existence of a Hobbesian world and was similarly convinced that the United States had to expend more energy in mastering it. "We have all of us been educated to isolation," wrote Lippmann, "and we love the irresponsibility of it. But that isolation must be abandoned if we are to do anything effective for internationalism . . . The supreme task of world politics is not the prevention of war, but a satisfactory organization of mankind."[37] The United States needed to assume its responsibilities as a leader of the international order—and do so without illusion. Internationalism was the only plausible and respectable foreign-policy course, but a sense of limits had to undergird the framing of diplomacy. The book's debt to Mahanian geopolitics is clear.

Yet aspects of Woodrow Wilson's foreign-policy vision also struck Lippmann as logical and necessary. The president had invited Lippmann to the White House in early 1916, and the young journalist had been impressed by the confidence Wilson possessed in his own judgment. On Mexico, for example, Lippmann recalled, "I remember Wilson's talking about how he believed in the Jeffersonian principle of the sacred right of revolution. It's something that no president would say today [in 1950]. He was defending his own policy and his belief that Huerta was a counter-revolutionist. He believed in the Madero Revolution."[38] A second meeting with Wilson, in the summer of 1916, moved Lippmann firmly into his camp of supporters. Aware that Lippmann's purpose was endorsement reconnaissance, Wilson welcomed him into the Oval Office with the words "So you've come to look me over?," rendering Lippmann mute. Wilson then said, "Let me show you the inside of my mind." Wilson had clearly taken the measure of the intellectualism that made Lippmann tick. The president delivered what Ronald Steel has described as "a dazzling monologue covering virtually every issue, from the Mexican imbroglio to German designs on Brazil, from TR's ambitions to dilemmas of neutrality."[39] Mightily impressed by Wilson's intellectual range, and the absence of any obvious idées fixes, Lippmann embarked on a campaign to convince his colleagues at *The New Republic* that supporting Wilson's re-election was the only sensible course in the midst of war: "We became more and more for Wilson. In 1916, we supported him in the campaign. It was a great struggle. Croly didn't want to do it. I did. Finally, by September I persuaded them that [Secretary of State Charles Evans] Hughes was taking a pro-German line with a feeling toward the pro-German vote, and that Wilson was the man for us."[40]

Lippmann's endorsement in *The New Republic* praised Wilson's potential more than his achievements to date. "I shall not vote for the Wilson who has uttered a few too many noble sentiments," Lippmann wrote, "but for the Wilson who is evolving under experience and is remaking his philosophy in the light of it."[41] In Lippmann's estimation, Wilson possessed "the most freely speculative mind we've had in Washington."[42] Firsthand experience had convinced Lippmann that the president's cognition was supple and that he was destined for greatness. But this path was realizable only if Wilson resisted the temptation to moralize. Nothing was more likely to undermine America's reputation with its hard-bitten Old World allies than cant. Lippmann believed that U.S. foreign policy should combine the best of both Mahan and Wilson, that realism and idealism work best in tandem.

In December 1916, Lippmann wrote a column titled "Peace Without Victory," which evenhandedly examined the peace overtures the president had made to the European belligerents, alongside the reasons for their rebuttal. Two weeks later, Wilson delivered a speech declaring his strong support for achieving "peace without victory," a rationale and compliment to Lippmann's phrasemaking that the journalist was quick to appreciate.[43] Yet there were clear differences between Wilson's and Lippmann's conception of the national interest—over what American aims should look like if war came. After Germany's declaration of unrestricted submarine warfare, for example, Lippmann penned an influential article titled "The Defense of the Atlantic World," which presented a straightforwardly realist rationale for an American declaration of war. Lippmann observed that there existed a virtuous "Atlantic Community," consisting primarily of the United States, Britain, and France, which were all threatened by German domination of the Atlantic, and a future combination of authoritarian states in Eurasia: "A victory on the high seas would be a triumph of that class which aims to make Germany the leader of the East against the West, the leader ultimately of a German-Russian-Japanese coalition against the Atlantic world. It would be utter folly not to fight now to make its hopes a failure by showing that in the face of such a threat the western community is a unit."[44] Lippmann wanted Wilson to be clearer about his war aims and present them with the clarity that was his own journalistic hallmark. The war should serve America's vital interests in preventing German naval domination of the Atlantic. But establishing war aims that redounded clearly to the nation's advantage was a task that Wilson, consumed by grander visions of the future, failed to discharge.

Lippmann performed significant wartime service for his nation. He first served as a special assistant to Secretary of War Newton D. Baker, next as the executive secretary of the president's "Inquiry," and finally as a member of the Inter-Allied Propaganda Board in London, where he drafted propaganda leaflets to be dropped behind enemy lines. Lippmann played an important role in drafting the Fourteen Points and elucidating their meaning for the benefit of perplexed French and British diplomats, unused to diplomatic gambits of such abstract ambition. Here, Lippmann was sympathetic to Wilson's idealism, which chimed with *The New Republic*'s perspective. Yet once the war ended, and peace negotiations commenced in Paris, Lippmann experienced a distinct sense of foreboding: "I remember very well Wilson's arrival in Paris. It was a great event—one of the greatest spectacles. I had the most gloomy feeling all day. Everybody was rejoicing, but I had an ominous feeling that something was very wrong already."[45]

Lippmann observed Wilson's performance despairingly from his vantage point as a little-used member of the American delegation. While conceding that the League of Nations could prove useful in providing "a temporary shelter from the storm," Lippmann could not fathom how the president could mortgage "peace without victory" for an untried international organization that had yet to clear the significant hurdle of Senate confirmation.[46] He also viewed concurrent participation in counterrevolutionary military action against the fledgling Soviet Union as counterproductive and clearly at odds with the much-trumpeted Versailles principle of national self-determination. In May 1919, Lippmann observed that "looked at from above, below, and from every side I can't see anything in this treaty but endless trouble for Europe, and I'm exceedingly doubtful in my own mind as to whether we can afford to guarantee so impossible a peace." In a letter to Norman Hapgood, Wilson's unofficial press liaison, Lippmann observed pointedly and accurately that the president had "bought the League from France and Britain with a bad peace instead of selling it to France and Britain for a good peace."[47]

When the Treaty of Versailles emerged into the harsh light of public view, Lippmann followed Beard in experiencing an acute sense of betrayal. He felt gullible for following President Wilson with such enthusiasm, hoping for the best in such a jejune fashion. Usually so accurate when judging the character of his interlocutors, Lippmann had erred in identifying Wilson as a pragmatist. Lippmann was so riled by what had transpired in Paris that he provided William Borah, Hiram Johnson, and other "irreconcilables" in the Senate with insider anecdotes and evidence that helped undermine the peace accords.

Lippmann suggested that the president had dissembled in denying personal knowledge of Allied secret treaties prior to his arrival in Paris. Wilson's concealment owed everything to his failure to use these revelations to his negotiating advantage. The Fourteen Points were partly conceived as a morally charged riposte to the treaties, made public by Lenin after the October Revolution in 1917. This made Wilson's denials appear ridiculous. Borah and Johnson used these revelations to damaging effect and implored Lippmann to testify before a Senate committee. Unwilling to go quite this far, Lippmann instead suggested that the diplomat William Bullitt, similarly angered by events in Paris, take his place. On the hearings, Lippmann observed that "Billy Bullitt blurted out everything to the scandal of the Tories and delight of the Republicans. When there is an almost universal conspiracy to lie and smother the truth, I suppose someone has to violate the decencies."[48] Lippmann's earlier preference for combining the best of Mahan and Wilson had ended with contempt for the latter. He would spend the remainder of his career tracking close to the worldview of the former.

Lippmann's break with Wilsonianism followed a similar pattern to that of Charles Beard. Reflecting on the role he had played supporting and advising

President Wilson, Lippmann confessed, "If I had it to do all over again, I would take the other side . . . We supplied the Battalion of Death with too much ammunition."[49] Though let down by Wilson, Lippmann was less than enthused by his presidential successors, however. He wrote to Graham Wallas, "Harding is elected not because anybody likes him or because the Republican Party is particularly powerful, but because the Democrats are inconceivably unpopular."[50] On Calvin Coolidge, Lippmann noted that his laconic reputation regrettably did not tally with his own experience:

> I . . . saw quite a lot of Calvin Coolidge in that period between 1922 and 1931, although we were opposing him rather strenuously. I used to go to lunch with him alone and we would have long interminable talks with him in his study. He did all the talking. He was far from a silent man . . . I had a strong impression with Coolidge that he really had nothing very much to do—that he was not at all a busy man. He always took a nap in the afternoon. His idea was, "Let the government drift."[51]

Yet in the sphere of foreign policy, Lippmann was relaxed about drift— compared to the misdirected energy of the war years, at any rate. Though never strictly isolationist, he welcomed U.S. detachment from the League of Nations. Like Beard, he denigrated the dollar diplomacy that undergirded Harding's and Coolidge's policies toward Latin America, and he opposed military intervention in Nicaragua and Mexico, especially when justified in reference to supposedly vital economic interests. In an article in *Foreign Affairs*, Lippmann examined "the conflict between the vested rights of Americans in the natural resources of the Caribbean countries and the rising nationalism of their peoples." He chided President Coolidge and Secretary of State Frank Kellogg for confusing nationalism with Bolshevism, for failing to comprehend the reality that Latin American nationalism mainly derived from the "desire to assert the national independence and the dignity of an inferior race." The worst of all policies would slavishly follow economic self-interest, impinge on national sovereignty, and lead to the "realization in Latin America that the United States had adopted a policy, conceived in the spirit of Metternich, which would attempt to guarantee vested rights against social progress as the Latin peoples conceive it."[52] Lippmann did not dispute that economic interests were present—he simply wanted them handled with greater sensitivity and sense of proportion.

Lippmann left *The New Republic* for Pulitzer's New York *World*—New York City's most important liberal daily—at the beginning of 1922. He wrote for the *World* for the next nine years, drafting twelve hundred editorials, of which about a third focused on foreign affairs, a notably high proportion given the parochialism of the American public sphere in the 1920s. It was during this time that Lippmann developed a truly national reputation. His profile was enhanced by the publication of two books, *Public Opinion* and *The Phantom Public*, which together caused a considerable stir.

In *Public Opinion*, Lippmann contended that the American people could not be trusted to make political decisions of high importance, and that more power should be placed in the hands of an administrative elite in respect to the framing of both domestic and foreign policy. In Lippmann's pessimistic view, democracy could function effectively only if politicians dismissed the "intolerable and unworkable fiction that each of us must acquire a competent opinion about all public affairs."[53] It was a brilliant and unsparing dissection of participatory democracy, which garnered glowing endorsements. John Dewey described *Public Opinion* as "perhaps the most effective indictment of democracy as currently conceived ever penned."[54] Justice Oliver Wendell Holmes observed that "there are few living, I think, who so discern and articulate the nuances of the human mind."[55]

Published in 1925, *The Phantom Public* pursued *Public Opinion*'s elitist logic to an even more discomfiting degree. Disregarding populist niceties, Lippmann wrote that viewing the average voter as "inherently competent" was a "false ideal" that had caused great damage.[56] The American polity was in fact divided between elite "insiders," with detailed contextual knowledge of salient political issues, and uninformed "outsiders," whose interests did not extend far beyond the everyday combination of work, sleep, family, and leisure. Lippmann had first trialed this distinction in *The New Republic* in 1915, when he wrote that "only the insider can make the decisions, not because he is inherently a better man, but because he is placed that he can understand and can act."[57] His ideal "democracy" would give insiders free rein to make important decisions, permitting the mass of "outsiders" to exercise a veto only if they felt the decision would unfairly injure the majority—a utilitarian calculation that few were capable of making. Hence Lippmann anticipated useful apathy.

The Founding Fathers recognized the dangers of extended suffrage. But democracy since the presidency of Andrew Jackson had labored under the illusion that the common man possessed virtue and sound judgment as an Aristotelian "political animal." Lippmann's purpose in *The Phantom Public* was to ensure that "each of us may live free of the trampling and the roar of a bewildered herd."[58] It was a postmortem on the corpse of his earlier idealism and Progressive faith in the capacity of people to self-govern and pursue a sage foreign policy. He had lost faith in Wilsonianism and the Universalist optimism that justified the attempt to make "the world safe for democracy." Democracy in the United States was clearly not safe in itself. Considerably more bracing and pessimistic than *Public Opinion*, the book met with an icy reception among reviewers and readers. Lippmann anticipated this when he observed that he was likely to be "put on trial for heresy by my old friends on *The New Republic*."[59] John Dewey's 1927 book *The Public and Its Problems*, conceived as a response to Lippmann, noted persuasively that the "world has suffered more from leaders and authorities than from the masses."[60]

Lippmann clearly diverged from Beard in these indictments of the political aptitude of the American people—although he shared his ambivalence toward unnecessary involvement in European affairs and opposition to interventionism in Latin America born of great power chauvinism. Sharp differences of opinion were becoming evident, though warm relations existed between the two men through the 1920s. On September 8, 1925, Lippmann wrote to Beard that "the answer, so far as I'm concerned, to the question about the collective capacity of democracy to plan a state is emphatically 'no.'" A few days later, Beard replied, "I shall wait with impatience the coming of your book on 'The Phantom Public' . . . At all events you always shoot every subject you touch full of holes and full of light." Lippmann thanked Beard for his letter, which "gave me a great deal of pleasure," before asking if he was available to meet in person: "I want lots of time and some solitude." Beard suggested that they meet at his house for an informal dinner, in order "to polish off the unfinished business of the universe. I suggest dining here because we can be as quiet and profane as we like in my lookout tower."[61] This intriguing flirtation is all we have to connect the two men during the 1920s. Regrettably, no record exists of their "survey of our little cosmos," as Beard poetically described it.

While Beard moved swiftly and purposefully toward his continental Americanism, Lippmann equivocated on the necessary dimensions of diplomatic retrenchment. Intellectually he was in flux. He became close with Senator William Borah, the retrenchment-inclined chair of the Senate Committee on Foreign Relations from 1924 to 1933. The two men collaborated in supporting naval disarmament and its attendant international agreements, and in opposing military intervention in Latin America. Yet they also joined forces in calling for a renegotiation of Allied war debts and supporting diplomatic recognition of the Soviet Union—policies that could not be characterized as isolationist in the orthodox sense. Their endeavors sometimes echoed internationalist goals and sometimes tended toward insularity. At one point Borah supported U.S. membership in the World Court. The next year he professed faith in the Kellogg-Briand Pact to outlaw war, which Lippmann found ludicrous in its detachment from reality. That "Europe should scrap its whole system of security based on the enforcement of peace," wrote Lippmann in *The World* in 1927, "and accept in its place a pious, self-denying ordinance that no nation will disturb the peace" was nonsensical. The support that Borah extended toward such folly represented an "extraordinary spectacle" in light of his own well-recorded contempt for the League of Nations.[62] Yet by 1930, Lippmann's foreign-policy views appeared as illogical in their entirety as Borah's. Ronald Steel captures this well: "During the 1920s, and much of the 1930s as well, Lippmann was neither consistent nor persuasive in his prescriptions for preventing war. Simultaneously espousing disarmament and American naval strength, international cooperation and an Anglo-American domination of the seas, American freedom of action and a 'political equivalent of war,' he reflected the confusions of the age."[63]

It took the onset of the Great Depression, the presidency of Franklin Roosevelt, and the rise of Germany and Japan to instill in Lippmann's diplomatic thought a realist consistency.

The World's circulation began to flag in the late 1920s. The newspaper had been drained of its capital (human and otherwise) by the feckless stewardship of Herbert Pulitzer, and there appeared little realistic prospect of recovery, in spite of a loyal readership. A variety of organizations began to bombard Lippmann with job offers. Impressed by his ability as a political scientist, despite the absence of a doctorate, Harvard offered Lippmann an endowed chair in government. Hamilton Fish Armstrong, the editor of *Foreign Affairs*, asked Lippmann to become director of studies at the Council on Foreign Relations. These were prestigious offers and destinations. Yet Lippmann decided that universities and think tanks were too far removed from the power that he so artfully cultivated. The solitude that lured certain intellectuals to the ivory tower discouraged this particular thinker, who thrived on flesh-and-blood relationships.

Politely declining these overtures, Lippmann instead accepted a job at the *International Herald Tribune*—a national Republican newspaper rather than a metropolitan Democratic one—which offered a significant salary of $25,000 a year in return for four columns a week. The paper also provided a personal assistant, generous travel budget, and two weeks' paid vacation in winter and six weeks over the summer. These vacations were essential to Lippmann in terms of business and pleasure. During his annual jaunt to Europe, he invariably met the continent's brightest intellectual and political lights.

Lippmann's first "Today & Tomorrow" column—or "T&T," as it became known among the cognoscenti—first rolled off the press in September 1931. A year later, the column was syndicated to a hundred papers with a combined circulation in excess of ten million.[64] Lippmann remained at the *Tribune* for the next thirty-six years. The column became a journalistic phenomenon, its author a trusted explanatory voice in a world changing fast for the worse. A rival of Lippmann's, the journalist Arthur Krock, observed bitterly that "to read, if not to comprehend, Lippmann was suddenly the thing to do."[65]

One of Lippmann's best-remembered "T&T" columns cast a critical eye on Franklin Delano Roosevelt. On August 1, 1932, Lippmann described FDR as "a highly impressionable person without a firm grasp of public affairs and without very strong convictions . . . He is an amiable man with many philanthropic impulses, but he is not the dangerous enemy of anything." So far, so conventional. FDR's lack of fixed ideological moorings had been noted by observers before. More damning was Lippmann's description of the Democratic presidential nominee as "a pleasant man who, without any important qualifications for the office, would very much like to be president." Lippmann had kept a close eye on Franklin Roosevelt since the Wilson administration and had arrived at a mixed conclusion. While admiring his rhetorical facility and keen political antennae, Lippmann found the generality and vagueness of FDR's policy interests unsettling, concluding that he was unqualified for high office. There was more to politics than merely winning elections: something meaningful had to be done with the accompanying power. While dismayed by the onset of the Depression, Lippmann could at least detect ideological constancy in President Hoover's response, resting on a substantial record as a public servant.

"The two things about him that worry me," Lippmann wrote Felix Frankfurter after FDR secured his party's nomination, "are that he plays politics well and likes the game for its own sake and is likely to be ultra-political almost to show his own virtuosity. The other fear I have is that he is such an amiable and impressionable man, so eager to please, and, I think, so little grounded in his own convictions that almost everything depends on the character of his own advisers." Roosevelt's forceful presidency proved Lippmann to be wide of the mark on this second point. Nonetheless, in the absence of any better options, Lippmann placed his reservations to one side, stating his intention come Election Day to "vote cheerfully for Governor Roosevelt."[66] Parlous domestic circumstances suggested to Lippmann that change was essential.

Lippmann met President-elect Roosevelt at a dinner in New York in honor of the retiring president of Harvard, A. Lawrence Lowell. Conscious of Lippmann's rapt national readership, Roosevelt brushed off the earlier criticism and invited Lippmann to visit him in Warm Springs, Georgia, where doctors attended annually to the paralysis caused by his childhood polio. It was a remarkable encounter by all accounts. In Roosevelt's private cottage near the medical facility, Lippmann reminded his host that Hitler had assumed power two days before, exploiting the ineffectiveness of a weak government that appeared incapable of dealing with economic meltdown. Roosevelt's most pressing task was to tackle America's economic malaise—a combination of low growth and high unemployment—head on and to forestall the threat of extremism. "The situation is critical, Franklin," Lippmann observed darkly. "You may have no alternative but to assume dictatorial powers." According to Ronald Steel, "The starkness of the phrase, particularly from Lippmann, took Roosevelt aback."[67] Over the space of a few months, Lippmann had gone from casting serious doubt on Roosevelt's suitability for high office to advising him to assume the necessary role of enlightened despot. Lippmann's 1920s mercurialness was continuing well into the 1930s.

Lippmann was enthralled by the executive energy of the early stages of Roosevelt's presidency, writing that the nation "had regained confidence in itself" and that "by the greatest good fortune which has befallen this country in many a day, a kindly and intelligent man has the wit to realize that a great crisis is a great opportunity."[68] His vote against Hoover had been vindicated in a short time. On foreign policy, Lippmann celebrated President Roosevelt's Good Neighbor Policy enunciated in his inaugural address—which promised noninterference in the affairs of Washington's Latin American neighbors—as a "radical innovation" and a "true substitute for empire."[69] On April 18, 1933, Lippmann called for the abandonment of the gold standard to inflate the money supply, combat deflation, and thus boost the economy. His column sparked a day of frantic trading on Wall Street; such was the expectation that Lippmann's positioning foreshadowed executive action. And so it came to pass when President Roosevelt denounced the logic of collaborative currency stabilization and removed the United States from the gold standard. British prime minister Ramsay MacDonald desperately called Lippmann from the London economic conference, imploring him to use his influence to revisit the decision to so brutally reject multilateral action—to no avail. An earlier discussion with John Maynard Keynes had convinced Lippmann that his position had been sound and the president's decision wise, so he politely rebuffed MacDonald's request. Keynes himself celebrated FDR's decision as "magnificently right."[70] Roosevelt could do little wrong during his first six months.

It was during the remainder of Roosevelt's first term that Lippmann found fault with his president, primarily in regard to the outsized statist ambitions of the New Deal. On domestic issues, Lippmann turned rightward as the president led the nation purposefully to the left. His disenchantment was such that in the presidential election of 1936, Lippmann endorsed Roosevelt's opponent, Governor Alf Landon of Kansas. Many liberals were appalled by Lippmann's strong move against Roosevelt and the New Deal. Writing in *The Nation*, Amos Pinchot dismissed Lippmann as an "obfuscator . . . who can be quoted on either side of almost any question." Pinchot compared Lippmann to the sometimes liberal bête noire Alexander Hamilton, who was "the first strong advocate of plutocratic fascism in America." Denigrating Lippmann's close links to lawyers and bankers, Pinchot described him as "an ambassador of goodwill to the philistines."[71] Unruffled by this assault, Lippmann welcomed *The Nation*'s scorn as proof that his rightward track was correct. He continued to denigrate the New Deal as an assault on political liberty and focused particular ire on FDR's ill-considered plan to pack the Supreme Court with sympathetic justices. In 1937, Lippmann published *The Good Society*, a frontal assault on what he viewed as Roosevelt's socialistic collectivism, which bore comparison to Italy, Germany, and the Soviet Union. Influenced by the conservative Austrian economist Friedrich von Hayek, Lippmann's polemic was criticized by previously supportive voices. John Dewey thought the book gave "encouragement and practical support to reactionaries."[72]

An aspect of the New Deal that Lippmann found particularly irksome was the participation of university professors. President Roosevelt evidently believed that law and the social sciences might assist the government in solving intricate problems in those arduous times—convening an august group of academics to assist his administration's efforts. FDR's original "Brain Trust," as they became known, consisted of a triumvirate of Columbia University law professors—Raymond Moley, Rexford Tugwell, and Adolf Berle—who combined to shape the first wave of New Deal reforms (1933–1934), which focused on practical measures to combat mass unemployment.[73]

Not to be outdone, Harvard Law School, smarting perhaps from Columbia's prominence in the policy process, offered teaching relief to three scholars—Benjamin Cohen, Thomas Corcoran, and Lippmann's friend Felix
Frankfurter—who helped shape the second wave of New Deal legislation
(1935–1936), which pursued the more ambitious goal of effecting fundamental reforms in American society. Some attacked the Brain Trust as a phalanx
of unaccountable ivory tower idealists. Others attacked them for lacking
intellectual substance. The British philosopher Bertrand Russell, for example, complained through the 1930s that it was not the intellectual but "the
technician . . . [who was] the really big man in the modern world."[74]

Lippmann declined to impugn the Brain Trust's intellectual substance,
instead delivering a pointed speech at the University of Rochester in June
1936 that cautioned professors against sullying their independence in the
pursuit of policy influence. Lippmann dwelled powerfully on the perils of
co-optation:

> Members of the university faculties have a particular obligation not
> to tie themselves to, nor to involve themselves in, the ambitions and
> pursuits of the politicians . . . Once they engage themselves that way,
> they cease to be disinterested men, being committed by their ambitions
> and their sympathies. They cease to be scholars because they are no lon-
> ger disinterested, and having lost their own independence, they impair
> the independence of the university to which they belong . . . If the pro-
> fessors try to run the government, we shall end by having the govern-
> ment run the professors.[75]

At the time of this speech, Lippmann was being routinely denounced by
liberals for his sympathy for reactionary causes and the absence of any value
system connecting his inchoate views on politics, society, and foreign policy. It is no stretch, therefore, to detect an element of catharsis in Lippmann's
words. But his opposition to Roosevelt's New Deal, and its irresponsible academic facilitators, remained constant through the remainder of his presidency. Lippmann just longed for a competent Republican to appear on the
national scene with the ability to oust the incumbent and take a hatchet to
the bloated government bureaucracy. One thing prevented Lippmann
from professing clear allegiance to the GOP: the party's views on foreign
policy, which tended toward muddle-headed isolationism. Lippmann was
deeply concerned by the socialistic nature of the New Deal. But he came
to view the rise of Germany and Japan as graver concerns, requiring an

emphasis on military preparedness that only Roosevelt appeared capable of delivering.

Reflecting on Adolf Hitler's rise to power, and the bellicosity displayed by irredentist Italy, Lippmann wrote in 1934, "As long as Europe prepares for war, America must prepare for neutrality."[76] Ostensibly, this entreaty might have been crafted by Charles Beard. But the operative word in Lippmann's sentence was "prepare," not "neutrality"—an important difference in emphasis. Lippmann believed that building a formidable American military was the surest way to repel predators. Like Beard, Lippmann harbored few illusions about the diabolical nature of the Nazi regime. Yet Lippmann thought that Hitler would pay little heed to professions of neutrality that were unsupported by serious military power. Avowedly neutral nations must also possess a big stick, to paraphrase Theodore Roosevelt.

While Lippmann believed that much more should be spent on military procurement, he did detect some cause for hope in Europe. In a bracingly amoral column of May 1933, he discerned two forces—well, one force and one persecuted minority—that might collectively restrain Hitler's territorial ambitions. The first was the French army, which still commanded respect from learned individuals steeped in Napoleonic history, oblivious of the hollowness of its contemporary military capabilities. The second phenomenon that Lippmann thought might localize German ambitions was the persecution of its Jewish population. In the spring and summer of 1933, Nazi thugs organized the burning of books written by Jews (and liberals) and perpetrated violence and intimidation on a national scale. The repression of Germany's Jews, Lippmann wrote, "by satisfying the lust of the Nazis who feel they must conquer somebody and the cupidity of those Nazis who want jobs, is a kind of lightning rod which protects Europe."[77] Here Lippmann displayed considerable callousness, and badly underestimated the extent of Hitler's ambitions. Felix Frankfurter recorded his understandable dismay about the "implications and attitude of feeling behind that piece."[78]

Though not as cruel as the logic undergirding his views on Germany's Jews, Lippmann's assessment of the Spanish Civil War was conditioned by a similar cold calculation. As Lippmann observed, "I never took a passionate, partisan interest in the Spanish Civil War. I feared it as a thing which was going to start a European war."[79] Notions of right and wrong never entered into Lippmann's reasoning on the conflict—Spain's Republicans were not worthy of U.S. support simply because they possessed greater legitimacy through the ballot box; the Nationalists' protofascist ideology was not sufficient cause for the United States to register meaningful disapproval. In this regard, of course, he was far from alone. The Popular Front government in France, the British government, and indeed President Roosevelt and Secretary of State Cordell Hull all prioritized the quarantining of the conflict ahead of saving democracy in Spain and preventing the rise of another dictator. With German and Italian assistance, therefore, General Francisco Franco established another fascist regime on continental Europe in 1939—after a brutal conflict in which approximately half a million died. Lippmann's final word was that Iberia was essentially tangential to the European balance of power.[80]

Continuing this logic of selective disengagement, Lippmann called for the United States to retreat from those Pacific interests that clashed most obviously with Tokyo's regional ambitions. In December 1936, he wrote that the "vital interests of Japan and the United States do not conflict," that war would be a "monstrous and useless blunder," and that this might be a "very opportune moment for the United States to withdraw gracefully from its Far Eastern entanglements." Uttering a sentiment that clashed with those of certain isolationists—Europe was beyond hope but China was very much a wronged party—Lippmann declared, "We can well afford to say plainly that the Chinese must defend their own country, and that we have no political interests whatever in Asia."[81] Retrenchment became imperative. Lippmann worried that the Philippines could become a source of contention with Japan. As Ronald Steel writes, "The 'blue water' strategy he had learned long ago from Alfred Thayer Mahan left him with a rule he held to all his life: the United States Navy should project American power in the Pacific, but the United States must never be drawn into military conflict on the Asian mainland."[82] Withdrawal from the archipelago should proceed forthwith. It took the Japanese attack on Pearl Harbor to convince Lippmann that war with Japan was unavoidable. Yet even then he continued to view the Pacific theater as secondary to the Atlantic and Mediterranean. Franklin Roosevelt would subsequently follow this prioritization, to Winston Churchill's great relief.

Lippmann knew where America should *not* invest resources and credibility. So what exactly did constitute the national interest? Lippmann partially answered this question in an article for *Foreign Affairs* titled "Rough-Hew Them How We Will," in July 1937, which resumed the "defense of the Atlantic world" rationale he had first developed during the Wilson presidency. Lippmann wrote that if Great Britain were to lose control of the Atlantic to Germany, then "all that is familiar and taken for granted, like the air we breathe, would suddenly be drastically altered." Echoing Mahan on the importance of Anglo-Saxon amity, Lippmann wrote: "In the final test, no matter what we wish now or now believe, though collaboration with Britain and her allies is difficult and often irritating, we shall protect that connection because in no other way can we fulfill our destiny." Assuring continued Anglo-American domination of the Atlantic thus remained the one cause clearly worth fighting for. Charles Beard predictably dissented—in this instance by quibbling with his mischaracterization of the Neutrality Act—cautioning Lippmann in a letter dated June 17, 1937, that "some things are not so rough hewn as they appear on the surface."[83] But Lippmann was moving far from Beard's worldview and was coming to fear that London underestimated the importance of this common purpose.

A visit to Europe in the summer of 1937 had left Lippmann despondent about Anglo-French complacency regarding the scale of the German threat. He was far ahead of his high-powered interlocutors in his understanding of the nature of Nazism and on the particularities of Hitler's psyche. In a farsighted "T&T" column, Lippmann observed perceptively that Hitler's continued dominance of German politics depended "not upon receiving tangible benefits by grace of his opponents, but upon taking things by the exercise of his own power . . . He cannot be placated by gifts; he must appear to conquer what he seeks."[84] If France and Britain continued on the track of denial and ignorance, Lippmann observed bleakly, "then the future of the Old World is once more in the hands of the warrior castes, and the civilian era, which began with the renaissance, is concluded."[85] In February 1938, during a meeting with Joseph P. Kennedy, the appeasement-inclined U.S. ambassador to the UK (and father of a future president), Lippmann insisted that "democracies must not delude themselves with the idea that there is any bloodless, inexpensive substitute for the willingness to go to war."[86]

Lippmann's prescience on the extent of Hitler's ambitions, and his critique of Anglo-French irresponsibility in the face of this threat, became more pointed through 1938 and 1939. In a letter to Harold Nicolson, Lippmann complained, "I don't see how Great Britain and France are going to hold their possessions or even preserve their independence if they go on living in peace when they are under the constant threat of three nations that are on a war footing all the time . . . While it was possible to surrender Czech territory, how is it going to be possible to surrender French territory . . . when I hear people talk about appeasement, I feel as if they were talking about a wholly imaginary and wholly incredible state of affairs."[87] Lippmann continued to make a case to the American people that military preparedness was the number-one political priority. Assistant Secretary of War Louis Johnson thanked Lippmann in December 1938 for his journalistic efforts to elucidate the national (Atlanticist) interest and his lucid warnings to Americans to reject the type of complacency and wishful thinking that so consumed Britain and France:

> I have just reread for the third time your comment which appeared a day or two ago in the *Washington Post* under the title "First Line and Preparedness for War" . . . Your views on this vital subject are so eminently sane and sound and your presentation of them is so forthright and so clear that I am impelled to the belief that if the country does not realize the situation as you have so admirably expressed it . . . in your column, I greatly fear that bitter days may be in store for us . . . You have told the country some straight-forward truths which, palatable or not, it should take to heart.[88]

Increasingly reconciled to the possibility of war, and of the likely necessity of material support for Britain and France, Johnson was delighted to have a journalistic ally as powerful as Lippmann.

In June 1939, as the unavoidability of war with Germany darkened the British mood—to the dissonant backdrop of summer's arrival—Lippmann met Winston Churchill for the first time. The art historian Kenneth Clark had arranged a supper with a guest list that included the evolutionary biologist Julian Huxley and Harold Nicolson and his wife, Vita Sackville-West, the author, poet, and lover of Virginia Woolf. This was a group not short on personality and opinion. Clark had convinced Churchill—suffering at that time from the periodic depression he labeled the "black dog"—to attend with the promise of Lippmann's attention. As Churchill sat quietly at dinner, Lippmann recounted the grim detail of a meeting with Joseph Kennedy earlier in the day. The gist of the ambassador's message was that Britain stood no chance of winning a war against Germany. Kennedy believed that London had to concede German freedom of action in Eastern and Central Europe—that no other choice was available. He had observed cuttingly to Lippmann that "all Englishmen in their hearts *know* this to be true, but a small group of brilliant people has created a public feeling which makes it impossible for the government to take a sensible course."[89]

Churchill was roused from his ennui by Lippmann's précis of the encounter. He regarded Ambassador Kennedy as a craven and credulous

Anglophobe—his Irish lineage rousing immediate suspicion—appointed by Roosevelt during one of his periodic (though grave) lapses in judgment. Harold Nicolson recounted that Churchill, "waving his whisky and soda to mark his periods, stubbing his cigar with the other hand," growled that while it was inevitable that "steel and fire will rain down upon us day and night scattering death and destruction far and wide," the British would endure the German assault stoically and return the "destruction" with interest. And in the unlikely event that Kennedy's "tragic utterance" was proved correct, Hitler would still have to pacify or defeat the world's most powerful nation. Churchill fixed Lippmann with a purposeful stare, imploring him to advise his fellow Americans to "think imperially" and continue their tradition of holding aloft the "torch of liberty."[90] Lippmann was mightily impressed by Churchill's bearing and eloquence. He came to view him as a colossal figure in Western civilization, whose significance and leadership qualities eclipsed even Theodore Roosevelt's.

As war edged closer, Lippmann observed events thoughtfully, mindful of historical analogies that illuminated the world's predicament. Responding to news of the Molotov-Ribbentrop Pact, Lippmann advised Lord Lothian—whom he knew in friendship as Philip Kerr—not to set too much store in professions of Russo-German friendship:

> So far as historical analogies hold at all . . . I recommend to you reading, if you haven't it in mind, the concluding chapter of Mahan's book on the French Revolution. There is, it seems to me, a striking resemblance between the policy of Russia then and now. Alexander, like Stalin, first wanted an all-embracing agreement against Napoleon, whereas the British held out for more specific and limited agreements. Then, having been totally against Napoleon, he turned around and made peace with Napoleon. In the Napoleonic analogy, I shouldn't be surprised now to see a series of wars with intervals of armistice and truce and shifting of the subordinate patterns in the new coalitions.[91]

With characteristic insight, Lippmann had laid bare the hollowness of alliance formation, particularly among despots of such brutal ambition. As the war progressed, Lippmann maintained his position that Britain and the United States should not give up on Stalin as a potential ally farther down the line—that Molotov-Ribbentrop was ephemeral. After Hitler reneged on his nonaggression agreement in 1941, Churchill followed the logic of the journalist's utilitarian views on Stalin's Soviet Union: as a useful force with which to crush Nazism. In an oft-quoted speech in Parliament, Churchill observed that "if Hitler invaded Hell, I would make at least a favorable reference to the Devil in the House of Commons."[92]

Lippmann was not surprised when Hitler's actions forced Britain and France to declare war in September 1939. Yet he understood that Allied military psychology was much more fragile than in 1914, when soldiers volunteered in droves to fight Germans to the backdrop of bunting and street parades. He wrote to Ronald C. Hood, the former editor of the *Birmingham Age-Herald*, that "even if a decisive military victory could be obtained by the sacrifice of, let us say, another million men, the Allied statesman would not seek such a decision as a matter of high political policy . . . I had a long talk in June with General [Maurice] Gamelin and I know that the problem of the French birth rate as affected by two great wars in one generation is a controlling element in his whole philosophy of war. The allies have to win the war by methods that do not cost that many lives."[93] In February 1940, Lippmann met again with Gamelin, commander in chief of the French army, during a tour of the Maginot Line. He asked France's military leader what might happen if Germany ignored Maginot and attacked through undefended Belgium. "Oh," said Gamelin, "we've got to have an open side because we need a *champ de bataille*. We're going to attack the German army and destroy it. The Maginot Line will narrow the gap through which they can come, and thus enable us to destroy them more easily."[94] Gamelin's failure of imagination was shown up a few months later when German troops poured through Belgium, little concerned by the narrowness of their route, and defeated the French army soon after.

After the fall of France, President Roosevelt, unshackled from his usual caution, declared that it was a "delusion" to believe that America might remain "a lone island in a world dominated by the philosophy of force."[95] Lippmann reveled in the speech's power and clarity. In his column, Lippmann developed the president's reasoning by observing that isolationists had been "duped by a falsification of history" and "miseducated by a swarm of innocent but ignorant historians." Lippmann's quarry is easy to identify here. It was a grave misreading of history, he continued, to believe that America entered the First World War "because of British propaganda, the loans of the bankers, the machinations of President Wilson's advisors, and a drummed up patriotic ecstasy." Wilson had failed to identify the primary reason the United States went to war: because the "safety of the Atlantic highway is something for which America should fight." To shirk in this task twenty years later would be to invite German aggression.[96] And Lippmann was at pains to ridicule isolationists who believed that the Atlantic was some form of magical barrier that no belligerent nation could cross. To the economist Edmund E. Lincoln, Lippmann wrote that "given command of the seas, the landing of troops in this hemisphere is a perfectly conceivable operation . . . If our navy is bottled up by superior navies in both oceans, it would be no more difficult for Germany to land troops in Venezuela, Colombia or Brazil than it has been for Great Britain to land Australian troops in Egypt. Distance as such is no barrier if the seas are under control."[97]

Lippmann played a major role in assuring congressional passage of the destroyers-for-bases deal, and he offered strong support for its more ambitious successor, Lend-Lease. Acknowledging that sophistry and loopholes were no longer required in rationalizing significant material support for Great Britain, Lippmann wrote, "With aid to Britain, this country passes from large promises carried out slightly and partially by clever devices to substantial deeds openly and honestly avowed."[98] Unlike destroyers-for-bases, Lippmann "had nothing to do with the idea, except by writing articles explaining the need of making a contribution to aid the Allies." Yet a national syndicated audience of ten million of America's wealthiest and most influential readers meant that his persuasive role was significant. Having opposed FDR through the New Deal, Lippmann became a staunch supporter of his diplomacy toward the Second World War. The author of *Public Opinion* even paid homage to the genius of the president's phrasemaking: "The name Lend-Lease was Roosevelt's own invention. It didn't mean anything, but it sounded as if we weren't giving the money."[99] Best of all was the president's magnificent Fireside Chat of December 29, 1940. Speaking to the largest radio audience in history—three-quarters of Americans tuned in to listen to the president—Roosevelt observed that the time had come for the United States to serve as "the great arsenal of democracy."[100] London endured a devastating bombing raid over the course of the night, but its markets rallied to FDR's speech the following day.

Lippmann grew to admire FDR's deft and purposeful leadership over the course of World War II. Roosevelt's keen political skills—his caution, optimism, and eloquence—allowed him to prepare the American public for participation in a world war *and* for a pivotal role in world affairs thereafter. After the Japanese attack on Pearl Harbor, the president responded stirringly to this shocking turn of events, identifying "a date which will live in infamy" that America would never let stand. His prioritization of defeating Germany first was sound and his appointment of senior Republicans to his administration was tactically adroit and appropriate in the circumstances. Aside from Roosevelt's hostile views toward the grandstanding leader of the Free French, Charles de Gaulle—whom Lippmann regarded as a major figure in world affairs—Lippmann viewed the president's management of American participation in the Second World War in a favorable light. Indeed, Lippmann even supported Roosevelt's most controversial action in wartime: the internment of Japanese Americans. In an infamous "T&T" column on February 12, 1942, Lippmann warned of "imminent danger of a combined attack from within and from without" if a fifth column of Japanese ancestry were allowed to roam free.[101] On February 19, President Roosevelt authorized the War Department to remove and intern any citizen of Japanese descent it deemed a threat: some 120,000 people in total. Lippmann cheered this mutilation of habeas corpus—sustained by a notorious ruling by the Supreme Court—in subsequent columns.

Lippmann's views on the Republican Party, conversely, were scathing. Writing to Congressman John M. Vorys of Ohio in February 1941, Lippmann observed that "there is nothing in the record of the Republicans, either on questions of national defense or on our relationship to the Allies, to justify any belief that they have had foresight. If they had had it, they would now be compelled to reverse themselves so completely that the only issue left between them and the Administration is one of procedure."[102] Wendell Willkie had proved a major disappointment during the 1940 campaign, declining to adopt a clear pro-Allied position and instead accusing FDR of harboring cynically concealed interventionist goals. Willkie had refused to follow Lippmann's earlier advice that "you have nothing to lose . . . by being the Churchill rather than the Chamberlain of the crisis, and by charging Roosevelt with being the Daladier, the weak man who means well feebly and timidly."[103] But Lippmann detected graver problems with Willkie than his refusal to assume the Churchillian mantle.

After his election defeat in 1940, Willkie showed admirable grace in supporting President Roosevelt's foreign policies. It was too late to make a political difference, but Willkie had surmised that Lippmann's campaign advice to him had been sound: U.S. support for Great Britain was a just cause and Churchill was the model statesman in such tumultuous times. Willkie thus gave his strong support to Lend-Lease, before going one step further in calling for the unlimited supply of Britain's war effort in the summer of 1941. Delighted to have his support, FDR asked Willkie to travel the world on a goodwill mission as the president's personal envoy. Willkie promptly agreed, visiting Great Britain, the Middle East, the Soviet Union, and China throughout 1941 and 1942. Impressed by the commonality of human experience he encountered in these diverse nations and regions, Willkie surmised that it was possible and preferable to govern the postwar world through a global peacekeeping organization. Woodrow Wilson had been correct, Willkie decided, to believe that human progress had no geographical limits and that universal peace was attainable if the right kind of multilateral organization was established to lead the way.

Willkie began the process of writing up his travel experiences in a book, published in 1943 under the title *One World*. Drawing on his fresh, cosmopolitan understanding of nationalities and ethnic groups, Willkie contended that the altruistic, sociable traits that unite humanity are far stronger than those that divide it. Under these circumstances, imperialism must be rejected, racial divisions should be addressed as a priority at home, and all nations must cede some sovereignty to live in one world—not many—in which mature, open diplomacy would eliminate the bloodletting that had so scarred human affairs. The book captured a transitory moment of multilateral idealism in the history of U.S. diplomacy. Willkie had channeled Woodrow Wilson, and then some. An opinion poll in 1942 had found that 73 percent of Americans believed that Wilson had been correct about joining the League of Nations, up from 33 percent in 1937.[104]

Having recanted such idealism through painful experience during the First World War, Lippmann was adamant that the United States must avoid repeating the blunder of substituting concrete goals with platitudes born of wishful thinking rather than comprehension of history. Lippmann wrote that "I felt that the One World doctrine was a dangerous doctrine . . . I felt it wasn't possible to make one world, and the attempt to do it would produce a struggle . . . that the right line was to recognize the pluralism of the world and hope for an accommodation among many systems."[105] There were certain geopolitical phenomena that could not be transcended: nationalism and the naked pursuit of commercial self-interest were at the top of the list.

Writing to Henry Cabot Lodge Jr. (who had followed his distinguished grandfather in representing Massachusetts in the Senate), Lippmann poured scorn on his self-righteous and self-deluding observation that the United States, unlike Great Britain, was not an imperial nation. "In this respect," Lippmann wrote, "we have exactly the same definite practical aim as Britain: we too intend to maintain our prewar position—in Alaska, Hawaii, the Philippines, in the Caribbean, and in South America." Lodge had also made a rash remark regarding the utility of international collaboration, which Lippmann took to task: "I think that the first point in your summary—

about 'effective international collaboration'—is an example of the cosmic transcendentalism which you deplore. It is too late in the day for any man to use such empty phrases: the time has come to particularize and to be practical by defining the strategic positions, the commitments, the alliances which give substance to the phrase."[106] Lippmann had embarked on this process of particularization by writing a book of his own. He halved the frequency of his weekly column to write the book in just four months, aware of the advanced stage of his adversary's book in progress. While "Willkie's *One World* helped to educate the people of this country to a participation in world affairs," Lippmann wrote, "it also helped . . . to miseducate them to an expectation about things which caused a furious resentment when it didn't come true."[107] America's world position would be gravely harmed by the unchallenged dissemination of such ignorance. Lippmann's contribution to public education, *U.S. Foreign Policy: Shield of the Republic*, was published in the spring of 1943, at the same time as *One World*. Rarely have two foreign-policy books combined so perfectly to capture the public's imagination.

U.S. Foreign Policy was Lippmann's best book on diplomacy. Writing with his typical elegance and sustained by pertinent references to America's historical experience, Lippmann interrogated foreign policy with a sharpness and accessibility that few writers before or since have achieved. Consider Lippmann's presentation of his core argument: "The thesis of this book is that a foreign policy consists in bringing into balance, with a comfortable surplus of power in reserve, the nation's commitments and the nation's power. The constant preoccupation of the true statesman is to achieve and maintain this balance."[108] The essence of realism has rarely been captured so well.

A central target in *U.S. Foreign Policy* is Woodrow Wilson, whom Lippmann lambasts for failing to enunciate America's war aims clearly—a familiar theme throughout his interwar journalism. "The reasons he did give," wrote Lippmann disapprovingly, "were legalistic and moralistic and idealistic reasons, rather than the substantial and vital reason that the security of the United States demanded that no aggressively expanding imperial power, like Germany, should be allowed to gain the mastery of the Atlantic Ocean."[109] In Lippmann's opinion, Wilson had entered World War I "without a foreign policy," and that "it was made to seem that the new responsibilities of the league flowed from President Wilson's philanthropy and not from the vital necessity of finding allies to support America's vast existing commitments in the Western Hemisphere and all the way across the Pacific to the China Coast."[110] In this respect Wilson operated in a regrettable tradition that sanctimoniously misread the nation's history. The cause of this diplomatic naïveté was miscomprehension of the Founding Fathers' views and actions. George Washington decried "entangling alliances" only because fixed allegiances did not suit the young republic at that time. The Louisiana Purchase and the Monroe Doctrine proved beyond doubt that U.S. foreign policy was not conceived in a vacuum, unsullied by consideration of the Old World. And nineteenth-century America nearly always possessed sufficient military power to serve its limited purpose: subjugating a continent and winning territory from weak adversaries in the form of Mexico and Spain. "Though Jefferson had some odd ideas about the navy," Lippmann wrote, "the Founders never thought of making unpreparedness for war a national ideal."[111] Thinking otherwise was America's original diplomatic sin.

It was the dawn of the twentieth century that compelled the United States to reconsider its foreign-policy responsibilities with a clearer head: "As soon . . . as Britain no longer ruled all the oceans—which was after about 1900—our own strategic doctrine ceased to be adequate."[112] In respect to the Spanish-American War, Lippmann quotes Mahan's view that the United States was fortunate to face such an incompetent enemy. This scenario was unlikely to be repeated during future conflicts, making it essential that America's vital interests be firmly established. Lippmann did so in observing that "we are committed to defend at the risk of war the lands and the waters extending from Alaska to the Philippines and Australia, from Greenland to Brazil to Patagonia."[113] That this represented a major commitment—nearly half the world's surface—was not lost on Lippmann. But hostile encroachment into any of these areas could pose a mortal threat to the nation's independence. Germany's quest for hegemony in Europe, for example, made the continental United States considerably more vulnerable:

> The fall of France laid Spain and Portugal open to the possibility of invasion and domination. This in turn opened up the question of the security of the Spanish and Portuguese island stepping-stones in the Atlantic. The fall of France gave Germany the sea and air bases from which Britain was besieged and American shipping along our Eastern shore and in the Caribbean subjected to a devastating raid.[114]

It was this reality of American vulnerability—little appreciated across a parochial nation—that compelled participation in the Second World War.

The book's other purpose was to identify the alliances most likely to sustain a stable postwar world. In this respect, Lippmann expected the core relationship among the United States, Great Britain, and the Soviet Union—the so-called Big Three—to prove as indispensable in peacetime as it had proved in fighting Germany. To maintain cordial relations with Moscow, it was imperative that Washington accept that the land to the east of Germany was firmly within the Soviet sphere of influence: "To encourage the nations of Central and Eastern Europe to organize themselves as a barrier against Russia would be to make a commitment that the United States could not carry out . . . the region lies beyond the reach of American power, and therefore the implied commitment would be unbalanced and insolvent."[115] Ensuring peace after the defeat of the Axis depended on acceptance by the great powers in general—and America in particular—that traditional diplomatic cooperation was a surer bet to avoiding war than vesting faith in a world parliament or binding arbitration. Maintaining close postwar relations with its two major wartime allies, furthermore, required Washington to look beyond behavior that clashed with cherished norms and values—whether in respect to Churchill's determination to preserve the British Empire or Stalin's heavy-handed creation of a cordon sanitaire in Eastern Europe.

U.S. Foreign Policy was a work of stark political realism that struck a resonant chord across the United States—a nation prone to gazing admiringly at its innocent self-image. Lippmann is better than anyone else at capturing the reasons for its remarkable popular success: "I think *U.S. Foreign Policy* has had by all odds the greatest circulation of anything I've ever written. It's been translated into almost every language. Its virtue was that it had certain very simple and fairly obvious ideas which just happened to be apropos. It was a time when people were beginning to take foreign affairs seriously."[116]

This short volume of "simple and fairly obvious ideas" sold close to half a million copies. A condensed version was published in *Reader's Digest*, while the *Ladies' Home Journal* published a remarkable rendering of Lippmann's thesis in the form of seven pages of cartoon strips—unique testament to his accessibility. The U.S. Army distributed a version to its troops, priced at 25¢.[117] On June 14, 1943, Lippmann appeared on the cover of *Time*, which hailed the quality of the analysis provided by the "pundit Lippmann." *Newsweek* praised Lippmann as "perhaps the foremost editorial voice of enlightened conservatism in this country." A review even appeared in the French Resistance magazine *Les Cahiers Politiques*, published under the perilous circumstances of German occupation.[118] In November 1943, Charles Beard complained that Lippmann was the "Dean of the World Savers," and that he was keen to "take a whack . . . [But] I haven't the time or strength"—a prospect that would have cheered Lippmann immensely.[119] Yet in spite of the global attention and review plaudits, Lippmann viewed the book as a failure. In the final calculation, *U.S. Foreign Policy* simply did not make good on its ambition of educating Americans out of their tendency to view the world immodestly through an idealistic lens. As Lippmann noted, "The theory that the nation's commitments and its power must be in balance is really an obvious idea, but it was a new one. It's one that we haven't learned of course. The book is a complete failure in that respect, because we proceeded right away to make more commitments than we had power to fulfill after the war."[120]

Through the spring and summer of 1943, the first rumblings of grand alliance fracture had become audible. Stalin believed that Britain and the United States had been purposefully tardy in refusing to sanction a cross-channel invasion to carve open a second front and relieve pressure on the Red Army, which bore the overwhelming burden of fighting Germany. For his part, Churchill had grave misgivings about the Soviet Union's territorial intentions in Eastern Europe. The prime minister had no desire to sacrifice Polish independence—for which Britain had declared war on Germany in the first place—for the sake of hypothetical postwar unity. At this stage Churchill did not view Eastern Europe as a sacrificial lamb. At the Tehran Conference of November–December 1943, Churchill and Roosevelt agreed to launch a cross-channel invasion the following spring. But Stalin was relentless in holding the line that Moscow would assume a "special" stake in the nations the Red Army occupied on its path to Berlin. The Soviet Union would swallow the Baltic states, and Poland would never again fall into hostile hands. At Tehran the disagreements that lurked beneath Allied bonhomie presaged new rivalries, which Lippmann was keen to avoid.

After Roosevelt returned from Tehran to reports of growing discord among the Allies, Lippmann wrote in his column that "we must not make the error of thinking that the alternative to 'isolation' is universal 'intervention.' A diplomacy which pretended that we were interested in every disputed region everywhere would easily disrupt the alliance." All nations throughout history have possessed spheres of influence and it was fallacious to believe that the creation of a United Nations—a term first used by FDR in January 1942—might allow something more equitable to take its place. Indeed, stability and peace were often predicated on powerful nations dominating the geographical region in which they resided—repelling predators and ensuring "stability." Lippmann observed that it was "not only unavoidable but eminently proper that each great power does have a sphere in which its influence and responsibility are primary," and that One World disciples engage in "the pretense, wholly illusory and dangerously confusing, that every state has an identical influence, interest, power and responsibility everywhere."[121] Lippmann was concerned that U.S.-Soviet postwar cooperation might founder on the marginal issue of Polish or Czech independence. He began writing a follow-up to *U.S. Foreign Policy* to warn the public of the dark consequences that might flow from well-intentioned miscalculations.

The sequel, *U.S. War Aims*, was published as Allied troops poured onto Normandy's beaches, establishing with considerable bravery, and grave human cost, the second front promised at Tehran. It was a propitious moment for the book to appear, as the Second World War in Europe was clearly entering its endgame. As with *U.S. Foreign Policy*, Lippmann criticized Wilson: "The Wilsonian principles are prejudices formed in the Age of Innocence, in the century of American isolation. Wilson wished America to take its place in a universal society. But he was willing to participate only if the whole world acted as the United States acted when it enjoyed isolationism during the nineteenth century . . . He supposed that international relations could then be conducted verbally by meetings at Geneva."[122] Lippmann believed Roosevelt should closely examine Wilson's diplomatic performance during and after the First World War and then do the opposite. Driven forward by abstract Kantian theories, Wilson forgot about the enemy and the fundamental Hobbesian nature of the world. Victorious nation-states, not untested world peacekeeping institutions, should make and keep the peace. People live for "their families and their homes," Lippmann wrote, "their villages and lands, their countries and their own ways, their altars, their flags, and their hearths—not charters, covenants, blueprints, and generalities."[123]

Lippmann's contempt for the worldviews presented by Wilson and Beard inform the book at every juncture. Instead, Lippmann championed Mahanian causes of realism, alliance-driven diplomacy, and hostility to arbitration:

> The argument developed in this book is that we should reverse the Wilsonian principles: that we should seek to conserve the existing political states, rather than to dismember them on the ground of self-determination, and that we should approve, not forbid, should perfect and not dissolve, the regional groupings of national states . . . We have to reverse the Wilsonian pattern of collective security. We cannot build a universal society from the top downwards. We must build up to it from the existing national states and historic communities.[124]

It was vital that America secure something concrete from hard-won victories on the battlefield. "We shall not squander the victory," Lippmann wrote, "as we did twenty-five years ago, if we hold fast to this simple idea: that the fundamental task of diplomats and public men is to preserve what is being accomplished by the war."[125] To "preserve" the fruits of war—the final and decisive defeat of militarism in Germany and Japan—Lippmann proposed that international affairs henceforth stem from "a nucleus around which order can be organized." This nucleus would consist of four centers of power, comprising the "Atlantic Community," spearheaded by the United States, Britain, and France, the "Russian Orbit," including a Soviet sphere in Central and Eastern Europe, and two other "constellations": China and the other forming in "the Hindu and in the Moslem worlds, but that is more distant."[126] In combination, these four powers would serve a police function. All would possess a vital economic stake in avoiding conflict and maintaining stability both within and outside the "orbits." Constituent nations were free to join the United Nations, but peace was served best by Lippmann's transnational alliance system, not through countless atomized nation-states arguing their selfish case to an impotent deliberative body.

In dispensing instruction on how best to shape the postwar world, Lippmann was farsighted on some issues but unduly pessimistic on a host of others. Insightfully, Lippmann observed that Germany should be weaned off notions of autarky—or continental Germanism—and encouraged to forge a new economic identity as an exporting nation: "It will be safer for all of Europe, and also for Russia, if Germany becomes dependent upon maritime commerce. The less self-sufficient Germany is, the better for her neighbors whom she has sought to dominate, and for the Atlantic nations which will emerge from this war with the command of the seas."[127] Channeling Germany's formidable economic potential in this export-led direction made sound geopolitical sense and anticipated the nation's remarkable journey from militarized, authoritarian aggressor to war-averse, export-led superpower. On Japan, conversely, Lippmann's usual perspicacity was hindered by a failure of imagination. He wrote, "The American objective will have been attained if Japan is incapable of recovering the military force to strike again. The reform and reconstruction of Japan are beyond our ken, and we shall be wise to solidify our relations with China by being in these matters her second . . . we cannot manage a Japanese revolution."[128] The United States has enjoyed few foreign-affairs successes comparable to its occupation of Japan, which indeed amounted to a revolution of sorts in the nation's polity and external bearing.

On potential sources of conflict with Moscow, Lippmann appeared blithe. He downgraded the significance of ideology and focused instead on the positive aspect of geographical remoteness. "The two strongest states in the world will be as widely separated as it is possible to be," Lippmann wrote. "The core of the Soviet power is at the Urals in the deep interior of the Eurasian continent; the American power is in the Mississippi Valley in the heart of the island continent of North America. Not since the unity of the ancient world was disrupted has there been so good a prospect of a settled peace."[129] Here, Lippmann was guilty of viewing events through a nineteenth-century paradigm, failing to anticipate that a divided Europe would become a source of considerable friction between Moscow and Washington, and that liberalism-capitalism and Marxism-Leninism represented not just antagonistic ideologies in theory but also proactive rationales for intervening across the world to steer "progress" in the right direction.

The important thing to note is that Lippmann's realism was a theory. It assumed permanent trends in the structure of world affairs. It held that the "true statesman" balances resources and commitments, and eschews reckless adventurism, in pursuing policies that redound to the nation's advantage. It was a social scientific insight. But Stalin was not motivated simply by material concerns. Soviet foreign policy required a wider ideological purpose; it was bound tightly into the nation's raison d'être. In a pugnacious speech delivered at the Bolshoi Theatre in 1946, Stalin observed that the First and Second World Wars had broken out "as the inevitable result of the development of world economic and political forces on the basis of present-day monopolistic capitalism." He pondered whether such wars were avoidable in the future but concluded that only the universal victory of Marxism-Leninism made this possible: "Perhaps catastrophic wars could be avoided if it were possible periodically to redistribute raw materials and markets among the respective countries in conformity with their economic weight by means of concerted and peaceful decisions. But this is impossible under the present capitalist conditions of world economic development."[130]

Stalin's reading of Marx and Lenin blinded him to the reality that conflict between liberal-capitalist states was not inevitable. Under American leadership the West cohered rapidly and effectively in opposing the spread of communism. But in holding that Stalin's rationality outweighed his ideological convictions, Lippmann similarly misread the taproots of Soviet foreign policy.

Lippmann was also unduly optimistic about Stalin's capacity to evolve in a more humane direction, writing that "since we became allies in war, the Soviet Union has been committing itself more and more definitively to a foreign policy based on democratic, and not totalitarian, principles . . . The fact is that Marshal Stalin has now repeatedly affirmed the democratic principle in respect to his dealings with his neighbors within the Russian Orbit."[131] Thinking the best of Stalin was forgivable to someone less informed; the despot had been presented to the American public in a flattering light—as "Uncle Joe"—due to the pressing concern of defeating Hitler. As someone with privileged political access and a wealth of published information, however, Lippmann might have known better.

Lippmann's purpose in writing the book was to elevate the importance of a close working relationship with the "Russian Orbit" and steer Americans away from their habitual tendency to view their place in the world through a moralistic lens. But *U.S. War Aims* failed to achieve the desired impact. Some people liked it, certainly. Within the Roosevelt administration, Secretary of the Interior Harold L. Ickes described the book as "an outstanding piece of work . . . novel and extremely interesting."[132] John Foster Dulles, then a foreign affairs adviser to the Republican presidential candidate, Thomas E. Dewey, complimented Lippmann on performing "a most able and constructive job," particularly in identifying the limitations of the proposed United Nations.[133] Like *U.S. Foreign Policy*, it appeared on the bestseller list and was serialized in *Reader's Digest*.

But hostility outweighed praise. Henry Luce, the publisher of *Life* magazine, considered serializing the book, then declined after reading the galleys. Luce viewed Lippmann's book as "too anti-Russian" for describing the Soviet Union (accurately) as a "totalitarian state," even though Lippmann was crystal clear in detailing the diplomatic benefits of a close working relationship between the orbits.[134] A former colleague at *The World*, John L. Balderston, complained to Lippmann that the book's underlying pessimism left him with a "feeling of despair." Lippmann defended his portrait of the postwar world as both accurate and reasonably optimistic:

> There's a great deal of confusion among our friends who think that war, which is a destructive process, can create the brave new world. The brave new world, in my view, can be created only if and when the threat of great war had disappeared for two or three generations. In other words, I think we shall get a peace as conclusive as that which followed the Napoleonic Wars and a century as free from great wars as was the Nineteenth. That's a devil of a lot when you think about it.[135]

The "friend" who had detailed a path to creating "a brave new world" from the ashes of war was Sumner Welles, FDR's undersecretary of state and an architect of his Good Neighbor Policy. In 1944, Welles published *The Time for Decision*, which restated Woodrow Wilson's ambitions in calling for the creation of a much-strengthened League of Nations. The book was driven by the idealism that Lippmann's book set out to denigrate, and it captured the public's mood of optimism much more successfully. The book sold a million copies and garnered critical plaudits from across the spectrum of opinion. Welles also reviewed *U.S. War Aims* critically. As Lippmann recalled, "Sumner Welles reviewed the book and opposed it because he said it was old-fashioned belief in the balance of power . . . all of which we had to get away from in one word—the United Nations."[136] In 1944, foreign policy appeared to be running away from Lippmann's modest spheres-driven realism, as he well realized: "The whole trend of our policy went in the other direction. The first theory was that we were going to unite everybody, including the Russians, in one world, and all were going to think alike. When that broke down, then we were going to unite everybody *but* the Russians in one world . . . The book came out as Roosevelt was in his last phase, and Truman, of course, never read a book."[137]

As Lippmann had cautioned in *Public Opinion* and *The Phantom Public*, the "outsider" American population, "served" by weak political leadership, was driving the nation toward needless confrontation with the one power with which America should remain on reasonably good terms. Worst of all was the notion that the United Nations should assume the essential role of arbiter. Lippmann complained later that "I can't help feeling that Welles's book did enormous damage in diverting the American people from an understanding of the historical realities . . . I might have accomplished more by a running criticism of him than I did by my own book."[138] Lippmann's plans had been frustrated by a population swayed by the Wilsonian sophistry of Sumner Welles and Wendell Willkie. If only, he lamented, "the public, and particularly the idealistic public, were not so stubbornly naïve."[139]

Sumner Welles's collaborative ideas were put to the test from August to October 1944, when representatives from the United States, United Kingdom, Soviet Union, and China met in Dumbarton Oaks, Washington, D.C., to draw a blueprint for a successor organization to the League of Nations. During these discussions the four major components of the United Nations were established: the Security Council, the General Assembly, the International Court of Justice, and a Secretariat. Significantly, the four delegations agreed that the United Nations should possess a military capability. This would be created through member states placing their militaries at the disposal of the Security Council at moments of crisis. Woodrow Wilson's dreams were being realized. As were Mahan's and Lippmann's nightmares.

In a long letter to his friend Grenville Clark, chairman of the Citizens Committee for a National War Service Act, Lippmann poured scorn on events at Dumbarton Oaks. He complained that "the Dumbarton Delegates have sought to create a universal society to enforce peace before the world has been sufficiently pacified . . . With these conventions to pacify and unite, we should not be quarrelling with Russia over the conundrum of legal equality, but should be bound together with Russia to make and keep the peace in the critical generation ahead of us." Lippmann thought that the creation of the United Nations was a foolish distraction at a time of profound global flux. When world peace became reality was the right time to vest faith in a new geopolitical experiment. It was "a false major premise" to believe that Dumbarton Oaks could conjure up "a universal society to pacify the world."[140] On this count, Lippmann's skepticism was well founded.

Remarkably, the creation of a United Nations was not even a campaign issue during the general election of 1944. Both Roosevelt and the Republican candidate, New York governor Thomas Dewey, agreed on the wisdom of establishing a new global organization to keep the peace. Lippmann had grown mightily tired of FDR's presidency—then in its twelfth year—but Dewey struck him as a worse prospect. Dewey had criticized Roosevelt for refusing to confront Stalin over his future plans for Poland. In "Today & Tomorrow" Lippmann criticized Dewey's support for those "reactionary Poles" who were foolish enough to resist compromise with Stalin over the nation's frontiers and political composition.[141] John Foster Dulles was furious with Lippmann, writing that "the basic issue between you and the governor is that you do not believe that the United States should have any policies at all except in relation to areas where we can make those policies good through material force. The governor, on the other hand, believes in moral force." Unwilling to accept a sanctimonious attack from a man who previously favored the appeasement of Hitler—even after the fall of France—Lippmann penned a cutting retort: "I wonder if it would be profitable to argue about who is more aware of the moral issues involved in this war, for that would involve examination of the record, whereas I for one prefer to let bygones be bygones."[142]

Lippmann did not so much endorse Roosevelt as eviscerate Dewey. In "T&T," he wrote, "I cannot feel that Governor Dewey can be trusted with responsibility in foreign affairs. He has so much to learn, and there would be no time to learn it, that the risk and cost of change during this momentous year seems to me too great."[143] The voting public appeared to agree with Lippmann, reelecting Roosevelt with 432 electoral college votes to Dewey's 99—a winning margin of 3.5 million cast ballots. Isolationists such as Hamilton Fish and Gerald P. Nye were voted from office. Self-declared "internationalists" entered Congress in considerable number, including a young, well-traveled Rhodes scholar from Arkansas named J. William Fulbright. Lippmann was pleased with the outcome at both the executive and legislative levels. But he remained concerned by the administration's still buoyant enthusiasm for the United Nations and the prospect that growing U.S.-Soviet discord might derail his hopes for postwar stability. Roosevelt's new vice president, Harry S. Truman, did not inspire much confidence in this regard. On June 23, 1941, Truman had observed, "If we see that Germany is winning we ought to help Russia and if Russia is winning we ought to help Germany and that way let them kill as many as possible."[144]

Engaging in diplomatic cynicism of a different kind, Winston Churchill visited Moscow in October 1944 to propose to Stalin a "percentages deal," whereby Eastern, Central, and Southern Europe (excluding Poland) would be divided into distinct spheres of interest. The Soviet Union would secure a preponderant stake in Romania, for example, while Britain would play the dominant role in Greece. This was a diplomatic gambit of which nineteenth-century prime ministers such as Disraeli and Palmerston would have been proud. Churchill appeared oblivious of how the times had changed, however, so when his proposal went public, a significant backlash ensued—FDR was compelled to disown his ally's proposal. In Lippmann's opinion, Churchill had displayed considerable skill in extracting a quid pro quo from a relatively weak diplomatic position. He was dismayed by such a violent response to sensible diplomacy. Lippmann wrote in December 1944 that American troops had not died to "have a plebiscite in eastern Galicia or to return Hong Kong to Chiang Kai-shek."[145] The irrational passions of the masses were again skewing the pursuit of sound diplomatic strategy driven by those privy to "insider" knowledge.

Roosevelt, Churchill, and Stalin met for a final time at the Crimean resort town of Yalta in February 1945. While Germany stood on the cusp of defeat, the daunting prospect of a sea invasion of Japan remained likely. The U.S. atomic bomb was still in development. It is in this context that we must comprehend FDR's primary goal of securing Soviet support for continued military action against Japan—to which Stalin agreed at a fixed point three months after Germany's unconditional surrender. The Big Three also hammered out a Declaration on Liberated Europe, which called for free elections in those nations liberated from Nazi occupation. This read well on the page, but the terms were ambiguous and effectively unenforceable.

Attempting to extract a Soviet concession on Eastern Europe, Churchill made clear that an independent Poland for him was a matter of honor. Stalin retorted testily that for the Soviet Union a friendly Poland was a matter of security. Roosevelt interjected that free elections in Poland "should be as 'pure' as Caesar's wife." Ominously, Stalin replied, "They said that about her, but in fact she had her sins." Five days of grueling negotiations had produced cloudiness on the fate of Eastern and Central Europe. When Admiral William Leahy, serving as the president's chief of staff, complained that the common declaration was so elastic that it could be stretched from the Black Sea to Washington without fear of rupture, FDR replied, "I know, Bill. But it's the best I could do for Poland at this time."[146]

Lippmann agreed. Yalta was as good an agreement as could have been made in the circumstances. In "T&T" he wrote that "there has been no more impressive international conference in our time, none in which great power was so clearly hardened to the vital, rather than the secondary, interests of nations."[147] Lippmann was as enthusiastic about Roosevelt's presidency as he had ever been. Then, at this high point of goodwill, reports began circulating about the fragile state of FDR's health. The long trip to Yalta had taken a severe physical toll on a man with serious and long-standing health problems. Upon his return, Roosevelt had retreated swiftly to Warm Springs for rest and medical attention. The prognosis was not good, as photographs of a visibly frail Roosevelt at Yalta testified. "Fearing that the president might not live much longer," Ronald Steel writes, "Lippmann, as a final gesture to the man toward whom he had such conflicting feelings, decided to write a tribute to FDR—in effect an obituary—while the president was still able to read it."[148] Having subjected Roosevelt to scathing critical treatment throughout the 1930s, Lippmann graciously observed that his performance during the Second World War had been exemplary. In this respect, the warmth of Lippmann's assessment was aided by the fact that Roosevelt's narrow conception of the national interest had come to converge so closely with his own. Painful concessions to Stalin at Yalta had proved beyond doubt that "[President Roosevelt's] estimate of the vital interests of the United States has been accurate and far-sighted. He has served these interests with audacity and patience, shrewdly and with calculation, and he has led this country out of the greatest peril in which it has ever been to the highest point of security, influence, and respect which it has ever attained."[149]

It was an accurate and generous premortem eulogy. America's greatest twentieth-century president died from a cerebral hemorrhage five days later.

Lippmann had emerged from war as the nation's most powerful journalist-analyst of foreign policy. *U.S. War Aims* had failed to hit its intended target, but his "Today & Tomorrow" column went from strength to strength in terms of its national and international readership. Losing a president devoted to a friendly relationship with the Soviet Union, however, was a major blow to Lippmann's persuasive aspirations regarding the postwar world. President Harry Truman's blunt, straight-talking style and provincial roots concerned Lippmann. Yet there were other political problems that commanded Lippmann's attention. Foremost was the imperative that the Republican Party be prevented from turning lethal fire on FDR's legacy—in the same way as Woodrow Wilson's diplomatic goals were crushed after the First World War.

Senator Arthur Vandenberg of Michigan was the likeliest candidate to emulate Henry Cabot Lodge's spoiling role in 1919. Participation in the Nye Committee in the 1930s had convinced Vandenberg that participation in the First World War had been a colossal error of judgment. Vandenberg argued that the Neutrality Acts did not go nearly far enough and that Roosevelt had been misguided in condemning Japanese aggression toward China. He was equally adamant that the rise of Hitler did not threaten America's vital interests. The Japanese attack on Pearl Harbor gave him little option but to abandon isolationism, but it was a reluctant recantation. As war commenced, Vandenberg offered a despairing appraisal: "We have tossed Washington's Farewell Address into the discard. We have thrown ourselves squarely into the power politics and the power wars of Europe, Asia, and Africa. We have taken the first step upon a course from which we can never hereafter retreat."[150] Lippmann was determined to keep him to his elegiac word.

Vandenberg was unenthused at the prospect of the United States assuming a central and proactive world role, but he possessed thinly disguised presidential ambitions, which Lippmann adeptly manipulated. Lippmann advised Vandenberg that running for the presidency in 1948 required a conversion to a responsible internationalism. The United States was the world's most powerful nation by a vast margin—controlling approximately 50 percent of all world trade—and this came with grave responsibilities in respect to maintaining benign international conditions to sustain this dominance. Lippmann and James Reston of *The New York Times* collaborated in drafting a major speech that Vandenberg delivered to the Senate on January 19, 1945.

In an address that bore Lippmann's distinctive authorial mark, Vandenberg declared, "I do not believe that any nation hereafter can immunize itself by its own exclusive action. Since Pearl Harbor, World War II has put the gory science of mass murder into new and sinister perspective. Our oceans have ceased to be moats which automatically protect our ramparts."[151] His congressional colleagues were stunned at this volte-face. For their part, Reston and Lippmann complimented Vandenberg (and their own phrasemaking) in their respective columns the following day. Lippmann later spotted Vandenberg at a diplomatic reception, striding from one admirer to the next "just like a pouter pigeon all blown up with delight at his new role in the world." A keen student of psychology and a seasoned observer of politicians, Lippmann knew exactly how to deal with this "vain and pompous and really quite insincere man."[152]

President Truman would prove less susceptible to Lippmann's bag of persuasive tricks. He never invited Lippmann to the White House, and their correspondence was limited to a few stiffly formal notes. Truman's first order of business was to preside over the creation of the United Nations at the San Francisco Conference that commenced on April 25, 1945. Addressing the fifty national delegations whose job was to revise the Dumbarton Oaks agreements and devise a foundational Charter, Truman remarked that the moment had come to give "reality to the ideal of that great statesman of a generation ago—Woodrow Wilson."[153] Such words were never likely to rouse Lippmann's enthusiasm—or indeed those of a continental Americanist like Charles Beard. When the United Nations Charter was signed on June 26, Beard joined realist skeptics in rubbishing the UN's decision-making procedures. "It gives Russia, Britain, and the United States a veto on everything they do not like," Beard complained. "How people with any knowledge and intelligence can be taken in by it passes my understanding."[154] Predictably, Lippmann took the opposite tack, contending that the Charter foolishly empowered smaller nations and failed to appreciate the centrality of great power relationships and systems of "orbits" that better reflected reality. The negotiations also brought sharp disagreements with the Soviet Union into the open.

One of the goals of the U.S. delegation, led by Edward R. Stettinius Jr., was to prevent the seating of the so-called Lublin delegation, a grouping of mainly pro-communist Polish political leaders favored by Stalin. This caused considerable strain in the Moscow-Washington relationship. The Soviet delegation had also been greatly irritated by American and British efforts to seat Argentina—a nation openly sympathetic to Germany during the war and a home to Nazi war criminals thereafter—as a founding member of the United Nations. Lippmann was dismayed that both issues had combined to sour relations between the world's two greatest powers. Midway through negotiations, he wrote to James F. Byrnes—an influential foreign-policy adviser to Truman who was appointed secretary of state in July—to register his displeasure:

> I have been more disturbed about the conduct of our own policy than I have thought it expedient during a great conference of this sort to say in print . . . There is a far deeper conflict of interest between the British and the Soviets than between the U.S.A. and the Soviets, but we have allowed ourselves to be placed in a position where instead of being the moderating power which holds the balance, we have become the chief protagonists of the anti-Soviet position. This should never have happened. It would never have happened, I feel sure, if President Roosevelt were still alive, and it will lead to great trouble not only over such matters as the Polish question but throughout the Middle East if we do not recover our own sense of national interest about this fundamental relationship.[155]

In paying insufficient attention to the balance of power, the United States had behaved naïvely and irresponsibly. As Lippmann recalled, Moscow "had a good case on Argentina and we wouldn't listen to it."[156] But Argentina and Poland were of little material significance in the larger scheme of things—unlike the prospect of antagonizing Moscow.

The San Francisco Conference, then, was a distressing affair for Lippmann. He complained to John Maynard Keynes that the preparations were "amateurish and second rate" and that "I do wish we'd had the foresight to make some kind of security pact as underpinning between Britain, France, and North America."[157] The United Nations had been signed into existence, meaning the maintenance of world peace would once again rest upon an illusion. The United States had lost sight of what mattered most, clinging doggedly to idealist diplomacy born of self-delusion about the nation's purpose in the world. Great Britain did not make such cardinal errors during its century of dominance. Lord Palmerston phrased it best when he remarked, "We have no eternal allies and no permanent enemies. Our interests are eternal, and those interests it is our duty to follow."[158] The Truman administration appeared intent on making an eternal enemy to promote peripheral interests. As Lippmann wrote to a former colleague at the *New York Herald Tribune*: "There are no direct conflicts of vital interest as between the Soviet Union and the United States, and in fact none as between the United States and any other of the four big powers. This seems to me to indicate clearly our role as mediator—that is, intercessor, reconciler, within the circle of the big powers."[159] Yet Lippmann had strayed from the mainstream. This became abundantly clear when he attended an off-the-record briefing delivered by the U.S. ambassador to the Soviet Union, W. Averell Harriman. Convinced that nothing good would come from vesting faith in efforts to maintain the prewar alliance with Moscow, Harriman remarked baldly that "our objectives and the Kremlin's objectives are irreconcilable." Stunned by the irresponsibility of the message and the bluntness of the language, Lippmann rose from his seat and strode angrily from the room.[160]

Just as Lippmann became strongly opposed to the Truman administration's reckless actions, he received a surprising job offer from the State Department. Archibald MacLeish, a distinguished poet and librarian of Congress from 1939 to 1944, had resigned from his position as assistant secretary of state for public information. Secretary of State Byrnes identified in Lippmann the ideal successor to MacLeish. He was respected across the political aisle, was tremendously persuasive in print, and had written two important books on public opinion. Lippmann rebuffed the offer, questioning the logic of the role:

> The office itself is a new one, and it is founded, I believe, on the misconception—quite common these days—that public relations are a kind of advertising which can be farmed out to specialists in the art of managing public opinion. At the higher levels of government this is certainly an error: the conduct of public relations is inseparable from leadership, and no qualified public official needs the intervention of a public relations expert between himself and the people.[161]

One wonders if Lippmann was dodging the issue by questioning the necessity of the office rather than the policies of the administration. It is conceivable that Lippmann's reluctance to serve his nation was conditioned by an aversion to selling President Truman's foreign policy. Regardless, Lippmann continued to avoid government service, embracing his dual position as an insider-outsider throughout the remainder of his distinguished career. To his death in 1974, he remained insistent that America act responsibly in pursuit of achievable goals that were incontrovertibly in the national interest. The ideological crusade against the Soviet Union offended Lippmann's pragmatic instincts and provoked the writing of some magnificent and polemical journalism. As George Kennan observed in 1995, Lippmann was "a man who had carried journalism into something much greater than what the term generally describes, a fine writer with a brilliant mind and an impressive store of what I might call liberal erudition."[162] He would coin a term—"the Cold War"—to describe the bipolar hostility that would divide Europe, brutalize the developing world, and make thermonuclear war over Cuba conceivable in 1962. Lippmann's term defined the age, which in turn would shape the strategic thought of his successors.

5

THE ARTIST

GEORGE KENNAN

A month after Lippmann turned heel at the prospect of government service, a congressional delegation traveled to Moscow, in September 1945, to meet with Josef Stalin. When the State Department instructed the embassy's number two to prepare for their arrival, George Kennan's mood darkened. Fluent in Russian and German, a voracious reader of Chekhov and Tolstoy, conservative in diplomatic sensibility and modus operandi, Kennan doubted whether elected politicians could behave intelligently and responsibly overseas. For Kennan there was a clear demarcation of responsibility between politicians and civil servants. Professional diplomats with linguistic and historical skills should cultivate America's external relations. Members of Congress, meanwhile, should focus their limited attention spans on the domestic sphere. Politicians rarely acted in accordance with the national interest but in their district or state interest, with primary focus on boosting reelection prospects. Kennan agreed with Lippmann that democracies were poor at pursuing a measured long-term foreign policy. American political life was disturbingly provincial, meaning the diplomatic service, a selfless intellectual elite, carried a grave burden of responsibility. "Sometimes I've been charged with being an elitist," Kennan remarked. "Well, of *course* I am.

What do people expect? God forbid that we should be without an elite. Is everything to be done by gray mediocrity?"[1]

The day after the delegation's arrival, a meeting with Stalin was organized for 6:00 p.m., leaving the visitors a full day to explore the city. Their Muscovite hosts took them on a tour of the recently extended subway system—a remarkable feat of engineering and design—and plied them with a liquid of undisclosed provenance. At 5:30 Kennan, waiting anxiously near the exit of the Mossovyet station, received word that "the party was being entertained at 'tea' somewhere in the bowels of the subway system . . . To my horror, I discovered that the 'tea' served to them [contained] . . . varying amounts of vodka, depending on the stoutness of character and presence of mind of the individual concerned." Swaying as they approached their limousines, the vodka had shorn the congressmen of their inhibitions. As the convoy neared the Kremlin gates, one shouted, "Who the hell is this guy Stalin, anyway? I don't know that I want to go up and see him. I think I'll get out." As adrenaline coursed through his body, Kennan, a naturally reticent man, exclaimed, "You'll do nothing of the sort; you will sit right there where you are and remain with the party." Crisis averted, the cars continued their journey. Then the same drunken voice broke a tense silence: "What if I biff the old codger one in the nose?" In Kennan's recollection, "My heart froze. I cannot recall what I said, but I am sure that never in my life did I speak with greater earnestness." During a mercifully short meeting with Stalin, the congressional provocateur "did nothing more disturbing than to leer or wink once or twice at the bewildered dictator, thus making it possible for the invisible gun muzzles, with which the room was no doubt studded, to remain sullenly silent."[2] So went the trials of life in the diplomatic service.

The next day Kennan was charged with a similarly irksome task: serving as a translator for a bilateral meeting between Stalin and Senator Claude Pepper of Florida, a member of the Foreign Relations Committee. Nicknamed "Red Pepper" for his left-wing politics, the senator was a declared admirer of Stalin's economic achievements. In the friendliest of discussions, Kennan was compelled to translate Pepper's fawning questions and Stalin's happy replies. Pepper later wrote up his experience in an article for *The New York Times*, noting that "the generalissimo is a realist, notwithstanding the fact that he is engaged in the mightiest effort ever made in a single nation to raise the standard of living of some 200,000,000 people."[3] The experience was highly discouraging for Kennan. Unaware that each translated word had emerged through gritted teeth, Stalin complimented Kennan on his excellent Russian before returning to his chamber and the daily grind of foreign-policy brinkmanship and domestic repression.

At the end of the interview, Pepper asked Stalin whether he had a message for the American people. Stalin's reply was simple and apropos: "Just judge the Soviet Union objectively. Do not either praise us or scold us. Just know us and judge us as we are." This was a task that Kennan believed few Americans were capable of completing. The drunken belligerence of the first day and Pepper's obsequiousness on the second mirrored America's schizophrenia on how best to approach the Soviet Union. Walter Lippmann epitomized this strain of well-intentioned wishful thinking that viewed Stalin as a rational actor and the Soviet Union as an indispensable ally.

General George Patton, the colorful commander of the Seventh United States Army, conversely, personified the kind of reckless saber rattling that might facilitate a seamless transition to a third world war. In a discussion with Undersecretary of War Robert Patterson in May 1945, for example, Patton, entering his final months as general of the Third Army, complained that "we have had a victory over the Germans [but] we have failed in the liberation of Europe . . . We must either finish the job now—while we are here and ready—or later under less favorable circumstances."[4] Kennan recoiled from the two extremes, believing it vital to chart a middle course. Still, he believed that complacency was a bigger problem in Washington than pugnacity.

In January 1945, Kennan declared his intention to leave the Foreign Service in a letter to his friend and colleague Charles "Chip" Bohlen. Perplexed by the brouhaha generated by Churchill's percentages deal, Kennan wondered, "Why could we not make a decent and definite compromise with it—divide Europe frankly into spheres of influence—keep ourselves out of the Russian sphere and keep the Russians out of ours?" He bemoaned the fact that "we have refused to name any limit for Russian expansion and Russian responsibilities, thereby confusing the Russians and causing them constantly to wonder whether they are asking too little or whether it was some kind of trap." Kennan believed that the correct diplomatic course was clear enough. Washington should "bury Dumbarton Oaks as quickly and quietly as possible," as multilateral agreements involving an expansionist Moscow were simply untenable. America's political leadership should then "accept as an accomplished fact the complete partition of Germany along the line of the Russian zone of occupation . . . The west must be integrated into the Atlantic economy as independently as possible of the east." The Soviet and

Western spheres of influence in Europe were readily apparent to Kennan, as they should have been to anyone with clear vision. The United States had to recognize this division as fact and repulse any Soviet effort to foment discord beyond this by now established sphere. This defensive end should be achieved through deploying the most appropriate available means: political, economic, diplomatic or, as a last resort, military. "The above is admittedly not a very happy program," Kennan conceded. "It amounts to a partition of Europe. It renounces—and for very good reason—all reliance on cooperation with Russia. But beggars cannot be choosers. We have lost a large portion of our diplomatic assets in Europe."[5]

For Kennan, the main culprit was Woodrow Wilson's sirenical legacy, which had been reenergized during the Roosevelt presidency. Indeed, Wilsonianism threatened to do as much damage in 1945 as it had 1919—as Kennan explained to Bohlen:

> The program I have outlined is bitterly modest. But it has the virtue of resting on the solid foundation of reality. If we insist at this moment in our history on wandering about with our heads in the clouds of Wilsonian idealism and universalistic conceptions of world collaboration, if we continue to blind ourselves to the fact that momentary peaceful intentions of the mass of inhabitants of Asia and eastern Europe are only the products of their misery and weakness and never the products of their strength, if we insist on staking the whole future of Europe on the assumption of a community of aims with Russia for which there is no real evidence except in our own wishful thinking, then we run the risk of losing even that bare minimum of security which would be assured to us by the maintenance of humane, stable and cooperative forms of human society on the immediate European shore of the Atlantic.[6]

Resignation letters are often prescriptive; rarely are they so farsighted. The ideas presented in the letter, born of deep frustration at the author's marginality, mostly became policy over the next five years.

Kennan was so far ahead of the curve, however, that he was virtually out of sight. While Bohlen appealed successfully to Kennan's sense of duty in convincing him to remain in his post, his substantive response to his letter was broadly skeptical, observing that "foreign policy of [your] kind cannot be made in a democracy. Only totalitarian states can make and carry out such policies."[7] Still hopeful that the ends-focused wartime alliance with Stalin could survive the peace, Bohlen believed Kennan was temperamentally inclined to envision the worst-case scenario, discounting the possibility of collaboration with Moscow much too readily. When the worst case became unchallenged fact a year later, however, the force and logic of Kennan's counsel swept all before it. "We should gather together at once," he wrote, "all the cards we hold and begin to play them for their full value."[8] Through 1946 and 1947, Kennan would play a great hand devising "containment": America's central strategy toward a divided Europe until the collapse of the Soviet Union. But a different kind of geostrategic game materialized as the Cold War assumed larger dimensions, one that was scarred by zero-sum mentalities on both sides. And at that point Kennan would walk from the table.

The original Kennans were named McKennan and had arrived from Scotland or Northern Ireland in the late eighteenth century.[9] George Frost Kennan was born on February 16, 1904, in Milwaukee, Wisconsin. Tragically, his mother died of a burst appendix just two months later. According to his older sister, Jeanette, the absence of his natural mother instilled in George a deep melancholy. He was team raised by a collection of mostly indifferent substitutes: several aunts and a stepmother who conformed to the fairy-tale rendering. His father Kossuth "Kent" Kennan was a placid, laconic tax attorney, fifty-two years old when his wife died. His advanced age and solitary nature ensured that no significant bond developed between father and son. Through his early childhood, George was quiet, dreamy, and lonely in his pursuits. He retreated to the attic of the family home to devour books and contemplate the unhappy course of his life. An aunt once chastised him with a counterintuitive demand: "George, stop thinking."[10]

Kennan's preference for his own company hampered his socialization but it also made him a dedicated student. He attended the Fourth Street School in Milwaukee, where swift progress allowed him to skip eighth grade. He was next dispatched to St. John's Military Academy because Kent hoped the experience might compel his son to shed his retiring, poetic disposition in favor of something more masculine. The result was predictable: George was bullied relentlessly, which failed to bring him out of his shell. He just about survived the experience—although two escape attempts suggest it was a close-run thing—and applied to Princeton with an unconventional rationale. One of Kennan's favorite contemporary novels—for he generally preferred the greater historical and philosophical ambition of nineteenth-century Russian writers such as Tolstoy and Dostoevsky—was F. Scott Fitzgerald's *This Side of Paradise*. The book's main character is an ambitious young midwesterner, Amory Blaine, who abandons his provincial roots to attend Princeton, with naïve hopes of societal acceptance and wider success. Blaine was a thinly disguised Fitzgerald, and Kennan, in turn, was happy to become either. The full course of Blaine's journey—he ends the book penniless and exhausted, observing that "I know myself, but that is all"—appeared not to have given the young romantic pause.

Princeton proved to be a challenging adjustment for Kennan, just as it was for his literary models. Woodrow Wilson's reformist platform had not survived his departure—dining-club snobbery still reigned, and the intellectual environment remained unexacting for the brightest students. Only one academic truly commanded Kennan's attention, Professor Joseph Green, who taught that climate and geography had an unalterable impact on the formation of nations and peoples. This insight stayed with Kennan and would shape his skeptical views on the utility of sending foreign aid to poorer nations—and of the developing world's tangential connection to American security. Nations shed geopolitical significance, Kennan came to believe, the closer they were to the equator. Beyond that Kennan skipped lectures and read widely in history, philosophy, and literature, gaining much from Oswald Spengler's *The Decline of the West*, which identified through history an inexorable process through which civilizations rise and fall.[11] Spengler observed that the "West"—by which he meant Europe and North America—was approaching a civilizational "winter" and that something more ominous was primed to take its place. He instilled in Kennan's diplomatic thought a preference for the minor key. That Kennan read *Der Untergang des Abendlandes* in the original German testifies to an impressive linguistic talent; he learned the basics of the language of Goethe, for example, during a six-month family residence in Kassel, Germany, in 1912.[12]

Kennan's analytical abilities grew sharper at college, and his range of reading grew wider—although his development was only vaguely connected to the education provided by Princeton itself. Kennan later observed that "Princeton had prepared my mind for further growth. It had not stimulated in that mind any great latitude of curiosity." The institution's stifling social hierarchies did not exactly encourage the life of the mind. Kennan joined a dining club but resigned soon after as he found its showboating, pride in family connections, and witty sophistry crass. He was an elitist who believed instinctively in meritocracy. It was only when Kennan had become surer of his literary and diplomatic gifts that he accepted Princeton as an appropriate home for someone of his delicate sensibilities—he lived there, primarily, from 1950 until his death in 2004. Socially, Kennan recalled of his undergraduate years, "I was hopelessly and crudely Midwestern. I had no idea how to approach boys from the East. I could never find the casual tone. My behavior knew only two moods: awkward aloofness and bubbling enthusiasm."[13] Something had to give, because adjusting to the company of "boys from the East" was sine qua non for his preferred career.

Kennan read and admired Fitzgerald but disapproved of his flamboyant and feckless lifestyle. It typified the materialism that poisoned American life in the Roaring Twenties. Departing Princeton in 1925 for a career in investment banking, say, was unappealing to Kennan, who believed in such a thing as a "calling" and did not covet the accumulation of wealth. Status born of lucre bestowed no particular distinction, he believed. He felt no great attachment to home comforts, abhorred flag-waving patriotism, and wanted to develop his observational antennae through living in other countries. A diplomatic career was thus a logical option for an aspiring cosmopolitan, although securing even entry-level acceptance to the Foreign Service was notoriously difficult. It was as true a meritocracy as existed at that time—which was part of its appeal.

After Kennan excelled in his written examination, Undersecretary of State Joseph C. Grew presided over his oral interview: "I was . . . so petrified by the experience that in my first words . . . my voice broke into a falsetto on the second syllable of Wisconsin and set the board roaring with laughter."[14] Kennan overcame his early nerves and was accepted to the service along with just seventeen other exceptional prospects. After seven months intensive study at the Foreign Service School in Washington, D.C., he took his first job, as a temporary vice consul in Geneva, in the spring of 1927. Set on a distinguished service career, Kennan would observe Europe's descent into war and division from Prague in 1938, Berlin in 1939, Paris in 1940, and Moscow in 1944. Kennan was a bona fide intellectual, yet his most enduring ideas did not emerge simply from the vacuum of his study. They were mined from the darkest of coal faces.

After a short stint in Geneva, Kennan moved to Hamburg, which he adored. "Why is that while other cities become empty and boring, Hamburg always sings its multi-sonic, buzzing song in which all hope and all fear of humankind finds its expression?"[15] He moved to Germany's capital in 1929, where the State Department funded his Russian studies at the University of Berlin's *Seminar für Orientalische Sprachen*, an institution founded during the chancellorship of Otto von Bismarck to prepare diplomats for entry to the Foreign Service. Kennan spent two years in Berlin as an engaged and attentive foreign student, and was tutored primarily by Russian émigrés, all of whom were implacably hostile toward the Marxist experiment that had cast them into Teutonic exile. His tutors mourned the passing of the tsarist ancien régime, emphasized the virtues of benevolent authoritarianism, and castigated Marxism-Leninism for destroying the centuries-old values of a cultured and necessarily hierarchical Russia. So began a lifelong fascination with Russian history, culture, and society—and an enduring antipathy toward any form of collectivism. He had read some Marx at Princeton and found it unpersuasive. Hearing from cultured and elegant émigrés about the ideology's grotesque realization under Lenin and Stalin was an important moment in Kennan's career. As he later wrote, echoing Edmund Burke's critique of the French Revolution, "I was never able to accept or to condone the stony-hearted fanaticism that was prepared to condemn to the loss of all civil rights, to ignominy, persecution, and 'liquidation as a class' entire great bodies of people—the 'bourgeoisie' and large portions of the peasantry, the majority, in fact, of the Russian population—for no other reason than that their members had been born into certain stations in life."[16]

Ironically enough, Kennan's movement toward Burkean conservatism was spurred by reading Charles and Mary Beard's *The Rise of American Civilization* in Berlin in 1930. He was cheered to discover that the Founding Fathers were not the paragons of liberty portrayed by Jeffersonians and Jacksonians but were actively hostile to giving the people too much of a say. Kennan posed a provocative question: If Washington, Madison, and their cohort were hostile to democracy "for a population predominantly white, Protestant and British, faced with relatively simple problems, would they not turn over in their graves at the mere thought of the democratic principle being applied to a population containing over ten million Negroes, and many more millions of southern Europeans, to whom the democratic principle is completely strange and incomprehensible?"[17] This was not the reaction the Beards would have hoped for.

Through the 1930s Kennan continued to ponder the limitations of participatory democracy—particularly in regard to its dismal effect on foreign policymaking—and the nature and intentions of the Soviet Union. Stationed in Moscow from 1934, Kennan amused Ambassador William Bullitt by carrying on his person at all times a well-thumbed copy of Edward Gibbon's *The Decline and Fall of the Roman Empire*, from which he would read aloud when the situation demanded. When discussing the challenges confronting Stalin in holding together a vast Soviet Empire, for example, Kennan would quote Gibbon's observation that "there is nothing more contrary to nature than the attempt to hold in obedience distant provinces." He later rendered this wise injunction in his own words, applicable to all nations consumed by hubris: "No one people is great enough to establish a world hegemony."[18] For the historian Anders Stephanson, indeed, Gibbon "was perhaps the most important source of guidance in Kennan's life." Gibbon's view that "under a democratical government the citizens exercise the powers of sovereignty; and those powers will be first abused, and afterwards lost, if they are committed to an unwieldy multitude" lay at "the heart of my political philosophy," as Kennan recalled.[19] *The Decline and Fall of the Roman Empire* contained enough cautionary tales to last a diplomatic lifetime.

Kennan kept a diary from the beginning of his diplomatic career to the end of his life, gifting a significant resource to scholars when it was finally processed and opened in 2009. The diary is replete with prescient geopolitical analysis, unsentimental reflections on the human frailties that lead to conflict, and some bitter denunciations of modernity, mass media, and multiculturalism. Some days Kennan's entries ran to multiple pages; for weeks he wrote nothing at all. Some days he wrote poetry that was conventional in form; at other points he painted cityscapes that were almost Joycean in their free-form lyricism. In 1935, for example, Kennan recorded the following observations:

> Back in Moscow—and extremely unhappy. Boulevards on summer nights. In it and not of. The stark reality of Soviet life compared to the neurotic unreality of our own. The almost theatrical vividness and directness of all things human. Here human flesh lives in one seething intimate mass—far more so, even than in New York. It streams slowly, guilelessly, in thick, full currents, along the boulevards, between the dark trees, under the gleam of the street lights; it is carried—as herded, tired animals are carried, in box-cars—in the long trains of street-cars. And it is human life in the raw, humanity brought down to its fundamentals—good and evil, drunk and sober, loving and quarrelling, laughing and weeping—all that human life is and does anywhere—but all much more simple and direct, and therefore stronger.[20]

These are the observational skills of a novelist. Much of Kennan's intellectual identity became vested in the quality of his writing, for it gave him his greatest sustenance. A year later in Moscow, for example, Kennan composed another neo-Burkean view—finished with an Orwellian flourish—on the Russia the revolution had created:

Has not the Russian experiment proven—if it has proven anything—
that the proletariat, once given power, does not necessarily exercise it
with any particular altruism or intelligence by virtue of its own economic chastity, but readily hands it over to the most ruthless and determined political element, which in turn, as a consequence of its ruling
position, only inherits the fears and interests of former regimes and ex-
ploits the people, under appeals to their patriotism, for the maintenance
of its own foreign and domestic position.[21]

This is a marvelous description of Marxism-Leninism in practice. Kennan had the skills to offer the most penetrating and elegant insights on the
phenomena he observed. In Germany and Russia, his fluency in those languages allowed him to assimilate and read these societies from a perspective
that most foreigners were incapable of assuming. His close and vast reading
of history enabled him to draw linkages across eras and empires that a novelist might miss. Yet his written English was also magnificent. This combination of attributes ensured that Kennan was promoted faster than any of
his colleagues in the Foreign Service.

In September 1938, on the same day as Chamberlain and Daladier
served up the Sudetenland to Hitler, Kennan arrived in Prague. He was
sanguine about the appeasement that took place in Munich, reasoning
that the nations of Central and Eastern Europe—the feeble progeny of
Versailles—were easy prey for predators. He blamed their plight on Wilson,
who facilitated the dissolution of the Habsburg Empire in the spurious
name of "self-determination," raising hopes of a meaningful future for its
constituent members. Doubtful of the viability of small states like Czechoslovakia, Kennan nonetheless sympathized with its people and viewed Nazism
as an abomination. Ultimately, however, he believed that Czechoslovakia's
incorporation into a larger German or Russian-ruled empire was in the natural order of things. His conservative views were challenged five days into
his job when a striking midwestern woman entered his office and berated
him for doing nothing to protect a helpless nation. Her name was Martha
Gellhorn, and it was fortunate for Kennan that she was not accompanied by
her combustible lover, Ernest Hemingway. Gellhorn subsequently became
one of the world's most celebrated war correspondents: brave, dedicated,
and insightful. Kennan found her passion admirable in a way, but he ultimately dismissed her as an idealist with a shallow understanding of history.[22] He was similarly unimpressed by a young man named John F.
Kennedy, whose father—the U.S. ambassador to the United Kingdom—had

sent him on a "fact-finding" mission to Czechoslovakia. According to Kennan, Kennedy was "obviously an upstart and an ignoramus," and he resented having to waste time attending to his needs. But with the "polite but weary punctiliousness that characterizes diplomatic officials required to busy themselves with pesky compatriots," Kennan secured Kennedy safe passage through German lines to Prague and then back to London.[23]

It was around this time that Kennan entertained a flirtation with authoritarianism. Through his reading of history, and firsthand experience, the nations and eras for which Kennan had developed firmest appreciation included Victorian Britain and Bismarckian Germany. The innocent virtues of the New World did not stand comparison to the best of the Old; Kennan found little in the American tradition of diplomacy that was worth retaining. Alexander Hamilton was a rare voice of geopolitical reason in the early republic, but few American diplomatists since then struck Kennan as particularly convincing. A painful return visit to the United States in 1936 had convinced him that his home had become a materialistic, self-satisfied, and philistine nation. A refrain throughout Kennan's written work is a lament that America should abstain from instructing others on the paths to progress and liberty until it creates a society of substantive, enduring value.

After departing the United States in a sorrowful state, Kennan had taken a diplomatic posting in Austria, where he had been impressed by the reactionary regime led by Kurt von Schuschnigg. In a manuscript titled "The Prerequisites: Notes on Problems of the United States in 1938," Kennan lauded Schuschnigg's success in implementing a comprehensive law unifying medical and financial procedures drafted entirely by "experts," a process from which the Austrian parliament had been excluded. Kennan thought that America would do well to learn from this success, its fidelity to democracy and transparency was hurting the consistency of its foreign policy and its ability to deal with acute social problems. Kennan's belief in the efficacy of government by experts, his abhorrence of the messy business of democracy and interest-group activity—particularly those ethnic lobbies that can so distort foreign-policy priorities—is presented with particular force in "The Prerequisites" and in his diary, echoing Lippmann's *The Phantom Public*. It was fortunate for Kennan that he failed to find a publisher for his manuscript. It was a fair indication of the reactionary turn of his thinking in the late 1930s and would almost certainly have ended a promising diplomatic career.

Kennan often took his disaffection with American society to remarkable extremes. On March 21, 1940, for example, as Nazi Germany subjugated and terrorized the European continent, Kennan composed a diary entry comparing European civilization favorably to American primitivism:

> When they [America's forefathers] turned their backs on Europe, they closed their eyes to the lessons of that continent's past; and their backwoodsmen wisdom was not adequate to the building of anything but the most primitive social scene. It is now too late to remedy the situation. The United States is, for better or for worse, a Latin American rather than a European state. Those of us who were given an old-fashioned bringing-up will scarcely ever adapt ourselves to the situation. The best we can do is to try and adapt our children to it.[24]

That these remarks coincided with Europe's historical nadir testifies to Kennan's powerful alienation from American societal and cultural mores.

Yet while Kennan was disappointed by American societal development, he found Nazism repugnant. He blamed the rise of Hitler on Germany's ignorant and clawing middle classes, newly empowered by the post-Versailles dissolution of the Junker elite. Even after Hitler's death, Kennan believed that the restoration of monarchy, "limited by an efficient bureaucracy and a powerful upper class," represented Germany's best hope for postbellum stability.[25] While Kennan's pseudo-aristocratic prejudices were unappealing, he was also sharp in identifying Nazism's weaknesses. After being transferred from Prague to Berlin in 1939, Kennan visited the nations that had recently fallen under the Nazi yoke. In Poland, Denmark, Holland, Norway, Belgium, and France, he found Nazi rule to be brutal and self-defeating in its disrespect of each nation's proud history and identity. Here was an empire of shallow foundation that surely was not built to last. For Kennan it was obvious that "the Nazi ideology, based on nothing other than a glorification of the supposed virtues of the German people themselves, had no conceivable appeal to people, and especially young people, outside Germany itself."[26] In Finland on March 13, 1940, Kennan recorded that it was "a black day . . . it was hard to think that another place where life was decent and healthy and cheerful had succumbed to the darkness and misery brought over the world by small-souled and ruthless men who control the engines of destruction."[27] In similarly evocative prose, Kennan described Paris after Hitler's triumphant, goading arrival:

> Could one not say to the Germans that the spirit of Paris had been too delicate and shy a thing to stand their determination and had melted

away before them just as they thought to have it in their grasp? Was there not some Greek myth about the man who tried to ravish the goddess, only to have her turn to stone when he touched her? That is literally what has happened to Paris. When the Germans came, the soul simply went out of it; and what is left is only stone . . . The Germans had in their embrace the pallid corpse of Paris.[28]

In Kennan's estimation, Stalinism was as baleful a force as Nazism. After the German invasion of the Soviet Union, he argued strongly against embracing Stalin as a future wartime ally. On June 24, 1940, Kennan wrote to Loy Henderson, head of the State Department's Bureau of Eastern European Affairs:

> It seems to me that to welcome Russia as an associate in the defense of democracy would invite misunderstanding of our position and would lend to the German war effort a gratuitous and sorely needed aura of morality. In following such a course I do not see how we could help but identify ourselves with the Russian destruction of the Baltic states, with the attack against Finnish independence, with the partitioning of Poland and Rumania, with the crushing of religion throughout Eastern Europe, and with the domestic policy of a regime which is widely feared and detested throughout this part of the world and the methods of which are far from democratic.

Reflecting on this letter in his memoirs, Kennan recalled that his reaction "embodied the essence of the disagreement that was to hold me in opposition to our governmental policy for some five years to come . . ."[29] He believed quite simply that the Soviet Union was unworthy of American support at any cost. Although primarily a realist in his diplomatic thought, Kennan was intermittently driven by strong considerations of morality, which often trumped notions of narrow self-interest. The logic of the adage "The enemy of my enemy is my friend" did not hold true when applied to a leader as heinous as Stalin.

Kennan remained at the heart of Hitler's empire through 1941, writing to his Norwegian wife, Annelise, that "life in Berlin has been much as you knew it. The major change has been the wearing of the star by the Jews. That is a fantastically barbaric thing. I shall never forget the faces of people in the subway with the great yellow star sewed onto their overcoats, standing, not daring to sit down or to brush against anybody, staring straight ahead of them with eyes like terrified beasts—nor the sight of little children running around with those badges sewn on them."[30] Berlin was becoming almost unbearable for Kennan, particularly as it was the capital of a nation whose history and achievements he greatly admired. After Germany declared war on the United States in the aftermath of Pearl Harbor, Kennan and his embassy staff were arrested and sent to an internment camp in Bad Nauheim, a fashionable spa town near Frankfurt. The retiring Kennan now found himself in charge of some 130 men, women, and children of the U.S. embassy, a fatherly role in which he did not thrive. To make things worse, the government stopped paying Kennan and his staff during the six months of their confinement. "We had not, you see, been working," recalled Kennan drolly.[31]

Kennan returned to the United States in a diplomatic swap in the early summer of 1942. One of the first things he read upon returning home was an article by Walter Lippmann, published on June 6, 1942, which opined that "if there is to be peace in the world, that peace has to be made in full partnership between the English-speaking sea and air powers and the massive land power of Russia." It struck Kennan that America's intelligentsia remained as delusional about Stalin as it had been ten years previously, when Walter Duranty of *The New York Times* reported gushingly on Stalin's grand success in lifting a nation out of agricultural poverty and propelling it toward the panacea of large-scale industrialization.[32] A few (hundred thousand? million?) missing kulaks, Duranty rationalized, constituted a bearable cost when placed against some remarkable strides in pig iron production. Such was the warped logic of the Grand Alliance, in Kennan's view. Defeating Germany at the cost of the independence of Eastern and Central Europe—and America's reputation as a decent nation—was not a price worth paying. Not for the first or last time, despondency descended.

Kennan's next move was to Lisbon, where he served as ambassador. Throughout the course of 1943, he began to consider the most appropriate way to defeat and rehabilitate Germany. Kennan disliked the "unconditional surrender" formula that President Roosevelt had crafted during the Casablanca conference in January 1943, testily observing that this was "only another way of saying that the war had to be fought until the Allied and Russian armies met *somewhere*."[33] American and Soviet troops might meet in bonhomie, but it was unlikely to end well, for advancing armies, flushed with victory, tend to abandon their reverse gear. Land captured at a steep blood cost is a painful thing to relinquish. On Germany itself, Kennan was mindful of the lessons of Versailles. Before the aggressor had even been defeated, he was sensitive to the need for its swift rehabilitation:

> Let the impact of defeat, therefore, be as tremendous as possible. Let the immediate impressions of failure be so vivid and unforgettable that they become a part of the national consciousness of the German people for all time. But having done this, let us then abandon the concept of punishment in the treatment of Germany—for prolonged punishment can never be effective against an entire people.[34]

Strongly opposed to a rigorous policy of denazification, Kennan viewed a robust and viable West Germany as an essential bulwark against Soviet expansionism. Like it or not, members of the Nazi party were so large in number that their removal from public life would hamper the nation's prospects for recovery. Devoid of wartime camaraderie—Churchill, Stalin, and Roosevelt went to great pains to bond with each other, bringing their publics with them—Kennan was thinking coldly in the longer term, prioritizing stability ahead of justice.

From Lisbon, Kennan was posted to London for a brief stint in January 1944 and then on to Moscow in the spring, where he was appointed minister-counselor, second in rank to Ambassador W. Averell Harriman. Placed close to the heart of a regime he reviled, Kennan would never have a better opportunity to persuade his superiors to abandon the pipe dream of collaboration with a man such as Stalin and accommodation with an ideology as insidious as Marxism-Leninism. It was from the embassy in Moscow that Kennan drafted the telegram that would transform his career and, with it, world affairs.

When Kennan arrived in Moscow in May 1944, the essentials of his foreign-policy philosophy had mostly been established. The process of their cohering was fascinating and iconoclastic. A compulsive writer, Kennan kept a conventional diary, composed poetry, started an ambitious biography of Anton Chekhov in the 1930s that he never completed, and at one stage recorded a remarkable "dream diary" in which he detailed and unpicked the scenarios that had intruded on the preceding night's sleep. Kennan had read Sigmund Freud attentively while recuperating from illness in Vienna in 1938. But he also followed the great thinkers of the Scottish Enlightenment in lavishing attention on his "inner life."[35]

Regarding external stimuli, Kennan was generalist in the mode of the Founders, reading widely in history, literature, philosophy, and certain of the natural sciences that pertained to land economy. Like Woodrow Wilson, he abhorred the narrow specialization of scholarship that had become de rigueur in the modern American research university. An elegant accessibility was his hallmark as a writer, and he wrote for the general reader throughout his career inside and outside government. In that respect he followed Lippmann in vesting little faith in the discipline of political science—and its subfield international relations—which encouraged in its faithful pupils a futile and damaging tendency to view the causes of war and peace as a puzzle waiting to be solved with the right formula.

From such misguided premises come rigid and utopian visions. Wilson was right to reject narrow scholarship during his academic career, but he pursued a fatally singular vision as president, which suggested to Kennan that he had failed to read widely and attentively in a variety of sources. (This was in fact an accurate characterization, connected to Wilson's efforts to overcome dyslexia.) Makers of foreign policy should avoid offering one answer to an infinite variety of conundrums—no matter how consistent and laudable that answer appeared. The ideal diplomat should read Spengler and Gibbon, to be sure, but also Plato, Plutarch, Shakespeare, Dickens, the great Russian novelists, and the Bible. From this variegated feast should emerge skepticism and a desire for pure experience, leading ultimately to the accumulation of an old-fashioned attribute: wisdom. "For people who think as I do, the judgment and instinct of a single wise and experienced man," Kennan wrote to a social science–inclined correspondent in 1950, "whose knowledge of the world rests on the experience of personal, emotional, and intellectual participation in a wide cross-section of human effort are something we hold to be more valuable than the most elaborate synthetic structure of demonstrable fact and logical deduction." Putting it even more bluntly in "great man" terms, Kennan wrote, "The perception of the most competent individual intelligence is thus our absolute ceiling in the development of ideas related to foreign policy."[36] The United States should forget about modish theories and educate the cleverest freethinkers to the best of the nation's ability. It was these men—Kennan did not entertain the possibility that women might have something meaningful to contribute to the making of diplomacy—who would rise meritoriously and infuse America's external relations with modesty, civility, and farsightedness, redounding always to the nation's advantage.

"I have always been regarded by the United States establishment as an odd-ball," recalled Kennan in an interview with *Encounter* in 1976, "and I *am* a strange mixture of a reactionary and a liberal. In this philosophical sense, I do consider myself a lonely person." There were many sources of his disillusionment, but the overarching cause can be condensed into one word: modernity. Rather than viewing the Industrial Revolution as an unalloyed blessing for nations seeking to outrun the Malthusian trap of population outstripping food supplies—leading to famine and brutal demographic realignment—Kennan was impressed by Charles Beard's damning portrayal of the endemic dehumanization of the modern age. "I am persuaded that the Industrial Revolution itself was the source of most of the bewilderments and failures of the modern age," Kennan observed.[37] Industrialization facilitated the growth and sustenance of a larger population. This larger population necessarily congregated in cities where jobs were plentiful; these jobs in turn were largely demeaning and purposeless, producing fripperies that previous generations had largely lived without, fomenting the alienation of labor that Marx and Engels identified and their political champions exploited.

A small population scraping a living through tilling the land was preferable to a large urban population engaged in labor that created substantially more wealth but robbed people of the essentials of how to live. The single-minded pursuit of "economic growth" was a risible imperative that by now afflicted all nations. Kennan was a keen farmer who followed Jefferson in believing a close connection to the soil was vital for anyone seeking purpose and emotional stability in the modern world: "I don't trust human beings to live successfully too far away from nature." With pride and regret, he conceded to his interviewer that "I am, I suppose, an 18th-century person, and I'm persuaded that those of our forefathers who had their roots really back in the 18th century had more convincing values and better tastes than those whose roots were in the society that issued from the industrial revolution."[38] He followed the sociologist Thorstein Veblen in deploring the "conspicuous consumption" that blighted the nation.[39] Accompanying this was profound regret at the environmental and societal degradation caused by the proliferation of the automobile and the ugly urban sprawl that was erected to facilitate the demographic shift to the suburbs.

From this variety of fascinating sources came a manner of diplomatic thinking that combined important elements of Mahan, Beard, and Lippmann; Wilsonianism would always remain an ideational adversary of regrettable resilience. Kennan shared with Mahan a sense of proportion and balance, agreement on the vital importance of the Atlantic Alliance, a deep ethnocentrism, and opposition to arbitration and multilateral institutions. Kennan was at one with Beard in believing that the United States should attend to its own problems before attempting to export its values. He also shared with the revisionist historian a strong belief that there were actually few foreign-policy crises that required a direct military response. The historian Bruce Kuklick puts it well when he detects in Kennan a "quietist if not pacifist dimension."[40] Later in his life, Kennan would go so far as to describe himself "with some qualifications" as an "isolationist."[41]

Finally, Kennan followed Lippmann in bemoaning the dangers that participatory democracy posed to the making of a wise foreign policy. He viewed public opinion as a grave impediment to elected politicians and professional diplomats doing their jobs effectively. Like Lippmann, Kennan also viewed himself as operating in the realist tradition and shared a common contempt for the fledgling United Nations. On August 4, 1944, Kennan had written, "International political life is something organic, not something mechanical. Its essence is change . . . An international organization for preservation of the peace and security cannot take the place of a well-conceived and realistic foreign policy."[42] These words could have been Lippmann's. Yet there was, at the time, a major difference of opinion between the two men on what constituted a "realistic foreign policy." Put simply, Lippmann favored an accommodation with Moscow whereas Kennan preferred nonmilitary confrontation. The latter strongly believed that the success of the D-day landings had created a propitious moment for the United States to issue a stern warning to Stalin to respect majority opinion in Eastern and Central Europe:

> We no longer owed them anything, after all (if indeed we ever had). The second front had been established. The Western Allies were now on the European continent in force. Soviet territory had been entirely liberated. What was now at stake in Soviet military operations was exclusively the future of non-Soviet territory previously overrun by the Germans. We in the West had a perfect right to divest ourselves of responsibility for further Soviet military operations conducted in the spirit of, and with the implications of, the Soviet denial of support for the Warsaw uprising.[43]

This was no simplistic anticommunism. Kennan believed the Kremlin's expansionist designs were driven not by Marxian ideology but by traditional concerns about security and vulnerability. But this did not make Moscow's goals any more palatable or acceptable to the West. He had met with the exiled Polish prime minister Stanisław Mikołajczyk at the British embassy in Moscow in July 1944. Detecting hopeful naïveté on the part of Mikołajczyk, and cynical bonhomie on the part of his British hosts and American guests, for Kennan the dinner and reception were excruciating. "I found the evening a hard one," he recorded in his diary. "I wished that instead of mumbling words of official optimism we had the judgment and the good taste to bow our heads in silence before the tragedy of a people who have been our allies, whom we have saved from our enemies, and whom we cannot save from our friends."[44] Kennan could not abide lies among friends. If America and Britain were to force the issue over Polish independence, so be it, although it needed to happen quickly to make any difference. Encouraging false hope was dishonorable.

False hope it was, as Kennan believed Yalta's obfuscations amply displayed. Where Lippmann celebrated President Roosevelt's clear-sighted delineation of the national interest in the Crimea, Kennan detected unworthy and deliberate ambiguity over the fate of Eastern Europe: "The Yalta declaration, with its references to the reorganization of the existing Polish-Communist regime 'on a broader democratic basis' and to the holding 'of free and unfettered elections . . . on the basis of universal suffrage and secret ballot,' struck me as the shabbiest sort of equivocation, certainly not calculated to pull the wool over the eyes of the Western public but bound to have this effect."[45]

Kennan had made repeated attempts to warn Averell Harriman, his superior at the embassy, of the nature of Moscow's intentions and the need for a swift and forceful diplomatic response, but each had been met with indifference. A scion of the railroad dynasty, Harriman was a multimillionaire who consciously rejected ostentation and pomp. Tall and conventionally handsome, a naturally commanding presence, Harriman was worldly born, whereas Kennan had discovered the world, such as it was, with no natural advantages. These were two men of very different backgrounds and sensibilities. No reclusive poet, or Freudian dissector of dreams, Harriman's worldview was closely aligned with that of his similarly wellborn president, Franklin Roosevelt, cognizant as he was of the larger gentlemanly stakes involved in defeating Hitler. Hence Harriman did not yet view Stalin as beyond the pale. That his perspective would change throughout the course of 1945 owed much to Kennan's persistence in dispatching one skillfully crafted entreaty after another, until the message finally conformed to events in the eyes of the besieged recipient.

The first of Kennan's persuasive broadsides was launched on September 1944, a long paper titled "Russia—Seven Years Later," which offered a searing critique of both Soviet intentions and the complacency that undergirded America's effective nonresponse. Kennan wrote that "we should realize clearly what we are faced with . . . the Soviet government has never ceased to think in terms of spheres of interest." Kennan offered up a solution:

> Instead of going as supplicants to the Russians, we should go to them as one bringing a friendly warning. Our position should be as follows: We would regret to have to make it plain to our public that Russia alone, of all the great powers, was unwilling to submit her future actions to the judgment of international society. We would regret this because it would only fortify and widen in our public opinion those very suspicions of Russia which we ourselves have been helping to eliminate.[46]

An impassive Harriman did not reply to his exercised subordinate, although he cabled sections of Kennan's paper to Washington, where they were met with a similarly deafening silence. It was a discouraging snub that led to Kennan's abortive attempt to leave the service in 1945. But he never held these slights personally against Harriman, whom he respected in spite of their differences. "I often think," Kennan recalled with winning self-deprecation, "what a trial I must have been to him, running around with my head in the usual clouds of philosophic speculation, full of interests other than my work, inclined to delegate responsibility and to forget about it cheerfully so long as all went well, bombarding him with bundles of purple prose on matters which, as I am sure he thought, it was the business of the president to think about, not mine—and all this when there was detailed, immediate work to be done. Small wonder that he was often peremptory."[47]

In his memoirs, Kennan recorded a vivid account of Moscow's celebrations following the declaration of victory in Europe. News traveled slowly to Russia, so it was not until May 10—two days after VE-day—that crowds began to congregate on the streets. Tens of thousands of Muscovites gathered in a "commodious" square outside the U.S. embassy to express appreciation for their wartime ally. "We were naturally moved and pleased by this manifestation of public feeling," Kennan recalled, "but were at a loss to know how to respond to it. If any of us ventured out into the street, he was immediately seized, tossed enthusiastically into the air, and passed on friendly hands over the heads of the crowd, to be lost, eventually, in a confused orgy of good feeling somewhere on its outer fringes." As Kennan was unwilling to "court this experience," he and his staff assembled on the balcony and waved in a friendly fashion to the delirious masses below. But to get into the spirit of things, he arranged for the Hammer and Sickle to be hung alongside the Stars and Stripes. As the crowds cheered for more, Kennan delivered a short speech in Russian, which consisted in his shouting, "Congratulations on the day of victory. All honor to the Soviet allies!" He recalled that this "seemed to me to be about all I could suitably say." The crowd grew larger with each passing hour, stirring disquiet among the Soviet authorities. The United States was a valued wartime ally, to be sure, but it also represented capitalism in its most unvarnished form: a vile, exploitative ideology anathema to all good Soviet citizens. The crowds, the cheers, the touchingly instinctive and unmediated affection—all were a slap in the face for Soviet propagandists. As Kennan recalled, "It is not hard to imagine what mortification this must have brought to both party and police. Without their solicitous prearrangement not even a sparrow had fallen in a Moscow street for twenty-seven years, and now, suddenly—this!" Efforts to break up the celebrations were to no avail. The authorities even set up a brass band on the other end of the square, hoping to create a Pied Piper effect. But the crowds stayed put, instilling in Kennan an ephemeral cheer.[48]

Near the end of the day, Kennan received a phone call from Ralph Parker, a former *New York Times* journalist who had married a Russian, settled in Moscow, and was known to him as being politically "far to the left." The two men nonetheless enjoyed semicordial relations, and Kennan readily consented to Parker's request that he visit the embassy to enjoy the balcony view of the square's cheering occupants. As Parker gazed at the remarkable scene, he observed to Kennan, "Isn't this wonderful?" Kennan agreed that in a way it was, but that the scene also made him sad. "Asked to explain," Kennan recalled, "I observed that these people out there in the crowd had been through so much, and they naturally now hoped for so much from victory; yet the world was still full of troubles; Russia faced major problems of reconstruction; things would not be put back together again all at once; peace could scarcely be what these people dreamed of it as being." Parker identified something more sinister. Four years later a book was published in Russia under Parker's name titled *Zagovor protiv Mira* (Conspiracy Against Peace). Parker recounted his evening trip to the embassy in starkly different terms from Kennan: "I noticed on Kennan's face, as we watched this moving scene, a strangely unhappy and irritated expression. Then, casting a last glance at the crowd, he moved away from the window and said bitterly: 'They

rejoice . . . They think the war has ended. But it is really only beginning.'"
An angered Kennan later described the book as "the most unscrupulous,
mendacious, and nauseating sort of Stalinist propaganda."[49]

Parker's retelling was a fabrication, although it captured something of
his interlocutor's unspoken thoughts. Kennan did favor a confrontation with
Moscow, just so long as it wasn't a military one. Throughout 1945, as Truman
strained to master the presidency following FDR's sudden death, Kennan
continued to craft strong critiques of the complacent tenor of U.S. policy
toward Moscow, all with little appreciation, or indeed acknowledgment, of
his efforts. In the early months of his presidency, Truman had not impressed
Kennan. The president was a machine politician from Missouri, partial to
guttural language, who poked fun at what he described as the "striped pants
brigade" at the State Department. He appeared only dimly aware of the
world beyond America's shores. This was assuredly not a combination of
traits to instill much confidence in an elitist professional diplomat and
cosmopolitan. Clark Clifford recounted of Truman that he had a "black-and-
white" view of world affairs, "and, by God, he was going to see to it that the
men in the white hats prevailed."[50] This Wilsonian echo was worrying, as
was the appearance of parochialism and obtuseness. But there was more to
Truman than met the eye. Surveying biblical scenes of destruction in Berlin
on July 16, 1945, Truman recorded in his diary that "I thought of Carthage,
Baalbeck, Jerusalem, Rome, Atlantis, Peking, Babylon, Nineveh; Scipio,
Rameses II, Titus, Hermann [Arminius], Sherman, Jenghis Khan, Alexander, Darius the Great."[51] Truman was clearly a devoted reader of history.[52]

Soon after assuming the presidency, Truman confided to his wife that
"I like Stalin. He is straightforward. Knows what he wants and will compromise when he can't get it."[53] At the Potsdam Conference of July 16 to August 2,
however, President Truman proved himself to be less sympathetic than
his predecessor to Stalin's "defensive" perspective on Eastern Europe's
"independence"—asking some hard questions of the Soviet Union's ultimate designs. At the beginning of the conference, the Red Army wielded
effective control over Poland, Czechoslovakia, Hungary, Bulgaria, Romania, and the Baltic states. Soviet troops were also positioned in northern
Iran, and Stalin had indicated to Churchill at Yalta that he had no intention
of withdrawing them.[54] Having missed the ideal opportunity to confront
Stalin twelve months before, Kennan believed that President Truman should
abandon hope of influencing events in Eastern Europe and engage with
Stalin on the more honest level of "spheres of influence," just as Churchill
had proposed to a mindless chorus of American disapproval.

Fighting a losing battle over Eastern Europe was merely a distraction, albeit one that wasted valuable time. It was Truman's naïve views on collaboration with Moscow over Germany's future that Kennan believed were truly detached from reality—posing serious risks to a situation that was unfolding, not one that had unfolded. A communiqué summarizing the agreement made at Potsdam was regrettably peppered, as Kennan described it, with "such words as 'democratic,' 'peaceful,' and 'justice' [which] went directly counter to everything I had learned, in seventeen years of experience with Russian affairs, about the technique of dealing with the Soviet government." The notion that Germany would be jointly run through a quadripartite control mechanism—with the United States, Britain, France, and the Soviet Union each controlling stakes of variable size—was folly. As early as May 1945, Kennan believed that the Western powers had no choice but to combine their areas of control to form a legitimate, noncommunist "West German" state. In dispensing futile protests about the sanctity of Eastern Europe, mainly to placate a domestic audience, and entertaining the illusory possibility of collaboration with Stalin over Germany, the Truman administration was "in danger of losing, like the dog standing over the reflecting pool, the bone in our mouth without obtaining the one we saw in the water."[55]

Potsdam was eventful for other reasons. On July 16, the opening day of the conference, a military test, supposedly shrouded in secrecy, took place near Alamogordo, a small town in New Mexico's vast desert, that had vast repercussions for the conference—and indeed for the world. As J. Robert Oppenheimer, the head of the Manhattan Project, looked on nervously from a bunker some seventeen miles away, an implosion-type plutonium device was detonated for the very first time. Informal bets were taken among researchers and observers on a range of possibilities: Would the device actually detonate? Would it conform to its projected maximum explosive yield of twenty kilotons? Would it destroy Alamogordo, the state of New Mexico, or indeed the face of the planet? The answer arrived when a searing flash illuminated the lunar landscape and a vast fireball was thrown high into the sky, eventually darkening to form a sullen, gray, mushroom-shaped cloud eight miles high. (Its yield was eighteen kilotons, and the earth, beyond a one-thousand-foot crater, fortunately retained its crust.) The roar of the shock wave took forty seconds to hit Oppenheimer and his fellow creators; its reverberations were felt two hundred miles away. Surveying a surreal scene, the director of the test, the Harvard-based professor of physics Kenneth Bainbridge, turned to Oppenheimer and remarked, "Now we are all sons of bitches." Oppenheimer shunned the profane, remembering a line from the Bhagavad Gita that followed Vishnu as he assumed a multiarmed form in order to impress a prince. Vishnu exclaims, "Now I am become death, the destroyer of worlds."[56]

At Potsdam, on July 24, 1945, President Truman informed Stalin in deliberately anodyne terms that the United States was now in possession of "a new weapon of unusual destructive force." In his memoir, Truman recalled that "the Russian Premier showed no special interest. All he said was he was glad to hear it and hoped we would make 'good use of it against the Japanese.'"[57] Observing the same scene, Soviet marshal Georgii Zhukov realized that Stalin's apparent lack of interest belied a detailed understanding of the significance of Truman's message. Following Truman's announcement, Zhukov joined Stalin for a private meeting with Molotov, where Stalin briefed his foreign minister on the substance of the brief exchange. "Let them," said Molotov impassively. "We'll have to talk it over with Kurchatov and get him to speed things up." Igor Kurchatov was head of the Soviet A-bomb project, so it was immediately obvious to Zhukov that his superiors were discussing the detonation of the world's first atomic bomb, and they weren't at all flustered.[58] This was because Soviet spies, such as the German-born British citizen Klaus Fuchs, had penetrated the Manhattan Project. They had kept their paymasters fully apprised of developments, who in turn had fed blueprints and formulas to Soviet atomic scientists. Truman need not have bothered informing Stalin about the A-bomb.

On August 6 and 9, 1945, the world's second and third atomic bombs were dropped on two Japanese cities. In Hiroshima, an area of approximately five square miles was incinerated in a flash—80,000 people were killed instantly. The bomb dropped on Nagasaki killed approximately 40,000 people within seconds of detonation. In the months and years that followed, as Japanese citizens who were in and around the blast zone died from burns and radiation sickness, the combined death toll rose to approximately 225,000.[59] Walter Lippmann was disgusted that Truman made the decision to drop the bombs, observing that "one of the things I look back on with the greatest regret, as an American, is that we were the ones that first dropped atomic bombs."[60] Kennan said little of this new weapon at the time, recording nothing in his memoir on his reaction to Truman's decision. As the months and years passed, however, it became clear that Kennan viewed the existence of nuclear weapons as an affront to the notion of civilization. In creating the bomb, Oppenheimer and his colleagues had made "a philosophical mistake," as Kennan described it, and interestingly this was an assessment with which Oppenheimer came to agree.[61] "Even the tactical atomic weapon," Kennan wrote in later years, as lower-yield variations on the device were tested, "is destructive to a degree that sickens the imagination."[62] A pure morality had entered Kennan's calculus once again, conditioning his views on a weapon that made the job of the diplomatist vital in the existential sense.

While Kennan was troubled by Truman's decision to use the atomic bomb, he was gladdened by his decision to cancel Lend-Lease aid to the Soviet Union after Japan's surrender on August 15—the day on which the Second World War formally ended. Typically, Kennan believed the United States had played tough with Moscow about a year too late, observing that "we should have considered at least an extensive curtailment of this program at the time of the Warsaw uprising in the summer of 1944."[63] Nonetheless, Truman had acted correctly on this matter, and a firmer sense of purpose was becoming evident in the White House.

But it was not yet pervasive, and Kennan blamed this delay in Truman grasping reality on Secretary of State James F. Byrnes, whom he suspected was still enthralled by the notion of peacetime collaboration with Stalin at the expense of America's core relationship with Great Britain. In his diary, Kennan recalled the substance of the Moscow Conference in December 1945, attended by the emissaries of the wartime Big Three: Byrnes, British foreign secretary Ernest Bevin, and Molotov. Bevin had not wanted to attend, believing that Moscow, through its aggressive and contemptuous actions in Eastern Europe and Iran, did not deserve the respect a conference bestowed. Byrnes thought otherwise. The process and personalities were captured nicely by Kennan:

> As for Byrnes, Bevin saw in him only another cocky and unreliable Irishman, similar to ones that he had known in his experience as a docker and labor leader. Byrnes had consistently shown himself negligent of British feelings and quite unconcerned for Anglo-American relations . . . When Harriman raised his glass to the future success of the conference, Bevin assented and added: "And let's hope we don't all get sacked when we get home." Molotov left the minute luncheon was over.[64]

Later that evening, Kennan attended a special performance of *Zolushka* (Cinderella) at the Bolshoi. Perplexed as to why such a first-rate performance had fallen flat on the large audience, Kennan discovered that Stalin had been part of the audience. "For this reason," Kennan wrote, "the audience, except for the diplomatic corps, was apparently composed almost exclusively of secret police people, who were doubtless afraid that any excessive display on their part of enthusiasm for the performance might look as though they were being diverted from their duties."[65] Kennan was appalled at the regimentation of thought and action demanded by the Soviet system; that it scarred a Russian cultural event of the highest artistic merit made it all the more insidious. But a small part of Kennan yearned for a similar measure of disciplined uniformity in the U.S. government. There was something unsettling about the haphazard nature of foreign policymaking, and Byrnes was particularly susceptible to departing from the script. Truman ultimately came to share Kennan's belief that Byrnes had performed abysmally at the conference, failing to warn Stalin of serious repercussions if the Red Army did not retreat from Iran. "I do not think we should play compromise any longer," wrote Truman in reference to Byrnes on January 5, 1946. "I am tired of babying the Soviets."[66] Prospects of exerting influence appeared to be improving for the embassy's resident Cassandra.

In February 1946, Kennan had taken ill with "cold, fever, sinus, tooth trouble, and finally the aftereffects of the sulpha drugs administered for the relief of these other miseries." Languishing in his sickbed, with Harriman out of town, Kennan had no choice but to field the relentless deluge of incoming telegraphic mail. "Among the messages brought up on one of these unhappy days," Kennan wrote, "was one that reduced us all to a new level of despair—despair not with the Soviet government but with our own." This telegram, dispatched from the Treasury Department, invited the embassy to make sense of Moscow's unwillingness to cooperate with the World Bank and the International Monetary Fund. Kennan recalled that "the more I thought about this message, the more it seemed to me obvious that this was 'it.' For eighteen long months I had done little else but pluck people's sleeves, trying to make them understand the nature of the phenomenon with which we in the Moscow embassy were daily confronted . . . So far as official Washington was concerned, it had been to all intents and purposes like talking to a stone." Kennan's ailments, low mood, and visceral reaction to Treasury's ignorance combined to instill a firm resolution to read them the riot act: "It would not do to give them just a fragment of the truth. Here was a case where nothing but the whole truth would do. They had asked for it. Now, by God, they would have it." Kennan summoned his secretary, Dorothy Hessman, to transcribe his thoughts, a process that would take quite some time. The telegram—or "Long Telegram" as it subsequently became known—amounted to some fifty-five hundred words. This "outrageous encumberment of the telegraphic process," as Kennan described it, arrived in Washington on February 22.[67] Its remarkable impact testified to the new reality that Washington and Kennan were finally in accord over the nature of the Soviet threat: "My official loneliness came in fact to an end," Kennan recalled, "at least for a period of two or three years."[68]

Kennan's Long Telegram was insightful and measured, and it took care to assail the Soviet Union as a system, not Russia as a nation. The population trapped inside Stalin's dystopia, Kennan wrote, "are by and large, friendly to [the] outside world, eager for experience of it, eager to measure against it talents they are conscious of possessing, eager above all to live in peace and enjoy [the] fruits of their own labor." But these people have little option but to privilege survival over principle in a state ruled through savage internal repression. "At bottom of Kremlin's neurotic view of world affairs is [the] traditional and instinctive Russian sense of insecurity," Kennan observed, but this flaw in the nation's historical consciousness was ruthlessly exploited by an ideology that fed off paranoia and insularity. He continued:

> Only in this land which had never known a friendly neighbor or indeed any tolerant equilibrium of separate powers, either internal or inter-national, could a doctrine thrive which viewed economic conflicts of society as insoluble by peaceful means. After establishment of Bolshe-vist regime, Marxist dogma, rendered even more truculent and intoler-ant by Lenin's interpretation, became a perfect vehicle for sense of insecurity with which Bolsheviks, even more than previous Russian rulers, were afflicted. In this dogma, with its basic altruism of purpose, they found justification for their instinctive fear of outside world, for the dictatorship without which they did not know how to rule, for cru-elties they did not dare not to inflict, for sacrifice they felt bound to de-mand. In the name of Marxism they sacrificed every single ethical value in their methods and tactics. Today they cannot dispense with it. It is fig leaf of their moral and intellectual respectability.

The combination of Marxian ideology and Russia's peculiar psychology had created a perfect anti-Western, anticapitalist storm.

In regard to the actual threat posed to American interests, Kennan be-lieved that Stalin was naturally cautious, taking what was possible where "it is considered timely and promising," but temperamentally disinclined to push to the point of open conflict. Thus "these efforts are restricted to cer-tain neighboring points conceived of here as being of immediate strategic necessity, such as Northern Iran, Turkey, possibly Bornholm." Soviet grand strategy, unlike the expansionist dogma of Nazi Germany, "is neither schematic nor adventuristic. It does not work by fixed plans . . . [It is] impervious to the logic of reason, and it is highly sensitive to the logic of force." Moscow was always likely to desist from adventurism in the face of serious Anglo-American resistance, making Stalin a rational actor in this one important respect. Here was cause for hope, because if Moscow's "adversary has sufficient force and makes clear his readiness to use it, he rarely has to do so. If situations are properly handled there need be no prestige-engaging showdowns." Give Stalin an opening and he will exploit it ruthlessly. Communicate a clear sense of boundaries, however, and the postwar world could be as peaceable as the era that followed the Congress of Vienna.

In reference to multilateral institutions such as the World Bank, IMF, and United Nations, Kennan believed that "Russians will participate officially in international organizations where they see the opportunity of extending Soviet power or of inhibiting or diluting power of others. Moscow sees in UNO [United Nations Organization] not the mechanism for a permanent and stable world society founded on mutual interest and aims of all nations, but an arena in which aims just mentioned can be favorably pursued." In this sense Kennan did not believe that Moscow was exceptionally culpable; rather, the creators of the United Nations had declined to heed the self-serving proclivities of all states. Soviet policy toward "colonial areas and backward or dependent peoples," meanwhile, "will be directed toward weakening of power and influence and contacts of advanced Western nations, on theory that in so far as this policy is successful, there will be created a vacuum which will favor Communist-Soviet penetration." The Third World would become a battleground only if the West vested in it sufficient prestige to make it a proxy fight worth having. Best of all was to ignore what Kennan would later dismiss as the "periphery."

The tone of Kennan's telegram was generally dispassionate, shielding the reader from the anger he clearly felt when dictating it to Hessman. But Kennan failed to present the entirety of his case with scholarly detachment. The prescriptive part of the telegram was condensed in the following terms: "In summary, we have here a political force committed fanatically to the belief that with US there can be no permanent *modus vivendi*, that it is desirable and necessary that the internal harmony of our society be disrupted, our traditional way of life be destroyed, the international authority of our state be broken, if Soviet power is to be secure."

This line has been often quoted by scholars keen to identify in Kennan a visceral anticommunism.[69] But words such as "fanatically," "broken," and "destroyed" are the exceptions rather than the rule. To take just one example, Kennan was careful to stress that the United States had vexing issues of its own to address. Paramount was the requirement that policymakers apprehend the Soviet threat with "courage, detachment, objectivity, and same determination not to be emotionally provoked or unseated by it . . . We must see that the public is educated to realities of the Russian situation." This vital pedagogical undertaking had to be completed in sober terms and with a cool head, a manner of comprehension and communication that Americans, a people tending toward absolutes, had historically found challenging. "I am convinced," Kennan wrote, "that there would be far less hysterical anti-Sovietism in our country today if realities of this situation were better understood by our people. There is nothing as dangerous or as terrifying as the unknown." If America heeded his warning, and ignored its sorry history of simplifying complex events and relationships, then the nation, and its allies, had nothing to fear, and civil liberties would be protected. If extremism was given free rein, however, then the newly atomic world would become incredibly dangerous: "We must have courage and self-confidence to cling to our own methods and conceptions of human society. After all, the greatest danger that can befall us in coping with this problem of Soviet communism, is that we shall allow ourselves to become like those with whom we are coping."

This was a bravura performance that justly found an influential audience. Before Kennan's telegram, nobody in the employ of the U.S. government had articulated a cohesive American strategy toward Moscow in the postwar world—Lippmann had performed this role from the outside. As Truman's aide, George Elsey, remarked, "Kennan tied everything together, wrapped it together in a neat package, and put a red bow around it."[70] Kennan's gift to American grand strategy was circulated quickly and widely upon its arrival—championed by Harriman, who was in Washington at the time—and was read by the secretaries of war and the Navy, and later by Truman himself. Secretary of the Navy James Forrestal was bowled over by its force of argument. He had the telegram copied and sent to other members of the cabinet, also insisting that it become required reading for senior members of the armed forces. The telegram was cabled to America's embassies and missions abroad. Kennan was soon receiving glowing endorsements from the audience he respected most: professional diplomats.

The U.S. ambassador to Cuba, Henry Norweb, wrote to Kennan, describing the telegram as "about the best piece of political reporting I have seen in my thirty years in the Service . . . It is a masterpiece of 'thinking

things out,' realism devoid of hysteria, of [a] courageous approach to a problem."[71] It met with near universal acclaim from fellow diplomats, politicians,
and members of the military. A rare dissenting voice was that of General
Lucius Clay, the American military governor in Germany who was still
managing to get along with his Soviet counterparts. Of course, the connected Walter Lippmann also soon got the gist of Kennan's telegram, which
caused him considerable concern. He redoubled his journalistic efforts to
convince Americans of the merits of U.S.-Soviet collaboration. Lippmann
also wrote to General Dwight D. Eisenhower to compliment him on "the
speech you made the other day in which you spoke of how vicious it is to be
thinking of another war . . . I almost feel that the soldiers are going to have
to save the peace which the diplomats and politicians will, if they don't look
out, most surely wreck."[72] Lippmann was depressed that Kennan's telegram
had engendered such unity of anti-Soviet purpose.

The main problem with Lippmann's championing of "closer diplomatic
contact" with Moscow, Kennan told Forrestal, was that it "reflects a serious
misunderstanding of Soviet realities."[73] The growing closeness between Kennan and Forrestal—who bonded for reasons beyond a common dismay with
Lippmann's apparent naïveté—was the critical spur to Kennan becoming a
person of influence. Forrestal had enjoyed a spectacularly successful career
with the venerable investment bank Dillon Read before becoming secretary of the Navy in 1944. He was ambitious, drove himself and his subordinates to the point of exhaustion, and was a formidable presence in Truman's
cabinet, gaining influence vis-à-vis the fading Byrnes. Forrestal had become
Kennan's champion in Washington, and the transformative effect on the
diplomat's career, which had stalled through the war years after starting so
brightly, was immediate. Within three months, Kennan, now age forty-two,
was hurried back to Washington (with his young family) to become deputy
commandant for foreign affairs at the National War College, an institution
established that same year to educate diplomats and midranking military
officers. In the summer of 1946, Kennan was dispatched on a nationwide
speaking tour, before being instructed to deliver seventeen lectures at the
college in the autumn—detailing at greater length the strategic purpose of
the Long Telegram. Like Mahan, Kennan had secured for himself a happily
contemplative setting on the northeastern seaboard. The Truman administration tasked Kennan with performing the function he had deemed essential in his telegram: educating the public and the military, in measured
tones, on the actual threat posed by the Soviet Union to American interests.

This threat, Kennan maintained, was surmountable if the right type of knowledge was applied.

Kennan spoke to a variety of audiences over the summer, ranging from atomic scientists in California, captains of industry in New York City, and academics at the elite universities. Among the intellectuals and scientists he encountered, across the full range of disciplines, Kennan detected two worrying trends: first a Lippmannesque tendency to view Moscow as a credible ally; second a Beardian inclination to view the Soviet Union as a noble experiment that the United States, scarred by poverty and societal discord, had no special right to judge. Kennan nonetheless generally impressed his audiences, and the State Department, with the clarity of his message, which focused on America's failings as well as the USSR's. Anticipating the development of a significant domestic problem, he told an audience at the University of Virginia, "I deplore the hysterical sort of anticommunism which, it seems to me, is gaining currency in our country."[74]

After concluding his national tour, Kennan delivered a series of lectures at the National War College, their contemporary focus illuminated by telling references to Gibbon and Clausewitz. Kennan had neglected to mention the atomic bomb—or the potential benefits of the U.S. monopoly on that weapon—in the Long Telegram. It was a peculiar omission given the weapon's vast geopolitical ramifications. Kennan addressed this lacuna by observing that the destructiveness of atomic weaponry made it vital that the United States confront the Soviet Union with nonmilitary means, so as to avoid fighting a third total war with consequences for humanity far graver than those of the two that preceded. It was inevitable that Moscow would develop and test a similar device. And there was no question of America pressing its atomic advantage during the interregnum. The reputational damage would be too severe, the very notion offensive. "Does not [the] significance of atomic weapons," Kennan observed hopefully, "mean that, if we are to avoid mutual destruction, we must revert to strategic political thinking of [the] XVIII century? Total destruction of enemy's forces can no longer be our objective." Here was the nuclear age's silver lining, reasoned Kennan, who was of course fond of the eighteenth century. His affinity for eras that predated the establishment of representative democracy (and factories, roads, large cities, etc.) was made clear in his observation that "there is a little bit of the totalitarian buried somewhere, way down deep, in each and every one of us."[75]

On September 16, 1946, Kennan delivered an important speech, "Measures Short of War (Diplomatic)," which detailed a full spectrum of U.S. strategies for the atomic age. Kennan first dwelled on the totalitarian repertoire, in which "no holds are barred." Stalin could apply or threaten a combination of any of the following: "persuasion, intimidation, deceit, corruption, penetration, subversion, horse-trading, bluffing, psychological pressure, economic pressure, seduction, blackmail, theft, fraud, rape, battle, murder and sudden death." Some of these options clearly fell outside Truman's executive purview, hence American strategy had to draw from three less diabolical nonmilitary strategic clusters: psychological, economic, and political.

In reference to psychological warfare, Kennan included "informational activity like propaganda, or radio broadcast or distribution of magazines." Thankfully, Kennan observed, "our government has begun to appreciate the fact that anything it does of any importance at all has a psychological effect abroad as well as at home." Second, America's economic arsenal included trade embargoes, aid programs, and the granting or refusal of trading preferences. Finally, Kennan defined political warfare broadly, which he took to mean "the cultivation of solidarity with other like-minded nations on every given issue of our foreign policy." These were the nonmilitary weapons at America's disposal. But Kennan understood that maintaining a strong conventional military held everything together. "You have no idea," Kennan told his audience to appreciative laughter, "how much it contributes to the general politeness and pleasantness of diplomacy when you have a little quiet armed force in the background."[76]

This was a diplomatic toolbox with implements to suit nearly all occasions. The communist parties in Western Europe had to be opposed with energy and purpose. This might entail the surreptitious funding of anticommunist political parties, infiltrating trade unions, or brandishing the "armed force in the background" to achieve the desired effect. (This was certainly the case during the Italian general election of 1948, when the U.S. Navy's Sixth Fleet made its presence felt in various ports.)[77] The purpose of American strategy was not to confront the Soviet Union directly or provoke war over any of its "allies" in Central and Eastern Europe. Rather, America had to ensure that Moscow's influence spread no farther on the European continent—and military action was the last possible resort, unlikely to be required given Stalin's sensitivity to the "logic of force." To counter communist subversion in Greece, for example, Kennan recommended that the United States dispatch "about three ships all painted white with 'Aid to Greece' on the sides, and to have the first bags of wheat driven up to Athens in an American jeep with a Hollywood blonde on the radiator."[78] Five decades before the Harvard political scientist Joseph Nye coined the term, Kennan understood the meaning of "soft power."

In January 1947, President Truman delivered his second State of the Union address, a speech infused with idealistic Wilsonian energy, rejecting by association Kennan's subtle geopolitical particularism: "Our goal is collective security for all mankind . . . The spirit of the American people can set the course of world history. If we maintain and strengthen our cherished ideals . . . then the faith of our citizens in freedom and democracy will be spread over the whole earth and free men everywhere will share our devotion to those ideals."[79]

A presidential vignette on a "little bit of totalitarianism" residing in all of us clearly would not have worked. Nor would any number of Kennanisms on America displaying justified modesty in its interactions with other nations, on Poland, Hungary, and Czechoslovakia being lost causes, and on the pernicious effects of universal suffrage. Kennan's conservative style of thinking was poisonous to the ambitions of presidential speechwriters. Nonetheless, the sweeping commitments detailed in Truman's speech worried him all the same; the president didn't have to channel Kennan directly to talk some sense. At this juncture Kennan and his government were happily as one on the practicalities of how best to combat Marxism-Leninism. But as long as Wilson's rhetorical ghost lingered, this unity of purpose was likely to be short-lived.

In *Anti-intellectualism in American Life*, Richard Hofstadter observed that 1947 was the year when America's international preeminence—economically, militarily, culturally, politically—was established beyond doubt. He wrote that it "was no longer possible to look at any foreign political system for moral or ideological illumination." To reinforce his point, Hofstadter quoted Edmund Wilson's remarks upon returning from Europe that "the United States at the present time is politically more advanced than any other part of the world." That this "least provincial of writers" could endorse the nation's political system without qualification, further observing that the postwar world had witnessed "a remarkable renascence of American arts and letters," testified to a special moment in time for the United States.[80] Not that there was any time to celebrate. Kennan was disinclined to revel in self-congratulation; the worrisome world situation kept his mood somber. There was a full-blown communist insurgency in Greece, acute political instability in Turkey, escalating U.S.-Soviet tension over a divided Germany, and a protracted civil war in China—tilting discernibly in Mao Zedong's favor—which ensured that its FDR-bestowed status as a fourth "global policeman" was now fully detached from reality. Kennan could see that America's view from the geopolitical summit was far bleaker than Britain's in 1815.

Some good news arrived to cheer Kennan in January 1947, when General George Marshall replaced James Byrnes as secretary of state. Winston Churchill had described Marshall as the West's "organizer of victory," in reference to the pivotal role he played as army chief of staff during the Second World War. An awe-inspiring presence, Marshall knew and liked Kennan—well, as much as this taciturn man could show—and the feeling was reciprocated. In his memoir, Kennan observed that there was "no one whose memory has less need of a eulogy from me than George Marshall." He composed a warm and affecting one all the same:

> Like everyone else, I admired him, and in a sense loved him, for the qualities I saw in him . . . for his unshakable integrity; his consistent courtesy and gentlemanliness of conduct; his ironclad sense of duty; his imperturbability—the imperturbability of a good conscience—in the face of harassments, pressures, and criticisms . . . his indifference to the whims and moods of public opinion, particularly as manifested in the mass media; and his impeccable fairness and avoidance of favoritism in the treatment of subordinates (there was no one in the Department of State whom he called by the first name; every one of us, from top to bottom, was recognized simply by his surname, with no handle to it).[81]

Marshall emerges through Kennan's writings as the one unimpeachable figure in public life, a giant among men. And counted among his many achievements was a farsighted decision to follow Kennan's advice in establishing a Policy Planning Staff at the State Department, and to appoint the author of the Long Telegram to head it.

On January 31, 1947, Kennan had sent a letter to Dean Acheson, Marshall's number two at the State Department, which emphasized the merits of creating a distinct policy-planning function. "What is important," wrote Kennan, "is that somewhere in the government there should be an honest, detached, and authoritative assessment of what constitutes national interest in foreign affairs and of how the national interest might be best promoted." The machinery of U.S. foreign policymaking was fundamentally reactive in its operational method. A separate detachment of policy planners at State would redress this problem in being afforded the space and time to think proactively. "The planner must accept the responsibility of defining overall purpose and approach," Kennan wrote. "The advisory quality of his function," he continued, "relieves him of any presumption of immodesty in this undertaking."

On the planning staff's ultimate purpose, Kennan identified two broad "objectives of United States policy." The first was "to assure to the people of the United States physical security and freedom to pursue in their own way the solution of the problems of their national life." The second was to "bring into existence that pattern of international relationships which will permit the people of the United States to derive maximum benefit from the experiences and achievements of other peoples and to make the maximum contribution to human progress anywhere." All of which was laudable and uncharacteristically vague. Kennan did offer more detail on America's economic goals, concurring with Charles Beard that the United States would be a much safer place if the nation reduced its "dependence" upon "the exchange of commodities."[82] Thus the global economy cannot be counted among the many topics about which Kennan was farsighted—Mahan had anticipated the patterns of world trade much more accurately a half century before. Regardless of this misstep, Kennan offered more specifics on the planning staff a fortnight later, observing to Acheson that it "should be started with a minimum of personnel," and that "these officers should be chosen, without regard to grade, on the basis of their official record, stress being laid on general intelligence, educational background, analytical capability, breadth and depth of experience, political judgment, and imagination."[83] Nothing less than the truest meritocracy was fit for purpose. The policy planning staff was formally convened in the State Department some two months later. Secretary Marshall's one piece of operational guidance to Kennan was pithy: "avoid trivia."[84]

On February 24, Acheson summoned Kennan to discuss an urgent problem. The British government, which counted Greece and Turkey within its protective sphere, no longer had sufficient resources to safeguard their independence. Could the United States assume this burden? Kennan instinctively thought yes in respect to Greece but no in respect to Turkey—where no armed insurgency actually existed (and whose connection to America's national security was less certain than that of Greece). President Truman said yes to Britain on both counts, and a draft presidential speech was composed and circulated across government on March 9.

Three days later, Truman delivered the speech to a joint session of

Congress; it announced a set of foreign-policy principles that became known as the Truman Doctrine. Kennan disliked the speech as soon as he saw it, and its key sentence allows us to understand why. About two-thirds of the way through the speech, which was mostly measured in tone and narrow in focus, Truman said, "I believe it must be the policy of the United States to support free peoples who are resisting subjugation by armed minorities or by outside pressures." Instead of addressing the specific problems of Greece and Turkey, Truman had summoned universals. Kennan's calibrated diplomatic gradations had seemingly been discarded for a blank Wilsonian check. The speech "placed our aid in the framework of a universal policy rather than in that of a specific decision addressed to a specific set of circumstances. It implied that what we had decided to do in the case of Greece was something we would be prepared to do in the case of any other country, provided only that it was faced with the threat of 'subjugation by armed minorities or by outside pressures.'"[85]

A foundational stone had been laid on the path to American involvement in Vietnam—and to many other destructive, purposeless tangents.

The critical substance of Walter Lippmann's reaction to Truman's speech was identical to Kennan's. But declining the State Department's job offer meant he could record his concerns publicly. In "T&T" on March 15, Lippmann observed that a "vague global policy, which sounds like the tocsin of an ideological crusade, has no limits. It cannot be controlled. Its effects cannot be predicted. Everyone everywhere will read into it his own fears and hopes, and it could readily act as incitement and inducement to civil strife in countries where the national cooperation is delicate and precarious." A few weeks after the column appeared, Lippmann and Dean Acheson clashed at a dinner party when the latter accused the former of "sabotaging" the nation's foreign policy. Lippmann and Acheson exchanged fierce rhetorical blows, creating "a very unpleasant evening," in the journalist's recollection.[86]

Lippmann had actually come around to the logic of resisting Soviet expansionism. His disagreement with Acheson was on means and parameters. On April 5, Lippmann had published one of his most influential columns, widely reprinted under syndication, titled "Cassandra Speaking"—a Kennanesque piece of historical self-identification. Lippmann observed that Europe was on the verge of economic collapse. This was not hyperbole, he maintained, but "only what responsible men say when they do not have to keep up appearances in public." It was now imperative that the Truman administration devise measures to shore up political and economic stability in Europe "on a scale which no responsible statesman has yet ventured to hint at."[87] The proposal of a large-scale intervention to save the center of the geopolitical universe garnered Kennan's instant approval. This was precisely the type of nonmilitary measure envisioned and prioritized in the Long Telegram. Others in the State Department were similarly impressed. The speechwriter Joseph Jones paraphrased Lippmann's column for an important address delivered by Dean Acheson, of all people, a few weeks later.

James Forrestal also liked Lippmann's column and suggested that he and George Kennan should meet in person to sketch out the basics of a recovery program for Europe on the appropriate grand scale. Facing the men were two considerable challenges, described by Ronald Steel: "how to sell such a costly program to a suspicious Congress, and how to organize it so that it did not seem either an American ploy to dominate Europe or a blatant anti-Soviet maneuver."[88] Lippmann and Kennan shared a political philosophy, seriousness of purpose, and diplomatic style. It was no surprise, then, that they devised an elegant and logical plan. They met for a long lunch at the National War College and made two substantive proposals. First, the Soviet Union would be invited to participate in the recovery program, and be offered advantageous loan terms. Its participation, however, should be made contingent upon acceptance that the encouragement and facilitation of free trade was sine qua non—recovery would proceed on broadly liberal-capitalist lines. Second, Kennan and Lippmann recommended that the United States encourage the European nations to request assistance themselves.

This would place the onus on Congress to simply accept or reject a European plea for help, a precedent that had met with recent success. It would also compel the European nations to collaborate, which would be useful in developing their political and economic cohesion, ensuring their longer-term vitality, and negating the potential for future conflict within the continent itself. Encouraging greater European unity—with a carrot worth billions of dollars—would also ask some hard questions of Soviet dominance in Eastern and Central Europe. Were Poland, Czechoslovakia, and Hungary gaining anything from residing in the Russian orbit? If Stalin forced the satellite nations to refuse to participate in a generous U.S. aid program, seeds of discord would be successfully sown. Durable empires are not made by cowing nations, crushing their spirit, and then hampering their development. (The architects of the British Empire understood that some degree of co-opting was required.) Kennan better understood the logic of this than Lippmann, because the latter genuinely believed that Moscow would participate in the program, bringing along its neighbors. Lippmann did not view the plan as a ruse to develop one part of Europe at the expense of the other but as a noble attempt to part what Churchill had described in 1946 as the "iron curtain." The journalist wanted to rekindle a form of ends-oriented U.S.-Soviet cooperation that had fallen into abeyance since Yalta.

Lippmann was of course duly thwarted. On June 4, 1947, while delivering a commencement address at Harvard, Secretary of State Marshall presented the broad sweep of a plan designed to assist the recovery and reconstruction of Europe. During the planning stage, the State Department had decided that creating the impression of a European-requested endeavor would have stretched credulity a little too far. The bulk of the speech was drafted by Kennan's friend Charles Bohlen, and it drew on Kennan's and Lippmann's insights as well as those from other State Department sources, William Clayton most notably. The Marshall Plan, as it became known, had a broad purpose tailored to the chaotic economic circumstances of the time:

> It is logical that the United States should do whatever it is able to do to assist in the return of normal economic health in the world, without which there can be no political stability and no assured peace. Our policy is directed not against any country or doctrine, but against hunger, poverty, desperation, and chaos. Its purpose should be the revival of a working economy in the world so as to permit the emergence of political and social conditions in which free institutions can exist.[89]

At the end of the month, Molotov and some eighty advisers, including a retinue of hopeful representatives from Eastern Europe, attended a conference in Paris to discuss Marshall's offer. Lippmann was delighted by this promising news; Kennan, aghast. Fortunately, Molotov behaved as expected in declining Washington's offer, taking the leaders of Moscow's unhappy satellites back east with him. Marshall's seemingly gregarious observation that U.S. "policy is not directed against any country, but against hunger, poverty, desperation and chaos" did not dupe Vyacheslav Molotov. Superpower rivalry was ideological, above all, and accepting the Marshall Plan also meant accepting the superiority of capitalism over communism. There was not enough cash in the world to sweeten that pill.

Over the next four years, $12.4 billion in aid was disbursed to the sixteen nations of the Organisation for European Economic Co-operation—including Great Britain, France, Italy, West Germany, and Austria—freshly created to administer the Marshall Plan from the recipient end. Lippmann had floated an early rationale and played his usually significant role in respect to guiding and illuminating public opinion. But this was George Kennan's achievement, perhaps his finest policy hour. The Marshall Plan was the perfect realization of logic contained in the Long Telegram. (Few policies henceforth came close to satisfying Kennan.) It was also successful in achieving its declared goals. Tottering on shaky economic and political foundations in 1947, Western Europe regained its footing following Marshall's speech and embarked upon a remarkable period of sustained growth. The Marshall Plan also presaged closer European economic and political cooperation—in the fashion that Lippmann and Kennan anticipated. Historians and economists continue to debate the actual utility of the plan. The $12.4 billion figure was not vast in the wider scheme of things; America's GDP in 1948 was $258 billion. Western Europe had greater latent economic potential than any other region on earth. But one need not enter this scholarly debate to observe that the Marshall Plan made an enormous contribution—psychologically at the least and economically transformative at the most—to the rehabilitation of Western Europe. It instilled hope and unity of purpose, which was enough.

A few months before the creation of the Marshall Plan, the editor of *Foreign Affairs*, Hamilton Fish Armstrong, invited Kennan to redraft the Long Telegram for publication. Here was an ideal opportunity for Kennan to reach a much larger audience than the National War College lectern could provide. *Foreign Affairs* was not the *International Herald Tribune*, but its readership was influential and its circulation respectable. Kennan replied with a caveat: "I really cannot write anything of value on Russia for publication under my own name. If you would be interested in an anonymous article, or one under a pen name, I would be glad to know this." An undeterred Armstrong replied that "the interest of the projected article more than outweighs from our point of view the disadvantage of anonymity. This letter is an invitation to you, then, to put into the form of an article the ideas you expressed so well in your memorandum and in your talk here at the Council."[90]

An article titled "The Sources of Soviet Conduct" by an author identified as "X" appeared in July's *Foreign Affairs*. Nothing published in that journal since—and that includes seminal pieces by Henry Kissinger, Richard Nixon,

Samuel Huntington, Paul Wolfowitz, and many others—has had a comparable impact. *The New York Times* and *Newsweek* reported on the article's
meaning and wider significance, and mused on the likely identity of its
author—"X" was intriguing, an unintended marketing masterstroke. *Reader's
Digest* and *Life* printed long excerpts, riling Kennan with their brutal edit-
ing, which he believed damaged the article's integrity. It took less than a
month for Arthur Krock to reveal X's identity in the *Times*. Perturbed by
this media storm, George Marshall summoned Kennan for a dressing down,
growling in admonishment that "planners don't talk." Kennan protested
that he had secured all necessary clearances, which mollified Marshall.[91]
The secretary of state and others understood that the publicity could serve
a useful purpose. James Forrestal, for one, was thrilled that the X Article
had secured such a large readership, and that its connection to U.S. policy
had been established. The danger posed by the Soviet Union would, he
hoped, become evident to all who read the article. The making of a resolute,
and costly, foreign policy would become simpler if the public and their
political representatives understood the stakes involved in containing
Moscow.

"The Sources of Soviet Conduct" covered much of the same ground as the
Long Telegram. It begins by re-creating Stalin's warped perspective on diplomacy: that there could be no meaningful collaboration between the Soviet
Union and "powers which are regarded as capitalist." "This means," Kennan
wrote, "that we are going to continue for a long time to find the Russians
difficult to deal with." It is impossible to engage meaningfully with a totalitarian regime because "truth is not a constant but is actually created, for all
intents and purposes, by the Soviet leaders themselves." Russian history, ad-
ditionally, provides ample evidence that communist "precepts are fortified
by . . . centuries of obscure battles between nomadic forces over the stretches
of a vast fortified plain." Assaulted in various eras by Mongol hordes from the
east, and Napoleon's and Hitler's formidable land armies from the west,
Russia had a complicated relationship with the outside world, to say the
least. Invading armies had visited death and destruction on Russia on a
scale experienced by no other nation on earth. In these circumstances, the
coupling of Russian history and Marxism-Leninism had real chemistry.

To ensure that this abused child was restrained in the extent of abuse it
could mete out, Kennan crafted a seminal strategic concept:

> In these circumstances it is clear that the main element of any United
> States policy toward the Soviet Union must be that of a long-term,

patient but firm and vigilant containment of Russian expansionist tendencies . . . It will be clearly seen that the Soviet pressure against the free institutions of the Western world is something that can be contained by the adroit and vigilant application of counter-force at a series of constantly shifting geographical and political points, corresponding to the shifts and maneuvers of Soviet policy, but which cannot be charmed or talked out of existence.

The next eight presidents would all subscribe to variations on this policy. The containment of Soviet expansionism was designed to ensure that the free world remained inoculated from Marxist contagion. In the meantime, the Soviet Union would wither on the vine:

> Russian communists who speak of the "uneven development of capitalism" should blush at the contemplation of their own national economy . . . It is difficult to see how these deficiencies can be corrected at an early date by a tired and dispirited population working largely under the shadow of fear and compulsion . . . The possibility remains (and in the opinion of this writer it is a strong one) that Soviet power, like the capitalist world of its conception, bears within it the seeds of its own decay, and that the sprouting of these seeds is well-advanced.

If the United States remained resolute and kept its head, the Soviet Union would not pose as serious a challenge as promised by Stalin's and Molotov's bluster. "For no mystical, messianic movement—and particularly not that of the Kremlin—can face frustration indefinitely without eventually adjusting itself in one way or another to the logic of that state of affairs."[92]

Kennan's article evoked a strong reaction in Walter Lippmann. Aware of the article's vast potential impact, he wrote twelve successive "T&T" columns, all of which appeared in the late summer of 1947, criticizing X's rationale, prescriptions, and predictions. Lippmann accused X of making some egregious errors: downplaying Russia's history at the expense of Marxist ideology, proposing a strategy so broad in application that it would lead to perpetual conflict in areas of marginal significance, and misplaced confidence in the fallibility of the Soviet system. In the most damning indictment, Lippmann accused Kennan of authoring a "strategic monstrosity" that was likely to cause geopolitical exhaustion: "The Americans would themselves probably be frustrated by Mr. X's policy long before the Russians were." The articles were published collectively as a book titled *The Cold War* in the fall.

With "the Cold War" and "containment," Kennan and Lippmann had provided the language that defined the postwar era.

Lippmann's twelve-stage critique of Kennan's article was brilliant at times and garnered a lot of publicity. His first column impugned X for observing that Soviet power "bears within itself the seed of its own decay." "Do we dare to assume as we enter the arena and get set to run the race," asked Lippmann sarcastically, "that the Soviet Union will break its leg while the United States grows a pair of wings to speed it on its way?"[93] In Lippmann's mind, the Soviet Union was an established fact that was here to stay. Both assessments had some merit, but Kennan more accurately identified the process through which the Marxist-Leninist experiment would unravel; Lippmann had been duped by a Soviet economic and political system that resembled a Potemkin village. Containment was entirely appropriate because Russian communism would prove evanescent. The Soviet Union's economic virtues bore no serious comparison to those of the United States and the West; Moscow's reluctant empire was not likely to remain quiescent.

Lippmann was on surer ground in following through on the faulty logic contained in Kennan's advocacy of the "adroit and vigilant application of counter-force at a series of constantly shifting geographical and political points." "The Eurasian continent is a big place," wrote Lippmann, "and the military power of the United States, though it is very great, has certain limits which must be borne in mind if it is to be used effectively." Of particular concern to Lippmann was containment's apparently broad application, unencumbered in presentation by any clearly established hierarchy of American interests. This made the Third World a battleground of dubious worth: "The policy can be implemented only by recruiting, subsidizing and supporting a heterogeneous array of satellites, clients, dependents and puppets." The problem with lavishing resources, and vesting credibility, on such areas and regimes is that "satellite states and puppet governments are not good material out of which to construct unassailable barriers. We shall have either to disown our puppets, which would be tantamount to appeasement and defeat and loss of face, or must support them at incalculable cost on an unintended, unforeseen and perhaps undesirable issue."[94] With this observation, Lippmann had peered into the future.

In the last of the twelve articles, Lippmann identified a continuity of aims between X and the authors of the Truman Doctrine. All had been foolishly driven by Wilsonianism, disregarding the Mahanian tradition in American diplomatic history that understood that certain values do not travel well. Washington policymakers should protect the security and interests of the nation and its closest strategic partners—not treat the world as a single battleground on which the champions of John Locke should be pitted against those of Karl Marx. Any poor nation should be free to opt for the latter just as it might prefer the former. Their decision was irrelevant, as weak and peripheral nations did not affect the West's core economic and security interests. And fighting proxy wars in such places was foolish on multiple levels:

> Our aim will not be to organize an ideological crusade. It will not be to make Jeffersonian democrats out of the peasants of eastern Europe, the tribal chieftains, the feudal lords, the pashas, and the warlords of the Middle East and Asia, but to settle the war and to restore the independence of the nations of Europe by removing the alien armies—all of them, our own included . . . Alien armies are hateful, however well behaved, just because they represent an alien power and are, therefore, a perpetual reminder that the people on whom they are quartered are not masters of their own destiny.[95]

Lippmann's polemic was highly impressive. In fact, Kennan mostly agreed with him, which made its ferocity harder to dismiss or absorb.

Of course, Kennan's first reaction was anger. He too abhorred the Truman Doctrine but was unable to vent his frustrations to millions of avid readers in the way Lippmann could. After Lippmann's first article went to press, Kennan asked permission to publicly respond, which Marshall denied. Kennan was annoyed that Lippmann had emphasized the perils of containment's military application, when its author in fact viewed war as an absolute last resort. Kennan began to wonder whether he had made his meaning clear, eventually conceding that the ambiguities and gaps contained in the article had invited Lippmann's critique. In his memoirs he confessed his "failure to make clear what I was talking about when I mentioned the containment of Soviet power was not the containment by military means of a military threat, but the political containment of a political threat." In identifying a "series of constantly shifting geographical and political points," Kennan had erred in proposing a strategy that was "at best ambiguous, and lent itself to misinterpretation." This led him to identify another "great deficiency"—his "failure to distinguish between various geographic areas, and to make clear that the 'containment' of which I was speaking was not something which I thought we could, necessarily, do everywhere successfully, or even needed to do everywhere successfully, in order to serve the purpose I had in mind." In April 1948, Kennan composed a long letter to Lippmann, from his sickbed at Bethesda Naval Hospital (it should be noted here that Kennan, who lived to 101, was more robust than his complaints suggest):

> I wrote a long letter to Mr. Lippmann, protesting the misinterpretation of my thoughts which his articles, as it seemed to me, implied. I never sent it to him. It was probably best that I didn't. The letter had a plaintive and overdramatic tone, reflecting the discomfort of flesh and spirit in which it was written. I took a more cruel but less serious revenge a year or two later when I ran into him on a parlor car of the Pennsylvania Railroad, and wore him relentlessly down with a monologue on these same subjects that lasted most of the way from Washington to New York.

The core of Lippmann's critique had been justified in these circumstances. Of this "misunderstanding almost tragic in its dimensions," Kennan graciously said, "I accept the blame for misleading him. My only consolation is that I succeeded in provoking from him so excellent and penetrating a treatise."[96] Lippmann and Kennan became close allies as the former's prophesies came to pass. On the X Article, Kennan later wrote that he felt "like one who has inadvertently loosened a large boulder from the top of a cliff and now helplessly witnesses its path of destruction in the valley below, shuddering and wincing at each successive glimpse of disaster."[97]

At the end of 1947, his annus mirabilis, Kennan's policy influence began to follow the same trajectory as the boulder. At the Policy Planning Staff meetings he chaired, and across government in general, Kennan began to notice that his views were now in the minority. In January, Kennan registered reservations about the Truman administration recognizing Israel as an independent state. He was concerned that the United States agreeing to serve as Israel's chief supporter would inevitably inflame Arab nationalism in the region. This was not a controversial opinion in 1947–1948—indeed, Henry Kissinger, a freshman at Harvard at that time, also believed that U.S. interests would be injured by supporting Israel's creation.[98] Yet President Truman (if not Secretary of State Marshall and Secretary of Defense Forrestal, who shared some of Kennan's doubts) declared his support for Israel's path to nationhood, and of America's vital interest in ensuring its long-term survival. Unconvinced by this reasoning, Kennan had drafted a paper on

Palestine for the Office of United Nations Affairs, which cautioned against America taking a strong position on the Arab-Israeli conflict. As Kennan recorded in his diary, it "came back with a long memorandum attacking it." He was particularly irritated that contained in this critical reply "was no hint of criticism of the Zionists, who were apparently blameless. The solutions toward which the memorandum pointed were all ones which would have put further strain on our relations with British and Arabs, and on the relations between British and Arabs. Such a policy could proceed only at the expense of our major political and strategic interests in the Middle East." Sensitivity to the Holocaust did not enter Kennan's analysis at any point. He believed Washington should step back and allow events to take their natural Darwinian course, irrespective of outcome:

> Unless the inhabitants of Palestine, both Jews and Arabs, and the international elements which stand behind them, are finally compelled to face each other eye to eye, without outside interference, and to weigh, with a sense of immediate and direct responsibility, the consequences of agreement or disagreement, I think they will continue to react irresponsibly . . . We Americans must realize that we cannot be the keepers and moral guardians of all the peoples in this world. We must become more modest, and recognize the necessary limits to the responsibility we can assume.[99]

The final two sentences distilled Kennan's worldview. It was America's obligation, as the world's single most powerful nation, to protect Western Europe from the Soviet Union, an abhorrent regime. Beyond that, Washington should learn from history's other great empires and resist the temptation to assume unsustainable burdens in volatile regions. Zionist attempts to found a nation in the Middle East should live or die by Jewish resources alone.

Elsewhere the geopolitical augurs were similarly gloomy. In February 1948, a Soviet-backed coup in Czechoslovakia removed the last remnants of independent-mindedness from its government. Foreign Minister Jan Masaryk died in mysterious circumstances two weeks later. President Edvard Beneš, who had initially accepted a strong communist presence within a coalition government, and who had been forced to sign off on the coup d'état under threat of Soviet invasion, resigned in June and died, from natural causes, at the end of the year. From Berlin, General Lucius Clay informed Washington that while he had previously believed a war with the Soviet Union was unlikely "for at least ten years . . . within the last few weeks, I have felt a subtle change in Soviet attitude which I cannot define but which now gives me a feeling that it may come with dramatic suddenness." Kennan found this assessment alarmist in the extreme. His response to Czechoslovakia's humbling was a repeat of ten years earlier. The nation was destined to fall under the domination of a larger neighbor; Kennan had given up hope of an independent Czechoslovakia soon after the D-day landings, when the Roosevelt administration missed the opportunity to confront Stalin over his wider intentions in Eastern Europe. Kennan recalled that "Washington, particularly the military establishment and intelligence fraternity (where the military predominated) . . . overreacted in the most deplorable way to the combination of Clay's telegram and the Czech coup." On March 16, the newly formed Central Intelligence Agency prepared an analysis that held that war was "not probable within the next sixty days." The notion of waging war over Czechoslovakia—which had been a dead man walking since the summer of 1944—appalled Kennan. The worst aspect was that few policy advisers appeared capable of understanding Stalin's perspective, which Kennan identified as "defensive reactions . . . to the initial successes of the Marshall Plan initiative and to the preparations now being undertaken on the Western side to set up a separate German government in Western Germany."[100] In a letter to Walter Lippmann, now a firm friend, Kennan observed that "the Russians don't want to invade anyone. It is not in their tradition . . . The violence is nominally *domestic*, not *international*, violence. It is, if you will, a police violence, not a military violence. The policy of containment related to the effort to encourage other peoples to resist this type of violence and to defend the *internal* integrity of their countries."[101] Walter Lippmann's response to the coup, meanwhile, was unimpeachable: he discarded any residual hope of America getting along with Stalin.[102]

Germany had become a major bone of contention between Kennan and the Truman administration. Having initially supported the creation of a distinct West Germany, to consolidate America's strategic position on the continent, Kennan had come to oppose the establishment of a sovereign separate state. On June 18, the Western occupying nations had announced that the zone would have a new currency—the deutsche mark—to assist its economic rehabilitation. In response, Stalin ordered the immediate closure of all access routes to West Berlin, leaving the zone's residents about a month's food supplies. To get around these restrictions, the United States and Great Britain began to operate a round-the-clock airlift, which successfully supplied the west of Berlin until May 1949, when Stalin simply gave up.

It was a stirring victory for Truman and the West, although the airlift was fraught with danger. On August 12, 1948, an anxious Kennan submitted document PPS 37 to Secretary Marshall:

> We can no longer retain the present line of division in Europe and yet hope to keep things flexible for an eventual retraction of Soviet power and for the gradual emergence from Soviet control, and entrance into a free European country, of the present satellite countries . . . If we carry on along present lines, Germany must divide into eastern and western governments and western Europe must move toward a tight military alliance with this country which can only complicate the eventual integration of the satellites into a European community.[103]

In the midst of this grand confrontation with Stalin, Kennan's emollient proposal, anticipating happier times, sank without a trace. Dean Acheson, in particular, began to harbor serious doubts about the quality of Kennan's counsel and even identified in him a form of defeatism or pacifism. Acheson later said that Kennan reminded him of his father's horse, "which used to startle itself with the noise of its own hooves when it crossed wooden bridges."[104] Acheson turned out to be a primary author of Kennan's policy decline.

Meanwhile, James Forrestal, a catalyst for Kennan's rise, had set out on a path to self-destruction. Truman appointed Forrestal as the nation's first secretary of defense in 1947, combining the War and Navy Departments. This reshuffle was part of a wider reorganization of U.S. government, enshrined in the National Security Act of 1947, which established the National Security Council and the Central Intelligence Agency. The United States was girding itself for a long and costly struggle with the Soviet Union. This was effectively a promotion for Forrestal, but his tendency to work unforgiving hours, combined with a fragile temperament, began to affect his mental equilibrium, setting alarm bells ringing in the goldfish bowl that was Washington. In 1948, Forrestal made the unwise decision to meet secretly with Thomas Dewey, the Republican presidential candidate, where he agreed to serve as his secretary of defense in the likely event that Dewey beat Truman. Drew Pearson, a syndicated journalist with a nose for political scandal, publicized the details of this meeting, and Truman forced his secretary of defense to resign, which happened on March 31, 1949. Forrestal suffered a nervous breakdown soon after and was hospitalized a few weeks later. After a series of unsuccessful medical interventions, which likely exacerbated his mania, Forrestal committed suicide on May 22 by throwing himself from the sixteenth floor of Bethesda Naval Hospital.[105]

Dean Acheson, conversely, was about as stable a public servant as ever drew a government salary—and his career was on the up. A product of Groton and Yale, ramrod straight in his bearing, with a well-tended pencil-line mustache, Acheson cut an impressive and imposing figure. The British journalist Alistair Cooke described him wonderfully as a "six foot two Velasquez grandee who has submitted, with a twinkling eye, to his present reincarnation in fine tweeds as a Connecticut Yankee."[106] This well-tailored WASP also had a sting in his rhetorical tail. His acid descriptions of those who crossed him were legendary. In fact they were so unpleasant, and often unfair, that they form a blot on his substantial record as secretary of state. Reasonably, Acheson once observed that the "task of a public officer seeking to explain and gain support for a major policy is not that of the writer of a doctoral thesis. Qualification must give way to simplicity of statement, nicety and nuance to bluntness."[107] But there was no merit in Acheson's barbed observations that Kennan had a "marshmallow mind" and that it surprised him in later years that this "footnote of the Truman presidency" would "masquerade as an important policymaker."[108] Similarly abrasive were his views that Kennan had only an "abstract" sense of the national interest and that he vested too much faith in his "Quaker gospel."[109] Acheson lacked the self-doubt that might have tempered his vitriol. In 1945, for example, Acheson still entertained Lippmannesque hopes of collaborating with Stalin when Kennan was leading the charge for confrontation. In his memoir, *Present at the Creation*, Acheson writes that Kennan "mingled flashes of prophetic insight [with] suggestions . . . of total impracticality."[110] This was a valid critique in many respects. Yet Acheson was not an original thinker in his own right, and he lacked Kennan's flair for "prophetic insight." It was on issues of "practicality" that Acheson felt he bested Kennan.

These disagreements of "practicality" took on added importance after it became clear, near the end of 1948, that Acheson would replace Marshall as secretary of state due to the latter's health problems. For example, Acheson played an important role in the creation of the North Atlantic Treaty Organization, an alliance that connected Western Europe's security with North America's through the binding commitment that an attack on one signatory was an attack on all. At best, Kennan viewed NATO as a form of useful "psychotherapy for nervous Europeans"—in Anders Stephanson's apt description—and at worst it was a meaningless "legalistic commitment" with no bearing on international diplomatic realities. Of particular concern to Kennan was the possibility that NATO—all of whose original signatories were nations with an Atlantic link—might expand to include nations unconnected to Western security. So, "beyond the Atlantic area, which is a clean-cut concept, and which embraces a real community of defense interest firmly rooted in geography and tradition, there is no logical stopping point in the development of a system of anti-Russian alliances until that system has circled the globe and has embraced all the non-communist countries of Europe, Asia, and Africa."[111] Kennan was largely correct in his diagnosis: Turkey came first, and then a flood of nations joined NATO during the 1950s and beyond. Whether NATO was a diplomatic masterstroke, instilling anticommunist unity during the Cold War, or an albatross around America's neck is a matter for debate. But there is no doubt that Kennan's skepticism was and is the minority view.

On January 3, 1949, Kennan wrote a long letter to Dean Acheson detailing his concerns with current policy. "Please ascribe it . . . to reason . . . ," wrote Kennan, "when I say that I am not really interested in carrying on in government service unless I can feel that we have at least a sporting chance of coping with our problem:—that we are not just bravely paddling the antiquated raft of U.S. foreign policy upstream, at a speed of three miles an hour, against a current which is making four." In a wide-ranging letter, Kennan took aim at the administration's reckless saber-rattling, sustained by a pugnacious and irresponsible Congress and held "accountable" by a bewildered public:

> The thesis of the X article, you will recall, was that our main problem was a political one and that we had a good chance of coping with it by political means—(at least means short of a full-scale shooting war)—if we would stop moping, face up to the situation cheerfully and realistically, and conduct ourselves rationally, in terms of our own epoch. I still feel that way. When I took my present job in the Department, I thought there was a good chance that this could be accomplished. Today, I am skeptical. I am afraid that we are not really getting anywhere.

Kennan identified problems at multiple levels. The Truman administration had to "accept propaganda as a major weapon of policy," and the State Department "must not hesitate to get out and participate in the intellectual debate on U.S. foreign policy." Communicating the proper purpose of U.S. diplomacy required eschewing "both the arrogance of trying to 'go it alone' and the neurotic satisfaction of striking of idealistic attitudes . . . In this concept, there is no room for self-delusion and for lofty announcements about peace and democracy." The existence of the United Nations, "and the general current vogue for multilateral international negotiation," was making America's task in containing the Soviet Union all the more difficult. Stalin did not take the organization seriously—except as a useful device for easy wins, where applicable—but a guileless swell of world opinion viewed it as a bastion of collaborative altruism, beyond reproach and cynical carping. This delighted Moscow, for "it is fatuous to expect them to deal seriously in the UN . . . They would be fools, from their standpoint, to do so; and we would be greater fools to expect them to." Kennan had begun to give up hope of America communicating with a firm but modulated voice in world affairs: "And if this is the set-up, I'd rather be at Yale, or where-you-will,—any place where I could sound-off and talk freely to people,—than in the confines of a department in which you can neither do anything about it nor tell people what you think ought to be done."[112] Kennan had crafted a declaration of independence conditioned by frustration with his government and envy at Walter Lippmann's independence and influence. There was no point remaining in a government that had veered away so drastically from Kennan's worldview. Yet he still retained a little hope that the secretary of state would come around to his way of thinking.

It was not to be. Kennan's letter simply confirmed Acheson's doubts about the absence of "practicality" in his diplomatic thought, informed by antidemocratic sentiments and a yearning for a halcyon age that never was. Through the course of 1949, Kennan continued to languish on the periphery—as Truman's rhetoric grew fiercer, as a virulent anticommunism gathered strength under Senator Joe McCarthy's crudely effective direction—pining for the happier days of 1946 and imagining the pleasures that might accompany scholarly retreat. A spring visit to Hamburg, Kennan's favorite German city, had brought home to him the importance of preserving peace. The indiscriminate Allied bombing campaign had created a scene of devastation that even Kennan, with his imaginative gifts, could scarcely have visualized. The realist snapped and the artist took over:

> Here, for the first time, I felt an unshakable conviction that no momentary military advantage . . . could have justified this stupendous, careless destruction of civilian life and of material values . . . And it suddenly appeared to me that in these ruins there was an unanswerable symbolism which we in the West could not afford to ignore. If the Western

world was really going to make valid the pretense of a higher moral departure point . . . then it had to learn to fight its wars morally as well as militarily, or not fight them at all.[113]

Here was a sentiment remarkable in its moral force, about as detached from Acheson's perspective as one could imagine. In two mournful diary entries, Kennan confronted the obvious fact that his perspective on world affairs had become a lonely one. On November 19, 1949, he wrote that "it is time I recognized that my planning staff, started nearly three years ago, has simply been a failure, like all previous attempts to bring order and foresight into the designing of foreign policy by special institutional arrangements within the Department." Three days later, he lamented that "my concept of the manner in which our diplomatic effort should be conducted is not shared by any of the other senior officials of the Department . . . If I am ever to do any good in this work, having the courage of my convictions, it must be outside the walls of this institution and not inside them."[114] In Kennan's mind, America's Soviet policy had fluctuated wildly from 1943 to 1949: from accommodation, to surety of purpose, to overreaction, to something else entirely. It was he who had remained constant and in command of his faculties—a baseline on a volatile graph.

6

⋆

THE SCIENTIST

PAUL NITZE

> We must not write into the constitution of the world society a license to universal intervention. For if we license it, we shall invite it. If we invite it, we shall get it. —WALTER LIPPMANN

Paul Nitze was one of the first Americans to visit the spectral ruins of Hiroshima and Nagasaki in 1945. But the experience affected him in a very different way from George Kennan's visit to Hamburg four years later. Nitze had a specific job to do: "measure as precisely as possible the exact effects of the two bombs—in other words, to put calipers on the problem so that people back home would have a factual frame of reference within which to draw conclusions about the bomb's true capabilities as well as its limitations."[1] He had arrived in Hiroshima from Tokyo, where the U.S. Air Force had deployed incendiary devices to create a firestorm that destroyed sixteen square miles of the city and killed upwards of eighty thousand people. For Nitze, the devastation visited upon Tokyo, Hiroshima, and Nagasaki was indistinguishable—the differences between atomic and conventional weapons were not as surprising as the similarities in outcome. It was as if Nitze had traveled from Sodom to Gomorrah to Admah in the aftermath of Yahweh's final judgment. Each biblical city had been utterly destroyed. Did it really matter whether this was achieved by fire or brimstone? In those abnormal times, during a pitiless war, the atomic bomb struck Nitze as a weapon like any other in the modern era.[2]

There were other aspects of the atomic bombings that Nitze found particularly noteworthy. While the firebombing destroyed a large radius of Tokyo, the atomic bombing had a more intense but localized effect. "The significance of the atomic bomb," Nitze wrote, "was that it compressed the explosive power of many conventional bombs into one and thus enormously enhanced the effectiveness of a single bomber."[3] Beyond the immediate blast radius, Nitze noted that Nagasaki's railroads were operating after only forty-eight hours. People sitting by closed windows were hurt by broken glass but protected from the radiation. Residents who had retreated to subterranean air raid tunnels, even within ground zero, had survived the blast. The atomic bomb was not just a usable weapon—its impact could even be mitigated by civil defense. He took this lesson home with him, proselytizing on the issue of nuclear preparedness. When Nitze returned to New York City, he asked the powerful urban planner Robert Moses to encourage property developers to include nuclear bunkers in all new structures. Moses cut him off mid-sentence: "Paul, you're mad, absolutely mad. Nobody will pay attention to that."[4]

Nitze would encounter more occasions where his conception of the national interest would run aground on the rocks of what was domestically practicable. Throughout his career, Nitze ascribed consistently malevolent intentions to Moscow and insisted doggedly that its military capabilities were more fearsome than the intelligence community believed. Combining a keen interest in psychology, systems analysis, and the academic discipline of international relations, Nitze believed that America's political leaders had a marked tendency to systematically underestimate the magnitude of the threat posed by Moscow. Nitze was particularly hostile toward presidents Eisenhower, Nixon, Ford, and Carter, believing that each had endangered the nation in a different way. To dissuade Soviet aggression, Nitze recommended that the United States devote a far higher proportion of its GDP to military spending. He recognized that this course would prove a hard political sell, but he believed that the American people were willing to pay higher taxes, and sacrifice a little material comfort, to better safeguard their nation. Nitze's seminal contribution to U.S. grand strategy, NSC-68, dangled worst-case scenarios, then rationalized a vast expansion of the national security state to meet and repulse them; his scientism and certainty were a potent combination.[5]

Paul Henry Nitze was born in 1907 in Amherst, Massachusetts, where his father, William Albert, was a professor of philology. His family was of German extraction and had made a fortune in the nineteenth century during the boom in railway construction. The security of inherited family wealth and the elite university settings in which the family resided made for a rarefied childhood. A year after Paul's birth, William Nitze accepted a position as head of the department of Romance languages at the University of Chicago, where he remained for four decades.[6] Paul's best friend at school was Glenn Millikan, the son of a Nobel prize–winning physicist who lived across the street.[7] The Nitzes spent long summers in Europe, taking advantage of Chicago's generous sabbatical arrangements.

His father was a quiet man, though he came down volubly on any intellectual shoddiness displayed by his son. His mother, Anina Hilken, was different: flamboyant, socially confident, consumed by myriad interests—and utterly devoted to Paul. At dinner parties she drank, smoked, and engaged in passionate scholarly debate with her many academic guests. She read Kafka, admired the music of Richard Strauss, became friends with the dancer Isadora Duncan and the actress and burlesque dancer Sally Rand, and once remortgaged the family home to assist Clarence Darrow, as her son recalled, "in order to provide bail for a left-wing agitator he was defending." Anina was an irresistible presence in her son's life, filling the parental vacuum left by his father's taciturnity. "By far the greatest influence in my life was my mother," Nitze wrote. "At times the intensity of her love was overwhelming."[8]

Paul was a capable student at school. Indeed, he had little choice but to perform or face William's wrath, remembering later that none of his friends had such a demanding father.[9] But when he left John Dewey's University of Chicago Laboratory School for one of the nation's elite prep schools, Hotchkiss, he rebelled and took full advantage of the attendant freedoms, observing that his years in Connecticut "were full of camaraderie, athletics, girls, and studies—pretty much in that order."[10] Nitze remained true to these priorities when he joined Harvard's class of 1928, reflecting later on America's preeminent university with a strong dose of self-exculpation: "In those days grades didn't count. Harvard was more like a European university. You just tried to absorb wisdom. We all drank too much, had girls, and a rich, glorious life."[11]

He joined the highly exclusive Porcellian Club, contravened the strictures of Prohibition at every available opportunity, and generally had a riotous time. The Porcellian's motto is *Dum vivimus vivamus*—"While we live, let us live"—which in Nitze's case appeared not to refer to the life of the mind. His performance his first two years was abysmal, though the jolt to the system provided by these results spurred him on to perform well through the rest of his studies. After his slow start, it was in fact miraculous that Nitze only narrowly missed graduating magna cum laude. His talent was clearly present even if the application was harder to discern. Nitze and Kennan's experiences of college could scarcely have been more different.

Nitze was struck down by a serious bout of hepatitis upon graduation—his immune system compromised, perhaps, by his champagne-fueled decision the previous week to canoe from Boston to New York with only two cans of beans and a pocket knife for company. It took Nitze some months to recover from his illness, which derailed his initial plans to enter Harvard's doctoral program. Then, to his father's chagrin, Nitze changed tack and decided against pursuing an academic career. He had always found academia's detachment from public affairs troubling. One episode that struck home with young Paul was an erudite discussion that his father and his colleagues had about the Treaty of Versailles. Each agreed, with good reason, that the treaty was fundamentally flawed, but each, Nitze later observed, was "powerless to influence events . . . I wanted to be in a position where I could participate in world events, and be close to the levers of influence. Distinguished scholarship did not appear to offer that opportunity."[12]

Instead Nitze made some serious money. A Harvard urban legend holds that if a member of the Porcellian has not made a million dollars by the time he is forty, the club would cover the shortfall. Paul Nitze required no such largesse. In October 1929, the New York investment bank Dillon Read hired him. He decided to specialize in economics because it "was a field where one could be close to the levers of power—to put it frankly the levers of influence."[13] Nitze was conscious of his luck in landing a plum job with a storied firm at that vertiginous moment in world economic affairs: "I was very likely the last man hired on Wall Street for many years thereafter."[14] He took full advantage of this good fortune. While Nitze's father disapproved of his career as a shallow "money lender," Nitze made a million dollars by 1935 through an astute investment in a laboratory based in the United States, run by two French scientists, which developed a vitamin-mineral supplement called Visyneral and a "pill for certain types of diabetes," both of which turned out to be "smashing success[es]."[15] From Nitze's perspective, the marvelous thing about making so much money was that it allowed him to ignore quotidian matters like earning a salary. Instead he could now devote all his time to pondering issues that really mattered—like the precarious balance of power in Europe. This life of the mind had a distinct advantage over the university-based version. Nitze's financial success meant he could pursue his intellectual interests without attending to teaching or university service.

The book that transformed Nitze from banker into aspiring diplomat was Oswald Spengler's *The Decline of the West*, which had also weighed on Kennan: Nitze read it during a fishing trip in 1937 "with care, word by word, while waiting for a fish to appear."[16] The book evoked in Nitze deep concern about America's place in the international system, tilting inexorably away from the years of Western advantage, although he had mixed feelings about Spengler's analysis:

> It had all the faults of the German temperament; it was brilliant, full of profound feeling and thought, but dogmatic, rough, tactless. Along the peaceful banks of the Upsalquitch River, I pondered the flaws in its logic. How could the tendencies toward cultural delay, socialistic Caesarism and war, which he saw as being irreversible, be countered and reversed? I knew of no one who had a lucid and persuasive opinion on those issues.[17]

In search of remedies to Spengler's gloomy prognoses, Nitze resigned from Dillon Read and enrolled in Harvard as a graduate student in sociology, taking supplementary seminars in philosophy and international law. Nitze's second sojourn in Cambridge was significantly more diligent than the first—he drafted a well-received thesis on Spengler supervised by the eminent sociologist Pitirim Sorokin—but he ultimately found the experience frustrating, complaining that he "received almost no answers about Spengler, the trends of the future, and what could be done to affect those trends."[18] The discipline of history still dominated the teaching of international affairs at Harvard—and this was not enough. Nitze believed that foreign policy had to be reconceived and practiced on a more scientific basis.

Having received no assistance in identifying a strategic worldview at Harvard, Nitze joined Charles Beard and other isolationists in favoring a passive one: neutrality from European affairs. Indeed, his frequent trips to Germany, his Teutonic ancestry, and his respectful appraisals of Hitler's success in rebuilding a strong Germany led some critics to suspect him of harboring Nazi sympathies.[19] These whispered allegations were off the mark; Nitze was a consistent if apathetic "America Firster" in the absence of any better alternatives. Hitler was a serious threat to American interests; Nitze was sure of that. He simply held to this view while at the same time holding a grudging respect for Hitler's success in reenergizing his nation.

The fall of France led Nitze to abandon his isolationism, never deeply felt, and his hope that someone else might answer Spengler; he would have to do this under his own steam. James Forrestal, a former colleague at Dillon Read, hired Nitze to serve as one of six "administrative assistants" with links to the business community; their purpose was to co-opt the private sector in an era of total war. Forrestal asked Nitze to serve his government on June 22, 1940—in those pithier days the entire cable ran: "Be in Washington Monday morning. Forrestal"—but it took awhile for the government to grant him the necessary security clearances, largely due to persistent rumors circulating about Nitze's admiration for the Third Reich. He had not helped his cause when at a dinner party in 1940 he joked that he would rather live under Hitler's rule than that of the British Empire—a remark that clearly made its way to the wrong audience.[20] Nitze was eventually cleared of wrongdoing, though he accumulated a weighty FBI file in the process. Once added to the government payroll, Nitze was charged with sourcing materials needed for the war effort, including Mexican prairie dog bones, required for making glue, and dried cuttlefish, for making bombsight lenses.[21] Nitze performed adeptly in this role, even if the duties were somewhat infra dig for a Wall Street millionaire. What Nitze found harder to accept was the lackluster way the State Department went about its business:

> As Forrestal and I began to dig into the matter, we found the State Department under Cordell Hull almost totally lacking an organization for strategic policy-making. Most of the people in the State Department at that time had been brought up in the school of diplomacy that emphasized reporting; few were oriented toward the formulation and execution of strategic policy per se. We concluded that the State Department was inadequately staffed and not intellectually equipped to deal with the radically new situation brought about by the war.[22]

This disturbing geopolitical vacuum was of course addressed by Walter Lippmann in *U.S. Foreign Policy* and *U.S. War Aims*, and by Kennan in the Long Telegram and the X Article. Nitze first began to ruminate seriously on foreign policy in the summer of 1944, when he was invited to participate in the United States Strategic Bombing Survey, established to ascertain the effectiveness of Allied strategic bombing in the Atlantic and Pacific theaters during the Second World War. The USSBS boasted a remarkable staff, including a young Canadian economist named John Kenneth Galbraith and a future undersecretary of state and critic of the Americanization of the Vietnam War, George Ball. It was a rich experience, from which aspects of Nitze's "theory of international relations," as he later described it, began to emerge.

The survey drew mixed conclusions about the effectiveness of Allied bombing in reducing the ability of German factories to produce munitions. In the summer of 1943, for example, an RAF-led bombing raid code-named "Gomorrah" targeted the center of George Kennan's beloved Hamburg with conventional ordnance and incendiary devices, unleashing a firestorm that reached a thousand degrees, killing some thirty thousand people in hideous circumstances. The historic and commercial center of the city—home to its restaurants, shops, and museums—was razed to the ground. But the factories and shipyards on the city's perimeter were untouched by the inferno. This was a dark day in German history: the heart of a great city was destroyed at appalling human cost. But the unintended consequences could hardly have been worse from an Allied strategic perspective. An exodus of waiters, bank clerks, and shopkeepers, "forcibly unemployed by the bombers," as Galbraith recalled, "flocked to the war plants to find work . . . The bombers had eased the labor shortage." The USSBS found that strategic bombing did not critically hinder Germany's military capabilities.

The bombing did accrue advantages, but they were as unintended as the disadvantages. Allied bombers forced German fighters to scramble, where they were overwhelmed in dogfights through Anglo-American weight of numbers. Dominating European airspace, George Ball recalled, "gave us command of the air for the [D-day] invasion."[23] Nitze took note of the limitations and unintended benefits of strategic bombing. More important, however, he was deeply impressed by the fact that the much larger defense budget of the United States, and that of Stalin's Soviet Union, had allowed the Allies to simply outproduce and outlast the German war machine. Berlin could not keep pace with its enemies in production terms, despite Albert Speer's best efforts. Once this fact was established, and it became clear that "Hitler's Empire" was not an imperial system—like Great Britain's—that could be co-opted and worked to the homeland's advantage, its military prospects were greatly diminished.[24] Nitze extrapolated that America should seek to build a permanent military advantage through devoting a higher proportion of national wealth to defense spending than any peer competitor. He described this goal as achieving for the United States in perpetuity a favorable "correlation of forces"—the strategic imperative that guided him through the entire Cold War.

From Harvard to Wall Street to World War II, Nitze was a committed Republican: cool toward Franklin Roosevelt's presidency and seriously concerned about his successor's leadership potential. Nitze's wartime appraisal of Truman was "less than favorable . . . When he became president I had visions of this country being turned over to political cronies of his . . . My wife Phyllis caused me to change my mind about Mr. Truman. When I came home from Europe in 1945 I found her convinced that the Trumans— Mrs. Truman in particular—were wonderful people of great integrity."[25] Throughout the early stages of the Cold War, Nitze came to warmly support the president's hard-edged diplomacy and was particularly impressed by the Truman Doctrine, caring little whether or not the commitments enunciated were open-ended. Truman had proved himself to be a leader of "courage and guts," in Nitze's estimation, who intuitively understood that the United States had to assume the preponderant burden "of leadership of the free world, no matter what was required."[26] The Wilsonian elements of Truman's approach that worried Kennan—linking America's liberty to the extension of freedom to all nations—roused only the warmest support in Nitze.

Nitze was based in the State Department's Office of International Trade Policy during the genesis of the Marshall Plan. After Kennan and Lippmann had thrashed out the basics of a reconstruction program, Nitze found himself in disagreement with its sole European focus. He suggested to his close friend Will Clayton, undersecretary of state for economic affairs, that the government disburse $5 billion of aid per annum, over a five-year period, to offset a balance of payments of surplus of a similar amount. But Nitze wanted this funding allocated "on a worldwide basis rather than concentrating it all in Europe." Kennan was hostile to the idea of spreading aid thinly, and to areas of the world whose prospects he deemed tangential to America's national interest. Nitze's view was, "Why Europe? The problem [of the communist threat] was a worldwide problem. Why not do it on a broader scale? But the decision finally was in favor of Kennan's approach of just an aid program to support Europe, not worldwide."[27] Nitze was forming a strong difference with Kennan on what constituted an appropriate range of America's overseas interests.

After he lost this debate, Nitze picked himself up with little fuss or self-recrimination and started adding substance to the Marshall Plan's bare outline. He called in favors to borrow some protocomputers from Prudential Life Insurance and began figuring out exactly what each European nation required. Nitze was in his quantitative element, compiling charts and graphs, identifying each nation's economic strengths and weaknesses, predicting the likely agricultural productivity of each, matching American surpluses in raw materials to European shortfalls. This paragon of Wall Street was a splendid statist, warming to the powers and certainties of centralized planning. Clayton described Nitze as "young, able and a hard worker. Moreover he knows more about the Marshall Plan than perhaps any other individual around here." Nitze was called to testify before a hostile Congress on the Marshall Plan's substance and purpose. It was a rough ride, but he managed to convince many Republicans of its merits, including Arthur Vandenberg, who observed that it was "backed by more hard work and careful research than almost any other bill to come before Congress."[28] Kennan's ideas and Nitze's logistical prowess had worked well in tandem.

On balance, however, discord between Nitze and Kennan was a more common response than concord to the salient geostrategic issues. President Truman's Point Four Program, for example, designed to deploy American science, industry, and aid to modernize the underdeveloped world, garnered Nitze's strong support. He was concerned that U.S. policy in Asia focused so intently on China and Japan, to the exclusion of a vast area: "The rest of Asia, except for the Philippines, stretching from the Persian Gulf to the Pacific, was generally unfamiliar territory that festered with problems—anticolonialism, social unrest, overcrowded populations, and economies that despite their resources and potential wealth remained underdeveloped."[29] Kennan evinced little concern for the Third World, for it mattered little to Washington if those nations continued to stagnate or flourished. It was preferable if poorer nations became richer, but it did not fall upon the United States to facilitate this process, the costs of which would eventually outrun its resources. Nitze believed that the range of America's overseas interests had no geographical boundaries, and that its latent capabilities would simply have to expand to take the strain. If that required a tax hike or the restructuring of the American economy—well, so be it.

Of course, Kennan's conception of the national interest had not diverged only from Nitze's but from every senior figure in the Truman administration. He liked Nitze personally, found him highly capable, and was relaxed at the prospect of him succeeding him. When Nitze joined PPS as his deputy in the summer of 1949, Kennan vacated his office for him and moved to work in a conference room down the hall. There could hardly have been a clearer signal that Kennan had anointed his successor. Then the H-bomb debate intervened, Kennan fell farther to the margins, and he began to have second thoughts. He wrote to Chip Bohlen that the "question must soon be faced as to who should succeed me. My own inclination would be to say that unless you yourself would feel like coming home . . . they should leave it vacant for a while."[30] But the die had already been cast. Nitze had momentum and had forged a close working relationship with Dean Acheson. After relocating to the Institute for Advanced Study at Princeton—where he eventually won over the mathematicians who were skeptical about his lack of academic bona fides—Kennan found it difficult to accept the manner of his eclipse. In the summer of 1950, Kennan half joked to Nitze and Acheson that "when I left the department, it never occurred to me that you two would make foreign policy without having first consulted me."[31]

Upon taking the reins at the PPS, Nitze effected a transformation in its manner of operation. Alluding to his predecessor's foibles, Nitze observed, "There was no point in producing a marvelous piece of paper if it didn't get read."[32] The main problem with Kennan's PPS was that it resembled an artist's studio in Renaissance Florence. Each of the staffers gained valuable experience and proximity to a genius, and many, in turn, went on to become substantial figures in their own right. But the papers that emerged were unmistakably Kennan's—as the paintings and sculptures were Donatello's or Michelangelo's. True collaboration was not possible in the master-apprentice relationship favored by Kennan, meaning all documents that emerged from the PPS had a single voice. This was hardly surprising, as Kennan's mode of operation was to discuss an issue with his staff and then sequester himself away to write alone without interruption. All policy papers had literary consistency, but when the audience became uncongenial, as happened with Acheson, the papers ceased to matter in the policymaking crucible. The Policy Planning Staff's output throughout 1949 came to consist primarily of minority reports and dissenting opinions—valuable for posterity but peripheral to the times.

Reporting on Nitze's appointment, *The Washington Star* quoted an unnamed source at the State Department who observed perceptively that "Kennan's leadership of the Policy Planning Staff was a little like a gallant cavalry charge with George brandishing a saber in the lead, astride the most spirited horse in the regiment. Nitze operates more like a chief of staff—or like the editor of a great research project. He presides, listens, and suggests.

He organizes, deputizes, and supervises. He weighs, balances, analyzes, and sums up."[33] This marked difference in style owed a lot to Nitze's career on Wall Street, as well as to the logistical nature of his wartime service and his work on the Marshall Plan. But due to his disciplinary preferences, it also stood to reason that Nitze would prefer the collaborative model of research common to the natural and social sciences, ahead of the lone scholar version common to the arts and humanities.

Nitze had developed many close links with the RAND Corporation (an acronym for research and development), which was established in 1946 to offer quantitative analysis to the U.S. Air Force, but which struck out as a nonprofit think tank in 1948 with seed money from the Ford Foundation. RAND's motto is simple: "To help improve policy and decision-making through research and analysis." According to the historian Alex Abella, its headquarters in Santa Monica, California, were "designed to be like a campus without students, just faculty thinking about the vicissitudes of their specialty."[34] RAND's approach was interdisciplinary, bringing together natural and social scientists to offer recommendations informed by the fledgling discipline of systems analysis. Nitze had long sought to quantify problems, eradicating the requirement for subjective value judgment in the process. He believed that the practice of international relations could be made more scientific, reducing the margin for error.

Nitze was given an opportunity to deploy these RAND-favored methods when President Truman issued a directive on January 31 that the State and Defense Departments "undertake a re-examination of our objectives in peace and war and of the effect of these objectives on our strategic plans, in the light of the probable fission bomb capability and possible thermonuclear capability of the Soviet Union."[35] Acheson delegated this task to Nitze, who immediately gathered an abundance of numerical data, which included predictions by the Joint Chiefs of Staff that the Soviet Union could have in its armory some 135 atomic bombs by mid-1953. If the figures were correct, the response was clear: the United States had to spend much more on both its nuclear and conventional deterrents. Nitze identified the likeliest opponents of military expansion and hired them as consultants to the project, persuading the likes of Robert Oppenheimer and James Conant—the president of Harvard University and consultant to the Atomic Energy Commission—that the Soviet threat was as ominous as the JCS suggested. Nitze also convinced Deputy Secretary of Defense Robert Lovett to abandon the Pentagon's plans for a separate review and instead collaborate with his team at the PPS. Through a deft bureaucratic sleight of hand, Nitze used new classification rules to shield his deliberations from the Treasury and budget bureau.[36] Through force of personality and example, Nitze inspired his team to work unrelenting hours in preparing a comprehensive response to Truman's request. The report that emerged, NSC-68, was very much a team effort, with PPS staffers such as John Paton Davies crafting some of its most memorable phrases. But its primary author and booster was Paul Nitze.

The manner of NSC-68's planning and execution was far removed from the style favored by Kennan. Its contents were too. NSC-68's estimate of threat assessment was influenced by Nathan Leites, a RAND social scientist who would write the important book *The Operational Code of the Politburo*. Nitze came to know Leites's work through his connections with RAND, and he was impressed by his insights, drawn mainly from psychology and psychoanalysis, regarding the relentless expansionary instincts of the Politburo. NSC-68 follows Leites in identifying a series of "rules" or "codes" that drove Soviet behavior—referred to in the document as the drivers behind a cohesive Soviet "design." Indeed, the word "design" is used some fifty times in NSC-68 and is deployed to imply malevolence, rather than "purpose" or "strategy," which suggest normality in diplomatic intention. So the third section of NSC-68, "The Fundamental Design of the Kremlin," describes Soviet intentions in the following terms:

> The design . . . calls for the complete subversion or forcible destruction of the machinery of government and structure of society in the countries of the non-Soviet world and their replacement by an apparatus and structure subservient to and controlled from the Kremlin. To that end Soviet efforts are now directed toward the domination of the Eurasian land mass. The United States, as the principal center of power in the non-Soviet world and the bulwark of opposition to Soviet expansion, is the principal enemy whose integrity and vitality must be subverted or destroyed by one means or another if the Kremlin is to achieve its fundamental design.[37]

A very different manner of expression had entered the American diplomatic lexicon.

Interpretative certainty conveyed in searing language courses through NSC-68's seventy-one pages. The following sentences provide a good example: "The implacable purpose of the slave state to eliminate the challenge of freedom has placed the two great powers at opposite poles. It is this fact which gives the present polarization of power the quality of crisis." The violence of the language was designed to carve out latitude in implementing a response. Defeating the designs of a "slave state," the ultimate purpose of which is to eliminate "freedom," justifies recourse to just about anything in whatever location the threat arises. And this is what Nitze demanded. Kennan's Long Telegram and X Article were imprecise in delineating the full range of vital American interests. There is no such ambiguity in NSC-68. The document identifies and confronts a major problem: that Marxism-Leninism holds the greatest appeal to underdeveloped nations emerging from colonial rule, hostile to a "West" synonymous not with progress and freedom but with exploitation:

> The ideological pretensions of the Kremlin are another great source of strength . . . They have found a particularly receptive audience in Asia, especially as the Asiatics have been impressed by what has been plausibly portrayed to them as the rapid advance of the USSR from a backward society to a position of great world power . . . The Kremlin cynically identifies itself with the genuine aspirations of large numbers of people, and places itself at the head of an international crusade with all of the benefits which derive therefrom.

To remedy this situation, Nitze advocated greater "assistance in economic development," but that on its own is insufficient. "The assault on free institutions is world-wide now," he wrote, "and in the context of the present polarization of power a defeat of free institutions anywhere is a defeat everywhere." The Cold War had been truly transformed into a zero-sum game, in which few Soviet provocations—real or perceived—could be ignored. Here was a doctrine of considerable force. In combating a broad-front Soviet assault, NSC-68 cautions against letting anything slip:

> The shadow of Soviet force falls darkly on Western Europe and Asia and supports a policy of encroachment. The free world lacks adequate means—in the form of forces in being—to thwart such expansion locally. The United States will therefore be confronted more frequently with the dilemma of reacting totally to a limited extension of Soviet control or of not reacting at all . . . Continuation of present trends is likely to lead, therefore, to a gradual withdrawal under the direct or indirect pressure of the Soviet Union, until we discover one day that we have sacrificed positions of vital interest. In other words, the United

States would have chosen, by lack of the necessary decisions and actions, to fall back to isolation in the Western Hemisphere.

This dilemma can be rephrased as an old adage: give an inch and Moscow will take a mile. NSC-68 calls for the creation of a flexible U.S. capability to respond to all manner of provocation at all geographical points.
American credibility was at stake everywhere, for ignoring transgressions
would invite subsequent aggression on a larger scale. All citizens needed to
realize that "the cold war is in fact a real war in which the survival of the
free world is at stake."

Despite its militant language, NSC-68 did not countenance waging a
premeditated war against the Soviet Union—America reserved the right to
respond symmetrically or asymmetrically depending on circumstances. "It
goes without saying," Nitze clarified, "that the idea of 'preventive' war—in
the sense of a military attack not provoked by a military attack upon us or
our allies—is generally unacceptable to Americans . . . Although the American people would probably rally in support of the war effort, the shock of
responsibility for a surprise attack would be morally corrosive." Instead
NSC-68 called for a "more rapid build-up of political, economic, and military strength," to a point of sufficiency where the United States had "the
military power to deter, if possible, Soviet expansion, and to defeat, if necessary, aggressive Soviet or Soviet-directed actions of a limited or total
character."

Defensive capabilities of this sort were not likely to come cheap, and
Nitze, before submitting the report, asked Acheson for advice on whether to
include a realistic cost estimate. "Paul," Acheson said, "don't put any such
figure into this report . . . One first ought to decide whether this is the kind
of policy one wants to follow. The extent to which one actually implements
it with appropriations is a separate question which involves the domestic
economy and other considerations. So don't get into that hassle at this stage."[38]
Acheson later commented that the purpose of NSC-68 was to "bludgeon the
mass mind of government."[39] Nitze wielded the bludgeon, certainly, but
Acheson was wise to counsel against revealing the true cost of waging
the global Cold War. The actual cost was arguably more frightening than
the presentation of an expansionist Soviet slave state. The U.S. defense budget quadrupled from 1950 to 1951: from $13.5 billion to $48.2 billion.[40] In
some ways Nitze was following Alfred Mahan in emphasizing the need for
greater military preparedness. But Mahan made his case when the United

States was a second-tier military power; Nitze did so when the United States was utterly dominant at sea and in possession of the world's most advanced weaponry. NSC-68 truly created what Dwight Eisenhower would later identify with concern as the "military-industrial complex."

Senator Arthur Vandenberg had told Truman and Acheson that they would "have to scare hell out of the American people" to secure the necessary support for the containment strategy.[41] NSC-68 was written for a supposedly less credulous and twitchy audience: the government and bureaucracy. But it scared people all the same. Nitze submitted the report to President Truman on April 7, 1950, who passed a copy to his chief domestic adviser, Charles Murphy, for his assessment. Murphy took the report home, read it, and was so shaken by Nitze's diagnosis of Soviet intentions that he took the following day off work, reading key passages again and again, worrying about the war that was all but certain to visit the world.[42]

Secretary of Defense Louis Johnson was less impressed. A thrifty man, Johnson immediately understood that the document's planning prescriptions, though unspecified in cost terms, would require a fundamental restructuring of the American economy. At a March 22 meeting called to discuss the report, Johnson stormed in, accused Nitze of hatching a "conspiracy" designed to undermine his efforts to control the budget, and stormed out again. News of the meeting spread throughout the Truman administration, generating sympathy for Nitze—a rare occurrence—and scorn for Johnson's supposedly intemperate stance. A few weeks later, while Johnson was in Europe on NATO business, the report made its way to the president. Nitze recalled that Johnson "made kind of an ass of himself."[43] The secretary of defense had also lost control of the planning process and, with it, the budget.

George Kennan took a predictably dim view of NSC-68: "With the preparation of NSC-68 I had nothing to do. I was disgusted about the assumptions concerning Soviet intentions."[44] It was histrionic, adjective laden, belligerent, and informed by insights from the social sciences, and contained an explicit rebuttal of his containment doctrine. It had taken just weeks for Nitze to jettison Kennan's cautious and carefully calibrated diplomatic legacy. Chip Bohlen joined Kennan's side in decrying the manner in which the report "gave too much emphasis to Soviet ambitions for expansion." Acheson stepped in to arbitrate the dispute but found Bohlen's critique unpersuasive. The language stood; all that remained was a presidential signature.

But this was no formality. Truman sympathized with Louis Johnson in his desire to limit American defense spending and balance the books. The president placed NSC-68 in a holding pattern, concerned that Nitze's grand strategic vision might derail his domestic agenda and his party's political prospects. Chances for presidential approval appeared slim until a conflict intervened that vested the report with decisive momentum. When North Korea invaded South Korea, Nitze's supposedly alarmist portrayal suddenly appeared accurate and measured.

At the close of the Second World War, Korea had been divided at the 38th parallel, with a Soviet occupation zone to the north and an American one to the south. The fiercely doctrinaire communist Kim Il-Sung ruled northern Korea in the manner of Josef Stalin. In the south, the corrupt, conservative Syngman Rhee wielded power. Rhee had studied for his doctorate at Princeton with Woodrow Wilson, was strongly pro-Western in political and economic preferences, Christian in spiritual matters, and as determined as Kim to reunify the nation on his own terms. The United States was unwilling to sanction or support Rhee's desire to launch a preemptive strike north of the 38th parallel. But Kim was more fortunate—if that is the word—in his superpower patron. Having been pestered for months with requests for support, Stalin reluctantly agreed to support Kim's invasion plans in April 1950, warning his zealous young comrade that "if you get kicked in the teeth, I shall not lift a finger."[45] Stalin's qualified consent was more than enough encouragement for Kim. On June 25, a hundred thousand North Korean troops poured across the 38th parallel, forcing the enemy into full-scale retreat.[46] The shock felt in Washington was palpable. Nitze's NSC-68 began to look as farsighted in 1950 as Kennan's Long Telegram had appeared in 1946.

The speed and purpose of America's reaction startled Stalin, whose support for Kim presupposed that the Western response would be limited to nonmilitary channels. Instead, Truman came out fighting to a degree that surprised even Nitze, who described his president as "a very feisty fellow [who] was prepared to fight anybody and everybody as long as he was convinced he was right." And so it was with the Korean War. The president took advantage of the Soviet Union's absence from the United Nations Security Council to secure UN approval for military action to repulse the northern offensive. Within days, the United States had committed itself to liberate South Korea. And as NSC-68 had recommended, America's range of strategic interests widened considerably. The Seventh Fleet was deployed to the Taiwan Strait. The Truman administration increased its financial support for the French effort to put down a communist insurgency in Indochina.

Hard realities compelled Truman to conclude that his fiscal caution had been misplaced, that NSC-68 was correct in identifying Marxism-Leninism as expansionary and insatiable. Nitze recalled that "when the attack took place, [Truman] felt that really did settle the matter in his mind. He came to the conclusion that what NSC-68 basically said . . . was true."[47] Containment had truly shed its European focus.

Nitze's and Kennan's responses to the war were in fact identical. Both shared a common belief that the United States should respond forcefully to this gross violation of the postwar status quo; this was a clear example of what NSC-68 identified as "piecemeal aggression." Kennan was immediately summoned to Washington from rural Pennsylvania in an advisory capacity—the summoning process hindered by Kennan's refusal to have a telephone installed at the farm. At a meeting in Dean Acheson's office on June 26, Kennan "stated it as my deep conviction that the U.S. had no choice but to accept this challenge and to make it its purpose to see to it that South Korea was restored to the rule of the Republic of Korea. The question of what we should commit to this purpose was simply a question of what was required for the completion of the task."[48] Nitze was of a similar mind, though Kennan confided to his diary that he was worried about working with his successor, as "my whole framework of thought . . . was strange to Nitze, and . . . he would be apt to act on concepts of his own which would differ from those I had put forward."[49] Kennan need not have worried. NSC-68's bluster and unwillingness to countenance opportunity costs was not to Kennan's taste, but confronting a clear-cut case of communist aggression—an internationally recognized boundary was breached, after all—was a different matter.

In September 1950, United Nations troops, composed primarily of U.S. Marines, executed an audacious amphibious landing at Inchon on the northwestern part of the Korean Peninsula. General Douglas MacArthur devised the plan and led the assault, which ultimately enabled the UN forces to divide and scatter its enemy. After Inchon, first Seoul and then the remainder of South Korea were liberated in a matter of weeks. This major battlefield victory led MacArthur to pose the question of what to do next. The primary goal of restoring Korea's 1945 boundary at the 38th parallel had been achieved. But building on this momentum to liberate North Korea from Kim Il-Sung was an enticing prospect for a man of MacArthur's outsized ambitions, which included a likely run at the presidency in 1952. Truman was fully aware of MacArthur's megalomania, describing him privately as "Mr. Prima Donna, Brass Hat, Five Star MacArthur."[50] Yet the president understood that MacArthur had momentum, and that liberating North Korea might quiet Republican attacks that he had "lost China" in 1949—when forces loyal to the communist Mao Zedong defeated Chiang Kai-shek's Nationalist army, so ending the Chinese Civil War. MacArthur and Truman both discerned political advantage in removing a communist regime from the face of the earth.

During a debate in the State Department on the merits or otherwise of attempting to liberate North Korea, Nitze and Kennan collaborated on a paper that argued strongly against it. The gist of their opposition was that moving north might provoke Chinese intervention, which in turn would lead to a much larger and more dangerous conflict. John M. Allison, director of the Office of Northeast Asian Affairs at State, presented a strong case to the contrary, criticizing Nitze and Kennan for recommending "appeasement"—that dread word which summoned worst-case scenarios to conceal argumentative deficiencies—and the abdication of "moral principles." Instead, Allison advised that MacArthur be permitted to lead his troops "right on up to the Manchurian and Siberian border," a crushing hypothetical victory that would facilitate a "UN-supervised election for all of Korea."[51] Caught up in the fervor, Acheson, George Marshall—who had been recalled to replace Louis Johnson as secretary of defense—and Truman all decided to support the "sorcerer of Inchon," as Acheson nicknamed MacArthur upon more sober reflection. On September 29, Marshall sent MacArthur a cable that read: "We want you to feel unhampered tactically and strategically to proceed north of the 38th parallel."[52]

Kennan and Nitze called it correctly. As MacArthur edged northward, hundreds of thousands of Chinese troops crossed their border to assume well-concealed defensive positions, hiding themselves in mine shafts and tunnels, not lighting fires that might alert their enemy, and preparing themselves to strike if MacArthur's UN force came too far north. After testing the water with a series of minor skirmishes, on November 25, 1950, the People's Volunteer Army launched a massive surprise attack that forced the advancing UN army into a swift and embarrassing retreat. By January 4, 1951, Chinese and North Korean troops had recaptured Seoul. China's shock entry to the Korean War had forced the U.S. military into its longest retreat in history.

The UN force eventually recovered its poise and Seoul was recaptured. But General MacArthur again wanted to expand the war's parameters, placing him on a collision course with Washington. In March 1951, Truman received word from the National Security Agency that MacArthur had been musing openly on launching a wider war against Red China to restore Chiang Kai-shek to power. Late that month, MacArthur supplied the Republican leader in the House of Representatives, Joseph William Martin Jr., with a speech criticizing Truman's leadership, which Martin read out on the floor of the House. The concluding paragraph brought to mind NSC-68's stridency:

> It seems strangely difficult for some to realize that here in Asia is where the Communist conspirators have elected to make their play for global conquest, and that we have joined the issue thus raised on the battlefield; that here we fight Europe's war with arms while the diplomats there still fight it with words; that if we lose the war to communism in Asia the fall of Europe is inevitable; win it and Europe most probably would avoid war and yet preserve freedom. As you have pointed out, we must win. There is no substitute for victory.[53]

Nitze had authored, or at least superintended the drafting of, similar sentiments. Yet he was appalled by this rank insubordination. On April 10, he helped draft President Truman's announcement that MacArthur was to be relieved of his command. MacArthur returned home to a ticker-tape parade in New York City, and Senator Joseph McCarthy was given yet more material for his campaign to purify the nation. Privately, McCarthy said of President Truman that the "son of a bitch ought to be impeached." Publicly, McCarthy predicted during a speech in Milwaukee that MacArthur's dismissal would produce a situation where "red waters may lap at all of our shores." He further opined that "unless the public demands a halt in Operation Acheson, Asia, the Pacific, and Europe may be lost to communism."[54] After observing an enthusiastic audience applaud McCarthy's histrionics in Milwaukee, his hometown, Kennan committed a long, mournful entry to his diary:

> For the first time in my life I have become conscious of the existence of powerful forces in the country to which, if they are successful, no democratic adjustment can be made: people in other words, to whom there is no reasonable approach, to whom the traditions of tolerance and civil liberty are of no real importance, people who have to be regarded as totalitarian enemies . . . I am now in the truest sense of the word an expatriate. As an individual, my game is up in this part of the world.[55]

Two days later, Kennan observed that "McCarthyism has already won, in the sense of making impossible the conduct of an intelligent foreign policy. The result is that there is no place in public life for an honest and moderate man."[56]

The Korean War was effectively stalemated near the 38th parallel from the summer of 1951 to the summer of 1953. It had been waged for sound reasons—to repulse clear-cut aggression—but had expanded into a much wider conflict, with the potential to expand even farther, and had caused painful ruptures in the American polity. The way MacArthur and McCarthy excoriated Truman's handling of the conflict—his refusal to invade China and/or use nuclear weapons for fear of provoking the Soviet Union—testified to the dangers of open-ended fidelity to strategic blueprints. Nitze himself advocated an unerringly cautious approach to the Korean War. But rationalizing the Cold War in NSC-68 as a struggle between "slave states" and the forces of "freedom" raised the stakes to a dangerous level, contributing to the creation of a febrile environment conducive to demagoguery. As Kennan wrote on August 4, 1951, "There is no escaping the vulgarizers, the detractors, the dismantlers, the strident over-simplifiers of our generation."[57] Diplomacy was no place to pander to the lowest common denominator. The Korean War was a truly terrible conflict in which upwards of two million soldiers died, including nearly forty thousand Americans. The reckless way the conflict was waged on the battlefield, and debated on the American home front, was a foretaste of worse to come.

Fearsome as it was, the Korean conflict coincided with Paul Nitze's optimum moment of professional satisfaction: "The happiest and most productive years of my life were those from 1947 to January 1953, when I was among those working closely with Dean creating the modern world."[58] Acheson was similarly inclined—he titled his subsequent memoir *Present at the Creation*—viewing Nitze as the exemplary strategist: hard-nosed, steadfast, but aware that full-frontal war with the Soviet Union offered no answers. Nitze and Acheson formed a very close friendship. George Kennan, meanwhile, continued to view both men, and the vast geostrategic commitments promised by NSC-68, with alarm. He wrote a long letter to Acheson on September 1, 1951 detailing his continued desire to avoid government service. Kennan noted that his high regard for the State Department, and his personal friendships with those who labored there, "have served to obscure the full measure of divergence between my own views and those that have been, and are, current in the shaping of policy and in the administration of the process of external relations. I say that quite without bitterness, and in the full realization that in many of these differences it is entirely possible that I may be the one farthest from wisdom."[59] Nitze and Acheson had no doubt of the truth conveyed in Kennan's final sentence.

But Nitze's service to the Truman administration had to come to an end. In February 1951, the ratification of the Twenty-second Amendment—which limited American presidents to two terms, or to one term and more than two years of a previous president's term—made it likely that this would occur after the general election of 1952. In a study in contrasts, the election pitted the Democrat Adlai Stevenson against the Republican Dwight D. Eisenhower—the intellectual versus the war hero. Weighing each candidate's merits, Walter Lippmann decided to endorse Eisenhower. Considering the national interest first and foremost, Lippmann believed that the Democratic Party's stranglehold on the executive branch had created a harmful imbalance in the political system: "Eisenhower appeared as a possibility, and a national hero—and that had other advantages. It not only virtually insured [sic] that the Republicans would come back to power, as you might say, respectably . . . but also because Eisenhower, due to his position as a national hero, was, in my view, bound to attract McCarthy and destroy him. And that is, as a matter of fact, what happened."[60]

Nitze's view of Eisenhower was less favorable. He had actually supported Eisenhower through the primary campaign—having remained a registered Republican through his service to the Truman administration—but Nitze switched allegiances following the Republican National Convention in Chicago in July 1952. Nitze watched in disgust as one speaker after another lambasted the Truman administration for a litany of supposed misdeeds: losing China; firing General MacArthur, one of the nation's greatest patriots; harboring communists; engaging in corruption; and so on and so forth. Eisenhower, who should have known better, was guilty of some of the worst slurs. Nitze recalled that "he said the most outrageous things that I was fully persuaded that he knew to be untrue or else he was the stupidest man in the world. I couldn't imagine he was that stupid, therefore I came to the conclusion that he was basically a fraud." Eisenhower's acceptance speech accused the Truman administration of corruption and malfeasance. "To have Eisenhower call [Democrats] a bunch of crooks, carpetbaggers, and so forth," Nitze fumed, "was absolutely the worst kind of demagoguery."[61]

Eisenhower, who had served an unhappy tenure as president of Columbia University, was generally skeptical of the utility of hiring intellectuals to advise politicians. Responding to an aide's proposal that a group of academics might be convened to review U.S. nuclear policy, Eisenhower replied that he did not want a "lot of long-haired professors" to examine matters of such national significance, exclaiming, "What the hell do they know about it?"[62] In 1954, Eisenhower described the "intellectual" acidly as "a man who takes more words than necessary to tell more than he knows."[63]

Adlai Stevenson, the Democratic Party's Princeton-educated, pointy-headed candidate—and a Unitarian, to boot—may well have been Eisenhower's intended target. The columnist Stewart Alsop coined the word "egghead" to categorize the type—of bulging cerebra—who swooned at Stevenson's erudition. Academic luminaries such as John Kenneth Galbraith and Arthur Schlesinger Jr., drafted Stevenson's speeches, which were peppered with classical allusions and quotations from Shakespeare.[64] George Kennan, delighted to have the chance to vote for a politician who did not resemble an irredeemable philistine, was charmed and offered Stevenson his support. But Stevenson himself recognized that his intellectual disposition, and devoted following among the nation's intelligentsia, was unlikely to provide a real advantage. Responding favorably to one of Stevenson's elegantly crafted speeches, a campaign supporter reportedly gushed, "Good for you, Governor, you're the thinking man's candidate!" "Thanks," replied Stevenson, "but I need a majority to win."[65] And so it turned out. Eisenhower won with 442 electoral votes to Stevenson's 89. As a consolation prize, which distilled both his virtues and his predicament, Stevenson was elected a fellow of the American Academy of Arts and Sciences.

Paul Nitze was disappointed at the outcome of the election, but he remained hopeful that his advisory services might be retained. To this end Nitze, in collaboration with others, including Assistant Secretary of Defense Frank Nash, drafted a long paper titled "Reexamination of United States Programs for National Security," which was presented to the National Security Council as NSC-141 on President Truman's last day in the White House. The paper called for a vast buildup of nonnuclear forces to allow the United States to properly meet the range of challenges delineated in NSC-68. The report placed no price tag on its recommendations, which amounted to a significant expansion of a military budget that had already quadrupled over three years. But the report made clear the severity of the challenges that lay ahead:

> A capability for varied and flexible application of our striking power
> is essential both because of the wide variety of situations which may

confront us and because such a capability offers the best chance to convince the Soviets that they cannot hope to destroy our striking power
by surprise attack.[66]

Nitze's valedictory advice to the Eisenhower administration was uncompromising: continue implementing the expansionary logic of NSC-68,
funding nuclear and nonnuclear capabilities at ever-increasing levels, or invite Soviet aggression. "Flexibility" in response was the key word, a capability
that would come at a substantial price.

It all started so promisingly. President Eisenhower's inaugural address could
have been filched from NSC-68, declining as it did to impose any hierarchy
of interest upon a concept as pure as freedom. "Conceiving the defense of
freedom, like freedom itself, to be one and indivisible," Eisenhower said,
"we hold all continents and peoples in equal regard and honor. We reject
any insinuation that one race or another, one people or another, is in any
sense inferior or expendable." Uttering a sentiment that chimed melodically
with Nitze's worldview, and jarred discordantly with Kennan's, Eisenhower
reinforced the universalism of his inaugural address six months later: "As
there is no weapon too small, no arena too remote, to be ignored, there is no
free nation too humble to be forgotten."[67]

These sentiments cheered Nitze, but they were not matched by the necessary corollary: increased defense spending. In fact, Eisenhower had told
Senator Robert Taft, his main challenger throughout the Republican primaries, that he planned to cut $5 billion from the Truman defense budget in
1954—the reverse of what Nitze had recommended in NSC-68 and NSC-141.
Indeed, Eisenhower was as good as his word, cutting the defense budget
from $41.3 billion to $36 billion in his first year in office, taking the largest
share from the Air Force—as any good soldier should. Eisenhower's public
stance was that America's foreign-policy interests were theoretically limitless. Privately, he opposed increasing the defense budget "excessively under
the impulse of fear," which "could, in the long-run, defeat our purposes by
damaging the growth of our economy and eventually forcing it into regi-
mented controls."[68] As Nitze was sympathetic to such government controls—
believing that living standards could stand to fall and taxes could certainly
rise, in the pursuit of an unchallengeable military machine—he did not
look kindly upon the Eisenhower administration's defense policies.

Prior to assuming office, Eisenhower actually considered appointing
Nitze as his secretary of defense. John Foster Dulles talked him out of

this idea, observing that it was unwise to appoint "an Acheson man" to such an important post, particularly as Eisenhower's hawkish running mate, Richard Nixon, had described Acheson as the "red dean of the cowardly college of containment."[69] But Eisenhower had been impressed by Nitze's anti-Soviet mettle and remained keen to find a place for him in his administration.

To this end the president drafted Nitze to advise the administration on how to respond to Stalin's death in March 1953. Did the dictator's demise present any opportunities for U.S.-Soviet rapprochement? If so, how might they be pursued without appearing weak? Nitze's advisory role began inauspiciously when he walked into the president's quarters midway through a change of outfit: "I caught him standing in nothing but his undershorts. His wife Mamie, who was sitting in a chair near the window, grinned, but the President flushed with annoyance . . . Thus ended my only claim to intimacy with Dwight Eisenhower."[70] Their relationship had not started well, but Nitze made a substantial contribution to the president's speech, advising Eisenhower to convey optimism but to temper this with a clear statement of U.S.-Soviet disagreements. Only if these differences were bridged could a truly meaningful dialogue with Moscow commence. Titled "The Chance for Peace," Eisenhower's speech offered a cautiously hopeful response to Stalin's death that was reported favorably in *Pravda* and *The New York Times*. Nitze had proved his worth to the new president.

As a reward, Nitze was finally offered a job—assistant secretary of defense for international security affairs—in June 1953. But the *Washington Times Herald*, a conservative paper sympathetic to Senator Joe McCarthy, made a devastating intervention. It ran a story that read: "Paul H. Nitze, 46 and wealthy, one of the principal shapers of the European recovery plan, is the latest Truman-Acheson lieutenant contemplated for retention in a powerful position under the Eisenhower administration." The article impugned Nitze "for pouring billions into Europe" through which "enormous profits were reaped by Wall Street." The *Times Herald* had characterized Nitze as a moneyed, liberal northeasterner out for personal gain—sufficient to torpedo his prospects. Eisenhower's Defense Secretary Charles E. Wilson informed Nitze that a change in the political climate made his position no longer tenable. Appalled, though not particularly surprised, that the administration had caved to a piece of defamatory reporting, Nitze replied, "Very well, Mr. Secretary. I didn't ask for this job."[71]

It is likely that Nitze would have resigned from the administration regardless, for there was much in Eisenhower's presidency that he disagreed with. The president and his hawkish secretary of state, John Foster Dulles, viewed the Soviet threat in similar terms to those presented in NSC-68: Moscow's expansionary instincts were insatiable and wholly nefarious. Indeed, Dulles went further than Nitze (and much further than Kennan), arguing that "liberation" should replace "containment" as America's default goal. But the administration's bark turned out to be worse than its bite. President Eisenhower's frugality made sure of that. At the Council on Foreign Relations on January 12, 1954, Dulles presented the logical conclusion of espousing strong anticommunism on the cheap. Recounting the substance of a meeting called to survey the Eisenhower administration's first year in office, Dulles said, "The President and his advisers, as represented by the National Security Council, had to take some basic policy decisions. This has been done. The basic decision was to depend primarily upon a great capacity to retaliate, instantly, by means and at places of our choosing."

Nitze sat next to the banker and diplomat—and later John F. Kennedy's treasury secretary—Douglas Dillon during Dulles's speech. He recalled, "We looked at each other in amazement as his words sank in."[72] Dulles had unveiled the policy of "massive retaliation," whereby the United States seemed to promise to confront all gradations of Soviet provocation—from meddling in a civil war in Congo to invading West Germany—with a massive American nuclear response. George Kennan was even more horrified, writing to Adlai Stevenson that "if we were to attempt to use the atomic bomb because—let us say—Italy might go communist in an election, we would be taking upon ourselves a most hideous moral responsibility for the sake of an extremely questionable issue. I cannot believe that our allies would bear with us in such an act of petulance."[73] Eisenhower and Dulles disagreed, viewing massive retaliation as the best way to keep Moscow in check at minimal financial cost.

Nitze was relieved to discover that massive retaliation was merely the scariest hollow threat in history. In fact, Dulles allegedly told Nitze and Kennan, in separate meetings, that "rollback," "liberation," and "massive retaliation" were political slogans designed to distinguish Eisenhower from his much-maligned predecessor and they shouldn't be taken too seriously. The truth of the matter was that Eisenhower's foreign policies were not so different from Harry Truman's. In October 1953, for example, Eisenhower approved NSC 162/2, which affirmed many of NSC-68's precepts—though not those that vastly increased the defense budget. As Nitze himself observed, "By 1955 it became clear that Foster's doctrine of massive retaliation was merely a declaratory policy, while our action policy was graduated deterrence."[74] Of course, George Kennan viewed both Nitze's and Dulles's strategic approaches as alarmist and needlessly provocative. He continued to lick his wounds, finding some solace in the fact that "the American people . . . would certainly not know brilliant and perceptive diplomacy if they saw it."[75]

Kennan did not like the substance of Eisenhower's foreign policies, but he had played a significant role in devising one of the president's major innovations: CIA covert action in the Third World. When designing his containment doctrine in the mid-1940s, Kennan had emphasized the merits of political warfare, covert action, and espionage—the dark arts of international relations—as Cold War weapons. Because Kennan's version of containment viewed war against the Soviet Union as inconceivable except as a last resort, deploying the talents of the CIA, as a coercive and supposedly undetectable tool, was greatly appealing. Kennan expended a lot of effort during the Truman years arguing first for the creation of the CIA, and second that it be funded more generously and deployed more frequently. So if a nation was susceptible to communist-inclined revolution—whether through force of arms or at the ballot box—America should neutralize this threat by funding Western-inclined individuals and groupings, while surreptitiously undermining their opponents, using whatever worked.

The Eisenhower administration deployed this rationale in extremis. It used the CIA to orchestrate the overthrow of Mohammad Mossadegh, the independent-minded, democratically elected prime minister of Iran who had irritated the United States and United Kingdom by nationalizing British oil interests in Iran and displaying a clear preference for socialistic solutions to endemic poverty in Iran. But the Iranian prime minister was no communist—not that this mattered much to Eisenhower, Dulles, and Winston Churchill. The CIA, led by Allen Dulles, John Foster's brother, began plotting Mossadegh's overthrow in the fall of 1952. The following summer the CIA hired a large group of Iranians to behave thuggishly—smashing windows and monuments, starting fights, and the like—while chanting pro-Mossadegh slogans. Counterdemonstrations were also organized, creating what the CIA viewed as the perfect storm of chaos and instability—optimal conditions for a coup d'état.

In August 1953, Mossadegh resigned under duress and the pro-American shah Reza Pahlavi took his place. The shah would remain in power until he was violently deposed by Islamist supporters of Ayatollah Khomeini in the Iranian Revolution of 1979—which had a much broader base of support than that of 1953. President Eisenhower's intervention was a success in that it showed that the CIA was entirely capable of toppling distasteful leaders in the right circumstances. But deposing Mossadegh and installing the shah was a strategic error—it led, among other things, to a vast increase in anti-American resentment in a volatile region. It was also remarkably callous and undemocratic. The CIA's actions in 1953 set a disturbing if seductive precedent, which encouraged illusions of consequence-free omniscience. A year later, the CIA intervened to depose Jacobo Arbenz in Guatemala, who had the temerity to pursue land reform policies that damaged the American multinational company United Fruit. Again a statist-inclined leader with broad popular support was deposed in the spurious name of anticommunism. The sanctity of democracy had been grievously damaged—not by the Soviet Union but by the United States. Kennan later described his role establishing the CIA's covert action capability as "the greatest mistake I ever made."[76]

Nitze was nonplussed by the ouster of Mossadegh, whom he had met and liked in 1952. Following a series of meetings in the latter stages of the Truman administration, Nitze had concluded that the Iranian leader "was neither a Marxist nor a Communist. He was . . . a shrewd and tricky politician, but, in my view, far preferable to the Shah and his regime."[77] But NSC-68's overheated rhetoric—which vested large stakes in ignoring any leader or crisis incommodious to U.S. interests—appeared to justify covert actions such as those that deposed Mossadegh and Arbenz. Like "massive retaliation," Nitze was a more fearsome prospect in theory than he was in reality. But other policymakers were not so queasy about following NSC-68's interventionist formula through to its logical conclusions. In deploying the CIA in Iran and Guatemala, Eisenhower and Dulles believed they were pursuing an unremarkable course of action—justified by framework precedents established by their predecessors. A State Department official named Joseph Jones captured this imperative when posing and answering the question "What indeed are the limits of United States foreign policy?" "The answer is that the limits of our foreign policy are on a distant and receding horizon; for many practical purposes they are what we think we can accomplish and what we think are necessary to accomplish at any given time."[78]

In opposing President Eisenhower's policies, Nitze seemed not to realize that he was partly reneging on the logic of NSC-68, which rationalized open-ended responses to communist threats. Nitze would go on to voice opposition to a series of foreign-policy misadventures to which his writings actually lent sanction. George Kennan was shocked by the damage that his loosened boulder, containment, had wreaked on the mountain and valley below. NSC-68, meanwhile, was an avalanche. But Nitze refused to accept that his blueprint harmed America's ability to ascertain which threats were mortal and which were ignorable.

The presidential election of 1956 reprised the 1952 candidates with Eisenhower again trouncing Stevenson. George Kennan again lent his support to Stevenson, although he was generally unimpressed by the Democratic Party. "I found myself disgusted by everything about the Democratic convention," Kennan wrote Nitze in September, "except Stevenson himself. The impression I get is that the only aspects of the Administration's performance that the Democratic professionals approve and do not intend to criticize are the conduct of foreign affairs and the security program. In these circumstances it seems obvious that the party has no need for anyone like myself at this juncture."[79] Kennan had expressed his ambivalence toward the Democratic Party in a speech for the Princeton Stevenson for President Committee earlier in the year. In the remarkable address, which must have met with a bemused response, Kennan observed that "I've never been able to believe that the Democrat Party has a monopoly or wisdom . . . I regard myself, actually, as a conservative." What kept him in the Democratic fold was disgust "over the naked and undiluted materialism that is so rampant in our country today" and despair at the GOP's anti-intellectualism, exemplified by John Foster Dulles's simplistic Cold War shibboleths. In such bleak circumstances, Adlai Stevenson was the only national political leader possessed of sufficient "intellectual and moral conscience" to enable him to communicate hard truths: "to say to our people what ought to be said to them by their own government, which is not necessarily always what they would most like to hear."[80] It is safe to assume that Kennan's speech did not produce a flood of checks.

That Kennan disliked the Democratic Party's foreign-policy plank was unsurprising given that Nitze was one of its authors. Kennan had earlier conveyed his own foreign-policy preferences in a letter to Stevenson:

I am actually inclined to question the utility of the whole concept of "bipartisan foreign policy." I wouldn't want to sponsor, or share responsibility . . . for, anything that Foster did, even if I were able to write the ticket. This particular administration may be justly criticized for smugness; for talking big and doing little; for acting in such a way as to frighten our friends and reassure our adversaries. One could talk about the grievous over-militarization of thought and statement.[81]

Stevenson wrote an appreciative note in return, but it was Nitze who commanded his attention. And Nitze disagreed with everything in Kennan's letter, except for the part that shunned bipartisanship. Nitze developed a close working relationship with Stevenson and advised him to attack the Eisenhower administration for complacency in the face of a *global* communist offensive that could not be deterred by brute nuclear force. In particular, Nitze wrote that the United States had to devote much more attention to the Third World, which he described as "a fertile field for communist exploitation." Scores of nations had been freed from European colonial rule or were close to doing so. If this new generation of leaders were to embrace Marxism-Leninism, spurning the West, then "peace can be lost without a shot being fired."[82] Nitze advised the reticent and bookish Stevenson to attack the four-star general and architect of the D-day landings for being an irresolute Cold Warrior. While Stevenson could not carry it off against General Eisenhower, John F. Kennedy found electoral success with this approach four years later.

The problem with the activism of Nitze—the archetypal liberal Cold Warrior—was that ducking challenges was not an option, for the right wing was ever poised to attack and exploit any foreign-policy irresolution. In the aftermath of Stevenson's defeat, Nitze joined the Democratic Advisory Council (DAC), similar in broad purpose to a British shadow cabinet, alongside Dean Acheson, Averell Harriman, Adlai Stevenson, John Kenneth Galbraith, and Arthur Schlesinger Jr. Galbraith recalled that the discussions on foreign policy, dominated by Nitze and Acheson, "were the true portents" of disasters to come. At each meeting, Nitze and Acheson would distribute a paper "attacking whatever John Foster Dulles had done in the preceding weeks. The attack was always for being too lenient toward Communism and the Soviet Union." Galbraith found it disturbing that Nitze's and Acheson's perspectives were treated almost as holy writ:

> Here, early and in miniature were the fatal politics of Vietnam. It was not that the decision was debated and the wrong decision taken; it was rather that there was no debate. The old liberal fear of being thought soft on Communism, the fear of being attacked by professional patriots and the knowledge of the political punishment that awaits any departure from the Establishment view . . . all united to eliminate discussion. Democracy has, as ever, its own forms of authoritarianism."[83]

Nitze's NSC-68 had played a major role in shaping America's basic Cold War posture. Out of office, he was exerting comparable influence shaping the foreign-policy priorities of the Democratic Party. Having suffered sca-brous McCarthyite attacks on the sincerity of his own anticommunism, Nitze was pleased to return fire on a Republican administration shirking the full spectrum of its Cold War responsibilities. Nitze was coming to be-lieve that the Cold War would be won or lost in the underdeveloped world, in nations and regions dismissed by Kennan as inconsequential hinter-lands. "Flexible response" to communist encroachments would become his mantra—a stick with which to beat Republicans. It is little wonder that Kennan declined Nitze's invitation to join him on the DAC, writing that "it is a tempting prospect—to merge one's efforts once again with so many other people after so many years of working alone—but sober reflection forces me to doubt that any very useful purpose would be served by my association with this Committee."[84]

Nitze was given a further opportunity to assault the Eisenhower admin-istration in 1957 when he was invited to join a committee, led by H. Rowan Gaither of the Ford Foundation, established to provide an independent as-sessment of national security policy. The NSC had convened the committee to report on whether the United States should embark on a large-scale civil defense program to mitigate the human costs of nuclear war, a course that Nitze viewed as imperative. The committee was composed largely of RAND analysts, including the Columbia University–trained nuclear strategist Albert Wohlstetter, who firmly believed in the utility of nuclear deterrence and was deeply concerned by the consequences of the Soviet Union secur-ing parity with the United States. Wohlstetter convinced Gaither to expand the committee's remit to examine American vulnerability to a Soviet preemp-tive nuclear attack. Gaither in turn hired Nitze as a consultant, who found that the committee's alarmist perspective chimed with his own. Wohlstetter reported to the steering committee that his analysis, drawn largely from Air Force intelligence, showed that the Soviet Union could have in its posses-sion some five hundred intercontinental ballistic missiles by 1960. This would allow Moscow to obliterate America's retaliatory nuclear capability—organized under the auspices of the Strategic Air Command (SAC)—with a devastating first strike, leaving American cities vulnerable to subsequent annihilation. Wohlstetter had identified a hypothetical missile gap—though he did not use those exact words—which the United States had to remedy as the highest, existential priority.[85] Nitze, Wohlstetter, and the other mem-bers of the committee critiqued Eisenhower and Dulles for failing even to get the "massive" part of their strategic linchpin right. Nitze's vast expe-rience in this field, allied to his skills as a coordinator and a draftsman, ensured that he became the primary framer of the Gaither Report: NSC-68 Redux.

Nitze recalled that the report's primary recommendation was that "maintaining an effective second strike force should be our first priority." This meant the United States had to "improve its early warning network, train its SAC bomber crews so that the portion of bombers on alert could take-off within the available warning time, accelerate our missile production program, and phase in hardened bases for our ICBMs as rapidly as possible."[86] In the event that America's nuclear deterrent failed to deter, the report urged contingency planning in the form of a large-scale civil defense program. Like NSC-68, the Gaither Report recommended a course of action that was astronomically expensive and that invited the military to assume an ever-larger role in the life and economic health of the nation.

On October 4, 1957, the Soviet Union launched Sputnik, the world's first artificial orbital space satellite. Having a Russian-made object whiz unseen across the continental United States every ninety-eight minutes was a worrying development—to put it mildly. If the Soviets were able to launch a satellite, did they also have the capability to launch ICBMs that could reach New York or Washington? Nitze hoped that this was a watershed moment and that Eisenhower would approve the Gaither Report in all its aspects. But this was not to be. During a meeting on November 7, Eisenhower described the report's recommendations as "far-fetched"—as well as ridiculously, unsustainably expensive.[87] "You know, you recommend spending a billion dollars for something in here," Eisenhower informed the report's authors. "But do you know how much a billion dollars is? Why, it's a stack of ten-dollar bills as high as the Washington Monument."[88] Nitze was appalled by the president's grade-school reasoning—preventing nuclear war was surely worth any cost, and a billion dollars was not what it used to be—but he reserved special scorn for John Foster Dulles, whom he was beginning to view as a chickenhawk. To vent his frustration, Nitze wrote Dulles a remarkably hostile letter. He pointed out that without a "much more vigorous defense program," a Soviet nuclear attack could "destroy the fabric of our society and ruin our nation." For presiding over such complacency, Nitze advised Dulles to take the honorable course and fall on his sword: "Finally, assuming that the immediate crisis is surmounted, I should ask you to consider, in the light of events of recent years, whether there is not some other prominent Republican disposed to exercise the responsibility of the office of Secretary of State."[89] Unsurprisingly, Dulles did not resign and Eisenhower did not relent. As a weapon of final resort, Nitze leaked the Gaither Report to Chalmers

Roberts of *The Washington Post*. The front-page article observed: "The still top-secret Gaither Report portrays the United States in the gravest danger in its history."[90]

Nitze was clearly not angling to secure a special place in Eisenhower's heart. George Kennan and Walter Lippmann, meanwhile, were as hostile toward the Gaither Report's rationale as was the president. The British Broadcasting Corporation had invited Kennan to deliver its prestigious annual series of Reith Lectures, in which prominent intellectuals are gifted six hours of radio time to reflect on a significant contemporary issue. Kennan's topic was "Russia, the Atom, and the West," and his arguments were antithetical to Nitze's. Kennan heaped scorn on those nuclear strategists who "evidently believe that if the Russians gain the slightest edge on us in the capacity to wreak massive destruction at long range, they will immediately use it, regardless of our capacity for retaliation." He also identified serious problems with the notion of civil defense: "Are we to flee like haunted creatures from one defensive device to another, each more costly and humiliating than the one before, cowering underground one day, breaking up our cities the next, attempting to surround ourselves with elaborate electronic shields on the third, concerned only to prolong the length of our lives while sacrificing all the values for which it might be worthwhile to live at all?"[91]

In a letter to Walter Lippmann in the summer of 1951, Kennan had earlier complained that foreign policy had become excessively quantified and mechanized and that wise diplomatic strategy required the touch and insight of a "gardener," not a "mechanic." Strategists like Nitze "do not understand the difference between working in a mechanical medium, where you can translate direct impulses in a mechanical way, and working in an organic medium, where the living impulse is beyond your own doing and you achieve your effects by altering the environmental stimuli to which a given growth is subjected or, if you cannot do this, then adjusting yourself as best you can to whatever unpleasant quality it may have."[92]

Kennan's implied critique of Nitze was deep but opaque. Lippmann's scorn was presented with hallmark clarity in a 1959 column titled "The Tired Old Men." The article blamed three individuals—Nitze, Dean Acheson, and ex-President Truman—for devising a confrontational blueprint from which U.S foreign policy still recklessly operated. Nitze was appalled by the article and attributed its genesis to a heated dispute he had with Lippmann five days earlier. Over the course of a wine-fueled lunch, Nitze had grown increasingly tired of Lippmann's sanctimonious call for a more "reasoned" approach to U.S.-Soviet relations. "You know, Walter," said Nitze, "it's possible to be too G-D impartial." "Paul, when you say that," replied Lippmann, "to whom are you referring?" Nitze replied, "Walter, if you press me, I have to admit that I have you in mind." According to Nitze, Lippmann "turned purple and then pink and then white and then black . . . [He was] absolutely outraged by that remark."[93] Lippmann and Kennan had come to view Nitze's foreign-policy recommendations with genuine concern.

Nitze cared not a jot for their poor opinion because he was developing warm relations with a more significant personage: Senator John F. Kennedy of Massachusetts, who was all but certain to run for the presidency in 1960. Nitze first met Kennedy in 1959, when he testified before the Senate Subcommittee on African Affairs on a fact-gathering trip he had taken to the continent for the Council on Foreign Relations. Nitze was impressed by the young senator's focus: "He listened carefully, absorbing information and ideas for use when the occasion arose."[94] Nitze's testimony on the vital importance of the unaligned, developing world to America's Cold War prospects found a receptive audience in Kennedy. He firmly believed in the necessity of a vastly increased foreign aid program, and for deploying a more varied set of diplomatic tools. The one tool currently in the box—the mallet of "massive retaliation"—was not designed for close work like undermining communism's appeal in the Third World. As early as 1954, Kennedy had delivered a speech in the Senate in which he observed that "our reduction of strength for resistance in so-called brush-fire wars, while threatening atomic retaliation, has in effect invited expansion by the Communists in such areas as Indochina."[95] Kennedy's and Nitze's views were closely aligned on a variety of issues, as the latter recalled with satisfaction:

> I thought he was very quick. In fact, he had independently come to some of the ideas that seemed to me to be very important. He was concerned about the massive retaliation doctrine. He was concerned that we were not putting enough emphasis upon defense options rather than the strategic nuclear attack option. He was concerned about the military support which we were able to give in crisis spots in Africa, the Middle East, and the Far East.[96]

A few months after their first meeting, Nitze was furnishing Kennedy with foreign-policy advice and contributing to the drafting of his speeches. They were an excellent match. Kennedy liked tough-minded advisers who got to the point; Nitze admired leaders who emphasized the possibilities, rather than the limitations, of American power.

Similarly attuned to the senator's potential, George Kennan had attempted to win Kennedy's favor when he wrote him a long letter detailing his own foreign-policy views. Kennan began by emulating Nitze's Paul Revere approach, observing that "the Russian and Chinese Communists are obviously determined to bring about, before a new administration can take over and get into the swing, an extensive and decisive undermining of our world position, with a view to isolating us politically and militarily and to eliminating us as a major factor of resistance to their ambitions and undertakings." The purpose and vitality of the prose might have surprised seasoned Kennan watchers. But after this tub-thumping buildup, Kennan reverted to type:

> One of the most dangerous elements in our present world position is that we are greatly over-extended in our commitments, political and military. I have felt this for years; so, I believe, has Lippmann. This provides our adversaries with one opportunity after another for badgering us and thrusting us onto the defensive. To get ourselves back into a sound position, there should be a careful appraisal of our existing commitments and a ruthless elimination of those which are unsound, super-annuated, or beyond our strength to support.[97]

At this moment of supposedly "maximum danger," to borrow Nitze's phrase from NSC-68, Kennan recommended "ruthlessly" hacking away at America's overgrown defense commitments. JFK was not won over. Kennan and Nitze did not so much disagree about foreign policy as inhabit different planets.

After securing the Democratic nomination ahead of Adlai Stevenson, Kennedy was keen to solicit the best—which for him meant the most robust—foreign-policy advice. He did not turn to Kennan, needless to say, and instead sought out the engineer of NSC-68. On August 30, 1960, Nitze and Kennedy held a joint news conference. The Democratic presidential candidate announced that he had appointed Nitze to convene and chair a Committee on National Security Policy. Its purpose was not to furnish Kennedy with partisan debating points but to provide concrete foreign-policy recommendations that would permit the new administration to hit the ground running. Kennedy informed the assembled press that he wanted Nitze to "consult . . . on national security problems with the ablest and most experienced authorities in the nation, without regard to party."[98] Nitze was given an office in the Russell Senate Office Building, right next to Senator Henry "Scoop" Jackson of Washington, where he sat down with his team—David K.

Bruce, Roswell Gilpatric, and James Perkins—to prepare his report. With his usual diligence, Nitze took soundings from RAND and some of the nation's elite universities, including the Center for International Studies at MIT, which had developed a distinctive research program emphasizing the centrality of the struggle with communism in the Third World.

While Nitze worked on his report, Kennedy had an election to win— against Eisenhower's vice president, Richard Milhous Nixon. One of Kennedy's most effective campaigning strategies was to portray the Eisenhower-Nixon years as a period in which the big stick of massive retaliation actually encouraged drift and irresolution, which had allowed the Soviet Union to narrow the gap in nuclear capabilities and project power and influence beyond the European theater. Even Cuba, just ninety miles from Florida, had been "lost" to communism in 1959. For hawkish Democrats with painful memories of McCarthyism, attacking Nixon and the GOP for foreign-policy weakness was cathartic. Drawing on Nitze's and Wohlstetter's dark Gaither scenarios, Kennedy blasted the Nixon-Eisenhower team for allowing a "missile gap" to develop, which imperiled American security: "Whether the missile gap—that everyone agrees now exists—will become critical in 1961, 1962, or 1963 . . . the point is that we are facing a gap on which we are gambling with our survival . . . Unless immediate steps are taken, failure to maintain our relative power of retaliation may in the near future expose the United States to a nuclear missile attack."[99]

This inflammatory allegation was taken right from Nitze's playbook. Never mind that the missile gap did not actually exist; the mere allegation was damaging enough. And Nixon could not decisively rebut the charge without revealing the full extent of America's surveillance operation over the Soviet Union. On this and other issues, Kennedy had Nixon on the hook.

Partly assisted by these foreign-policy advantages—as well as Walter Lippmann's priceless endorsement—Kennedy defeated Nixon on Election Day by the slimmest of margins. Across the nation he secured just 100,000 more popular votes, which translated as 303 votes to Nixon's 219 in the electoral college. Nitze submitted his report to President-elect Kennedy on November 9, the day after his victory. It called for an "early decision" on whether the United States should "attempt to achieve a politically meaningful 'win' capability in general nuclear war, or settle for the more modest goal of being able to deny the Soviets such a capability through assuring ourselves secure retaliatory capability." It also focused on the sheer weight of crises that would confront Kennedy upon entering the White House, in "Cuba, the Congo, Laos, and the 'smoldering guerrilla war in South Vietnam.'" "Because of limitations of time and space," Nitze recalled, "our report made only brief stabs at sorting out the multitude of problems inherent in these global time bombs."[100] An appreciative Kennedy directed that a copy of the report be sent to all cabinet appointees as the starting point for their subsequent recommendations. The main question that remained was where would Nitze—an architect of Kennedy's main diplomatic campaigning advantage—land?

President-elect Kennedy offered Nitze three jobs during the transition, in a brief phone conversation. He informed Nitze that the incoming secretary of state, Dean Rusk—a man Nitze had recommended for the job—wanted him to serve as his undersecretary for economic affairs. "Before you respond to this, however," said Kennedy, "you should know that I would like you to become either my national security adviser or deputy secretary of defense." Nitze asked, "How long do I have to make up my mind?" to which Kennedy answered, "Thirty seconds." His mind set to gallop, Nitze immediately dismissed the job at State because he had already worked in economic affairs during the Truman administration. He liked the proximity to power that the office of national security adviser provided, but worried that he would be continuously "stalemated by a Pentagon unsympathetic to the type of policy I thought was required." To truly grapple with the issues that mattered most—primarily pertaining to strategic vulnerabilities and the conventional and unconventional means to address them—Nitze believed it was vital to work in the Pentagon. "I choose the post of deputy secretary of defense," replied Nitze within the thirty seconds. "Fine," said Kennedy, who hung up without saying goodbye and crossed another job off his long to-do list.

Nitze made a major error in declining the job of national security adviser. The position had lacked clout during the Eisenhower years, certainly, but the Kennedy, Johnson, Nixon, and Carter appointments—McGeorge Bundy, Walt Rostow, Henry Kissinger, and Zbigniew Brzezinski—used the office to construct independent power bases in the White House, exerting an influence on presidential decision making that often exceeded the supposedly more powerful cabinet appointments. Nitze's mistake was compounded when Kennedy appointed Robert S. McNamara as his secretary of defense and his position immediately became insecure.

McNamara and Nitze shared many traits. A graduate of Berkeley and the Harvard Business School, McNamara had enjoyed a spectacularly successful business career, rising to the presidency of the Ford Motor Company. He also held a strong belief in deploying quantitative methods to assess a whole range of issues—from automobile production in Detroit to military progress in Indochina. Once described memorably as an "IBM machine with legs," McNamara was a formidable presence whose crisp analyses, impatience with prolixity, and unforgiving work ethic kept his subordinates in a state of perpetual tension and exhaustion. He accepted Kennedy's job offer on one condition: that he would have total control over subsequent Pentagon appointments. McNamara decided that he did not want another McNamara (with actual foreign-policy experience) serving as his number two. He wanted a loyal lieutenant to carry out his orders without demur. This person turned out to be the hardworking and selfless Roswell Gilpatric. "I had never met Bob McNamara," Nitze later recalled, "but he knew of me and my reputation for hard-nosed determination. He told Mr. Kennedy that he would prefer a deputy who would be his alter ego and carry out his programs without argument or confrontation."[101]

Nitze was instead forced to take the position of assistant secretary of defense for international security affairs—the job he had accepted in 1953 before the forces of McCarthyism had intervened. It was not a bad compromise move, as it turned out, because the Office of International Security Affairs (ISA), known as the "little state department," offered Nitze considerable autonomy and some three hundred staff. The ISA's primary function was to coordinate the disbursement of foreign military aid, but Kennedy wanted the office to do more. On Christmas Day, *The New York Times* endorsed Nitze's appointment, noting that the ISA's scope had been "widened" to allow Nitze to contribute to policy on multiple levels. President-elect Kennedy remarked that "I cannot too strongly stress the importance of the post which Mr. Nitze has accepted . . . His wealth of experience will be of great assistance to both Defense Secretary McNamara and to me."[102] Kennedy's warm words were likely conditioned by some guilt at the retraction of his initial job offer. In fact, Nitze's influence on the Kennedy administration turned out to be significant. But this owed less to the job he assumed than to the geopolitical principles he bequeathed. John Kennedy was the first president to fully embrace the maximalist crisis logic of NSC-68: "We cannot simply sit by and watch on the sidelines. There are no sidelines."[103]

In January 1961, Presidents Eisenhower and Kennedy delivered seminal speeches: the first a farewell address, the second an inaugural. They were opposite in purpose. Eisenhower's speech repudiated Nitze's foreign-policy vision; Kennedy's embraced it. Eisenhower was bidding farewell to the nation. Foremost on his mind was the manner in which the military had come to assume an outsized place in national life. He observed that the "conjunction of an immense military establishment and a large arms industry is new in the American experience. The total influence—economic, political, even spiritual—is felt in every city, every State house, every office of the federal government." Eisenhower was referring to the quadrupling of America's defense budget ushered in by NSC-68 and the Korean War—and the problems he had faced in trimming a budget once it had been established. "In the councils of government," Eisenhower warned, "we must guard against the acquisition of unwarranted influence, whether sought or unsought, by the military-industrial complex." This complex did not only threaten "our liberties or democratic processes," Eisenhower said, but could also sully the nation's reservoir of intellectual capital:

> Today, the solitary inventor, tinkering in his shop, has been overshadowed by task forces of scientists in laboratories and testing fields. In the same fashion, the free university, historically the fountainhead of free ideas and scientific discovery, has experienced a revolution in the conduct of research. Partly because of the huge costs involved, a government contract becomes virtually a substitute for intellectual curiosity. For every old blackboard there are now hundreds of new electronic computers. The prospect of domination of the nation's scholars by Federal employment, project allocations, and the power of money is ever present—and is gravely to be regarded.[104]

Eisenhower's presidency had ended in the most remarkable fashion.

Kennedy delivered his inaugural address three days after Eisenhower's elegiac farewell. It was a typically frigid January day in Washington, and Kennedy chose not to wear an overcoat or scarf so as to emphasize his youthful vitality. Flanked on each side by two well-wrapped former and future presidents, Dwight Eisenhower and Lyndon Johnson, Kennedy spoke with conviction and purpose, his words given exclamation points by visible puffs of exhalation. It took just two and a half minutes for Kennedy to commit U.S. foreign policy to anything and everything: "Let every nation know, whether it wishes us well or ill, that we shall pay any price, bear any burden, meet any hardship, support any friend, oppose any foe, to assure the survival and the success of liberty. This much we pledge—and more."[105]

The speech was one of the most gracefully written inaugurals in history. It contained myriad other themes presented with artistry: a pledge of assistance to "those people in the huts and villages of half the globe struggling to break the bonds of mass misery"; an entreaty to remember that "civility is not a sign of weakness, and sincerity is always subject to proof. Let us never negotiate out of fear, but let us never fear to negotiate"; a challenge to American citizens to "ask not what your country can do for you; ask what you can do for your country." The speech became the unavoidable point of comparison for all subsequent inaugurals; its primary author, Theodore Sorensen, set the highest literary bar. Yet lurking behind the ornate words was a fierce commitment to Cold War confrontation and activism every bit as pungent as that presented in NSC-68. "In the long history of the world," Kennedy said near the end of the speech, "only a few generations have been granted the role of defending freedom in its hour of maximum danger. I do not shrink from this responsibility—I welcome it." The inaugural address synthesized Woodrow Wilson's idealism—"defending freedom"—and Paul Nitze's alarm-fueled pugnacity: "its hour of maximum danger." The United States had arrived at a high point in its confidence in muscular foreign-policy idealism. For Kennedy to remain true to his inaugural word, America's diplomatic commitments would have to expand in precisely the way Nitze had earlier proposed.

Many of the young president's appointments were precisely the type of policy-oriented academics that Eisenhower identified with alarm. McGeorge Bundy, Kennedy's national security adviser, was old-money Boston and a star in the academic firmament. Harvard had elected Bundy to its prestigious Society of Fellows in 1941, when he was just twenty-two, and made him dean of the college in 1953, when he was thirty-four—the youngest man so honored in Harvard's history. Walt Rostow, Bundy's deputy assistant for national security affairs, was a Yale Ph.D. and a Rhodes scholar at Oxford. He joined the administration from MIT's CIA-funded Center for International Studies, where he had participated in numerous government-sanctioned research programs. In 1960, Rostow "answered Karl Marx" with his seminal book *The Stages of Economic Growth: A Non-Communist Manifesto*. Rostow claimed that the United States was destined to best the Soviet Union in "modernizing" the Third World, thus sealing the West's victory over Marxism-Leninism—which Rostow dismissed as a mere "disease of the transition" to modernity.[106] Rostow borrowed from NSC-68—and expanded upon it—in rationalizing a vast increase in America's Cold War commitments. Finally, Robert S. McNamara moved from the presidency of Ford to assume control of the Pentagon—an even larger organizational behemoth. Nonetheless, his academic credentials, from the University of California, Berkeley, and Harvard Business School, were highly impressive. Indeed, McNamara made his cerebral proclivities clear when he chose to live in the college town of Ann Arbor rather than buy a mansion in Grosse Point, the more conventional housing choice of Ford executives. He was a voracious reader, possessed of preternatural self-assurance, and devoted to RAND's pioneering work in quantitative analysis. McNamara was set on rationalizing his department, on making it bow to his will.

Kennedy himself was a gifted student at Harvard and the London School of Economics, although he followed Nitze in succumbing to extracurricular temptations that brought down his grades. His gilded childhood and early adulthood involved a significant amount of European travel, which included a trip to Prague in 1938, where he had roused the ire of George Kennan, then serving as the U.S. ambassador. Kennedy summarized the method behind his hiring policy when he remarked, "There's nothing like brains, you can't beat brains."[107] Rostow, in turn, was impressed by Kennedy's intellect, observing, "Ideas were tools. He picked them up easily like statistics or the names of local politicians. He wanted to know how ideas could be put to work."[108] Having been rejected for his preferred position as secretary of state—this vital position went to another Rhodes scholar, Dean Rusk—Adlai Stevenson accepted as a consolation prize the ambassadorship to the United Nations. Casting a jaundiced eye over the bright young things hired ahead of him, Stevenson observed: "They've got the damndest bunch of boy commandos running around . . . you ever saw."[109] Speaker of the House Sam Rayburn relayed his own concerns in memorable terms to his friend and protégé, Vice President Lyndon Baines Johnson: "Well, Lyndon, you may be right and they may be every bit as intelligent as you say, but I'd feel a whole lot better about them if just one of them had run for sheriff once."[110]

Rayburn's meaning was clear: running for elected office imparts a cautionary sense of what will fly that might elude the most brilliant thinkers, unused to real-world constraints on their process of thinking and strategizing. Rayburn suspected that the Kennedy administration was committed to too many bold, transformational ideas—rendered vital by the backdrop portrayal of acute crisis presented by Nitze and others—and seemed to have only trace understanding of what was meant by the art of the possible. The Kennedy era truly witnessed the social sciences entering the "crucible of circumstance," as Charles Beard had prophesied in 1917.

During the televised presidential debates with Richard Nixon, Kennedy had criticized the Eisenhower administration for allowing Cuba to turn communist on its watch. It was a damning charge, which consciously echoed

Republican attacks on Truman for "losing China" in 1949. What Kennedy did not know was that Eisenhower and Nixon had already laid plans to oust Castro through a CIA-orchestrated counterrevolution—the gambit that had apparently worked so well in Iran and Guatemala. Yet Nixon could not reveal these plans in response to Kennedy's charge without giving Castro notice of America's intentions. Holding his tongue must have been agonizing for Nixon in the circumstances. But he had some kind of revenge when it fell to President Kennedy to implement the optimistic plans already laid. Having hammered Eisenhower and Nixon for complacency, Kennedy could hardly refuse to sanction the ouster of Castro. Indeed, many of Kennedy's "best and the brightest" welcomed the opportunity. A few weeks prior to the invasion, McGeorge Bundy complained, "At this point we are like the Harlem Globetrotters. Passing forward, behind, sideways and underneath. But nobody has made a basket yet." Here, Bundy reasoned, was a chance to put some points on the board.[111]

Unfortunately, implementing the CIA's plan was akin to attempting a half-court hook shot with a beach ball. In the early morning of April 7, 1961, approximately fifteen hundred CIA-trained Cuban exiles boarded agile landing craft and moved toward Playa Girón—the Bay of Pigs. Their purpose was to establish a beachhead and foment a popular rebellion that would lead in neatly cascading stages to Castro's removal. A tragic series of events ensued. As the boats approached the Bay of Pigs, some of their engines failed, leaving the occupants sitting ducks. Some of the other boats crashed into a coral reef that the CIA advance operation had misidentified as seaweed. Castro's regular army had little trouble subduing this bedraggled insurgent force as it eventually made landfall. Presented with the option of deploying the Air Force to strafe Castro's forces, Kennedy declined, deeming it wiser to cut losses and regroup than to risk a wider conflict. It was an inglorious episode for which the president accepted full responsibility—although it was CIA director Allen Dulles who lost his job. Kennedy was shocked to discover that this misadventure had not dented his high approval ratings, which remained true at 82 percent. He commented wryly, "It's just like Eisenhower. The worse I do, the more popular I get." It fell to Dean Acheson to capture the flawed logic undergirding the operation, observing that it did not take "Price-Waterhouse to discover that 1,500 Cubans weren't as good as 25,000 Cubans."[112]

Nitze was torn about the merits of invading Cuba with CIA-trained exiles. Major General Edward Lansdale, a counterinsurgency adviser based in the Pentagon, had serious doubts about the viability of the operation. He relayed them to Nitze, who also found them sobering. He confessed to his "uneasiness about the operation," although he ultimately kept those doubts to himself, supporting the action in a meeting called by President Kennedy. "In my mind," Nitze stated, "our moral right to try to stop the Communist menace from invading our hemisphere was not the issue. The Soviet Union had inserted itself in our backyard by stealth and deception in the form of the Castro regime in Cuba. Like a spreading cancer, it should, if possible, be excised from the Americas."[113] The logic of Kennedy's activism did not faze Nitze—indeed, he had encouraged it. But he would increasingly find himself at odds with the administration on the best means to implement NSC-68's precepts. Nitze liked military assertiveness in principle—his career to date had been devoted to maintaining and extending U.S. strategic dominance over the communist world. While "throw-weights"—the combined weight of each side's ballistic missile payloads—were calculable, however, civil wars in distant theaters were unknowable, impervious to charting, a law unto themselves. And Nitze disliked uncertainty.

In the aftermath of the Bay of Pigs disaster, Walt Rostow suggested that the president focus more intently on combating the fast-growing communist insurgency in South Vietnam—a crisis that had been festering for some time. After the nationalist Viet Minh had defeated France at the Battle of Dien Bien Phu in 1954, the contours of the newly independent nation were thrashed out at the Geneva Conference: Vietnam was divided at the 17th parallel on a temporary basis. The communist Ho Chi Minh led North Vietnam while South Vietnam was governed by the pro-Western combination of President Bao Dai and his prime minister, Ngo Dinh Diem. The treaty stipulated that the division was temporary and that the 17th parallel should not be "interpreted as constituting a political or territorial boundary."[114] Nationwide reunification elections were scheduled to take place in 1956, but realizing that Ho Chi Minh was likely to win a national ballot, South Vietnam, with Washington's full support, refused to participate. From that point a civil war in the weaker South Vietnam became virtually certain. In December 1960, the Democratic Republic of Vietnam (North Vietnam, or DRV) approved the establishment of the National Liberation Front (NLF) in South Vietnam. Its avowed aim was "to overthrow the dictatorial . . . Diem clique, lackey of the U.S. imperialists, to form a . . . coalition government in South Vietnam, to win national independence and . . . to achieve national reunification."[115] In little time, the NLF insurgency began to ask hard questions of South Vietnam's continued viability as a state. On April 21, 1961, Rostow advised Kennedy that "Viet Nam is the place where . . . we must prove we are not a paper tiger."[116] He believed that the conflict in South Vietnam was precisely the type of Third World crisis that the United States had to step in and resolve. Even history needed a nudge sometimes.

Nitze had served on Truman's Policy Planning Staff as the rebellion against French rule intensified under Ho Chi Minh's leadership. Nitze had participated in strategic discussions through two and a half years of the Korean War. It was a conflict that had highlighted serious operational deficiencies in the U.S. military, which had struggled on alien terrain against a well-drilled opponent. Unlike Rostow, McNamara, and Bundy, Nitze had already advised a president on how to respond to conflict in Southeast Asia. The experience was not one Nitze thought warranted repeating. He had supported the Korean War because a communist nation had invaded its neighbor, crossing an internationally recognized boundary in the process. This casus belli did not apply to the conflict in Vietnam. Nitze found plenty of reasons not to stake American credibility in fighting Vietnamese communism. So when Rostow and others began recommending an escalation in the U.S. commitment to South Vietnam, Nitze generally took the opposite view.

In October 1961, for example, Rostow and General Maxwell Taylor, a special military adviser to Kennedy based in the White House, embarked on a fact-finding tour to South Vietnam. Upon their return they submitted a report that recommended the dispatch of six to eight thousand U.S. combat troops—disguised as "flood relief workers"—to South Vietnam.[117] Taylor and Rostow also pointed out that Ho Chi Minh "not only had something to gain—the South—but a base to risk—the North—if war should come."[118] They believed that the insurgency in South Vietnam might be choked off by an attack on the North, cabling Kennedy on October 23 that "NVN is extremely vulnerable to conventional bombing, a weakness which should be exploited diplomatically in convincing Hanoi to lay off South Vietnam."[119] Nitze's experience with the USSBS led him to treat such claims with skepticism. He also worried about the jauntily upbeat nature of Rostow's escalatory advice—he described him as "the most irrepressible optimist you can find any place"—which he felt was abstract and untested by hard diplomatic experience. Nitze later elaborated on this theme: "Walt and Max Taylor were more on the side of 'let's do it,' and less on the side of how do we do it, can it be done, are there crevasses there, how passable are they, should we put some pitons in the mountain wall in order to make it safe to go up the goddamn thing or we're going to fall flat on our face if we don't put those pitons in. That wasn't their mood."[120]

In a meeting called to discuss Taylor-Rostow, Nitze argued strongly against sending U.S. troops to South Vietnam. "There was no such thing as being a little bit pregnant," Nitze observed, "and an open-ended commitment could well lead to American involvement in another major ground war in Asia under unfavorable political and logistical circumstances."[121] In earthier language, Nitze suggested that the dispatch of American combat troops "wouldn't be decisive, it would just get our tit in the wringer."[122] Critically, Nitze managed to persuade Robert McNamara, an early supporter of the Taylor-Rostow report, that it was in fact based on a dangerously uncontrollable rationale. "I think I was the one who persuaded him to reverse his position," Nitze recalled with satisfaction. "I'm sure I did. This was one of the things that really got my dander up and I was absolutely convinced that this was a bad idea so I held forth with acerbity and carried the day."[123]

While Nitze and the skeptics of escalation won this particular skirmish, the American commitment to South Vietnam increased steadily during the Kennedy years. Nitze was correct in predicting that even a modest detachment of U.S. combat troops generated an escalatory momentum that was difficult to reverse. If eight thousand troops were unable to protect South Vietnam from communists, why not double the number? In fact, why not keep doubling until an optimum number is reached? In striving to locate an illusory tipping point—when each additional American soldier would supposedly have a decisive effect in quelling the insurgency—the United States would find itself with half a million troops stationed in South Vietnam in 1968. Nitze's "little bit pregnant" captured an essential truth. And his anticommunist credentials meant his cautionary advice could not be dismissed as dovish irresolution. Nitze had great instincts about certain things.

Important as his ideas were to the administration, Nitze never hit it off with President Kennedy. He found socializing with the "Kennedy set" tiresome—the demands made on Camelot's courtiers were unreasonable. "There was a certain difficulty with the Kennedys," Nitze noted. "Either you became very much a part of the Kennedy set, you know, went to all their functions at Hickory Hill and played touch football . . . McNamara did that. He was very much part of the Kennedy set. Mrs. N[itze] and I knew them all, and from time to time went to these things, but you know we don't like to become part of somebody else's group." This independent-mindedness partly explained why Nitze declined the position that McGeorge Bundy accepted. There was a constant pressure on national security advisers to "become the president's man and not an independent soul. And I hate the business of being somebody's man."[124] Nitze's isolation from the Kennedy circle became more pronounced during the Cuban missile crisis and the postmortem that followed.

In October 1962, an American U-2 spy plane photographed Soviet nuclear missile sites being constructed in Cuba. Moscow had embarked on an audacious attempt to equalize the nuclear balance of power. The United States had to do something—but what exactly? The stakes were unimaginably high, with no margin for error. An American air strike could destroy the sites, but what if the missiles were operational and a zealous communist managed to fire one away? What if Moscow decided to up the ante in response to a strike on Cuba? And if the United States did nothing, would not Moscow interpret this as a sign of weakness, an invitation to future mischief?

To coordinate the administration's response to the Cold War's most perilous crisis, the president convened an Executive Committee (ExComm) comprising his most significant and trusted foreign-policy advisers. Nitze was the only person authorized to take notes at the meetings, which he compared unflatteringly to "sophomoric seminar[s]." He soon grew tired of Kennedy's glacially slow consultative approach. On October 19, three days after the crisis began, he and U. Alexis Johnson, undersecretary for political affairs, sketched a range of possible American responses moving upward in intensity from a naval blockade to an air strike to a full-blown invasion. The following day ExComm arrived at a consensus view that a blockade was the most appropriate first response. But then two days later, Nitze reneged on his earlier recommendations and advised the immediate launching of an air strike to "eliminate the main nuclear threat."[125] He believed it was unlikely that the Soviet Union would order a strike in response while the American Strategic Air Command was mobilized, primed, and geographically dispersed. A Russian retaliatory strike would merely invite its own annihilation.

Nitze's change of heart on the supposed necessity of destroying the missile sites led to his marginalization. Kennedy implemented the quarantine, and it worked. Meanwhile Attorney General Bobby Kennedy and Soviet ambassador to the United States Anatoly Dobrynin worked a secret bilateral channel to thrash out a quid pro quo. President Kennedy's public posture was one of indefatigability—nothing would be gifted to Moscow as a reward for its misdeeds—but behind the scenes his younger brother offered as bargaining chips the removal of obsolete Jupiter nuclear missiles in Turkey and an assurance that the United States would never invade Cuba again.

Nitze viewed this kind of horse trading as unbecoming of a nation as powerful as the United States. He was upset that the Jupiter missiles had been traded in this fashion, observing, "Our NATO partners—Turkey, in particular—would be outraged at our weakness in the face of an immediate threat to our security." Thanks in part to Nitze's efforts, Washington had a far greater nuclear capability than Moscow. His retrospective assessment of the Cuban missile crisis was that it was America's superior deterrent that allowed it to prevail—Khrushchev realized there was no point pushing on toward a war of self-immolation. Kennedy had a very strong hand and gave up too much in the process:

> I believed that we should have pushed our advantage with greater vigor. We had achieved our objective of getting offensive weapons removed from Cuba with a minimum amount of force. With the nuclear balance heavily in our favor, I believed we should have pushed the Kremlin in 1962 to give up its efforts to establish Soviet influence in this hemisphere. As it turned out, while the resolution of the crisis was seen as a triumph for the West, the Soviet Union achieved its goal of securing a guarantee from the United States to respect the territorial integrity of a socialist state in the hemisphere.[126]

It is impossible to know whether Nitze's plan to push America's advantage "with greater vigor" would have resulted in Soviet concessions or a third world war. We do know that it was a high-risk stratagem that led Bobby Kennedy and others to view Nitze as reckless. He came out of the missile crisis badly, and in the late summer of 1963 Kennedy transferred him from the Pentagon to a position he did not want: secretary of the Navy. For Nitze, being eased out of policymaking and placed back in management was something like purgatory. Richard Nixon remarked brutally that "the service secretaries, well, they're just warts. I like them as individuals, but they do not do important things."[127] Nitze did come to enjoy aspects of the job, but he longed to return to an advisory role. Kennedy reassured Nitze that his stint as Navy secretary would be short; within six months the president would return him to a job appropriate to his talents. But Kennedy was unable to keep his promise. Lee Harvey Oswald murdered the president in Dallas on November 22, 1963. A distraught George Kennan, who admired Kennedy's intuitive diplomatic style—if not the advisers he hired—composed a eulogy that lauded the president's understanding of the two fundamental principles of statecraft: "First, that no political judgments must ever be final; and second, that the lack of finality must never be an excuse for inaction." Kennan hailed the fallen president as "an extraordinarily gallant and gifted man" whose vast potential had barely been realized when "the hand of the assassin reached him."[128]

A few weeks after assuming the presidency in those traumatic circumstances, Lyndon Baines Johnson called Nitze to a one-on-one meeting in the White House. Here was an ideal opportunity for Nitze to convince LBJ of his merits as an adviser—the first step to his coming in from the cold. Nitze prepared assiduously, anticipating a series of questions on various Cold War flashpoints. Instead, Nitze was disappointed to find that the meeting was merely a test of his endurance and loyalty. LBJ asked Nitze no questions. Instead, he went about his presidential business: he made phone calls, took notes, signed documents, dictated letters, and watched news reports on his television. "From time to time," Nitze remembered, "he would look at me out of the corner of his eye to see whether I was duly impressed, and then would continue his work."[129] Nitze, whose presence was scarcely registered, was forced to endure this spectacle for four hours before the president dismissed him. He ruminated on Johnson's motives: "He was trying to satisfy himself as to whether or not I was capable of being a wholly dedicated supporter, or whether I really was an incorrigibly independent man. In other words, would I become one of his boys or would I refuse to become one of his boys. And I was clear in my mind that I would never give up being an independent man."

Nitze attributed Johnson's coolness toward him to his dim view of the "Eastern Establishment," of which Nitze was assuredly a member. "He had this grave suspicion of anybody part of the Eastern Establishment. [He] felt that they looked down upon him, didn't have a true appreciation of his merits."[130] There was truth to Nitze's suspicions, although Johnson managed to get over his alleged phobia in respect to McGeorge Bundy—who was as Eastern Establishment as they came. The main reason LBJ kept Nitze at the Navy Department was that he remembered his opposition to the Taylor-Rostow report and viewed him as a potential irritant on the Vietnam War. President Johnson wanted everyone on the same page—he disliked arbitrating disagreement among his advisers. But singing in harmony was not Nitze's thing. He believed that Johnson's insistence on unity was part of his tragedy:

> I found President Johnson, in spite of his occasional lapses into coarse behavior, to be a man with drive, humanity, and depth of sensitivity,

struggling with too large an ego and too little solid confidence. He felt a need wholly to dominate those around him, but those who could really be helpful to him would not let themselves be dominated. He thus came to rely on those not worthy of his own stature.[131]

This was a gracious and perceptive assessment of the Johnson presidency. Kennan failed to muster similar evenhandedness at the time. He wrote in 1965 that "what this man represents—this oily, folksy, tricky political play-acting, this hearty optimism, this self-congratulatory jingoism, all combined with the whiney, plaintive, provincial drawl and the childish antics of the grown male in modern Texas—this may be the America of the majority of the American people but it's not *my* America."[132]

The foreign-policy crisis that came to define, and eventually crush, Johnson's presidency was the Vietnam War. Three days after Kennedy's assassination, LBJ informed his advisers that he was not going to be "the president who saw Southeast Asia go the same way China went." "Tell those generals in Saigon," he said, "that Lyndon Johnson intends to stand by our word."[133] The only thing that matters in South Vietnam, Johnson said bluntly, is to "win the war."[134] This tough talk did not necessarily stem from a sincere commitment to South Vietnam's inviolability; rather, it was a means to an end. The new president's all-consuming passion was to create the Great Society, a radical reshaping of the United States on socially progressive lines. All other matters came a distant second on the president's list of priorities. But creating the Great Society required Johnson to protect his right flank from the GOP. He had seen firsthand how Republicans, emboldened by the president's supposed foreign-policy weaknesses, had derailed Harry Truman's Fair Deal: "I knew that Harry Truman and Dean Acheson had lost their effectiveness from the day that the communists took over in China. I believed that the loss of China had played a large role in the rise of Joe McCarthy. And I knew that all these problems, taken together, were chickenshit compared with what might happen if we lost Vietnam."[135]

Building the Great Society meant winning the Vietnam War—or at least doing enough not to lose. So President Johnson secured congressional authorization, in the form of the Gulf of Tonkin Resolution, to combat Vietnamese communism in whatever way he deemed fit. The first step was a program of aerial bombing to hurt Hanoi and stem north–south infiltration: on March 2, 1965, the Rolling Thunder bombing campaign against North Vietnam commenced. Next was the introduction of U.S. combat troops: on

March 8–9, nine thousand men from the Ninth Marine Expeditionary Brigade made landfall in South Vietnam. These modest early commitments snowballed in precisely the way Nitze feared. By the end of the following year, there were 365,000 American troops in Vietnam. By 1968, the total number of American troops had reached half a million. Making good on NSC-68's strictures, and protecting the president's right flank, was a vastly expensive business.

While he had devoted relatively little time to considerations of foreign policy, there was also a clear Wilsonian aspect to Johnson's worldview. The president liked to quote Wilson's observation that "I hope we shall never forget that we created this nation, not to serve ourselves, but to serve mankind."[136] Like Kennedy, LBJ hoped that the combination of U.S. foreign aid and expertise might help solve the perennial global problems of "ignorance, poverty, hunger, and disease."[137] Johnson would later expend a lot of energy considering how New Deal–style public works programs might be applied to South Vietnam. During a celebrated speech at Johns Hopkins University in April 1965, Johnson announced his intention to build a new Tennessee Valley Authority in the Mekong Delta. NSC staffer Robert Komer recalled that Johnson would drive him "up the wall" on the issue of rural electrification in South Vietnam.[138] Exporting the New Deal would modernize countries in the Third World, allowing the United States to realize Wilsonian dreams. Banished at the Navy Department, Nitze played no role in the key escalatory meetings of the Vietnam War. But NSC-68's portrait of communist intentions tended to frame discussions on the efficacy of escalation. Nitze would find himself torn over whether to support the Americanization of the conflict.

Walter Lippmann and George Kennan both believed that it was foolish to invest American credibility and resources in preserving South Vietnam's independence. The faux nation was so insignificant in the grand scheme of things that any American effort to prop it up was little more than a fool's errand. Lippmann initially welcomed Lyndon Johnson's accession to the presidency. The two men enjoyed warm relations in the first couple of years when the esteemed journalist was a regular visitor to the White House. In September 1964, Johnson awarded Lippmann the Presidential Medal of Freedom for his role in educating his fellow Americans about the complexities of world affairs. But the president's escalation of the Vietnam War through 1964 and 1965 caused Lippmann to reassess. He went from hailing LBJ as "a man for this season" to describing him as a "primitive frontiersman" who had "betrayed and abandoned" his worthy domestic ideals.[139] On October 14, 1965, Lippmann wrote to Allan Nevins, a history professor at Columbia, "I do not doubt Johnson's sincerity and fervor for these domestic reforms, but when he looks abroad, he is filled with a simple-minded chauvinism of the good-guy, bad-guy thought, and I doubt very much if he has the kind of moral courage to liquidate an unprofitable war."[140] Lippmann began to attack Johnson's Vietnam policies in his "Today & Tomorrow" column. In response, administration officials established what became known as the "Lippmann Project," parsing the journalist's voluminous writings for egregious inconsistencies and errors of counsel. "An acceptance of Lippmann's doctrine [in Vietnam]—as in the cases of Greece, Berlin, Korea, and the Cuban Missile Crisis," reassured Walt Rostow in a memo to Dean Rusk, "would undermine the stability of the Free World everywhere and endanger our own safety by making the mainland of Europe and Asia safe hunting ground for the Communists."[141]

George Kennan joined Lippmann in attacking the president's policies in private and in print—and similarly earning LBJ's enmity. On February 7, 1965, the NLF had attacked Pleiku air base in South Vietnam, killing nine Americans and injuring five hundred. McGeorge Bundy was in South Vietnam at the time and, upon visiting Pleiku, he fell under what General William Westmoreland described as "field marshal psychosis." On Bundy's recommendation, the president ordered reprisal bombing raids against North Vietnam.[142] Kennan recorded his concerns in his diary the following day: "The provocation, admittedly, was great; but this bombing of points in Vietnam is a sort of petulant escapism, and will, I fear, lead to no good results."[143] On December 12, 1965, Kennan wrote the lead article in the Outlook section of *The Washington Post* on U.S. involvement in Vietnam. His critique was typically elegant and searing:

> I would not know what "victory" means . . . It seems to me the most unlikely of all contingencies that anyone should come to us on his knees and inquire [about] our terms, whatever the escalation of our effort . . . If we can find nothing better to do than embark upon a further open-ended increase in the level of our commitment simply because the alternatives seem humiliating and frustrating, one will have to ask whether we have not become enslaved to the dynamics of a single unmanageable situation—to the point where we have lost much of the power of initiative and control over our own policy, not just locally but on a world scale.[144]

Lippmann was thrilled to have a fellow dissenter, writing warmly to his former adversary: "[I] read your article in the *Washington Post* on Sunday. It is very illuminating and profoundly true, and I am very much afraid that the President has got beyond the point of no return in the distortion of our foreign policy by this Vietnamese War."[145]

Kennan's article in *The Post* annoyed LBJ, as was expected, but worse was to come. In February 1966, Senator J. William Fulbright called Kennan to testify before his Foreign Relations Committee. Fulbright, a cerebral and imposing presence in the Senate, had become increasingly frustrated by Johnson's escalation of the war, which he had come to view as unwarranted. He made arrangements for the hearings to be televised live to maximize the impact of his star witness's testimony. It certainly made for powerful theater. The White House could hardly impugn the architect of America's containment doctrine as weak willed—a man interned by the Nazis and banished from Moscow by Josef Stalin. In clipped, elegant sentences, Kennan eviscerated the shibboleths that served to sustain America's escalating commitment to South Vietnam. Kennan observed that President Eisenhower's "domino theory"—which held that if one nation falls to communism, its neighbors will soon follow—had recently been proved nonsensical by events in Indonesia, where a brutal anticommunist insurrection in 1965 had wiped a protocommunist regime off the map. The rebellion marked a vicious period of bloodletting in which half a million Indonesians—those of Chinese origin were targeted in particular—were killed. But the toppling of Sukarno's Jakarta regime showed that some dominoes could pop back up with minimal American interference (the CIA was involved only in a secondary capacity). Sukarno's ouster certainly seemed to show that East Asia was not quite the region on the brink of communist revolution that crisis-driven Vietnam hawks liked to maintain.

Kennan devoted much of his testimony to explaining how the United States should extricate itself from the mess in which it found itself. The United States was sufficiently strong and respected, Kennan insisted, that a tactical withdrawal from Vietnam in 1966 would scarcely register among allies and enemies: "There is more respect to be won in the opinion of this world by a resolute and courageous liquidation of unsound positions than by the most stubborn pursuit of extravagant or unpromising objectives." Kennan suggested that the United States withdraw incrementally by limiting tactical engagements and defending strategically important enclaves. The important thing was to melt away quietly without instilling too much consternation or conveying a sense of panic. Thereafter, Saigon's fate would be entirely in its own hands. If the nation failed to stand unaided on its own two feet—well, then, Charles Darwin had a theory about that.[146]

Senator Wayne Morse of Oregon, one of only two senators to vote against the Gulf of Tonkin Resolution, was smitten by Kennan's coolly rational logic, observing that "words simply fail me in expressing the degree to which this testimony of yours has moved me this morning . . . It is going to be referred to for generations to come." Senator Frank Lausche of Ohio pushed a little harder, asking Kennan how the architect of containment could so readily abandon his own theory. Kennan replied simply that "the situation has changed"—America had to choose where to spend its finite resources, and South Vietnam was not sufficiently important to warrant the investment. Angriest of all was Senator Stuart Symington of Missouri, who had recently returned from Vietnam mightily impressed by the morale of U.S. troops and appalled by tales of atrocities perpetrated by the Viet Cong. "Morally," Symington demanded, "do you think we have the right to desert them by going into coastal enclaves?" Kennan, impassive during the tirade, replied slowly and patiently:

> Senator, if their morale is so shaky that without an offensive strategy on our part they are simply going to give up the fight, I do not think they are worth helping anyway. And, as for the question of our having a moral obligation to them, they have had enormous help from us to date. I mean, goodness, they have had help in billions and billions of dollars. How many countries are you going to give such a claim on our resources and on our help? If they cannot really do the trick with this, I feel strongly that the trouble lies somewhere with them and not with us.[147]

Kennan's testimony caused a remarkable stir. NBC broadcast the hearings live in their entirety, but CBS opted to air a rerun of *I Love Lucy* instead. The network's decision led its news president, Fred Friendly, to resign in protest. Meanwhile Kennan was swamped with a barrage of fan mail from across the nation. His secretary recalled that the mailman would arrive at his Princeton home every day "hauling sacks like Santa Claus."[148] One poll revealed that in the month after Kennan's testimony, public support for LBJ's handling for the war dropped from 63 to 49 percent.[149] For a man of Kennan's self-critical disposition, the acclaim and validation must have been pleasurable—though the warm feeling did not last long.

As Lippmann and Kennan presented formidable public critiques of President Johnson's Vietnam policies, Nitze continued in his struggle to master his views on the conflict. He had visited Vietnam in June 1965 in his capacity as secretary of the Navy and was unimpressed with the field commander, General William Westmoreland. He had queried the general on some of the data he presented on troop numbers—with a little too much certainty, in Nitze's opinion—and Westmoreland "took deep umbrage and said I was accusing him of inflating enemy strength in order to justify lifting the ceiling on American forces in Vietnam."[150] Upon his return, Nitze warned McNamara about Westmoreland's cavalier methods for calculating enemy strength— perhaps, Nitze ventured cautiously, the United States should consider withdrawing its forces from Vietnam. McNamara asked whether withdrawal would lead communists to escalate their efforts elsewhere. Nitze replied yes. McNamara then asked where this might happen. Nitze didn't know. "Well," McNamara observed, "under those circumstances, I take it you can't be at all certain that the difficulties of stopping them in the next area that they may choose won't be greater than the difficulties of stopping them in South Vietnam." When Nitze replied "no, I can't" to the second consecutive question, McNamara killed the discussion: "You offer no alternative."[151]

The following month, Nitze was given an unambiguous opportunity to voice his concerns when Johnson called a meeting to discuss Vietnam with the cabinet secretaries, service secretaries, and the Joint Chiefs of Staff. Midway through the meeting, LBJ asked Nitze directly what he thought of American prospects in South Vietnam—should he agree to Westmoreland's request for more troops? Nitze replied that the situation was challenging but that adding more troops would commensurately increase prospects for success. "Would you send in more forces than Westmoreland requests?" interrupted the president. "Yes. Depends on how quickly they—" LBJ cut him off. "How many?" the president demanded. "200 [thousand] instead of 100?" "Need another 100 in January—" replied Nitze. "Can you do that?" Johnson cut in again. "Yes," said Nitze obligingly.[152] Over the course of a minute-long presidential interrogation, Nitze had lent clear support to a war he had found troubling for so long. In a room of can-dos, the principal author of NSC-68 had decided to take ownership of its logic.

Nitze lived to regret the advice he dispensed under pressure at the meeting, although his support for the war certainly improved relations with the president. When McGeorge Bundy left the White House to assume the presidency of the Ford Foundation, LBJ briefly contemplated appointing Nitze as his replacement. Robert McNamara was open to just about anyone taking the job so long as it wasn't the relentlessly hawkish Walt Rostow. So he told Johnson that Nitze "could do it all right," though he added a caveat: "I don't know if you'd find it pleasant to work with him; he's an abrasive charac-ter."[153] Takes one to know one, Nitze might have replied.

Rostow got the job, the Vietnam War escalated apace, and Nitze's isola-tion continued until June 1967, when he was appointed deputy secretary of defense. This was the job he had accepted from Kennedy until the caustic, superconfident Bob McNamara had blocked it. In the summer of 1967, how-ever, McNamara was a different man: emotionally broken over his part in escalating a war that he now viewed as unwinnable.

That times had changed from the optimistic Kennedy era might be seen in the fact that Nitze's first job as deputy secretary was to prepare the Penta-gon for a massive antiwar protest. Among the hundred thousand protesters who marched on the Pentagon on October 21 were three of Nitze's children, "more out of curiosity than for protest," he observed hopefully. Nitze made absolutely sure that the troops that defended the Pentagon carried no live ammunition in their rifles. Nonetheless, scuffles broke out, tear gas was de-ployed, red paint was poured on the Pentagon steps to simulate blood, and Yippies (members of the Youth International Party) led by Abbie Hoffman and Jerry Rubin failed in their attempt to surround and "levitate" the Penta-gon in a bid to cast out evil spirits. The marchers included the writer Nor-man Mailer, the godfather of intuitive parenting Benjamin Spock, and the poet Robert Lowell. Mailer wrote the fine "nonfiction novel" *Armies of the Night* based on his experience of the march and his subsequent arrest. Re-viewing the book in *The New York Times*, Alfred Kazin wrote that "only a born novelist could have written a piece of history so intelligent, mischie-vous, penetrating and alive, so vivid with crowds, the great stage that is American democracy, the Washington streets and bridges, the Lincoln Memorial, the women, students, hippies, Negroes and assorted intellectuals for peace."[154] Nitze did not record his views of Mailer's stylized depiction. He did mock the protesters for getting het up by "vaguely Marxist authors whom they then considered inspirational, such as Dr. Herbert Marcuse and Noam Chomsky, [who] are no longer read."[155] George Kennan was ostensibly on the same side as the protesters, but he wrote a mean-spirited book, *De-mocracy and the Student Left*, mocking their methods and pretensions: "If the students think *they* are gloomy about the American scene, and fearful of America's future, I must tell them that they haven't seen anything yet. Not only do my apprehensions outclass theirs but my ideas of what would have to be done to put things right are far more radical than theirs."[156]

Kennan's assault on the student protesters was wide-ranging: they were naïve, work shy, drug addled, nihilistic, and spewed cant informed by an alarmingly shallow pool of knowledge. Writing in *Commentary,* the conservative Norman Podhoretz hailed Kennan as a resolute truth teller. Elsewhere he was denounced by the playwright Lillian Hellman, Columbia professor Zbigniew Brzezinski, and the poet W. H. Auden. "There is no one in public life for whose integrity and wisdom I have greater respect than Mr. George Kennan," Auden wrote, but denigrating the protesters' potential and purpose "is to deny that human history owes anything to martyrs."[157]

Antiwar dissent grew fiercer throughout 1968 as it became obvious that the United States was killing and maiming its enemy to no political effect. A watershed moment arrived on January 30, 1968, when a combined force of eighty-four thousand NLF troops launched a coordinated assault on every significant town, city, and U.S. military facility in South Vietnam. In its greatest propaganda coup, NLF troops infiltrated the U.S. embassy in Saigon and killed two U.S. military policemen. It was a suicide mission—they were all eventually killed—but they stayed alive long enough for their efforts to make it onto American television screens, presenting a distressing image of the war that jarred with President Johnson's hitherto upbeat assurances of steady progress. For the first time, the major newsweeklies—*Time, Life, Newsweek*—criticized the war. America's most trusted news anchor, Walter Cronkite, observed with genuine surprise, "I thought we were winning the war."[158]

Nitze was not as surprised as Cronkite by the Tet Offensive—so-called because the assault was launched on the eve of Tet, the lunar New Year. He had been consistently unpersuaded by the insistence of Walt Rostow and other optimistic hawks that the vast U.S. military effort had the southern insurgency on the back foot—that there was "light at the end of the tunnel." Clark Clifford had officially replaced a broken Robert McNamara as defense secretary on March 1, and Nitze began to lobby Clifford for a fundamental reappraisal of the war. Clifford had served as a naval aide to President Truman in the latter stages of the Second World War and played a key role in drafting the seminal 1947 National Security Act. He had served President Kennedy on the Foreign Intelligence Advisory Board, and advised President Johnson on the Vietnam War in 1965—when he sided with George Ball in opposing escalation. But after LBJ made the decision to Americanize the war, Clifford became one of the president's staunchest supporters—a fierce advocate of winning wars once established. At the point of his replacing McNamara, Nitze described him as a "fire-breathing hawk." But then Tet compelled him to change tack completely, as Nitze later described:

Clark's [views] changed first and Clark switched 180 degrees, so Clark came to the conclusion the thing to do was to cut and run right away. Having been a "bomb 'em to pieces" fellow, he suddenly became "get out at all costs, any costs, just get out." And that I thought was also wrong, so from that point on suddenly I found myself being not on the dove side, but on the firmer side. I thought it was just dreadful to just pull out.[159]

On March 4, Clifford briefed the president on his post-Tet recommendations and cast what he described as "grave doubts" on the sharp escalatory route—the dispatch of a further 206,000 American troops—urged by Walt Rostow and General William Westmoreland. Clifford observed that the president's war policies had already done "enormous damage" to the country "we are trying to save."[160] He doubted whether "we can ever find a way out if we continue to shovel men into Vietnam."[161]

Clifford's assessment shocked President Johnson. Nitze was glad for his change of heart—he had threatened to resign from the administration rather than defend the Vietnam War before Senator Fulbright's committee— but he now came to view the new defense secretary as mercurial and untrustworthy. So followed a remarkable month in American politics. On March 12, the liberal antiwar senator from Minnesota, Eugene McCarthy, won 42 percent of the presidential primary vote in New Hampshire. Sensing LBJ's political weakness, Robert Kennedy joined the race—on a similarly antiwar platform—to secure the nomination ahead of the sitting president four days later. Previously steadfast supporters of Johnson's efforts in Vietnam shifted their position to outright opposition in the aftermath of Tet. During a tense meeting with Walt Rostow, Dean Acheson told the national security adviser "to tell the president—and you tell him in precisely these words—that he can take Vietnam and stick it up his ass."[162] During a meeting of the so-called Wise Men—establishment types like Acheson, Robert Lovett, John McCloy, and Charles Bohlen—on March 25, each member counseled the president to disengage from Vietnam. After the meeting, Rostow wrote mournfully, "The American Establishment is dead."[163] The logic of NSC-68 had been given its last rites. On March 31, President Johnson announced a unilateral restriction on the U.S. bombing, called for substantive peace negotiations, and added, finally, that he would not seek a second elected term in office.

The remainder of Nitze's service to the Johnson administration consisted largely of opposing Clifford's efforts to concede too much to North

Vietnam in the search for peace. President Johnson had appointed Averell Harriman to lead peace negotiations with North Vietnam in Paris beginning May 1. Both Clifford and Harriman wanted the president to order further restrictions on the bombing to facilitate discussions. Nitze joined Rostow in arguing strongly to the contrary. "I was convinced," Nitze wrote, "that we would achieve nothing in Paris that was not won on the battlefield."[164] And so Nitze's peculiar relationship with the Vietnam War continued right to the end of the Johnson administration. Advocates of escalation had always spoken the language of NSC-68, the hallowed text of Cold War interventionism. Yet Nitze was as indecisive in person as he was unambiguous on the page. Some conflicts cannot be refracted through a crystalline doctrine, offering a clear path to success. His scattershot take on Vietnam reflected this dilemma. Nitze refused to connect the amped-up language of NSC-68—a theory designed to guide the United States through the Cold War—to any foreign-policy misadventure that followed.

Richard Nixon defeated Hubert Humphrey—Johnson's vice president, who fended off Eugene McCarthy's challenge following Robert Kennedy's assassination in June—in the general election of November 1968. Nitze yearned for a job in the new administration, but he had gathered too many enemies on the left and the right during the 1960s to make him a viable choice. Nixon's defense secretary, Melvin Laird, sounded out senators from both sides of the political aisle on their willingness to confirm Nitze to an appropriate second-tier position. Senator Barry Goldwater of Arizona, the 1964 GOP presidential candidate, said no way. He blamed Nitze, unfairly, for the Democratic Party's success during the election in portraying him as unhinged and quick on the trigger. Laird asked Senator Fulbright his thoughts on the same question, particularly in regard to Nitze becoming U.S. ambassador to West Germany. "My comment is that Nitze is an imperialist at heart," replied Fulbright, "and would not be a good person to support U.S. troop withdrawals and, therefore, might be a good ambassador to Mali or some other equivalent position—but not Bonn."[165]

Congenitally incapable of sitting around in a funk, in the spring of 1969 Nitze established a pressure group with Dean Acheson. The Committee to Maintain a Prudent Defense Policy lobbied for the continued development of Safeguard, a missile defense program that would allow the United States to shoot down incoming Soviet ballistic missiles. In the mood to reassert itself after being made peripheral through the Americanization of the Vietnam War, Congress had threatened to cut off funding for the program. Nitze was aghast that sore feelings about Vietnam might be allowed to imperil America's defensive capabilities. He hired three of Albert Wohlstetter's most talented graduate students at the University of Chicago to assist his lobbying efforts: Richard Perle, Peter Wilson, and Paul Wolfowitz.[166] They combined well and Safeguard was spared by one vote in the Senate in August 1969. Thereafter Nitze's team remained united in their opposition to defense cuts and any needless kowtowing to the Soviet Union. They began sketching a new strategic agenda for the next generation. When a year later Kennan met with Nitze in Washington, D.C., he found him "as serious as ever about the mathematics of destruction."[167]

7

★

METTERNICH REDUX

HENRY KISSINGER

Henry was too tricky to get along with—nobody in the U.S. government liked him at all because he tricked and deceived everybody.

—PAUL NITZE

Henry understands my views better than anyone at State ever has.

—GEORGE KENNAN

By the fall of 1967, Robert McNamara was absolutely certain that the Americanization of the Vietnam War had been a mistake. Determined to halt a debacle that was largely of his own making, the secretary of defense urged Lyndon Johnson to appoint Henry Kissinger to lead third-party negotiations to end the conflict. Kissinger was a noted scholar and public intellectual, the author of acclaimed books on nuclear strategy and the Congress of Vienna, a Harvard professor with a fierce ambition for government service. McNamara reasoned that Kissinger's deliberative style, moderation, and varied international connections made him the ideal person to move negotiations forward. On September 12, President Johnson's advisers gathered to consider McNamara's suggestion. Secretary of State Dean Rusk endorsed Kissinger's "trustworthiness and character," noting that his centrist politics and seemingly orthodox Cold War views means that he is "basically for us." The hawkish Walt Rostow conceded that Kissinger was a "good analyst" but worried that "he may go a little soft when you get down to the crunch."[1]

McNamara won the argument—for the last time in the Johnson administration—and Kissinger began meeting in Paris with two French intermediaries with Hanoi connections, Herbert Marcovich and Raymond Aubrac, through September and October. The negotiations—code-named

"Pennsylvania"—foundered on Hanoi's reluctance to talk until the United States stopped bombing North Vietnam. While McNamara lauded Kissinger as "a very shrewd negotiator . . . the best I have seen in my seven years," Johnson grew increasingly impatient as the weeks passed.[2] During a tense telephone conversation in which the president addressed Kissinger as "Professor Schlesinger," LBJ issued a blunt final warning in the style of Al Capone: "I'm going to give it one more try," said Johnson, "and if that doesn't work I'm going to come up to Cambridge and cut off your balls."[3]

The channel quietly expired late in 1967 (though the president declined to carry out his threat). Kissinger drew at least two conclusions from this dismal affair. First, he needed to serve a president who trusted his judgment and was willing to give his diplomacy some time to work. Second, he would boost his prospects of securing a powerful position in the next administration if both major parties viewed him as a potential appointment. Having previously worked for the centrist Republican Nelson Rockefeller, Kissinger turned swiftly to advise the victorious Nixon campaign after Rockefeller was defeated in the summer of 1968. His contact was Richard Allen, a thirty-two-year-old member of the Hoover Institution at Stanford University whom Nixon had appointed his principal foreign-policy aide. Allen and Kissinger worked together on the Vietnam platform plank. Allen was sufficiently impressed to invite Kissinger to join Nixon's foreign-policy advisory board.

Assuming this position would have required Kissinger to break cover, however, so he declined and continued his dual-focus charm offensive. Kissinger also rationalized that he could better serve Nixon by retaining the Johnson administration's confidence, securing access to whatever useful information might come his way. So Kissinger reached out to members of the administration with whom he had previously worked and who considered him an ally. One was Daniel Davidson, one of Kissinger's former students at Harvard, who served as a member of Averell Harriman's delegation in Paris and who kept his old tutor up to date with what was happening. Kissinger then forwarded this information to Nixon via Allen, unbeknownst to Harriman and Davidson. As Allen described it:

> Henry Kissinger, on his own, volunteered information to us through a spy, a former student, that he had in the Paris peace talks, who would call him and debrief, and Kissinger called me from pay phones and we spoke in German. The fact that my German is better than his did not at all hinder my communication with Henry and he offloaded mostly every night what had happened that day in Paris.[4]

Kissinger was brazen in carrying out this task. On August 15, 1968, for example, he wrote to Harriman that there "is a chance that I may be in Paris around September 17, and I would very much like to stop in and see you then. I am through with Republican politics. The party is hopeless and unfit to govern."[5] A few weeks later, Harriman replied, "All is forgiven. Welcome back to the fold."[6] When Kissinger's double-dealing was publicized in later years, through the publication of Seymour Hersh's exposé, *The Price of Power*, Harriman's team in Paris was appalled. Richard Holbrooke, who would later embark on a celebrated diplomatic career, was one member of the Paris delegation who found Kissinger's behavior tawdry. "Henry was the only person outside of the government we were authorized to discuss the negotiations with," Holbrooke said bitterly. "We trusted him. It is not stretching the truth to say that the Nixon campaign had a secret source within the U.S. negotiating team."[7]

Kissinger's devious method of gathering intelligence was not nearly as problematic as what Nixon chose to do with it. In late September, Kissinger informed John Mitchell, Nixon's campaign manager, "that something big was afoot regarding Vietnam." A few weeks later, Kissinger fleshed out this insinuation, predicting that the Johnson administration would announce a bombing halt in mid to late October. On October 30, LBJ confirmed Kissinger's expectation and announced that a unilateral U.S. bombing halt would take effect the following day—meeting Hanoi's substantive precondition for peace talks. As the skies above North Vietnam cleared of American B-52s, Mitchell got in touch with Anna Chennault, a prominent Chinese-American businesswoman who headed the nationwide Republican Women for Nixon, and who had close links to the South Vietnamese ambassador to the United States, Bui Diem. Mitchell said, "Anna, I'm speaking on behalf of Richard Nixon. It's very important that our Vietnamese friends understand our Republican position and I hope you have made this very clear to them."[8]

The "Republican position" was as follows: South Vietnamese President Thieu should refuse to attend peace negotiations under a Democratic president and instead wait to secure more generous terms under a Nixon administration. The advice was received loud and clear. On November 1, Thieu delivered a belligerent speech that disassociated himself from LBJ's speech and Harriman's efforts in Paris. The next day, Ellsworth Bunker reported that Thieu had "closeted himself in his private apartment in independence palace" and was refusing to meet with him. Bunker surmised correctly that Thieu was "convinced that Nixon will win and will follow a hawkish policy, and therefore he can afford to wait."[9] Wait Thieu assuredly did.

The margin of Nixon's victory on November 5 was wafer-thin. Nixon secured 43.4 percent of the popular vote compared to Hubert Humphrey's 42.7—this translated into a wider victory of 301 to 191 electoral votes. The segregationist third-party candidate, former Democratic governor of Alabama George Wallace, won 13.5 percent of the popular vote, providing an early portent of how LBJ's greatest domestic achievements—in the sphere of civil rights—had destroyed Franklin Roosevelt's uneasy coalition of northern liberals, African Americans, college professors, blue-collar workers, and southerners of all stripes, including bigots. Nixon also used Johnson's progressive legislation as a useful foil, pursuing the so-called Southern strategy of exploiting the racism and fears of lawlessness of many southern voters, whose world LBJ had upended. In appealing to "states' rights" and "law and order," Nixon deployed euphemisms that resonated through the history of the South and that would serve the Republican Party well in the future. The year 1968 was pivotal in American political history—a defining moment for modern conservatism. But George Wallace got it wrong when he crowed that the "great pointy heads who knew best how to run everyone's life have had their day."[10]

The election was seminal in regard to foreign policy too, where pointy-heads like Kissinger were much in evidence. Nixon made two major decisions after defeating Humphrey. First, the president-elect decided to marginalize the State Department and concentrate foreign policymaking in the White House, ensuring that he could pursue his agenda without excessive interference from an arm of government he viewed as an adversary: a competing power base with an institutionally liberal bent. Second, Nixon appointed Henry Kissinger as his national security adviser, with all the power that Nixon's first goal promised this position. The appointment marked a grand strategic break with the escalation and broadening of the Cold War since 1950. Kissinger was allergic to Woodrow Wilson's moral certainties and viewed the Kennedy and Johnson years as an era in which American commitments were expanded—in accordance with Paul Nitze's NSC-68—to unsustainable levels. Kissinger's geopolitical views held important points of convergence with those of Alfred Mahan, Walter Lippmann, and George Kennan.

Yet the manner of Nixon and Kissinger's coming together created problems that bedeviled their working and personal relationships. Both were adept at secrecy and duplicity, and they viewed their assuming power as an essential good in itself, regardless of the means used to achieve it. Kissinger was thus willing to lie to Averell Harriman, one of America's most distinguished public servants, in the hope that he might gain useful information to win favor with Nixon. At the same time, he flirted with the Humphrey campaign, whispering enticing promises—such as one to present the Humphrey campaign with a large incriminating file on Nixon that he'd prepared while advising Nelson Rockefeller—without actually delivering. He was so skilled at convincing people that he was on their side that Humphrey acknowledged, "If I had been elected, I would have had Kissinger be my assistant. That fellow is indestructible—a professional, able and rather unflappable. I like the fact that he has a little fun too."[11] The flappable Kissinger—for Humphrey misread him on that score—would have been pleased by this endorsement, which validated his acting skills as well as his bipartisan credentials.

For his part, Nixon was comfortable sacrificing a peace settlement in 1968 to the greater good of his assuming power. Passing advice to Chennault via Mitchell that he knew would reach Bui Diem was technically treasonous: frustrating the declared intentions of the U.S. government in concert with a foreign nation. Kissinger and Nixon's first meaningful collaboration therefore laid bare the worst of their traits. Even Nixon's announcement of Kissinger's appointment was presented with a glaring untruth. On December 2, Nixon unveiled his new national security adviser and "announced a program that was substantially at odds with what he had told me privately," Kissinger admitted. Nixon said that Kissinger's role would be limited to planning and that he "would not come between the President and the Secretary of State."[12] Yet that was precisely where Nixon wanted Kissinger—a like-minded barrier to the State Department.

Observing each other in action throughout 1968, Nixon and Kissinger must have struggled to discern when one was lying or being sincere. Indeed, during the 1972 election campaign, Nixon worried (in needlessly paranoid—or "Nixonian"—fashion) that Kissinger might jump ship and offer sensitive information to whoever was likeliest to promote his career prospects. "Remember," Nixon said to White House Chief of Staff H. R. Haldeman, "he came to us in '68 with tales."[13] These first actions evidently left a lasting impression. Nixon and Kissinger paired up after some scandalous infidelities—Kissinger betrayed Harriman; Nixon, his country. This was clearly not a solid foundation on which to base a long-term relationship. In combination the two men scored some remarkable achievements. But it was little wonder that each would habitually suspect the other of cheating on them.

Heinz Alfred Kissinger was born in Fürth, Germany, on May 27, 1923, where his father, Louis, was a teacher at the local school. A refined and articulate—though reticent—man, Louis Kissinger read and collected great books, revered classical music, played the piano, and proselytized on the pleasures of intellectual endeavor—reminding his children that they were engaged in a perpetual exercise in self-improvement, or *Bildung*.[14] Bavaria, however, was a hostile environment for Jews. Louis's Judaism barred him from serving his country during the First World War. Young Heinz himself was prevented from attending the gymnasium, or state-run high school, because of his religion. Instead he was enrolled at the Israelitische Real-schule, a fine Jewish school where history, philosophy, and religion were taken very seriously; each student studied the Bible and Talmud for two hours every day.[15]

As Hitler consolidated power after 1933, it became increasingly clear that the Nazis viewed segregation as insufficient in itself. The Nuremberg Laws of 1935 dissolved Jews' German citizenship, forbade intermarriage, and barred Jews from numerous professions, including teaching. Heinz's childhood friend Werner Gundelfinger described the suffocating nature of Nazi repression: "We couldn't go to the swimming pool, the dances, or the tea room. We couldn't go anywhere without seeing the sign: *Juden Verboten*. These are things that remain in your subconscious."[16]

When Walter Lippmann observed in 1933 that Germany's Jews might serve as a conveniently placed lightning rod, deflecting Hitler's attention from the rest of Europe, he was thinking of families like the Kissingers and the Gundelfingers.

State-sanctioned persecution and the volatile passions of the masses were the dark mainstays of Heinz's formative years. The rise and fall of Weimar Germany had exposed democracy's deficiencies when confronted by a ruthless and opportunistic adversary; Hitler's Germany illustrated the brute force of totalitarianism and the effectiveness of propagating simple and poisonous lies. Kissinger drew the attendant conclusions. Paraphrasing Goethe, Kissinger later observed that "if I had to choose between justice and disorder, on the one hand, and injustice and order, on the other, I would always choose the latter."[17] Though their points of departure were different, Kissinger, Walter Lippmann, and George Kennan all shared grave concerns about the naïveté of the masses. All were troubled by democracy's gaping blind side.

After the passage of the Nuremberg Laws in 1935, Heinz's tenacious and farsighted mother, Paula, wrote to her first cousin, who lived in Manhattan's Washington Heights, asking if her sons, Heinz and Walter, could come and live with her. Fearing for Paula and Louis's safety, the cousin suggested that the whole family emigrate, not just the children. It proved to be lifesaving advice for Paula and her husband. On August 30, 1938, the Kissingers departed Bavaria for New York via London. A brave and defiant Heinz, who Anglicized his name to Henry upon arrival in the United States, told a German customs inspector at the border: "I'll be back someday."[18]

Heinz was prophetic, though his pluck could not mask a wrenching experience for a family that had venerated German culture only to have the nation turn on them. Louis was forced to leave behind his beloved library, the focal point of the family's erudition and ambition. Henry later responded stoically to questions that addressed the traumas of his childhood. In 1971, for example, he said, "That part of my childhood is not the key to anything. I was not consciously unhappy. I was not acutely aware of what was going on. For children, these things are not that serious."[19] Whether Kissinger's response was brave or genuine, Hitler's Germany took a terrible toll on the extended family members who chose to remain or were too old or infirm to leave. Thirteen perished in Nazi concentration camps.

Fürth and New York City were different worlds. America's largest city was ethnically heterogeneous, entrepreneurial rather than hierarchical, and expanded at breakneck speed throughout the 1930s, serving as a haven for European Jews and as a magnet for the world's brightest minds. After passing through Ellis Island, the Kissingers effectively started again with a blank slate. Paula Kissinger worked long hours as a housekeeper and a caterer to support her family. But her husband struggled to adjust to losing the status accrued through his refined tastes and teaching accomplishments in Bavaria. Louis Kissinger could not find the right map to navigate the New World.

Henry had no such status to lose and so managed the transition to living in New York City more comfortably. He attended George Washington High School—an excellent public school—and established himself as an outstanding student. He mastered English swiftly, though never losing his strong Bavarian accent; this part of his identity—conveying a seriousness of thought and purpose—was inviolable. Henry took a part-time job in a brushmaking factory, providing additional resources for a family living in straitened circumstances. The comparison in life experience with Paul Nitze, who by that time had made all the money he could ever need, is stark. After graduating from high school, Henry embarked on an accountancy degree at City College, attended by many émigré Jews in New York. It did not charge tuition and the students could continue to live at home, the professors were excellent, and the students at this time—Jews in particular—became highly respected and well known in all fields of endeavor. Henry recalled, "My horizons were not that great when I was in City College. I never really thought of accounting as a calling, but I thought it might be a nice job."[20]

After he had completed just a year at City College, the U.S. Army drafted Kissinger in February 1943. He was a serious and hardworking youth of just nineteen years when he left Manhattan for basic training at Camp Croft in Spartanburg, South Carolina—another jolting change in environment. In Fürth and Washington Heights, Henry had been immersed in an orthodox German Jewish milieu. The Army's all-consuming demands of training— the drills, early starts, communal eating, cajoling, and bullying—ironed out the religious diversity of the draftees and ripped up the comforting routines of many recent immigrants. This had a positive dimension as well as a disorienting one, and Kissinger found that "the significant thing about the army was that it made me feel like an American . . . It was the first time I was not with German Jewish people. I gained confidence in the army." Yet life in Spartanburg was not without difficulty, and he endured prejudice. After he scored exceptionally well on aptitude tests, the Army denied Kissinger the opportunity to become a doctor because of its quota on the number of Jews permitted to train as physicians. Impermanence, insecurity, and anti-Semitism—of different orders of magnitude—had been constants throughout his life: "Living as a Jew under the Nazis, then as a refugee in America, and then as a private in the Army isn't exactly an experience that builds confidence."[21] But Kissinger secured one prize through his Army service that bolstered his sense of permanence and place: at Camp Croft he became a naturalized American citizen.

While Kissinger's Judaism prevented him from becoming an Army doctor, his fluency in German and experience of life under Hitler made him a valuable commodity to the U.S. Army. He was assigned to the Army Specialized Training Program and given the brief of educating his fellow soldiers on the reasons why America was at war with Nazi Germany. Kissinger moved to Camp Claiborne in Louisiana, where he met Fritz Kraemer, another German émigré—though of aristocratic Prussian origin—whose job was to explain the peculiar evils of Nazism to American soldiers. Kissinger observed Kraemer in action and was impressed by the forcefulness of his speech and the quality of his insights. He wrote him a fan note: "I heard you speak yesterday. This is how it should be done. Can I help you somehow?" Kraemer met with Kissinger and was deeply impressed by his intellectual depth and seriousness of purpose, noting that Henry had "a sixth sense of musicality—historical musicality." The two men became close; Kissinger had discovered his first mentor and won his patronage, marking an important stage in his career and intellectual development. Kraemer was deeply versed in philosophy and history—he had a bachelor's degree from the London School of Economics and doctorates from the universities of Frankfurt and Rome—and Kissinger drew all the insight he could. "He would squeeze me for my ideas the way one would squeeze a sponge," Kraemer recalled. "He hankered for knowledge, for truth. He wanted to know everything."[22]

Kraemer recommended Kissinger for assignment to Germany as a translator for the division's general. He informed his superiors that he had been thoroughly impressed by "this little Jewish refugee [who] as yet knows nothing, but already he understands everything."[23] And so, making good on his promise to the Nazi customs official in 1938, Kissinger returned to Germany in November 1944 as a translator for General Alexander Bolling. He was soon after promoted to a much larger role as the administrator of Krefeld, a small city in Westphalia, where he was instrumental in restoring order. Henry was promoted again to serve as a sergeant in the Counter Intelligence Corps, assuming control of a large district in the state of Hesse. What an empowering experience this must have been: returning to the scene of an awful crime visited upon him, his family, and millions of fellow Jews, and bringing some of its perpetrators to justice. With his keen insight into the German psyche, Kissinger was particularly effective at smoking out former Gestapo. As Jeremi Suri observes in *Henry Kissinger and the American Century*:

> Decades later, Kissinger enjoyed recounting how he manipulated German habits for American purposes. In 1945 he posted signs in occupied areas requesting job applications from men with "police experience." When an applicant arrived at Kissinger's office, "I asked him what he had been doing, and he said *Staats polizei* [state police]. I then asked him in a joking manner, *Geheim Staats Polizei* [Gestapo]? And he said yes. So I locked him up . . . I locked up more Gestapo than the entire rest of the U.S. Army."[24]

Though highly effective at his job, Kissinger had no appetite for the coarser aspects of revenge and scolded those who crossed the line in the interview room. He was awarded the Bronze Star for distinguished service.

Kissinger abandoned his religion during this time. He met many Jews who had survived Nazi concentration camps and was at a loss to find solace in the faith in which he had been immersed. "How could a benevolent God have allowed such horrors against his worshippers?" was Kissinger's unanswered question, and that of many others beside.[25] His vast energy and the self-reliance of the talented immigrant propelled his career forward while a deep pessimism about human nature cautioned him against trusting people too easily, or hewing too closely to the Wilsonian strain of thought regarding the world's perfectibility. God was dead to Kissinger, and his worldview became accordingly fatalistic, anticipating worst-case scenarios. In this regard Fritz Kraemer is insightful on Kissinger's experiences of Germany: "Kissinger is a strong man, but the Nazis were able to damage his soul . . . For the formative years of his youth, he faced the horrors of his world coming apart, of the father he loved being turned into a helpless mouse . . . It made him seek order, and it led him to hunger for acceptance, even if it meant trying to please those he considered his intellectual inferiors."[26]

As his Army service in Germany approached its end, Kissinger pondered what he would do in the United States upon his return—the study of accountancy had lost all its limited appeal. Kraemer was on hand to dispense typically bracing advice to his protégé in 1947. Responding to Kissinger's complaints regarding the shallowness of his education—"I know nothing," Henry despaired—Kraemer said, "Go to a fine college. A gentleman does not go to the College of the City of New York."[27] Kissinger followed this advice and applied to Columbia, Princeton, and Harvard. His application letter read: "In order to adequately prepare myself for a literary carreer [sic] with political history as the main field of interest, I consider it essential to acquire a Liberal Arts education."[28] Columbia and Princeton rejected him, but Harvard—at that time making a concerted effort to recruit veterans of exceptional promise— accepted him with a scholarship attached. This was a wonderful opportunity for a young man who only seven years before had been assembling shaving brushes after school to make ends meet. The Second World War gave a mighty boost to male social mobility; Henry Kissinger benefited from meritocratic principles taking deeper root in U.S. society.

Kissinger led a monastic life in Cambridge, working sixteen-hour days to make the most of the gilt-edged opportunity that was a Harvard education. The class of 1950 was the largest in Harvard's history, and some three-quarters of the incoming sophomores were veterans who had benefited from the GI Bill. The class was more socially than racially diverse, however. James Conant's presidency had made Harvard somewhat more accommodating to Jewish and nonwhite students, but many of the institutional slights present in Lippmann's day remained. University administrators believed that housing Jewish students separately would better suit both Jews and

Gentiles. So Kissinger was housed in Harvard's oldest dormitory, Claverly Hall, where he shared accommodations with two fellow Jews. Henry kept these men at a distance, shunned extracurricular activities, and immersed himself in his courses, preparing assiduously for class. As his friend and biographer Stephen Graubard writes, "For the first time in his life, Kissinger experienced the exhilaration that came from habitual reading and writing, he became something of a recluse."[29] To relax, Kissinger set aside the assigned books and instead read novels or *The New York Times* and *The Boston Globe*. He avoided reading the editorials—"He said he had to form his own opinions," remembered one of his roommates, "not learn those of the editors."[30]

Professor William Y. Elliott performed a similar role at Harvard to Fritz Kraemer in the Army—swiftly identifying Kissinger's gifts and encouraging his ambition. A magnetic presence, Elliott did not conform to the stereotype of a Harvard professor. A native of Tennessee and all-American football player at Vanderbilt, Elliott staged cockfights in the basement of his Cambridge town house and delighted in his nickname, "Wild Bill." More conventionally, Elliott had been a Rhodes scholar at Balliol College, Oxford, and from that experience drew great pleasure in teaching students of uncommon ability on an individual basis. To test Henry's mettle, he sent him off to the library with a reading list of twenty-five books, inviting him to compare Immanuel Kant's critiques of pure and practical reason. When Kissinger returned, three months later, with an outstanding paper, Elliott was bowled over. He began meeting with Kissinger frequently, lavishing attention in the Oxbridge style on his thinking and writing. Elliott later wrote to the Phi Beta Kappa selection committee that "I have not had any students in the past five years, even among the summa cum laude group, who have had the depth and philosophical insight shown by Mr. Kissinger." Yet there was still work to be done. Elliott noted that Kissinger's "mind lacks grace and is Teutonic in its systematic thoroughness."[31]

Kissinger's undergraduate dissertation became something of a Harvard legend. Whereas most students narrow their topic to boost the originality of their contribution—and to be able to finish more quickly—Kissinger chose to write on "The Meaning of History: Reflections on Spengler, Toynbee and Kant." At 388 pages, the dissertation was the longest submitted in Harvard's history and led to the creation of a "Kissinger rule," which limited subsequent students to one-third of this length. The dissertation discussed the ways Oswald Spengler, Arnold Toynbee, and Immanuel Kant grappled with the meaning of history, but also contained lengthy digressions on Homer,

Virgil, Dante, Milton, Spinoza, Goethe, Rousseau, Hegel, Dostoevsky, and others, proving to readers the breadth and ambition of Kissinger's reading.

Given that the dissertation assessed Spengler, and was written by a Jewish refugee from Nazi Germany, it is perhaps unsurprising that a deep vein of pessimism informed the argument: "Life is suffering. Birth involves death. Transitoriness is the fate of existence. No civilization has yet been permanent . . . This is necessity, the fatedness of history, the dilemma of mortality . . . The generation of Buchenwald and the Siberian labor camps cannot talk with the same optimism as its fathers."[32] One of the dissertation's most important themes, however, pertained to the inadequacies of theory testing when applied to politics and international relations. Or as Kissinger phrased it, "It does not suffice to show logically deduced theorems, as an absolute test of validity. There must also exist a relation to the pervasiveness of an inward experience which transcends phenomenal reality."[33] There were no "merely technical" solutions to "the dilemmas of the soul," Kissinger cautioned, and "political scientists should cease condemning their profession for not living up to their misnomer." Kissinger was developing a line of thought that Mahan, Lippmann, and Kennan would have cheered: politics and diplomacy are better understood and practiced as an art—requiring skill, craft, creativity, and intuition—than as a science, requiring prediction, hypothesis testing, and the application of theory. Clues to Kissinger's later inclinations thus abound. The intellectual historian Bruce Kuklick believes that insufficient respect has been accorded Kissinger's "The Meaning of History," judging it "the most intellectually creative and sustained piece of work that he wrote, and a key exposition of his concerns."[34] If this is true, though, Kissinger hit his intellectual peak in his midtwenties.

After graduating summa cum laude and as a member of Phi Beta Kappa in 1950, Kissinger was urged by Elliott to embark on doctoral work under his supervision. It took some persuasion, as Kissinger—like Kennan after his graduation—was keen to study for a graduate degree overseas, to broaden his range of experience, and then to join the Foreign Service. A major factor that convinced Kissinger to stay put was Elliott's establishment of an International Seminar at Harvard, assisted by funding from the Ford and Rockefeller Foundations as well as the CIA. The seminar was established to fund visits by exceptionally promising academics, politicians, and journalists from across the world. Here was a way to showcase the best of America—its premier research university and a bustling city—to the world's embryonic elite. No wonder, then, that the program attracted lavish financial support.

Some six hundred foreign students participated in the seminar up to 1969, including Yasuhiro Nakasone of Japan, Valéry Giscard d'Estaing of France, Yigal Allon of Israel, Bülent Ecevit of Turkey, Leo Tindemans of Belgium, and Mahathir Bin Mohamad of Malaysia. American participants in the program were similarly distinguished, and included Eleanor Roosevelt, Reinhold Niebuhr, Christian Herter, Walter Reuther, Arthur Schlesinger Jr., and William F. Buckley Jr. To serve as his executive director, Elliott appointed Kissinger, who leapt at the opportunity to identify and cultivate remarkable domestic and global contacts. Some scholars at Harvard disliked the manner in which Kissinger used the seminar as a vehicle to serve his career goals. The eminent game theorist and nuclear strategist Thomas Schelling accused Kissinger of exploiting the seminar "to make Henry known to great people around the world."[35] This seems unfair, however, for who could have resisted such temptation?

Kissinger was based in Harvard's government department but he continued to shun political science methods as inadequate to the task of drawing insight from the disordered world of international relations. As his doctoral cohort focused intently on U.S. Cold War strategy, identifying and testing the theories that best fitted their topics and emerging worldviews, Kissinger instead chose to write on the aftermath of the Napoleonic Wars. In "A World Restored: Metternich, Castlereagh and the Problems of Peace, 1812–1822," Kissinger studied the way Napoleon's adversaries fashioned a stable and enduring structure of peace (by European standards) at the Congress of Vienna in 1815. In Kissinger's telling, Metternich of Austria had the star turn. Metternich was subtle and devious, and he eschewed morality as a guide to diplomatic action. It was through manipulating the balance of power in Europe that Metternich was able to create stability and a concert of mutual interests—without recklessly needling the defeated France—sufficient to sustain a commerce-facilitating peace through the nineteenth century in which all of Europe's constituent nation-states were invested. Kissinger's descriptions of Metternich were vivid and subconsciously autobiographical:

> Napoleon said of him that he confused policy with intrigue . . . With his undeniable charm and grace, subtly and aloofly conducting his diplomacy with the circuitousness which is a symbol of certainty . . . He excelled at manipulation, not construction. Trained in the school of eighteenth-century cabinet diplomacy, he preferred the subtle maneuver to the frontal attack, while his rationalism frequently made him mistake a well-phrased manifesto for an accomplished action.

Walter Isaacson describes the dissertation as, "at its core, a tribute to Metternich's mastery of complex diplomacy and his ability to play a game of sophisticated linkage among different negotiations."[36]

This paean to Metternich and nineteenth-century balance-of-power diplomacy certainly caught Kissinger's fellow students by surprise. One wondered aloud if Kissinger had heard of the atomic bomb; another suggested a transfer to the history department. As his biographer Walter Isaacson observes, "Kissinger rebutted coldly. Hiroshima had not created a new world; it merely showed that man had yet to learn history's lessons about shaping a stable balance of power. So it made sense to explore the Congress of Vienna, one of the few successful peace conferences of the modern era."[37] The insights contained in "A World Restored" truly informed the policy career that followed. But Kissinger also penned his own elegy in the concluding chapter of the dissertation: "A statesman who too far outruns the experience of his people will fail in achieving a domestic consensus, however wise his policies."[38] Cold War America's transparent, idealistic political context was vastly different from the closed arena in which Castlereagh and Metternich had plied their trade. Kissinger understood this only too well:

> This book has dealt with conservative statesmen of countries with traditional social structures, of societies with sufficient cohesion so that policy could be conducted with the certainty conferred by the conviction that domestic disputes were essentially technical and confined to achieving an agreed goal. This enabled Metternich to pursue a policy of "collaboration" between 1809 and 1812 without being accused of treason and Castlereagh to negotiate with Napoleon without being charged with "selling his country."[39]

Twenty years later, Paul Nitze accused Kissinger of committing these very same crimes.

Though Elliott regarded Kissinger's thesis as first-rate, some of his colleagues worried about its shallow archival base, heavy reliance on secondary sources, and the sweep and generality of his conclusions—the same criticisms directed at Alfred Mahan's *The Influence of Sea Power upon History*. For this reason and others, Kissinger did not secure tenure at Harvard in the years after completing his doctorate. While gaining tenure at Harvard was a Herculean task for anyone, Kissinger was disappointed nonetheless. Part of the problem was the sheer number of high-quality Ph.D.s vying for a permanent position at the same time, an imposing list that included Zbigniew Brzezinski, Samuel Huntington, and Stanley Hoffmann. But many at Harvard also detected in Kissinger a variety of unendearing traits: transparent ambition and the haughtiness and obsequiousness that sustained it. A significant problem was that Harvard—white, Anglo-Saxon, and Protestant to its very core—was not a conducive environment for Jews to prosper. McGeorge Bundy, whose parents' families were both listed in the *Social Register*, was made dean of Harvard College in 1953. Bundy worked hard to reform Harvard on meritocratic lines. But Kissinger's relationship with him was strained from the beginning, and he suspected prejudice played a part. In his 1979 memoir, Kissinger wrote that Bundy "tended to treat me with the combination of politeness and subconscious condescension that upper-class Bostonians reserve for people of, by New England standards, exotic backgrounds and excessively intense personal style."[40] Bundy, in fairness, actually deployed a different ethnic stereotype when criticizing Kissinger; he sensed a "certain Germanic cast of temperament which makes him not always an easy colleague."[41] Too Jewish *and* too German—here was a cruel twist of fate.

In 1955, Kissinger published an article in *Foreign Affairs* criticizing Eisenhower's policy of massive retaliation. In a similar vein to Paul Nitze, Kissinger lambasted the strategy for being recklessly all-or-nothing. The gap between waging nuclear war and doing nothing was dangerously capacious. This would invite Sino-Soviet adventurism in the developing world, over which Moscow and Beijing knew Washington was unlikely to risk World War III.[42] The article was Kissinger's first foray into the contemporary foreign-policy debates and it raised his profile considerably. Hamilton Fish Armstrong, the long-standing editor of *Foreign Affairs*, invited Kissinger to direct a new Council on Foreign Relations study group on nuclear weapons and foreign policy. Kissinger was thrilled to accept the job, which provided a wonderful entrée into the American foreign-policy establishment. It was quite an accolade for an untenured thirty-one-year-old instructor at Harvard.

The first meeting of the study group took place on May 4, 1955, and witnessed a testy exchange between Kissinger and Nitze, whose common concern about Eisenhower's foreign policies appeared to unite them. In reference to the demarcation line between conventional and nuclear weapons, Nitze observed that "while the services still have a conventional ability of high order, some of their leaders seem to feel that non-nuclear methods may not be adequate to the tasks which have been outlined for the services to perform." To fill the gap between the most powerful conventional bomb and the least powerful atomic one, Nitze suggested that low-yield tactical nuclear weapons could be developed to serve an important battlefield function. Kissinger was unconvinced by the merits of Nitze's proposal, observing that "once a war becomes nuclear it is much harder to set any effective limits."[43] Nitze left the meeting with a distinctly bad impression, and relations would deteriorate from there.

The primary cause of their antagonism was Kissinger's conversion to the merits of tactical nuclear weapons and the successful book he wrote based on the study group's findings. On August 17, 1957, Kissinger wrote to Hamilton Fish Armstrong that "in a war among nuclear powers I have come to the conclusion—and this represents a big change in my own thinking—that limited nuclear war may actually prove to be a more stable situation than conventional war: thus, if we are concerned with avoiding all-out war, limited nuclear war might be the most effective strategy."[44] Kissinger published *Nuclear Weapons and Foreign Policy* that same year. The book took square aim at Eisenhower's massive retaliation, advocated more flexible means of response to Sino-Soviet adventurism, and urged defense planners to devote more time to gaming scenarios in which low-yield nuclear weapons played a role. Kissinger was not exactly urging everyone to stop worrying and love the bomb—though he soon after earned the nickname "Dr. Strangelove East," sharing the title with Stanford-based Edward Teller—but rather that the weapon should be normalized and rendered usable, in a similar fashion to certain hawkish Democrats.[45] But rather than showering praise on Kissinger—a brother in nuclear arms—Nitze savaged the book.

In a long review in *The Reporter*, Nitze assailed Kissinger for misunderstanding weapons types, miscalculating blast effects, and engaging in vague generalizations that did not stand up to scrutiny. He even deployed the criticism that Kissinger had used against him the previous year, chiding Kissinger for failing to appreciate that waging "limited" nuclear war was incredibly challenging and dangerous. "If the limitations are really to stand up under the immense pressures of even a 'little war,'" Nitze wrote, "it would seem something more is required than a Rube Goldberg chart of arbitrary limitations."[46] He found little of merit in Kissinger's book, asserting that "I read the book with complete distaste. I felt that Henry had not really understood the discussion, he hadn't been in this field. He didn't understand thoroughly what we were talking about. The argumentation in the book was puerile and fallacious in many of its aspects."[47] Yet even the combative Nitze was surprised when Kissinger threatened to sue him for libel.

While vacationing in Maine, Nitze received a call from Philip Horton, the editor of *The Reporter*, who worriedly asked him if he was absolutely sure that his facts were correct. When Nitze said yes and asked why, Horton replied that Kissinger and the Council on Foreign Relations had threatened *The Reporter* with a libel suit. So Nitze took another look at the review, deleted a section that accused Kissinger of being contemptuous of democracy—in that the only historical figures Kissinger praised were Napoleon, Mao, and Stalin—and sent it back to Norton. The review was published, Kissinger remained silent, and the CFR's lawyers stood down. A few months later, Kissinger spotted Nitze in Rome at a meeting of the Bilderberg Group—the secretive annual meeting of Western Europe's and North America's political and business elite—and told him what had happened: "Concerning that review you wrote of my book," said Kissinger, "I made a deal with *The Reporter* that they could go ahead and publish it but I would be entitled to publish a rebuttal of any length. For the last couple of months I have been working, off and on, on that rebuttal. And you know what? I got to page 147 of my rebuttal and decided that if the rebuttal took that many pages there must be something wrong!"[48] Kissinger had discovered the self-deprecating humor that would serve him so well in later years.

Nitze's hostility toward Kissinger's *Nuclear Weapons and Foreign Policy* was informed by many factors, one of which was simple jealousy. One reviewer observed cattily, "I don't know if Mr. Kissinger is a great writer, but anyone finishing his book is a great reader."[49] But this was a rare note of criticism. Reviewing the book for *The Washington Post*, Chalmers Roberts hailed it as "the most important book of 1957, perhaps even of the past several years."[50] Writing in *The New York Times Book Review*, Edward Teller wrote, "In a limited nuclear war, as in any limited war, it is possible to avoid big-scale conflict if our aims remain moderate and our diplomacy skillful."[51] The Christian Realist thinker Reinhold Niebuhr endorsed Kissinger's central argument in *Christianity and Crisis*: "No book in recent years promises to be so influential in recasting traditional thinking about war and peace in a nuclear age. We must be ready to fight limited wars in terms of our objectives and to win them with appropriate weapons. This circumspect and wise analysis of possibilities makes more sense than anything that has come to our notice in recent times."[52]

The book stayed on the bestseller list for fourteen weeks and sold a remarkable seventy thousand copies in hardback. Vice President Richard Nixon was photographed carrying a copy and President Eisenhower ordered that a twenty-four-page synopsis of the book be prepared and distributed to members of his administration. The combination of a highly technical subject matter and leaden prose made the book an unlikely runaway success.

Kissinger recognized this, observing that "I am sure that it is the most un-read best-seller since Toynbee." Nitze found the book's success hard to ac-cept, and Kissinger knew why: "Nitze wanted to do some work on the topic and maybe write a book of his own. He thought I should help him. I didn't want to be a research assistant to Nitze. It got very personal. He should not have reviewed the book."[53]

Regardless, *Nuclear Weapons and Foreign Policy* won Kissinger a na-tional and an international reputation as an important foreign-policy thinker. Though he finally secured tenure at Harvard in 1959, Kissinger had no de-sire to live the contemplative life in a gilded Cambridge cage. He wanted to work for government. In 1959, he wrote a long essay in *The Reporter* on "The Policymaker and the Intellectual." It was a thoughtful piece that made some important cautionary points. For example, Kissinger observed that "intel-lectuals with a reputation soon find themselves so burdened that their pace of life hardly differs from that of the executives whom they advise . . . In his desire to be helpful, the intellectual is too frequently compelled to sacrifice what should be his greatest contribution to society: his creativity." He also cautioned against the impossibility of achieving policy certainty:

> The quest for certainty, essential for analysis, may be paralyzing when pushed to extremes with respect to policy. The search for universality, which has produced so much of the greatest intellectual effort, may lead to something close to dogmatism in national affairs. The result can be a tendency to recoil before the act of choosing among alternatives which is inseparable from policymaking, and to ignore the tragic aspect of policymaking which lies precisely in its unavoidable component of conjecture.[54]

It was a nuanced and impressive piece, an open job application to who-ever won the presidential election. He followed this up with essays in *Dae-dalus, Foreign Affairs*, and *The New Republic*, also publishing a book, *The Necessity for Choice: Prospects of Foreign Policy*, which repeated and sharp-ened his criticisms of the Eisenhower/Dulles era. While engaged in this writing campaign, Kissinger had been on retainer as an adviser to Nelson Rockefeller, with whom he had developed a strong bond of affection. But this most moderate and passive of Republicans stood little chance of wrest-ing the Republican nomination from Nixon in 1960. And so presented with a straight choice between Nixon and Kennedy, Kissinger voted for JFK on Election Day. Nixon's anticommunist stridency jarred with Kissinger's moderation, while Kennedy's advocacy of flexible response chimed with many of the policy recommendations in *Nuclear Weapons and Foreign Policy*. Kissinger appeared well positioned to secure a spot in an administration intent on laying out the red carpet for policy-facing academics.

In February 1961, President Kennedy invited Kissinger to the Oval Office, praised *The Necessity for Choice*—"or at least a long review of it in *The New Yorker*," in Kissinger's view—and invited him to join his White House staff.[55] Kennedy's national security adviser, McGeorge Bundy, was less pleased at the prospect of having Kissinger back in his life. He persuaded the president to employ Kissinger instead as a "part time consultant," subsequently making sure that he had little face time with the president. Their fellow Harvard colleague Arthur Schlesinger Jr. remembered that "Bundy pretty much blocked his access. Whenever Henry had a pretty interesting idea, I'd help perform an end run on Bundy. I'd bring him in to see Kennedy." Eventually Kennedy grew tired of the small deceptions used to bring Kissinger into his office. "You know, I do find some of what Henry says to be interesting," Kennedy told Schlesinger, "but I have to insist that he report through Bundy, otherwise things will get out of hand." Carl Kaysen, a White House staffer, remembered: "Henry was not the president's style. He was pompous and long-winded. You could be long-winded if the president liked you. But I never heard anyone say that Kissinger was likable."[56] Schlesinger was more generous, noting that it was "a great error not to put him into the center of political/diplomatic planning."[57] Looking back on his service to the Kennedy administration, Kissinger was clear as to where he had erred: "With little understanding then of how the presidency worked, I consumed my energies in offering unwanted advice and, in our infrequent contact, inflicting on President Kennedy learned disquisitions about which he could have done nothing even in the unlikely event that they roused his interest."[58]

Kissinger did not help his cause with Kennedy when he responded belligerently to the building of the Berlin Wall in 1961. JFK understood the objections to the Wall, but he believed it would defuse tensions between East and West. Kissinger, on the other hand, favored a showdown in which he fully expected Khrushchev to cave. Kissinger believed that a nonresponse to Khrushchev's decision would threaten America's credibility as guarantor to West Germany, and thus Europe. "If present trends continue," Kissinger predicted, "the outcome will be a decaying, demoralized city with some access guarantees, a Germany in which neutralism will develop, and a substantially weakened NATO."[59] Kennedy disagreed, and was quite content to lose a little face if it meant preventing a larger war. Kissinger's marginal levels of influence and access waned sharply thereafter. The coup de grâce was applied in 1962 when, during a trip to Israel, Kissinger made some maladroit statements regarding Soviet adventurism in the Middle East.[60] "If you don't keep your mouth shut," warned Bundy, "I'm going to hit the recall button."[61] After Kissinger returned in February, Bundy declined to renew his appointment as a consultant. Kissinger's first experience of government service, his ultimate career goal, had ended in failure. He returned to Cambridge and the everyday demands of teaching.

The Johnson presidency brought similar disappointments, though he sensibly lowered his expectations. Kissinger accompanied Nelson Rockefeller, with whom he had resumed his advisory relationship, to the Republican National Convention in San Francisco in 1964. Barry Goldwater's observation that "extremism in the defense of liberty is no vice" was never likely to persuade a politically moderate Jewish refugee from Nazi Germany.[62] More noxious was the manner in which zealous supporters of Goldwater verbally abused Rockefeller during the convention. Kissinger voted for Johnson, and was relieved when he beat Goldwater so comfortably on Election Day. So began Kissinger's fraught relationship with the right wing of the Republican Party.

When President Johnson Americanized the Vietnam War during the first few months of 1965, Kissinger lent his full support: "I thought the President's program on Vietnam as outlined in his speech was just right," he wrote McGeorge Bundy, "the proper mixture of firmness and flexibility." Bundy had an awkward relationship with Kissinger, but this was an endorsement he could accept: "It is good to know of your support on the current big issue," he replied, "[although] I fear you may be somewhat lonely among all our friends at Harvard." In December 1965, Kissinger defended the Vietnam War in a televised CBS debate with Michael Foot, an influential figure on the left of the British Labour Party. "We are involved in Vietnam," Kissinger declared, "because we want to give the people there the right to choose their own government." Soon after, he joined a petition of 190 academics lending support to President Johnson's policies in Vietnam.[63]

Although Kissinger was publicly supportive of the Vietnam War, privately he was ambivalent. In October 1965, the U.S. ambassador to Saigon, Henry Cabot Lodge, invited Kissinger to tour South Vietnam and record his impressions. Kissinger's private views echoed those of George Kennan:

We had involved ourselves in a war which we knew neither how to win
nor how to conclude ... We were engaged in a bombing campaign powerful enough to mobilize world opinion against us but too halfhearted and
gradual to be decisive ... No one could really explain to me how even on
the most favorable assumptions about the war in Vietnam the war was
going to end ... [South Vietnam had] little sense of nationhood.[64]

In his formal report to Lodge, Kissinger kept his doubts to himself,
observing that "you are engaged in a noble enterprise on which the future of
free peoples everywhere depends," and that Vietnam was "the hinge of our
national effort where success and failure will determine our world role for
years to come." Perhaps Kissinger felt that divulging his unvarnished thoughts
would harm his chances of securing a more significant role in the Johnson
administration. In this he was undoubtedly correct. When the *Los Angeles
Times* printed some unguarded remarks Kissinger made to journalists at
the Saigon embassy, President Johnson was furious.[65] When McNamara
asked Johnson in 1967 that Kissinger lead third-party negotiations with
North Vietnam, LBJ took a lot of convincing and never really gave him a
chance to succeed.

Like Nitze, Kissinger struggled to formulate a consistent line on the Vietnam War. In June 1968, he took part in an academic panel on the war with
Arthur Schlesinger Jr., Daniel Ellsberg, Stanley Hoffmann, and Hans
Morgenthau. Kissinger downplayed South Vietnam's geostrategic significance,
observing that the "acquisition of Vietnam by Peking would be infinitely less
significant in terms of the balance of power than the acquisition of nuclear
weapons by Peking."[66] The People's Republic of China had tested its first nuclear device in 1964, suggesting that Kissinger did not think the fall of South
Vietnam would be significant at all. A few months later, Morgenthau wrote an
essay in *The New Republic* that, among other things, criticized Kissinger for
lending the Johnson administration his support. Kissinger was stung by the
critique, not least because he and Morgenthau viewed so many issues
through a common realist lens. The letter he drafted in response to Morgenthau was forceful but disingenuous:

I never supported the war in public. Before 1963, this was because I did
not know enough about it and because I tended to believe the official
statements. After the assassination of Diem I thought the situation was
hopeless. In 1965 when I first visited Vietnam I became convinced that
what we were doing was hopeless. I then decided to work *within* the

government to attempt to get the war ended. Whether this was the right decision we will never know, but it was not ineffective. My view now is not very different from what you wrote in the *New Republic*, commenting about Bundy, though as a practical matter I might try to drag on the process for a while because of the international repercussions.[67]

Dragging out the process of U.S. withdrawal from Vietnam because of the "repercussions"—which sometimes he seemed to believe were negligible— would consume Kissinger for much of the next four years.

When Nixon defeated Nelson Rockefeller to secure the GOP presidential nomination in August 1968, Kissinger was distraught. He told Emmett Hughes, Rockefeller's speechwriter, that Nixon was "of course, a disaster. Now the Republican Party is a disaster. Fortunately, he can't be elected—or the whole country would be a disaster."[68] So when Nixon offered Kissinger the national security job after his election victory, "We were shocked," said Rockefeller adviser Oscar Ruebhausen. "There was a sense that he was a whore."[69] Reactions such as these, and the anticipation of worse to come, led Kissinger to ask the president-elect for more time to consult with friends and colleagues at Harvard before accepting the offer. He told Nixon that he "would be of no use to him without the moral support of his friends and associates," subsequently observing that this was "a judgment that proved to be false." Fearing that Kissinger's Harvard circle was unlikely to shower him with praise, Nixon "rather touchingly . . . suggested the names of some professors who had known him at Duke University and who would be able to give me a more balanced picture of his moral standards than I was likely to obtain at Harvard."[70]

Unsurprisingly, Kissinger's friends and colleagues, including Arthur Schlesinger Jr. and Nelson Rockefeller, all urged him to accept—at the very least he could serve as a moderating influence on Nixon. Declining the offer, of course, would have been unimaginable under any circumstances; Kissinger's deliberations had a strong element of theater. But these parting endorsements had some value. Though he was not firmly connected or committed to Harvard, he did worry that he might follow his predecessor, Walt Rostow, in burning bridges with academia. Rostow's previous employer, MIT, had not invited him back to his professorship after his hawkish stint as LBJ's national security adviser. Instead he moved to Austin, Texas, where Lyndon Johnson created a job for him at the LBJ School of Public Affairs. When Rostow discovered that Kissinger had made a dinner party joke about

the probability that he would subsequently be "exiled in Arizona," he failed
to see the humor. During a painful telephone conversation in January 1970,
Kissinger tried to salve Rostow's hurt feelings: "That was not a crack at
you . . . I said it at a party, it was meant to be a sarcastic remark. I love Arizona.
In fact my desire to go back to Cambridge is practically zero."[71] This last
sentence actually turned out to be true.

To say that Nixon was complex is to observe that rivers are wet. A self-made
man—his father owned a grocery store, his mother was a homemaker, and a
Quaker—Nixon was smart, driven, ruthless, and unable to transcend the
insecurities born of his humble origins. Though marred by snobbery, Paul
Nitze's characterization of Nixon is perceptive:

> Nixon could simultaneously kid himself into believing [three] different
> propositions concurrently . . . One, that he was a good and competent
> realistic analyst of foreign affairs and devoted pursuer of a foreign pol-
> icy that was dedicated to U.S. security and he was the wisest, not only
> [as] an analyst, but also [as] the conductor of [a] foreign policy consis-
> tent with our security. The other was that he rather inherited from his
> mother, the passionate religious preacher, a lay preacher, this idea that
> because he could deliver sermons, he was holier than thou, somehow or
> another, and he could do this through the word regardless of what the
> facts were. The third role was that of being a lower middle class person
> who greatly admired those who had success, and the way in which you
> achieve success was to climb through every kind of trick you could
> think of, with no respect for any moral restraints as long as you climbed,
> as long as you made it. When you keep all those balls in the air concur-
> rently, you can trip yourself up.[72]

Nixon displayed shocking levels of brutality toward his enemies—
imagined and real—and could be spiteful toward those who worked for
him. Yet he shrank from direct confrontation. In fact, he was stilted in most
people's company, with the exception of a small circle of long-standing
friends—whom Kissinger described as a "gang of self-seeking bastards . . . I
used to find the Kennedy group unattractively narcissistic, but they were
idealists. These people are real heels." Kissinger was scarcely less scathing
about Nixon himself, describing him as "a very odd man, an unpleasant man.
He didn't enjoy people. What I never understood is why he went into politics." His working theory was that Nixon leapt at the opportunity to "make

himself over entirely," to transform himself through force of will into some-one he was not—gregarious, charismatic, dominant, larger than life. Yet, Kissinger noted, this was "a goal beyond human capacity" and Nixon paid "a fearful price for this presumption."[73]

While Nixon normally preferred abusing people from a distance, Kissinger proved to be an exception to this rule. Kissinger's Ivy League background, his connections to the northeastern establishment, his ambition, and his love of the limelight constantly riled the president and provided abundant vituperative fodder. Nixon rarely missed an opportunity to put him in his place, attacking supposed points of vulnerability. The president would muse aloud about his Jewish enemies in the media, the business world, and aca-demia, mouthing hateful conspiracies that Kissinger felt unable to chal-lenge. At one point Nixon called Kissinger in a rage, deploying ethnic slurs against blacks and Jews as one of Kissinger's aides, Winston Lord, listened in, aghast, on another phone. "Why didn't you say something?" Lord asked afterward. Kissinger replied, "I have enough trouble fighting with him on the things that really matter; his attitudes toward Jews and blacks are not my worry."[74] A basic dynamic emerged in their relationship: Nixon meted out abuse and sought validation in equal measure. Kissinger ignored the barbs and focused on bolstering Nixon's confidence through his many hours of need.

Following a time-honored pattern, the bullied Kissinger took out his frustrations on his staff, who witnessed some remarkable tantrums. It was said that Kissinger treated aides like mushrooms: they "were kept in the dark, got a lot of manure piled on them, and then got canned."[75] His care-fully selected staff included future luminaries such as Lawrence Eagleburger, Alexander Haig, Anthony Lake, Hal Sonnenfeldt, and Morton Halperin. Each man was expected to work fourteen- to sixteen-hour days seven days a week, all were prevented from enjoying any presidential access, a privilege (if this is the right word) that Kissinger closely guarded. Unsurprisingly, not everyone was willing to stay the course—Eagleburger, Halperin, and eight others resigned before the year was out. Eagleburger, in particular, suffered under Kissinger's brutal regimen. Alexander Haig, a future White House chief of staff and secretary of state, describes one occasion when "after many hours of uninterrupted work, Kissinger asked Eagleburger to get him a cer-tain document. Larry stood up, turned deathly pale, swayed, and then crashed to the floor unconscious. Kissinger stepped over his prostrate body and shouted, 'Where is the paper?' "[76] One aide observed that when "he stamps a foot in anger, you're OK. It's when both feet leave the ground that you're in trouble."[77] The turnover in staff was becoming so problematic that Kissinger turned to humor to lighten the mood. He joked, after moving to a larger office, that it now took so long to march across the room and slam the door that he tended to forget who had committed the original offense.

The press was unanimous in praising Nixon's appointment of Kissinger as national security adviser. The conservative columnist William F. Buckley Jr., whom Kissinger had been courting for a number of years, observed, "Not since Florence Nightingale has any public figure received such public acclamation."[78] *The Washington Post* described the appointment as "welcome," while James Reston in *The New York Times* called it "reassuring." A common journalistic theme emerged: Kissinger was a good choice because he would keep Nixon under control and thus the world a little safer. Adam Yarmolinsky, a Harvard colleague of Kissinger's who would serve in the Pentagon, observed that "we'll all sleep a little better each night knowing that Henry is down there."[79] Reveling in this positive attention, Kissinger peddled this scenario to the press on a recurring off-the-record basis. He was the one indispensable man in the administration, preventing this "lunatic," this "madman," as he sometimes described his president, from wreaking merry havoc.

The reality was of course more complicated. Nixon's nuanced presidential incarnation differed markedly from his hawkish vice presidency. Throughout the 1950s Nixon had served as a firm and vocal anticommunist on the world stage: Eisenhower's respectful nod to the right wing of the GOP. He had performed this role effectively, haranguing Khrushchev on liberal capitalism's superiority to Marxism-Leninism during the "Kitchen Debate" of 1959—so-called because the clash occurred in a model kitchen at the American National Exhibition in Moscow. He went after Democrats with relish, attacking their lackluster dedication to winning the Cold War on American terms. As president, however, Nixon left his attack-dog persona behind. Instead he delegated this role to his vice president, the hyperaggressive Spiro Agnew, whose wordy vitriol directed at political and ideological enemies—"a spirit of national masochism prevails, encouraged by an effete corps of impudent snobs who characterize themselves as intellectuals," to give one example—made Nixon's vice presidency appear decorous in comparison.[80]

Nixon's hawkish credentials were thus unimpeachable in 1969. This gave him the flexibility to pursue policies that were difficult for Democrats, such as reaching out to Beijing and Moscow in the spirit of reconciliation. As Nixon observed to Mao Zedong a few years later, "Those on the right can do what those on the left can only talk about."[81] Like Kissinger, Nixon believed that Nitze's NSC-68 no longer worked as a Cold War blueprint; something more cost aware and better tuned to the world's fluid power dynamics should take its place. In light of the nation's failure to quell the insurgency in South Vietnam, the fast-rising economic power of Western Europe and Japan, and America's relative economic decline, the president-elect sought to recast the nation's geostrategic posture. Nixon deemed it essential that the United States delegate peace- and warmaking responsibilities to increasingly wealthy regional allies; the diffusion of global power meant that assuming the entire burden of waging the Cold War was now economically unsustainable as well as strategically foolhardy. He also believed that the nation had to recognize the existence of the People's Republic of China, particularly now that its path had diverged so violently from its supposed Marxist-Leninist brethren. The Soviet Union and China almost went to war in 1968 over a border dispute. In a seminal, widely discussed article for *Foreign Affairs* in 1967, Nixon wrote, "We simply cannot afford to leave China forever outside the family of nations, there to nurture its fantasies, cherish its hates and threaten its neighbors." Nixon believed that Sino-American "dialogue" was essential to his Cold War restructuring.[82]

Engaging in meaningful dialogue with Brezhnev, reaching out to Mao, transferring power and responsibility to regional actors—all these policies were devised to facilitate one essential task: withdrawal from Vietnam without critically undermining U.S. credibility. For Nixon, closing down the Vietnam War made sound strategic and political sense. Indeed, he believed that his reelection in 1972 hinged on his signing a peace accord with Hanoi. "I've got to get this off our plate," Nixon told Kissinger in the early months of his administration.[83] Driven by such grand and vexatious goals—the plate was clearly overfull—Nixon accorded relatively little attention to domestic politics. The one constant throughout his vice presidency and presidency was his clear preference for matters of foreign policy, once dismissing the passage of domestic legislation as "building outhouses in Peoria."[84] Richard Nixon was Charles Beard's negative image; their values, politics, and priorities were diametrically opposed.

That Nixon chose Kissinger to help implement his strategic vision made sense in spite of their differences. Kissinger also believed that the nation's relative decline necessitated a strategic rethink. Kissinger would complain that Americans "never fully understood that while our absolute power was growing, our *relative* position was bound to decline as the Soviet Union recovered from World War II."[85] In August 1971, Kissinger met with a collection of conservative intellectuals, including William Rusher, the editor of *The National Review*, and Allan Ryskind, the editor of *Human Events*. Finding them locked in quite a different era—when Paul Nitze's and Walt Rostow's expansionary doctrines retained luster—Kissinger reminded them that Nixon was elected following "the collapse of foreign policy theory. A new frontier of the 1960s had ended in the frustration of Vietnam, a divided country, and vicious isolationism clamored [for] by liberals."[86]

While Nitze and his ilk had badly erred, Kennan's notion of containment, though admirable in certain ways, lacked the specifics to wage effective diplomacy in a multipolar world. As Kissinger observed in *White House Years*, "Containment treated power and diplomacy as two distinct elements or phases of policy. It aimed at an ultimate negotiation but supplied no guide to the content of those negotiations. It implied that strength was self-evident and that once negotiations started their content would also be self-evident."[87] Like Kennan, Kissinger strongly believed in the necessity of negotiating with America's enemies—ignoring powerful nations was reckless and pointless, engagement brought significant rewards. But Kissinger was more comfortable deploying the military—to maintain and enhance U.S. "credibility," a geostrategic attribute he valued above all others—where he deemed it necessary. So the United States intervened forcefully, and in many cases calamitously, in North Vietnam, Cambodia, and Laos, and significant credibility was vested in the outcome of conflicts on the Indian subcontinent, in sub-Saharan Africa, and in Latin America. Kissinger longed to liberate American foreign policy from the expensive demands of waging the global Cold War on the lines suggested in NSC-68. But he struggled to control his tendency to view all conflicts through a zero-sum lens, which artificially inflated the stakes involved. Kissinger's Cold War perspectives were conventional in many respects.

Though Kissinger viewed containment as underdeveloped, George Kennan was delighted that a realist thinker partial to nineteenth-century European history had assumed such a prominent position. In 1966, Kennan met Kissinger for lunch in Cambridge and found him "now fully recovered from the militaristic preoccupations of earlier years," a reference to *Nuclear Weapons and Foreign Policy*, which Kennan predictably abhorred.[88] When Kennan called a few days after Nixon's victory to offer his congratulations, Kissinger assured Kennan that the president-elect regarded him as "a leading example of people whose possibilities were not being used by the last administration."[89] Here Kissinger might have hurt Kennan in his kindness, building unrealistic expectations that his counsel would again be sought out, which proved not to be the case. Nonetheless, Kennan and Kissinger corresponded frequently and appreciatively, the older man advising the younger to hold to a steady course as Wilsonian-inclined criticism of his foreign policy sharpened from 1973 onward.

Paul Nitze, meanwhile, was not sure what to make of Nixon's victory and Kissinger's appointment. In the first few months of 1969, he was consumed by his campaign to save Safeguard—the antiballistic missile system designed to shoot down incoming nuclear missiles—from an emboldened and increasingly cost-obsessed Congress. While Kissinger supported his efforts, Nitze also learned that one of the Nixon administration's primary objectives was to improve relations with Moscow and to embark upon strategic arms limitation talks, a process soon known as SALT. Nitze supported nuclear arms limitation talks in theory, but only if they preserved America's advantage. As he recalled, "I doubted Mr. Nixon's interest in negotiating an arms control agreement with the USSR; other matters crowded his agenda. The major problems facing him were the country's growing disillusionment with its involvement in Vietnam, a general weakening of our relative strategic military posture and capabilities vis-à-vis the Soviet Union, a worsening of our economic position relative to Japan, South Korea, Taiwan, and the European Community, and a loosening of our ties to our allies and friends." Nitze was surprised and delighted, therefore, when Secretary of State William Rogers invited him to join the administration as an arms control negotiator in a team led by Gerard Smith: "I assured Rogers that I was indeed interested in the job."[90]

After Rogers informed the president of Nitze's enthusiastic response, a meeting was arranged with Nixon and Kissinger in July 1969. The president came to the point with uncharacteristic clarity. "Paul," he said, "I very much want you to take this job. I have no confidence in Rogers nor do I have complete confidence in Gerry Smith . . . So I want you to report anything you disapprove of directly to me." Nitze could scarcely believe what he was hearing. The president wanted him to serve as a spy in an operation that would marginalize the State Department and the man Nixon had chosen to lead it. "If I am to be a member of the delegation," Nitze replied, "it will be as a member of Gerry Smith's team and not as someone reporting to someone else. And in any case, Smith reports to the secretary of state, who must have complete confidence in what Smith reports. That's the way it has to work!"[91] Nixon grew irritated: "God damn it, I've told you what the channel of communication is and if anything comes up, I want you to use it." After negotiations began in Helsinki in November, a private line was installed to allow Nitze to communicate discreetly with the White House. Nitze never dialed the number. They "knew that I was not going to do anything like that," he said, an assessment that underestimated Nixon and Kissinger's views on the fallibility of man.[92]

Kissinger was exasperated, though not surprised in light of experience, by Nitze's refusal to do as instructed. Clearly the only way to keep SALT under Nixon and Kissinger's full control was to lead the process themselves. And as it happened, the architecture to do so was already in place. Soon after Nixon's inauguration, Kissinger had established a secret back channel with the Soviet ambassador to the United States, Anatoly Dobrynin. Nixon told the ambassador that conventional State Department channels left sensitive communications "open to an excessively broad range of officials."[93] Instead, Dobrynin should communicate all important messages from Moscow directly to Kissinger, the president's point man.

Dobrynin and Kissinger met frequently; as often as once a week when the situation demanded. The ambassador would enter the White House through a discreet entrance on the East Wing and meet Kissinger in the Map Room. Their conversations were remarkably free-flowing and familiar, interspersed with jokes and inquiries about family and mutual friends and acquaintances in Washington. Substantively, both men reveled in being indispensable to their political masters. The Soviet political scientist and U.S. specialist Georgy Arbatov observed that "the Channel was done largely to feed Kissinger's ego and grandeur, if I may be so blunt. And perhaps for Dobrynin's ego, too."[94]

Although Arbatov's assessment contains a measure of truth, it fails to do justice to the scale of their achievements. As Jeremi Suri observes, "In an unprecedented manner, Moscow and Washington cooperated to implement agreements on the permanent division of Berlin (the Four Power Agreement), nuclear non-proliferation (the Nuclear Non-Proliferation Treaty), arms limitation (the Strategic Arms Limitation Treaty and the Anti-Ballistic Missile Treaty), security and cooperation in Europe (the Helsinki Accords), and even basic principles of international conduct."[95] Kissinger would discover that there were significant costs, though, to brokering agreements in a manner that excluded—in order of importance—Congress, the State Department, the press, and the general public. And each group in time would turn on him. Like Kennan before him, there is little doubt that Kissinger envied the latitude afforded Soviet diplomats serving a totalitarian government.

Nitze discovered only after the fact that his negotiating efforts in Helsinki, and later Vienna, were a sideshow; the serious business was being done by Kissinger and Dobrynin in the Map Room. It infuriated Nitze, and with good reason. During a back-channel meeting on April 9, 1970, Nitze discovered that "Kissinger had effectively repudiated our initial Vienna proposals even before we offered them, telling Dobrynin that if the Soviet Union preferred something more limited, he would be happy to entertain it. Knowing in advance that the delegation's proposals were not backed at the top, the Soviets lost nothing by stalling." The executive branch was inadvertently sabotaging the delegation's carefully calibrated efforts, and Nitze railed against this impotency: "For all practical purposes, this meant that there had been two sets of parallel negotiations—those between the officially designated delegations, and those between Kissinger and Dobrynin. I suspected that that was happening, but like the rest of the members of the delegation, I was kept in the dark."[96]

In 1971, Kissinger attempted to use the back channel as a bargaining tool with Nitze, promising to divulge details of his discussions with Dobrynin in exchange for his keeping tabs on Gerald Smith. Nitze again declined to serve as a spy, though he promised Kissinger that he would not tell Smith about the back channel's existence. This established a pseudoconspiratorial bond between them, though one NSC staffer observed that "it was not clear who was using who."[97] Nitze continued to fume about being left out of the loop. Kissinger grew ever more irritated by Nitze's obstinacy. Relations between the two men, never warm, continued to deteriorate.

Nixon and Brezhnev signed the SALT I agreement in Moscow in May 1972 to the reassuringly bright glare of blanket media coverage. It was a historic occasion. The summit marked the first time since Roosevelt's presidency that an American president had set foot in the Soviet Union. It was a high point of détente and of Nixon's presidency. The substance of the summit, and the process it portended, followed Kissinger's views on the importance of removing Wilsonian precepts from the nation's diplomacy. Both Kissinger and Nixon agreed that morality and human rights were out of bounds. In a discussion about speeches on May 22, Kissinger observed: "I don't think it is proper for you to start lecturing them about freedom of speech." Nixon replied, "oh no, no, no, no, no, no, no."[98] Those seven "nos" told quite a story. An enemy previously characterized as hell-bent on global conquest had been normalized, the repressiveness of its system purposely downplayed. Castlereagh and Metternich would have cheered this infusion of cold reason into America's external relations.

The summit made for great theater. After signing the world's most significant nuclear arms control agreement in the splendor of the Kremlin's St. Vladimir Hall—formalities were exchanged under a two-ton chandelier, which hangs from a glorious fifty-four-foot cupola—Brezhnev and Nixon retreated to the former's dacha just outside Moscow, where they exchanged warm toasts and drank heroic quantities of cognac over the course of a two-hour caviar-laden dinner. After returning to Washington, an elated Nixon convened a joint session of Congress and delivered a nationally televised speech. Though Nixon cautioned that he did not "bring back from Moscow the promise of instant peace," he added incautiously, "We do bring the beginning of a process that can lead to lasting peace." There was much to be happy about. A major element of Nixon and Kissinger's grand strategy—improved relations with Moscow—had been pursued with style, reaping a significant achievement. A major arms control agreement, laying down an important marker for the future, had been reached. Plus the State Department had been frozen out of the process and thus denied the credit that Nixon and Kissinger gathered solely for themselves. The president's good spirits evaporated, however, when he began to notice that Kissinger was being accorded the lion's share of the credit. In June 1972, the *Chicago Sun-Times* declared that Kissinger "had become a legend."[99] Kissinger could have done without such headlines, although he enjoyed them all the same.

Nitze had worked long, hard hours on the SALT negotiations in Helsinki and Vienna, and their essentials had been thrashed out elsewhere. This was a painful reality to accept, and Nitze's assessment of the agreement was correspondingly harsh. SALT I comprised two parts: an ABM Treaty and the inelegantly phrased and capitalized "Interim Agreement Between The United States of America and The Union of Soviet Socialist Republics on Certain Measures With Respect to the Limitation of Strategic Offensive Arms." The ABM Treaty limited each nation to just two sites where an antiballistic missile system could be located, foreclosing the possibility of a defensive race potentially more costly than the armed version. Unlike with the interim agreement, Nitze had played an important role in thrashing out its provisions: "I thought that the ABM treaty, which I had some hand in fashioning, was a definite step forward in arms control, a model perhaps for future agreements . . . The Interim Agreement covering offensive weapons, on the other hand, was flawed in that . . . it tended to accentuate the asymmetries that already existed in favor of Soviet land-based missiles."[100]

Rather than safeguarding the United States, then, Nitze believed that the SALT I treaty had entrenched the Soviet Union's advantage in "throwweight" capability—the combined weight of each side's ballistic missile payloads. In fact, one important missile technology that SALT I failed to ban was the development of Multiple Independent Reentry Vehicles (or MIRVs), which critically undermined the treaty's ceilings on permitted missile numbers. A MIRVed missile was a single rocket carrying multiple nuclear warheads capable of striking different targets. Critics of the treaty observed with some justification that SALT I—symbolically important as it may have been—actually started a new arms race hidden within the carapace of the superpowers' missile arsenals. George Kennan found the whole affair mystifying and distressing. After the Moscow Summit, Kennan wrote in his diary that Washington and Moscow should be working to eliminate nuclear weapons, not puttering around with "the wretched ABMs and MRVs and MIRVs and SALTs and what not."[101]

For different reasons, Nitze believed that SALT I was an almighty mess, but he chose not to resign in protest. Instead he joined forces with Admiral Elmo Zumwalt Jr., chief of naval operations and a member of the Joint Chiefs of Staff, in an effort to undermine Kissinger from within the administration. Zumwalt was a highly decorated veteran who feared, as Nitze did, that Kissinger was frittering away America's military advantage. Zumwalt's perception was that no one "knew better than Paul the way Henry Kissinger and his apparatus filtered all communications to the President so that, on the whole, Mr. Nixon only saw and heard what Kissinger wanted him to see and hear."[102] Whether true or false—and this assessment fails to comprehend the essential point that Nixon and Kissinger were on the same page— Zumwalt joined Nitze in viewing Kissinger as a threat to national security. Their anti-Kissinger machinations soon took something of a McCarthyite hue. Both men referred to Kissinger privately as a "traitor" and, as David Callahan observes, "gave credence to rumors that Kissinger had been recruited by the KGB when he worked for army intelligence in Germany. Nitze once even called a friend in the intelligence world to ask about Kissinger's loyalty. No evidence ever emerged linking Kissinger to the Soviets, but Nitze remained suspicious."[103]

Nitze's assault on Kissinger's loyalty was perhaps the ugliest, most dishonorable chapter of his foreign-policy career. And his rancor did not abate with the years. In 1985, Nitze registered a jarring assessment of Kissinger, comparing him unfavorably with Averell Harriman:

> Harriman is the son of a very wealthy man, an aristocrat, an American-type patrician, very much imbued with the American liberal point of view, while Henry Kissinger, of course, is a European Jew, who had no such background whatsoever. Therefore he was not inhibited by any of the inhibitions someone brought up with the American liberal tradition

had . . . So that Averell wouldn't have thought of doing the tricky kinds
of things that Kissinger did.

Worrying with good reason that his assessment might be interpreted
as anti-Semitic, Nitze qualified his remarks, observing that "it wasn't just
Henry. There was the distinction between what I would call the climbers—
the lower segments of the middle class were climbing up and their standards of what is proper are somewhat different than those in the patrician
element in the United States."[104] Nitze disliked the substance of Kissinger
and Nixon's diplomacy and the equanimity with which they accepted Soviet
nuclear parity. But it reflected poorly on him that he identified as explica-
tory the background of those at the helm: an émigré Jew and the son of a
California grocer.

The Moscow Summit was certainly momentous, but the opening to China
was the signature foreign-policy achievement of the Nixon presidency—and
a hinge moment in modern world affairs. During the 1960s, few believed
such a rapprochement was possible, or even desirable. How could Washington engage with Mao Zedong, the author of the Cultural Revolution, a program of state-sanctioned persecution that brutalized millions of alleged
"revisionists" and "enemies of the revolution"?[105] Yet some Americans were
quite content to ignore China's domestic tyranny in the name of a larger geostrategic good. Restoring relations with the world's most populous country
had been on George Kennan's mind at least since 1963, when he observed in
an interview—echoing Churchill's oft-quoted remarks on endorsing the
devil if Hitler invaded hell—that "we should be prepared to talk to the devil
himself if he controls enough of the world to make it worth our while."[106]
Nixon himself had recorded a similar view, albeit in more guarded prose, in
his 1967 *Foreign Affairs* article "Asia After Viet Nam."

Yet Kissinger was skeptical when Nixon told him of his desire to normalize relations with Beijing and to visit the nation in person. When in July
1969, H. R. Haldeman informed the national security adviser that Nixon
"seriously intends to visit China before the end of the second term,"
Kissinger could barely suppress laughter, replying "fat chance."[107] Perhaps
Kissinger suspected that Nixon had taken flight into a Walter Mitty–type
imagining; a pointed reference Kissinger sometimes made to the fantastical
daydreams of an unremarkable man. If so, Kissinger was wrong, for the president's hopes were firmly grounded in reality.

It did not take long for Kissinger to take Nixon's ambitions more seriously, particularly as he quickly realized that establishing relations with communist China could reap significant diplomatic benefits. Indeed, Jeremi Suri argues that "Kissinger's thinking was distinctive for its effort to integrate China in a systematic global strategy. Improved relations with Beijing were part of a fundamental structural shift from bipolar containment to multipolar federalism." Here, Suri perhaps underappreciates the quality of insight contained in Nixon's *Foreign Affairs* article. But he does marshal some compelling evidence to suggest that Kissinger deserves significant credit for pioneering what he defined in 1968 as "triangular diplomacy," a three-point relationship that promised Beijing and Moscow an equal stake in improving relations with Washington. In 1968, Kissinger had advised Nelson Rockefeller that the "chances of peace are increased as we are able to develop policy options toward both Communist powers."[108] He was surprised when Nixon indicated his desire for a China opening, for he was no Rockefeller. But once the novelty of "Richard Nixon, Red China enthusiast" wore off, Kissinger joined his president in pushing vigorously for rapprochement with Beijing. And in time he would develop an enduring fascination with and admiration for the "middle kingdom," one of history's great civilizations.

The events leading to the normalization of Sino-American relations proceeded first in small steps, then a canter, and then at a gallop. These ranged from an invitation to the American table tennis team to play in China—a clear signal of Beijing's willingness to begin the process of restoring relations, later characterized as "Ping-Pong diplomacy"—to Nixon's use of Romania and Pakistan as channels through which to communicate his administration's desire for engagement.[109] Eventually, on June 2, 1971, a letter arrived from China's premier, Zhou Enlai—Mao's second in command—offering to host Kissinger as a prelude to a presidential visit. Rather than focusing solely on Taiwan's contested status, which had earlier been a sticking point, Zhou indicated his willingness to discuss a broad range of issues, including the war in Vietnam. An elated Kissinger informed Nixon about Zhou's letter. In a rare moment of bonhomie, Kissinger and Nixon celebrated with a fine bottle of vintage Courvoisier. Nixon proposed a toast: "Let us drink to generations to come who may have a better chance to live in peace because of what we have done."[110] William Rogers and the State Department, meanwhile, grew yet more frustrated at their isolation from the main events of the administration. "It was painful enough to see me and the NSC staff dominate the policy process in Washington," observed Kissinger. "It was harder still to accept the proposition that I might begin to intrude on the conduct of foreign policy overseas."[111]

Kissinger's most galling intrusion occurred the following month when, using stomach complaints as subterfuge to fall off the accompanying media's radar, he hopped on a Chinese aircraft and traveled to Beijing. Over the course of the long flight, Kissinger had time to mull over Nixon's parting advice. In a two-hour briefing the previous day, Nixon had cautioned against abstract philosophizing. "I've talked to communist leaders," Nixon reminded Kissinger. "They love to talk philosophy, and, on the other hand they have enormous respect if you come pretty directly to the point." Nixon attributed his success with Khrushchev et al. to the fact that "I don't fart around . . . I'm very nice to them—then I come right in with the cold steel . . . You've gotta get down pretty crisply to the nut-cutting . . . the stuff that really counts."[112] Kissinger decided that what worked for Nixon with the brusque Soviets might not necessarily impress his Chinese interlocutors. So he declined to apply the "cold steel" and instead engaged in a fascinating discussion with Zhou on America's reluctant world role and how he and Nixon were recalibrating in the direction of modesty.

Kissinger and Zhou held a series of long meetings on July 9 that began at 4:00 p.m. and concluded seven hours later. Kissinger's preliminary remarks were suitably charming:

> For us this is an historic occasion. Because this is the first time that American and Chinese leaders are talking to each other on a basis where each country recognizes each other as equals. In our earlier contacts we were a new and developing country in contrast to Chinese cultural superiority. For the past century you were victims of foreign oppression. Only today, after many difficulties and separate roads, have we come together again on the basis of equality and mutual respect."[113]

Kissinger and Zhou thrust and parried on issues such as Taiwan and the Vietnam War until the latter mentioned the blanket anticommunist hostility of America's early Cold War posture. Kissinger reassured him that times had changed: "We do not deal with communism in the abstract, but with specific communist states on the basis of their specific actions toward us, and not as an abstract crusade."[114] Responding to this, Zhou reiterated China's default diplomatic stance—noninterference in the affairs of other nations—and compared it unfavorably to America's frenetic activism that had served to create so much conflict. Surprisingly, Kissinger agreed, blaming many of America's missteps on a misguided "liberal" activism:

We didn't look for hegemony as we spread across the world; this was an undesirable consequence and led us into many enormous difficulties. In fact, our liberal element, very often because of missionary tendencies, got itself even more involved, for example, as in the Kennedy administration, than the more conservative element. (Zhou nods.) So here we are. When President Nixon came into office, we found ourselves, as you say, extended around the world without a clear doctrine under enormously changed circumstances.[115]

Kissinger's critique of U.S. Cold War strategy was thus as far removed from "nut-cutting" as it is possible to imagine. His exposition on his and Nixon's strategic priorities was crystal clear and similarly cognizant of the limits to American power: "At any rate, this administration has had a very difficult task of adjusting American foreign policy to new realities at the same time we also have to conclude a very painful and difficult war. (Zhou nods.) We have established the principle that the defense of far away countries cannot be primarily an American responsibility . . . This has been our philosophy since we came into office."[116]

Unsurprisingly, Kissinger and Zhou's first meeting was an unalloyed success. Kissinger had thoroughly dismantled the confrontational logic of the early Cold War, which was much appreciated by his hosts.

Yet while Kissinger had succeeded in impressing Zhou Enlai, American conservatives were becoming increasingly hostile toward the policy of engaging with Moscow and Beijing. In August, a group of conservative businessmen close to Governor Ronald Reagan of California signed a public statement in the *National Review* expressing concern at the way Nixon's America had bowed so obsequiously to its communist competitors. Governor Reagan called Nixon to register his strong opposition to the UN's October decision to remove Taiwan (or the Republic of China) from the Security Council and replace it with the People's Republic of China—a decision that Kissinger's visit appeared to invite. But this was a rare discordant note across a near-unified chorus of adulation. Nixon poked fun at Reagan's "typical right wing simplicity" and continued to enjoy the spectacle of Democrats puzzling over how to react.[117]

In October, Kissinger traveled to China again, where he warned Zhou of the media circus that would accompany Nixon on his visit. He observed that *The New York Times* viewed itself as a "sovereign country" and that he was "afraid the Prime Minister [would have] to deal with Walter Lippmann and James Reston in one year; and that is a degree of invasion no country should be required to tolerate." Zhou replied with good humor that he "was not afraid of that"—and in fact he welcomed the intrusion. The Chinese policy elite were keenly aware that making a good impression on the American home audience, following events on television, was vitally important.

And so it was. Nixon's visit took place in February 1972, and it produced indelible images of the Forbidden City, Tiananmen Square (which was not yet infamous), and the Great Wall—which Nixon described in underwhelming but accurate fashion as a "great wall."[118] The grand theater of the visit inspired the American composer John Adams to write his first opera, *Nixon in China*. In one of its memorable scenes, Nixon sings the following aria after disembarking Air Force One. It captures perfectly how laden with meaning this visit was:

> News has a kind of mystery
> When I shook hands with Chou En-lai
> On this bare field outside Peking
> Just now, the whole world was listening
> Though we spoke quietly
> The eyes and ears of history
> Caught every gesture
> And every word, transforming us
> As we, transfixed,
> Made history.[119]

The real Nixon made absolutely sure that he was alone when making history. He firmly instructed Kissinger and Rogers to stay in the plane—on twelve occasions over the course of the flight, by Kissinger's reckoning—until he had reached the bottom of the stairs and shaken Zhou Enlai's hand, something John Foster Dulles had famously refused to do when he met Zhou in Geneva in 1954.[120] This moment was achieved in near-perfect solitude; Nixon permitted his wife, Pat, to tag along. "Your handshake," Zhou told Nixon, "came over the vastest ocean in the world—twenty-five years of no communication."[121]

Soon after Nixon's arrival, Mao issued an invitation to Nixon and Kissinger—William Rogers was not on the list, and Kissinger failed to make his case—to visit his quarters in the Imperial City. Nixon opened discussions by mentioning nations and regions of common concern—Japan, the

Soviet Union—hoping to draw Mao into a substantive discussion. The chairman demurred, replying, "All these troublesome questions, I don't want to get into very much." Instead, Mao indicated a preference for engaging in "philosophic questions"—which were not Nixon's natural forte. Taking his cue, Nixon replied gamely, "I have read the Chairman's poems and speeches, and I knew he was a professional philosopher." Mao pointed at Kissinger, asking, "He is a doctor of philosophy?" Nixon replied, with irritation, "He is a doctor of brains"—and whatever Nixon meant by that, it probably was not good.

Pleased nonetheless to have an entrée into the discussion, Kissinger—referencing his Ivy League pedigree—added that he "used to assign the Chairman's collective writings to my classes at Harvard." Immune to the flattery, Mao said, "Those writings of mine aren't anything. There is nothing instructive in what I wrote." Nixon interjected: "The chairman's writings moved a nation and have changed the world." Mao disagreed, observing that "I haven't been able to change it. I've only been able to change a few places in the vicinity of Peking." Several moments later, Kissinger delivered an encomium to China's brand of Marxism-Leninism that had recently wreaked such havoc: "Mr. Chairman, the world situation has also changed dramatically . . . We've had to learn a great deal. We thought all Socialist-Communist states were the same phenomenon. We didn't understand until the President came into office the different nature of revolution in China and the way revolution had developed in other Socialist states."[122]

It was a good thing that none of the embarrassing details leaked out. Ronald Reagan and his ideological cohort would have found Nixon's and Kissinger's "slobbering" over Mao—a word Kissinger often used to mock Anatoly Dobrynin's warm and familiar diplomatic style—deeply troubling.[123]

In his memoir, Kissinger effusively summarizes the impact of the China opening: "In one giant step we had transformed our diplomacy. We had brought new flexibility to our foreign policy. We had captured the initiative and also the imagination of our own people."[124] This observation is hard to dispute. Downplaying ideological differences and restoring relations with a nation of China's size and latent economic potential was a deft diplomatic move. Moscow was horrified, as one might expect, and Soviet fears of what this unexpected rapprochement portended added value to American diplomacy. It allowed Nixon and his successors to play the communist antagonists against each other. It gave China a direct stake in the timely resolution of the Vietnam War. For Kissinger, a devotee of balance-of-power diplomacy, China's entry to the concert of nations was an absolute gift. If the Cold War resembled a game of chess, as some strategists opined, then the United States had acquired at least a third rook.

Yet Kissinger's regard for China and its leadership was almost too high. In February 1973, he informed Nixon that the United States "was now in the extraordinary situation that, with the exception of the United Kingdom, the PRC might well be closest to us in its global perceptions."[125] How does one take this seriously? As a cosmopolitan student of history, Kissinger was probably more susceptible than others to romanticizing China, a civilization whose diplomatic traditions he admired. The military strategist Sun Tzu, for example, held a prominent place in his pantheon of exemplary strategists, alongside Metternich, Clausewitz, and Bismarck. Kissinger later hailed Sun Tzu's masterpiece *The Art of War* as possessing "a degree of immediacy and insight that places [Sun Tzu] among the ranks of the world's foremost strategic thinkers."[126] Kissinger's Sinophilia was laudable in many ways, but it led him to overestimate China's geopolitical significance, as well as its ability and willingness to help the United States achieve its goals; this was glaringly apparent in respect to Vietnam. In describing Zhou Enlai as "one of the two or three most impressive men I have ever met" and succumbing to something close to awe upon meeting Mao, Kissinger looked and acted more like a fan than a hard-nosed realist.[127] Metternich and Sun Tzu would not have approved.

One thing about the China opening was incontestable. The "liberal" American media that Nixon reviled—but whose good opinion he craved—had little choice but to hail his breakthrough as epoch defining. "An opening exists where there has not been one for 22 years," went an editorial in *The Washington Post*. "A beginning has been made; the potential is vast and for this much the President is entitled to great credit for it was a bold stroke . . . It was something like going to the moon."[128] Such endorsements thrilled Nixon. Yet as with the Moscow Summit, he was angry when he discovered that the media was praising Kissinger in at least equal measure. Nixon viewed the China gambit, with some justification, as a sole-authored breakthrough; this was clearly an affront. The cartoonist Bill Mauldin was ruthless in hitting the president's (admittedly numerous) psychological weak spots. One of his cartoons showed an excited boy pointing at the presidential motorcade, exclaiming: "Look! It's Dr. Kissinger's associate!"[129] When in 1972 *Time* magazine declared Nixon *and* Kissinger its joint "Men of the Year," Nixon fumed and sulked. Ahead of publication, Kissinger implored the editor to remove his name and bestow the honor on Nixon alone, but to no avail. Kissinger described the designation a "nightmare" and said that accepting the honor was "almost suicidal."[130] Surrounded by silver lining, Nixon fixated on a cloud called Henry.

Détente with the Soviet Union and the opening to China were significant breakthroughs in their own right. Indeed, a positive appraisal of the Nixon administration's foreign policies is predicated on our viewing them this way. But Nixon and Kissinger did not view them in isolation at the time. Instead, both men believed that Moscow and Beijing, keen to extract economic and strategic benefits from an improved relationship with Washington, would apply pressure on Hanoi to agree to peace terms permitting a full American withdrawal. On this topic their reasoning was misguided. It did not accord sufficient respect to North Vietnam's fiercely guarded status as an independent actor, or indeed to the ideological solidarity that existed on at least a bilateral basis between Hanoi and its two Marxist-Leninist patrons.

So when the United States withdrew from Vietnam in January 1973, when "peace" was finally achieved, it came at a horrendous cost. Cambodia was dragged directly into the fray, leading ultimately to the rise of the Khmer Rouge and a genocide that killed approximately 1.7 million people— 20.1 percent of Cambodia's population.[131] Hundreds of thousands of North and South Vietnamese soldiers and noncombatants lost their lives. Of the fifty-seven thousand American soldiers who died on or above Vietnamese soil, twenty thousand perished during Nixon's presidency.[132] During the 1968 presidential campaign, Nixon had stated his intention to achieve "peace with honor."[133] In 1971, a returning veteran named John Kerry testified powerfully before the U.S. Senate Foreign Relations Committee. He indicted the war as "the biggest nothing in history" and posed a powerful question: "How do you ask a man to be the last man to die for a mistake?"[134]

Kissinger's best answer to Kerry's question was "for the sake of credibility." The national security adviser understood that the United States could not "win" the Vietnam War and largely agreed with Kerry that the Americanization of the conflict had been a mistake. But he was adamant that the nation could not be seen to "lose" it either. In a widely noted essay in *Foreign Affairs* in January 1969 titled "The Viet Nam Negotiations," Kissinger placed greatest emphasis not on the tangible ramifications of withdrawal but on the amorphous psychological ones:

> The commitment of 500,000 Americans has settled the issue of the importance of Viet Nam. What is involved now is confidence in American

promises. However fashionable it is to ridicule the terms "credibility" or "prestige," they are not empty phrases; other nations can gear their actions to ours only if they can count on our steadiness . . . In many parts of the world—the Middle East, Europe, Latin America, even Japan—stability depends on confidence in American promises.[135]

Kissinger's plan for a staged withdrawal from Vietnam was thus sustained by the logic of keeping up appearances. "We could not simply walk away from an enterprise involving two administrations, five allied countries, and thirty-one thousand dead," Kissinger observed in his memoir, "as if we were switching a television channel."[136] More would die to display America's continued potency to friends and enemies. The nation would not slink away under cover of darkness but depart with all guns blazing.

Credibility was important to nineteenth-century diplomats like Metternich and Bismarck. (The latter established extensive German colonies in Africa primarily for reasons of credibility, not because he believed that an African empire added much to Berlin's strategic or economic strength.) But its logic was harder to sell in twentieth-century America, where battlefield deaths born of prestige-driven actions were tolerated less well by political elites beholden to mass democracy and subject to media scrutiny. In Paris in March 1969, President Charles de Gaulle asked Kissinger, "Why don't you get out of Vietnam?" Surprised by de Gaulle's bluntness, Kissinger answered, "Because a sudden withdrawal might give us a credibility problem." "Where?" demanded de Gaulle. Kissinger specified the Middle East. "How very odd," said de Gaulle. "It is precisely in the Middle East that I thought your enemies had a credibility problem."[137] De Gaulle understood something that Kissinger did not: America's allies—even ambivalent ones like France—believed Washington's credibility would be enhanced, not diminished, by casting aside fictions, cutting its losses, and pursuing an expedited withdrawal.

Kissinger's ostensible peace goals were twofold: that North Vietnamese troops leave South Vietnam at the point of armistice, and that North Vietnam respect South Vietnam's independence after America's withdrawal. Kissinger was not so naïve that he believed either goal was realistically attainable. Rather, as he observed to Hans Morgenthau in 1968, he would "drag on the process" of withdrawal "for a while because of the international repercussions."[138]

This dragging effect would be achieved with multiple weights and pulleys. First, the withdrawal of American troops would commence at a steady rate—twenty-five thousand American troops left Vietnam in 1969 and hundreds of thousands soon followed. Second, the Army of the Republic of Vietnam (ARVN), whom the Americans would train and equip to the highest standards, would fill the gap left by the departing American troops—a strategy described as "Vietnamization." Third, the United States would escalate the war in the most efficient (read destructive) manner possible. As the ground war was being deescalated, the U.S. bombing campaign increased sharply in intensity—and secretly, for such actions were always likely to create a firestorm of protest. Nixon and Kissinger expanded the U.S. bombing campaign in the spring of 1969 to include targets in Cambodia. This action caused two of Kissinger's assistants, Anthony Lake and Roger Morris, to resign in protest. A year later, American troops began their "incursion" (read: invasion) of Cambodia in the hope—forlorn, as it turned out—of destroying North Vietnamese command facilities.

The bombing of Cambodia encapsulated all of Nixon's and Kissinger's failings regarding transparency, strategy, and morality. The bombings were conducted in total secrecy and were falsely designated as attacks on North Vietnam. Congress and the public were not informed. As per usual, many within the administration knew as little as Congress: the State Department, inevitably, and even the secretary of the Air Force. Yet keeping a large-scale bombing campaign under wraps was impossible. On May 9, 1969, *The New York Times* ran a front-page story publicizing this expansion of the war into Cambodia. Nixon was furious, exclaiming to Kissinger, "What is this cocksucking story? Find out who leaked it, and fire him." Without foundation, Kissinger pinned the blame on Defense Secretary Melvin Laird and confronted him directly: "You son of a bitch. I know you leaked that story, and you're going to have to explain it to the president." Laird simply hung up. Kissinger subsequently conceded that he had accused the wrong man. To identify the real culprit, he and Nixon requested the director of the FBI, J. Edgar Hoover, to install a series of wiretaps on three of Kissinger's NSC staff: Daniel Davidson, Morton Halperin, and Hal Sonnenfeldt, as well as one of Melvin Laird's assistants at the Pentagon, Colonel Robert Pursley. The number of wiretaps Nixon and Kissinger authorized on administration staff eventually totaled seventeen, but none captured anything incriminating. Nixon lamented that the wiretaps "never helped us," they merely comprised "gobs and gobs of material. Gossip and bullshitting."[139] Only one recording device captured a detail that led to a high-level resignation. It was voice-activated and whirred into action whenever the president opened his mouth.

The bombing of Cambodia killed thousands of people and destabilized a sovereign nation to little if any discernible effect. The secret bombing raids—for the administration persisted in denying their existence in spite of compelling evidence to the contrary—continued for fourteen months, during which U.S. B-52s flew 3,875 sorties and dropped 108,823 tons of bombs.[140] The objective of the raids was to destroy North Vietnam's political and military headquarters—the Central Office for South Vietnam—and in this it failed. Kissinger felt no moral qualms about escalating the war in this fashion. The fact that the primary strategic objective had not been met seemed not to faze him. This was because the bombing had a negligible impact on the United States beyond the cost of the tonnage—and the lives of the airmen who died delivering their payloads.

Kissinger was as hawkish as Walt Rostow when it came to bombing, observing, "I refuse to believe that a little fourth-rate power like Vietnam does not have a breaking point."[141] Unsurprisingly, Rostow was on hand to encourage Kissinger to stay the course, that the bombing was having its desired effect. In November 1970, he told Kissinger, "On Vietnam, I suggest you give some thought in light of intelligence coming from Hanoi, that they are having some difficult morale problems in the field as well as at home . . . I get word that for the first time in the whole thing leaflets saying go home, work the farms, grow some rice, raise some kids—that's something the army in the field and the people at home may be ready to listen to."[142] Rostow's words were an echo from the previous administration; he had told LBJ the same story for months in 1967 and 1968. It is hard to say whether Rostow's observations pepped up Kissinger or depressed him.

Throughout this process of escalation, Kissinger was concurrently engaged in peace negotiations with the North Vietnamese in Paris. As Le Duc Tho, the chief North Vietnamese negotiator, well understood, "Vietnamization" was a patchy device designed to cloak an inevitable U.S. withdrawal. So he was not particularly amenable to granting concessions prematurely. The South Vietnamese president, Nguyen Van Thieu, was vehemently opposed to Nixon and Kissinger's withdrawal strategy and drew only limited succor from the expansion of the war into Cambodia. Kissinger could not decide which side he disliked more. Thieu was "this insane son of a bitch," and the North Vietnamese were "bastards . . . [who] have been screwing us." Broadly speaking, he concluded that his Vietnamese interlocutors on both sides of the 17th parallel were "just a bunch of shits."[143]

Thieu and Le Duc Tho understandably formed a similar view of Kissinger. Thieu's South Vietnam was being given up for dead—this was the reality. The United States was bombing North Vietnam, meanwhile, to preserve Kissinger's pool of "credibility" and as a parting gift to Thieu. In May

1972, the White House tried to solicit support from George Kennan for an escalation in the bombing campaign. Kennan's "I thought it was inordinately costly in terms both of extraneous destruction and of our international reputation," was not at all the hoped-for reply.[144] The Christmas bombing campaign of December 1972 marked the first occasion that B-52 bombers, incapable of precision strikes, wreaked destruction on the centers of Hanoi and Haiphong—the destroyed wing of Bach Mai hospital was just one example of collateral damage.[145] America's allies and enemies universally condemned the campaign.

On the other side of the equation, in order to secure Thieu's agreement, Nixon and Kissinger threatened to cut off all aid to South Vietnam and cast the nation adrift. The pursuit of "honor" thus played little role in any of Kissinger's Vietnam gambits. The peace that came a few weeks later was not so much sullied as disfigured beyond recognition. On January 8, Kissinger shook Le Duc Tho's hand and told him, "It was not my fault about the bombing." Tho replied, "You have tarnished the honor of the United States. Your barbarous and inhumane action has aroused the general and tremendous indignation from the world peoples." John Ehrlichman later asked Kissinger how long South Vietnam was likely to last. Kissinger predicted, "I think that if they're lucky, they can hold out for a year or two."[146]

For making peace in January 1973, Kissinger and Le Duc Tho were jointly awarded the Nobel Peace Prize later in the year. Knowing what was around the corner, Tho refused the award. Kissinger had no such qualms, although he understood as well as Tho that the "peace" was stopgap—a sham. Edwin Reischauer, the Harvard scholar and former U.S. ambassador to Japan, observed that the award "shows either that the people of Norway have a very poor understanding of what happened out there or a good sense of humor."[147] The critic and humorist Tom Lehrer famously announced his retirement on the grounds that reality had rendered satire obsolete. Kissinger and Nixon complained that insufficient respect was being accorded to what was a significant achievement. On October 17, 1973, Kissinger asked Nixon if he had seen "*The New York Times* blasting the Nobel Prize." "Why have they blasted it?" asked Nixon. "Because they can't bear the thought the war in Vietnam has ended," replied Kissinger. After Nixon observed, "that's amusing," Kissinger elaborated: "They can't bear the thought— you know, Mr. President, when they said the détente wouldn't work. They never say the détente enabled us to settle the Vietnam War because that's the thing they cannot bear—with honor." Nixon replied, "Yeah, that's right. When we stick to the honor—that's the last straw."[148]

There was in fact a connection between détente and the settlement of the Vietnam War, and it had occurred six months previously at the Moscow Summit. Over the course of a wide-ranging discussion, Brezhnev recounted to Nixon an earlier conversation he had had with his national security adviser, during which "Dr. Kissinger told me that if there was a peaceful settlement in Vietnam you would be agreeable to the Vietnamese doing whatever they want, having whatever they want after a period of time, say 18 months. If that is indeed true, and if the Vietnamese knew this, and it was true, they would be sympathetic on that basis" to reaching an agreement.[149] Brezhnev had outed Kissinger's acceptance of a "decent interval" between American withdrawal and a North Vietnamese invasion of the South.[150]

This interval lasted a little longer than Kissinger had estimated. In March 1975, North Vietnam army regulars crossed the 17th parallel and advanced rapidly on Saigon, encountering token resistance along the way. The ARVN collapsed or melted from view, Saigon fell within a month, and a murderous final reckoning ensued. The abiding image of those harrowing events is an American helicopter perched precariously atop one of the embassy's auxiliary buildings, a ladder dangling below providing last-gasp deliverance for a fortunate few. A little farther down, at ground level, thousands of desperate South Vietnamese citizens besiege the embassy's gates, unable to escape, soon to enter a very different world.

George Kennan was pleased that the United States had terminated a meaningless conflict and shed an unreliable ally. "They won. We lost. It is now their show . . . our attitude should be: you are heartily welcome to each other; it serves you both right."[151] The callousness of Kennan's appraisal is perhaps mitigated by the fact that his opposition to the Vietnam War was long and consistently disinterested in morality. Kissinger's record is harder to defend. He had inherited a debacle, the escalation of which he supported from afar, and had failed to achieve any of his declared aims beyond a compromised peace agreement and U.S. withdrawal, on terms similar to those Averell Harriman had proposed in 1968. American credibility was already low when the nation took its gloves off and bombed Cambodia and North Vietnam with few restrictions; the world's most powerful nation deploying its heavy bombers against tightly packed cities did not make for edifying viewing. American credibility was almost undetectable in 1975 as Saigon burned.

In an ideational sense, the Vietnam War combined the worst of two worlds. The conflict was made and escalated by liberal Cold Warriors—in the name of ideals that can be traced to Wilson—and was terminated by devotees of realpolitik at a deliberately glacial pace for reasons of credibility.

Like the Civil War, Vietnam would cast a pall over American society, and its foreign policy, for decades. Like the Civil War, its history and meaning are fiercely contested to this day. In recent years, orthodox critics and revisionist defenders of the war have clashed over issues such as whether the war was ever winnable, and whether the United States really lost. So Ngo Dinh Diem was a disaster unworthy of American support; Diem was a heroic leader whom the United States fecklessly destroyed. South Vietnam lacked the wherewithal to stand alone; South Vietnam was pro-Western, growing in strength, and badly betrayed. LBJ's bombing campaign was brutal; LBJ's bombing campaign was timid. The United States losing the Vietnam War was inevitable; America would have won had its political leaders shown greater fortitude. So go the lessons of history—or not.

Kissinger followed his hero Metternich in focusing most of his energy on great power politics. The affairs of smaller nations did not arouse his interest— unless, of course, their patrons were using them as part of a larger game. In language redolent of George Kennan, Kissinger in June 1969 upbraided Chile's foreign minister, Gabriel Valdés, for having the temerity to critique U.S. economic policy toward Latin America. Kissinger told him, "Nothing important can come from the South. History has never been produced in the South. The axis of history starts in Moscow, goes to Bonn, crosses over to Washington, and then goes to Tokyo. What happens in the South is of no importance. You are wasting your time." With some justification, Valdés replied, "Mr. Kissinger, you know nothing of the South." Kissinger agreed, before adding in the style of a sarcastic teenager, "And I don't care." An infuriated Valdés replied, "You are a German Wagnerian. You are a very arrogant man."[152]

As it happened, Kissinger cared more about the "South" than he realized. Chile was a case in point. Kissinger once dismissed the 2,700-mile-long, 200-mile-wide nation as a "dagger pointed to the heart of Antarctica."[153] Yet on September 4, 1970, when the socialist Salvador Allende won Chile's presidential election by a narrow margin, Kissinger stirred into action, visualizing only the worst-case scenarios. He saw, "Allende's election [as] a challenge to our national interest . . . [Chile] would soon be inciting anti-American policies, attacking hemisphere solidarity, making common cause with Cuba, and sooner or later establishing close relations with the Soviet Union."[154] Kissinger chaired the Forty Committee, which oversaw the covert operations executed by America's intelligence agencies. He informed the committee, tongue in cheek, "I don't see why we have to let a country go Marxist just because its people are irresponsible." Nixon and Kissinger instructed the CIA to foment instability in Chile to prevent Allende taking power in October. The Agency's point man in Chile, Henry Hecksher, duly obliged, assisting a simple scheme to assassinate the commander in chief of Chile's armed forces, René Schneider, and pinning the blame on the left. Schneider was duly murdered, but few Chileans swallowed the line that Allende's supporters were responsible—foul play was immediately suspected.[155] Alternative plans would have to be made.

On September 15, 1970, Nixon had ordered the CIA to "make the economy scream," inviting its agents to try anything "your imagination can conjure."[156] So the CIA disbursed funding to opposition political groups, newspapers, and agitators for hire, and generally embarked upon a pervasive campaign of disinformation. Yet none of these ploys achieved the desired results, primarily because Allende was not the protocommunist hobgoblin of Nixon and Kissinger's imagining. Land reform proceeded cautiously and compensation was efficiently arranged for private landowners. The constitution remained sacrosanct and civil liberties continued to be protected—at least when the CIA was not conspiring to violate them.[157] It took three full years for the CIA's destabilization campaign to produce a tipping point. The Chilean military overthrew Allende on September 11, 1973, and soon after he was found dead—he had either committed suicide, or had been murdered, with an AK-47 assault rifle.

While Kissinger did not accept full responsibility for this bloody denouement, he did concede that "we helped them" and was personally delighted with the outcome: the rise to power of Augusto Pinochet's repressive pro-Western military junta.[158] Historians estimate that the first, and most brutal, stage of Pinochet's reign of terror resulted in nearly two thousand summary executions, tens of thousands of instances of torture, and upwards of eighty-two thousand politically motivated imprisonments.[159] Kissinger— who had been promoted to secretary of state by that time, becoming the first man to concurrently head the State Department and serve as national security adviser—informed his colleagues that "however unpleasant [they] act, the [new] government is better for us than Allende was." Indeed, Kissinger poked fun at America's spineless diplomatic elite during his first meeting with Chile's new foreign minister: "The State Department is made up of people who have a vocation for the ministry. Because there are not enough churches for them, they went into the Department of State."[160]

Depending on taste, there are two ways to interpret the 1973 Chilean coup. It was either a big win for U.S. foreign policy in that a new Castro-type regime had been killed during its infancy, or an egregious example of a superpower blundering into a sovereign nation, hypocritically trampling its democratic will, and installing a regime capable of demonstrable evil. Although the administration was following a precedent set by the Eisenhower administration in Iran and Guatemala in the 1950s, one might have hoped for better from Kissinger, who claimed to understand that U.S. diplomacy required a more sober sense of what was vital and what was not.

Kissinger's response to the 1971 Indo-Pakistani War displayed similarly skewed threat perception, and possibly looked worse to neutral observers of events. Pakistan and India had been at loggerheads for years because East Pakistan sought independence from West Pakistan—East and West were separate territories, some eight hundred miles apart, with quite different identities—and Lahore refused to grant it. In the election of 1970, the pro-secession Awami League won 167 out of 169 seats in East Pakistan. In response, in March 1971, the Pakistani president, Yahya Khan, dispatched 40,000 troops to quell "disorder" and bring the region to heel. Within two months, 2.8 million residents of East Pakistan had fled across the border into India, creating a vast refugee crisis with which India—a painfully poor country—was ill equipped to cope. The Pakistani military crackdown on the breakaway region had been brutal, and its army committed widespread atrocities, including the targeted rape of Bengali women on a mass scale.[161] On December 3, Pakistani troops crossed into India, sparking war, a decision that turned out to be as foolish as it was rash. It took India only thirteen days to defeat Pakistan. On December 16, Pakistan surrendered and East Pakistan became Bangladesh.[162]

This simple recounting of fact might lead one to conclude that the United States had no horse in this race—that, if anything, India and the emerging Bangladesh were on the side of natural justice. In fact, Kissinger and Nixon instinctively supported Pakistan in its struggle with India. While the CIA could not conclude with certainty which side commenced hostilities, Nixon and Kissinger blamed India—and its prime minister, Indira Gandhi, whom Nixon detested—for starting the war. The president complained to Kissinger that Indian aggression "makes your heart sick," particularly given that he had "warned the bitch." "We have to cut off arms," Nixon demanded. "When India talked about West Pakistan attacking them, it's like Russia claiming to be attacked by Finland." The less excitable William Rogers wanted nothing to do with the conflict and argued strongly against cutting off supplies to India. Rogers's well-judged caution provided further impetus for Kissinger to side with his bellicose and emotionally volatile boss. He reported to Nixon that "it's more and more certain it's India attacking and not Pakistan." In concrete terms, the two men secretly urged China to move troops to the Indian border and dispatched a U.S. aircraft carrier to the Bay of Bengal. On December 12, Nixon used the hotline to warn the Soviet Union of dark consequences if it became involved directly. Kissinger hailed the move as "a typical Nixon plan. I mean it's bold. You're putting your chips into the pot again. But my view is that if we do nothing, there is a certainty of disaster. This way there is a high possibility of one, but at least we're coming off like men."[163]

Credibility—"coming off like men"—was the reason Nixon and Kissinger sided so strongly with Pakistan. As Nixon recalled, Kissinger explained his reasoning to him in even starker language: "We don't really have a choice. We can't allow a friend of ours and China to get screwed in a conflict with a friend of Russia's."[164] It is difficult to improve upon William Bundy's sharp assessment of Nixon's and Kissinger's actions, which were profoundly reckless:

> The fundamental point is that a naked balance-of-power policy, going beyond recognized and accepted U.S. interests, was (and is) simply not possible under the American system, which compels concern for public opinion, for the separation of powers, and for the role of Congress. In the Indo-Pakistan crisis and war of 1971, the policy pursued by Nixon and Kissinger was not merely contrary to these American principles or misjudged at almost every turn: it was an excellent example of the weakness of any American policy that is based heavily on balance-of-power considerations without proper weight to other factors.[165]

In supporting Pakistan, come what may, Kissinger believed he was acting in accordance with Metternich's precepts on the balance of power.[166] Yet the great Austrian strategist did not have to deal with hotlines, nuclear weapons, and public opinion. And he certainly did not direct the diplomacy of a nation born of an idea—whose foreign policy through infancy, adolescence, and adulthood was driven by idealistic self-regard. And so as the trauma of Vietnam faded slowly, powerful elements of the Democratic and Republican Parties joined forces in labeling Kissinger's worldview a tumor amid healthy tissue. They moved swiftly to purge it from the body politic.

———

First came Watergate. In conversation with Kissinger in November 1973, Mao Zedong dismissed the fast-spiraling controversy surrounding the botched burglary of the Democratic National Committee headquarters in May 1972—and Nixon's increasingly desperate attempts to mask his involvement in the cover-up—as "a fart in the wind." If only the stakes involved were so infinitesimal. Rather gracelessly during the same conversation, Kissinger had observed to Mao, "For me there is no issue at all because I am not connected with it at all."[167] This was strictly true, although Kissinger's enthusiasm for wiretapping explains a certain jumpiness. Watergate cast a dark shadow over the Nixon administration from then on.

Yet there were large pockets of light in which to work, exemplified by Kissinger's deft handling of the Yom Kippur War in October 1973, during which an Arab attack on Israel, spearheaded by Egypt and Syria, was repulsed; Israel was victorious, thanks in no small part to U.S. arms, and then prevented from winning too huge a victory; and the Soviet Union was rendered largely inconsequential. This was one of Kissinger's finest moments, alternating between the antagonists, offering inducements and threatening reprisals. He ensured that the war did not spill over into a larger conflict and, crucially, restrained Israel's desire to press its advantage. He followed this up with some adroit shuttle diplomacy through which he brokered a remarkable rapprochement between Tel Aviv and Cairo. And most of this was achieved as Nixon languished in alcohol-soaked isolation—Kissinger made some crucial decisions without the president's participation. In 1974, however, Watergate became a total eclipse, plunging Kissinger's one-man diplomacy, and Nixon's wounded presidency, into darkness.

As the possibility of impeachment proceedings moved closer in the first few months of 1974, Nixon's foreign-policy options narrowed. In January 1974, Secretary of Defense James Schlesinger—who had succeeded Melvin Laird in 1973—offered Paul Nitze, still serving the administration unhappily as an arms control adviser, his old job as assistant secretary of defense for international security affairs. Nitze was pleased to accept the job—in spite of his contempt for Kissinger and Nixon—but then Barry Goldwater called a halt to proceedings. A powerful member of the Senate Armed Services Committee, Goldwater declared himself "unalterably opposed" to Nitze's nomination, as he belonged to "a group interested in bringing about our unilateral disarmament."[168] That Goldwater's fears were comically off the mark—Kissinger attributed his opposition to the "liturgical implacability of the conservatives"—did not matter in the scheme of things.[169] As *The New York Times* reported on March 22, "As analyzed by White House officials,

Senator Goldwater is so strongly opposed to Paul Nitze that he could well switch on the impeachment issue if the White House insisted on proceeding with the nomination."[170] This was clearly a risk not worth running. Nitze was told that he had to remain where he was. This was quite a disappointment, and he did not stay in the post for long. On May 28, as the Watergate scandal approached its denouement, Nitze resigned from the Nixon administration. Receiving no reply to his letter, he released a public statement on June 14:

> In my view it would be illusory to attempt to ignore or wish away the
> depressing reality of the traumatic events now unfolding in our nation's
> capital and of the implications of those events in the international arena.
> Until the office of the Presidency has been restored to its principal func-
> tion of upholding the Constitution and taking care of the fair execution
> of the laws, and thus be able to function effectively at home and abroad,
> I see no real prospect for reversing certain unfortunate trends in the
> evolving situation.

Kissinger was courteous in detailing his high regard for Nitze in his memoirs. Yet he could not hide his dismay at this "blistering public attack on Nixon."[171]

On July 27, the House Judiciary Committee voted to impeach President Nixon for obstructing justice. After some prevarication—during which Kissinger advised Nixon that his options were now limited to a graceful exit—Nixon concluded he had little option but to resign. As George Kennan noted in his diary, Nixon's resignation speech was "rather odd, since it showed appreciation neither of the real reasons for his personal disaster nor of the significance of it for his future career."[172] Vice President Gerald Ford, who had replaced Spiro Agnew following his involvement in a tax and bribery scandal, now replaced a president deep in denial. "Gerry Ford, fond as I am of him," Kissinger told Nixon in October 1973, "just doesn't have it."[173]

Worrying, perhaps, for the soul of a relative innocent like Ford, Nixon briefed his successor on how to handle Kissinger. Crucially, Nixon urged Ford to retain Kissinger in his present role: he was "the only man who would be absolutely indispensable to him . . . His wisdom, his tenacity, and his experience in foreign affairs" were vital attributes at this volatile juncture. Yet he also cautioned Ford against giving Kissinger "a totally free hand." As Nixon later observed, "Ford has just got to realize there are times when Henry has to be kicked in the nuts. Because sometimes Henry starts to think he's president. But at other times you have to pet Henry and treat him like a child."[174] One of Nixon's last actions as president was to ask Kissinger to cut off all military aid to Israel until it left the occupied territories. A surprised Gerald Ford rescinded this order as soon as he discovered its existence. Kissinger could not help but wonder if this was Nixon's attempt at "retaliation" for advising him to resign, and for a multitude of other perceived disloyalties.[175]

Over the course of Nixon's decline and fall, Kissinger's enemies continued to assault him. The Democratic senator from Washington, Scoop Jackson, was a particularly resolute adversary. A liberal on most domestic issues, Jackson followed Paul Nitze's hawkishness on matters of national security. Indeed, Jackson's belligerence surpassed that of the author of NSC-68 in many respects—he joined Nitze in assailing Eisenhower for permitting the appearance of a missile gap but was consistently supportive of Johnson's escalation of the Vietnam War. In August 1972, the Soviet Union introduced an "exit tax" on departing citizens that affected Jewish emigrants disproportionately. Appalled by this policy, Jackson joined with the Ohio Democrat Charles Vanik in proposing an amendment to a proposed trade bill with the Soviet Union granting the nation most favored nation (MFN) status.

The Jackson-Vanik Amendment—successfully attached to the Trade Act of 1974—linked the granting of MFN status to the transparency and fairness of that nation's emigration policies. Kissinger viewed the amendment as a sneaky attempt to involve the United States in the domestic affairs of another nation. Jackson-Vanik lay well outside the purview of Kissinger's conception of proper diplomacy, and he believed that the amendment would limit Jewish emigration as Moscow dug in its heels. Observing these dispiriting events from afar, George Kennan began to fear for Kissinger's political future: "with opportunists like Scoop Jackson around, he could go at any moment."[176] With good reason, Nixon had described Jackson as "our most formidable opponent."[177] And in Kissinger's estimation, Jackson's retinue were even worse. In 1975, the secretary of state described Richard Perle, Jackson's most stridently anti-Soviet intern, as "a psychopath."[178]

In conversation with J. William Fulbright in September 1973, Kissinger mused on his most vocal critics: "It's a weird combination of right-wingers and intellectuals and Jewish pressure groups."[179] Some even technically worked for him. In May 1974, to mark the fiftieth anniversary of Woodrow Wilson's death, the U.S. ambassador to India, Daniel Patrick Moynihan, delivered a rousing speech that was reprinted in the influential journal *Commentary*, edited by the self-identified "neoconservative" Irving Kristol.

Moynihan hailed Wilson's "singular contribution" as establishing America's core duty "to defend and, where feasible, to advance democratic principles in the world at large." Moynihan wondered if Wilson's inescapable legacy had been forgotten along the way by strategists who followed a different god: "We must play the hand dealt us: we stand for liberty, for the expansion of liberty. Anything less risks the contraction of liberty: our own included." Moynihan's article was titled "Was Woodrow Wilson Right?" and his answer was an unequivocal yes. Rather than slapping him across the wrist, however, Ford promoted the popular Moynihan to become the U.S. ambassador to the United Nations the following year. Though they had common academic roots—Moynihan had been a Fulbright scholar at the London School of Economics and had taught at Harvard—he and Kissinger shared little affection for each other. Moynihan observed that "Henry does not lie because it is in his interest. He lies because it is in his nature." As Walter Isaacson writes, "Moynihan would say that Kissinger's conspiratorial nature 'helped bring on' Watergate."[180]

In his memoirs, Kissinger laments the strategic naïveté of Irving Kristol, Norman Podhoretz, and Moynihan:

> Tactics bored them; they discerned no worthy goals for American foreign policy short of total victory . . . The radical opponents of the Vietnam War had ascribed the failures in Indochina to a moral defect and had preached the cure of abdication to enable the United States to concentrate on self-improvement. The neoconservatives reversed the lesson, seeing in moral regeneration the key to reengagement. Nixon and I agreed with the neoconservative premise, but we also believed that the simple Wilsonianism of the early 1960s had lured us into adventures beyond our capacities and deprived us of criteria to define the essential elements of our national purpose . . . The neoconservatives . . . put forward not so much a new dispensation—as they claimed—but a return to a militant, muscular Wilsonianism. The fundamental aim of foreign policy as they saw it was the eradication of the evil represented by the Soviet Union without confusing the issue with tactics.[181]

This was a penetrating assessment of the neoconservative movement. Kissinger well understood their desires and influences and was correct to critique the way their overarching goals—eradication of evil, spread of democracy, and rejection of moral relativism—were effectively unattainable.

What Kissinger failed to recognize, however, was the degree to which his diplomatic worldview, and its five-year period of dominance, was a historic aberration created by a unique confluence of events. The popularity of Kissinger's diplomacy is hard to imagine without the harrowing military stalemate in Vietnam, the election of a nuanced president with an unnuanced history of anticommunism, the first stirrings toward sociability from post–Cultural Revolution China, the Soviet Union's attainment of nuclear strategic parity, and the Democratic Party's leftward move toward unelectability, which selected the genuinely liberal George McGovern as its candidate in 1972, whom Nixon crushed by the margin of 61 to 37 percent in the popular vote and 520 to 17 in the electoral college. All these factors gave Kissinger the latitude to ape his hero Metternich on the world stage, focus unerringly on the balance of power, and downplay ideology as a factor in America's external relations. But the end of the Vietnam War, Nixon's fall from grace, the post-McGovern resurgence of the Democratic Party, the rightward turn of the GOP—all these brought the United States back to a default Cold War position that was inhospitable to realpolitik. Nixon and Kissinger had achieved a great deal in their narrow window of opportunity. By mid-1974, however, it had been slammed shut.

Although Kissinger's diplomatic options were more limited in 1974, a significant compensating factor provided cheer: the ascension of Gerald Ford to the presidency. Kissinger's boss had morphed overnight from John Gotti into Johnny Carson, which was enough to please anyone. Ford was light in spirits and unburdened by self-doubt—assuredly not the type to detect dark portents in all events, whether good or bad. Kissinger describes a sense of palpable relief after their first meeting:

> When I left his office after an hour and a half, I suddenly realized that for the first time in years after a Presidential meeting I was free of tension . . . No single conversation with Nixon ever encapsulated the totality of his purposes. It was exciting but also draining, even slightly menacing. With Ford, one knew that there were no hidden designs, no morbid suspicions, no complexes . . . I could think of no public figure better able to lead us in national renewal than this man so quintessentially American, of unquestioned integrity, at peace with himself, thoughtful and knowledgeable of national affairs and international responsibilities, calm and unafraid.[182]

In an interview with Walter Isaacson, David Kissinger—Henry's son—identified another reason his father drew such pleasure from the transition: "President Ford made it clear that he considered my father intellectually superior to him, but he was comfortable with that."[183]

Ford's deference to Kissinger was clearest in the first year of his presidency. Critics of détente had long argued that Soviet dissidents such as the scientist Andrei Sakharov and the writer Alexander Solzhenitsyn had received insufficient encouragement from Washington. In September 1973, George Kennan had called Kissinger to lend him his support over what he denigrated as the "hysteria of the western press" in highlighting their plight. After noting that "nothing as yet has actually happened to either [Sakharov] or Solzhenitsyn"—"You know what would have happened to them under Stalin," added Kissinger—Kennan observed that "many of the issues that they have with them are simply ones that they have provoked. So I just want you to know that I'm strongly with you. And I don't think in any case that it's right for a great country such as ours to try and adjust its foreign policy in order to work internal change in another country."[184] Pleased by this endorsement, Kissinger certainly followed Kennan's logic when he advised President Ford against meeting Solzhenitsyn in early 1975 during his visit to the United States. "I decided to subordinate political gains to foreign policy considerations," President Ford admitted in a matter-of-fact style that concealed much regret.[185]

In the pantheon of political missteps, the president's decision was not quite as misguided as granting Nixon a full pardon and thus immunity from prosecution—as Ford did immediately after coming to office, with disastrous electoral consequences—but it came pretty close. An editorial in *The New York Times* asked, "Does President Ford know the difference between détente and appeasement?"[186] One of Gerald Ford's assistants, Dick Cheney, expressed his unease to Donald Rumsfeld, the president's chief of staff:

> I think the decision not to see him is based upon a misreading of détente . . . At most, détente should consist of agreements wherever possible to reduce the possibility of conflict, but it does not mean that all of a sudden our relationship with the Soviets is all sweetness and light. I can't think of a better way [than meeting Solzhenitsyn] to demonstrate for the American people and for the world that détente with the Soviet Union . . . does not imply also our approval of their way of life or their authoritarian government.[187]

Cheney was absolutely right. And it hardly needs emphasizing that any decision capable of uniting Dick Cheney and *The Times* in well-reasoned opposition was likely to either have some serious flaws or be touched by a peculiar genius. The furor that engulfed the administration made clear that it was the former. Kissinger conceded so much in his memoir, lamenting that "our ability to conduct a balanced Soviet policy was far more damaged than it would have been had we found some way to meet with this great and courageous champion of freedom."[188]

A month after the Solzhenitsyn snub, in Minneapolis, Kissinger responded to his legion of critics in a speech titled "The Moral Foundation of Foreign Policy." The speech followed a familiar post-political-fiasco pattern in that regret appears to be expressed, critics appear to be disarmed, and then the essential point is made at the end: my critics are wrong and my approach is not just correct but unavoidably so. Thus Kissinger began by saying, "We have never seen ourselves as just another nation state pursuing selfish aims. We have always stood for something beyond ourselves—a beacon to the oppressed from other lands." And he ended with a staunch defense of détente and brand Kissinger, reinforcing the advantages of engagement:

> As a consequence of improved foreign policy relationships, we have successfully used our influence to promote human rights. But we have done so quietly, keeping in mind the delicacy of the problem and stressing results rather than public confrontation. Therefore, critics of détente must answer: What is the alternative that they propose? What precise policies do they want us to change? Are they prepared for a prolonged situation of dramatically increased international danger? Do they wish to return to the constant crises and high arms budgets of the Cold War? Does détente encourage repression—or is it détente that has generated the ferment and the demands for openness that we are now witnessing?[189]

The final sentence was a reference to the Helsinki Final Act, signed that same month, which confirmed Europe's postwar borders, regulated and facilitated East-West exchanges on science, tourism, the environment, and trade, and devoted a discrete third section—or basket—to "humanitarian and other fields." This final category committed all signatories to respect the inviolability of its citizens' human rights. The first basket, formally recognizing Soviet domination of Eastern Europe, attracted the most attention. And at the time, Kissinger could scarcely imagine what that third basket would portend a generation later. But some historians now believe that Brezhnev effectively signed the Soviet Union's death warrant in Helsinki. As John Lewis Gaddis writes:

> Challenging authoritarian rule ... was now a legitimate enterprise, because Brezhnev's signature on the Helsinki Final Act formally endorsed the argument that the Soviet Union's adversaries had been making throughout the Cold War: that the people, not the party and its leaders, had the right to organize, vote, and thereby determine their own future. Dissidents who had long hoped for reform could now claim it as their right, and within months their demands were sweeping the Soviet bloc.[190]

In an act of creative self-destruction, the full text of the Helsinki Accords—technically the Conference on Security and Cooperation in Europe—was printed in *Pravda*. Soon after the conference ended, Helsinki Groups sprang to life in the nations of the Warsaw Pact, including Václav Havel's Charter 77 in Czechoslovakia and Lech Wałęsa's Solidarity in Poland. Kissinger could not finesse the full significance of the Helsinki Accords at the time—how could he?—but the secretary of state was sharp enough to identify "ferment and the demand for openness" as an early reality. Gerald Ford's speech at Helsinki represented his finest hour. The president focused particular attention on the human rights provisions, addressing Brezhnev directly: "To my country, they are not clichés or empty phrases ... It is important that you recognize the deep devotion of the American people and their government to human rights and fundamental freedoms ... History will judge this conference not by what we say here today, but by what we do tomorrow; not by the promises we make but by the promises we keep."[191] Yet Kissinger's and Ford's critics missed all this, assailing Helsinki as if it were Yalta's second coming—without the mitigating factor of the wartime alliance.

George Kennan was never likely to warm to a diplomatic treaty signed by thirty-five states with domestic politics at its heart. He dismissed Helsinki as "a lot of nonsense ... none of it committing anyone specifically to anything."[192] Alexander Solzhenitsyn, smarting from the presidential snub, described Helsinki as "the betrayal of Eastern Europe" and predicted darkly that "an amicable agreement of diplomatic shovels will bury and pack down corpses still breathing in a common grave." Honing his forthcoming primary strategy of blaming the world's ills on Kissinger, Governor Ronald Reagan said, "At Kissinger's insistence, Mr. Ford snubbed Alexander Solzhenitsyn, one of the great moral heroes of our time. At Kissinger's insistence, Mr. Ford flew halfway around the world to sign an agreement at Helsinki which placed the American seal of approval on the Soviet Empire in Eastern Europe."[193] "I think we lost in Helsinki," chimed in Governor Jimmy Carter, readying himself for his tilt at the presidency. "We ratified the takeover of Eastern Europe. We got practically nothing in return."[194] Kissinger and Ford understood that Soviet dominance of Eastern Europe had been ceded in 1945. The genius of Helsinki was that it grasped a validated, cocksure Brezhnev in a warm embrace—placing official imprimatur on a long-standing reality— and then planted a time bomb on his person.

Post-Helsinki validation was a long time away. The year 1975 was generally miserable. South Vietnam and Cambodia both fell to communist onslaughts in April. As Kissinger recalled, passively, "As for Indochina, I observed it with the melancholy shown toward a terminally ill relative, hoping for a long respite and miracle cure I was unable to describe."[195] Kissinger favored a military intervention, which Ford swiftly refused to sanction, leaving him to lament, "I'm the only secretary of state who has lost two countries in three weeks." During an NBC interview with Barbara Walters, which garnered a large viewing audience, Walters asked what this loss meant to the United States. Where had we gone wrong in Vietnam? Kissinger began to answer the question conventionally, observing that there "is in almost every major event a domino effect" that one can attribute to "the general psychological climate that is created in the world as to who is advancing and who is withdrawing." Then he paused, took a deep breath, and added that "we probably made a mistake" in believing such canards. "We perhaps might have perceived [the war] more in Vietnamese terms, rather than as the outward thrust of a global conspiracy." Watching Kissinger channeling David Halberstam was an exhilarating moment for *The Washington Post*'s Stephen Rosenfeld, who hailed "a burst of historical revisionism fit to make his bitterest critics weep for joy."[196]

There were few other validations for Kissinger during the remainder of his tenure as secretary of state. During the so-called Halloween Massacre of 1975, Ford ruthlessly restructured his administration, ceding the most significant gains to the right wing of the GOP. Ford's chief of staff, Donald Rumsfeld, became secretary of defense. Dick Cheney was promoted to replace Rumsfeld. Ford's vice president, and Kissinger's friend and patron, Nelson Rockefeller, was persuaded to eliminate himself as a running mate in the forthcoming election. Finally, Kissinger's national security brief was taken from him and handed to Brent Scowcroft. This was positive in the sense that Scowcroft and Kissinger had similar worldviews. But Kissinger had enjoyed the power vested in his unprecedented dual role and struggled to adjust to losing his White House perch. Kissinger retreated into a sulk and contemplated resignation. He soon concluded, however, that the prospect of a Rumsfeld or a Cheney replacing him was sufficiently horrifying for him to stay the course. "Don," Kissinger said to Rumsfeld during a cabinet meeting to audible laughter, "your wife was over measuring my office today."[197]

The massacre was not bloody enough for Ronald Reagan, who delivered an ominous threat: "I am not appeased." Rather than challenging Reagan, Ford gave appeasement another chance. In November 14, 1975, Ford's campaign adviser, Robert Teeter, warned the president that "détente is a particularly unpopular idea with most Republican primary voters . . . We ought to stop using the word wherever possible."[198] Ford agreed, and "détente" joined "liberal" in its lexical journey from descriptor to epithet. Kissinger's grand strategy was being picked apart in full view.

Scenting more blood that same year, Paul Nitze and Eugene Rostow—Walt's more belligerent older brother—gathered together a selection of prominent anti-Kissinger Democrats and Republicans to form a Committee on the Present Danger. The roster of members was highly impressive, ranging from Dean Rusk to Richard Perle to Saul Bellow. Jeane Kirkpatrick, a well-regarded professor of international relations at Georgetown University, was an important member of the committee, and she was highly effective at assailing Kissinger's worldview: "[A] culture of appeasement which finds reasons not only against the use of force but denies its place in the world is a profoundly mistaken culture—mistaken in the nature of reality."[199] The executive committee was divided equally between Democrats and Republicans and its public stance was nonpartisan. This worked well in 1976 when Jimmy Carter and Ronald Reagan both assailed Kissinger in more or less equal measure. When their piñata departed the scene, however, and the GOP found a charismatic Cold Warrior in Ronald Reagan, the membership of the committee was almost unified in its support for the Republican Party.

Throughout 1976, Ford faced a fierce primary challenge from Ronald Reagan, which he only narrowly overcame, while Jimmy Carter, the governor of Georgia, secured the Democratic nomination. When it came to foreign policy, Reagan and Carter had near identical messages. "Henry Kissinger's stewardship of United States foreign policy," Reagan repeated on the primary campaign trail, "has coincided precisely with the loss of United States military superiority." He and Ford had presided over "the collapse of the American will and retreat of American power."[200] Reagan's insurgent campaign ended in defeat when Ford secured the nomination in August at the party convention. But Reagan had won the GOP's soul.

Jimmy Carter, meanwhile, picked up where Reagan left off. During the second presidential debate, for example, he name-checked Kissinger's "secrecy" and "secret" diplomacy eleven times. During his powerful opening remarks, Carter observed that "our country is not strong anymore; we're not respected anymore . . . We've lost, in our foreign policy, the character of the American people. We've ignored or excluded the American people and the Congress from participation in the shaping of our foreign policy. It's been one of secrecy and exclusion." Yet the principal architect of this dismal state of affairs was not the incumbent: "As far as foreign policy goes, Mr. Kissinger has been the president of this country," Carter noted.[201]

Later in the debate, a weak-looking Ford made the worst gaffe in the history of presidential debates. In defending his policy of engaging with Moscow, Ford observed, "There is no Soviet domination of Eastern Europe and there never will be under a Ford administration." When gently asked for a clarification, Ford simply made matters worse:

> I don't believe, Mr. Frankel, that the Yugoslavians consider themselves dominated by the Soviet Union. I don't believe that the Romanians consider themselves dominated by the Soviet Union. I don't believe that the Poles consider themselves dominated by the Soviet Union. Each of those countries is independent, autonomous; it has its own territorial integrity. And the United States does not concede that those countries are under the domination of the Soviet Union.[202]

Few Cold War–era presidents have sounded quite so much like a Soviet propagandist. As well as being flat-out wrong, Ford's remarks appeared to vindicate Reagan's and Carter's charges regarding his indifference to the Soviet menace and acceptance of its worst excesses. The opinion pollster George Gallup observed that the president's gaffe was "the most decisive moment of the campaign. It fatally stalled Ford's comeback."[203]

Carter defeated Ford in the election of 1976 by two percentage points in the popular vote and by 297 to 240 electoral votes. With Ford's defeat, America's curious relationship with European balance-of-power politics came to a swift and ignominious end. It was a passionate and volatile affair—a holiday romance, perhaps. After the fling ended, however, the nation sheepishly returned to its long-standing spouse: Woodrow Wilson. Kissinger departed the scene with his wit and self-confidence intact. "Can you tell me," one reporter asked him after his departure, "what you consider to be your greatest success and greatest failure?" "I don't quite understand your second point," said Kissinger.[204]

A little after leaving office, Kissinger made some unguarded remarks about Richard Nixon that were picked up on an open microphone. He described his former boss as an "odd," "unpleasant," "nervous," and "artificial" man. Word got back to Nixon, who was predictably angered—though probably not surprised. It made for an awkward reunion in 1977 when the two men exchanged words at the funeral of Hubert Humphrey, who might have been president had events taken a different course in 1968. "You as mean as ever?" Nixon asked Kissinger. "Yes," replied Kissinger, "but I don't have as much opportunity as before."[205] When Nixon died in 1994, Kissinger quoted Hamlet during an elegant and affecting eulogy: "He was a man, take him for all in all. I shall not look upon his like again."[206] The same might be said of Kissinger.

8

★

THE WORLDMAKER

PAUL WOLFOWITZ

Sometimes people call me an idealist. Well that is the only way
I know I am an American. America is the only idealistic nation in
the world. —WOODROW WILSON

Paul Wolfowitz worked dutifully for the Nixon and Ford administrations,
but with no real enthusiasm for their policies. When Fred Iklé, a hawkish
RAND strategist, invited Wolfowitz to join the Arms Control and Disarmament Agency in 1973, the young scholar dropped his tenure-track job
at Yale as if it were a paper route. Wolfowitz was not excited by the thought
of making a university career as a political scientist, even at an institution as
venerable as Yale. What he wanted was proximity to power and the opportunity to put theory to practice. And he had to start somewhere.

Unfortunately for Wolfowitz, Henry Kissinger had the final say on
which theories became practice—and they were usually his own. While
Wolfowitz enjoyed the process and detail of his work on missile launches,
early-warning systems, and other cutting-edge technologies, he soon grew
frustrated with the wider context in which he operated. Wolfowitz viewed the
Nixon administration's strategy of détente as morally wrong and tactically
deficient. Instead of taming America's principal adversary, détente legiti-
mated and vitalized the Soviet Union—plus the accompanying SALT negotiations ceded Moscow significant tactical advantages. Kissinger was
incapable of accepting this possibility, as it contradicted his Metternichian
focus on dealing dispassionately and constructively with allies and enemies.

Waylaid by specious historical analogies, Kissinger was a lost cause. But the CIA also appeared blasé about the Soviet threat, and this was a real worry.

At the end of every year, the CIA compiles a top-secret National Intelligence Estimate (NIE), which provides a comprehensive assessment of the most pressing threats facing the United States. During the Nixon and Ford administrations, a growing number of critics—including Paul Nitze and Albert Wohlstetter—began complaining that the CIA was underestimating Soviet military strength. Some wondered whether these sanguine NIEs had been so designed to bolster the administration's policies of engagement with Moscow. During his bruising primary battle with Ronald Reagan, Ford buckled under severe pressure from the right of his party and instructed George H. W. Bush, the president's recently appointed director of Central Intelligence, to launch an independent review into these allegations. Bush assembled an external team of experts—designated Team B—to review the CIA's classified data and determine whether the agency's view of Moscow was indeed complacent. Team B was led by the Sovietologist Richard Pipes, a professor of Russian history at Harvard University, who oversaw a team of sixteen analysts and defense intellectuals that included two Pauls: Messrs. Nitze and Wolfowitz.[1]

After completing their deliberations, Team B launched a lacerating attack on the CIA. Their report criticized the agency for leaning too heavily on satellite imagery and signals intelligence. They alleged that the agency paid insufficient attention to the actual speeches made by members of the Politburo—much more than mere bluster—and to the increasingly aggressive manner in which the Soviet proxies across the world, whether in Angola, Afghanistan, or Vietnam, actually behaved.[2] As Nitze explained in a letter to Zbigniew Brzezinski, "The Soviet leaders are totally frank in saying that they believe the correlation of forces has moved dramatically in their favor over the last five to ten years. They attribute this to their growing military preponderance and to détente."[3] The aggressiveness and certainty with which Pipes and Nitze made their case left the fresh-faced, undermanned CIA "Team A" reeling. "It was like putting Walt Whitman High versus the Redskins," said one CIA analyst of the meeting between both "teams" in October 1976. Another recalled, "People like Nitze ate us for lunch."[4]

Participation in the Team B exercise was a formative experience for Wolfowitz. The group's conclusions appeared to show that the core component of Kissinger's diplomacy—that improved relations with Moscow increased America's range of diplomatic options—rested on a fallacy. The Soviet Union was as committed to extinguishing liberal capitalism as it had been under Josef Stalin. How does one interact with an entity subscribing to such a worldview? Team B's answer: one doesn't. Wolfowitz's assessment was that "the B-Team demonstrated that it was possible to construct a sharply different view of Soviet motivation from the consensus view of the analysts, and one that provided a much closer fit to the Soviets' observed behavior."[5] He departed the exercise convinced that threats to the United States were often worse than they appeared, that Washington should plan on the basis of the worst-case scenario, that arms spending should be sharply increased, and that the CIA was essentially untrustworthy, conditioned by the same systemic biases—reliance on objectively verifiable evidence, moral relativism, an unwillingness to cite ideology as causative factor—that also blighted the State Department. It was all bracing stuff, although Team B's alarmist assessments turned out to be factually wrong.[6]

Team B, and Wolfowitz's geopolitical awakening, was something of a hinge moment in the history of U.S. foreign policy. Kissingerian realism was soon to be eclipsed by moralism, stridency, and instinctual certainties about American virtue and its duty to combat evil. In the summer of 1976, as James Mann recounts in *Rise of the Vulcans*, Wolfowitz invited two graduate students—one of whom was Francis Fukuyama—to assist his work on Team B as unpaid interns. At dinner at his home, Wolfowitz ruminated on the strengths and limitations of Henry Kissinger's *A World Restored*. It was a well-researched and interesting book, Wolfowitz said, but Kissinger had identified the wrong exemplar. That craftsman of realpolitik, Metternich, projected a vision that was lacking in scruple and substance; the "peace" he helped secure was unsustainable in the long term. Tsar Alexander I, who had advocated fierce resistance to Napoleon Bonaparte on moral and religious grounds, was the true hero of the tale. Fukuyama recalled "him saying the thing that's wrong with Kissinger is that he does not understand the country he's living in, that this is a country that is dedicated to certain universalistic principles."[7] On Kissinger's preference for amoral, balance-of-power diplomacy, Wolfowitz was fond of quoting a sardonic Polish phrase that emphasized its insidiousness: "the stability of the graveyard."[8] Wolfowitz's values-led universalism marked a clear break with Kissinger, owed a large debt to Woodrow Wilson, and would dominate the foreign-policy debate for the next thirty years.

Paul Dundes Wolfowitz was born in Brooklyn on December 22, 1943, the second child of Lillian Dundes and Jacob Wolfowitz. Paul's paternal grandparents had fled Poland in 1920, fearing that their Judaism made them a target for discrimination and violence. Their instincts spared their lives. As was the case with the Kissingers, those family members who remained perished during the genocidal Nazi occupation.

Like so many talented, cash-poor Jewish immigrants, Jacob Wolfowitz attended City College, where he received a first-class education. He then moved to New York University for his graduate work, where he completed his doctoral dissertation in mathematics. Jacob's interests were myriad. He was highly cultured, a steadfast supporter of Franklin Roosevelt's New Deal, a dedicated Zionist, and an organizer of protests against the Soviet Union's brutal treatment of minorities and dissidents. In 1951, Jacob moved the family from New York City to Ithaca, where he took a professorship at Cornell in mathematics and statistics.

Paul's childhood in Ithaca—an attractive if isolated college town in up-state New York—was idyllic and directed by his father toward serious purposes. The family library was well stocked, and Paul consumed his father's histories of the Second World War and the Holocaust—of which he confessed he read "probably too many"—George Orwell's oeuvre, and John Hersey's *Hiroshima*, a visceral account of the atomic bombing of that city.[9] Paul was a precocious student at Ithaca High School. During his senior year, the school gave him dispensation to attend a calculus class at Cornell in the morning before completing his school lessons in the afternoon.[10] Cornell recognized Paul as a student of uncommon ability and offered him a university place with a full scholarship, too good an opportunity for him or his family to decline. He majored in mathematics and chemistry and appeared poised to follow in his father's disciplinary footsteps.

Paul's exemplary scholastic record qualified him for membership in the Telluride Association, a select group of Cornell and University of Michigan undergraduates from various disciplines united only by their smarts. Telluride was a self-governing entity founded in 1910 with seed money from an unorthodox Colorado businessman named Lucien Lucius Nunn. Telluride encouraged the free exchange of ideas and compelled a large degree of self-reliance and responsibility. It was the students, not administrators, who hired kitchen and cleaning staff, organized basic maintenance, invited guest speakers, and oversaw admissions. And it was at Telluride in 1963 that Wolfowitz first encountered Professor Allan Bloom, a charismatic classicist and political theorist who had moved to Telluride as a faculty adviser.[11] Bloom's tutoring style was Socratic, the classical philosophers were his lodestars, and his pleasures tended toward the bacchanalian—he lived a full and joyful life. Bloom was close to Alexandre Kojève, Raymond Aron, Leo

Strauss, Susan Sontag, and the great novelist Saul Bellow, a fellow graduate of the University of Chicago, who later wrote a novel around him, *Ravelstein*, in which a thinly disguised Wolfowitz (named Philip Gorman) also makes a cameo appearance. Telluride was not a cult—much as it might have appeared that way—but the magnetic Bloom attracted a cult following.[12]

Wolfowitz changed direction at Cornell, moving away from natural science and toward political science. By Wolfowitz's own admission, Bloom had a role in inspiring this shift: "He had a lot to do with my coming to appreciate that the study of politics could be a serious business, even though it wasn't science in the sense that I understood science to be. That was an important eye-opener." Sensing the appearance on the scene of a dangerous influence, Jacob Wolfowitz took a rather dim view of Bloom's grandiose philosophizing; indeed, both were suspicious of the other's subject areas. Wolfowitz remembered that "Bloom was somewhat disdainful of hard science in general because it left out the philosophical dimension."[13] His father viewed the social sciences as inferior disciplines; their presumption to deliver verifiable truth was unconvincing.

Jacob was fighting a losing battle with his son. It was not just Bloom's charisma and passion for political theory he had to counteract but also momentous world events that drew Wolfowitz closer to those disciplines that promised to make sense of them. "I was a Cuban Missile Crisis kid," Wolfowitz said. "I was a sophomore in college when all that happened. There were other things in it as well. It was kind of a passion for history and politics even though I was good in math and science."[14] The combination of Bloom and the Cold War conspired to frustrate the father's hopes for his son. Paul was accepted to the prestigious Ph.D. program in biophysical chemistry at MIT. Unbeknownst to his father, however, he had also applied to doctoral programs in political science at Harvard and the University of Chicago. When both offered him places, Wolfowitz chose Chicago largely because Leo Strauss, a major thinker with close links to Bloom, was on the faculty. "I told my father I had to try political science for a year," Wolfowitz said. "He thought I was throwing my life away."[15]

Strauss was a major figure in twentieth-century political philosophy. He was devoted to Plato and Aristotle and taught classes through meticulous reading of their major works. Strauss (and indeed Bloom) believed that twentieth-century philosophy was blighted by two failings: moral relativism and ahistorical liberalism. The first philosopher Strauss designated (and damned) as "modern" was Niccolò Machiavelli, whose callous worldview fitted neatly in the former category. That seminal rejection of classical and biblical morality, *The Prince*, represented all that Strauss abhorred. On the failings of modern liberalism, Strauss came down hard on Karl Popper, whose 1945 work *The Open Society and Its Enemies* was a strong attack on Plato's *Republic*, which Popper condemned as "totalitarian." As the intellectual historian Melissa Lane observes, Strauss viewed the *Republic* very differently: as "secretively and ironically an anti-totalitarian text, a text which warns against the danger of being sanitized by exegetes as a utopian ideal."[16] Or as Strauss said of one of Popper's lectures in 1950: It "was beneath contempt: it was the most washed-out, lifeless positivism trying to whistle in the dark, linked to a complete inability to think 'rationally,' although it passed itself off as 'rationalism'—it was very bad."[17] Plato was a hero to Strauss because he asked fundamental questions about justice and order; the issues and dilemmas he confronted were timeless. Popper had distorted Plato's prescriptions to pursue his own agenda, and this was dishonest. Strauss spoke frequently of the "crisis of liberalism . . . a crisis due to the fact that liberalism has abandoned its absolutist basis and is trying to become entirely relativistic."[18] Like George Kennan, Strauss was conservative in the most literal sense.

Drawn in by the clarity of his worldview and seductiveness of his classroom technique, and of course by Bloom's endorsement, Wolfowitz took two classes with Strauss at Chicago—on Plato and Montesquieu. Wolfowitz gained much insight from both courses and found that Strauss lived up to his laudatory advance billing. Yet Wolfowitz was later dismissive of those scholars who drew linkages between Strauss and his subsequent foreign-policy views: "It's a product of fevered minds . . . I mean I took two terrific courses from Leo Strauss as a graduate student. One was on Montesquieu's spirit of the laws, which did help me understand our Constitution better. And one was on Plato's laws. The idea that this has anything to do with U.S. foreign policy is just laughable."[19] Of course Strauss did not have to write on U.S. foreign policy—and, indeed, he wrote nothing on this subject—to exert an influence on its makers. Strauss's idealization of the strong leader—Churchill was a hero of his—and firm moral convictions were certainly present in Wolfowitz's subsequent career. But the professor at Chicago whom Wolfowitz cited as his true mentor was his Ph.D. supervisor, Albert Wohlstetter.

The urbane, whip-smart Wohlstetter worked at the RAND Corporation throughout the 1950s, where he developed a global reputation in the field of nuclear strategy.[20] He and Paul Nitze were close; both were alarmed by U.S. vulnerability to the Soviet Union's fast-improving nuclear capabilities and believed that the Eisenhower administration was recklessly sanguine on this point. Wohlstetter moved to the University of Chicago in the 1960s, where he taught political science. Here he developed a strong focus, which remained throughout his career, on the best means to forestall the proliferation of nuclear weapons. A visit to Israel in the late 1960s left him fearful that its hostile neighbors were hell-bent on acquiring a nuclear capability, and that America's duty to Israel (and the world) was to use whatever means necessary to prevent this from happening.[21] Wohlstetter's influence was clearly evident in Wolfowitz's doctoral dissertation, which examined and critiqued Israel's desire to develop nuclear-powered desalination stations near its borders with Egypt and Jordan.

Desalination served a laudable function, Wolfowitz conceded, but he also feared that the plutonium by-product of such plants could find its way into the wrong hands and eventually pose an existential threat to Israel itself. The dissertation warned of these dire consequences and emphasized the difficulties of instituting an international nuclear inspection regime truly capable of assuring the technology remained devoted to peaceful purposes. While Woodrow Wilson's idealism inspired Wolfowitz, he found the former president's views on the peacemaking potential and capabilities of multilateral institutions and international law far less persuasive.

Wolfowitz's thesis criticized not only the wisdom of building these desalination plants but also the very notion of Israel acquiring a nuclear weapons capability:

> The fundamental point is that any Israeli nuclear force would have to depend on relatively simple delivery systems, which would be vulnerable even to conventional attack . . . An Israeli nuclear threat against Arab cities would weaken Israel's conventional military position by cutting her off from friendly countries in the West, and by encouraging, if not forcing, the Soviet Union to intervene more actively on behalf of the Arabs . . . Israeli nuclear weapons would push the Arabs into a desperate attempt to acquire nuclear weapons, if not from the Soviet Union, then at a later date from China or on their own.[22]

We know that Wolfowitz's nuclear-free Middle East did not come to pass. Israel developed an atomic weapon capability during the 1970s, while adhering to a stance of so-called nuclear ambiguity—also known as keeping schtum.[23] Just as Wolfowitz predicted, other regional powers, such as Saddam Hussein's Iraq, laid plans to counterbalance Israel's advantage and develop a nuclear insurance policy. Whether declared or not, the new reality of a nuclear-armed Israel was never likely to go unchallenged by its hostile neighbors. Wolfowitz could scarcely have realized this at the time, but issues of nuclear proliferation—and "weapons of mass destruction" more broadly—in the Middle East would dominate much of his subsequent career. Whether events would have turned out differently if Israel had followed Wolfowitz's cautionary advice is impossible to know. What we do know is that Wolfowitz produced a fine dissertation that was grounded in multiple Hebrew-language sources and propelled by nuanced and sharp analysis.[24]

Wolfowitz cut a fascinating figure during his time at Cornell and Chicago, alternating between civil rights–inspired liberalism and hawkish iconoclasm through the upheavals of the 1960s. In August 1963, Wolfowitz hitched a ride with some Ithaca church congregations that had chartered buses to Washington to attend a major civil rights demonstration. Wolfowitz thus became one of a quarter of a million people on the National Mall who witnessed Martin Luther King Jr. deliver his "I Have a Dream" speech from the steps of the Lincoln Memorial. This road trip was no one-time progressive aberration. Wolfowitz was a strong supporter of John Kennedy and Lyndon Johnson, and of the civil rights movement more generally. Indeed, throughout his career, he shared little with the Republican Party on domestic politics. "The most surprising thing about Wolfowitz," Christopher Hitchens said of his frequent dinner companion, "is that he's a bleeding heart. His instincts are those of a liberal democrat, apart from on national security."[25]

But Wolfowitz also supported Kennedy and Johnson's foreign policies, and this is where he departed company with the civil rights movement and indeed the mainstream left. During his final year at Cornell, for example, Wolfowitz was one member of a three-person demonstration (if this designation can be applied to a trio) supporting U.S. intervention in the Vietnam War. A founder member of Cornell's Committee for Critical Support of the United States in Vietnam, Wolfowitz fully agreed with President Johnson's logic for escalating the conflict. Following the fall of Saigon in 1975, Wolfowitz was not dispirited, believing that America's military effort had served an important function, even when the immediate objective had not been met. He agreed with Singapore's president Lee Kuan Yew and Walt Rostow that fighting communism in Vietnam ultimately saved its neighbors from Marxist-Leninist revolutions.[26]

Wolfowitz was clearly an atypical college student in that volatile and socially experimental era when political differences burned with uncommon intensity. Yet in the midst of this tumult, Wolfowitz was incapable of making enemies; he was as gracious to his ideological opponents as he was to his (fewer) like-minded allies. As George Packer observes in *The Assassins' Gate*, Wolfowitz was "always a good boy, the kind on whom adults fasten their dreams, with a yeshiva student's purity about him, though his education was entirely secular." One of Wolfowitz's fellow students at Telluride observed that there was "a certain public-spirited prudery about him. Paul is sort of the good citizen."[27] Wolfowitz may have chosen the wrong subject, in his father's estimation, but any parent would have been proud of the dedication with which he pursued those studies, his active political life, and the easy way he interacted with others.

In 1969, as Wolfowitz was working on his dissertation in Chicago, Wohlstetter invited him to set it aside for a while and take a job with him in Washington, D.C., conducting research for the Committee to Maintain a Prudent Defense Policy, a pressure group established by Paul Nitze and Dean Acheson to protect the development of an antiballistic missile system from congressional sequestration. Wolfowitz was more than willing to put his dissertation on ice. Indeed, he soon found himself hooked on real-world politics. Nitze and Acheson were inspirational figures, and both warmed to the idealistic and energetic Wolfowitz. The Safeguard ABM program was saved by a vote of 51 to 50 in the Senate (as the vote was tied, the extra vote came from Vice President Spiro Agnew). Wolfowitz's return to Chicago and his doctoral research was something of a comedown. After Wolfowitz accepted the lottery win that was a tenure-track position at Yale in 1970, his default career focus tended toward job opportunities in Washington rather than journal articles, promising doctoral students, and grant applications. In 1973, he joined the Nixon administration and remained there through Nixon's protracted waltz with oblivion, Gerald Ford's ascension to the Oval Office, and Ford's defeat in 1976 to Jimmy Carter. At that point Wolfowitz faced a stark choice: Leave with Ford, or remain in post and work for Carter?

Jimmy Carter rose to political prominence as the governor of rural Georgia—he made his wealth as the owner of a peanut-warehousing business—and his presidential campaign was driven by this well-cultivated outsider status, by the purity that supposedly accrues through avoiding direct contact with Washington, D.C.[28] Carter was a born-again Christian, and while he did not lead with his religiosity, there is little doubt that a clear sense of right and wrong informed his worldview. Carter lambasted Kissinger, Nixon, and Ford for too narrowly defining America's national interests and insisted that the nation's foreign policy should pay greater heed to human rights. Carter pointedly exchanged warm letters with Andrei Sakharov, encouraged post-Helsinki dissidents across the Soviet Bloc, and established a Bureau of Human Rights and Humanitarian Affairs at the State Department that graded each nation on how well it treated its citizens. During his inaugural address in 1977, Carter declared, "Our commitment to human rights must be absolute."[29]

The new president's words and actions reassured an admiring Wolfowitz, who accepted the position of deputy assistant secretary for defense for regional programs. It was a midlevel job that invited Wolfowitz to contemplate and identify future trends, a function he was pleased to perform. But there was no job in the Carter administration for Paul Nitze, who had reason to expect better. In the summer of 1976, Nitze met and unnerved Carter— one witness described the meeting as "a disaster"—with his dark warnings about Soviet nuclear intentions and American vulnerability.[30] Carter described Nitze as "typically know-it-all. He was arrogant and inflexible. His own ideas were sacred to him. He didn't seem to listen to others, and he had a doomsday approach."[31] That the two men did not hit it off was not all that surprising. A few months previously, Nitze had written to Zbigniew Brzezinski that Carter's human rights emphasis was "based upon a Wilsonian approach, an approach that was impracticable even in Wilson's day, and which seems even more out of tune with today's realities. I further question whether *mea culpas* about the United States as a nation are helpful. We have not, as a nation, ignored Latin America or the third world or engaged in military adventurism; we acted imprudently in Vietnam, but not from evil motives."[32] Not a man to be slighted without consequence, Nitze became one of Carter's fiercest critics. (Nitze was generally more hawkish when unemployed.)

Wolfowitz's new job at the Pentagon required him to identify parts of the world where American interests were present, to a hitherto underestimated extent, and threatened. Broadening the geographical remit of his doctoral studies, Wolfowitz identified the Persian Gulf as a particularly nettlesome region for Washington, and Baathist Iraq—the pan-Arab Baathist movement was driven by nationalism and a variant on socialism, dedicated to achieving an Arab renaissance, thus reducing the region's susceptibility to the whims of larger nations—as a likely future threat. The vast oil reserves in the region, combined with dwindling U.S. domestic capacity, made the Persian Gulf an economically vital region, one where Wolfowitz suspected the Soviet Union would attempt to make mischief. Yet even without direct adventurism on the part of Moscow, an assertive and nationalist Iraq—implacably opposed to Israel, flush with high-tech Soviet weaponry—posed a clear threat to regional stability.

Wolfowitz presented his report—titled "Capabilities for Limited Contingencies in the Persian Gulf," more commonly known as the "Limited Contingency Study"—to Secretary of Defense Harold Brown in 1979. It was a fascinating and accurate piece of futurology:

> The emerging Iraqi threat has two dimensions. On the one hand, Iraq may in the future use her military forces against such states as Kuwait or Saudi Arabia (as in the 1961 Kuwait crisis that was resolved by timely British intervention with force). On the other hand, the more serious problem may be that Iraq's *implicit* power will cause currently moderate local powers to accommodate themselves to Iraq without being overtly coerced. The latter problem suggests that we must not only be able to defend the interests of Kuwait, Saudi Arabia and ourselves against an Iraqi invasion or show of force, we should also make manifest our capabilities and commitments to balance Iraq's power—and this may require an increased visibility for U.S. power.[33]

What looks farsighted today, however, appeared quirky in 1979. The military brass did not favor a partial redeployment of its assets to the Persian Gulf; Harold Brown worried that Wolfowitz had created a threat where none existed. A confident young Baathist named Saddam Hussein was at that juncture outmaneuvering his rivals to consolidate power at the apex of Iraqi politics. Fearful that Wolfowitz's report might be leaked, and Saddam recklessly and needlessly antagonized, Brown ordered that the study be buried deep in the Pentagon's archive. Iran was America's primary regional ally in the Middle East, and the Nixon Doctrine held that surrogates such as the shah should bear the preponderant burden of safeguarding the region. Farther down the line, Wolfowitz could not resist a little sarcasm: "Well, we don't plan forces for the Persian Gulf. The Shah [of] Iran takes care of the Persian Gulf for us."[34]

During his service to the Carter administration, Wolfowitz was given the opportunity to engage in ambitious blue skies thinking—if not the power to execute those ideas. Yet even as Wolfowitz mulled the future, the Carter present frustrated him. After assuming the presidency, Carter had needled Moscow with his human rights emphasis—which Brezhnev viewed as an aggressive intrusion into Soviet domestic affairs—but he was dedicated

to achieving a second, more comprehensive nuclear arms control agreement with the Soviet Union: SALT II. In August 1978, Carter had vetoed
a $37 billion arms bill because it provided for a $2 billion nuclear aircraft
carrier that the president deemed unnecessary. A member of Carter's White
House staff correctly predicted that his veto would "make you look weak on
defense issues at a time when public attitudes are shifting to the right." On
November 18, Carter's pugnacious national security adviser, Zbigniew
Brzezinski, identified "a growing domestic problem involving public perception [of foreign policy] . . . To put it simply and quite bluntly, it is seen as
'soft.'" To reestablish his bona fides as a resolute Cold Warrior, Brzezinski
advised the president to do something that "has a distinctively 'tough' quality to it."[35]

Carter did get tough, but only after the United States suffered some serious foreign-policy reverses. In January 1978, Carter visited Iran, where
he paid warm homage to the shah, Mohammad Reza Pahlavi, identifying
among the choreographed crowds in Tehran the "respect . . . admiration
and love" that ordinary Iranians supposedly felt toward him. As the historian Odd Arne Westad notes, "It was perhaps the worst possible moment
for a presidential visit; just as the shah needed to shore up his nationalist
credentials to confront the opposition."[36] Over the remainder of 1978, protests against the shah's rule grew more fervent and widespread—December
witnessed a remarkable two-million-person demonstration in Tehran.[37]

In January 1979, the shah fled the country and Ayatollah Ruhollah
Khomeini returned from his exile in France, wasting little time in establishing a theocracy that looked (way) backward, not forward, for inspiration. On
November 4, 1979, Iranian students stormed the U.S. embassy in Tehran and
seized sixty-six American hostages, fifty-two of whom remained captive for
the next 444 days. Carter launched a disastrous helicopter-led rescue attempt in April 1980 that resulted in the destruction of two aircraft, the
death of eight American servicemen, and the resignation of his courtly
secretary of state, Cyrus Vance, whose trepidation had been ignored. The
United States lost its major regional ally in the Middle East, its prestige
took a significant hit, and its vaunted military failed to rescue its own
citizens. Such were the dark consequences of "America's first encounter with
radical Islam," as David Farber describes the episode in the subtitle of his
2006 book.

The Iranian Revolution was a crushing blow to U.S. interests in the
Middle East, alone sufficient to cast a Democratic presidency into fatal
disrepute. But Iran was just the beginning. Other foreign-policy "losses"

combined to cast Carter's presidency into almost Stygian gloom. In July 1979, a leftist insurgent group, the Sandinistas, toppled the repressive but reliably anticommunist government of Anastasio Somoza—whose family had ruled Nicaragua since 1936. And then on December 25, the Soviet Union invaded Afghanistan in a desperate attempt to prop up a Marxist-Leninist government struggling to quell an Islamist insurgency riled by secular efforts to reduce the influence of political Islam on Afghan society. Carter's response was fierce. He withdrew the SALT II treaty from consideration in the Senate, increased defense spending, reinstituted registration for the draft, embargoed grain and technology shipments to the Soviet Union, and ordered an American boycott of the 1980 Olympic Games in Moscow. The president also authorized the CIA to begin funneling arms and supplies to the Afghan insurgent movement, the mujahideen, although Zbigniew Brzezinski later allegedly claimed that covert support commenced as early as July 1979, predating the invasion by some six months.[38]

George Kennan faulted nearly all of Carter's responses. During testimony before the Senate Foreign Relations Committee on February 27, 1980, Kennan was asked for his thoughts on how to resolve the Iranian hostage crisis. His reply was simple and somewhat surprising: declare war on Iran. This remarkable suggestion showed that there was nothing predictable or doctrinal about Kennan's thinking—he clearly possessed the ability to shock. The crisis evoked bad memories of Kennan's own internment during the Second World War, and he believed that only an official declaration of war would permit a fruitful resolution of the crisis. When asked about the Soviet invasion of Afghanistan, however, Kennan counseled a moderate response and chided President Carter for his belligerence. Moscow's move southward was not the first stage of a wider gambit to dominate the Persian Gulf, as Carter and Brzezinski appeared to be suggesting; rather, it was a weak and defensive move that portended little except a protracted and enervating conflict for Moscow.[39]

Wolfowitz viewed the Soviet invasion of Afghanistan as the consequence and culmination of Kissinger and Nixon's détente policy, which had encouraged Soviet adventurism. Brezhnev was actually surprised when Carter withdrew the SALT II treaty from Senate consideration. That is how comfortable the Politburo had become in its "normalized" relationship—Moscow believed it could invade another nation and assume the continuation of business as usual. The Iranian Revolution, meanwhile, reinforced Wolfowitz's view that the Persian Gulf would become a major area of crisis and contestation. And again, it laid bare the Nixon-era fallacy of recruiting regional powers to serve American interests. During Jimmy Carter's 1980 State of the Union address, Wolfowitz could have been forgiven for claiming vindication for the contentious logic presented in his "Limited Contingency Study." In a pugnacious speech, the president warned that "an attempt by any outside force to gain control of the Persian Gulf region will be regarded as an assault on the vital interests of the United States of America, and such an assault will be repelled by any means necessary, including military force."[40] The Carter Doctrine was the Wolfowitz Doctrine melted down and recast. The Persian Gulf was now deemed a vital area of American concern.

At the close of 1979, as Carter reeled from this three-part succession of bad news, Fred Iklé called his former staffer and advised him to leave the administration with all due haste. Iklé was now advising Ronald Reagan's presidential campaign and anticipated a decisive victory for his man in the next election. "Paul, you've got to get out of there," Iklé warned. "We want you in the new administration."[41] Republican hawks like Jesse Helms had viewed Paul Nitze warily for his service to Truman, and Iklé worried that these same men would dismiss Wolfowitz as a Carter man. By remaining in an administration whose policies he disliked through a misguided sense of loyalty, Wolfowitz ran the clear risk of sabotaging a future job in a more accommodating administration. He did not need to be told twice. At the beginning of 1980, Wolfowitz resigned from the Carter administration and took a job as a visiting associate professor at the Paul H. Nitze School of Advanced International Studies at Johns Hopkins University—the institution Nitze had founded with Christian Herter in 1943. Here Wolfowitz bided his time, dearly hoping that Iklé's confidence about Reagan's electoral prospects was well placed.

Though it did not necessarily appear that way to the electorate in 1980, Carter had scored some notable achievements as president. In 1977, the United States and Panama signed a treaty that promised to return the Canal Zone to Panama at the end of the century but that permitted the United States to unilaterally deploy its military if the canal was ever imperiled by external threats. In 1978, Carter presided over successful negotiations between Menachem Begin and Anwar Sadat at Camp David that led to their signing an Egypt-Israel peace treaty the following year—ending the technical state of war between the two nations that had existed for the previous thirty years. (Wolfowitz was so impressed by Sadat's bravery and the quality of his speechmaking that he taught himself Arabic to "appreciate the valor of Sadat's speech in the original."[42]) And while Nixon and Kissinger had pioneered the opening to China, it was Jimmy Carter who officially normalized relations with Beijing in 1979. The positives in Carter's foreign-policy record, however, were largely obscured by events in Iran, Nicaragua, and Afghanistan. Ronald Reagan won a crushing victory in November 1980, winning 489 votes in the electoral college to Carter's 49 (of which 11 came from his home state of Georgia).

Reagan was the most conservative Republican presidential candidate since Barry Goldwater, and his victory suggested a major political realignment in the United States. George Kennan was initially unsure of what to make of Reagan's ascension. Although he abhorred the unsophisticated right wing of the Republican Party, he was more concerned by what he viewed as Jimmy Carter's reckless saber-rattling following the Soviet invasion of Afghanistan. In 1980 Kennan wrote, "Never since World War II has there been so far-reaching a militarization of thought and discourse in the capital. An unsuspecting stranger, plunged into its midst, could only conclude that the last hope of peaceful, nonmilitary solutions had been exhausted." Perhaps, Kennan mused, Reagan's campaigning bark would be worse than his governing bite—he could scarcely be more belligerent than Carter in the summer of 1980. Reagan's first presidential press conference swiftly disabused Kennan of this notion. Casting an eye over the Soviet leadership, Reagan informed the assembled press corps that "the only morality they recognize is what will further their cause, meaning they reserve unto themselves the right to commit any crime: to lie, to cheat, in order to attain that."[43] Kennan became a fierce critic of President Reagan's moral certainties, which he viewed as simplistic and dangerous.

In 1976, Paul Nitze and Eugene Rostow had formed a pressure group called the Committee on the Present Danger (CPD). The group was hostile to détente and positive that the Soviet Union was building an ominous strategic superiority in the field of nuclear weapons. Its membership included former treasury secretaries Henry H. Fowler and Charles Walker, and national security hawks Jeane Kirkpatrick, Norman Podhoretz, Richard Pipes, and Nitze himself. The CPD became a bane of Carter's presidency. After Carter and Brezhnev signed the SALT II treaty in June 1979, Nitze quickly mobilized the committee to block its ratification in the Senate. One concerned Carter adviser confided to *The Washington Post* that "Paul Nitze is worth 100 bureaucrats." Another staffer gamely observed, "Henry Kissinger we will have to stroke; Paul Nitze we will have to beat."[44]

Some chance. While the Soviet invasion of Afghanistan applied *estocada* to SALT II, Nitze's deftly managed lobbying effort had already mortally weakened the bill. The CPD was a highly effective advocacy organization, a shadow foreign-policy establishment in many respects, making it unsurprising when Reagan made so many national security appointments with a CPD affiliation. Richard Allen became national security adviser, William J. Casey became the director of Central Intelligence, Jeane Kirkpatrick became the U.S. ambassador to the United Nations, and Richard Pipes became a senior staff member on the National Security Council. Nitze returned to policy prominence as an arms control negotiator. The hawks had finally found their roost.

But finding a job for Wolfowitz proved problematic. He had worked for the Carter administration for too long and was viewed by some as guilty by association—just as Iklé had feared. Richard Allen again headed the president-elect's foreign policy advisory team and Wolfowitz's résumé worried him. His assessment was, "He was a goner, as far as I was concerned. He'd just been at the Pentagon. He had worked for Carter. I thought he was a Carter guy." John Lehman, a friend who had worked with Wolfowitz in the Nixon administration, urged Allen to look beyond happenstance, meet with Wolfowitz in person, and form his own opinion. Allen agreed, met with Wolfowitz, reversed course, and never again doubted his foreign-policy credentials.[45] He suggested that he become director of policy planning at State, and Wolfowitz gladly accepted.

On the Senate Foreign Relations Committee, Jesse Helms raised the same objections to Wolfowitz as he had to Nitze: He was a Democrat and hence soft on national security. Helms's colleagues convinced the elderly senator otherwise, however, and Wolfowitz assumed his position, hiring promising young scholars from America's elite universities, including Francis Fukuyama from Cornell and Zalmay Khalilzad, another former Telluride student, from Chicago. He also reached out to one of his former students at Yale, a conservative lawyer named I. Lewis "Scooter" Libby, and to the conservative African American activist (and Telluridian) Alan Keyes. While Wolfowitz's team also included moderates like Dennis Ross, who later served in the Clinton administration, and Stephen Sestanovich (yet another Cornell contemporary), there is no doubt that Wolfowitz, and the majority of his twenty-five-person staff, were on the hawkish, neo-Wilsonian end of the spectrum.

Wolfowitz's first year certainly proved as much. He led studies that challenged 1970s orthodoxies: the value of détente with Moscow, engagement with China, and the vital importance of resolving the Arab-Israeli conflict. So Wolfowitz argued that the United States did not need any arms control agreements with the Soviet Union *and* that their absence actually improved Washington's strategic position. He attempted with some success to stall a growing momentum in the State Department toward interacting meaningfully with the Palestinian Liberation Organization. He was a steadfast supporter of Israel and was strongly opposed to providing new military hardware to Saudi Arabia—such as the Airborne Warning and Control System (AWACS)—that might undermine Israeli military dominance. Finally, Wolfowitz repudiated Kissinger's assertion that the existence of a multipolar world made it essential that Washington engage respectfully with Beijing. Wolfowitz viewed the People's Republic of China as a repressive state devoted to upending the status quo in East Asia that America had devoted so many resources to underwriting. President Reagan's announcement of a massive arms buildup negated the supposed requirement that Beijing be cultivated as a counterweight against the Soviet Union. Even in the most hawkish presidential administration of the Cold War, Wolfowitz's PPS stood apart in its bellicosity and desire to challenge conventional wisdom.

On the issue of China, Wolfowitz clashed bitterly with Secretary of State Alexander M. Haig Jr., who had previously served as Kissinger's deputy at the NSC and who held no doubts about China's strategic importance to the United States in the Cold War. In the spring of 1982, Wolfowitz drafted a memo that strongly criticized Haig's State Department for making unnecessary concessions to China on the subject of arms sales to Taiwan. As Wolfowitz's biographer Lewis Solomon writes, "In view of the growing friction between the two, the Secretary of State snubbed other proposals for Wolfowitz's policy planning staff and attempted to cut them out of the communication loop."[46] Wolfowitz's willingness to push the envelope had turned out to be counterproductive—he lacked the bureaucratic guile of a Kissinger or a Nitze. In Scooter Libby's judgment, Wolfowitz's assemblage of conservative talent achieved virtually nothing that was concrete and enduring. In March 1982, *The New York Times* reported that Secretary Haig "has notified Paul D. Wolfowitz, the director of policy planning, that he will be replaced . . . Associates reported that Mr. Haig found Mr. Wolfowitz too theoretical."[47]

The Times was a little ahead of the mark, though it did accurately characterize Haig's basic view. But Haig's own problematic relationship with President Reagan—his high self-regard and thinly disguised desire to aggregate power at Foggy Bottom—led to the secretary of state's downfall in June. Reagan appointed George P. Shultz to replace him. Shultz, in turn, promoted Wolfowitz to become assistant secretary of state for East Asia and the Pacific. Through sheer good luck Wolfowitz had survived another day.

"Paul, this is an administrative job," Shultz cautioned. "It's not just thinking. It's a big area. You've got to get around, get to see a lot of people."[48] Wolfowitz had been given a wonderful opportunity to manage relations with a pivotal region. The job also required him to sharpen his bureaucratic acumen and relational skills and to better recognize when the gap between theory and reality was unbridgeable.

Ronald Reagan was a remarkable figure in many respects: a former B-movie actor, president of the Screen Actors Guild, Democrat, Goldwater protégé, governor of California, and devotee of supply-side economics and small government. He was also a presidential communicator par excellence.[49] Yet contemporary bipartisan consensus on Reagan's varied attributes—his virtually uncontested status as one of America's ten to fifteen "great" presidents—can obscure how polarizing a figure he was, particularly during his first few years in office. George Kennan certainly did not pull his punches when assessing the administration at the time, identifying in Reagan and his advisers a "childishness and primitivism" that could serve only to damage America's global standing. "I love certain old fashioned values and concepts," Kennan recorded in his diary, "but not *his*." While Kennan recognized that the Soviet Union was not averse to hawkish bluster, he queried whether it was really necessary for the United States to follow suit; dignified silence was surely more elegant *and* diplomatically astute. Politburo posturing was "as Russian as boiled cabbage and buckwheat kasha. But what about my own government and its state of blind militaristic hysteria?" Kennan's level of despair would sink below anything he had felt during the wretched Eisenhower-Dulles era, though at least he was not alone in finding serious fault with Reagan's foreign policies. "I am only a small part of the resistance in the U.S. to the madness of the present-Am[erican] administration," Kennan wrote hopefully in the spring of 1982.[50]

So how had the Reagan administration managed to rile Kennan quite so intensely? By offering a comprehensive repudiation of Kennan's strategy of containment. Eschewing the protocol diplomacy of civility and moderation, the president excoriated the Soviet Union as "the focus of evil in the modern world" during a speech to the National Association of Evangelicals in 1983. More substantively—and vexingly, from Kennan's Atlanticist perspective—Reagan offered military support to any insurgent group in the developing world dedicated to overthrowing a leftist government; the initiative that became known as the Reagan Doctrine.[51] Rather than "containing" communism behind the Iron Curtain, Reagan sought to extinguish it far beyond the European theater through supporting insurgencies in Nicaragua, Afghanistan, Angola, Cambodia, Mozambique, and Ethiopia.[52]

Allied to this rhetorical and proxy-supporting escalation of the Cold War was a vast increase in America's defense expenditures. In collaboration with Secretary of State Caspar Weinberger, Reagan set his first annual defense budget at $220 billion, the largest ever in peacetime. Reagan planned for annual increases in the budget of 7 percent, which ultimately led to the 1987 defense budget weighing in at a colossal $456.5 billion. He devoted significant resources to the B-1 stealth bomber, F-14 and F-15 fighter jets, and the new generation of MX intercontinental nuclear missiles.[53] And then in March 1983, Reagan announced the development of the Strategic Defense Initiative, a satellite based, laser-armed system designed to shoot down incoming nuclear missiles that was soon dubbed "Star Wars" by incredulous critics. Wolfowitz's friend and ally Richard Perle embraced the nickname. "Why not?" he asked. "It's a good movie. Besides, the good guys won."[54]

Wolfowitz applauded Reagan's rapid defense buildup and his willingness to lambast the Soviet Union on moral grounds—evil it assuredly was, why the fuss? But the aspect of Reagan's foreign policy that pleased him the most was his clearly stated desire to spread democracy. In a speech to the House of Commons, greeted enthusiastically by Prime Minister Margaret Thatcher and her front bench but more cautiously by the rest of the chamber, Reagan observed that democracy promotion was one of America's principal goals, proposing a concerted effort to "foster the infrastructure of democracy" the world over. One passage on the world's vast capacity for democratic enlargement must have sounded to Wolfowitz like the final movement of Beethoven's Ninth:

> This is not cultural imperialism, it is providing the means for genuine self-determination and protection for diversity. Democracy already flourishes in countries with very different cultures and historical experiences. It would be cultural condescension, or worse, to say that any people prefer dictatorship to democracy . . . Let us now begin a major effort to secure the best—a crusade for freedom that will engage the faith and fortitude of the next generation. For the sake of peace and justice, let us move toward a world in which all people are at last free to determine their own destiny.[55]

Reagan was deploying the Wilsonian language of democracy promotion—but applied without exception. According to Lou Cannon, a Reagan biographer, "The Westminster speech expressed more cogently than any other address of his presidency Reagan's belief that the forces of freedom would triumph over communism."[56] His words set off a chain of events that included the creation of the National Endowment for Democracy in November 1983—a nongovernmental organization funded by Congress devoted to supporting democratic institutions worldwide—and to a hardening of policy toward undemocratic but steadfast allies such as the Philippines, South Korea, and Taiwan.

This democracy-promoting yin was counterbalanced to some degree, however, by a realist yang. In 1979, Jeane Kirkpatrick published an influential article in *Commentary* titled "Dictatorships & Double Standards." While her preference in ideal conditions was the Wilsonian proliferation of virtuous democracies, Kirkpatrick cautioned that the Cold War world was not so simple. The article launched a strong attack on the Carter administration for pushing autocratic leaders, such as the shah in Iran and Anastasio Somoza in Nicaragua, to liberalize and democratize their governments too quickly. Kirkpatrick faulted Carter for encouraging far-reaching changes only in nations "under pressure from revolutionary guerrillas . . . We seem to accept the *status quo* in Communist nations (in the name of 'diversity' and national autonomy), but not in nations ruled by 'right-wing' dictators or white oligarchies." Here was the double standard of Kirkpatrick's title. Instead of pursuing laudable but self-defeating pipe dreams, she recommended that political leaders be patient with authoritarian governments that support U.S. policy. These regimes are more likely to evolve gradually in the direction of liberal democracy than Marxist-Leninist totalitarianism. Allied to this was Kirkpatrick's contempt for ahistorical wishful thinking. Wilsonianism was clearly the intended target:

> Although most governments in the world are, as they always have been, autocracies of one kind or another, no idea holds greater sway in the mind of educated Americans than the belief that it is possible to democratize governments, anytime, anywhere, under any circumstances . . . Decades, if not centuries, are normally required for people to acquire the necessary discipline and habits [of democracy].[57]

Kirkpatrick's article made an immediate impression on Reagan, who read it soon after publication and sent her a note expressing admiration for her logic. After assuming the presidency, Reagan appointed Kirkpatrick as ambassador to the United Nations, the first woman ever to serve in that position.

In 1983, Secretary of Defense Caspar Weinberger and CIA Director William Casey both urged Reagan to appoint Kirkpatrick his national security adviser, which would have been another first for a woman. Secretary of State Shultz persuaded Reagan otherwise, however, later observing, "I respected her intelligence, but she was not well suited to the job. Her strength was in her capacity for passionate advocacy." Shultz remarked that the role of national security adviser required the temperament of a "dispassionate broker," which he believed did not describe Kirkpatrick. He may have been right. But then again, few national security advisers have historically resembled dispassionate brokers, a criterion that certainly would have excluded Walt Rostow, Henry Kissinger, and Zbigniew Brzezinski from service. Perhaps the more likely explanation is that the path-breaking Kirkpatrick hit a glass ceiling. Yet while Kirkpatrick was prevented from hitting the heights, her distinction between useful right-wing and irredeemable left-wing versions of authoritarianism had a significant influence on the policies pursued by the Reagan administration, much to Wolfowitz's chagrin.[58]

One of Wolfowitz's primary goals at the State Department was to deploy U.S. influence in East Asia to compel various authoritarian governments—in the Philippines, South Korea, and Taiwan, most notably—to transition to democracy. In collaboration with Richard Armitage, based at the Pentagon, and Gaston Sigur, on the NSC staff—the so-called troika—Wolfowitz began to consider how democratic change might be effected. They began with the Philippines, where Ferdinand Marcos had led the nation in dictatorial style since 1965—and whose wife, Imelda, was known globally for her extravagant tastes and spending. They had quite a task ahead of them. When Vice President George W. Bush visited Manila in 1981, he told a glowing Marcos, "We love your adherence to democratic principles and democratic processes," a statement that rather underplayed his tendency to declare martial law whenever his regime was electorally threatened. When Jeane Kirkpatrick visited Manila a few years later, the savvy Marcos quoted verbatim from "Dictatorships & Double Standards" during a banquet toast. He thanked her ostentatiously for providing such a compelling rationale for continued U.S. support for anticommunist regimes such as his.[59]

Yet slowly but surely, aided by the support of Secretary of State George Shultz—who viewed the removal of Marcos as a strategic victory for Washington regardless of Wilsonian niceties—U.S. policy toward the Marcos regime hardened. In January 1985, Wolfowitz, accompanied by his aide Scooter Libby, traveled to Manila, where they met and encouraged Marcos's principal political opponents. During congressional testimony, Armitage and Wolfowitz stated their clear preference for policies that would apply pressure on Marcos to liberalize the political system of the Philippines. In late 1985, the opposition leader Corazon Aquino appeared to win a snap general election, but Marcos refused to accept the result. Washington soon learned that Aquino was the fair winner, and that Marcos was clinging to power through the traditional recourse to electoral fraud. Shultz urged Reagan to threaten to cut off military aid to Marcos if he continued to refuse to accept the popular verdict and step down.

Reagan agonized over this for a while—such a move certainly contradicted Jeane Kirkpatrick's theory—before following his secretary of state's counsel and dispatching the ultimatum. This led inevitably to the end of Ferdinand Marcos, who was flown out of the Philippines with his wife on an American Air Force plane. A precedent had been set. A year later, massive street demonstrations demanded the removal of Chun Doo Hwan's authoritarian government in South Korea. Reagan again urged the leader of a flailing, unloved autocracy to step aside and allow history—marching toward a liberal-democratic endpoint—to run its course.[60]

Henry Kissinger was distressed to witness the repudiation of yet another of his strategic maxims. Détente was a dead accented letter, balance-of-power diplomacy had been dismissed as anachronistic and contrary to American values, and now "better the devil you know" had been rent asunder. He attacked the Reagan administration for its democracy-promotion agenda: "Are there no other overriding American interests?" he asked despairingly. What would other American allies with an authoritarian coloring (and there were many) make of Reagan's shabby treatment of Marcos? "Whatever else may be said about the Marcos regime," wrote Kissinger, "it contributed substantially to American security and had been extolled by American presidents for nearly two decades." Kissinger closed his article by recording "grave concerns" about this Wilsonian resurgence.[61]

Wolfowitz held Kissinger's logic in contempt, for it highlighted a damaging paradox: "You can't use democracy, as you appropriately should, as a battle with the Soviet Union, and then turn around and be completely hypocritical about it when it's on your side of the line." Values and morality were an integral part of the struggle with the Soviet Union; the Cold War was nothing if not an ideological battle. The United States had to be on the side of the angels as often as possible.

Wolfowitz's aspirations were of course laudable, but they were applied inconsistently by the administration he served. In Chile, the Reagan administration continued to lend Augusto Pinochet's brutal regime its material and political support. U.S. policy toward El Salvador, Guatemala, Costa Rica, Honduras, and Nicaragua was sullied by egregious human rights abuses perpetrated by insurgent groups challenging leftist governments. These were ignored by the Reagan administration in the name of a wider anticommunist good, and people certainly noticed.[62] Wolfowitz's assertion that "the best antidote to communism is democracy" was catchy, but it failed to capture the full spread of the administration's foreign policies, which were often just as callous and amoral as those pursued during the Nixon-Kissinger era.[63]

Secretary of State Shultz appointed Wolfowitz to serve as the U.S. ambassador to Indonesia in 1986. It was a position Wolfowitz coveted for personal reasons; his wife, Clare, was an anthropologist with research interests there. But this was also an important nation in world affairs. Indonesia was the world's most populous Muslim country and had been a steadfast ally to the United States following the bloody rise in 1967 of Suharto, who ruled the nation until 1998 as a repressive anticommunist. Suharto was precisely the type of leader whom Jeane Kirkpatrick viewed as essential to U.S. interests. There was never any danger of the United States applying political pressure on Suharto à la Marcos—the strategic stakes were much higher. Nonetheless, Wolfowitz politely chided Suharto for failing to encourage greater "openness in the political sphere" and established a bond of friendship with Abdurrahman Wahid, a critic of Suharto who led one of Indonesia's largest Muslim political parties. One of the most notable aspects of Wolfowitz's stay in Jakarta, however, was the degree to which he imbibed Indonesian culture. As the historian Richard Immerman writes, "Over the next three years he learned the language; he studied the culture; he toured the neighborhoods. He even won a cooking contest."[64]

The three-year stint in Indonesia was an enriching period for Wolfowitz, clearly, but there was also a downside—he was far removed from the momentous events that occurred during the final two years of Reagan's presidency. In 1985, Mikhail Gorbachev became the general secretary of the Communist Party of the Soviet Union. His youth (he was fifty-four) and vigor cast Gorbachev in vivid contrast to the decrepit gerontocracy—Leonid Brezhnev, Yuri Andropov, and Konstantin Chernenko—that preceded him. Indeed, Ronald Reagan once joked, "How am I supposed to get anyplace with the Russians if they keep dying on me."[65] In 1986, a hale and hearty

Gorbachev announced a new policy of perestroika, roughly translated as "restructuring," designed to liberalize the Soviet economy and remedy deficiencies in regard to supply and demand. Gorbachev followed this up in more radical fashion in 1988 with glasnost, or "openness," which delivered on the promise of the Helsinki Accords, extending political freedoms, including freedom of speech, to the Soviet citizenry.

George Kennan was thrilled by Gorbachev's ascension but fretted that the Reagan administration was incapable of grasping this opportunity, just as Eisenhower had failed to act decisively following Stalin's death in 1953. In October 1986, Kennan recorded a diary entry that imagined him in conversation with this new leader: "You could give in to us on every point at issue in our negotiations; you would still encounter nothing but a stony hostility in official American circles; and your concessions would be exploited by the President as evidence that he had frightened you into compliance; and that the only language you understood was the language of force."[66]

Kennan was correct in one sense. Many conservatives did indeed attribute Gorbachev's shift in direction to the pressure Reagan applied on Moscow through the radical hike in U.S. defense spending and the launch of the SDI. But he was wrong in another. Reagan's actual response to Gorbachev's ascension was far removed from the "stony hostility" that Kennan feared inevitable.[67]

Over the course of a brief but historic encounter in Reykjavik, Iceland, in October 1986, Reagan and Gorbachev established sufficient trust to propose the elimination of *all* nuclear weapons by the year 2000.[68] The suggestion was quickly scuppered—to the relief of Prime Minister Margaret Thatcher and many within the administration—by Reagan's refusal to shelve the SDI program, which Gorbachev fairly pointed out was not in the spirit of things. That such an idea was even seriously discussed was remarkable all the same, and it paved the way for nuclear arms negotiations of a more substantive nature than SALT I. The 1987 INF (Intermediate-Range Nuclear Forces) Treaty was the first ever to deliver a real cut in the superpowers' nuclear arsenals: Moscow dismantled 1,836 missiles and the United States 859. This caused a predictable outcry from conservatives, among them Richard Perle, William Buckley, and Jesse Helms. Howard Phillips of the Conservative Caucus derided Reagan as "a useful idiot for Soviet propaganda."[69]

More to their liking was Reagan's rousing demand in front of Berlin's Brandenburg Gate in June 1987: "Mr. Gorbachev, open this gate! Mr. Gorbachev, tear down this wall!" Both Secretary of State George Shultz and

National Security Adviser Colin Powell had pleaded unsuccessfully with Reagan to delete these words, which they viewed as unnecessarily provocative in light of Gorbachev's moderation.[70] But "tear down this wall!" was an increasingly rare bit of cheer for the ideologues. Moscow and Washington cooperated in the UN Security Council on the issue of arranging a cease-fire in the Iran-Iraq War, East-West cultural exchanges proliferated, and Moscow raised the cap on Jewish emigration quotas. Gorbachev drew huge crowds of admirers when he visited the United States in December 1987, creating a phenomenon soon tagged "Gorby fever." In May 1988, Reagan visited Moscow, informing his hosts that his earlier characterization of the Soviet Union as an "evil empire" no longer held true.[71] Remarkable things stemmed from the warm personal relations that developed between the two men, described by Reagan as a "kind of chemistry."[72] Anatoly Dobrynin's laudatory assessment captures a truth: "Ultimately, Reagan's achievements in dealing with the Soviet Union could certainly compare favorably with, and perhaps even surpass, those of Richard Nixon and Henry Kissinger."[73] Reagan launched his political career by attacking détente as defeatist; it closed with his surpassing Henry Kissinger's most optimistic assessments of what dialogue with Moscow might achieve.

The year 1988 ended in remarkable fashion. On December 7, Gorbachev delivered a speech at the United Nations that had seismic repercussions. He began by conceding that Moscow—and thus Marxism-Leninism—had no monopoly on wisdom and truth, which was akin to the pope suggesting the Bible was fiction. He followed this remarkable admission of ideological doubt by declaring that the Soviet Union would not deploy military force as a means to achieve its aims and observed that his goal was much more modest than that of his predecessors—to attain "reasonable sufficiency for defense," which in practical terms meant demobilizing half a million troops from the Red Army. He ended by promising that Moscow would henceforth respect the right of all the constituent nations of the Warsaw Pact to self-determination: "the principle of freedom of choice is mandatory," he declared.[74] With remarkable grace and efficiency, Gorbachev had ended the Cold War—so far as he was concerned, at least.

So what had happened? Who deserved the acclaim? In a 1993 essay for the *National Review*, Wolfowitz identified Reagan's confrontational tactics as the catalyst for Gorbachev's radical reforms and Moscow's military retreat: "It is striking how many of Russia's new democrats give Ronald Reagan much of the credit for the Soviet collapse."[75] George Kennan believed that such extrapolations, common among Reagan's hawkish supporters, were illusory and indeed dangerous; the cause and effect, if any, was impossible to establish. As he observed to his friend the historian John Lukacs, "The suggestion that any American administration had the power to influence decisively the course of a tremendous political upheaval, in another great country on another side of the globe is intrinsically silly and childish."[76]

During a 1996 interview with John Lewis Gaddis—an admirer of Reagan's foreign policies—Kennan slightly revised his opinion. When Gaddis asked Kennan who had ended the Cold War, he predictably named Gorbachev. "But then he added," Gaddis recalled, "watching carefully to see whether his interviewer, who came close, would fall off his chair: 'also Ronald Reagan, who in his own inimitable way, probably not even being quite aware of what he was really doing, did what few other people would have been able to do in breaking this log jam.'"[77] Perhaps the truth was simply that Reagan's instincts were good at identifying something substantively different in Gorbachev compared to his predecessors.[78] The president sensed Soviet weakness during his first term and acted accordingly, and when he detected a meaningful change in direction in the second, he did the same. The fact that Reagan antagonized liberals *and* conservatives during his presidency certainly suggests the existence of a more flexible and pragmatic style than critics like Kennan, and indeed Kissinger, were capable of discerning. But Kennan's fundamental point, that Mikhail Gorbachev was the principal actor in the Cold War's final act—delivering the most important soliloquies—is a compelling one.

The election of 1988 pitted Reagan's experienced, cautious, and uncharismatic vice president, George H. W. Bush, against Michael Dukakis, a similarly stilted communicator whom the Bush campaign damned as the stereotypical Massachusetts liberal: weak on crime and foreign policy, with an unsteady grasp of economics. The Dukakis campaign did their candidate no favors when they arranged for him to be photographed atop an M1 Abrams tank. The contrast between Dukakis's strained gesture and the machine guns, the oversized helmet with MIKE DUKAKIS lettered on the front and the blue shirt–claret tie combo peeking through the khaki, created an iconic image of electoral desperation. The photo op failed to convince Americans that proximity to a tank made Dukakis a more plausible commander in chief—just as proximity to Henry Kissinger failed to do the same for Sarah Palin in 2008. Instead, Republicans used the Dukakis tank footage in devastating campaign advertisements, superimposing the words "America Can't Afford That Risk" underneath his grinning visage. The election was a blowout: Bush won 53.4 percent of the popular vote to Dukakis's 45.7 percent, which translated into a 426-to-111 victory in the electoral college. The fact that Bush won in Vermont, New Jersey, and Connecticut says it all.

George Kennan was glad to see the back of a presidential administration whose cant he abhorred. He declared himself delighted to have "new and more intelligent people in and around the White House," though he worried that the peaceable momentum with Gorbachev might be lost.[79] For his part, Paul Wolfowitz lamented Reagan's departure and was much more ambivalent about Bush than was Kennan. The new president nominated Dick Cheney, a colleague from the Ford administration, to serve as his secretary of defense. Cheney recalled Wolfowitz from Indonesia to serve as his undersecretary of defense for policy. In his memoir, *In My Time*, Cheney recalled, "Paul had the ability to offer new perspectives on old problems. He was also persistent. On more than one occasion, I sent him on his way after I had rejected a piece of advice or a policy suggestion, only to find him back in my office a half hour later continuing to press his point—and he was often right to do so."[80] They made a close and like-minded duo, but a clear ideological gap divided Cheney and Wolfowitz, the two most hawkish members of the Bush administration, from the rest of the national security team.

President Bush appointed Brent Scowcroft, a former deputy to Henry Kissinger who shared much of his former boss's worldview, to serve as his national security adviser. Bush nominated another realist-inclined figure, James A. Baker III, to serve as secretary of state. For these staffing reasons, Wolfowitz deliberated for a while before accepting Cheney's job offer. The man who gave Wolfowitz his first job in Washington, Fred Iklé, observed that his friend "hesitated a long time. He couldn't make up his mind. He talked about going back to academia."[81] Perhaps he remembered his marginality during the incommodious Nixon-Ford years and did not want to repeat the experience in his prime with another "moderate" Republican. Regardless, Wolfowitz's friends and colleagues convinced him to accept the job; the administration needed more men of conviction to counter the renascence of Kissingerian realism. His new job asked Wolfowitz to turn away from the multicultural vibrancy of Indonesia and refocus his intellectual energies on the regions and issues that had consumed him during the 1970s: arms control, forward planning, the Persian Gulf, and the wider Middle East.

On the first two of these issues, Cheney charged Wolfowitz with the task of reviewing defense policy in light of Gorbachev's historic actions through 1988. The report that emerged counseled caution with a simple justification— it was too early to ascertain with certainty what was actually happening within the Soviet Union. On April 4, 1989, George Kennan repudiated this caution during testimony before the Senate Foreign Relations Committee. In an effusive article for *The Washington Post*, titled "Kennan—A Prophet Honored," Mary McGrory depicted a remarkable scene:

> Grandeur on Capitol Hill? Yes, it sometimes happens. George F. Kennan, the world's greatest authority on the Soviet Union, appeared last week before the Senate Foreign Relations Committee and discoursed with such lucidity, learning and large-mindedness that the senators did not want to let him go. Kennan is 85 now. His back is as straight as a young man's, his jaw as chiseled. Only the cloudy voice bespeaks age. What made his appearance more remarkable was that the speaker was as grateful as the audience.[82]

Kennan's gratitude likely stemmed from the fact that he had been provided a high-profile forum from which to criticize present policy. His opening statement announced unequivocally that the Soviet Union was no longer a threat to American interests:

> What we are witnessing today in Russia is the breakup of much, if not all, of the system of power by which that country has been held together and governed since 1917 . . . The arsenals of nuclear weapons now in the possession of the Soviet Union and the United States are plainly vastly redundant in relation to the purpose they are supposed to serve . . . In summary, it appears to me that whatever reasons may once have been for regarding the Soviet Union primarily as a possible, if not probable, military opponent, the time for that sort of thing has clearly passed.[83]

So while some in the Bush administration had doubts about the sincerity and durability of Gorbachev's actions, Kennan had none. The committee and the audience rose at the end of Kennan's testimony to deliver a standing ovation. They liked his optimism and implicit message: the United States had won the Cold War because a weary Soviet Union had decided not to fight any longer. A month later the president declared his agreement. In a commencement address at Texas A&M University on May 13, Bush paid warm tribute to Kennan and the other architects of America's containment policy. Concurring with the gist of Kennan's testimony—rejecting the caution of Wolfowitz and others—Bush declared that it was time to move "beyond containment." "We seek the integration of the Soviet Union into the community of nations," he declared. "Ultimately, our objective is to welcome the Soviet Union back into the world order."[84] Outlining his general approach to foreign policy—and lack of interest in pursuing grandiose strategies— Bush had remarked in 1980, "I am a practical man. I like what's real. I'm not much for the airy and abstract. I like what works. I am not a mystic, and I do not yearn to lead a crusade."[85] For the first time in a long time, Kennan and a president were largely in sync.

The foreign-policy crisis that defined Bush's presidency for posterity was the Gulf War, which was either a model of diplomatic élan or a missed opportunity depending on one's point of view.[86] On August 2, 1990, Saddam Hussein ordered the invasion of Kuwait to forcibly wrest back a territory— and the oil reserves and access to the sea it provided—that he viewed as historically Iraq's. Saddam did not anticipate a strong American response, which perhaps was understandable. Eight days prior to the invasion, April Glaspie, the U.S. ambassador to Iraq, told him directly: "We have no opinion on your Arab-Arab conflicts, such as your dispute with Kuwait . . . I have direct instructions from President Bush to improve our relations with Iraq. We have considerable sympathy for your quest for higher oil prices, the immediate cause of your confrontation with Kuwait."[87]

The chairman of the Joint Chiefs of Staff, Colin Powell, appeared to confirm Saddam's confidence as well-founded the day after the invasion. He told General H. Norman Schwarzkopf, head of U.S. Central Command, "I think we'd go to war over Saudi Arabia, but I doubt we'd go to war over Kuwait." Powell was wrong. When he counseled caution during the first National Security Council meeting called to discuss the crisis, Dick Cheney slapped him down: "Colin, you're chairman of the Joint Chiefs. You're not secretary of state. You're not the national security adviser. And you're not secretary of defense. So stick to military matters."[88] Twelve years later, Colin Powell *was* secretary of state. And his call for caution in Iraq was similarly ignored, trailing off into the vacuum of inconsequence that separates Foggy Bottom from the White House.

Powell was out of step with idealists *and* realists on how to respond to

Iraq's aggression in the summer of 1990; his voice was a lonely one. Dick Cheney argued that Iraq's annexation of Kuwait had transformed the nation into the major oil power in the Middle East—a transformation that intolerably threatened U.S economic interests and the regional stability that sustained them. Brent Scowcroft and James Baker focused on what the former described as "the ramifications of the aggression on the emerging post–Cold War world."[89] The Soviet Union was no longer a threat to the United States, but for Washington to ignore this crisis was unthinkable. Its credibility as a guarantor and peacemaker would be seriously harmed, and this might embolden other second-tier adversaries. This was certainly the view of Prime Minister Margaret Thatcher, who famously urged President Bush "not to go wobbly" when America's prestige was so clearly at stake.[90] Paul Wolfowitz's Carter-era prophecies, meanwhile, had apparently been vindicated in dramatic fashion. Saddam Hussein was fulfilling the early bellicose promise that Wolfowitz had been the first to identify. With Powell the sole dissenting voice within the administration, some form of military intervention was never really in doubt. "This will not stand," President Bush declared, "this aggression against Kuwait."[91] Sensing the worst, as was his wont, George Kennan wrote on December 16, "Mr. Bush continues to entangle us all in a dreadful involvement in the Persian Gulf to which no favorable outcome is visible or even imaginable . . . At the moment, it is hard to see anything ahead but a military-political disaster."[92]

As it turned out, the president and his advisers managed the conflict more skillfully than Kennan could have imagined. The first thing Bush did in preparation for war was assemble a vast coalition to assist the United States in removing Iraq from Kuwait. Some partners, such as Japan and Germany, contributed treasure, not blood. Some, such as the Soviet Union, lent neither, but crucially did not oppose military action against a traditional ally of Moscow—real evidence that Gorbachev was true to his peacemaking word. Across the Middle East, Syria, Egypt, and Saudi Arabia all endorsed U.S. military action, while Israel, crucially, promised to hold fire in response to inevitable Iraqi missile attacks using outdated but dangerous Soviet-supplied Scuds. Convincing Israel of the need for patience, which Wolfowitz played a significant role in achieving through a series of trips to Tel Aviv, reduced the possibility of direct Israeli involvement, a wider war, and the destruction of the coalition. In total, President Bush assembled an alliance of nearly fifty nations to help wage and finance the war and secured a UN resolution authorizing the use of force. He also rejected Dick Cheney's advice that congressional authorization was unnecessary, winning a majority of 250 to 183 in the House and 52 to 47 in the Senate. The preparatory diplomacy was exemplary. So what of the military campaign itself?

Operation Desert Storm was launched on January 16, 1991, in dramatic style, with a devastating salvo of Tomahawk missiles and laser-guided bombs dropped by Stealth F-117 aircraft that targeted Iraq's air bases and electrical and communications networks. This aerial bombardment lasted until February 24, when forces from the U.S.-led coalition entered Kuwait from Saudi Arabia and engaged Iraqi troop concentrations. The land invasion spanned only one hundred hours, the time it took for the demoralized Iraqi army to cut, run, and concede defeat in the face of overwhelming odds—Goliath won this particular matchup. American fatalities amounted to just over one hundred, Iraqi losses numbered between twenty thousand and thirty-five thousand. This one-sided war was similar in its decisiveness to America's crushing defeat of Spain in 1898.

In advance of the cease-fire, tens of thousands of Iraqi troops fled Kuwait down the so-called highway of death. Colin Powell urged Schwarzkopf, for reasons of honor and civility, not to destroy these fleeing troops, as easy and as injurious to Saddam Hussein's rule as that would have been.[93] Secretary of State James Baker had a vivid recollection of Powell's objections to continuing the slaughter: "I remember Colin Powell saying with a trace of emotion, 'We're killing literally *thousands* of people.'"[94] Deputy National Security Adviser Robert Gates remembered "very clearly Colin Powell saying that this thing was turning into a massacre. And that to continue it beyond a certain point would be un-American, and he even used the word 'unchivalrous.'"[95] President Bush heeded Powell's advice and ordered the coalition forces to stand down.

Wolfowitz was unhappy that the war ended so swiftly, having fewer qualms than Powell—his lack of military experience might have limited his imagination—about strafing the departing Iraqi troops. He was certainly correct to a point in believing that a medium-scale slaughter might have prevented a larger one later. Wolfowitz's deputy, Scooter Libby, said, "We objected to it. I was floored by the decision. Neither of us liked it." But neither man was close enough to the action to make a difference. A few days after hostilities ceased, the CIA reported that many of Saddam's elite fighting forces, the Republican Guard, had escaped Kuwait with significant supplies: at least 365 Soviet T-72 tanks crossed back into Iraq, and an entire division, the Hammurabi, remained intact. General Schwarzkopf also granted a foolish concession to Iraq by permitting its helicopters to transport Iraqi officials across Kuwait and Iraq. Saddam ruthlessly exploited this loophole, ordering helicopter gunships to crush Shiite and Kurdish forces that were assembling to launch a revolution, encouraged by the earlier words of President Bush and Secretary Baker suggesting that they rise in revolt.

Wolfowitz observed, "Simply by delaying the ceasefire agreement— without killing more Iraqi troops or destroying more Iraqi military assets— the United States might have bought time for opposition to Saddam Hussein to build and to act against him."[96] But while delay appeared a savvy option with the benefit of hindsight, it was never actively considered at the time. Scowcroft and Baker believed that civil war in Iraq would have negative un-intended consequences, including a substantial strengthening of Iran's po-sition in the Middle East. Employing a rationale that Kissinger and Kennan would have cheered, Powell explained, "Our practical intention was to leave Baghdad enough power to survive as a threat to an Iran that remained bit-terly hostile toward the United States."[97]

As for an invasion of Iraq and the ouster of Saddam Hussein, this was viewed at the time as implausible: vexing in design and execution, and un-knowable in consequence. As Bush wrote in his memoir, coauthored with Scowcroft, "Had we gone the invasion route, the United States could con-ceivably still be an occupying power in a bitterly hostile land. It would have been a dramatically different—and perhaps barren—outcome."[98] Many hawkish Republicans, including the president's own son, would challenge this classically realist interpretation. Donald Rumsfeld, for example, presents a strong case against Bush-Scowcroft pragmatism: "For his part, Saddam Hussein came to believe that the United States lacked the commitment to follow through on its rhetoric. He saw America as unwilling to take the risks necessary for an invasion of Iraq."[99] But public opinion at the time in the United States and across the world saw things rather differently—the Gulf War was a resounding success for America and the coalition. Clear-cut aggression, the crossing of an established international border, had been met with a resolute response, sanctioned by the United Nations and carry-ing the crucial support of Moscow, Cairo, and Damascus. It was a remark-able achievement all considered. Rumsfeld's assessment was not so much written as bloated with hindsight. Nonetheless, Cheney, Rumsfeld, and Wolfowitz all learned a lesson that they applied to the Second Iraq War: Colin Powell and similarly risk-averse generals had to be detached from decision making.

On August 19, 1991, hard-line communists launched a coup against Mikhail Gorbachev, placing him under house arrest at his dacha in the Crimea and ordering tanks and infantry to assume strategic positions in Moscow. Boris Yeltsin became the focal point of resistance, famously standing atop a tank across from Russia's White House in a catalyzing act of defiance. The coup collapsed in the face of popular antipathy and Gorbachev returned to Moscow, though not in triumph. On August 21, Yeltsin requested that Gorbachev read a statement outlining details of the coup against him—a request that was hard to turn down in the circumstances. The following day, Gorbachev resigned as general secretary of the Soviet Communist Party, though he retained his position as the Soviet Union's titular president. Over the course of the next few months, Ukraine, Armenia, Georgia, and Moldova moved swiftly to secure their independence from Moscow. On December 8, political leaders from Russia, Ukraine, and Belarus met at Belovezh Forest, near Minsk, to form a Commonwealth of Independent States—others would soon join. On December 25, Gorbachev resigned as president of the Soviet Union. The Soviet Hammer and Sickle was lowered from the Kremlin and the blue, white, and red tricolor of the Russian Federation was raised to take its place. Boris Yeltsin was now assuredly in charge. The once solid Soviet Union had melted into air.

As Gorbachev departed office, he warned that something terrible had just happened to the United States—it had been deprived of an enemy.[100] A huge vacuum certainly had been created in the enemy column. It fell to Paul Wolfowitz, as undersecretary of defense for policy, to launch an effort to ascertain which nations were most likely to step up and take Moscow's place as the bad guy. In a speech in early 1992, Wolfowitz vowed to learn from the aftermath of earlier conflicts, when Washington downsized its military capabilities too quickly. "We've never done it right in the past," he complained. After securing victory in 1945, for example, the Truman administration had erred in cutting defense spending—Nitze's NSC-68 was prescient but arrived too late to swiftly repulse North Korea, resulting in a painful, protracted war: "It only took us five short years to go from having the strongest military establishment in the world, with no challengers, to having a force that was barely able to hang on to the Korean Peninsula against the attack of a fourth-rate country."[101] Wolfowitz's assessment underestimated the Red Army—enough of a "challenger" for Washington to essentially give up on Eastern Europe—but the gist of his message was clear. The lessons of history teach that the cashing of a "peace dividend" is invariably premature.

The United States should remain vigilant by normalizing the high levels of defense spending introduced by Reagan.

Like NSC-68, the Defense Policy Guidance (DPG) document of 1992 was a seminal statement of intent. Wolfowitz directed the study but delegated its drafting to Zalmay Khalilzad, who in turn took advice from Richard Perle, Albert Wohlstetter, and Scooter Libby.[102] The DPG resembled NSC-68 in that it was a collective enterprise inspired by the vision of one individual. It also assumed worst-case scenarios, emphasizing the necessity of the United States maintaining an insurmountable lead in military and power-projection capabilities. Someone in the Pentagon, desirous of a wider debate, leaked the document to the foreign-affairs journalist Patrick Tyler, who published excerpts in *The New York Times* on March 8, 1992. Tyler reported that the forty-six-page document stated, "America's political and military mission in the post-cold-war-era will be to insure that no rival superpower is allowed to emerge in Western Europe, Asia, or the territory of the former Soviet Union."[103]

The DPG offered a clear-cut repudiation of the collectivist aspirations of the United Nations—"ad hoc assemblies" was the preferred alliance model. This was the principal policy area where Wolfowitz disagreed fundamentally with Woodrow Wilson. The former feared that America's enemies would use a well-intentioned but dangerous institution like the UN to curtail the nation's freedom of action. Wilson was more hopeful that the proclivities and interests of nations could harmonize, instilling vitality and unity of purpose into his cherished League of Nations. He was more optimistic, ultimately, than Wolfowitz that the world could have a peaceable future. The DPG identified a whole series of threats to American interests: "European allies, Arab dictatorships, Muslim terrorists, resurgent Russians, Chinese and North Korean Communists, weapons proliferators," as George Packer described them.[104]

In reference to the ominous threat posed by hostile nations with weapons of mass destruction, the DPG detailed the potential necessity of "preempting an impending attack with nuclear, chemical or biological weapons." The report jarred with Colin Powell's more sanguine state of mind—he joked during a contemporaneous interview with the *Army Times*: "I'm running out of demons. I'm running out of villains, I'm down to Castro and Kim Il-Sung . . . I would be very surprised if another Iraq occurred."[105]

Tyler's article provoked outrage among America's allies, who were not thrilled at the vassal status bestowed on them by Wolfowitz and his colleagues. The reaction from old-school Republicans and mainstream

Democrats was similarly hostile. Pat Buchanan, a retrenchment-inclined Republican who struggled to identify many "good" wars in American history, observed that the DPG was "a formula for endless American intervention in quarrels and war when no vital interest of the United States is remotely engaged." He urged Bush, whom he was challenging for the GOP presidential nomination, to disown it. George Stephanopoulos, an influential adviser to the fast-rising Democrat Bill Clinton, described the draft as "one more attempt to find an excuse for big budgets instead of downsizing." Bush's national security adviser, Brent Scowcroft, later remarked of the DPG: "That was just nutty. I read a draft of it. I thought, 'Cheney, this is just kooky.' It didn't go anywhere. It was never formally reviewed."[106] Scowcroft is correct on the absence of presidential imprimatur but wrong to observe that it "didn't go anywhere." It went through various drafts and emerged as a remarkable and durable strategy document. On May 5, 1992, Wolfowitz sent the final draft to Dick Cheney and added a PS: "We have never had a defense guidance this ambitious before."[107] While the document fell into partial abeyance for eight years, the next President Bush resuscitated it. And his administration would reintroduce the idealistic Wilsonian dimension that Wolfowitz felt was lacking in the original DPG drafts: a strong emphasis on America's role in fostering democratization.[108]

The election of 1992 pitted the incumbent Bush against Bill Clinton, a charismatic and politically gifted former governor of Arkansas. For James Carville, a key Clinton adviser, the election was about one thing, "It's the economy, stupid," and his reductionism was apposite—Clinton won the election largely on those terms, aided by the candidacy of the center-right third-party candidate Ross Perot, who siphoned votes from the unfortunate Bush. But foreign policy did figure significantly in the campaign—how could it not, just one year after the collapse of the Soviet Union?—and many Wilsonians on both sides of the political aisle found that there was much to like about Clinton. For starters, Clinton criticized Bush's narrow realism on multiple fronts. He accused Bush of issuing a weak, un-American response to the Tiananmen Square massacre of 1989, when Chinese troops attacked prodemocracy demonstrators in Beijing, and across the nation, killing hundreds and injuring thousands. He attacked Bush for failing to engage seriously with the looming crisis in the former Yugoslavia, where Slobodan Milošević's Serbia posed a serious threat to regional stability, and whose army had Bosnia's Muslim population in its sights. Clinton believed that James Baker's callous assessment of the crisis in the Balkans—"We don't have a dog in that fight"—revealed a distressing truth about the Bush administration's human rights deficiencies.

Wolfowitz was sympathetic to the sweep of Clinton's critique of Bush, as his appraisal of the Bush administration attests:

> That impressive victory [in Iraq], coming on top of the victory in the Cold War, contributed to a widespread feeling that the United States no longer faced serious dangers in the world or else that the problems we faced could be handled by a newly invigorated United Nations. Rhetoric from the administration about "A New World Order"—or comments that we had "no dog" in fights such as those in the former Yugoslavia—did nothing to counter that complacency.[109]

But while he found Bush's foreign policies largely wanting, Wolfowitz had learned a painful lesson in the Carter era: it was difficult to work for a Democrat without burning bridges with the GOP. And besides, Clinton could criticize Bush's timidity all he wanted on the campaign trail. The real test was how he would act in office. Wolfowitz doubted, with good reason, that Clinton was nearly as hawkish and values-led as he appeared. So he left the Pentagon and took up the position of dean of the Johns Hopkins School of Advanced International Studies. The policy school that Paul Nitze had cofounded was an appropriate place for Wolfowitz to begin his assault on an irresolute Democratic president. He began assailing Clinton's foreign policies on largely the same grounds as Clinton had attacked those of Bush.

Clinton was the first Democratic president in twelve years, and he was acutely conscious of how Jimmy Carter's presidency had unraveled in the face of geopolitical calamities with which his divided advisory team had failed to cope. Clinton's foreign-policy team all had clear memories of that period. Secretary of State Warren Christopher had served as Cyrus Vance's deputy at the State Department. Clinton's national security adviser, Tony Lake, had been Carter's chair of policy planning. Madeleine Albright, Clinton's ambassador to the United Nations and later Christopher's successor as secretary of state, had worked in Carter's NSC as a congressional liaison under the direction of her Columbia Ph.D. supervisor, Zbigniew Brzezinski. Christopher, Lake, and Albright all understood that Clinton's diplomacy needed to display far greater unity of purpose than Carter's. So with this consideration in mind, Clinton's foreign-policy team began to search for a new name to define America's post–Cold War approach to world affairs—a process that they jokingly described as the "Kennan sweepstakes."[110] Secretary of State Christopher solicited advice from the source in 1994, when he asked Kennan what he thought of their quest. Kennan replied that "containment" had misled as much as it illuminated, and that a nation's foreign policy could not be reduced to fit onto a "bumper sticker." Clinton laughed when he learned of Kennan's response, observing, "That's why Kennan's a great diplomat and scholar but not a politician."[111]

But was Kennan so wrong? His cautionary words regarding single-word reductions and monotheories could also be construed as sound *political* advice. Clinton's foreign policies proved to be multifaceted and irreducible to a single word or concept. How could they be otherwise in the absence of an enemy like the Soviet Union? One theme emphasized repeatedly was the necessity for "democratic enlargement"—that the United States (and NATO) should extend security and political commitments to the emerging democracies in Eastern and Central Europe. A renewed dedication to free and open trade was also stressed as vital. On January 1, 1994, Clinton presided over the creation of a North American Free Trade Agreement (NAFTA) among Canada, the United States, and Mexico. So far, so Wilsonian. The collapse of the Soviet Union was akin to the collapse of the Habsburg Empire. Clinton, like Wilson, welcomed a significant increase in the number of independent nation-states and encouraged their long-suppressed democratic aspirations.

But purposeful American leadership of this democratically enlarged and economically liberalized world was taken as given. There would be no ceding of U.S. sovereignty in the manner Wilson envisioned in 1918. Bill Clinton did not view the United Nations as a practicable conduit through which to realize specific U.S. goals or, indeed, to keep the peace more generally—here Clinton hewed more closely to Mahan and Wolfowitz than to Wilson. Clinton promised to lead "an America with the world's strongest defense, ready and willing to use force when necessary."[112] During Clinton's second term, Secretary of State Albright declared herself comfortable "with the projection of American power." She pointedly observed that the historical analogy that motivated her worldview took place in the 1930s, not the 1960s: "My mind-set is Munich; most of my generation's is Vietnam. I saw what happened when a dictator was allowed to take over a piece of a country and the country went down the tubes. And I saw the opposite during the war when America joined the fight. For me, America is really, truly, the indispensable nation." Wolfowitz thrilled to Albright's words, observing that she "represents the best instincts of this administration on foreign policy."[113] Indeed, the Clinton administration appeared to be following the recommendations presented in the controversial 1992 DPG. Defense spending scarcely dipped in real terms from Reagan-era levels, the maintenance of primacy remained the principal goal, and the United States reserved the right to undertake unilateral action when necessary to protect its interests or right wrongs.

These sentiments were borne out in practice. In 1999, for example, the United States spearheaded NATO air strikes against Slobodan Milošević's Serbia to defend Kosovo against a brutal assault motivated by ethnic cleansing. The UN was not willing to authorize such an action, due to Russian objections, so Clinton operated through NATO instead. Serbia eventually desisted and Milošević's odious regime collapsed—a win on multiple levels. But the United States had indeed acted as "the indispensable nation" in sidestepping the UN when it deemed action necessary. And most allies, such as Prime Minister Tony Blair, recognized and encouraged this reality. Much of Clinton's foreign policy vindicated a document that roused such ire upon its publication in 1992. The playing was different—Clinton favored pianissimo; Wolfowitz, forte—but the notation was largely the same.

Yet Wolfowitz did identify serious flaws in the Clinton administration's policies toward other regions. First among them was Saddam Hussein's sullen and resentful Iraq, where Clinton's containment strategy relied on the enforcement of no-fly zones through intermittent air strikes and the maintenance of stringent UN sanctions. Wolfowitz viewed this combination as not up to the task of applying sufficient pressure on Saddam Hussein. In a widely discussed article in *The Wall Street Journal* in 1996, with the attention-grabbing title "Clinton's Bay of Pigs," Wolfowitz accused Clinton of neglecting the growing threat posed by Saddam. This was manifested in Iraq's invasion of a Kurdish "safe zone" in northern Iraq in August 1996 and a dishearteningly weak U.S. military response in the form of ineffectual cruise missile strikes. Wolfowitz lambasted the "pinprick" Tomahawk attacks favored by Clinton and accused the administration of "betraying" the Kurds in permitting Iraqi forces to strike northward against that restive region with impunity.

This was clearly bad news for America's reputation as a guarantor, and for its hard-won reputation as a military power without equal, but it also emboldened Saddam, whose military might pose a threat to the United States itself. Wolfowitz believed the stakes in Iraq could scarcely be higher: "Saddam is a convicted killer still in possession of a loaded gun—and it's pointed at us." Here was one of the first public references to Saddam's chemical and bacteriological weapons programs, and the potential that he might either use them against the United States or sell or gift them to a terrorist organization to do the same. As Derek Chollet and James Goldgeiger write, Wolfowitz urged Clinton to "go beyond the containment strategy and confront the Iraqi dictator once and for all."[114]

In the general election of 1996, Wolfowitz served as an adviser to the aged Republican candidate, Bob Dole. Iraq turned out to be one area where clear daylight could be detected between the candidates. While campaigning for Dole, Wolfowitz remarked to a reporter, "The U.S. has virtually abandoned its commitment to protect a besieged people from a bloodthirsty dictator."[115] But Dole and Wolfowitz struggled to land any meaningful blows on Clinton. Dole's campaign staked out positions that were considerably more hawkish than those of George H. W. Bush—the need for developing a missile defense system and his implacable hostility to the United Nations. But in the realm of foreign policy, Clinton's first term had been largely devoid of Carter-like disasters.

There had been some wretched moments, certainly. During a calamitous UN-sanctioned intervention in Somalia in October 1993, two U.S. Black Hawk helicopters were shot down and a brutal gunfight ensued on the streets of Mogadishu in which eighteen Americans and hundreds, perhaps thousands, of Somalis died.[116] This was a human tragedy and a public relations disaster—footage of American corpses being dragged down Mogadishu streets were relayed on cable news. This episode had a major impact on Clinton's willingness to deploy the nation's military in areas that George Kennan viewed as peripheral. Indeed, Kennan had warned against intervention in Somalia in December 1992:

> I regard this move as a dreadful error of American policy . . . The dispatch of American armed forces to a seat of operations in a place far from our own shores, and this for what is actually a major police action in another country and in a situation where no defensive American interest is involved—this, obviously, is something that the founding fathers of this country never envisaged or would ever have approved. If this is in the American tradition, then it is a very recent tradition.[117]

The debacle in Somalia was sufficient to relieve the Clinton administration of any latent impulse toward humanitarian intervention.

This became clear when the administration averted its gaze—for open eyes might have meant acting—from a well-documented genocide in Rwanda, when between five hundred thousand and one million Rwandans, mainly from the minority Tutsi ethnic group, were slaughtered by the Hutu majority.[118] Four years later, Clinton traveled to Kigali, Rwanda's capital city, and apologized for failing to act.[119] But there was no need to issue an apology to the American public. These dark episodes scarcely registered with the electorate in 1996. Somalia and Rwanda were two of the poorest nations in the world—what happened there clearly had little bearing on the United States' economic interests or indeed its prestige and credibility. The end of the Cold War had sharply reduced the attention that strategists afforded the poor nations (Angola, for example, interested Henry Kissinger only as a proxy, mineral-rich battleground.) With the technology bubble still in the inflating phase, the U.S. economy was motoring. Clinton was well liked by centrist voters, and Dole proved to be an uninspiring candidate. Clinton comfortably secured his reelection. It turned out that he didn't need a grand strategy that fit onto a bumper sticker.

Wolfowitz was profoundly disappointed that Dole had lost the election, his defeat hastened by the peripheral part that foreign affairs played in the overall outcome. He and Dole had certainly found it difficult to land significant blows on Clinton for being weak on national security in the absence of serious geopolitical threats. U.S. elections are not won or lost on the fate of the Kurds, Rwandans, Bosnians, or Kosovars. During the Cold War, the draft-dodging Clinton would likely have been easy prey for a decorated World War II veteran like Dole, who had only narrowly avoided death in 1945 after being seriously wounded by German machine gun fire. But times had changed, as the GOP foreign-policy establishment well understood.

The problem may have been complexity. The bipolar Cold War era often rewarded leaders with a Manichaean sensibility. The post–Cold War world did not. Gorbachev's warning that he had done a terrible thing to the United States by depriving it of an enemy lacked specificity. It turned out that the GOP was the damaged party. A relatively placid international environment certainly helped Clinton defeat George H. W. Bush—also a decorated World War II veteran, and with a formidable foreign-policy record—and Dole in successive elections. Voters traditionally favored the GOP over the Democrats to better protect national security. The end of the Cold War had neutralized this advantage.

Wolfowitz responded to this challenge by focusing most of his energies on a single enemy, Iraq, and by broadening the range of his ambition. In 1997, he wrote a chapter for an edited book, *The Future of Iraq*, in which he detailed three possible ways to deal with Saddam Hussein: containment, engagement, or replacement. Wolfowitz argued strongly for the final option, though he did not spell out what this might entail.[120] He followed this up with an article coauthored with his long-standing collaborator Zalmay Khalilzad titled "Overthrow Him." Wolfowitz and Khalilzad identified the primary strategic lesson of the Gulf War, "Military force is not enough," instead stating that a broad and effective U.S. policy toward Iraq "must be part of an overall political strategy that sets as its goal not merely the containment of Saddam but the liberation of Iraq from his tyranny."[121] In the absence of the Soviet Union, overthrowing Saddam Hussein and liberating Iraq became Wolfowitz's idée fixe.

That same year, Wolfowitz joined other hawkish Republicans declaring intellectual allegiance to the Project for the New American Century (PNAC), a think tank in Washington, D.C., founded by William Kristol and Robert Kagan. It released its Statement of Principles on June 3, 1997. The statement revealed a political party in deep dialogue with itself—rattled by Clinton's success in winning two consecutive elections—about its future foreign-policy direction:

> American foreign and defense policy is adrift. Conservatives have criticized the incoherent policies of the Clinton Administration. They have also resisted isolationist impulses from within their own ranks. But conservatives have not confidently advanced a strategic vision of America's role in the world. They have not set forth guiding principles for American foreign policy . . . We seem to have forgotten the essential elements of the Reagan Administration's success: a military that is strong and ready to meet both present and future challenges; a foreign policy that boldly and purposefully promotes American principles abroad; and national leadership that accepts the United States' global responsibilities.[122]

The Statement of Principles was a rousing declaration of allegiance to the style and substance of Ronald Reagan's first term in office, although it was short on policy specifics. Among the statement's signatories were Elliot Abrams, Dick Cheney, Eliot A. Cohen, Francis Fukuyama, Fred Iklé, Zalmay Khalilzad, Scooter Libby, Donald Rumsfeld, and Paul Wolfowitz—the shadow foreign-policy establishment.

Some of the specifics were fleshed out on January 26, 1998, when PNAC published an open letter to Bill Clinton, urging a change in U.S. policy toward Saddam Hussein's Iraq. The signatories rendered their concerns in simple prose, writing that the "current policy, which depends for its success upon the steadfastness of our coalition partners and upon the cooperation of Saddam Hussein, is dangerously inadequate." President Clinton needed to open his eyes to the fact that Iraq was working assiduously to develop weapons of mass destruction, which could destabilize the region and indeed the world. "It hardly needs to be added," stated the authors darkly, "that if Saddam does acquire the capability to deliver weapons of mass destruction, as he is almost certain to do if we continue along the present course, the safety of American troops in the region, of our friends and allies like Israel and the moderate Arab states, and a significant portion of the world's supply of oil will all be put at hazard."[123] After the letter was published, a small selection of its signatories, including Wolfowitz, Richard Perle, and Donald Rumsfeld, traveled to the White House to discuss Iraq with Clinton's national security adviser, Sandy Berger. After the meeting, Perle declared that he was "appalled at the feebleness of the Clinton administration."[124]

The clock was ticking on Bill Clinton's presidency, however. During 1998, the GOP foreign-policy brain trust began surveying the field in earnest to identify (and tutor) the Republican most likely to defeat Al Gore—Clinton's vice president, who was all but certain to win his party's nomination—in 2000. In the spring of 1998, the governor of Texas, George W. Bush, visited Stanford University's Hoover Institution to discuss foreign policy with an illustrious group that included George Shultz and Condoleezza Rice, Stanford's provost, who had worked for Bush's father and had coauthored a well-received book on the reunification of Germany with the University of Virginia's Philip D. Zelikow.[125] The meeting went well, with Bush and Rice striking up a rapport based on a common love of sports. A follow-up meeting was scheduled in Austin a few months later. Joining Bush, Rice, and Shultz in the heat of July were Dick Cheney—then head of the Halliburton Corporation, a vast oil field services company with a staff in excess of fifty thousand—and Wolfowitz. Bush informed the gathering that he was planning to run for the presidency and he wanted their help.

Bush was not uniformly popular across the GOP. Many preferred Senator John McCain, who had accumulated significant foreign-policy experience and whose willingness to deploy the U.S. military for humanitarian purposes had been broadly consistent. William Kristol warned his colleagues that "getting in bed with Bush" would be a mistake.[126] Kristol feared that Bush Jr. might turn out to be just as cautious and centrist as his father. And besides, he evinced no particular interest in foreign affairs and had accumulated no great accomplishments either in his business career—which was largely bankrolled by an indulgent father—or his political career, which was necessarily devoted to the sizable if parochial matter of governing Texas. Arizona's John McCain, with his thirteen years in the Senate as of 2000, was a titan compared to Bush. On nearly every level—intellect, experience, valor— McCain appeared the superior candidate. McCain had spent five and a half years as a prisoner of war in Vietnam, two of them in solitary confinement. Bush accepted a commission to the Texas Air National Guard and saw no active service. McCain had won over many neo-Wilsonian Republicans when he supported President Clinton's air strikes on Serbia to protect Kosovo. He was a man of principle and experience. William Kristol's choice was clear: "I preferred McCain, and Kosovo was what did it for me, where he bucked a large chunk of the Republican party."[127]

Others detected a lot more potential in Bush, largely because he was unafraid of declaring his own foreign-policy ignorance and asking simple exploratory questions. They discerned no overbearing ego and little of the bluster often commonplace among the politically ambitious. Richard Perle viewed Bush as an endearing tabula rasa, observing that he "didn't know very much . . . [but] had the confidence to ask questions that revealed he didn't know very much . . . He was eager to learn . . . You got the sense that if he believed something, he'd pursue [it] tenaciously."[128] Wolfowitz was even more enthusiastic. According to Jacob Heilbrunn, "In August 1999 an excited Wolfowitz told me over lunch at I Ricchi restaurant in Washington, D.C., that Bush had the ability to penetrate the dense fog of foreign-policy expertise to ask a simple question, 'Tell me what I need to know?' Bush, Wolfowitz said, was 'another Scoop Jackson.' "[129] So Perle and Wolfowitz both hailed Bush for his willingness to declare his own ignorance—a rare trait in Washington, admittedly—and seek advice from the likes of them. Put in those terms, Bush's appeal is not hard to comprehend.

Working alongside Condoleezza Rice, Wolfowitz became one of Bush's two principal foreign-policy advisers throughout the primaries and the campaign. Yet it was Rice, not Wolfowitz, who forged a closer bond with Bush. According to James Mann, Bush had distrusted bona fide intellectuals since his raucous undergraduate days at Yale (which made Paul Nitze's Harvard experience appear monastic in comparison). Condoleezza Rice was an intellectual, sure, but she could talk baseball, football, and basketball. She had the knack of making Bush feel at ease, which helped her immensely when it came to taking Bush through a crash course in international relations. Rice was close to Bush's father and viewed the arch-realist Brent

Scowcroft as her principal mentor. Her diplomatic worldview was quite different from Wolfowitz's, meaning her ascendancy had clear implications for the candidate's core foreign-policy message—which subsequently tended toward caution, not idealism. During the second presidential debate with Al Gore, Bush chided his opponent for his Wilsonianism. "The vice president and I have a disagreement about the use of troops," Bush said. "He believes in nation building. I would be very careful about using our troops as nation builders. I believe the role of the military is to fight and win war . . . I don't want to try to put our troops in all places at all times. I don't want to be the world's policeman."[130]

This was discouraging to Wolfowitz, needless to say. The policies he liked—such as Bush's dedication to building an effective national missile defense program and a willingness to abandon the 1972 ABM treaty—were being drowned out by realist mood music conducted by the multitalented Rice (who was a concert pianist as well as an academic). In the general election of 2000, Al Gore won a majority of the popular vote but eventually lost due to the vagaries of the electoral college and the nation's judicial system. In *Bush v. Gore*, the Supreme Court halted a protracted recount that was taking place in Florida, caused by myriad voting irregularities, and declared Bush the winner by a narrow majority of 271 to 266 electoral votes. It was one of the most controversial episodes in America's modern political history. Bush was president, but he lacked the legitimacy that accompanied a clear victory at the polls. When one combines this fact with Bush's openly expressed dedication to what he described as "compassionate conservatism," one might have expected Bush 43 to be a retread of Bush 41—with added humility and a renewed dedication to bipartisanship.

Wolfowitz's service to the Bush administration began inauspiciously when he failed to land the job he coveted: secretary of defense. His reputation as an original thinker and hopeless administrator endured. One high-ranking colleague observed, "Paul is a brilliant guy, but when you went down to his office . . . you couldn't even find Paul, the papers were piled so high."[131] Working habits like these more or less precluded his running a behemoth like the Pentagon. So Wolfowitz instead lobbied for what he viewed as the next best alternative, deputy secretary of state. This time Colin Powell, whom Bush had announced as his choice for secretary of state on December 16, 2000, intervened to block his path. Powell had described Cheney and Wolfowitz in his memoir as "right-wing nuts."[132] This was evidently a working relationship that never stood much of a chance, though Powell later described their incompatibility more judiciously in observing that they were not "ideologically in gear."[133] So Wolfowitz was eventually appointed to serve as deputy secretary of defense under Donald Rumsfeld—who was not entirely thrilled himself:

> I knew Wolfowitz would be an unusual pick. He did not have an industry background or deep management experience traditional for successful deputy secretaries of defense. I worried that a man with such an inquisitive, fine mind and strong policy instincts might not take well to many of the crucial but often mundane managerial duties—making the hundreds of nonpolicy related decisions—that would come with the deputy post.[134]

It is no challenge to comprehend Rumsfeld's unease. Wolfowitz was an ambitious thinker driven by a grand Wilsonian vision of what American power might achieve if deployed in an appropriately ambitious manner. Rumsfeld was a hard-hitter with a narrower conception of what his nation owed the world. But in spite of their differences, they became a potent combination. Colin Powell certainly came to regret their coming together. Perhaps he should have welcomed Wolfowitz to State and kept his ideological enemy close.

The Senate confirmed Wolfowitz's appointment unanimously after an illuminating hearing in which he clearly established his priorities. On the Middle East, he observed that the "whole region would be a safer place, Iraq would be a much more successful country, and the American national interest would benefit greatly if there were a change of regime in Iraq."[135] He quickly pushed the Joint Chiefs of Staff on how the United States might assist opposition groups in Iraq. As Saddam Hussein had ordered the draining of Iraq's southern marshes to deny Shiite rebels a safe haven, Wolfowitz asked the military brass if air strikes could destroy dams to flood the region and re-create them. Lawyers in the Pentagon stymied Wolfowitz's proposal as being inconsistent with "the rules of war." Wolfowitz countered that reinstating a sanctuary for Saddam's opponents was quite clearly a "humane" option.[136]

Wolfowitz appointed Douglas Feith, whose views on Iraq closely mirrored his own, as his deputy. Feith was even less organized than Wolfowitz, according to his critics, and was a believer in the necessity of deposing Saddam Hussein come what may—to the frustration of many in the military. General Tommy Franks, commander of the United States Central Command, memorably described Feith as "the stupidest fucking guy on the planet."[137] Colin Powell was more temperate in his language but, like Franks, he did not share Wolfowitz and Feith's obsession with Saddam Hussein. During his own confirmation hearings, Powell had observed that the sanctions against Iraq should be strengthened but a change of regime was not essential: "As long as we are able to control the major source of money going into Iraq, we can keep them in the rather broken condition that they are in now. Mr. Saddam Hussein can put a hat on his head and shoot a rifle in the air at an Army Day parade, but it is fundamentally a broken, weak country ... His only tool, the only thing he can scare us with are those weapons of mass destruction, and we have to hold him to account."[138] Powell was clear that this would be achieved through enhanced sanctions and the return of UN weapons inspectors. State and Defense were not on the same page. They were not even reading the same book.

Wolfowitz was broadly impressed by the first eight months of the Bush presidency. Bush withdrew the United States from the 1972 ABM treaty and moved forward with the development of a national missile defense program, resurrecting Reagan-era hopes of invulnerability to missile attack. He immediately repudiated Clinton's engagement policy and unveiled a hard line toward North Korea, undermining Seoul's so-called sunshine policy of courting Pyongyang with the prospect of greater economic interaction. On a personal level, Wolfowitz grew ever more admiring of Bush's simple, direct style. During a discussion about the relative merits of economic interests— focused engagement versus principled opposition to an authoritarian regime, Wolfowitz recalled (although he did not disclose the identity of the nations under discussion) that Bush interjected with real moral clarity: "We're talking about them as though they were members of the Chevy Chase Country Club. What are they really like? ... How brutal are these people?"[139] In Wolfowitz's opinion, Bush's words brought to mind Reagan at his best.

But there was an unevenness in implementation similar to Reagan's when it came to human rights. Bush declined to condemn Egypt's Hosni Mubarak, or Pakistan's Pervez Musharraf, or indeed China's leadership for their many human rights deficiencies. Bush's favorable snap appraisal of Russia's increasingly hard-line president, Vladimir Putin—"I looked the man in his eye. I found him to be very straightforward and trustworthy ... I was able to get a sense of his soul"—appeared alarmingly naïve to close observers of Putin and Russia.[140] Bush also contravened one of the central tenets of the 1992 DPG when he privileged a $1.2 trillion tax cut ahead of increased defense spending. William Kristol's *The Weekly Standard*, the most influential conservative weekly in Washington, editorialized that Rumsfeld and Wolfowitz should resign.[141] This was a particularly painful episode for Wolfowitz, who was one of the staunchest advocates of military prepared-ness in Washington.

One issue that was very much on Bill Clinton's radar when he departed office, but that appeared not to elicit the same interest in Bush, was the grow-ing threat posed by al-Qaeda, a global terrorist network dedicated to con-fronting Western encroachments in the Muslim world and, ultimately, to the establishment of a global Islamic caliphate. In 1993, Ramzi Yousef, an al-Qaeda operative, had detonated a truck bomb in the basement of tower one of the World Trade Center in New York City. Yousef's plan was that one tower would fall onto the other, killing upwards of 250,000 people. But the World Trade Center absorbed the explosion and the attack killed only 9. In August 1998, al-Qaeda claimed responsibility for simultaneous bomb attacks on the U.S. embassies in Nairobi, Kenya, and Dar es Salaam, Tanzania, which killed 223 and injured more than 4,000. Two years later, al-Qaeda militants used a small vessel loaded with explosives to launch a suicide attack on the USS *Cole*, docked in Aden, Yemen. The blast ripped through the ship's gal-ley, killing 17 and injuring 39. On December 19, 2000, Clinton met Bush in the White House and asked if his campaign literature was correct—that his two primary foreign-policy priorities were national missile defense and regime change in Iraq. When Bush replied yes, Clinton suggested that he instead address a wider range of challenges, with al-Qaeda at the top.[142]

Bush did not reply to Clinton, but he and Wolfowitz clearly did not share Clinton's concerns with stateless Islamist terrorism. During a depu-ties meeting on April 30, 2001, Wolfowitz pushed hard against those who identified terrorism as a major threat: "Well, I just don't understand why we are beginning by talking about this one man bin Laden . . . You give bin Laden too much credit. He could not do all these things like the 1993 attack on New York, not without a state sponsor. Just because FBI and CIA have failed to find the linkages does not mean they don't exist." Richard Clarke, the national coordinator for security, infrastructure protection, and national security, became instantly irritated by Wolfowitz's narrow focus on nation-states and his complacency on the threat posed by al-Qaeda. The CIA had discovered no link between Iraq and the 1993 attack on the World Trade Center, but Wolfowitz was talking as if such a link existed and the CIA simply hadn't detected it yet. "I could hardly believe it," Clarke later recalled. The low opinion Wolfowitz formed of the CIA during the Team B exercise clearly remained; the agency should not be trusted on matters of importance.

Wolfowitz was also upset that foreign-policy focus appeared to be shifting away from America's primary adversary: Saddam Hussein's Iraq.

Clarke replied that al-Qaeda's ambition to attack America was clearly expressed and entirely plausible. "Al Qaeda plans major acts of terrorism against the U.S.," Clarke warned. "It plans to overthrow Islamic governments and set up a radical multinational Caliphate, and then go to war with non-Muslim states." To illustrate this point he deployed a clumsy analogy: "They have published all of this and sometimes, as with Hitler in *Mein Kampf,* you have to believe that these people will actually do what they say they will do." Had Clarke referenced Brezhnev's speeches rather than Hitler, he might have struck a nerve. Instead, Wolfowitz replied testily, "I resent any comparison between the Holocaust and this little terrorist in Afghanistan."[143]

On the morning of September 11, 2001, Wolfowitz met with a congressional delegation at the Pentagon. They were discussing an issue that would soon appear beside the point: national missile defense. A colleague interrupted the meeting to inform the group that a passenger jet had crashed into the World Trade Center. They turned on the television and watched in horror as a plane struck the second tower. Black smoke enveloped lower Manhattan as an inferno, fed by thousands of gallons of aviation fuel, raged inside the towers. "There didn't seem to be much to do about it immediately and we went on . . . ," Wolfowitz recalled, "then the whole building shook. I have to confess my first reaction was an earthquake. I didn't put the two things together. Rumsfeld did instantly."[144]

What felt to Wolfowitz like an earthquake was a Boeing 757 crashing into the west side of the Pentagon, killing everyone on board and 125 in the building. Al-Qaeda terrorists had hijacked the plane, subdued or killed its pilots using primitive box cutters, and crashed it into the Pentagon. The plane was traveling at approximately 530 mph at the moment of impact.[145] It was one of a four-part suicide attack using hijacked commercial aircraft that had been many years in the making. The strikes on the WTC that Wolfowitz had observed on television were part of the same assault—this is what Rumsfeld had "put together." A fourth hijacked aircraft, destined for a second target in Washington—the Capitol or the White House, most likely—crashed into a field near Shanksville, Pennsylvania, following a struggle between the hijackers and the passengers. After learning through cell-phone conversations of what had happened in lower Manhattan, the thirty-three people on board bravely decided to author their own fate, saving hundreds of lives in the capital and preventing the destruction of another iconic building.

The revolt on Flight 93 was an inspiring act of defiance on a dark day—2,977 people were murdered. As the World Trade Center—where the majority died following the fire-induced collapse of both towers—was an international place of business, some 12 percent of those killed were foreign nationals: 373 people in total. One single company, Cantor Fitzgerald, whose offices were based above the impact zone in the north tower, lost two-thirds of its entire workforce, or 658 people. The New York City Fire Department lost 343 men and women, "the largest loss of life of any emergency response agency in history."[146] The scale and murderous intent of the attack took a long time to process; the harrowing images of that day, broadcast live on television, were searing. It was a traumatic event for the United States, the deadliest ever attack on its soil.

After the attack on the Pentagon, Wolfowitz had been separated from Rumsfeld, to ensure continuity at the Defense Department in the event of subsequent lethal attacks, and taken to a nuclear bunker for safekeeping outside the capital. In separate locations, Rumsfeld and Wolfowitz arrived at similar conclusions. According to Lewis Solomon, "On the afternoon of 9/11, Rumsfeld mused about going after not only Osama bin Laden, but also Saddam Hussein. He asked one of his aides, a Pentagon attorney, to talk to Wolfowitz about Iraq's connections with bin Laden."[147] Wolfowitz was thinking much the same thing:

> I think what September 11th to me said was this is just the beginning of what these bastards can do if they start getting access to so-called modern weapons, and that it's not something you can live with any longer. So there needs to be a campaign, a strategy, a long-term effort, to root out these networks and to get governments out of the business of supporting them. But that wasn't something that was going to happen overnight.[148]

Getting governments out of the business of supporting terrorism meant one thing: invading Iraq and deposing Saddam. Yet this reasoning was problematic, to put it mildly, given that no evidence existed connecting Iraq's emasculated, secular leader to the Islamist 9/11 attacks. And indeed, none would ever be found.

But the Bush administration pushed this line so insistently—Dick Cheney was a particularly effective salesman—that by the summer of 2003, seven out of ten Americans believed that Saddam Hussein was implicated in the 9/11 attacks.[149] Wolfowitz's post-9/11 push for regime change in Iraq was predicated on evidence that did not exist. But in those fearful circumstances, with the nation on a war footing and dissent steamrollered as unpatriotic, the public was willing to give him and the Bush administration the benefit of the doubt. Walter Lippmann and George Kennan's misanthropic views regarding the incompatibility of democracy with the making of a temperate foreign policy never looked more plausible than from 2001 to 2004. Let down by its politicians and print and television media—*The New York Times* later apologized for its supine coverage of the Bush administration's post-9/11 foreign policies—the U.S. public sphere became perilously misinformed.[150]

On September 12, the debate began in earnest on how to respond to al-Qaeda's brutal attack. Over the course of a fractious NSC meeting, Donald Rumsfeld echoed Wolfowitz in recommending Iraq as the primary retaliatory target. Colin Powell queried this reasoning, observing that the American people would expect—indeed, demand—its military to attack the actual perpetrators al-Qaeda, not Iraq, whose leader, while noxious, was hostile to radical Islam. Richard Clarke was pleased to have the secretary of state's support, observing privately to Powell that "for us now to go bombing Iraq in response would be like our invading Mexico after the Japanese attacked us at Pearl Harbor." Powell replied, "It's not over yet," and so it would prove. That evening, President Bush took Clarke aside for a quiet word. "Look," Bush said, "I know you have a lot to do and all . . . but I want you, as soon as you can, to go back over everything, everything. See if Saddam did this. See if he's linked in any way." Clarke replied, "But Mr. President, al Qaeda did this." Bush said, "I know, I know but . . . see if Saddam was involved. Just look." Clarke tried (and failed) to be "more respectful, more responsive," replying, "Absolutely, we will look . . . again. But, you know, we have looked several times for state sponsorship of Al Qaeda and not found any real linkages to Iraq. Iran plays a little, as does Pakistan, and Saudi Arabia, Yemen." Bush cut him off, saying, "Look into Iraq, Saddam," and walked away. Clarke recalled that one of his staff members, Lisa Gordon-Hagerty, "stared after him with her mouth hanging open." Paul Kurtz, a counterterrorism adviser, arrived at the scene, noticed the ashen faces, and asked, "Geez, what just happened here?" "Wolfowitz got to him," replied Gordon-Hagerty.[151]

The essentials of America's military response to the 9/11 attacks were thrashed out at Camp David on September 15. During a long day of meetings, it became clear that Bush's principal foreign-policy advisers held diverging views on how to respond. Colin Powell's preference was to attack al-Qaeda's training camps in Afghanistan, which would likely necessitate a full-scale war against the Taliban regime that hosted them. The secretary of state believed that this course was just and proportionate. Wolfowitz argued that the Afghan option was perilous and uncertain. Fighting in mountainous terrain was challenging and the Taliban was firmly entrenched. He countered that Saddam Hussein's Iraq was a much more inviting target and that there was at least a 50 percent possibility that Saddam was involved in the attacks.[152] During a coffee break, Wolfowitz lobbied President Bush directly on the merits of his plan, observing that it "would be very simple to enable the Iraqi opposition to take over the southern part of the country and protect it with American air power." This area would include the bulk of Iraq's oil fields, which could eventually be used to finance the costs of the operation.[153]

Secretary of State Powell and Vice President Cheney were not convinced by Wolfowitz and Rumsfeld's prioritization. Powell observed that the attacks had created a huge reservoir of international goodwill toward the United States—the headline in France's *Le Monde* on September 12 read "*Nous sommes tous Américains*" (We are all Americans), and NATO had invoked Article 5 of its treaty for the first time, committing its signatories to America's defense in this time of war. This reservoir would quickly dissipate, Powell reasoned, if the administration targeted Iraq ahead of al-Qaeda. Afghanistan first made sense on every conceivable level. "If we do that," Powell observed with a nod to Rumsfeld and Wolfowitz, "we will have increased our ability to go after Iraq—if we can prove that Iraq had a role [in 9/11]."[154] Cheney agreed with Powell: "If we go after Saddam Hussein, we lose our rightful place as the good guy."[155] The director of the CIA, George Tenet, agreed with Powell and Cheney: "Don't hit now. It would be a mistake. The first target needs to be al Qaeda."[156] The vice president took Wolfowitz to one side and bluntly told him to "stop agitating for targeting Saddam."[157]

During an NSC meeting on September 17, President Bush announced his decision: "I believe Iraq was involved, but I'm not going to strike them now. I don't have the evidence at this point."[158] The president's decision was a short-term disappointment to Wolfowitz, but there was little doubt that regime change in Iraq remained on the to-do list—and that his contribution to putting it there had been important. As Donald Rumsfeld wrote in his memoir, "Deputy Secretary Wolfowitz helped conceptualize the global war on terrorism as being broader than just Afghanistan. At that Camp David discussion Wolfowitz raised the question of Iraq, but Bush wanted to keep the focus on Afghanistan."[159] While strictly true, President Bush himself made it clear that Afghanistan was only the first stage of what he christened the "global war on terror." "This crusade, this war on terrorism," Bush declared in a televised speech, "is going to take a while, and the American people must be patient." The president subsequently retracted the clumsy reference to a crusade—which evoked civilizational, religious conflict between the West and Islam, of a type that Harvard's Samuel Huntington had prophesized in his book *The Clash of Civilizations*—but the speech honestly communicated the extent of his ambitions. On September 26, Wolfowitz spelled some of them out during a press conference in Brussels: "As the president has said over and over again, it's not about one man or one organization. It's about a network of terrorist organizations. It's about the support and sanctuary and harboring they receive from some states. And while we are going to try to find every snake in the swamp that we can, the essence of the strategy is to try to drain the swamp."[160]

Wolfowitz had in fact alluded to this broader strategy on September 13 during an interview on Fox News, when he talked of "ending states who sponsor terrorism." When later asked if the state he had in mind was Iraq, Wolfowitz replied that Saddam Hussein "is one of the most active supporters of state terrorism."[161] Wolfowitz was incisive and proactive in the week following the attacks, and his success in setting agendas would later become clear. His next task was to provide a coherent rationale for a second American war on Iraq, with all the complexities this posed in terms of locating a casus belli that didn't disintegrate upon first skeptical touch. This vexing task consumed Wolfowitz's intellectual energies through the fall of 2001, while the department he served prepared for war against another enemy in a different theater.

On October 7, 2001, less than a month after the attacks, the United States began the process of seeking justice and meting out retribution. As a consequence of the Taliban's refusal to meet President Bush's demand to hand over Osama bin Laden and dismantle al-Qaeda's training camps—to effectively stop serving as a haven for terrorists in learning mode—the United States, with strong support from the United Kingdom and other allies, began its war in Afghanistan. An ailing George Kennan registered strong disapproval in his diary: "Regarding the war in Afghanistan I find myself more of an isolationist than ever, reflecting that we, as soon as we can detach ourselves from that imbroglio, should concentrate our efforts on developing at home alternatives to the importation of Middle Eastern, and especially Saudi Arabian, oil—this, in place of further efforts to play a role in that particular region."[162] As Kennan aged, his views became increasingly aligned with those of Charles Beard.

The first wave of attacks, a high-tech salvo of cruise missiles and laser-guided bombs, destroyed thirty-one military targets such as anti-aircraft defenses and radar installations. A missile destroyed the Taliban Defense Ministry, in the center of Kabul, instantly killing twenty Afghans. The air war was necessarily brief. Sources in the military later said that it had taken only two nights to destroy every fixed Taliban target.[163] The basic strategy was to rely on the Northern Alliance, the Taliban's principal domestic foe, to fight the war on the ground, assisted by teams from the CIA's Special Activities Division and U.S. Army Special Forces, who could call in air strikes when necessary. In terms of ousting the Taliban, the strategy was successful. On November 9, the Taliban fled the city of Mazar-e-Sharif, and four days later Northern Alliance troops marched triumphantly into Kabul. On December 7, the Taliban fled the southern city of Kandahar, and its medieval rule over Afghanistan—given Cold War impetus by the Carter and Reagan administrations—finally ended.

In an interview with *The New York Times*, Wolfowitz recorded satisfaction that the Taliban had been removed without "creating an unnecessarily large footprint" and that "the benefits that come from these advanced capabilities and the ability to fuse them together in new ways I think has been very amply demonstrated in Afghanistan . . . [it was] almost a model demonstration."[164] This assessment was accurate in regard to the war against the Taliban, but not so much when it came to al-Qaeda. In late November, it was estimated that as many as fifteen hundred Arab and Chechen fighters affiliated with al-Qaeda had taken shelter in the Tora Bora cave complex high in the mountains of eastern Afghanistan and close to the border with Pakistan. Most now believe that Osama bin Laden was among them. The U.S. Air Force ferociously bombarded Tora Bora, but the majority of al-Qaeda, including bin Laden, successfully evaded death or capture, navigating a complex path through the mountains to Pakistan.[165] The perils of relying on air strikes plus proxies were laid bare during the Battle of Tora Bora. America's inability to press home its advantage against a cornered enemy that was actually connected to the 9/11 attacks was negligent bordering on shameful. Writing in *The New Republic* in 2009, Peter Bergen observed, "I am convinced that Tora Bora constitutes one of the greatest military blunders in recent U.S. history."[166] He argued convincingly that this failure stemmed directly from the faint military footprint favored by Rumsfeld and Wolfowitz.

The Bush administration deployed insufficient ground forces to Tora Bora when the mastermind of the 9/11 attacks was there for the taking—a monumental failure. Thereafter, the conflict in Afghanistan gathered intensity as the Taliban launched an insurgency against the new government led by Hamid Karzai. It was a war that rumbled on through the Bush administration, consuming more and more American lives and treasure. But the insurgency became largely tangential to Bush and his advisers, who were refocusing attention on grander equations elsewhere. Undersecretary of Defense (Comptroller) Dov Zakheim had responsibility for advising the Pentagon on budgetary matters. In his book *A Vulcan's Tale*, Zakheim laments the way Afghanistan became a back-burner issue:

> Paul Wolfowitz asked me to join him on what was my second trip to Afghanistan in January 2003. It was a one-day affair; we arrived late on January 14 and departed at the end of the following day. The purpose of Paul's visit was to inspect the road still under construction between Kabul and Kandahar and to reassure Afghans that the United States had not forgotten about them—when of course we really had.[167]

America's neglect of Afghanistan became a line of criticism that John Kerry deployed against George W. Bush and that Barack Obama used against Bush and John McCain. The charge was not without foundation.

At the moment Osama bin Laden was making his high-altitude escape into Pakistan—providing a mythic tale of greatness for his followers—Donald Rumsfeld began preparing Americans for the next project, the phase that he and Wolfowitz believed was far more significant than the first. On December 26, 2001, as U.S. Special Forces picked frustratingly through the rubble of Tora Bora, Rumsfeld told troops in Kabul to prepare for redeployment: "Your job certainly is not over. There are a number of countries that are known as being on the terrorist list."[168] This list included other desperately poor nations with weak governments and little by way of rule of law—places like Somalia, Sudan, and Yemen. But while each failing state had elements of al-Qaeda in situ, none was deemed worthy of a full-scale military campaign. None was as significant and inviting an enemy as Saddam Hussein's Iraq. The previous month, Bush had hinted at this during a news conference in the White House's Rose Garden. "Afghanistan is still just the beginning . . . ," he declared. "And as for Saddam Hussein, he needs to let inspectors back in his country to show us that he is not developing weapons of mass destruction." A journalist asked about the consequences for Saddam of noncompliance. Bush replied tersely: "He'll find out."[169]

Saddam Hussein's weapons of mass destruction—whether he had them, what he might do with them, where he was concealing them—was the foreign-policy issue of 2002. Here was a reason for toppling Saddam Hussein that did not rest on an illusory connection with al-Qaeda—although that angle was also developed regardless. And, crucially, it was eminently plausible; Saddam's possessing WMDs and potentially using them against the United States or its allies was not some wild imagining. In 1988, Iraq had used chemical weapons—a pitiless cocktail of mustard gas and the nerve agents sarin, tabun, and VX—to kill three to five thousand Kurds in Halabja.[170] Age ninety-eight, Kennan observed despairingly, as the Bush administration identified Saddam Hussein's WMDs as a compelling reason to invade Iraq, "The political arguments on TV, hoping against hope that the President will soon begin to be called to account for his grievous and abundant follies. God help us if he is not."[171]

Throughout the 1980s, as a bitter war with Iran raged, Iraq had plowed its scarce resources into developing a biological weapons program. Then following the 1991 Gulf War, the United Nations assumed the task of destroying these stockpiles and ensuring that no new programs were launched. This was achieved through the oversight of an inspections operation, the United Nations Special Commission (UNSCOM), created by UN Security Council Resolution 687. When UNSCOM was disbanded in 1998, following unsubstantiated Iraqi allegations of American spying—and the subsequent launch of air strikes against Iraq, Operation Desert Fox—it was succeeded by the United Nations Monitoring, Verification and Inspection Commission (UNMOVIC) led by Hans Blix. But Saddam consistently denied UNMOVIC entry into Iraq, claiming that the organization was subterfuge for American espionage. From 1998 to 2002, the United Nations had no one in Iraq able to assert convincingly and conclusively that Saddam was not developing WMDs. In the post-9/11 world, this uncertainty was intolerable to the Bush administration.

The problem was evidence. Just because Saddam was denying UNMOVIC inspectors entry into Iraq did not necessarily mean he was developing chemical and bacteriological weapons. This was broadly the view of the CIA, which did not possess any verifiable intelligence to suggest that Saddam had stockpiled or was developing WMDs. For this reason the agency could not identify Iraq as an immediate threat to the United States—or at least it couldn't in good faith.[172] Wolfowitz feared that the CIA's sanguine view of Saddam's Iraq in 2002 paralleled its too kind assessment of the Soviet Union in the 1970s, which he had challenged as part of Team B. He believed that Saddam and al-Qaeda were connected, and that Iraq's WMD program made that relationship potentially incendiary. With the support of Cheney and Rumsfeld, Wolfowitz set up an alternative intelligence-gathering operation in the Pentagon—the Policy Counterterrorism Evaluation Group (PCTEG)—and invited Feith to take charge. The value of PCTEG, as Wolfowitz described it, was that it was cognizant of "a phenomenon in intelligence work, that people who are pursuing a certain hypothesis will see certain facts that others won't, and not see other facts that others will. The lens through which you're looking for facts affects what you look for."[173] PCTEG certainly looked at Iraq through a different lens from the CIA. But it never turned up any "facts" to substantiate its innuendo. In 2003, Feith admitted to members of Congress that PCTEG was essentially an advocacy operation— its purpose was "to help me develop proposals for Defense Department strategies for the war on terror, which is a policy exercise, not an intelligence activity."[174]

Wolfowitz had no particular enthusiasm for using WMDs as the primary justification for invading Iraq: "The truth is that for reasons that have a lot to do with the U.S. government bureaucracy we settled on the one issue that everyone could agree on[,] which was weapons of mass destruction as the core reason."[175] So what did Wolfowitz truly believe? Certainly he thought that Saddam Hussein and al-Qaeda were linked in ways that the CIA had not fathomed and substantiated. CIA director George Tenet observed: "Wolfowitz genuinely believed that there was a connection between Iraq and 9/11."[176] But there was a measure of doubt on this issue—as even he recognized. Rather, Wolfowitz believed that an American invasion of Iraq could rid the world of a brutal despot, provide the United States with a strategic foothold in this pivotal, oil-rich region, and lead ultimately to the creation of a democratic and prosperous Iraq, which would serve as a model for the rest of the Middle East and make Israel's place in the region more secure. As Andrew Bacevich observes, Wolfowitz also wanted to "establish new norms governing the use of force . . . The objective was to lift any and all restrictions on the use of armed force by the United States."[177] There were potential "wins" right across the board. As Lewis Solomon appropriately notes, Wolfowitz's plan for regime change in Iraq "represented one of the most ambitious programs to transform a region in U.S. history."[178] Colin Powell's chief of staff, Lawrence B. Wilkerson, identified in Wolfowitz's plans a more dismal future: "I call them utopians . . . I don't care whether utopians are Vladimir Lenin on a sealed train going to Moscow or Paul Wolfowitz. Utopians, I don't like. You're never going to bring utopia, and you're going to hurt a lot of people in the process of trying to do it."[179]

Was Wolfowitz as utopian as Wilkerson suggests? When it came to Iraq, the available evidence suggests he was. Colin Powell's State Department was a continual source of irritation to Wolfowitz and his fellow war enthusiasts. Powell would stab at Wolfowitz's Wilsonian proselytizing on democratizing Iraq and the Middle East, observing that conditions in the region were not conducive to the implantation of "Jeffersonian Democracy." Wolfowitz took direct aim at Powell during an interview with *The New York Times*:

> You hear people mock [the goal of transforming Iraq into a democracy] by saying that Iraq isn't ready for Jeffersonian democracy. Well, Japan isn't Jeffersonian democracy, either. I think the more we are committed to influencing the outcome, the more chance there could be that it would be something quite significant for Iraq. And I think if it's significant for Iraq, it's going to cast a very large shadow, starting with Syria and Iran, but across the whole Arab world, I think.[180]

Wolfowitz's boss did not share his zeal. Testifying before a congressional committee in September 2002, Rumsfeld was asked what would happen after the fall of Saddam. He replied, "Going the next step and beginning to talk about democracy or things like that is a step I can't go."[181] Rumsfeld and Wolfowitz were united on the necessity of invading Iraq and deposing Saddam. But they had different scales of ambition as to what would come after. There was only one point on which the two men fundamentally agreed, and it happened to repudiate Woodrow Wilson's most cherished goal. The United Nations should not under any circumstances be permitted to constrain America's freedom of action. Washington reserved the absolute right to go it alone.

In this sense, Wolfowitz was as hostile as Kissinger toward Wilson's views on the potential for a collaborative world system. Does this not make it impossible to characterize him as Wilsonian? Well, yes and no. Wolfowitz and other so-called neoconservatives reject Wilson's multilateralism as wishful thinking, but they embrace his views on America's global role in spreading democracy. In 2004, the historian Max Boot, who later served as an adviser to John McCain's presidential campaign, drew a useful distinction between "hard Wilsonians," such as Wolfowitz, "who place their faith not in pieces of paper, but in power, specifically the power of the United States," and "soft Wilsonians," such as Jimmy Carter (this example does not entirely persuade), who "share a faith that multilateral organizations such as the League of Nations or the United Nations should be the main venues through which the United States promotes its ideals, and that international law should be the United States' main policy tool." Hard Wilsonians, Boot writes, "believe the United States should use force when necessary to champion its ideals as well as its interests, not only out of sheer humanitarianism but also because the spread of liberal democracy improves U.S. security, while crimes against humanity inevitably make the world a more dangerous place." It is a characterization that suits Wolfowitz well.[182]

In the fall of 2002, Albert Eisele, editor of the congressional daily, *The Hill*, landed quite a scoop. George Kennan, then aged ninety-eight, had agreed to an interview on the Bush administration's foreign policies. At a Georgetown senior citizens' home, Eisele questioned the esteemed diplomat on the headlong move to war with Iraq. Kennan was thoroughly distressed at the prospect, warning that "the history of American diplomacy" showed that "war has a momentum of its own, and it carries you away from all thoughtful intentions when you get into it. Today, if we went into Iraq, like the President would like us to do, you know where you begin. You never know where you are going to end." Kennan believed that a simple-minded Republican president deserved censure on this issue, but he also lambasted high-profile Democrats—particularly those eyeing a run for the presidency—for refusing to criticize President Bush's intentions on Iraq. He scorned their assent as a "shabby and shameful reaction. I deplore this timidity out of concern for the elections on the part of the Democrats." He closed the interview by cautioning that the United States cannot "confront all the painful and dangerous situations that exist in the world . . . That's beyond our capabilities."[183]

The interview was classic Kennan: plainspoken, sharply judgmental, historically literate, and hostile to overreach and ideology. That he delivered this prescient jeremiad just two years short of his hundredth birthday was testament to his intellectual lucidity and vigor. Yet as was so often the case, Kennan was somewhat isolated in his opinion, at least among the foreign-policy mainstream. He wrote in his diary, "I have been urged, by at least one friend, to write another X-article, urging patience and avoidance of violence even with regard to Saddam Hussein and his Iraq . . . But I am simply not in any position, at this stage in my life, to involve myself in public controversy. So the matter stops at that point."[184] Kennan's absence from the debate was a pity. Meanwhile, centrist supporters of Bush's unfolding policies toward Iraq included Hillary Clinton, John Kerry, Henry Kissinger—with the occasional qualification regarding the unlikelihood of the United States successfully "democratizing" Iraq—and Joe Biden. When President Bush's speechwriter Michael Gerson asked Henry Kissinger why he supported a war against Iraq, he replied, "because Afghanistan wasn't enough." America's radical enemies in the Muslim world wanted to humiliate the United States, Kissinger continued, "and we need to humiliate them." Gerson had drafted some of Bush's grandest phrases—about "ending tyranny" and "ridding the world of evil"—and he confessed to disappointment that Kissinger "viewed Iraq purely in the context of power politics. It was not idealism. He didn't seem to connect with Bush's goal of promoting democracy."[185]

Liberal intellectuals such as Michael Ignatieff, Anne-Marie Slaughter, Peter Beinart, and Christopher Hitchens also lent their support.[186] Wilsonianism was clearly a force that united aspects of the left and the right in admiration. But some devotees of realism departed from Kissinger in issuing strenuous objections. Kennan was joined in his dissent by three GOP heavyweights: Lawrence Eagleburger, James Baker, and Brent Scowcroft. In an op-ed titled "Don't Attack Saddam" in *The Wall Street Journal* on August 15, 2002, Brent Scowcroft observed that "Saddam's goals have little in common with the terrorists who threaten us." Deposing Saddam Hussein would be relatively straightforward but "it undoubtedly would be very expensive—with serious consequences for the U.S. and global economy—and could as well be bloody." Condoleezza Rice was upset that her mentor had turned on the administration she served: "Why didn't you tell me?" she asked.[187]

As widely respected and farsighted as they were, Scowcroft and Kennan were pitted against an administration that had locked on war with Iraq and had more or less destroyed the fail-safe mechanisms that might permit deviation from this path. They did not stand a chance in those circumstances, although they did have like-minded allies within the administration. Colin Powell, for example, had serious doubts about the efficacy of invading Iraq. He continued to view this course as a distraction from the main job of defeating al-Qaeda. But by the summer of 2002, Powell was coming to understand that the debate had left him behind—the decision to invade Iraq had more or less been made. "Our counterparts at the Pentagon and the vice president's office are too cocky," one State Department official complained. "It's like they know something we don't."[188]

The idea of not merely deposing Saddam but also democratizing and liberalizing Iraq and holding the nation aloft as an exemplar was becoming increasingly appealing to George W. Bush. Indeed, he came to think that a push for democratization could reap benefits elsewhere in the region—and he acted on that Wilsonian instinct with Wolfowitz's encouragement. During an important speech in the Rose Garden on June 24, 2002, Bush ended America's long-standing dialogue with Yasser Arafat. He instead urged "the Palestinian people to elect new leaders, leaders not compromised by terror," and "build a practicing democracy, based on tolerance and liberty."[189] In January 2006, the Islamist group Hamas, designated by most nations in the West as a terrorist organization, won a majority of the seats in Palestinian parliamentary elections. It has governed the Gaza Strip ever since, provoking a series of bloody short wars with Israel by firing rudimentary rockets toward Tel Aviv—and in so doing inviting a predictably asymmetrical response from the Israeli military. In this instance, "democratizing" Palestine was clearly no panacea when it came to resolving the world's most damaging and long-standing territorial dispute.

But the ascension of Hamas in Gaza was some way into the future. The potential for democratizing the Middle East appeared limitless in 2002—before theory made acquaintance with reality. This came through clearly in the Bush administration's most important policy document: the National Security Strategy of the United States, 2002—or NSS 2002, as it became commonly known. The first sentence declared with absolute conviction that there was "a single sustainable model for national success: freedom, democracy, and free enterprise." Thereafter the words "freedom" and "democracy" recur with a frequency that might have made President Wilson blush. Wolfowitz did not draft the document, but he can lay good claim to being its spiritual author. "We will defend the peace by fighting terrorists and tyrants . . . We will extend the peace by encouraging free and open societies on every continent." NSS 2002 fleshed out the Wilsonian elements that Wolfowitz believed were lacking in the 1992 DPG. It also provided a rationale for invading Iraq in the absence of a direct, verifiable threat to the American homeland: "While the United States will constantly strive to enlist the support of the international community, we will not hesitate to act alone, if necessary, to exercise our right of self-defense by acting preemptively against such terrorists, to prevent them from doing harm against our people and our country."[190]

The concept of preemptive or preventive defense—what came to be known as the Bush Doctrine—thus entered the foreign-policy lexicon. American presidents had always reserved the right to unilaterally neutralize a threat before its realization. John F. Kennedy's policy of "quarantining" Cuba loosely falls into this category, and John Lewis Gaddis claimed historical precedent for the Bush administration in the unilateral and preemptive foreign-policy doctrines of John Quincy Adams.[191] But reserving the privilege to strike before being struck—or not, as the case may be—had never been proclaimed so baldly. NSC-68, for example, had characterized preventive defense as a step too far.

On February 26, 2003, just a few weeks prior to the invasion of Iraq, President Bush delivered a speech at the American Enterprise Institute, a think tank that had provided Wolfowitz and his ideological allies a sheltered contemplative setting in which to think and strategize about foreign policy during the Clinton years. In this remarkable address, Bush rationalized the planned invasion of Iraq as a war to make the Middle East safe for democracy. It was informed by Wolfowitz's deeply felt belief in humanity's innate perfectibility (to a Western blueprint): "There was a time when many said that the cultures of Japan and Germany were incapable of sustaining democratic values. Well, they were wrong. Some say the same of Iraq today. They are mistaken. The nation of Iraq—with its proud heritage, abundant resources and skilled and educated people—is fully capable of moving toward democracy and living with freedom."

Bush, delighting his rapt, like-minded audience, riffed on this Wilsonian theme throughout the address. "The world has a clear interest in the spread of democratic values, because stable and free nations do not breed the ideologies of murder . . . A new regime in Iraq would serve as a dramatic and inspiring example of freedom for other nations in the region."[192]

An important question remained: How many American troops were necessary to effect such momentous change? On February 25, the chief of staff of the United States Army, General Eric Shinseki, gave an answer his political masters did not want to hear. During testimony before the Senate Armed Services Committee, Carl Levin, a Democrat from Michigan, asked Shinseki how many troops would be required to keep order after the fall of Saddam. Shinseki replied that he was not in the chain of command and not privy to such discussions. But if forced to hazard a guess, the number would be several hundred thousand. "We're talking about posthostilities control over a piece of geography that's fairly significant," Shinseki continued, "with the kinds of ethnic tensions that could lead to other problems. And so it takes a significant ground-force presence."[193] The defense secretary was furious and asked Wolfowitz to make a statement rebutting Shinseki's shoddy guesswork. Rumsfeld was keen to replicate the small-footprint model that he believed had worked so well in toppling the Taliban in Afghanistan. And so on February 27, Wolfowitz dismissed Shinseki's estimate as "wildly off the mark" and downplayed the prospect of sectarian conflict in the war's aftermath. "I am reasonably certain," said Wolfowitz, "that they will greet us as liberators, and that will help us to keep [troop] requirements down."[194] These words, epitomizing the hubris present in the Pentagon at that time, would return to haunt Wolfowitz.

The Pentagon had assumed complete control of both the invasion of Iraq and the occupation thereafter. This was a peculiar situation, given that the State Department was better served through experience and capability to direct the latter. State had previously expressed significant doubts about the logic of toppling Saddam. In late 2002, Colin Powell had instructed Assistant Secretary of State for Near Eastern Affairs William Burns and his assistant, Ryan Crocker, to analyze the risks involved in the invasion of Iraq. They produced a tightly argued eight-page memorandum titled "The Perfect Storm," which warned that Iraq's patchwork of ethnicities would be ripped apart and radicalized following the departure of the oppressive presence that tied them all together. They also warned that Iran, Syria, and Saudi Arabia would all intervene in postwar Iraq—with varying degrees of openness—further inflaming the Sunni-Shia divide. In 2004, Crocker pointed out that, "nearly everything we said would happen, did happen, particularly the insurgency."[195] But Rumsfeld, Cheney, and Wolfowitz dismissed the report as flat-out wrong and entirely predictable from such a risk-averse, liberal institution. Their ideology trumped caution. Colin Powell's State Department, America's principal repository of foreign-policy knowledge, was pushed further to the margins.

In her memoir, Condoleezza Rice expressed regret that the Pentagon led both the invasion and the occupation of Iraq. In late March 2003, the State Department provided a list of eight officials to assist with the pacification and administration of post-Saddam Iraq. Most were area specialists with particular expertise in the region. Some even knew Arabic. But the White House instructed this delegation to "stand down" until further notice on the advice of the Pentagon. As Rice recalled, "The State Department was prepared to deploy employees, many of whom were Arabists. Some were sent without incident, but Feith vetoed several State recommendations on what could only be called ideological grounds. When I learned of this, I went to the President and told him that it was an affront to Colin to act that way and we needed the expertise. But it was the Defense Department's show, and the president was reluctant to intervene."[196] As Stephen Glain writes in

State vs. Defense, Kenneth Keith, a former U.S. ambassador to Egypt and Qatar, compared the Pentagon's actions to a coup d'état: "Whether it was in the form of a memo or a phone call from the president, that coup did take place. It was part of the struggle led by Wolfowitz and the Secretary of Defense, who convinced the president that postwar Iraq should be in the hands of the Defense Department."[197]

Some numbers allow us to comprehend just how unrealistic the Bush administration's planning was prior to the invasion of Iraq. To liberate Kuwait, President George H. W. Bush had assembled a coalition of just under one million troops, of which 500,000 were American. To invade Iraq, depose Saddam Hussein, and preside over the democratization of that nation, President George W. Bush assembled a coalition of 265,000, of which 148,000 were American. It is tempting to conclude that the debacle that followed the invasion was foreseeable to anyone with basic numeracy and an open mind. The fiscal cost of the war was also badly underestimated. When invited during congressional hearings to assess the likely cost of invading Iraq, Wolfowitz declined to give a number but claimed that it would be "considerably" lower than the suggested $95 billion. A recent study led by Brown University suggests than the cost of the Iraq War has exceeded $2.2 trillion, and that the combined cost of the wars in Iraq and Afghanistan will rise to more that $4.4 trillion, excluding future interest costs on borrowing.[198]

Insights from the Nobel Prize–winning psychologist Daniel Kahneman also cast the Bush administration's lack of foresight—its blinkered unwillingness to contemplate negative repercussions—in a harsh light. Wolfowitz had a simple theory: the invasion of Iraq would proceed smoothly, the Iraqi people would greet Americans as liberators, and the unshackled nation would march toward free elections and prosperity. But there were other hypothetical scenarios, and most were not so sunny. In *Thinking, Fast and Slow*, Kahneman discusses the concept of "planning fallacy," whereby individuals "make decisions based on delusional optimism rather than the rational weighting of gains, losses, and probabilities." To correct this fallacy, Kahneman proposes the rigorous completion of what his fellow psychologist Gary Klein describes as a "premortem." This process consists in inviting the author or authors of a particular plan to "imagine that we are a year into the future. We implemented the plan as it now exists. The outcome was a disaster. Please take 5 to 10 minutes to write a brief history of that disaster."[199] There is no guarantee that this exercise would have changed a thing. But who knows? The exercise might have persuaded some to confront the notion of contingency. Or maybe not. A premortem might instead have been dismissed as defeatist and somehow unpatriotic. Cognitive suppleness was not a common trait among the planners of the second Iraq War.

On March 19, 2003, President Bush announced the launch of Operation Iraqi Freedom. As in 1991, the cruise missile and aerial bombardment was devastating, the progress after the ground invasion was swift, and most of Saddam Hussein's hopelessly outgunned Iraqi army prioritized self-preservation and melted away. Iraq did not use its alleged weapons of mass destruction—whether Saddam would have used them if he had them is a moot point—and did not fire missiles at Israel to lure it into the fray. On April 6, in the midst of the war, Wolfowitz talked ambitiously about the future: "I think Iraq can be an inspiration to the Muslim world and the Arab world that Arabs and Muslims can create a democratic country . . . Many people have done it in the latter part of the 20th century. It's time for the Arabs to do it now."[200] On May 1, President Bush donned a flight suit and landed on the aircraft carrier USS *Abraham Lincoln* aboard a Lockheed S-3 Viking to declare the "end of major combat operations" in Iraq. The backdrop to Bush's speech was a large banner that read MISSION ACCOMPLISHED.

A few days later, Dick Cheney held a party at his home to celebrate the liberation of Iraq. Included on the guest list were true believers such as Paul Wolfowitz and his deputy Scooter Libby. Excluded were Condoleezza Rice, whom Cheney viewed warily as an irritating competing influence on Bush, and Colin Powell, who had no discernible influence on Bush but was reviled for his geopolitical caution. It was a moment of great euphoria and self-congratulation, although Cheney and Wolfowitz differed on which cause the war was promoting. Cheney was primarily interested in invading Iraq for the chilling "demonstration effect"—as Cheney's adviser, the Princeton professor of international relations Aaron Friedberg, described it—on America's enemies.[201] The vice president's rationale was similar to Henry Kissinger's: display strength, crush an enemy, inspire fear and respect, and bolster the nation's credibility. For Wolfowitz, of course, it was a free and prosperous Iraq that would exhibit the "demonstration effect," inspiring its neighbors to democratize their political systems and liberalize their economies. But these differences did not cloud the bonhomie chez Cheney.

Condoleezza Rice later confessed that she found Cheney and Wolfowitz's triumphalism unedifying: "For a brief time there was a kind of hubris among those who had been the most persistent and long-standing advocates for the overthrow of Saddam. It was summed up by the Vice President who, when challenged on the need for interagency cooperation in the postwar period, said, 'The Pentagon just liberated Iraq. What has the State Department done?'"[202] Cheney's gloating was justified in that the liberation of Iraq *was* well executed. It was mostly everything that followed the fall of Baghdad that wasn't. And this would create a foreign-policy disaster that echoed the debacle in Vietnam.

A basic problem was lack of coalition troops on the ground. The historian Philip Bobbitt—a strong supporter of the Bush administration—casts most of the blame on the Pentagon for this critical flaw in planning: "Wolfowitz claimed that it was inconceivable that the Coalition would need more troops in Iraq after the fall of the Iraqi state—'after the war,' as it were—than during it. As a direct result of this inadequate conceptualization of war, as of November 2007 at least 80,000 Iraqis had died since May 1, 2003."[203] There was an insufficient troop presence in Iraq at the moment of its subjugation, but even the soldiers on the ground were unsure how to react to the resulting chaos. A calamitous collapse of authority followed the liberation of Baghdad on April 9. Looters ransacked nearly every public building in the capital. Lacking precise orders, U.S. troops did nothing. It is impossible to estimate how many Iraqis were instantly alienated by the invading army's inability to keep basic order. Rumsfeld's facile response to the looting that so badly undermined prospects of sound governance and national unity— "Stuff happens! . . . It's untidy and freedom's untidy"—likely did not allay the concerns of ordinary Iraqis about the casual incompetence of Saddam Hussein's successor.[204]

In the weeks that followed Bush's "Mission Accomplished" speech, it was becoming clear that America's problems as an occupying force went beyond the looting of Baghdad. At the Pentagon's behest, L. Paul Bremer—who had replaced Jay Garner as administrator of the Coalition Provisional Authority of Iraq—dissolved the Baath Party and the Iraqi National Army. In this instance it was not just Rumsfeld and Wolfowitz dispensing wisdom, but Ahmed Chalabi, a prominent U.S.-based Iraqi exile who had forged a close relationship with both men. It was he who insisted that the Americans would be met and celebrated as liberators. Chalabi had designs on returning from exile to rule Iraq, and the admiring Wolfowitz and Rumsfeld believed that removing all hints of Baathism would help clear his path, rooting out the last vestiges of loyalty to Saddam's regime.

In disbanding the Iraqi Army, however, the Bush administration also made some four hundred thousand Iraqis (mainly Sunnis) unemployed, affording them considerable time to nurse resentments. These men began to demonstrate volubly on the streets against the coalition authority, threatening retribution if their demands were not met. In May and June, U.S. troops were targeted and killed on the streets of Baghdad in greater number. Rumsfeld went to great lengths to characterize the violence as run-of-the-mill: "You got to remember that if Washington, D.C., were the size of Baghdad, we would be having something like 215 murders a month. There's going to be violence in a big city." Wolfowitz told the House Armed Services Committee that "these people are the last remnants of a dying cause" and coalition forces "have the sympathy of the population, not the surviving elements of the Baathist regime."[205] Wolfowitz's Wilsonian optimism about the advantages that accompany liberty impeded his ability to see clearly.

If only Wolfowitz had been correct. The insurgency against the American-led occupation began in earnest on August 7, 2003, with the suicide truck bombing of the Jordanian embassy in Baghdad that killed seventeen. On August 19, a similar attack on the United Nations headquarters in Baghdad killed at least twenty-two people, including the UN's special representative in Iraq, a widely revered champion of humanitarianism, Sérgio Vieira de Mello. A subsequent attack the following month led to the withdrawal of the United Nations from Iraq—the situation on the ground was simply too dangerous for the organization to remain. A bitter sectarian conflict was emerging in Iraq, pitting the newly emboldened Shia majority against former Baathists, foreign jihadists lured to Iraq by the prospect of killing Americans and Britons, and disempowered Sunni Arabs.

Not that this bleak outcome was necessarily foreordained. The political scientist Toby Dodge refuses to attribute the onset of civil war in Iraq to intractable ethnic divisions—there was nothing inevitable about what followed.[206] Instead, he identifies the critical moment as the collapse of the Iraqi state and the inability of the coalition to replace it with a binding authority that commanded respect, if not necessarily affection. Rumsfeld, Cheney, and Bremer's negligence at that juncture was appalling. But Wolfowitz's failure of imagination is more difficult to forgive. This is a man who genuinely believes in the project of building a vibrant, wealthy, pluralist Iraq. Yet the department he helped run did many things to frustrate the realization of an aspiration that already tended toward the utopian.

Instead, the Iraq that emerged in the first few post-Saddam years was dystopian. Ordinary Iraqis died in the tens of thousands as the cycle of sectarian bloodletting intensified through 2004 and 2005. Recent estimates suggest that at least 133,000 Iraqi civilians have been killed since March 2003, and that number continues to rise. In 2010, Dr. Haider Maliki, based at the Central Pediatric Teaching Hospital in Baghdad, estimated that 28 percent of Iraqi children suffer from post-traumatic stress disorder. Iraq remains one of the most unstable and dangerous nations on earth.

On the American side, some 6,800 troops have been killed in Iraq since March 2003. When Bush declared victory aboard the USS *Abraham Lincoln* in May 2003, the death toll stood at 128. More than 6,780 American military contractors have also been killed in Iraq. Some 970,000 veterans of the Afghan and Iraq wars have returned home and registered postcombat disability claims. The insurgencies in Afghanistan and Iraq had a profound psychological effect on the soldiers who battled them, and the spouses, children, and parents who lived with them. The human toll is a solemn one.[207]

There were grim strategic consequences too. Iran was perhaps the greatest beneficiary of the Bush administration's freedom agenda. To the west, Tehran's principal adversary was crushed and a Shia majority assumed political dominance. To the east, the hostile and unpredictable Taliban were removed from power. Iran was as safe in 2003 as it had been since the revolution. Indeed, if any national leader should have contributed financially to the Bush administration's war on terror it was surely Mahmoud Ahmadinejad. The "Great Satan" provided Ahmadinejad—a risible, Holocaust-denying blowhard—with a genuine free ride. And this was a nation actually developing weapons of mass destruction. Iran's emboldening certainly imperiled Israel, which was probably not what President Bush and the Pentagon had intended.

So what of the original casus belli? Not a lot, regretfully. Following months of scouring Iraq for weapons of mass destruction, an official government report concluded that Iraq "essentially destroyed" its stockpiles of WMDs after the 1991 Gulf War and that its final facility, devoted to developing biological weapons, was decommissioned in 1996.[208] With both WMDs and the al-Qaeda connection laid bare as fallacious, the principals instead reemphasized the democratization advantage. George Bush is confident that history will judge the Second Iraq War more generously than it has been judged in the present.

There were clear advantages to invading Iraq and toppling Saddam Hussein in 2003. In the most obvious and immediate sense, the United States and its allies had removed an unpleasant, dangerous, and erratic despot from power. As Bush describes it in his memoir:

As a result of our actions in Iraq, one of America's most committed and dangerous enemies stopped threatening us forever. The most volatile region in the world lost one of its greatest sources of violence and mayhem. Hostile nations around the world saw the cost of supporting terror and pursuing WMD. And in the space of nine months, twenty-five million Iraqis went from living under a dictatorship of fear to seeing the prospect of a peaceful, functioning democracy.[209]

The demonstration effect was indeed immediate. In December 2003, Muammar Gaddafi consented to give up his WMDs and abandon his decades-long quest to acquire a nuclear capability. This was a clear win. Gaddafi's decision stemmed directly from America's preemptive attack on Iraq. But other "rogue" states drew different lessons. The two remaining "axes of evil," Iran and North Korea, reasoned logically that it was the absence of a nuclear deterrent that made Iraq vulnerable and pushed harder to develop their own.

The democratization of Iraq can certainly be counted as a victory—at first glance, at least. The civil war that raged intensely from 2003 to 2006 cooled from 2007. In January of that year, Bush announced a new military strategy in Iraq, the "surge," which involved the dispatch of twenty thousand additional U.S. combat troops and the embrace of a comprehensive counterinsurgency strategy led by General David Petraeus. When combined with the so-called Sunni Awakening—whereby armed Sunni groups rose up and turned on al-Qaeda in Iraq—the surge served to reduce the harrowing levels of violence in Iraq. Endemic bloodletting and low levels of Sunni participation had marred the first national election of 2005. By 2010, the situation had improved in the sense that more Sunnis were willing to cast votes—although violence and electoral fraud had not abated.

The situation has deteriorated markedly since then. Up until August 2014, Iraq was led by a two-term prime minister, Nuri al-Maliki, with clear authoritarian tendencies. Al-Maliki reneged on earlier promises to build a unity government with Sunni political groups, undermined the freedom of the press, and built a government blighted by pervasive corruption. Freedom House, an American NGO founded by Wendell Willkie and Eleanor Roosevelt, offered a damning assessment in 2013: "Iraq is not an electoral democracy. Although it has conducted meaningful elections, political participation and decision-making in the country remain seriously impaired by sectarian and insurgent violence, widespread corruption, and the influence of foreign powers."[210] Throughout the summer of 2014, the extreme Islamist successor to al-Qaeda in Iraq, the Islamic State of Iraq and Syria—or ISIS—launched brutal assaults against Shia Muslims and other minorities. As of today, Iraq remains mired in violence. The Iraq War "positives" seem not so much when they are subjected to scrutiny.

In an interview with London's *Sunday Times* on March 18, 2013, Wolfowitz expressed regret at the way the war was conceived and executed. There "should have been Iraqi leadership from the beginning," Wolfowitz lamented, instead of a fourteen-month American occupation based on "this idea that we're going to come in like MacArthur in Japan and write the constitution for them." The decision to disband the Iraqi Army and pursue a rigorous policy of de-Baathification was clearly ill-conceived, Wolfowitz continued, and the Pollyannaish Ahmed Chalabi was not "completely straight with us." But Wolfowitz also provided a staunch defense of many decisions that stoked fierce criticism then and now. On General Shinseki's warning that America embarked on war with insufficient troops, Wolfowitz retorted that "this was not the kind of war you win by overwhelming force." On the misleading use of "evidence" to justify the conflict, Wolfowitz observed, "The falsehood that the president lied, which by the way is itself a lie, is so much worse than saying we were wrong. A mistake is one thing, a lie is something else." Ultimately, Wolfowitz protested hopefully that it was too soon to judge the invasion of Iraq as a failure: "We still don't know how all this is all going to end."[211]

In an open letter published in *Harper's* magazine a few days previously, the historian Andrew Bacevich invited Wolfowitz—a former colleague from the American Enterprise Institute—to give more serious thought to what had transpired in Iraq:

> Why did liberation at gunpoint yield results that differed so radically from what the war's advocates had expected? Or, to sharpen the point, *How did preventive war undertaken by ostensibly the strongest military in history produce a cataclysm?*
>
> . . . To be sure, whatever you might choose to say, you'll be vilified, as Robert McNamara was vilified when he broke his long silence and admitted that he'd been "wrong, terribly wrong" about Vietnam. But help us learn the lessons of Iraq so that we might extract from it something of value in return for all the sacrifices made there. Forgive me for saying so, but you owe it to your country. Give it a shot.[212]

One must hope that Wolfowitz rises to Bacevich's challenge, and not twenty-five years after the fact à la McNamara. For the Second Iraq War may eclipse Vietnam in terms of its shuddering impact on U.S. foreign policy. But the prospects for a Wolfowitzian self-reckoning do not appear to be promising. In an interview in June 2014, Wolfowitz observed that America had in fact "won" the Second Iraq War by 2009 but that this hard-earned victory had been squandered by the Obama administration in its headlong rush to withdraw.[213]

9

BARACK OBAMA
AND THE PRAGMATIC RENEWAL

With all respect to James and Dewey, it takes more than a common
sense instinct . . . to deal with the age of guided missiles [and] the
age of revolution in Asia, the Middle East and Africa.

—WALT ROSTOW

In the fall of 2002, John Mearsheimer, a well-known professor of international relations at the University of Chicago, pulled out of an antiwar rally
scheduled to take place in Chicago's Federal Plaza. To replace him, the orga-
nizers invited a young state senator named Barack Obama, who was scholarly, a fluent speaker, Chicago based, and available. Though the event was
billed as an "antiwar rally," suggesting a dovish unity of purpose, the ambitious Obama sensed an opportunity to present his foreign-policy views to a
national audience. It was a potential breakthrough moment in his fledgling
political career, though it was also fraught with danger. High-profile Democrats such as Hillary Clinton and John Kerry had supported the Bush administration's response to the 9/11 attacks, including the president's move
toward war against Iraq. Opposing the mainstream of his party and a popular incumbent wartime president was not the safest course for a politician
with national aspirations to take.

Obama spoke after the Reverend Jesse Jackson, the nation's best-known
African American political figure and a stalwart of the left of the Democratic Party. Here was a chance to lambast Bush's rush to war *and* present
an alternative paradigm of what a black Democratic politician might sound
like. Reverend Jackson's rhetorical prowess certainly made him a hard act to

follow. "This is a rally to stop a war from occurring," Jackson declared. He invited his audience to look into the sky and count to ten. When the time elapsed, and the crowd lowered their gaze, Jackson explained: "I just diverted your attention away from the rally. That's what George Bush is doing. The sky is not falling and we're not threatened by Saddam Hussein."[1]

Yet while Jackson's antiwar views were theatrically rendered, they were also predictable. On the eve of a major welcome-home parade in 1991, Jackson had characterized the first Gulf War as a costly failure waged by "public school children and foreign technology," the latter a quaintly protectionist reference to the Japanese computer components used in American munitions. "It's right to love the troops," Jackson said. "But the moral way is to love the troops when they are no longer troops."[2] In the tradition of Charles Beard, Jackson viewed war as a distraction from the essential job of correcting the grievous societal problems that scarred the United States. Americans came first, Jackson reasoned.

Barack Obama viewed America and the world differently, as his first sentence made clear: "Let me begin by saying that although this has been billed as an antiwar rally, I stand before you as someone who is not opposed to war in all circumstances." Indeed, Obama devoted the next eight sentences of his speech to explaining precisely why some wars were necessary. "The Civil War was one of the bloodiest in history," Obama said, "and yet it was only through the crucible of the sword, the sacrifice of multitudes, that we could . . . drive the scourge of slavery from our soil." His grandfather (a white Kansan) "signed up for a war the day after Pearl Harbor was bombed, fought in Patton's army . . . He fought in the name of a larger freedom, part of that arsenal of democracy that triumphed over evil . . . After September 11 . . . ," Obama continued, "I supported this administration's pledge to hunt down and root out those who would slaughter innocents in the name of intolerance, and I would willingly take up arms myself to prevent such tragedy from happening again."

What made the proposed war with Iraq so ill conceived, in Obama's view, was its passionate "ideological" nature and its disregard of the apparent facts of the matter: "that Saddam poses no imminent and direct threat to the United States or to his neighbors . . . and that in concert with the international community he can be contained until, in the way of all petty dictators, he falls away into the dustbin of history." For Obama, launching a war against Saddam Hussein was "a dumb war. A rash war. A war based not on reason but on passion, not on principle but on politics . . . What I am opposed to," he said, "is the cynical attempt by Richard Perle and Paul

Wolfowitz and other armchair, weekend warriors in this administration to shove their own ideological agendas down our throats, irrespective of the costs in lives lost and in hardships borne."[3] It was a good line, but the applause that met Obama's speech was less effusive than the acclaim that met Jackson's more "passionate" address.

It is interesting to compare the attributes Obama extolled—reason and principle—to those he impugned: passion, ideology, and politics. It was a speech that reveled in cold, hard thinking informed by reason and evidence, that decried the consequences of following theories and ideologies unshackled from historical precedent. He name-checked Paul Wolfowitz for a reason. Obama abhorred the grandiose utopianism that he and his allies embodied, preferring policies that test and probe, reaping incremental progress, rather than those that seek to unveil or validate universal truths. The world is uncertain and constantly evolving. Framing policies informed by modesty and provisionality is the best way to avoid needless conflict driven by skewed threat perception and grand, unattainable ambitions.

This intellectual method has a name: pragmatism—a word often misinterpreted to solely mean excessive compromise in pursuit of any given goal. In his classic book *Pragmatism*, William James observed that "at the outset, at least, it stands for no particular results. It has no dogmas, and no doctrines save its method . . . *The attitude of looking away from first things, principles, 'categories,' supposed necessities; and of looking towards last things, fruits, consequences, facts.*"[4] The Harvard-based intellectual historian James Kloppenberg argues persuasively that Obama's worldview and diplomatic method are informed by Jamesian pragmatism, writing admiringly that it is "a philosophy for skeptics, a philosophy for those committed to democratic debate and the critical assessment of the results of political decisions, not for true believers convinced they know the right course of action in advance of inquiry and experimentation. Pragmatism stands for openmindedness and ongoing debate."[5] The aftermath of the Second Iraq War rendered otiose grand Wilsonian thinking about America's ability to bend nations, regions, and indeed history to its will. The rise to power of Barack Obama, and America's diminished geopolitical circumstances, vitalized America's principal contribution to world philosophy as a guide to foreign policy.

Barack Hussein Obama was born on August 5, 1961, in Hawaii. His father, Barack Obama Sr., was Kenyan, and his mother, Stanley Ann Dunham, was from Kansas. But they shared many traits, including a restless yearning for varied intellectual and geographical experience. The couple had met in a

Russian class at the University of Hawaii in 1960 and had married just a few months before their son's birth. This exotic mixed parentage would have caused a stir had Barack been born in, say, Wichita. But as the biographer David Maraniss notes, during the week of Obama's birth in Honolulu's Kapi'olani Maternity and Gynecological Hospital, the other newborns were named Arakawa, Caberto, Kamealoha, Chun, Wong, Camara, Walker, Kawazoe, and Simpson.[6] To be mixed race, or *Hapa*, in Hawaii was unexceptional—a scenario that remained constant through Obama's peripatetic childhood. His parents divorced in 1964, following Barack Sr.'s departure for graduate school at Harvard, and Ann met and married an Indonesian graduate student named Lolo Soetoro in 1965. The family relocated to Indonesia in 1967, and from the age of six to ten Barack lived in Jakarta—joined by a half sister, Maya Soetoro—and attended Indonesian-language schools. The world's most populous nation was similar to Hawaii in its ethnic heterogeneity. It was only when Barack finished his schooling in Indonesia and Hawaii and attended college in California and later New York City that he truly began experiencing racial discrimination, his hand forced by the dismal realities of the mainland.

To provide her son with educational stability while she pursued a travel-heavy career as a research anthropologist, Ann enrolled Obama at the elite Punahou School in Hawaii, one of the best-performing schools in the United States. Barack—or Barry, as he was then known—was academically accomplished, although he also devoted a fair amount of time to playing basketball and smoking marijuana. After graduating from Punahou in 1979, Obama moved to Pasadena, California, and enrolled at Occidental College (or "Oxy"), a highly regarded liberal arts college, where he worked harder and played less basketball, having failed to make the team. Obama's college friend Phil Boerner recalled the range of topics that he and Barry discussed:

> . . . the CIA, El Salvador . . . whatever news was in the *L.A. Times*, Jimi Hendrix, Euro-communism, socialism . . . Marcuse's "An Essay on Liberation," Voltaire's *Candide*, how to bring change in the world, the right wing's control of the media, totalitarianism, Alexander Haig, poetry, James Joyce, Kafka, the Enlightenment, enlightened despotism of the eighteenth century . . . Frederick II, Richard C. Allen, the Soviet Union, gigantic traffic jams in L.A., arts of the avant-garde . . . the rise of apathy in America.[7]

If Boerner's recollections are accurate, then Obama's conversational tastes showed admirable range and heft.

After two years at a gilded college in the privileged environs of southern California—not dissimilar to Punahou in a cultural and climatic sense—Obama decided to transfer to Columbia University. His move to New York City was motivated by many factors, one of which was simply to find "a bigger pond to swim in."[8] But there was more to it than that. Oxy was small and parochial, inhabiting something of a bubble in a part of Los Angeles that was already detached from the everyday. And its total student body of sixteen hundred included only seventy-five African Americans, "and you could count the black faculty members on two fingers," a classmate recalled. "I was concerned with urban issues," Obama said, "and I wanted to be around more black folks in big cities."[9] He moved from Pasadena to Morningside Heights with his friend Phil Boerner and shared an apartment at 142 West 109th Street. Obama walked the city as often as he could, drinking in New York's myriad cultural attractions: a Sunday service at the Abyssinian Baptist Church, where he "was lifted by the gospel choir's sweet, sorrowful song," a conference on political ideology at Cooper Union, African cultural fairs in Brooklyn, a speech delivered by Jesse Jackson in Harlem. Obama went off the radar during his time at Columbia—few professors remembered him well—flying low to the ground of the world's greatest city.

In a manner reminiscent of Kennan at Princeton, Obama recalled in 2011 that during his two years at Columbia he was "deep inside my own head . . . in a way that in retrospect I don't think was really healthy." In a letter to his girlfriend Alexandra McNear in the fall of 1982, Obama confessed "large dollops of envy" for his Pakistani friends heading toward a career in business and his Hawaiian friends who were "moving toward the mainstream." Obama's mixed racial heritage, the absence of a stable family home, and financial insecurity placed strains on him. "Caught without a class, a structure, or tradition to support me," he wrote to McNear, "in a sense the choice to take a different path is made for me . . . The only way to assuage my feelings of isolation are to absorb all the traditions [and all the] classes; make them mine, me theirs."[10] Obama read, walked, observed, listened, wrote. His sensibilities were literary; notions of self, identity, and alienation were constants in his tangled thoughts. As he recalls in his memoir *Dreams from My Father*, "I spent a year walking from one end of Manhattan to the other. Like a tourist, I watched the range of human possibility on display, trying to trace out my future in the lives of the people I saw, looking for some opening through which I could reenter."[11]

Obama's reading habits corresponded with this inquisitive, identity-seeking voice. Like all students at Columbia, Obama studied Literature Humanities (or Lit-Hum), a great books course that required students to read up to five hundred pages of philosophy a week—from Plato, Locke, and Hume to Camus, Sartre, and Marcuse. A fellow student recalled that he "was really involved in the discussions . . . It was a fairly serious discussion about philosophy." Obama took a course with Edward Said but never warmed to the professor or the literary theory he taught. Boerner recalled that he and Obama would "rather read Shakespeare's plays than the criticism. Said was more interested in the literary theory, which didn't appeal to Barack or me." Obama later described Said as "a flake," a jibe that placed him in interesting company.[12] Allan Bloom, for example, would have enthusiastically agreed.

But Obama also read texts that would not have figured in Bloom's literary canon: Ralph Ellison's *Invisible Man*, Richard Wright's *Native Son*, W.E.B. Du Bois's *The Souls of Black Folks*, the poetry of Langston Hughes, Malcolm X's autobiography. In *Dreams from My Father*, Obama recalls the impact each made on him:

> In every page of every book, in Bigger Thomas and invisible men, I kept finding the same anguish, the same doubt; a self-contempt that neither irony nor intellect seemed able to deflect. Even [Du Bois's] learning and Baldwin's love and Langston's humor eventually succumbed to its corrosive force, each man finally forced to doubt art's redemptive power . . . Only Malcolm X's autobiography seemed to offer something different. His repeated acts of self-creation spoke to me; the blunt poetry of his words, his unadorned insistence on respect, promised a new and uncompromising order, martial in its discipline, forged through sheer force of will.[13]

After Obama concluded his studies at Columbia—he majored in political science but never warmed to that subject—he spent two unfulfilling years working in the business world. In 1985, he decided to emulate Malcolm X and embarked on a journey of "self-creation." He relocated to Chicago to take a job as a "community organizer" in its deprived African American neighborhoods for a salary of $10,000 a year.

Obama's move to community organizing in the same city that had awoken Charles Beard's social conscience a century before was inspired by his progressive politics and Harold Washington's election as that city's first black

mayor, which dealt a death blow to "machine" politics in the highly segre-
gated city. He worked on the city's poverty-scarred South Side, where he helped
establish a job-training program, a tutoring system to help underprivileged
children get to college, and an organization dedicated to protecting tenants'
rights in Altgeld Gardens, one of America's first public-housing projects.

The work was unrelenting, the challenges overwhelming, the disappointments legion, and the salary a pittance. But through community organizing
Obama found a home, a more fully realized identity, and a church that
helped with both: Reverend Jeremiah Wright's Trinity United Church of
Christ in Washington Heights. In 1988, however, Obama decided to move
on to the next stage of his career, focusing on law and politics, the metaforces
that created, taunted, and neglected places like Chicago's South Side. Obama
was accepted into Harvard Law School and moved to Cambridge in the
fall to commence his studies. But there was little doubt that Chicago had
become his city, an anchor for the remarkable journey that followed.

Obama was an outstanding student at Harvard Law School, where he attracted the attention of the faculty's professoriate. He was a quick study, of
course, and his ability to comprehend difficult concepts, and penetrate ab-
struse legalese, placed him at a distinct competitive advantage across a
high-achieving cohort. But what struck his teachers and contemporaries as
exceptional was his skill in navigating different legal perspectives—usually
deeply felt—and finding a path through the thicket that did not fundamentally alienate the protagonists. With the support of both liberals and
conservatives, Obama was elected editor of the *Harvard Law Review*, becoming the first African American to hold the position. Stilling passions,
defusing rancor with humor, finding points of agreement, no matter how
faint—all these skills permitted Obama to assume this position of leadership with the journal, and his editorship coincided with the journal publishing articles from multiple legal and philosophical perspectives. It was an
era of genuine intellectual pluralism that united conservatives like Richard A.
Posner and liberals like Laurence Tribe in admiration. Indeed, Tribe was
sufficiently impressed by Obama's rationality, work ethic, and intelligence
to hire him as a research assistant for a project with the forbidding subtitle
"What Lawyers Can Learn from Modern Physics."[14] Like Walter Lippmann,
Obama was a star turn in Harvard Yard. Great things were expected of him
and he would not disappoint.

After graduating from Harvard, Obama returned home to the Windy
City, where he taught constitutional law at the University of Chicago, whose

faculty was nearly as high profile as Harvard's—Richard A. Posner, Cass Sunstein, and Geoffrey R. Stone all became colleagues. In 1993, he joined Davis, Miner, Barnhill & Galland, a small law firm specializing in neighborhood economic development and civil rights, the issues that had consumed him as a community organizer. His legal and academic careers were soon to coexist with one in politics. Obama was elected to the Illinois State Senate in 1996 for the 13th District, which spanned the South Side and included Hyde Park, the vibrant, multicultural neighborhood surrounding the University of Chicago that he and his wife, Michelle, also an Ivy League–educated lawyer from a modest background, called home. He was reelected in 1998 but then suffered a significant blow when he ran in the primaries against incumbent Bobby Rush in Illinois's 1st Congressional District and lost by a margin of nearly two to one. In 2004, Obama drew the appropriate lessons from this humbling and outpaced an open field to win the Democratic nomination for election to the U.S. Senate. In the general election, he crushed his Republican opponent, Paul Wolfowitz's contemporary at Cornell, Alan Keyes, by a margin of 70 percent to 30 percent.

John Kerry lost the presidential election of 2004 after an ugly campaign in which GOP strategists built an unassailable lead on national security by tarring their opponent, a decorated Vietnam veteran, as unpatriotic. But Barack Obama was one of 2004's winners. Kerry had campaigned with Obama in April and had been hugely impressed by his skill and potential. Kerry's national finance chairman, Louis Susman, whispered to Kerry, "This guy is going to be on a national ticket someday." Kerry agreed but was less patient: "He should be one of the faces of our party now, not years from now." So Kerry invited Obama to deliver the keynote address at the Democratic National Convention in July. It was a remarkable vote of confidence in a junior senator of just two years' standing.

Kerry's choice turned out to be inspired. The speech met with acclaim in the hall and across the nation. Obama's simple recounting of his family tree was riveting enough. But it was his ability to transcend that bitter election—to stake a claim as the grown-up in the room—that was especially impressive. The emotional climax of the speech extolled the merits of unity and decried the corrosive effects of negativity and the false dichotomies of the culture wars:

Now even as we speak, there are those who are preparing to divide us, the spin masters and negative ad peddlers who embrace the politics of anything goes. Well, I say to them tonight, there is not a liberal America and a conservative America; there is the United States of America. There is not a black America and white America and Latino America and Asian America; there is the United States of America ... We coach Little League in the blue states and, yes, we've got some gay friends in the red states. There are patriots who opposed the war in Iraq, and there are patriots who supported the war in Iraq ... In the end, that's what the election is about. Do we participate in a politics of cynicism, or do we participate in a politics of hope?[15]

The convention hall rattled to a crescendo of applause. There were tears, whooping, stomping feet—all achieved without orchestration. Reflecting on Obama's remarkable performance the following day, Hillary Clinton was bowled over: "I thought that was one of the most electrifying moments that I can remember at any Convention."[16] Four years later, confronting Obama as a political adversary, Clinton would come to rue Obama's remarkable life story, rhetorical facility, and transcendent appeal. He embodied America's virtues and promise, its complex composition and the vibrancy it engendered. Running against Obama must have felt like running against fate.

A few weeks before announcing his presidential candidacy in 2006, Obama delivered an important speech on foreign policy. He announced his intention as commander in chief to follow a "strategy no longer driven by ideology and politics but one that is based on a realistic assessment of the sobering facts on the ground and our interests in the region. This kind of realism has been missing since the very conception of this war, and it is what led me to publicly oppose it in 2002."[17] Hillary Clinton, the overwhelming favorite to secure the Democratic nomination, had one principal line of attack against Obama's prospective foreign policies: he was inexperienced and hence might imperil national security. Obama had a devastating response: the "experienced" Clinton had voted in the Senate to authorize the Second Iraq War.

With similar lack of success, Clinton tried different lines of attack, chiding Obama for talking up the threat posed by instability on the Pakistan-Afghanistan border and for announcing that the United States should reserve the right to strike there unilaterally against al-Qaeda if the need arose. Obama's response was cool and robust: "I find it amusing that those who helped to authorize and engineer the biggest foreign policy disaster in our generation are now criticizing me for making sure that we are on the right battlefield and not the wrong battlefield in the war against terrorism." In the fall of 2007, Obama developed this line of reasoning, assailing "Washington group think," "the foreign policy elite," and "conventional thinking in Washington."[18] Obama could present a solid case that his foreign-policy judgment was sounder than Clinton's, based on the farsightedness displayed in his 2002 speech in Chicago. It rocked Clinton on her heels every time Obama pointed this out.

Obama eventually beat Clinton to the nomination, assisted in no small part by his early opposition to the Iraq War. In the general election, Obama faced John McCain, a four-term senator from Arizona. With good reason, perhaps, McCain believed that he could succeed with the "inexperience" jab where Clinton had tried and failed. So when Obama declared, "If we have actionable intelligence about high-value terrorist targets [in Pakistan] and President Musharraf won't act, we will," McCain chided him for this naïve bluster: an affront to Pakistani pride and an illegal threat to its sovereignty.[19]

White House press secretary Tony Snow made it similarly clear that President Bush had and would continue to respect Pakistan's borders and that Senator Obama was engaging in reckless politicking. Secretary of Defense Donald Rumsfeld had once rejected a proposed commando raid into Pakistan for the destabilizing effect it would have on Islamabad and for the damage it would wreak on bilateral relations. Weighing in with a rare admiring editorial, titled "Barack Obama, Neocon," *The Wall Street Journal* admitted, "Anyone who wants to run to the right of Rummy on counterterrorism can't be all bad."[20] John McCain observed on the campaign trail that he would "follow Osama Bin Laden to the gates of hell." Obama might have replied that McCain would not actually pass through those gates, however, because there was a risk that hell might be destabilized—and better the devil you know.[21]

Obama's foreign-policy views coalesced throughout election year, although they never hardened into an "ideology." He read popular books on foreign affairs by Fareed Zakaria and Thomas L. Friedman and met frequently with Democratic Party éminences grises like Tony Lake and Zbigniew Brzezinski. Jimmy Carter's former national security adviser praised Obama: "I thought he had a really incisive grasp of what the twenty-first century is all about and how America has to relate to it. He was reacting in a way that I very much shared, and we had a meeting of minds—namely, that George Bush put the United States on a suicidal course." A meeting of minds, maybe, but Obama's worldview was suppler than the reflexive anti-Soviet one Brzezinski displayed throughout the 1970s. He drew inspiration from a variety of sources that spanned the political and ideological divide. "The truth is that my foreign policy is actually a return to the traditional bipartisan realistic policy of George Bush's father," Obama observed at a campaign event in Pennsylvania, "of John F. Kennedy, of, in some ways, Ronald Reagan."[22]

But Obama's self-identification as a realist does not capture the totality of his worldview—as his qualified admiration for Reagan suggests. The Protestant theologian Reinhold Niebuhr exerted a significant influence on his thinking about foreign policy, and there was nothing narrowly realist about the complex architecture of thought expressed in works like *The Irony of American History* and *The Children of Light and Children of Darkness*. In a 2007 interview with the *New York Times* journalist David Brooks, Obama identified Niebuhr as a major inspiration: "[He] is one of my favorite philosophers. I take away [from his works] the compelling idea that there's serious evil in the world, and hardship and pain. And we should be humble and modest in our belief we can eliminate those things. But we shouldn't use that as an excuse for cynicism and inaction. I take away . . . the sense we have to make these efforts knowing they are hard."[23]

Niebuhr was sympathetic to the realist tradition, but his devout Christianity tempered the amorality engendered by its purest application. Obama, also a devout Christian, shared these sentiments on religious, moral, and tactical grounds.

As Andrew Preston observes in *Sword of the Spirit, Shield of Faith*: "Without religion, Niebuhr argued, realism would invariably lead the nation astray because it would lack a moral compass and thus lack moral purpose, but without realism, religion could also be damaging because of its tendency to veer off into destructive idealistic crusades."[24] This was a thinker who stood on his own terms. Obama read and came to admire Niebuhr while teaching at the University of Chicago Law School. Niebuhr's critique of John Dewey—for failing to comprehend that self-interest drove humanity more than any other single force, and for being led by his worthy pacific tendencies to ignore the reality that the existence of evil meant some wars had to be fought to complete victory—struck a resonant chord with Obama.[25] This amalgam of realism and contingent idealism defies neat categorization, but pragmatism is the category that comes closest. In March 2008, Obama's national security advisory team recommended that "pragmatism over ideology" serve as his foreign-policy tagline. As Jo Becker and Scott Shane wrote in *The New York Times*, "It was counsel that only reinforced the president's instincts."[26]

Throughout 2008, Obama provided details on how "pragmatism over ideology" might translate into practice. After defeating Hillary Clinton in the primaries, Obama traveled to Iraq to meet General David Petraeus. The architect of the "surge" recognized that Obama would withdraw U.S. forces from Iraq promptly if he was elected. So he pressed him for more resources while American forces remained in situ. "Look, if I were in your shoes, General," Obama replied, "I would be asking for everything you're asking for and more . . . But you have to understand that, from where I sit now as a senator, and from where I might sit if I'm elected president, we have ultimately different responsibilities."[27] Petraeus was not blindsided by this response. During the campaign, Obama had clearly stated that "by refusing to end the war in Iraq President Bush is giving the terrorists what they really want . . . a U.S. occupation of undetermined length, at undetermined cost, with undetermined consequences."[28] He proposed to withdraw all U.S. troops from Iraq within sixteen months of his election. But Petraeus did confide to an associate that he was surprised that Obama had talked more like a centrist than a liberal. Perhaps this was a reference to the fact that Obama had publicly indicated his desire to send more troops to Afghanistan, which he believed the Bush administration had misguidedly neglected in favor of its "ideological" war in Iraq. This reprioritization displayed Obama's tendency to frame foreign policy on a case-by-case basis. There were more dangerous Islamist militants in Afghanistan and Pakistan than in Iraq, and policy should reflect this reality.

Obama's pragmatism, then, meant the absence of doctrine and dogma. It was a modest foreign-policy vision that suited the temper of the times, framed by a financial crisis that threatened to wreak as much havoc as the Great Depression. On September 1, Lehman Brothers filed for bankruptcy. A combination of excessive exposure to the subprime mortgage market and egregious corporate malfeasance had gutted this venerable investment bank, founded in 1850. The Dow Jones fell off a cliff—experiencing a one-thousand-point drop, its worst in history—and world markets soon followed. House prices plummeted as credit withered on the previously abundant vine. The crux of the general election turned sharply in a direction that favored Obama. John McCain's forte was foreign policy, not economics, as was clear from his responses to questions on the financial crisis. His responses (and mien) ran the gamut from illogical to baffled to prickly. Obama was much more coherent on the subject, exhibiting greater authority than the man his senior by a quarter of a century. The economic crisis won Obama the election. But it also ensured that his fiscal inheritance was as toxic as Lehman Brothers' assets.

The election wasn't all about the economic crisis, however. There were foreign-policy question marks about McCain that similarly played to Obama's advantage. Sarah Palin, for example. In a desperate effort to invigorate the GOP base, McCain chose the governor of Alaska as his running mate. Her selection helped invigorate both parties' bases and alienated those in the middle. Palin's grasp of foreign policy turned out to be uncertain, a significant problem given that McCain was the oldest man ever to run for the presidency. To confer some gravitas on Palin, McCain's campaign arranged for her to meet with Colombian president Álvaro Uribe, Afghanistan's president Hamid Karzai, Iraq's president Jalal Talabani, and Georgia's president Mikheil Saakashvili over the course of two days in late September. Henry Kissinger was also drafted to provide Palin with what *The New York Times* described as a "broad overview of international affairs, focusing particularly on Russia, China and the Middle East."[29] The evidence suggests that this was not quite a meeting of minds. A few days later, over the course of a calamitous series of interviews with the journalist Katie Couric, Palin described the view that the United States should proceed to direct negotiations with Iran and Syria—which Kissinger supported—as "naïve." When fielding a question on U.S.-Russian relations, Palin claimed authority through proximity, observing, "You can actually see Russia, from land, here in Alaska."

The unfolding spectacle was too much for some moderate Republicans to take. Colin Powell might have endorsed Obama regardless of McCain's choice of running mate, but Sarah Palin made Powell's decision to vote against his party easier:

> Frankly, it was in the period leading up to the conventions, and then the decisions that came out of the conventions, and then just sort of watching the responses of the two individuals on the economic crisis. It gave me an opportunity to evaluate their judgment, to evaluate their way of approaching a problem, to evaluate the steadiness of their actions. And it was at that point that I realized that, to my mind, anyway, that Senator Obama has demonstrated the kind of calm, patient, intellectual, steady approach to problem-solving that I think we need in this country.[30]

Powell was not alone among independents and moderate Republicans in holding these views. That Obama had successfully wrested the center ground of American politics from the Republican Party was made clear on Election Day. Barack Obama defeated John McCain by a margin of 365 to

173 in the electoral college, turning blue traditionally GOP-leaning states such as Virginia, North Carolina, and Colorado.

After winning the election handsomely, Obama was inundated with advice from well-wishers. The Yale political scientist Ian Shapiro hopefully ventured that "containment is back," building on his 2008 book that called for the United States to "contain" al-Qaeda through better intelligence and defter diplomacy, rather than legitimize it, and indeed radicalize more Muslims, through invading secular countries like Iraq. Alan Brinkley, professor of American History at Columbia, recommended George Kennan's *Memoirs* when asked to identify one book that Obama should read before entering the Oval Office.[31] Realists located Obama in their own tradition, prophesying a sharp turn from the pseudo-idealistic excess of the Bush years.

Wilsonian-inclined scholars also tried to bring Obama around to their way of thinking. In 2004, two political scientists had formally established the Princeton Project on National Security: Anne-Marie Slaughter—whom Obama would appoint chair of policy planning at the State Department—and G. John Ikenberry. Its bold intention was to emulate George Kennan and draft "the collective X article" for the twenty-first century. But it did so by drawing inspiration from Wilson, not Kennan. Titled "Forging a World of Liberty under Law: U.S. National Security in the Twenty-First Century," the final report emphasized the merits of liberal internationalism, repudiated the Bush administration's unilateralism, and recommended that multilateral institutions such as the United Nations and NATO be transformed into more effective decision-making forums. Multilateralism was the Princeton Project's principal thread, but idealism and a devotion to humanitarian goals also drove the report. The intention was to rescue Wilsonianism from the tarnishing embrace of Obama's predecessor. For some participants, the final report was also an opportunity to turn in an extended job application.[32]

In time, Obama would prove himself to be his own man—neither narrowly realist nor identifiably Wilsonian. His staffing decisions certainly reflected this duality. The president appointed Hillary Clinton as his secretary of state, a masterstroke that united his party, allowed for a major (Bill) Clinton contribution to Obama's reelection campaign in 2012, and placed an energetic, thoughtful, and experienced politician—a truly significant figure—in an office that had too often been peripheral.

Obama appointed General James Jones as his national security adviser, a man similarly hard-nosed, results-oriented, and possessed of no fixed grand strategic convictions. In the Pentagon, meanwhile, Obama retained Robert Gates from the Bush administration as secretary of defense. Cut from the same cloth as Obama and Jones, Gates's views on most issues tracked closely to those of the president. "I'm not sure if he considers this an insult or a compliment," Obama said of his defense secretary, "but he and I actually think a lot alike, in broad terms."[33]

There were Wilsonians in his administration too. Susan Rice was appointed U.S. ambassador to the United Nations; Anne-Marie Slaughter followed Kennan, Nitze, and Wolfowitz in serving as chair of policy planning; and Samantha Power, author of the influential *A Problem from Hell: America in the Age of Genocide*, was appointed to an advisory position in the White House—she would have placed higher had she not described Hillary Clinton as a "monster" during the primaries. Each had proselytized on the need for the United States to move more quickly toward humanitarian interventions when evil is being perpetrated, and each believed that American foreign policy was nothing if it did not stand for Wilsonian values. But when assessing Obama's advisory team as a whole, it is the absence of ideology that stands out.

At the outset, though, Obama's energies were devoted to the chilling impact of the world financial crisis, not to geostrategic self-identification. In the first three months of 2009, the U.S. economy contracted by 6.1 percent, following a steep 6.3 percent drop the previous quarter. From its high-water mark of 14,198 in 2007, the Dow Jones had plummeted to 7,949 at the time of Obama's inauguration before hitting its low point of 6,443 in March. Lehman Brothers' demise was just the beginning, as the malaise moved from banks to manufacturing colossi. Chrysler and General Motors both declared bankruptcy in the president's first hundred days. The financier George Soros was not engaging in hyperbole when he described the scenario as an "economic Pearl Harbor."[34] Bruce Riedel, a former CIA analyst and adviser to his presidential campaign, briefed Obama on the major external threats that faced the nation. As Riedel outlined a grave scenario in which Pakistani nuclear weapons found their way to Islamist militants, the president interceded: "That's scary. But in the meeting I just had before this one, the Treasury people told me that virtually every bank in the United States could fail before the end of the month. Now, that's *really* scary."[35]

Which is not to say that Obama's foreign-policy inheritance was roseate in comparison. There were 161,000 American troops stationed in Iraq and 38,000 in Afghanistan. North Korea had tested a nuclear device and Iran appeared intent on acquiring a similar capability. China was becoming increasingly strident on the world stage; Russia, shored up economically by its bounty of natural gas, was at odds with Washington on various issues; relations with many European nations had become icily formal; goodness knows what al-Qaeda and its affiliates were hatching in the Pakistan-Afghanistan border areas; Osama bin Laden remained at large. As Obama confided to a close adviser, "I'm inheriting a world that could blow up any minute in half a dozen ways, and I will have some powerful but limited and perhaps even dubious tools to keep it from happening."[36]

When Obama did delve into foreign policy in those early days, it was mainly to repudiate the "dubious tools" his predecessor had employed. On January 22, just two days into his first term, the president signed an executive order banning torture (or "enhanced interrogation") and ordered that the prison at Guantánamo Bay be shuttered within a year and its inhabitants moved into the U.S. criminal justice system. The president stopped using the term "global war on terror" and made clear that he viewed his primary role as commander in chief—safeguarding the United States—in very different terms from Bush.

Yet Obama did not dispose entirely of his predecessor's tool kit. Guantánamo Bay remains open today. Moving its inhabitants into the American criminal justice system, or sending them back whence they came, has become an almost Sisyphean prospect. The CIA's program of rendition—the apprehension and extrajudicial transfer of a suspect from one country to another—remained in place. The "extraordinary" part of rendition, where the suspect is tortured by an illiberal regime at the end of the journey, was prohibited on paper. But it is impossible to verify with certainty whether this practice has ended. Attorney General Eric Holder's insistence on "assurances from the receiving country" that the suspect would not be tortured is not necessarily watertight, because details on how these assurances are verified are not yet in the public domain. Human Rights Watch hailed Holder's announcement as a clear move in the right direction—the organization paid testament to "some of the most transparent rules against abuse of any democratic country"—but expressed regret that ambiguity remained on implementation and oversight.[37]

Obama said little about foreign policy in his inaugural address, observing that "we are ready to lead once more" and that "we reject as false the choice between our safety and our ideals"—the first a reference to Bush's knack for losing allies and alienating neutrals, the second a pointed reference to Guantánamo, Abu Ghraib, waterboarding, and extraordinary rendition. But he had certainly said a lot about foreign policy on the campaign trail, and during the first few months he made good on some of these promises. In mid-February, the president dispatched seventeen thousand additional troops to Afghanistan, a 50 percent increase on the thirty-eight thousand already in post. Two weeks later, he announced that all U.S. troops would be withdrawn from Iraq by December 2011. Obama was winding down the war of choice and ramping up the war of necessity.

For his stated desire to engage with America's enemies, Obama had caught flak during the campaign. But the criticism did not deter him from pursuing this path as president. To coincide with Nowruz, the Persian New Year, Obama sent a videotaped message to Iran in March stating, "My administration is now committed to diplomacy that addresses the full range of issues before us." As part of a wider attempt to rehabilitate America's tattered image in the Middle East, and win the confidence of the president of the Palestinian National Authority, Mahmoud Abbas, Obama also insisted to Israel's president, Benjamin Netanyahu, that settlement construction in the occupied territories must immediately cease.[38] The president publicly stated his expectation that Palestinian statehood would be achieved by 2011, and said that hard concessions would be required from both sides. (Obama's confidence was wildly misplaced.) He gave his first foreign interview as president to the Arab television network Al Arabiya. During an early overseas tour that took in the major capitals of the Muslim world, Jakarta, Ankara, Riyadh, and Cairo, Obama declined (pointedly, according to his critics) to visit Jerusalem.

The defining moment of Obama's early engagement strategy was a landmark address at Cairo University in June. The administration had spent months crafting the speech, testament to the importance it attached to repairing America's image in the Middle East. In front of a crowd of three thousand, a black American president with the middle name Hussein began his speech with the words *Assalamu alaykum*, a traditional Muslim greeting that translates as "Peace be upon you." It was clear that Obama possessed points of connectivity to the non-Western world that were unavailable to his predecessors. He discussed his paternal lineage, described his roots in a "Kenyan family that included generations of Muslims," and spoke of the awe inspired by his "hearing the call of the *azaan* at the break of dawn and the fall of dusk."[39]

It was a frank performance that celebrated his cosmopolitanism and his nation's pluralism. It drew a line under the monism of the Bush administration: "I know there has been controversy about the promotion of democracy in recent years, and much of this controversy is connected to the war in Iraq. So let me be clear: no system of government can or should be imposed upon one nation by any other."

This was a critical moment in the speech, the point at which Obama's virtues and Bush's failings were starkly contrasted to the anticipated acclaim of the crowd. But the expected applause line did not materialize (although Hosni Mubarak was undoubtedly cheering on the inside). Human Rights Watch's Tom Malinowski, who had informally advised Obama's campaign, put his finger on the problem: "I don't think he was aware that the audience both despised George W. Bush and desperately wanted Bush's help in their cause."[40]

In an interview with *The Wall Street Journal* two years later, Paul Wolfowitz identified as significant the moment when Obama's modesty and preference for incremental change fell flat in a nation (and region) desperate to free itself from autocrats like Mubarak. It was the word "democracy"—not Obama repudiating his predecessor's operationalization of the concept—that had stirred applause. Wolfowitz re-created what must have been going through the president's mind at the end of that segment: "There's something not quite right here. I'm about to say it's controversial, and . . . they've applauded the mere mention of the topic."[41] But the significance of the moment became clear only subsequently. Obama's critics immediately after the speech were less nuanced and incisive. Frank Gaffney, an aide to Richard Perle through the 1970s and 1980s, observed that Obama "not only identifies with Muslims, but may actually be one himself."[42]

Obama's reluctance to hitch U.S. foreign policy to an unpredictable wagon like democratization was displayed clearly in the months that followed. A week after Obama's speech in Cairo, Iranians went to the polls to cast their votes for one of two primary alternatives: the hard-line incumbent Mahmoud Ahmadinejad or reformist Mir-Hossein Mousavi. Ahmadinejad won the contest, gathering a suspiciously high proportion of all votes cast: 63 percent. Mousavi's supporters took to the streets of Tehran—where Mousavi's popularity was highest—to protest the fraud that had clearly been perpetrated. Hundreds of thousands assembled in pursuit of a green revolution—the color of Mousavi's campaign, which was embraced subsequently by all who sought Ahmadinejad's removal—but the government moved swiftly to strangle the movement in its infancy.

The demonstrations were the largest seen in Iran since 1979, but the United States refused to get involved. Obama condemned the brutality of the government's response, in which scores of protestors were killed, observing that the "United States and the international community had been appalled and outraged by the threats, the beatings and imprisonments of the past few days." But the chastening aspect of the president's intervention ended there. "The United States respects the sovereignty of the Islamic Republic of Iran," Obama added reassuringly, "and is not interfering with Iran's internal affairs."[43] His caution was conditioned by two factors that were comprehensible in the context of that time. First, Obama was keen to engage Iran on its nuclear weapons program and did not want to derail the possibility of direct talks that could lead to meaningful progress. Second, history suggested that American intervention in support of the protesters might undermine the independence of that very movement, allowing them to be portrayed by Ahmadinejad and his lackeys as unpatriotic stooges of the United States.

Again, Paul Wolfowitz took strong exception to Obama's position, decrying his logic as devoid of values and, indeed, strategic merit:

> On Iran, it was just terrible. To me the analogy is in 1981, when martial law was declared in Poland . . . Reagan saw it as an opportunity to drive a wedge into this opening, and he and the Pope went at it . . . You had a similar opportunity in Iran in June of 2009 . . . What did we do? We sat on our hands. Why? [Because Obama] entertained this hope that we could negotiate with the regime, and therefore we didn't want to antagonize them . . . Which, by the way, isn't even a smart way to negotiate. It suggests such an eagerness to negotiate that the other guy knows he has you.[44]

Wolfowitz did not state precisely what the president should have done instead. Another U.S. intervention in the Middle East might have midwifed a permanent democratic revolution in Iran. Or it might have drawn the United States into a civil war as bitter and intractable as the one in Iraq. Or it might have raised and then dashed the expectations of ordinary Iranians—alienating everyone. What we do know is that Obama's inaction looked weak and unprincipled and Wolfowitz's critique was easy to make but difficult to own. Henry Kissinger strongly backed Obama: "I think the president has handled this well. Anything that the United States says that puts us totally behind one of the contenders, behind Mousavi, would be a handicap for that person. And I think it's the proper position to take that the people of Iran have to make that decision."[45]

In 1895, the Swedish chemist and armaments manufacturer Alfred Nobel established a peace prize in his will, to be awarded annually to individuals who have "done the most or the best work for fraternity between nations, for the abolition or reduction of standing armies and for the holding and promotion of peace congresses." Some believe that Nobel added peace to chemistry, physics, medicine, and literature as penance for the dynamite that his factories had brought to the world. Whatever its rationale, the Nobel Peace Prize became one of the most significant accolades in world affairs. Previous American recipients include Theodore Roosevelt in 1906, Elihu Root in 1912, Woodrow Wilson in 1919, Frank B. Kellogg in 1929, Jane Addams in 1931, Cordell Hull in 1945, Emily Balch in 1946, George Marshall in 1953, and Henry Kissinger in 1973. The Nobel Committee awarded prizes to each in homage to previous efforts and achievements—whether apparent or real, durable or ephemeral—in making the world more peaceable. But in 2009, the committee decided to reward promise rather than achievement. In recognition of "his extraordinary efforts to strengthen international diplomacy and cooperation between peoples," and for having "created a new climate in international politics," Barack Hussein Obama was awarded the Nobel Peace Prize.[46]

Obama's political opponents had some fun with the announcement, mocking the committee's ulterior motive—this was clearly a swipe at Bush, not a reward for Obama—and the president's slight achievements. The chairman of the Republican National Committee, Michael Steele, was not alone in expressing disbelief: "The real question Americans are asking is, 'What has President Obama actually accomplished.'"[47] It was a prize that Obama might have done without.

"To be honest," Obama said upon learning the news, "I do not feel that I deserve to be in the company of so many of the transformative figures who've been honored by this prize." But it was also impossible for him to decline such an honor. And besides, the award assisted certain of his aspirations, particularly in regard to the restoration of America's reputation. "I also know . . . that throughout history," Obama added, "the Nobel Peace Prize has not just been used to honor specific achievement; it's also been used as a means to give momentum to a set of causes."[48] The acceptance speech itself was a wonderful opportunity for the president to build momentum, to explain to a world audience what he wanted to achieve.

Obama's Nobel acceptance speech developed some of the themes present in his "antiwar" speech of October 2002. In Chicago he had to distinguish his opposition from that of Jesse Jackson. In Oslo he had to pay homage to Martin Luther King Jr. and Gandhi while dismissing the nonviolence they practiced as inapplicable to someone holding his office. Obama had to dim the crowd's ardor by asserting that while peace is the ultimate aspiration of humankind, meting out violence against "evil"—the precise word he used—is often necessary:

> We must begin by acknowledging the hard truth: We will not eradicate violent conflict in our lifetimes. There will be times when nations—acting individually or in concert—will find the use of force not only necessary but morally justified . . . I face the world as it is, and cannot stand idle in the face of threats to the American people. For make no mistake: Evil does exist in the world. A non-violent movement could not have halted Hitler's armies. Negotiations cannot convince al Qaeda's leaders to lay down their arms.

Obama spoke directly to the tension in America "between those who describe themselves as realists or idealists—a tension that suggests a stark choice between the narrow pursuit of interests or an endless campaign to impose our values around the world." The president maintained that there was fluidity across that boundary, that the pure application of either made for bad foreign policy. "I reject these choices," said Obama, and he celebrated those individuals in recent history who had transcended the dogmas conventionally ascribed to them—alienating many traditional supporters along the way—in pursuit of larger goals:

> In light of the Cultural Revolution's horrors, Nixon's meeting with Mao appeared inexcusable—and yet it surely helped set China on a path where millions of its citizens have been lifted from poverty and connected to open societies. Pope John Paul's engagement with Poland created space not just for the Catholic Church, but for labor leaders like Lech Walesa. Ronald Reagan's efforts on arms control and embrace of perestroika not only improved relations with the Soviet Union, but empowered dissidents throughout Eastern Europe. There's no simple formula here. But we must try as best we can to balance isolation and engagement, pressure and incentives, so that human rights and dignity are advanced over time.[49]

"There's no simple formula here" was the most revealing line in the speech. It signaled that the Obama Doctrine was the absence of one.

In the weeks after Obama's election victory in the fall of 2008, Doug Lute, a three-star general, briefed the transition team on Afghanistan. A tall and imposing man, Lute did not pull his punches. As Tom Donilon, who became Obama's deputy national security adviser, recalled, the very first Power-Point slide stated an uncomfortable truth: "It said we do not have a strategy in Afghanistan that you can articulate or achieve. We had been at war for eight years, and no one could explain the strategy." For Donilon and others, this was a startling revelation. What had the Bush administration been doing these past six years? What precisely was America trying to achieve in Afghanistan beyond the eradication of al-Qaeda training camps (which had been achieved by 2002)? As David Sanger asks in *Confront and Conceal*, Was it "a full-blown democracy with the rule of law and respect for human rights? A divided country in which every warlord runs his own piece of turf? A state-in-name-only that survived on revenue from opium, minerals, and foreign aid? Something else?"[50] No one in the Bush administration appeared to have figured this out. It fell to the Obama administration either to provide an answer or head for the exit.

Members of the administration had different answers to these questions. Vice President Joe Biden believed that the conflict between the Taliban and the corrupt Karzai government was unresolvable—he began with the requirement for a swift American withdrawal and worked from there. President Hamid Karzai was an Ngo Dinh Diem–type figure who lacked popular legitimacy and whose government would fall quickly without U.S. support. Biden feared that Afghanistan could become Obama's Vietnam, leading to a lingering foreign-policy death by a thousand cuts. Instead he recommended a strategy of "counterterrorism plus," requiring the withdrawal of conventional U.S. ground troops and the increased use of Special Forces–spotted drone and cruise missile strikes. America's focus should solely be on those individuals who seek to do the nation harm; anything more was fantastical. Biden was worried by those who did not care to remember their history. Susan Rice's observation that Vietnam "is not the frame of reference for every decision—or any decision, for that matter. I'm sick and tired of reprising all of the traumas and the battles and the psychoses of the 1960s" was a source of concern to Biden and other like-minded colleagues.[51] George Santayana's observation that "those who cannot remember the past are condemned to repeat it" seemed apposite in the circumstances.

Hillary Clinton rejected the Vietnam analogy as misleading—embedding gains rather than cutting and running was her goal. Her preference was for a policy of "sustained counterinsurgency," transferring General Petraeus's successful surge in Iraq to Afghanistan. She and Petraeus believed the United States could actually win over the Afghan people by protecting them, through pressuring Karzai to reform and delegitimizing the Taliban by displaying the competence and durability of an alternative. If Clinton had a time scale in mind, however, it was undoubtedly shorter than the two generations that Petraeus had identified as a possibility in private discussions: "You have to recognize . . . that I don't think you win this war. I think you keep fighting. It's a little bit like Iraq, actually . . . This is the kind of fight we're in for the rest of our lives and probably our kids' lives."[52] Her perspective was close to that of Petraeus but perhaps not that close. A key motive behind Clinton's preference for sustained counterinsurgency was her desire to render permanent the progressive gains that had permitted some 2.4 million Afghan girls to attend school for the first time since the communist era.

President Obama was placed in a quandary. There was no obvious median point between stay and go. The ranking commander in the field, General Stanley McChrystal, made the president's decision all the trickier in September when he requested forty thousand additional troops, noting that not doing so "will likely result in failure" in Afghanistan—namely, the collapse of the Karzai government and victory for the Taliban. More cheerily, McChrystal observed that while "the situation is serious, success is still achievable." All General McChrystal needed was what he wanted and all the time in the world to use it.[53] To older, more cautious hands, there was a distinct echo of General Westmoreland in March 1968.

But during the campaign, Obama had identified Afghanistan as the central theater in the ongoing fight against Islamist terrorism. It was well-nigh impossible for him to decline McChrystal's request without looking shabbily opportunistic. And besides, Obama's views on Afghanistan's importance were sincerely held. Bush *had* taken his eye off the ball; Afghanistan *was* the war of necessity. Yet the president did not want to be bounced into a decision by a pair of generals acutely aware of their political power. Colin Powell, with whom Obama met frequently during his first term, furnished some sound advice on this subject:

> Mr. President, don't get pushed by the left to do nothing. Don't get pushed by the right to do everything. You take your time and you figure it out . . . If you decide to send more troops or that's what you feel is

necessary, make sure you have a good understanding of what those troops are going to be doing and some assurance that the additional troops will be successful. You can't guarantee success in a very complex theater like Afghanistan and increasingly with the Pakistan problem next door.[54]

Powell had served in Vietnam, had strategized the first Iraq War, and had better cause than most to lament the origins and course of the second. He was a man who commanded Obama's respect. This made it doubly pleasing that Powell's advice amounted to a triangulation of sorts—it was a call to ignore both the left and the right and follow his own instincts. Maybe there was a plausible middle point between Stanley McChrystal and Joe Biden.

On December 1, 2009, at West Point, Obama announced his policy decision on Afghanistan and spoke broadly about America's role in world affairs, which the president believed had to become more modest. He would send thirty thousand additional troops to Afghanistan but on a strictly time-limited basis: they would begin leaving in the summer of 2011. Obama made clear that he would not accept "a nation building project of up to a decade" while at the same time rejecting the Vietnam comparisons that had been drawn frequently by the press—and indeed by members of his administration. The Vietnam analogy "was a false reading of history," Obama said. "Unlike Vietnam, we are not facing a broad-based popular insurgency. And most importantly, unlike Vietnam, the American people were viciously attacked from Afghanistan." On America's place in the world, Obama noted that since "the days of Franklin Roosevelt, and the service and sacrifice of our grandparents and great-grandparents, our country has borne a special burden in global affairs . . . We have not always been thanked for these efforts, and we have at times made mistakes. But more than any other nation, the United States of America has underwritten global security for over six decades." But times were changing and the nation had to refocus its energy on self-improvement: "That's why our troop commitment in Afghanistan cannot be open-ended—because the nation that I'm most interested in building is our own."[55]

This Beardian flourish was one of the few aspects of the speech cheered by the left of his party. The right, meanwhile, excoriated Obama for setting a deadline for withdrawal—surely the Taliban would now simply wait America out—and for not furnishing all the troops that McChrystal requested.

There was certainly something in the speech to annoy everyone, a quality that Obama shared with Henry Kissinger. But it was a typical Obama performance in its methodical nature, its precision, restraint, and apparent reasonableness. It was surge and withdrawal at the same time, a final roll of the dice before he pulled the troops home—come what may.

But there was also sufficient material there to stoke the concern of America's allies. One European journalist observed, "For the first time, I can envision the United States returning to isolationism."[56] It is no challenge to surmise why Obama's preference for rebalancing toward the domestic sphere caused this reaction. The president had approvingly quoted Eisenhower's farewell address on national security—"Each proposal must be weighed in the light of a broader consideration: the need to maintain balance in and among national programs"—before adding ominously, "Over the past several years, we have lost that balance. We've failed to appreciate the connection between our national security and our economy." The president did his best to bathe the speech in optimistic rhetoric and references to the American fundamentals: "freedom," "justice," "hope," "opportunity," which taken together form "the moral source of America's authority."[57] But the core message was jaded, its deliverer battle-worn.

The year 2010 was the deadliest of the conflict—499 American troops were killed in Afghanistan. The McChrystal surge was not replicating the Petraeus one in Iraq in terms of impact. How could it? The antagonists, political context, and terrain were so different. Obama began to worry that he had made a mistake in escalating the war, even on this time-limited basis. "You know," warned Strobe Talbott, deputy secretary of state during the Clinton administration, in the summer of 2010, "he could lose the presidency on this one."[58] On the decision to order a surge in Afghanistan, *New York Times* journalist David Sanger observed that Obama "regretted it almost instantly."[59]

In the summer of 2010, Obama was forced to put General McChrystal to the sword—for reasons quite unrelated to battlefield tactics. *Rolling Stone* had run an article titled "The Runaway General" in which McChrystal and his advisers were quoted deriding President Obama and Vice President Biden. After McChrystal's first meeting with the president, one aide noted that Obama "clearly didn't know anything about him, who he was. Here's the guy who's going to run his fucking war, but he didn't seem very engaged. The Boss was pretty disappointed." Biden was lampooned—"Biden? Did you say: Bite Me?"—and his hostility to counterinsurgency doctrine was rubbished. (Obama had earlier reprimanded McChrystal for stating that Biden's retrenchment would create "Chaos-istan.") More generally, according to McChrystal, Obama was unsure of himself when surrounded by military brass: "uncomfortable and intimidated." The impression the article conveyed was that President Barack Obama was weak-minded and effete, compared, at least, to that hard-headed, nunchuck-carrying leader of men: Stan "the Man" McChrystal.[60]

It is hard to believe that McChrystal did not realize by the end of the interview that the article might spell the end of his military career. No president could ignore that level of insubordination—a perspective that carried broad bipartisan support. Obama fired McChrystal the day after the article appeared, following a tense meeting at the White House. Afterward, Obama said, "I welcome debate, but I won't tolerate division," adding that it was essential that individual soldiers and officers—no matter what their rank—observe "a strict adherence to the military chain of command and respect for civilian control over that chain of command."[61] The president said that McChrystal's departure would not alter his strategic priorities in Afghanistan, appointing the like-minded David Petraeus to take his place. Others were not so sure, sensing a gradual disillusionment with the course the president had launched at West Point. Reflecting on the *Rolling Stone* article, Bruce Riedel observed, "The description that it portrays of how our commander in the field is operating, and how some of the people around him are behaving, will definitely undermine support for the war."[62]

By late 2010 there were one hundred thousand troops in Afghanistan, a significant increase over the thirty-eight thousand stationed there when Obama assumed the presidency. Throughout 2011, however, Obama moved sharply toward de-escalation in pursuit of a final withdrawal. Riedel's prediction had been right. On June 22, the president returned to West Point to make another major speech on Afghanistan. Over the course of the address, Obama did precisely what George Ball and others had urged LBJ to do in 1965 and 1966. He declared victory and announced his intention to get out: "When I announced this surge at West Point, we set clear objectives: to refocus on al Qaeda, to reverse the Taliban's momentum, and train Afghan security forces to defend their own country. I also made it clear that our commitment would not be open-ended, and that we would begin to draw down our forces this July. Tonight, I can tell you that we are fulfilling that commitment."

Obama's address also signaled a sharp break with the counterinsurgency doctrine propounded by McChrystal and Petraeus—at least in its Afghan incarnation—making clear that it was time for the Afghan people to step up and take control of their destiny. Addressing the camera directly, Obama said, "We won't try to make Afghanistan a perfect place. We will not police its streets or patrol its mountains indefinitely." He reiterated a theme that he had first introduced, to the vexation of some, during his speech announcing the surge eighteen months previously. "Over the last decade," Obama said in conclusion, "we have spent a trillion dollars on war, at a time of rising debt and hard economic times. Now we must invest in America's greatest resource—our people . . . America, it is time to focus on nation building here at home . . . Let us responsibly end these wars, and reclaim the American Dream that is at the center of our story."[63] In making his decision to wind down the war, Obama directly rebuffed David Petraeus. A year later, Secretary of Defense Leon Panetta (who replaced Robert Gates) announced that America's combat mission in Afghanistan would end at the close of 2013. Obama had drawn a line under his predecessor's wars in Iraq and Afghanistan. He had shown himself more than capable of reversing course when events on the ground counsel such a course. He appeared to agree with John Maynard Keynes's question to a dogmatic critic: "When the facts change, I change my mind. What do you do, sir?" Obama's critics called him a hypocrite; hawkish Republicans attacked his lack of spine. To his admirers the president was refreshingly flexible.

Over the course of his presidency, George W. Bush had ordered forty drone strikes: targeted assassinations of high-value targets using unmanned drones carrying Hellfire missiles, operated at a remove of thousands of miles by CIA "pilots" in Langley, Virginia.[64] Barack Obama's presidency witnessed a step change in the number of strikes—more than four hundred at the time of writing—a widening of the program's geographical remit, and a willingness to kill radicalized American citizens if the need arose and the opportunity presented itself. The CIA-led drone program was extended beyond Afghanistan, Pakistan, and Iraq to include the targeted killing of alleged terrorists (or aspirants) in Libya, Yemen, and Somalia. In September 2011 in Yemen, a Reaper drone, operated by the CIA, killed Anwar al-Awlaki, a firebrand Islamist cleric, al-Qaeda operative, and American citizen—along with three other Americans "not specifically targeted."[65]

Obama could not resist the temptation to celebrate a program that diminished and terrorized al-Qaeda without putting American boots on the ground. In one speech he observed, "We have had more success in eliminating al-Qaeda leaders in recent months than in recent years."[66] Drone strikes were the reason Obama shifted from supporting counterinsurgency in 2009 to rejecting it two years later. One foreign-policy adviser to Obama described the appeal of drone strikes succinctly: "precision, economy, and deniability."[67] Drone strikes also took no prisoners. And the last thing America needed was more of those in Guantánamo Bay.

These were advantages, but Obama's increased propensity to launch drone strikes also posed large ethical questions. This was a policy of high-tech assassination, after all, that flouted the sovereignty of other nations. The Bush administration elevated preventive defense to the status of official policy—invading states on the basis of potential threats. Obama rejected this strategy on the metalevel but was evidently comfortable applying it to the micro. Eliminating individuals on the basis of their prospective threat to a state sounds like a plotline from George Orwell's 1984 or Philip K. Dick's short story "The Minority Report." And because the United States was the first nation in the world to weaponize drones, Obama was setting a precedent that other nations will eventually follow. David Sanger asks the right question in Confront and Conceal: "What is the difference—legally and morally—between a sticky bomb the Israelis place on the side of an Iranian scientist's car and a Hellfire missile the United States launches at a car in Yemen from thirty thousand feet in the air? How is one an 'assassination'—condemned by the United States—and the other an 'insurgent strike'?"[68]

Even though the drone program officially did not exist—the "deniability" element of its appeal—Obama realized that he needed an intellectually plausible and convincing answer to searching questions such as Sanger's. The president certainly had a well-credentialed individual in-house to carry out this task. Harold Koh, the State Department's top lawyer, had clerked for Harry Blackmun, the author of Roe v. Wade, was a former dean of Yale Law School, and was well regarded among liberal Democrats and touted by many as a future appointee to the Supreme Court. Koh had his work cut out for him. It is difficult to conceive of a more challenging or important legal commission.

In a speech delivered in March 2010 at the annual conference of the American Society of International Law, Koh provided a carefully worded defense of the legality of drone strikes (without ever using the word "drone"). At the outset, Koh stated that he viewed his duty as to serve as the "conscience" of the Obama administration's counterterrorism policies, to ensure that the nation was "following universal standards, not double standards." Yet it was clear from his research, Koh stated, that "U.S. targeting practices, including legal operations conducted with unmanned aerial vehicles, comply with all applicable law, including the laws of war." How did Koh justify this assertion? Primarily through claiming that al-Qaeda had "not abandoned its intent to attack the United States, and indeed continues to attack us." In those circumstances the targeting of an individual possessed of such desires represents what the Obama administration defines as a "lawful extrajudicial killing"—one that is "consistent with its inherent right to self-defense" under international law. An "unlawful extrajudicial killing" takes place when the United States does not provide sufficient proof that a target is possessed of those same inclinations. Koh's case is logical in many respects. But it is also entirely predicated on trusting the government to make such determinations thoroughly, transparently, and without prejudice.

On the issue of breaching other nations' sovereignty, Koh presented a neat formulation. The United States may target individuals only in a country that has permitted them to do so; such as was the case in Iraq, Afghanistan, and Pakistan (or at least until May 2011). But the United States also reserved the right to act unilaterally where a nation in question is "unwilling or unable to suppress the threat"—a definition that would include anarchic nations with porous borders like Somalia and Yemen. Koh also made a final point that he believed critics of the drone program would do well to ponder: all war involves making mistakes that kill, but unmanned drones— which can hover above a target for hours on end—make fewer mistakes than even the most advanced bombers. As one operator told Koh, "I used to drop bombs from a flying airplane. I could not see the faces of the people . . . I am much, much more aware of the human concerns in these situations."[69]

Drone strikes have been at the heart of President Obama's counterterrorism strategy. Their success at eliminating major al-Qaeda figures explains why Defense Secretary Leon Panetta could state boldly in the summer of 2011 that the United States was "within reach" of winning the war against Islamist terrorism. But the policy has also created significant antipathy across the world. Do drone strikes eliminate high-value al-Qaeda targets? Absolutely. But it is impossible to gauge how many others have been radicalized by America's drone program. These invisible assassins inspire fear and dread. But it is impossible to secure the United States from attack with recourse to these tactics alone. And the Obama administration's silence did not help. Silence is understandably equated with sin.

In May 2013 at the National Defense University, Obama broke his vow of omertà. He delivered what an admiring *New York Times* editorial described as "the most important statement on counterterrorism policy since the 2001 attacks, a momentous turning point in post-9/11 America." The basic message was: mission nearly accomplished. "Our systemic effort to dismantle terrorist organizations must continue," Obama said. "But this war, like all wars, must end. That's what history advises. That's what our democracy demands." In the course of a speech of remarkable candor, the president admitted for the first time that he had ordered the killing of an American citizen, Anwar al-Awlaki, in a strike that also killed three other people, including al-Awlaki's sixteen-year-old son. The president provided strong evidence suggesting Awlaki was organizing terrorist attacks. Obama also stated his intention to transfer the drone program from the CIA to the Department of Defense and indicated his desire to discuss with Congress "options for increased oversight," which might include a "special court to evaluate and authorize lethal action" or "an independent oversight board in the executive branch." Crucially, Obama added that the only circumstance in which he would order a drone strike would be where there was a "continuing and imminent threat to Americans"—a tighter definition than existed previously.[70]

Less than a week after Obama's speech, Pakistan announced that a U.S. drone strike had killed Wali ur-Rehman, the deputy leader of the Pakistan Taliban. The strike illustrated the merits and demerits of the program in microcosm. It is alleged that Rehman, who had a $5 million U.S. bounty on his head, orchestrated attacks on U.S. forces in Afghanistan and helped plan a suicide bombing that killed seven CIA agents at Camp Chapman in 2009 (later dramatized in the movie *Zero Dark Thirty*). As the deputy leader of the Pakistan Taliban, Rehman helped organize multiple suicide attacks in Pakistan that had killed thousands. The Pakistani government certainly did not mourn his passing.[71] The U.S. government, of course, was pleased to have eliminated such a high-value target.

Yet the strike also infuriated the Pakistani government, a bystander to events, whose Foreign Ministry condemned the strike and where a consensus is emerging that American drone activity above its territory needs to be halted. The U.S. government refused to confirm that a strike had actually taken place, undermining Obama's claims regarding transparency. Indeed, the speech was still being cheered as the missile eviscerated its target. From President Obama's perspective, the tactical advantages far outweighed the reputational damage. It was bold, in many respects, to order a strike so soon after a speech that was hailed as a progressive landmark. But the strike laid bare the ethical quandaries that will face all future presidents in possession of this omniscience-encouraging technology. Imperiled nations that possess lethally effective weapons tend to use them.

At the beginning of 2009, the CIA briefed Obama on the agency's efforts to locate Osama bin Laden. Off-the-record observers of that meeting have indicated that the president was underwhelmed. He instructed his incoming CIA director, Leon Panetta, to make locating bin Laden the number-one priority. The additional resources that accompanied the reprioritization reaped dividends in the summer of 2010 when the agency made a significant breakthrough. They had been tracking an al-Qaeda courier named Abu Ahmed al-Kuwaiti, who had led them to a fortified compound in the Pakistani city of Abbottabad. The compound had some features that struck analysts as suspicious.

The three-story main building was custom built with large canopies to protect its inhabitants from satellite photography. High walls crowned with razor wire surrounded the compound. No phone lines were connected to the property. Many in the agency were convinced that the main building was home to Osama bin Laden. A false vaccination program was established in an attempt to secure DNA evidence from the compound's inhabitants, but to no avail. It ultimately fell to President Obama to choose one of three options: launch an air strike, dispatch ground forces, or wait longer to find corroborating evidence. A final complicating issue was whether to consult with Pakistan or decline to share this information, since their intelligence agency (ISI) leaked like a sieve.[72]

Obama's advisers were far from unanimous on how to proceed. Vice President Biden recalled that Obama "went around the table with all the senior people, including the chiefs of staff, and he said, 'I have to make a decision. What is your opinion?'" Few wanted to make a clear recommendation, fearing the consequences—far graver, hypothetically, than those stemming from the 1993 Black Hawk Down debacle in Somalia—if the decision turned bad. "Every single person in that room hedged their bet except Leon Panetta," Biden said. "Leon said go. Everyone else said, forty-nine, fifty-one."[73] As a salutary parallel, Robert Gates reminded them of Jimmy Carter's ill-fated decision to send U.S. helicopters to Iran to rescue American hostages. The term "shit show" began doing the rounds as a catchall descriptor of the potential consequences of a botched U.S. attempt to kill or capture bin Laden in Pakistan.[74]

Weighing these issues, Obama ultimately made a decision that was both bold and stemmed logically from previous remarks on the issue of bin Laden and Pakistani sovereignty. The president rejected his cabinet's caution and ordered implementation of the riskiest option. On the evening of May 1, 2011, two Black Hawk helicopters departed Jalalabad airfield in eastern Afghanistan and set out for Abbottobad. In addition to the pilots, the helicopters carried twenty-three Navy SEALs, an Urdu-English translator, and a Belgian Malinois dog to track anyone leaving or arriving on the scene. The SEALs penetrated the compound, killed bin Laden, stripped the property of hard drives and papers, and transported their bounty back to Afghanistan. In addition to bin Laden, the SEALs killed three men and one woman within the compound, including one of bin Laden's sons. All the Americans were unharmed. Bin Laden's body was identified and transported to the USS *Carl Vinson*, where his corpse was cleaned and wrapped, which was in accordance with Muslim custom, then dropped into the North Arabian Sea, which wasn't. At 3:00 a.m. on May 2, two hours after the architect of 9/11 was shot and killed, Chairman of the Joint Chiefs Mike Mullen informed his Pakistani counterpart that a military operation had been carried out in his country and that bin Laden was now dead. Relations between the two nations have never fully recovered. Islamabad viewed the raid as a flagrant betrayal of trust.

The dilemma that confronted Obama over how to react to bin Laden's apparent discovery did not lend itself to triangulation. The president quickly surmised that the choice was between going all in with ground forces—eliminating the uncertainty that would accompany a missile strike—or not going in at all. Keeping Pakistan out of the loop evidently caused Obama little angst. He was simply acting in accordance with what he had said during the campaign, and for which he had received significant flak from both Hillary Clinton and John McCain. It was an incisive decision that stemmed logically from previous remarks.

Paul Wolfowitz was impressed by Obama's decision. He hailed it as a "gutsy call" and implied that it ran against the grain of the president's default leadership style: "Obama has just made the toughest decision of his presidency, arguably. It wasn't a simple decision . . . He was in a position where he'd have to take responsibility for it if it went badly. It's gone well. I hope he's learned some of the virtues of boldness."[75]

The praise and the underhanded criticism were both genuine. But Wolfowitz rather misreads his subject. Barack Obama is utterly ruthless and decisive when it comes to eliminating enemies when it does not require the

deployment of significant military resources and where an exit plan is obvious. The president applies the Powell Doctrine to individual human enemies, who are dispatched with overwhelming force. It is on the larger matters
of war and peace among nation-states that he practices caution.

In December 2010, a twenty-six-year-old vegetable vendor named Mohamed
Bouazizi doused himself in gasoline and set himself alight in front of the
governor's office in Sidi Bouzid, a rural town in Tunisia scarred by endemic
corruption. Bouazizi couldn't afford to pay the bribes required to get a permit to sell his vegetables. He died a month later from his burns and became
a martyr and a catalyst to the cause of democratic reform across the Middle
East. No one could have anticipated the consequences that stemmed from
his desperate act.

Just the month previous, more than two hundred classified U.S. diplomatic
cables had been published on the WikiLeaks website. Many were reprinted
in high-circulation international newspapers such as *The Guardian*, *Le Monde*,
Der Spiegel, and *The Washington Post*. Over time, some 250,000 leaked State
Department documents were released into the public domain. Bouazizi's
self-immolation had followed a series of embarrassing disclosures about the
regime led by Tunisia's president, Zine El Abidine Ben Ali. It was Robert
Godec, the U.S. ambassador to Tunisia, who unwittingly revealed details of
the Ben Ali family's opulent lifestyle that firmly suggested they were detached from reality. Godec wrote that "it is the excesses of President Ben
Ali's family that inspire outrage among Tunisians," noting that these included Pasha, a pet tiger owned by Ben Ali's daughter, and the family's insistence on flying in yogurt and ice cream from the French Riviera. These
WikiLeaks revelations were repackaged by Sami Ben Gharbia, a Tunisian
activist for social justice, and placed on the website TuniLeaks, which experienced high traffic. As Secretary of State Hillary Clinton observed, "I'm not
sure the vegetable vendor killing himself all by itself would have been
enough. I think the openness of the social media, I think WikiLeaks, in
great detail, describing the lavishness of the Ben Ali family and cronies was
a big douse of gasoline on the smoldering fire."[76] It is a fire that burns to this
day. And the Obama administration remains undecided about whether to
fan or ignore it.

On January 14, Tunisian demonstrations acquired sufficient intensity
to force Ben Ali and his indulged wife and progeny to flee for Saudi Arabia,
a safe haven for oppressors. He became the first Arab leader in the modern

era to be bounced from office by street-level popular antipathy. President Obama welcomed his departure, calling for elections that "reflect the true will and aspirations" of the long-suffering Tunisian people. It was a remarkable moment. The combination of WikiLeaks, Twitter, Facebook, and cable television had unleashed a protest of remarkable force and intensity that resonated throughout the region. Moments after Ben Ali stepped down, one tweet would prove particularly farsighted: "Today, Ben Ali. Tomorrow Hosni Mubarak."[77]

The Egyptian president Hosni Mubarak had been a steadfast ally of the United States for thirty years. The American ambassador to Egypt, Margaret Sobey, provided an astute appraisal of Mubarak in 2009, publicized by WikiLeaks: "He is a tried and true realist, innately cautious and conservative, and has little time for idealistic goals." She added that he was not impressed by Obama's predecessor: "Mubarak viewed President Bush as naïve, controlled by subordinates and totally unprepared for dealing with post-Saddam Iraq, especially the rise of Iran's regional influence."[78] A sharp analyst of America's geostrategic foibles, Mubarak also sat in gilded isolation atop a tinderbox. Inspired by events in Tunisia, tens of thousands of Egyptians began to congregate in towns and cities across the nation—Cairo's Tahrir Square was the movement's focal point—to protest policy brutality, endemic corruption, economic malaise, and the absence of democratic accountability. It was clear to seasoned observers that Mubarak would not be able to ride out this storm, particularly while the army was ambivalent about his fate. But he was certainly going to give it a try.

It fell to Joe Biden to provide the administration's initial response to events in Egypt. On January 27, 2011, on PBS's *NewsHour*, Jim Lehrer asked the vice president if Mubarak should stand down in the face of these nationwide protests. Biden replied with an unequivocal no, adding that the long-standing Egyptian president had been a "very responsible" ally in a volatile region—a statement that was essentially true. As Mubarak ratcheted up the brutality of the government response—tear gas and live ammunition were used in a failed attempt to subdue and break up the crowds—Hillary Clinton changed tack a few days later and called for "an orderly transition" in Egypt. But she did not specify when she thought Mubarak ought to depart. By February 1, the reality of hundreds of thousands of protestors in Tahrir Square began to force the issue. Obama had to make a clearer decision: support a long-standing secular ally or embrace the protesters and the uncertainty that would follow Mubarak's departure. A significant concern was the prominence that the Islamist Muslim Brotherhood would likely assume in this new era.

The president felt he did not have much of a choice in the end. The revolution in Egypt was outside of American hands, its momentum near unstoppable. During a painful telephone conversation the following day, Obama advised Mubarak to step down immediately. The president was not convinced by Mubarak's assertion that the protesters would disperse given time: "With all due respect, we have a different analysis. We don't believe the protests are going to die down."[79] Mubarak continued to reject Obama's analysis, observing that he didn't understand Egyptian politics and that failure to support him would destabilize the region. Obama's reply was firm: "Mr. President, I always respect my elders. You've been in politics for a very long time. But there are moments in history when just because things have been the same in the past doesn't mean they'll be the same way in the future."[80]

Obama's abandonment of Mubarak vexed many nations and individuals. Saudi Arabia was disappointed, as it set a dismaying precedent for similarly repressive regimes and it greatly strengthened Iran vis-à-vis its neighbors. Israel was nonplussed because Hosni Mubarak's Egypt had been a friend in an unfriendly region. The potential rise to power of the Muslim Brotherhood was regarded with great trepidation in Tel Aviv. With Mubarak gone, Israel would likely have to add another enemy to an already long list.

For many of the same reasons, Henry Kissinger was alarmed by Mubarak's departure. Like Anwar Sadat, Mubarak had provided "an element of moderation in the region." There was so much uncertainty as to what would come next that celebrations were both premature and unwise. "We shouldn't delude ourselves that a moment of exultation is a foreign policy," Kissinger warned. The prospect of an Islamist-led coalition assuming power was chilling and momentous, "a fundamental change to the kind of world that we have known since the end of World War Two." Nonetheless, Kissinger realized that Obama had been dealt a poor hand and played it reasonably well. There was little that Washington could have done to save Mubarak, and supporting a military crackdown was unthinkable. Obama could not run the risk of placing the United States on the wrong side of history. "I think that the American government has behaved skillfully and thoughtfully during this immediate period," Kissinger observed, although he would have preferred that the Egyptian people had opted for evolution rather than revolution.[81]

Paul Wolfowitz claimed a degree of vindication for the Bush administration's democracy-promoting agenda. When asked whether the revolutions in Tunisia and Egypt—part of a wider process of popular reform across the Middle East that had become known as the Arab Spring—could be connected to the Bush administration's toppling of Saddam Hussein, Wolfowitz replied cautiously, "It's a fascinating question, and one should probably simply . . . say it's in the category of the unknowable." When pressed for elaboration, Wolfowitz duly obliged: "I think Iraq took so long and was so bloody and is still so uncertain that it would be hard to say that it has inspired people . . . [But] the last thing he'd [Saddam] want to see is democratic revolutions anywhere . . . [Because Saddam would likely be] actively supporting [fellow dictators,] we very likely would not be seeing what's happening . . . The absence of Saddam is a huge weight off the Arab World."

It was a thoughtful answer to an unknowable question. But Wolfowitz's critique of Obama's handling of Mubarak's departure was not so nuanced: "Egypt we just bungled completely. I mean, our position was always three days behind whatever was actually going on." Wolfowitz faulted Obama's caution toward the wave of reform rolling across the region. He called for the president to display more certainty in committing to the cause of democratization:

> When you have freedom sweeping the Arab world, and you have people willing to risk their lives not as suicide bombers to kill innocent people, but to save lives and to gain freedom, the United States, first of all, should recognize generally speaking which side of the issue we're on . . . There are all kinds of ways it can end badly, but that would seem to me to be even more reason to be deeply engaged—to find people who want it to end the right way and to support those people, rather than holding back.

Wolfowitz believed that America's response to the Arab Spring could be reduced to a monotheory: embrace "the freedom sweeping the Arab world" and identify and support the "people who want it to end the right way."[82] Wolfowitz thought that forming a strategy toward the Arab Spring was simpler than it appeared—just as he had with Iraq.

Obama's policies toward Libya followed the gist of Wolfowitz's advice. Five days after Mubarak was forced from office in Egypt, protestors in Libya took to the streets—and to social media—demanding the release of the writer and political activist Jamal al-Hajji, who had called for Libya to afford greater rights to its citizens. As Muammar Gaddafi—whom Reagan had described as "this mad dog of the Middle East"—unleashed his security forces, the demonstrators proliferated in cause and number. It was not just al-Hajji they wanted freed, it was everyone—their goal was the toppling of Gaddafi's repressive regime. Within days, Libya slipped into full-scale civil war as the rebellion cohered and its forces began advancing on Tripoli. During a bellicose speech in late February, Gaddafi indicated that his security forces would hunt opponents "house by house." His son Saif indicated that there would be "rivers of blood" if the uprisings continued: "We will take up arms, we will fight to the last bullet . . . fight until the last man, the last woman . . . the last bullet [to] destroy seditious elements."[83] Gaddafi chose a different path than Ben Ali and Mubarak, one that ended in a darker place.

Obama's advisers were deeply divided over how to proceed. Outgoing Defense Secretary Robert Gates believed that a U.S. military intervention in Libya—or indeed anywhere in the world beyond Europe and Latin America—was utter folly. In a widely reported speech at West Point on February 25, Gates said, "In my opinion, any future defense secretary who advises the president to again send a big American land army into Asia or into the Middle East or Africa should 'have his head examined,' as General MacArthur so delicately put it." During congressional testimony, Gates could not contain his contempt for the blasé way some of his colleagues were talking about instituting a no-fly zone: "Let's just call a spade a spade. A no-fly zone begins with an attack on Libya to destroy the air defenses. That's the way you do a no-fly zone."[84] Joe Biden agreed with Gates. Hillary Clinton was ambivalent on how to proceed.

The primary advocate for military intervention to assist the rebellion and oust Gaddafi was Samantha Power. But Obama was also under external pressure to do something—or at least help other nations do something. British prime minister David Cameron and French president Nicolas Sarkozy were both pushing strongly for American support to institute a no-fly zone— France and Britain possessed the will if not the resources to intervene alone. But the usual suspects were not all in agreement. In a remark that ran contrary to her reputation as an advocate of humanitarian intervention, but conformed with her reputation as a blunt talker, Susan Rice informed Gérard Araud, her French counterpart at the United Nations, "You are not going to drag us into your shitty war."[85] Yet there was one organization that did possess sufficient clout to persuade the United States to join the fray. On March 12, the Arab League—with twenty-two Middle Eastern and

African member states—came out in favor of a no-fly zone, calling for the UN to provide the rebellion in Libya with "urgent help."[86]

Enough was enough. During an NSC meeting on how to proceed on Libya, Obama was decisive. "If we don't act, if we put brakes on this thing," the president said, "it will have consequences for U.S. credibility and leadership, consequences for the Arab Spring, and consequences for the international community." Permitting Gaddafi to destroy the rebellion in Benghazi, its principal point of origin, was "just not who we are." Instead of imposing a no-fly zone, however, Obama instructed Susan Rice to secure from the United Nations a resolution stipulating that "all necessary measures" may be used to protect and assist the rebellion.[87] This went further than Cameron and Sarkozy had requested and "called a spade a spade," to use Robert Gates's formulation, making clear that under no circumstances would the United States and its allies allow Gaddafi to prevail. UN Security Council resolution 1973 was passed quickly, with Russia and China abstaining. President Obama was delighted: "This is precisely how the international community should work, as more nations bear both the responsibility and the cost of enforcing international law."[88]

Obama attracted criticism at the time for his slowness in making a decision to support the rebels in Benghazi and for his preference for multilateralism. It was surely an embarrassment that Britain, France, and the Arab League were out in front. Kori Schake, who had positions on the NSC and in the State Department in the George W. Bush administration, observed, "Stepping back and letting others do the work certainly isn't a bold or brave moment for American foreign policy."[89] Following her two-year stint on the Policy Planning Staff, Anne-Marie Slaughter returned to Princeton in February 2011, unimpressed by what she had observed. "On issues like whether to intervene in Libya there's really not a compromise and a consensus," she said. "You can't be a little bit realist and a little bit democratic when deciding whether or not to stop a massacre."[90]

Critiques like these tend to underestimate how complicated the situation in Libya was and is. There were clearly positives. When Obama deemed circumstances propitious, he made a clear decision and followed through to conclusion. (He also failed to seek congressional approval for his action, which stirred considerable anger across the political divide.) Throughout March, the U.S. Air Force and NATO forces destroyed Gaddafi's air defenses, a pivotal act that protected the rebellion. At the end of March, Britain and France took control of the air campaign, though technical deficiencies required them to be propped up now and again. At the loss of no American lives and at a cost of $1.1 billion—a small sum as these things go—the United States helped remove a noxious dictator in the Middle East. It was a military action, furthermore, that won the imprimatur of the Arab League and the United Nations.[91]

At the time it appeared as if the military intervention in Libya was everything the Second Iraq War was not: successful, swift, and legitimate. But there exists a strong possibility that "victory" there may also be Pyrrhic. On September 11, 2012, heavily armed militias attacked the U.S. consulate in Benghazi, killing Ambassador J. Christopher Stevens and three others. Embarrassment that the attack had been launched from the "friendliest" part of new Libya was one possible reason the Obama administration initially presented it as impromptu and provoked by an incendiary anti-Islamic video rather than a carefully planned operation. The instability and violence in Libya has got much worse since then, as militias—comprising many hundreds of different groups, including secessionists and Islamists—struggle for control. At the moment of writing, the nation is effectively lawless.

The election of 2012 pitted Barack Obama against Mitt Romney, a centrist Republican forced to behave like an ultraconservative to secure his party's nomination. It was the GOP candidate's misfortune to run against an incumbent who—through a step change in the frequency, audacity, and lethality of drone attacks—was able to argue persuasively that he had waged war on al-Qaeda more effectively than his predecessor (and at a lower human and financial cost). The locating and killing of Osama bin Laden, meanwhile, was a priceless electoral advantage, armoring Obama against Republican attacks on his lack of fortitude. How could Romney communicate a greater desire to confront America's enemies without sounding like Barry Goldwater in 1964?

The Republican candidate was rarely less convincing than when seeking to outhawk Obama on facing down Iran, Russia—"without question our number one geopolitical foe" (a designation that appears less hyperbolic now than it did then)—and China.[92] Romney's bluster was just that. There were in fact fewer differences between the candidates than either was willing to concede. In October 2011, Romney delivered a speech at the Citadel in Charleston, South Carolina, that was widely reported for its bellicosity on Iran. During the speech, however, he also made an important cautionary point: "Our next President will face many difficult and complex foreign policy decisions. Few will be black and white."[93] Obama could hardly dispute the wisdom of this remark. He voices a variation on the same theme regularly.

That there were few substantive differences between the candidates on foreign policy owed everything to the temper of the times. George W. Bush was an electoral pariah, his costly and adventurous foreign policies now were unpopular with the majority of Americans. A CNN poll in the summer of 2012 found that 54 percent of Americans viewed Bush unfavorably—the same proportion that viewed Jimmy Carter favorably.[94] For understandable reasons, Romney had to explain just how different he was from the previous Republican president. This meant he had to struggle to find substantive grounds on which to differentiate his own approach from Obama's.

On Iran, for example, during the final presidential debate Romney attacked Obama for allowing Tehran to move "four years closer" to acquiring a nuclear weapon. But when pressed to state precisely what he would do differently, Romney had little to say beyond generalities about toughening the existing sanction regime.[95] How could he? After trying to engage Iran and receiving nothing by way of a constructive response, President Obama had imposed suffocating sanctions and kept all military options firmly on the table. As David Sanger wrote in *The New York Times*, "The economic sanctions Mr. Obama has imposed have been far more crippling to the Iranian economy than anything President Bush did."[96]

That Romney failed to establish any clear differences with the president showed how much America's foreign-policy options were being narrowed by its economic distress. He never followed through on his vague criticism of Obama's approach toward Syria. A Republican presidential aspirant talking up another military engagement in the Middle East was not manna from electoral heaven. Foreign policy played a peripheral role in the election of 2012. There was no edge to the exchanges on any issue beyond the Obama administration's alleged obfuscation regarding the attack in Benghazi that killed Ambassador Stevens. Obama and Romney could find little to argue about. This scenario worked out fine for the incumbent. Handsomely assisted by Mitt Romney's varied political failings—including a series of remarks at a fund-raiser in which the presidential aspirant dismissed 47 percent of the American people as "dependent" on government handouts and stated that "my job is not to worry about those people"—Obama comfortably secured reelection.

Barack Obama has sharply reduced America's military commitments during one of the nation's most painful economic contractions. But this is no mere

temporary lull in the nation's global activism. Moderation and retrenchment is the present and the future. In December 2011, Obama withdrew the
last remaining American troops from Iraq. A month later, he unveiled a
new statement of intent, the Defense Strategic Guidance, which explicitly
repudiated the democracy-enlarging Wilsonian logic presented in the Bush
administration's NSS 2002. Obama announced that the standing army
would be cut from 570,000 to 490,000. The existing policy, which held that
the nation should possess sufficient military resources to win two concurrent wars in different theaters, was abandoned. America's declared policy
is now to be able to win one war while merely stymying a potential assault
elsewhere. "This country is at a strategic turning point after a decade of war,"
Obama's preface to the document declared, "and, therefore, we are shaping
a Joint Force for the future that will be smaller and leaner, but will be agile,
flexible, ready, and technologically advanced." The document called for
the Pentagon "to reduce the 'cost of doing business.' "[97]

A month in advance of the publication of the document—to prepare the
Pentagon for the pain that would inevitably follow—Obama invited the Joint
Chiefs and the military's most prominent figures to a ceremonial dinner at the
White House's State Dining Room. From 2001 to 2011, the Pentagon's budget
had grown by 67 percent in real terms. Its annual budget of $700 billion ex-
ceeded that of the next twenty nations combined. Obama told the assembled
brass that this was unsustainable, that the defense budget would contract by
$500 billion over the next ten years. He torpedoed the Pentagon's proposal to
keep one hundred thousand troops on standby to engage in "stability operations" of the type the United States had been engaged in in Afghanistan and
Iraq for close to ten years. Obama was indicating that the expensive business of
counterinsurgency and overseas nation-building was over. "This was the end
of an era," one commander told David Sanger afterward, "and that was a hard
concept for many in the room to accept."[98] Obama's decision not only ended
an era inaugurated by the second Bush administration, it also shut out the
maximalist crisis logic contained in Paul Nitze's NSC-68.

In his January 2012 State of the Union address, Barack Obama echoed
Madeleine Albright in emphasizing the nation's pivotal world role: "America
remains the one indispensable nation in world affairs—and as long as
I am President, I intend to keep it that way."[99] His words were both sincere
and accurate. Britain and France had agitated for intervention in Libya but
could do nothing without U.S. participation. The same is true in respect to
Syria. In spite of swinging cuts to the Pentagon's budget, the United States
has no genuine peer competitor in the military realm.

But there was something new. The concept of "opportunity cost" had become central to American decision making on matters of diplomacy. R. Nicholas Burns had served as a high-level diplomat for thirty years prior to Obama winning the presidency. Through that tumultuous era, he said, "No one ever stopped and asked, 'How much will this cost?'" Now it is the first question posed. In a major set piece speech on the Arab Spring in May 2011, Obama mooted the possibility of forgiving $1 billion of Egypt's debts and establishing a "Middle East Fund," seeded with another $1 billion to support reform across the region. This is small change in development terms. The Marshall Plan cost $150 billion in real terms. But how could Obama justify spending more to the American people?[100]

Further steep cuts in the defense budget were made in 2013 and 2014. In January 2013, Barack Obama nominated Chuck Hagel to replace Leon Panetta as secretary of defense. Senate Republicans objected strenuously to the appointment of Hagel, a Republican, to head the Pentagon. A decorated Vietnam veteran, Hagel had served on the Senate Committee on Foreign Relations and as cochair of the president's intelligence advisory board. In 2006, however, Hagel had caused controversy by observing that the "Jewish lobby intimidates a lot of people" in Congress. Hagel had also publicly supported the launch of meaningful dialogue with Iran on its nuclear capabilities and had voiced skepticism about the efficacy of a military strike against Iranian facilities.[101]

Fellow Republican Lindsay Graham observed that Hagel, if confirmed, would be "the most antagonistic secretary of defense toward the state of Israel in our nation's history." Senate Republicans filibustered his nomination— emboldened by Hagel's uncertain performance during his confirmation hearings—for as long as they could. Provocatively, Ted Cruz of Texas mused that if Hagel was unable to provide the source for some of his speaking fees, then it was "relevant" to wonder if those monies in fact came from America's enemies, such as North Korea. James Inhofe of Oklahoma suggested that Hagel was "cozy" with terrorist regimes such as Iran. But reality eventually caught up with the chamber, and the Senate voted for cloture on February 26, confirming Hagel by the narrow margin of 58 to 41.[102]

A year later, in February 2014, some of the GOP's fears regarding Hagel's alleged irresolution appeared to be realized. The Pentagon leaked a preview of its 2015 budget, which would necessitate a cut in the size of the Army from 522,000 to 440,000 troops, the lowest level since the Second World War—and 50,000 fewer than the proposal announced in 2011. Dick Cheney intemperately observed that this decision showed that President Obama "would much rather spend money on Food Stamps" than on keeping the nation strong. John McCain denounced the proposed reduction as a "serious mistake." But like most political disputes in Washington these days, this contretemps is blighted by histrionics. The United States still possesses eleven aircraft carrier groups—where Russia and China have just one each, fitted with significantly poorer technology. The United States still spends more on defense than the next ten nations combined. This remarkable scenario far exceeded the wildest expectations of any number of individuals who have strenuously advocated "preparedness" in recent history, including Alfred Thayer Mahan, Walter Lippmann, and even Paul Nitze. The "correlation of forces" is still strongly tilted in America's favor, even if the "correlation of economic forces" is more diffuse and complex. On the latter point, America's place in the world is substantively different from ten years ago, which Barack Obama clearly understands.

The civil war in Syria is one of the gravest crises confronting the Obama administration, and indeed the world. In February 2013, the UN high commissioner for human rights, Navi Pillay, confirmed that 70,000 had been killed in Syria since the uprisings began two years previously.[103] A year later, in March 2014, the British-based anti-Assad group the Syrian Observatory for Human Rights estimated that some 146,000 Syrians had died.[104] The humanitarian imperative is acute. But toppling Assad's regime could also bring numerous strategic benefits. Iranian influence in the region would be diminished; the Middle East would be shorn of another ruthless dictator; Israel's position would be strengthened.

China and Russia—the latter a long-standing ally of Damascus—were resolved to veto any Security Council measure to attack Assad's substantial military capabilities, the only action that would realistically stem the bloodshed. But even with Moscow and Beijing's abstention, Syria represents the most painful of dilemmas. The opposition to Assad contains a substantial extremist element. Were Assad removed from power, a bloody sectarian reckoning would inevitably follow. And Syria is a hugely challenging environment in which to launch a military campaign. It is doubtful that air strikes would be sufficient to topple Assad as they did Gaddafi. Reflecting on how the Libyan parallel flattered to deceive, one State Department official observed, "The only reason that we're not doing the same for the Syrians is that it is hard." A senior adviser to Secretary of Defense Leon Panetta told David Sanger, "There is no way to do this other than a full-scale war."[105]

In June 2013, with great reluctance, Obama decided to begin arming the rebellion in Syria, primarily through the provision of antiaircraft weaponry. Too many "red lines" had been crossed. After receiving disturbing intelligence for a number of months, the president had concluded with certainty that Assad had used chemical weapons "on a small scale against the opposition multiple times in the last year."[106] The likes of Paul Wolfowitz, John McCain, and Anne-Marie Slaughter had been urging the president to arm the rebels since the conflict commenced. A week before Obama made his announcement, in a "closed press" dialogue with Senator John McCain (subsequently published on *Politico*), Bill Clinton called for intervention in Syria to assist the rebellion. The former president observed that Obama ran the risk of looking "like a total wuss" if he heeded skeptical public opinion by refusing to intervene. "Sometimes," Clinton said, "it's just best to get caught trying, as long as you don't overcommit—like, as long as you don't make an improvident commitment." He elaborated on the reasons why a U.S. intervention might be provident in the circumstances, paying reference to his own procrastination in Bosnia and Rwanda, and reflected more broadly on the lessons of history:

> My view is that we shouldn't over-learn the lessons of the past. I don't think Syria is necessarily Iraq or Afghanistan—no one has asked us to send any soldiers in there. I think it's more like Afghanistan was in the '80s when they were fighting the Soviet Union . . . when President Reagan was in office [and] got an enormous amount of influence and gratitude by helping to topple the Soviet-backed regime and then made the error of not hanging around in Afghanistan.[107]

The former president's Afghanistan analogy was dramatic, suggesting a costly long-term U.S. commitment to Syria when Assad is removed from power. And for all Clinton's tough talk about ignoring public opinion, there is a good reason why sitting presidents—as opposed to ex-presidents—don't allow significant gaps to emerge between diplomacy and what the public can bear. It tends to end badly for the political party the president leads.

That Obama was mindful of this fact was borne out two months later. On August 21, rockets containing the odorless and invisible nerve agent sarin rained down on Eastern Ghouta, a suburb of Damascus. Médicins Sans Frontières reported at least 3,600 Syrians had been treated for "neurotoxic symptoms" at hospitals it supported, and 355 of them had died. A preliminary U.S. government assessment placed the death toll at 1,429 (including 426 children). The White House said that the relevant agencies had ascertained "with high confidence" that the Syrian government was responsible. A French intelligence assessment baldly stated that the attack "could not have been ordered and carried out by anyone but the Syrian government," observing that "the launch zone for the rockets was held by the regime while the strike zone was held by the rebels." For his part, Russian president Vladimir Putin described the American and French assessments as "utter nonsense," instead concurring with Assad's version of events: that the rebels had launched the chemical weapons attack to provoke a U.S.-led military intervention against his government.[108]

British prime minister David Cameron was determined to lend the United States his full support in any attack against Syria. On August 29, he recalled Parliament to vote to authorize British military action against Assad's regime if evidence became conclusive that it had used chemical weapons. The government was defeated by a vote of 285 to 272, ruling out any British involvement in U.S.-led strikes and leading some Cassandras to declare the special relationship dead. Obama's response to this setback was equally surprising. On October 31, he stated his desire to launch swift reprisal attacks against Assad but requested formal congressional approval before any action was taken. Pundits wondered about Obama's motives. Congressional support was not certain, given that both parties were deeply divided on the merits or otherwise of launching air strikes against Syria. "The moral thing to do is not to stand by and do nothing," Obama said, before posing the question: "I do have to ask people, well, if in fact you're outraged by the slaughter of innocent people, what are you doing about it?"[109]

But Obama's congressional gambit showed that the response to an atrocity could not simply be refracted through categories such as "right" and "wrong." The president had deployed a humanitarian casus belli for military action against Muammar Gaddafi's Libya in 2011, but he had not sought congressional approval in doing so. Syria was different; the strategic stakes and impediments to military action were higher, as was the potential for disaster if a radical Islamist group assumed power in the vacuum that would accompany Assad's fall. Paul Wolfowitz strongly supported a military assault against Assad's regime, noting, "It's not Iraq 2003. It's Iraq in 1991 . . . In 1991 we had an opportunity without putting any American lives at risk to enable the Shia uprisings against Saddam to succeed. Instead we sat on our hands and watched him kill tens of thousands. We did nothing and we could have very easily enabled those rebellions to succeed. I think if we had done so we could have gotten rid of Saddam Hussein and there would not have been a second war."[110] But Wolfowitz's historical analogy was dubious.

Air strikes alone would not have ousted Assad; that would have required a much larger intervention, with all the uncertainty that entailed.

Events took a bizarre turn a week or so after the vote in the House of Commons. During a press conference in London on September 9, a reporter asked Secretary of State John Kerry whether Assad could do anything to prevent a U.S.-led military strike against his regime. "Sure," replied Kerry with more than a hint of sarcasm, "he could turn over every single bit of his chemical weapons to the international community in the next week—turn it over, all of it without delay and allow the full and total accounting [of it], . . . but he isn't about to do it, and it can't be done."[111] Ignoring the tone, Russia immediately seized on Kerry's words, proposing that Assad should eradicate his chemical weapons under UN supervision. Obama's interest was immediately piqued. On September 14, John Kerry and Russia's foreign minister, Sergei Lavrov, agreed to put a plan into action that would charge the United Nations with the removal of Assad's chemical weapons.

A pragmatist to his core, Barack Obama handed the initiative to Russia in resolving the crisis and unemotionally pulled back from the brink of military action. On *This Week*, George Stephanopoulos quoted the critical assessment of Richard Haas, the president of the Council on Foreign Relations: "Words like 'ad-hoc,' 'improvised,' 'unsteady' come to mind. This is probably the most undisciplined stretch of foreign policy in your presidency." What do you make of that?" asked Stephanopoulos. "Well, you know, I think that folks here in Washington like to grade on style," Obama replied, "and so had we rolled out something that was very smooth and disciplined and linear, they would have graded it well, even if it was a disastrous policy. We know that, because that's exactly how they graded the Iraq war . . . [But] I'm less concerned about style points. I'm much more concerned about getting the policy right."[112] A survey commissioned by the Pew Research Center found that two-thirds of Americans approved of Obama's decision to support the Russian proposal, even though only a quarter believed that Assad would ultimately comply.[113] In August 2014, Rand Paul wrote an op-ed for *The Wall Street Journal* that staked out a significant difference of opinion with Hillary Clinton, who had expressed her frustration at Obama's unwillingness to take stronger action against Assad. "We are lucky Mrs. Clinton didn't get her way and the Obama administration did not bring about regime change in Syria. That new regime might well be ISIS." Moving well beyond Clinton, Paul noted acerbically, "Our so-called foreign policy experts are failing us miserably."[114]

Barack Obama confronts an increasingly risk-averse public and a series of crises that defy easy categorization, let alone solutions. At the outset, at least, the United States can weigh in decisively in certain theaters (Libya), but with far less certainty—and with unknowable repercussions in both cases—in others (Syria, Iraq). After the Second Iraq War, the public's appetite for supporting a policing function for the United States in the Middle East is vastly diminished. The debacle in Iraq demonstrated that fine-sounding plans and actual outcomes don't always match—that world-making in the Middle East is well nigh impossible. In twenty years' time, U.S. policymakers may well look back on the Mubarak era as halcyon. Obama's critics assail his weak strategic handle on the situation—his reactiveness and reluctance to announce a doctrine—but how does one devise a "grand strategy" toward the Middle East in such a tumultuous era? Is the Arab Spring merely a process whereby radical Islamism replaces secular despotism? Or will it lead to a cycle of sectarian violence and the withering of the rule of law? Will this wave of democratization lead to pluralism, economic modernization, and the dispersal of wealth and opportunity across the Middle East? Will active U.S. engagement assist or discourage one or the other? No one can possibly know, and expert predictions are confounded by events almost weekly. One can understand why Obama is reluctant to walk purposefully in a straight line across this minefield.

But the news has not all been bad in the region. A major breakthrough in U.S.-Iranian relations was achieved on September 26, 2013, when Barack Obama spoke on the telephone with Hassan Rouhani, a moderate who had been elected Iran's president on August 3, succeeding the hard-line Mahmoud Ahmadinejad. It was the first conversation between the presidents of Iran and the United States since 1979. The conversation followed from an announcement made the day previously that in-depth negotiations with Iran over its nuclear activities and capabilities would commence in Geneva on October 15. "We've got a responsibility to pursue diplomacy," Obama said, "and . . . we have a unique opportunity to make progress with the new leadership in Tehran."[115] The Israeli president Benjamin Netanyahu was less enthusiastic about this diplomatic breakthrough, the speed of which had largely blindsided him.

The October meetings in Geneva closed without a deal, but the mood music was promising. The breakthrough arrived on November 24, when a preliminary six-month nuclear agreement, brokered by the European Union's Catherine Ashton, was reached between Iran and six world powers: Britain, France, Germany, China, Russia, and the United States. Tehran agreed to suspend enriching uranium beyond the levels needed for its power stations. It also halted the installation of new centrifuges designed to enrich uranium and agreed to a cap on the amount of enriched uranium it is allowed to produce from existing devices. In a statement delivered from Washington, Barack Obama said that the measures make it virtually impossible for Iran to build a nuclear weapon without being detected. In return, international sanctions against Iran worth approximately $7 billion would be relaxed.

The deal vindicated Obama's dual policy of attempting to engage Iran while strengthening the sanctions imposed on the nation—which severely devalued Iran's currency and halved its oil exports. Some compared the breakthrough with Tehran to President Nixon's rapprochement with the People's Republic of China. Congressional Republicans were predictably less impressed, with some, such as Senator John Cornyn of Texas, suggesting that the deal was brokered to deflect attention from the Obamacare debacle— a remarkably parochial perspective, although not entirely surprising given the parlous state of contemporary political debate.[116] Ranking Republicans in the House and Senate also emphasized that the real threat Iran posed to Israel would not be mitigated by the agreement. To assuage such concerns, Secretary of State Kerry described the deal as a "serious step" toward resolving the crisis with Iran, observing that it "will make our partners in the region safer. It will make our ally Israel safer."[117]

Israel's president, Benjamin Netanyahu, was not placated by Kerry's soothing words. "What was achieved last night in Geneva," he said, "is not a historic agreement; it is a historic mistake . . . Today the world has become a much more dangerous place because the most dangerous regime in the world has taken a significant step toward attaining the most dangerous weapon in the world."[118] The Israeli minister of the economy, Naftali Bennett, went even further: "If in another five or six years, a nuclear suitcase explodes in New York or Madrid, it will be because of the agreement that was signed this morning."[119] U.S.-Israeli relations have never been warm during the Obama administration, but the agreement the United States made with Iran marked a genuine low point. Whether the interim deal can be translated into something more enduring is unknowable, though it certainly rests on precarious foundations. President Rouhani has come under repeated criticism in Iran for gifting too many concessions to Washington. Crucially, he retains the all-important support of Ayatollah Ali Khamenei. But the long-term prospects for U.S.-Iranian rapprochement depend largely on Khamenei's continued approval. In this respect, Israel's furious reaction to the deal has only helped Rouhani's cause.

Whether an overwhelmingly pro-Likud GOP—encouraged in this direction by the powerful American Israel Public Affairs Committee (AIPAC)—will tolerate Obama's diplomacy is another question entirely. But the signs are not good. On March 9, 2015, forty-seven Republican senators signed an open letter to "the leaders of the Islamic State of Iran," noting that any treaty signed by President Obama would require a two-thirds majority in the Senate to become law—an unlikely scenario: "We will consider any agreement regarding your nuclear weapons program that is not approved by the Congress as nothing more than an executive agreement between President Obama and Ayatollah Khamenei. The next president could revoke such an executive agreement with the stroke of a pen and future Congresses could modify the terms of the agreement at any time."[120] It was a rare partisan congressional intrusion into an ongoing diplomatic negotiation.

The irritation and obstructionism displayed by Senate Republicans toward the Obama administration's Iran diplomacy had many sources. Principal among them was the fact that Obama had responded to comprehensive electoral defeat at the November 2014 midterms—the GOP won a 54–46 majority in the Senate and increased its majority in the House—not with chastened humility but with a renewed sense of purpose. On December 17, Barack Obama made one of the most startling announcements of his presidency: "In the most significant changes in our policy in more than fifty years, we will end an outdated approach that, for decades, has failed to advance our interests, and instead we will begin to normalize relations between our two countries. Through these changes, we intend to create more opportunities for the American and Cuban people, and begin a new chapter among the nations of the Americas." Vowing to "cut loose the shackles of the past," Obama ordered the restoration of full diplomatic relations with Cuba and the opening of a U.S. embassy in Havana.[121] The president's policy shift was the result of eighteen months of intensive negotiations—involving a complex prisoner swap—in which Pope Francis had become involved. It was a remarkably bold move for a president contemplating the looming reality of a Republican-controlled House of Representatives *and* Senate from January 3, 2015.

Most Republicans in Congress announced that they would resist lifting the fifty-four-year-old trade embargo. Some denounced the policy shift with real vehemence. "This entire policy shift announced today is based on an illusion, on a lie, the lie and the illusion that more commerce and access to money and goods will translate to political freedom for the Cuban people," warned Senator Marco Rubio, Republican of Florida. "All this is going to do is give the Castro regime, which controls every aspect of Cuban life, the opportunity to manipulate these changes to perpetuate itself in power."[122] Yet the polls suggested that this harsh appraisal was not shared by a majority of Americans. A CNN/ORC poll conducted soon after the historic announcement showed that six out of ten Americans supported the restoration of full diplomatic relations and that two-thirds wanted the travel ban overturned.[123] In a press briefing on December 19, Obama said, "I share the concerns of dissidents there and human rights activists that this is still a regime that represses its people." But he also noted that the "whole point of normalizing relations is that it gives us greater opportunity to have influence with that government."[124] The restoration of U.S.-Cuban relations and the ongoing nuclear negotiations with Iran will provoke sharp disputes in 2015 and 2016 between President Obama and the Republican-controlled Congress. While his opponents portray the president as a spineless appeaser—the historically illiterate John Bolton described him as "worse than Neville Chamberlain"—Obama believes that his policy of engaging with Tehran and Havana will reap tangible results, making Israel and the region safer, and Cuba more prosperous and politically open.[125]

The People's Republic of China's swift economic rise makes it likely that the nation will surpass America's GDP sometime in the next thirty years. It is advancing its military capabilities faster than any other competitor nation. It is the world's biggest consumer of energy and producer of greenhouse gases. It is the world's largest holder of foreign-exchange reserves, including more than $1 trillion in U.S. treasury bonds.[126] And the largely U.S.-made global financial crisis has suggested to China's leadership that its centralized economic model is uniquely stable and virtuous—discouraging any latent momentum for political liberalization. At the World Economic Forum at Davos in 2010, Chinese premier Wen Jiabao chided "Western" economic practices "and their unsustainable model of development characterized by prolonged low savings and high consumption; excessive expansion of financial institutions in a blind pursuit of profit."[127] The combination of an emboldened China and an irascible America has the potential to make a lot of trouble for the rest of the world. "If we get China wrong," one senior Obama adviser remarked, "in thirty years that's the only thing anyone will remember."[128]

Obama has experimented with two approaches to managing relations with China: extending friendship and avoiding conflict; and pursuing a narrower, interests-driven approach that accepts some antagonism as inevitable. The former style predominated from 2009 to 2011 and was shaped by Deputy Secretary of State James B. Steinberg and National Security Council Senior Director for East Asia Jeffrey Bader. Its critics maintain that China sensed weakness and began behaving with remarkable haughtiness. During the Copenhagen Summit of December 2009, called to reach an international agreement on climate change, Premier Wen Jiabao declined to attend a heads of state meeting, sending a subordinate to sit opposite President Obama.[129]

Little wonder that the president's critics alleged that his friendly approach to China secured nothing but Beijing's scorn. In an opinion piece in *The Wall Street Journal*, Mitt Romney strongly attacked the administration:

> President Obama came into office as a near supplicant to Beijing, almost begging it to continue buying American debt so as to finance his profligate spending here at home . . . Now, three years into his term, the president has belatedly responded with a much-ballyhooed "pivot" to Asia . . . The supposed pivot has been oversold and carries with it an unintended consequence: It has left our allies with the worrying impression that we left the region and might do so again.[130]

Romney's damning critique was formulated by one of his principal foreign-policy advisers, Aaron L. Friedberg, a professor of politics and international relations at Princeton's Woodrow Wilson School of Public and International Affairs. His 2011 book, *A Contest for Supremacy*, issued a warning that the United States is "on track to lose" the strategic battle for power and influence in the Western Pacific. He chides Obama for focusing too intently on engagement with Beijing and not devoting sufficient resources to contingency planning if the worst-case scenario materializes in the form of armed conflict over any number of issues.

This line of criticism was persuasive when Friedberg wrote the book but was less so in the months after it was published. In November 2011, the president announced that the United States would station an additional twenty-five hundred troops in northern Australia: their strategic purpose was clear enough and China was predictably dismayed. In addition, Secretary of State Clinton was proactive in encouraging Myanmar to move in the direction of genuine independence and pull itself away from Beijing's orbit.

Finally, the Obama administration was steadfast in supporting the Philippines over China's strong-armed approach to their territorial dispute in the South China Sea. On the deck of a U.S. warship in Manila Bay—one need not be Freudian to discern a message—Secretary of State Clinton announced that "we are making sure that our collective defense capabilities and communications infrastructure are operationally and materially capable of deterring provocation from the full spectrum of state and nonstate actors." Ramon Casiple, executive director of the Manila-based Institute for Political and Economic Reform, observed that "Filipinos appreciate symbolism."[131]

Obama's "pivot" to Asia can be attributed to many sources. China's swift rise means it makes strategic sense for the United States to redeploy resources to the Pacific to better guard its interests and allies there. There are many friendly nations desperate for Washington's reassurance, and this has now been provided. But there is a personal element too. Obama grew up in Hawaii and Indonesia. He lacks the habitual eastward orientation of his predecessors. Most American presidents have had a strong Atlanticist perspective, believing that Europe is the continent in which the world's most significant geostrategic conflicts play out. America's Cold War strategy was predicated on this axiom. But Europe is clearly no longer the fulcrum. "The future of the United States is intimately intertwined with the future of the Asia-Pacific," wrote Secretary of State Clinton in an article to coincide with her Pacific tour. "A strategic turn to the region fits logically into our overall global effort to secure and sustain America's global leadership."[132]

The pivot toward Asia may be viewed as the Obama administration's principal foreign-policy legacy thirty years hence. It is clearly imperative that the United States responds skillfully to China's rise. The consequences are momentous if it does not. In placing U.S.-Chinese rivalry in historical context, the Harvard political scientist Graham Allison has identified a phenomenon he describes as "the Thucydides trap," fretting that precedent suggests that conflict between these two nations, moving in opposite directions, may be inevitable. In his *History of the Peloponnesian War*, Thucydides wrote, "It was the rise of Athens and the fear that this inspired in Sparta that made war inevitable." For Athens, read China; for Sparta, America. As Allison writes:

> For six decades after the Second World War, an American "Pax Pacifica" has provided the security and economic framework within which Asian countries have produced the most rapid economic growth in history. However, having emerged as a great power that will overtake

the U.S. in the next decade to become the largest economy in the world, it is not surprising that China will demand revisions to the rules established by others.[133]

The difference between now and then, of course, is that China and America are much more invested in each other's economic success than Sparta and Athens were in 431 B.C., or Germany and Great Britain were on the eve of the First World War. Economic interdependence—the colossal hybrid entity tagged "Chimerica" by the historian Niall Ferguson and the economist Moritz Schularick—is the strongest guarantee against a calamitous war between the two nations.[134]

The prospects for broadly harmonious U.S.-Chinese relations appear relatively bright. But a more familiar type of conflict, which brought to mind World War II and Yalta, visited the world in March 2014, when President Vladimir Putin ordered the invasion of Crimea, the southerly region of Ukraine that includes Sevastopol—and Russia's Black Sea fleet—and a large ethnic Russian majority. Putin explained that his hand was forced by the ousting of the pro-Russian president of Ukraine, Viktor Yanukovych, following a series of demonstrations against him, and the odious pro-European government that replaced him. Putin claimed that the opposition groups that had compelled Yanukovych to flee Kiev for Moscow on February 21 had far-right or fascistic tendencies and that he had intervened in Crimea to protect ethnic Russians from reprisals. Russia set up a referendum on March 16, in which 97 percent of Crimeans supported incorporation into Russia (the pro-Ukrainian Tatar minority refused to take part). That Wilsonian self-determination had been deployed to serve cynical purposes was made clear by the chair of Russia's upper house of parliament, Valentina Matviyenko: "Deciding to hold [a] referendum is a sovereign right of Crimea's legitimately elected parliament . . . the right of people to self-determination."[135] Clearly, the Obama administration possessed no realistic military options to discourage President Putin. But this did not stop critics from suggesting that his irresolution had invited Russian aggression and that his response to this flagrant Russian aggression was weak on substance and tepid in presentation.

America's foreign-policy commentariat weighed in with a series of editorials, and most were entirely predictable. Zbigniew Brzezinski suggested that the West should privately convey to Russia "that the Ukrainian army can count on immediate and direct Western aid so as to enhance its defensive capabilities" and recommended that "NATO forces, consistent with the organizations' contingency planning, should be put on alert."[136] Charles Krauthammer endorsed Brzezinski's approach eleven days later, but also suggested sending "the chairman of the Joint Chiefs to the Baltics to arrange joint maneuvers," and proposed that Obama should "order the Energy Department" to expedite the export of more gas to Europe to render crippling sanctions against Russia more palatable to Britain, France, and Germany.[137] On the left, Stephen Cohen, a professor of Russian history at New York University, criticized the United States for failing to comprehend Putin's strategic perspective and for needlessly inflaming the situation.[138]

Age ninety and liberated from his usual default position of pursuing or advising power—which had led to his awkward tête-à-tête with Sarah Palin in 2008—Henry Kissinger drafted one of the most nuanced analyses of the crisis. Writing in *The Washington Post* on March 5, Kissinger faulted Russia for failing to comprehend that forcing Ukraine into accepting a satellite status "would doom Moscow to repeat its history of self-fulfilling cycles of reciprocal pressures with Europe and the United States." But he also chided many in "the West" for failing to comprehend that "to Russia, Ukraine can never be just a foreign country. Russian history began in what was called Kievan-Rus. The Russian religion spread from there. Ukraine has been part of Russia for centuries, and their histories were intertwined before then." Historically literate, elegantly crafted, and eminently sensible, Kissinger offered a penetrating account of the misconceptions, and lack of empathy, blighting both sides:

> The United States needs to avoid treating Russia as an aberrant to be patiently taught rules of conduct established by Washington. Putin is a serious strategist—on the premises of Russian history. Understanding U.S. values and psychology are not his strong suits. Nor has understanding Russian history and psychology been a strong point of U.S. policymakers. Leaders of all sides should return to examining outcomes, not compete in posturing.[139]

For Kissinger, Obama's response to the Ukrainian crisis has little connection to credibility, which is at stake only in genuinely contested areas. Crimea falls within the Russian sphere of influence, and this has to be recognized. Managing the crisis requires understanding Putin's perspective, clearly communicating how damaging the annexation of Crimea will be to Russia's world position, and not needlessly inflaming the situation through reckless promises—Kissinger echoed Kennan in warning that Ukrainian membership in NATO is not an option.

President Obama appears to side with Kissinger on the best way to deal with Putin's aggression. On February 19, Obama had described Ukraine as a "client state of Russia" and cautioned that the region should not be seen as "some Cold War chessboard in which we are in competition with Russia."[140] On March 25, in response to a question on the magnitude of the threat posed by Moscow, Obama observed cuttingly, "Russia is a regional power that is threatening some of its immediate neighbors—not out of strength but out of weakness." The president understands that even if Russia is left largely alone, the lessons of history suggest that it will suffer in the long run for its belligerence. "I think it would be dishonest to suggest that there's a simple solution to resolving what has already taken place in Crimea," Obama observed. "Although history has a funny way of moving in twists and turns and not just in a straight line."[141]

On Ukraine, and a multitude of other issues, Obama's critics accuse him of fretting too much about alienating the public—that the president follows rather than leads, lacking as he does a grand strategy. Vali Nasr, a senior State Department adviser to Richard Holbrooke from 2009 to 2011 and the current dean of the Paul H. Nitze School of Advanced International Studies, published a book-length assault on Obama's foreign policies in 2013:

> In the cocoon of our public debate Obama gets high marks on foreign policy. That is because his policies' principal aim is not to make strategic decisions but to satisfy public opinion—he has done more of the things that people want and fewer of the things we have to do that may be unpopular. To our allies, however, our constant tactical maneuvers don't add up to a coherent strategy or a vision of global leadership. Gone is the exuberant American desire to lead in the world.[142]

Nasr's portrayal of Obama as weak and led by opinion polls underestimates the coherence and sincerity of his pragmatic worldview and his genuine desire to marshal resources in a fashion consistent with the enhancement rather than diminishment of America's world position. Obama finds complaints such as Nasr's unfair, noting that his critics seem to believe that he possesses a "joystick" with which he is able to maneuver precise outcomes.

Near the end of a series of interviews, which became the basis of a fascinating profile in *The New Yorker*, David Remnick asked Obama if he was "haunted" by his decision not to intervene in Syria. "I am not haunted by my decision not to engage in another Middle Eastern war," replied Obama. "It is very difficult to imagine a scenario in which our involvement in Syria would have led to a better outcome, short of us being willing to undertake an effort in size and scope similar to what we did in Iraq." Another Iraq-style military intervention, of course, is a fantastical prospect to Obama and, indeed, to the public he serves. But Obama provided Remnick with a description of his policymaking method:

> I have strengths and I have weaknesses, like every President, like every person. I do think one of my strengths is temperament. I am comfortable with complexity, and I think I'm pretty good at keeping my moral compass while recognizing that I am a product of original sin. And every morning and every night I'm taking measure of my actions against the options and possibilities available to me, understanding that there are going to be mistakes that I make and my team makes and that America makes; understanding that there are going to be limits to the good we can do and the bad that we can prevent, and that there's going to be tragedy out there and, by occupying this office, I am part of that tragedy occasionally, but that if I am doing my very best and basing my decisions on the core values and ideals that I was brought up with and that I think are pretty consistent with those of most Americans, that at the end of the day things will be better rather than worse.[143]

These words, extolling recognition of complexity and comprehension of the limits of what is achievable, could have been spoken by George Kennan. In contrast to Vali Nasr, Obama appears to believe that "exuberance" has caused some of the United States' most damaging foreign-policy missteps, that it is a trait best left to motivational speakers and sports announcers. Sobriety is much more in keeping with Obama's style. In thirty years or so, historians will be better placed to determine who is correct. But the past fifteen years suggest that Nasr's "exuberant American desire to lead" may well have destabilized the world more than it has steadied it. It is little wonder that the United States has a diminished capacity and inclination for worldmaking.

During a supposedly off-the-record discussion with reporters in the summer of 2014, Obama observed that his core strategic doctrine could be summarized simply as "Don't do stupid shit." During an on-the-record interview with *The Atlantic*, Hillary Clinton disagreed: "Great nations need organizing principles, and 'don't do stupid stuff' is not an organizing principle."[144] Yet when the interviewer invited Clinton to spell out her own organizing principle, she answered, "peace, progress, and prosperity," alliterative boilerplate that any American politician since the inception of the republic could have uttered. Clinton understands the problems with neat organizing principles all too well. As she wrote in her 2014 memoir, *Hard Choices*, "Although some may have yearned for an Obama Doctrine—a grand unified theory that would provide a simple and elegant road map for foreign policy in this new era, like 'containment' did during the Cold War—there was nothing simple or elegant about the problems we faced."[145] This was true when Clinton became secretary of state and it remains so today.

President Obama delivered an important speech at West Point in 2014 that set out a typically equivocal vision:

> It is absolutely true that in the 21st century American isolationism is not an option. We don't have a choice to ignore what happens beyond our borders . . . But to say that we have an interest in pursuing peace and freedom beyond our borders is not to say that every problem has a military solution. Since World War II, some of our most costly mistakes came not from our restraint, but from our willingness to rush into military adventures without thinking through the consequences—without building international support and legitimacy for our action; without leveling with the American people about the sacrifices required.[146]

The usual suspects assailed the speech as weak and unprincipled—"One can only marvel at the smallness of it all," wrote Charles Krauthammer.[147] Of course, no one seriously believes that every crisis has a military solution, and in this sense the president was disingenuous in setting up "a somber parade of straw men," as Krauthammer wittily phrased it. But Obama's observation that "some of our most costly mistakes came not from restraint, but from our willingness to rush into military adventures without thinking through the consequences" contains wisdom.

CONCLUSION

One of Woodrow Wilson's inspirations was Richard Cobden, the influential nineteenth-century British advocate of free trade and economic interdependence, whose "eloquence" and "genius," Wilson believed, made him a man of truly "exalted character."[1] Henry Kissinger's political hero was of course Prince Metternich, whose enduring fascination was with power and how to wield it. When Wilson's and Kissinger's lodestars met for dinner in Vienna in the summer of 1847, it quickly became clear that their differences on statecraft were unbridgeable. Cobden noted how troubled he was by the reactivity and pessimism of Metternich's worldview: his belief that peace was best realized though applying weight to the lighter side of a scale; his disbelief in the ability of powerful nations to make systemic changes to the world system:

> [Metternich] is probably the last of those State physicians who, looking only to the symptoms of a nation, content themselves with superficial remedies from day to day, and never attempt to probe beneath the surface to discover the source of the evils which afflict the social system. The order of statesmen will pass away with him, because too much light

has been shed upon the laboratory of Governments, to allow them to impose upon mankind with the old formulas.[2]

In Cobden's words lies a tension that is central to this book. Should the United States look to cure diseases in the international system through rendering nations democratic or liberal-capitalist, remedying the "source of the evils which afflict the social system"? Or should Washington seek to ensure that the threat of infection presented by hostile regimes, alliance systems, or ideologies does not spread, through defensive "remedies" such as George Kennan's containment. Should diplomacy be practiced as a science, unveiling new discoveries to effect enduring change, or as an art, responding creatively and intuitively to a world without pattern?

One can imagine Woodrow Wilson, Paul Nitze, and Paul Wolfowitz lobbing Cobden's charge of "superficial remedies" at Alfred Thayer Mahan, Walter Lippmann, George Kennan, Henry Kissinger, and Barack Obama—and indeed we have encountered such clashes in this book. A curative ambition was present in Wilson's view that the United States must move beyond Mahan's realism to devise and lead a new collaborative world system in the aftermath of the First World War, or in Wolfowitz's view that America must unfurl the Wilsonian banner in catalyzing the democratization of an entire region, the Middle East, to make the nation more secure in the aftermath of the 9/11 attacks. When Paul Nitze helped establish the School of Advanced International Studies in Washington in 1943, he surveyed the literature on international affairs and was disheartened to discover that "most of it was historical . . . [the books and articles would] have no theoretical background at all." This absence of scientific ambition suggested to Nitze that few took the subject seriously: "I complained to various people . . . why has United States academia been so deficient in addressing themselves from an experienced and theoretical view as to the practice of foreign policy?"[3] Nitze believed that a foreign-policy education dominated by the teaching of history encouraged amateurism rather than professionalism.

Cobden, Wilson, Nitze, and Wolfowitz were all susceptible to scientism, which in this context is the belief that the core elements of scientific method—theory testing, the detection of patterns, and the unveiling of new discoveries—can be emulated to discern objective truth and make fundamental changes to the structure of world affairs. The appeal of scientism is not difficult to comprehend. It holds out a promise of certainty—permitting a nation to understand and tame the world's volatility—that is highly seductive. It is an optimistic creed that resonates with America's self-image as exceptional and eminently capable of "making" the world it leads. Denying America's ability to cure the world's "evils" is thus viewed as defeatist and un-American—amoral, European, declinist, Metternichian—all charges that have been leveled at Mahan, Kennan, Kissinger, and of course Obama.

This grouping of artists (or pessimists, as their critics would have it), comprising Mahan, Lippmann, Kennan, Kissinger, and Obama, conversely, believe that "evil" is a permanent fixture in our morals and habits, and that the application of "superficial remedies" is often the best that any foreign policymaker can do. As Barack Obama had observed during his 2007 interview with David Brooks (a response that was later used to blurb a reissue of Reinhold Niebuhr's *The Irony of American History*, "I take away [from his works] the compelling idea that there's serious evil in the world, and hardship and pain. And we should be humble and modest in our belief we can eliminate those things. But we shouldn't use that as an excuse for cynicism and inaction."[4] Or as Alfred Thayer Mahan wrote in 1897, "Let us worship peace, indeed, as the goal at which humanity must hope to arrive, but let us not fancy that peace is to be had as a boy wrenches an unripe fruit from a tree."[5] As the Mahan scholar Jon Tetsuro Sumida observes, "The formulation of theory, or the construction of a philosophically complete system of explanation, was either secondary or hostile to the accomplishment of Mahan's primary task." Mahan believed that skilled diplomatists must possess an artistic temperament that facilitates creative responses to the world's essential unpredictability.[6]

In many ways, the contrasting visions offered by Mahan and Wilson represented the first great American foreign-policy debate. Significant clashes on matters of international relations had occurred many times before—such as that between Alexander Hamilton and Thomas Jefferson over whether the fledgling republic should support the French Revolution—but Mahan and Wilson lived during the era in which the United States surpassed Great Britain to become the world's most powerful nation.[7] This ensured that the ideas that prevailed would have global consequences.

Mahan believed that some problems were beyond America's ability to resolve and that interventions designed to effect change in other nations could end badly. This caution shaped Mahan's opposition to annexing the Philippines in 1898 and his unease at the American war against the Filipino insurgency that followed. In mid-1910, he observed that he had been a "personal witness of the extreme repugnance" with which America had seized the archipelago, and a year later he compared the hypothetical loss of the Philippines to "the loss of a little finger, perhaps a single joint of it. The Philippines to us are less a property than a charge."[8] Mahan focused ruthlessly on the policies that would serve the national interest and was unfazed by reputational damage wreaked by tactical retreat. The rest of the world's preferences and opinions were of scant concern to the United States, so long as its commercial interests were unaffected, its borders secure, its navy dominant, and its principal ally, Great Britain, free and unthreatened. Mahan focused on the big picture, which necessarily required an understanding of history. Those who lacked this detailed historical knowledge roused his ire:

> During my whole time on the [Naval Planning] Board, historical parallels to our positions were continually occurring to me. How many men in the Navy, do you suppose, know naval history, or think of naval operations in that way; or how many, if they read this, would fail to vote me an egotistic, superannuated ass! . . . The Navy—in my opinion—wants to stop grubbing in machine shops and to get up somewhere where it can take a bird's eye view of military truths, and see them in their relations and proportions.[9]

Woodrow Wilson disagreed with Mahan on the best means to discern such truth. The outbreak of the First World War had shown that enduring peace was not maintainable through balance-of-power politics. Wilson argued that a world in which disputes were arbitrated by a League of Nations had to be attempted instead. In time, Wilson believed that America had to make other nations more like America. A world of democratic, liberal-capitalist uniformity offered the best prospect of an enduring "scientific peace."

Charles Beard rejected a key assumption—that America's economic fate rested on the expansion of an export-led economy—that informed Mahan's and Wilson's worldviews. During the 1930s, as the Nye Committee pinned blame on bankers and industrialists for maneuvering the nation into the First World War, Beard argued that it was the taut economic threads that connected the United States to the world that ran the greatest risk of tearing the nation apart. His theory of "American continentalism" was designed to free the nation from those binds and leave it unencumbered. Beard hoped that FDR might be sympathetic to his "continentalist" blueprint—"the old possibility of a distinct national life and character" as "a living and vital force"—even if the hostility of his secretary of state, Cordell Hull (also known as the "Tennessee Cobden"), was all but guaranteed.[10]

In *The Idea of National Interest* and *The Open Door at Home*, Beard pitched self-reliance and Europe avoidance to President Roosevelt. In recommending a move toward autarky, Beard's training in political science instilled confidence in the efficacy of this method; he had run a statistical analysis that confirmed the dispensability of export markets and the feasibility of turning inward. "[A] thousand experiences of political life," Beard observed in 1908, "bear witness that a treatise on causation in politics would be the most welcome contribution which a scholar of scientific training and temper could make."[11] His theory was born of the best intentions regarding America's capacity for perfectibility. Beard made a strong argument that the short-term economic costs of isolation—he calculated that foreign trade accounted for just 10 percent of American economic output—would reap a much larger peace dividend.[12] Yet the rest of the world's ability to encroach upon American seclusion was a variable that his proposal failed to anticipate—Beard's imagination ultimately failed him. President Franklin Roosevelt was wise to reject American continentalism and chart a course of preparedness that drew on the appropriate Mahanian lessons from the past.

Elements of Beard's vision endure. The historian Walter McDougall is correct to observe that the "vaunted tradition of 'isolationism' is no tradition at all, but a dirty word that interventionists, especially since Pearl Harbor, hurl at anyone who questions their policies."[13] But as the impetus for Wilsonian democracy promotion has dissipated in recent years, so putting Americans first has come back into vogue—reconnecting with a long-standing foreign-policy tradition that McDougall traces to Washington and Jefferson. In July 2011, Barack Obama announced a withdrawal plan for Afghanistan, expressing his desire to "reclaim the American dream that is the center of our story . . . America, it is time to focus on nation-building here at home."[14] On April 7, 2015, Senator Rand Paul, Republican of Kentucky, announced that he would seek his party's presidential nomination. Critics from across the political spectrum rounded immediately on Paul's supposed "isolationism." Two days later, Paul delivered a speech in South Carolina that decried "frivolous" wars: "I see an America strong, strong enough to deter foreign aggression, yet wise enough to avoid unnecessary intervention." It is clear that Paul's Republican opponents won't find it difficult to connect his worldview with that of Barack Obama, and condemn each as declinist and isolationist.[15]

Beard was an admirer of Walter Lippmann in the 1910s and 1920s when the journalist was "expounding a socialist philosophy of a mild brand." But his opinion changed during the 1930s as Lippmann attacked the New Deal as perilously statist and Beard's views on foreign policy as hopelessly naïve. In 1937, Beard observed that "amid all his outpourings there are often flashes of insight and justice with which I sincerely agree. I do not think he is a bad man." Yet in Lippmann's supposed cozying up to entrenched elites, and in his support for a policy of military preparedness, Beard detected "the odor of a sickly humanism as thick as the smell of magnolia blossoms which apologists of the good old days in the South spread over the sweat of slave gangs."[16] Profoundly disillusioned by Wilson's performance at the Paris Peace Conference, during which the president vested too much hope in an untested abstraction, Lippmann embraced Mahan's realism from the mid-1930s, which was always likely to rouse Beard's hyperbolic ire. Lippmann viewed Nazi domination of the Atlantic Ocean as intolerable. The United States had a vital stake in ensuring the independence of Great Britain.

Rationalizing and encouraging American participation in the Second World War was essential, which Lippmann worked toward skillfully. But so too was ensuring that President Roosevelt did not botch the peace in the fashion of Woodrow Wilson. To avoid this happening, Lippmann advised that America should work with the world's other powerful nations to ensure postwar stability—not through vesting any serious hope in the League of Nations' successor. Roosevelt should certainly resist making grandiose claims connecting the spread of democracy to the maintenance of peace. And while the president should disagree with Moscow where necessary, he should always keep an eye on the ultimate goal of avoiding another global war, to which contentious issues of smaller stake—such as Soviet domination of Eastern Europe—could be sacrificed.

Like Mahan, Lippmann believed that peace was best achieved through strength, that idealism should be stripped from policymaking, that the arbitration of disputes was impossible to achieve, and that the nation-state remained the principal actor in world politics. It disappointed Lippmann that so many of his goals were dashed in the first few postwar years, as ideological hostility—not a dispassionate calculation of respective interests—began to sour U.S.-Soviet relations. Yet Lippmann overestimated the ability of the United States and the Soviet Union to maintain a credible and workable postwar alliance. It turned out that ideological differences between the two nations mattered profoundly.

Lippmann's 1943 thesis that "a foreign policy consists in bringing into balance, with a comfortable surplus of power in reserve, the nation's commitments and the nation's power," was a classic expression of realism, but its assumptions were scientistic. Lippmann's theory held that Josef Stalin was a rational actor acutely conscious of his nation's strengths and weaknesses, which meant the Soviet leader was unlikely to overstep the mark in projecting power if dispassionate analysis flagged the dangers of such a course. Lippmann was only partly right. While Stalin's goals in the early Cold War were not as expansionary as some have portrayed, ideology did play a causal role in shaping Soviet foreign policy.[17] Lippmann's theory blinded him to the possibility that Marxism-Leninism was not merely a wall of sanctimony deployed to dupe the people and lend grandiosity to a brutal despot, but rather that it animated Soviet action. And this made a modus vivendi between the two nations difficult to achieve.

George Kennan, whom Lippmann attacked in a series of influential articles, was the consummate foreign-policy artist. Kennan never intended that containment be applied as a rigid formula, he subsequently professed hostility to strategies that could fit onto a "bumper sticker." He was insightful in identifying the ideological and historical factors that drove Stalin's foreign policy and proposed largely measured policies to ensure that Western Europe avoid the fate that Marxism-Leninism intended for it. Yet Lippmann was correct to chide Kennan for failing to set clear limits on what containment entailed beyond the European theater—on where America's vital interests began and ended. Kennan lamented later that he yearned to "extricate himself from the tar baby of containment."[18] In the late 1960s, Kennan freely admitted that Lippmann's critique of the X Article had been valid: "much of it reads exactly like one of those primers put out by alarmed congressional committees or by the Daughters of the American Revolution, designed to arouse the citizenry to the dangers of the Communist conspiracy."[19]

Kennan was an impressive and subtle diplomatist, however, and this acuity was evident throughout his entire career. His keen historical perspective, remarkable linguistic ability, skill at assuming different identities and drawing insight from multiple epochs make him stand out as a scholar and diplomat. As a shaper of U.S. foreign policy, Kennan was constantly frustrated, with the exception of the period from 1946 to 1948 when his views and those of his political masters converged briefly on their path to divergence. As an analyst of U.S. foreign policy and of the foibles of politicians, however, he was exceptionally gifted, and history will likely view Kennan's post-1950 record as a public intellectual as farsighted on a great many counts. Like Walter Lippmann, his opposition to the Vietnam War, for example, was ahead of the curve and consistently insightful.

In 1989, during testimony before the Senate on the end of the Cold War, George Kennan delivered a rousing and unexpected endorsement of Wilsonianism as the only means to solve the world's most dangerous problems:

> I was long skeptical about Wilson's vision . . . But I begin today . . . to think that Wilson was very ahead of his time in his views about international organizations. You see, just as I feel that the Cold War is now ending, I feel that another great and tremendous problem is growing upon us—or a double problem. One is to get rid of the weapons of mass destruction which are too terrible to be permitted to rest in human hands . . . But the other is to face up to the planetary environmental crisis which is now, if we can believe the scientists, growing upon us . . . The general lesson of what [the scientists] are telling us is that we have a much shorter time than we think to put things to rights in this planet if our descendants are going to have any sort of a civilized life in it. Now this is to my mind going to require a realization of the dream of international collaboration which Wilson had. I don't see any other way out of it.[20]

Kennan appears to believe that some challenges—climate change and nuclear proliferation—are of sufficient magnitude and complexity that Wilsonianism is the only available course. And this is perhaps the only circumstance when foreign policy can truly be approached scientistically—when every nation is vested in solving a crisis with the potential to affect all. It is the closest the world can get to stable laboratory conditions.

Paul Nitze was a paradox. Like Kennan, he formulated a seminal foreign-policy strategy—NSC-68—before disavowing the conflicts that the document rationalized. Unlike Kennan, he never expressed regret for the document's alarmist style or the way NSC-68 recklessly expanded America's obligations to the world. Nitze's other significant contribution to the making of U.S. foreign policy—the notion of the "correlation of forces"—was a clear expression of faith in the model of foreign policy as science. More accurately, Nitze applied scientistic principles to build structures that performed particular functions. Through the entirety of his career, Nitze inflated Soviet military capabilities, pushed strongly for increased military spending, and lambasted administrations he disliked—those of Eisenhower, Nixon, Ford, and Carter—for allowing the Soviet Union to tilt the correlation of forces in Moscow's direction, encouraging future conflict. This assumption of worst-case scenarios led to many foreign-policy misadventures.

But Nitze was also prescient on many issues. He was often correct to assume the worst of the Soviet Union—that Stalin would behave rationally and seek to develop a fusion device—when recommending the development of an American hydrogen bomb. Throughout the Reagan administration, Nitze favored deep cuts in the superpowers' nuclear arsenals, earning the enmity of those who previously viewed him as an ideological ally. In fact Nitze was far from dogmatic; it was merely that NSC-68, the Gaither Report, and Team B made him appear that way. The disconnection between plan and action was often stark in the case of Nitze. He never successfully translated his often nuanced personal views into the blueprints he drafted, which built massive structures that were intimidating and awe-inspiring but difficult to move once locked in position.

Though his doctorate was in political science, Henry Kissinger was steeped in history. His dissertation focused on the Napoleonic era and identified lessons that the United States might draw from the adroit statesmanship displayed at the Congress of Vienna. Kissinger did not experiment in the Wilsonian fashion, viewing liberal idealism as his main ideological adversary. Instead he recommended policies that emulated his hero, an arch-exponent of balance-of-power diplomacy, Prince Metternich. Kissinger wanted to apply the lessons of history and had no interest in seeking new discoveries about the laws of international relations. Stability mattered more than justice.

But while Kissinger drew from historical precedent, he also followed some formulas. He *believed* in the balance of power and the domino theory. This explains his cautious support for the Americanization of the Vietnam War; his coming around to the logic of recognizing China; the value of pursuing a policy of détente with the Soviet Union; his tendency to vest American credibility in conflicts of tangential significance; the brutal manner in which he and Nixon escalated and deescalated the Vietnam War; his veneration of credibility as a priceless diplomatic commodity; his amorality. Kissinger was capable of profound diplomatic insight and the tawdriest recommendations. He was not an obvious practitioner of diplomacy as science. But he clung doggedly to his axioms and was rigid in his approach to many diplomatic crises. Metternich possessed a quality that Kissinger evidently lacked: a sense of proportion.

Paul Wolfowitz was second only to Woodrow Wilson in his scientism. His scholarly methods and foreign-policy career emphasized experimentation with a view to remaking the aspects of the world that he viewed as deficient. Following Wilson, Wolfowitz's worldview was undergirded by a single principle: substantive geopolitical stability is contingent upon the spread of democracy. Wolfowitz begins by imagining what a peaceable world looks like and works backward to realize that utopian aspiration. The abstraction is the starting point in matters of import; the primary goal is often vaulting and unprecedented.

Such ambition clearly has virtue. But it also resembles the self-righteousness shared by Wolfowitz's fiercest critics on the left. Who is more confident than the individual who understands the *true* nature of world affairs? Noam Chomsky and Paul Wolfowitz share many common traits; among other things, they both overstate America's actual or prospective ability to engage in worldmaking. Wolfowitz's stated belief that the invasion of Iraq might catalyze the democratization of the entire Middle East may be unfolding before our eyes. Or it may be that the causal connection is illusory or impossible to detect. Or more likely still: that the current unrest across the region is beyond both America's ken and its ability to "manage." But let there be no doubt that the invasion of Iraq led to bleak consequences that overwhelm the stock defense: "Isn't it better that Saddam is gone?" The human cost is harrowing and the financial cost continues to spiral upward as compound interest wreaks havoc. The war emphasized the limits of American power rather than the potentialities. Like Vietnam, this lesson has salutary value, but only if it is heeded.

Of all the individuals this book has surveyed, Barack Obama is the most intuitive and averse to ideology. The insight that the incumbent president drew from the Second Iraq War is similar to that which Oliver Wendell Holmes drew from the Civil War: "certitude leads to violence." According to Louis Menand, in his erudite history of the emergence of pragmatism, the harrowing conflict led Holmes to "lose his belief in beliefs," a phrase that could be attributed to the defiantly unideological Obama, who pointedly decried the proposed invasion of Iraq as an "ideological" war. As Menand writes, "Pragmatism was designed to make it harder for people to be driven to violence by their beliefs . . . Holmes, James, Peirce, and Dewey wished to bring ideas and principles and beliefs down to a human level because they wished to avoid the violence they saw hidden in abstractions."[21] Obama is identifiably pragmatic in responding to challenges on a case-by-case basis, shunning universal principles and doctrines.

After Barack Obama's election victory in 2012, Anne-Marie Slaughter wrote an op-ed in *The Washington Post* titled "Does Obama Have a Grand Strategy for His Second Term?" To help Obama locate his big idea, Slaughter observed, "First terms are about justifying your place in office. Second terms are about justifying your place in history," and helpfully pointed out that there were lots of places for Obama to seek inspiration in achieving this second goal (such as her employer, the Woodrow Wilson School of Public and International Affairs at Princeton): "In Washington, the period between an election and an inauguration is a fertile time for big, ambitious ideas, reports, and essays. Foreign policy wonks are partial to laying out 'grand strategies': sweeping statements of the means through which the United States should achieve its goals in the world."[22]

That Obama has not yet identified his doctrine was clearly a source of concern and frustration to Slaughter. But one suspects that the president does not view the quest as particularly useful or important. His observation to David Remnick in 2013 that "I don't really even need George Kennan right now" was an affront to scholars and analysts vested in the formulation of "big, ambitious ideas."[23] But Obama's approach exhibits a modesty and suppleness well suited to an age in which the dangers of "ideological" wars have become painfully apparent.

The ideas surveyed in this book have transcended their historical moment, some more obviously than others. There is useful instruction to be drawn—both positive and negative—from all the actual and aspirant worldmakers discussed herein. And as we move toward the presidential election of 2016, the legacies of Mahan, Wilson, Beard, Kennan, Kissinger, Wolfowitz, and others will fall into view during foreign-policy debates, with or without attribution. The identity of the next president will help answer a question that is currently impossible to answer: Will Obama's pragmatic method represent a short-lived aberration—akin to the Kissinger era—or does it mark the beginning of something more lasting?

The power capabilities and economic requirements of dominant nations at any given moment condition the strategies devised. Mahan counseled naval expansion to facilitate swifter economic growth at a time when the U.S. Census Bureau declared the American frontier closed, and restless eyes turned elsewhere for opportunity. At no other time, perhaps, than following a cataclysmic global war in which seventeen million people died could Wilson have proposed dismantling balance-of-power politics and elevating a League of Nations to take its place. Beard's continental Americanism was framed before a backdrop of acute economic distress and growing evidence that Wilson's idealistic justification for America's entry into the First World War was not all it seemed. Kennan's Long Telegram was shaped by frustration and anger that Washington seemed incapable of finessing Stalin's true nature; Nitze's NSC-68 by the notion that the Cold War was a zero-sum game in which Soviet adventurism had to be resisted everywhere. Kissinger believed he was cleaning up the almighty mess created by such blunt and obtuse thinking; Wolfowitz believed that America would shed what made it special if it followed Kissinger's path to great power normalcy. Barack Obama's foreign policy has been defined by an aversion to Wolfowitzian scientism and certainty, but also by recognition that finite resources have to be redirected from neo-Wilsonian interventionism to the more pressing requirement of renewing the United States itself.

History teaches that anything is possible, of course, and that historians are best advised to suppress any nagging inclination to prophesize. Following America's withdrawal from Vietnam in 1973 was a period of introspection as the nation became conflict averse. In October 1983, for example, an Islamist suicide bomber detonated a truck bomb in the lobby of a U.S. Marine barracks in Beirut, Lebanon, killing 241 servicemen—a tragedy and willful provocation. Yet President Reagan—commonly feted as the toughest of Cold Warriors—responded by withdrawing all U.S. forces from the region. Indeed, Reagan dispatched troops overseas only once during his presidency: during the 1984 invasion of tiny Grenada, Operation Urgent Fury, which did not bring the catharsis promised by its code name. The president was pleased to support anticommunist proxies wherever they fought, of course, and his anti-Soviet rhetoric was strident. Yet one can draw a significant line of continuity from Eisenhower to Reagan to Obama. All were reluctant to send U.S. troops overseas, and all felt the targeting of America's enemies was best achieved by deploying other dark arts: CIA covert action, the funding of anticommunist insurgents, and the expansion of lethal drone strikes.

In the 1970s, the United States seemed to be a nation in decline, chastened and humiliated by an insurgency ten thousand miles away and losing economic ground to Japan and Western Europe. Yet who would have predicted that America's withdrawal from the debacle in Vietnam would be followed by a disastrous war of choice in Iraq a generation later? Humility exited the stage in the interim, which could well happen again. It seems inconceivable at this juncture that the United States might again launch a war as misconceived as those in Vietnam and Iraq. But makers of foreign policy often forget the nation's traumas or reconceive them as foiled victories; if only different tactics had been tried, the outcome might have been different. Optimism is one of America's principal virtues, and it is a source of considerable strength. But the trait can cause significant damage when applied to foreign policy in a manner that is untroubled by historical memory.

There are clearly problems with narrowly conceiving of foreign policy as either an art or a science. And I do not believe that intuition and creativity, the traits of the artist, are the only diplomatic virtues, that presidents must simply react and that proactivity is an impossible dream. The sequence of foreign-policy innovations that the United States spearheaded from 1945 to 1949—the creation of the United Nations, the establishment of a rules- and institution-based financial system at Bretton Woods, the Marshall Plan, NATO—were a collective masterstroke. But they were also a series of strategies, plural, advocated by various individuals at different times with different motivations and goals. The process of their devising was organic and they did not follow a master plan. Led by the efforts of memoirists and historians, a sequence of discrete, single-shot initiatives spanning a presi- dency is often reconceived as something larger and more deliberate. But this omniscient narrator is not always discernable in the archival record.

While not a Rosetta stone, I believe that art and science is a binary worth considering. The uncertainty of history is the most significant obstacle to approaching foreign policy as a science. In his 2014 book, *World Order*, Henry Kissinger confessed that he was "brash" at Harvard to proclaim on the mean- ing of history, but "I now know that history's meaning is a matter to be dis- covered, not declared."[24] Unless every nation is united behind a common goal—as Kennan implied in urging a Wilsonian solution to the dangers posed by climate change and nuclear proliferation—nothing in international af- fairs is possessed of stable properties. Many experiments conceived as stark departures from historical precedent have failed abysmally, and the bolder the experiment, as this book has witnessed, the greater the failure. Ultimately it is through studying history and aspiring toward objectivity—it is the trying that counts, for its achievement is impossible—that foreign policymakers can study dilemmas, contextualize threats, compare their magnitude to the resources available, weigh humanitarian and reputational imperatives, and offer appropriately calibrated responses. It is perhaps the best that any nation can do.

NOTES

Abbreviations

ATMLP	Alfred Thayer Mahan Letters and Papers
FRUS	*Foreign Relations of the United States*
GFKP	George F. Kennan Papers
JFKL	John F. Kennedy Library
KD	*The Kennan Diaries*, edited by Frank Costigliola
Kissinger Telcons	Henry Kissinger Telephone Conversations on World Affairs
LBJL	Lyndon Baines Johnson Library
PP	*Public Philosopher: Selected Letters of Walter Lippmann*, edited by John Morton Blum
PWW	*The Papers of Woodrow Wilson*, edited by Arthur S. Link
"T&T"	Walter Lippmann, "Today & Tomorrow," *New York Herald Tribune*
WLP	Walter Lippmann Papers
WLR	Walter Lippmann Reminiscences

Introduction

1. Quoted in Morris, *Why the West Rules*, 534.
2. Miscamble, *George F. Kennan*, 303.
3. Memorandum from George F. Kennan, January 20, 1950, *FRUS*: 1950, 1:38. The memo appears in heavily edited form on pp. 22–44.
4. Ibid., 43–44. For an excellent discussion of the debate, see Thompson, *The Hawk and the Dove*, 98–108.
5. Quoted in Beisner, *Dean Acheson*, 119.

6. Nitze, *From Hiroshima to Glasnost*, 89.
7. Nitze, "The Role of the Learned Man in Government," 277.
8. Nitze, *From Hiroshima to Glasnost*, 89.
9. On Teller's life and career, see Goodchild, *Edward Teller*. On Oppenheimer, see Bird and Sherwin, *American Prometheus*.
10. Thompson, *The Hawk and the Dove*, 106.
11. Beisner, *Dean Acheson*, 233.
12. Herken, "The Great Foreign Policy Fight," 73.
13. Galison and Bernstein, "In Any Light," 311.
14. "Realism" is of course a loaded term that contains multiple gradations and types. Kennan is often characterized as a "classical realist"—in his focus upon the self-interested verities of human nature—as opposed to, say, "neorealists" or "structural realists" like Kenneth Waltz, Stephen Walt, and John Mearsheimer, who focus on structural constraints and incentives that shape international relations. See Waltz, *Theory of International Politics*.
15. Zubok and Pleshakov, *Inside the Kremlin's Cold War*, 151.
16. Several fine histories of American foreign policy have adopted an ideational frame. See, for example, Immerman, *Empire for Liberty*; Kuklick, *Blind Oracles*; Brands, *What America Owes the World*; and Hunt, *Ideology and U.S. Foreign Policy*. Preston's *Sword of the Spirit, Shield of Faith* traces with great skill the influence of religion on U.S. foreign policy.
17. George F. Kennan, March 12, 1949, *KD*, 213.
18. I am grateful to Joel Isaac for his insights on this subject.
19. The analytic philosopher Nelson Goodman used the word "worldmaking" in his *Ways of Worldmaking*, an erudite and wide-ranging discussion of art, science, literary criticism, and psychology. I use it here in a very different, specifically foreign-policy context.
20. See Kahneman, *Thinking, Fast and Slow*, 129–36.
21. Ambrosius, *Wilsonian Statecraft*, 87.
22. Nichols's *Promise and Peril* is particularly successful in rescuing isolationism from the condescension of history.
23. George F. Kennan, July 30, 1982, *KD*, 542.
24. On Roosevelt's personal diplomacy, see Costigliola, *Roosevelt's Lost Alliances*.
25. Kimball, *The Juggler*, 7.
26. See Steel, *Walter Lippmann*, 385, and WLR, 178.
27. www.fas.org/irp/offdocs/nsc-hst/nsc-68.htm.
28. Quoted in Stephen Wertheim, "A Solution from Hell: The United States and the Rise of Humanitarian Interventionism, 1991–2003," *Journal of Genocide Research* 12, no. 3–4 (September–December 2010).
29. Partial audio of the speech (and a full transcript) is available at www.npr.org/player/v2/mediaPlayer.html?action=1&t=1&islist=false&id=99591469&m=99603945.
30. Zachary A. Goldfarb, "Obama Says Iran Shouldn't Misinterpret U.S. Response to Syria," *The Washington Post*, September 15, 2013.
31. President George W. Bush, second inaugural address, January 20, 2005, www.npr.org/templates/story/story.php?storyId=4460172.
32. Stephanson, *Kennan and the Art of Foreign Policy*, 181.
33. David Remnick, "Going the Distance," *The New Yorker*, January 27, 2014, www.newyorker.com/reporting/2014/01/27/140127fa_fact_remnick.
34. Quoted in Guyatt, *Providence and the Invention of the United States*, 319.
35. See, for example, Paul Wolfowitz, "Obama Needs to Change Stance on Iran," *The Washington Post*, June 19, 2009; Anne-Marie Slaughter, "Obama Should Remember Rwanda as He Weighs Action on Syria," *The Washington Post*, April 26, 2013; and Nasr, *Dispensable Nation*.

36. Quoted in Hyde, *Common as Air*, 187.

37. Dallek, *Nixon and Kissinger*, 346.

38. Jeane J. Kirkpatrick, *Legitimacy and Force: Political and Moral Dimensions* (New Brunswick, NJ: Transaction, 1988), 1:461.

39. I am grateful to Andrew Preston for this comparison. See Preston, *The War Council*, 246.

40. Quoted in Mistry, *The United States, Italy, and the Origins of the Cold War*, 207.

1. The Philosopher of Sea Power: Alfred Thayer Mahan

1. Seager, *Alfred Thayer Mahan*, xi.

2. Schlesinger quoted in J. Simon Rofe, "Europe as the Nexus of Theodore Roosevelt's International Strategy," in Krabbendam and Thompson, *America's Transatlantic Turn*, 191.

3. Beard, *A Foreign Policy for America*, 41.

4. See James R. Holmes and Toshi Yoshihara, *Chinese Naval Strategy in the 21st Century: The Turn to Mahan* (New York: Routledge, 2008).

5. Zachary Keck, "Alfred Thayer Mahan with Chinese Characteristics," *The Diplomat*, August 1, 2013, http://thediplomat.com/2013/08/alfred-thayer-mahan-with-chinese-characteristics.

6. Beard, *A Foreign Policy for America*, 39–44.

7. Kennan, *American Diplomacy*, 11–12. See also Adams, *America's Economic Supremacy*.

8. Beard, *A Foreign Policy for America*, 45.

9. Dennis Hart Mahan's most important works include *A Complete Treatise on Field Fortifications* (New York: Wiley and Long, 1836), *Summary on the Cause of Permanent Fortifications and of the Attack and Defense of Permanent Works* (Richmond, VA: West and Johnson, 1850), and *An Elementary Course of Military Engineering*, 2 vols. (New York: John Wiley, 1866–1867).

10. As his biographer Robert Seager notes, "There is no evidence that Alfred Mahan ever read any of D. H. Mahan's books. Nor, in spite of his great respect for his father and his strong sense of pride in family, did he ever number his father among those men he later identified as having had a major influence on the evolution of his own ideas." Seager, *Alfred Thayer Mahan*, 4. This lack of recognition is perhaps unsurprising given the manner of his father's death.

11. Ibid., 89.

12. Ibid., xii.

13. Mahan, *From Sail to Steam*, x.

14. Ibid., xiv.

15. Ibid.

16. Zimmermann, *First Great Triumph*, 104.

17. Mahan, *From Sail to Steam*, xvii.

18. Alfred Thayer Mahan to Elizabeth Lewis, October 16, 1857, ATMLP, 1:3–4.

19. Seager, *Alfred Thayer Mahan*, 14.

20. Mahan, *From Sail to Steam*, 91, 92.

21. Ibid., 187, 192.

22. Quoted in Seager, *Alfred Thayer Mahan*, 52.

23. Alfred Thayer Mahan, "A Statement on Behalf of the Church Missionary Society to Seamen in the Port of New York," April 10, 1897, ATMLP, 3:590.

24. Alfred Thayer Mahan, "Woman's Suffrage: A Speech," 1914, ibid., 713.

25. Alfred Thayer Mahan to Mary Helena Okill Mahan, May 10, 1867, ibid., 1:102.

26. Ibid., December 29, 1867, and January 2, 1868, 118, 120.

27. Alfred Thayer Mahan to *The Times* (London), June 13, 1913, ibid., 3:497–498.

28. Seager, *Alfred Thayer Mahan*, 54.

29. This story is recounted in May, *Imperial Democracy*, 3.

30. Morgan, *America's Road to Empire*, 2.

31. Seager, *Alfred Thayer Mahan*, 38.

32. Widmer, *Ark of the Liberties*, 145.

33. Robert Kagan's provocative *Dangerous Nation* argues that aggressive continental and overseas expansion has been central to the American story since the inception of the republic. In this respect the conservative Kagan pursues an argument that is strikingly similar to that proposed by New Left historians such as William Appleman Williams and Walter LaFeber throughout the 1960s and 1970s. But even Kagan concedes that following the Civil War, "The expansive-reactive quality of American foreign policy, and the vagueness of American foreign policy goals, did determine the comparatively limited size and pace of the naval buildup" (355).

34. Ibid., 359.

35. Alfred Mahan to Samuel Ashe, July 26, 1884, ATMLP, 1:574.

36. Mahan, *The Gulf and Inland Waters*.

37. Seager, *Alfred Thayer Mahan*, 135.

38. Alfred Thayer Mahan to Stephen B. Luce, September 4, 1884, ATMLP, 1:577.

39. Alfred Thayer Mahan to Stephen B. Luce, May 16, 1885, ibid., 606–607.

40. Alfred Thayer Mahan to Stephen B. Luce, September 2, 1885, ibid., 613.

41. Alfred Thayer Mahan to Samuel A. Ashe, February 2, 1886, ibid., 625.

42. For a detailed account of the Mahan-Roosevelt relationship, see Turk, *The Ambiguous Relationship*.

43. "New Publications: Our Navy in 1812," *The New York Times*, June 5, 1882.

44. In "The Nature of Influence," Peter Karsten argues that Mahan's influence on Roosevelt has been greatly exaggerated, and that TR was an original naval thinker in his own right, requiring little tutoring from the overestimated Mahan. He contends that Roosevelt used Mahan—and his intellectual respectability—to serve his own expansionary ends. Karsten's article makes some fine cautionary points, but he both overestimates the depth of Roosevelt's historical insight and underplays Mahan's originality.

   In 1886, Roosevelt, while engaged in writing a shallow, cursory biography of Missouri senator Thomas Hart Benton, wrote to his friend Henry Cabot Lodge, "I have pretty nearly finished Benton, mainly evolving him from my inner consciousness; but when he leaves the Senate in 1850 I have nothing whatever to go by; and being by nature a timid and, on occasions, by choice a truthful man, I would prefer to have some foundation of fact, no matter how slender, on which to build the airy and arabesque superstructure of my fancy—especially as I am writing a history." Zimmermann, *First Great Triumph*, 172.

45. Zimmermann, *First Great Triumph*, 92.

46. Alfred Thayer Mahan to Charles Scribner's Sons, September 4, 1888, ATMLP, 1:657–58.

47. Alfred Thayer Mahan to Stephen B. Luce, September 21, 1889, ibid., 707–708.

48. Mahan, *Influence of Sea Power upon History*, 26. Walter LaFeber is particularly astute in identifying the commercial imperative driving Mahan's theories. See, "A Note on the 'Marcantillistic Imperialism' of Alfred Thayer Mahan."

49. Figures cited in Michael Cox and Doug Stokes, eds., *US Foreign Policy* (New York: Oxford University Press, 2008), 301.

50. Mahan, *Influence of Sea Power upon History*, 33.

51. Ibid., 34.

52. Ibid., 42.

53. Ibid., 43.

54. Ibid., 45–46.

55. Ibid., 52–53.

56. Seager, *Alfred Thayer Mahan*, 466.

57. Mahan, *The Influence of Sea Power upon History*, 53–54.

58. Ibid., 56.
59. Ibid., 57.
60. Ibid., 57–58.
61. Ibid., 58–59.
62. Ibid., 82–83.
63. See, for example, Johnson, *The Sorrows of Empire*; Ferguson, *Colossus*; Bacevich, *Limits of Power*; Hobsbawm, *On Empire*; Gaddis, *The Cold War*; Hoffman, *American Umpire*.
64. Figure cited in Johnson, *Nemesis*, 5–6.
65. Jonathan Freedland, "A Black and Disgraceful Site," *The New York Review of Books*, May 28–June 10, 2009, 27.
66. Wimmel, *Theodore Roosevelt and the Great White Fleet*, 48.
67. Morris, *Rise of Theodore Roosevelt*, 434.
68. Both reviews are quoted in Seager, *Alfred Thayer Mahan*, 210–11.
69. Ibid., 213.
70. Wimmel, *Theodore Roosevelt and the Great White Fleet*, 57.
71. Karsten, "The Nature of 'Influence,'" 590.
72. Seager, *Alfred Thayer Mahan*, 295.
73. Ibid., 291.
74. Alfred Mahan to Ellen Evans Mahan, July 13, 1893, ATMLP, 2:122.
75. Alfred Mahan to Theodore Roosevelt, June 6, 1894, ibid., 281.
76. John Hay, "John Hay's Years with Roosevelt," *Harper's Monthly Magazine* 131, no. 784 (June 1915): 578.
77. Hofstadter, *Anti-Intellectualism in American Life*, 208.
78. Zimmermann, *First Great Triumph*, 236.
79. Karsten, "The Nature of 'Influence,'" 590.
80. For a deft portrait of Lodge, see Nichols, *Promise and Peril*, 22–25.
81. Zelizer, *Arsenal of Democracy*, 13.
82. Seager, *Alfred Thayer Mahan*, 328.
83. Alfred Mahan to Samuel A. Ashe, November 7, 1896, ATMLP, 2:470.
84. Seager, *Alfred Thayer Mahan*, 338.
85. Roosevelt quoted in Kagan, *Dangerous Nation*, 385.
86. Alfred Thayer Mahan to Theodore Roosevelt, May 6, 1897, ATMLP, 2:507.
87. Alfred Thayer Mahan to Theodore Roosevelt, May 1, 1897, ibid., 506.
88. Alfred Thayer Mahan to Theodore Roosevelt, May 6, 1897, ibid., 507.
89. Zimmermann, *First Great Triumph*, 240.
90. Roosevelt quoted in Karsten, "The Nature of 'Influence,'" 590.
91. May, *Imperial Democracy*, 94.
92. Ibid., 73.
93. Ernest May offers an elegant pen portrait of McKinley ibid., 112–13.
94. Kagan, *Dangerous Nation*, 387.
95. See Zimmerman, *First Great Triumph*, 236.
96. Quoted in Foner, *The Spanish-Cuban War*, 237.
97. Ibid., 238.
98. Halper and Clarke, *The Silence of the Rational Center*, 36–37. See also Thomas, *The War Lovers*.
99. Foner, *The Spanish Cuban War*, 239.
100. May, *Imperial Democracy*, 143.
101. Seager, *Alfred Thayer Mahan*, 361.
102. "The Sinking of the USS Maine," remarks to the New Jersey chapter of the Society of the Cincinnati, February 22, 1898, ATMLP, 3:592.
103. On McKinley's reluctance to wage war against Spain, see Offner, *An Unwanted War*.
104. May, *Imperial Democracy*, 130, 268.

105. Seager, *Alfred Thayer Mahan*, 364.
106. Foner, *The Spanish-Cuban War*, 263.
107. Zimmermann, *First Great Triumph*, 262.
108. May, *Imperial Democracy*, 159.
109. Kristin Hoganson believes that a crisis of masculinity—provoked by mass unemployment, which deprived American men of the means to support their families—contributed to a popular mood of bellicosity. See *Fighting for American Manhood*.
110. On the festive popular mood on the eve of war, see Morgan, *America's Road to Empire*, 65.
111. Quoted in John Braeman, *Albert J. Beveridge*, 22–25.
112. Seager, *Alfred Thayer Mahan*, 363.
113. Ibid., 357; for a discussion of the lopsided military balance, see 354–58.
114. Zimmermann, *First Great Triumph*, 271.
115. Seager, *Alfred Thayer Mahan*, 375.
116. May, *Imperial Democracy*, 221.
117. Traub, *The Freedom Agenda*, 13.
118. Seager, *Alfred Thayer Mahan*, 393.
119. Herring, *From Colony to Superpower*, 323.
120. Alfred Thayer Mahan to Henry Cabot Lodge, July 27, 1898, ATMLP, 2:569.
121. Alfred Thayer Mahan to Henry Cabot Lodge, February 7, 1899, ibid., 627.
122. Seager, *Alfred Thayer Mahan*, 409.
123. Alfred Mahan to Samuel Ashe, September 23, 1899, ATMLP, 2:658.
124. Seager, *Alfred Thayer Mahan*, 410.
125. Ibid., 413.
126. Ibid., 414.
127. Alfred Thayer Mahan to Theodore Roosevelt, March 12, 1901, ATMLP, 2:706–707.
128. Morris, *Theodore Rex*, 3.
129. Cooper, *The Warrior and the Priest*, 69.
130. Safire, *Safire's Political Dictionary*, 154.
131. On the building of the canal, see McCullough, *The Path Between the Seas*.
132. Zimmermann, *First Great Triumph*, 436.
133. See Hannigan, *The New World Power*, 19–24.
134. Baer, *One Hundred Years of Sea Power*, 41.
135. Wimmel, *The Great White Fleet*, xiv.
136. See Cooper, *The Warrior and the Priest*, 65.
137. Figures cited in Jacoby, *The Age of American Unreason*.
138. See Darwin, *After Tamerlane*, 320–21.
139. On Taft's presidency and distinguished wider career, see Anderson, *William Howard Taft*; Coletta, *The Presidency of William Howard Taft*; and Burton, *William Howard Taft*.
140. Theodore Roosevelt, speech in Louisville, April 3, 1912, in Hagedorn, *The Works of Theodore Roosevelt*, 17:169.
141. Alfred Thayer Mahan to Henry White, June 28, 1912, ATMLP, 3:468.
142. Alfred Thayer Mahan to Bouverie F. Clark, October 28, 1912, ibid., 484.

2. Kant's Best Hope: Woodrow Wilson

1. On the election, see Gould, *Four Hats in the Ring*.
2. Quoted in Cooper, *The Warrior and the Priest*, 154. On the arbitration dispute, see Campbell, "Taft, Roosevelt, and the Arbitration Treaties of 1911."
3. Cooper, *The Warrior and the Priest*, 157.
4. Ibid., 208.
5. Woodrow Wilson to Mary Allen Hulbert Peck, August 25, 1912, *PWW*, 25:55–56.

6. Cooper, *Woodrow Wilson*, 168.

7. See Hofstadter, *Anti-intellectualism in American Life*, 207–22.

8. Ibid., 209–10.

9. Thompson, *Woodrow Wilson*, 16.

10. Nordholt, *Woodrow Wilson*, 95.

11. Cooper, *Woodrow Wilson*, 159.

12. Freud and Bullitt, *Thomas Woodrow Wilson*, 4.

13. See Widmer, *The Ark of the Liberties*, 169.

14. Brands, *Woodrow Wilson*, 5.

15. Raymond D. Fosdick, Personal Recollections of Woodrow Wilson, January 30, 1956, Henry Allen Moe Papers, 2.

16. Ibid., 10.

17. Link, *Wilson the Diplomatist*, 12.

18. Freud and Bullitt, *Thomas Woodrow Wilson*.

19. Thompson, *Woodrow Wilson*, 19.

20. Samuel G. Blythe, "Mexico: The Record of a Conversation with President Wilson," *Saturday Evening Post*, May 23, 1914, 4.

21. Link, *Wilson the Diplomatist*, 15.

22. Brands, *Woodrow Wilson*, 15.

23. Woodrow Wilson to Charles A. Talcott, December 31, 1879, *PWW*, 5:267.

24. Cooper, *Woodrow Wilson*, 35–36.

25. Cooper, *The Warrior and the Priest*, 44.

26. Ibid., 53.

27. Brands, *Woodrow Wilson*, 11.

28. Thompson, *Woodrow Wilson*, 28.

29. Quoted ibid., 27.

30. Gunnell, *The Descent of Political Theory*, 82.

31. Wilson, *Constitutional Government in the United States*, 77–78.

32. Cooper, *The Warrior and the Priest*, 52.

33. Cooper, *Woodrow Wilson*, 68.

34. See Cowley and Williams, *International and Historical Roots of American Higher Education*, 35.

35. Thompson, *Woodrow Wilson*, 43.

36. Speech, March 22, 1906, *PWW*, 16:341.

37. Wilson, *Constitutional Government in the United States*, 59, 78.

38. Wilson, "The Law and the Facts," 8–11.

39. Thompson, *Woodrow Wilson*, 49.

40. Ibid., 50.

41. Cooper, *The Warrior and the Priest*, 221.

42. White, *Woodrow Wilson*, 264.

43. Cooper, *Woodrow Wilson*, 182.

44. Walworth, *Woodrow Wilson*, 265.

45. Wilson quoted in Lim, *The Anti-Intellectual Presidency*, 19.

46. Cooper, *Woodrow Wilson*, 210.

47. Halper and Clarke, *The Silence of the Rational Center*, 46.

48. See Herring, *From Colony to Superpower*, 381.

49. Cooper, *Woodrow Wilson*, 212.

50. Cooper, *The Warrior and the Priest*, 272.

51. Cooper, *Woodrow Wilson*, 211.

52. Herring, *From Colony to Superpower*, 386.

53. Cooper, *The Warrior and the Priest*, 272.

54. Ibid., 382.

55. Widmer, *Ark of the Liberties*, 172.
56. Quirk, *An Affair of Honor*, 77.
57. Woodrow Wilson, remarks at a press conference, November 14, 1914, *PWW*, 31:351.
58. Herring, *From Colony to Superpower*, 395.
59. See Katz, "Pancho Villa and the Attack on Columbus, New Mexico."
60. Herring, *From Colony to Superpower*, 397.
61. Seager, *Alfred Thayer Mahan*, 595–96.
62. Woodrow Wilson, Address to Women in Cincinnati, October 26, 1916, *PWW*, 38:531, quoted in John A. Thompson, "Wilsonianism: The Dynamics of a Conflicted Concept," *International Affairs* 86, no. 1 (2010):32.
63. A fine recent history of the origins of the First World War is Clark, *The Sleepwalkers*.
64. Russell, "Alfred Thayer Mahan and American Geopolitics," 130.
65. Seager, *Alfred Thayer Mahan*, 598–99.
66. Woodrow Wilson to Lindley Miller Garrison, August 6, 1914, *PWW*, 30:352.
67. Alfred Mahan to Josephus Daniels, August 15, 1914 (two letters), ATMLP, 3:540–42.
68. Seager, *Alfred Thayer Mahan*, 600.
69. Alfred Mahan to the Editor of *The New York Times*, August 31, 1914, ATMLP, 3:542.
70. Seager, *Alfred Thayer Mahan*, 602.
71. Cooper, *The Warrior and the Priest*, 273.
72. See Herring, *From Colony to Superpower*, 399.
73. Woodrow Wilson, speech to joint session of Congress, December 8, 1914, *PWW*, 31:423.
74. Herbert B. Brougham, Memorandum of Interview with the President, December 14, 1914, ibid., 458–59.
75. Franklin D. Roosevelt to Eleanor Roosevelt, August 3, 1914, quoted in Widmer, *Ark of the Liberties*, 197.
76. See Cooper, *The Warrior and the Priest*, 277.
77. See Herring, *From Colony to Superpower*, 401.
78. Ibid., 402.
79. Theodore Roosevelt to Hugo Münsterberg, October 3, 1914, in Morison, *Letters of Theodore Roosevelt*, 8:824–25.
80. Cooper, *The Warrior and the Priest*, 303.
81. See Herring, *From Colony to Superpower*, 403.
82. Figures cited in Geoffrey Wheatcroft, "Hello to All That," *The New York Review of Books*, June 23, 2011.
83. Knock, *To End All Wars*, 107.
84. See, for example, Doyle, *Ways of War and Peace*.
85. Woodrow Wilson, address to a joint session of Congress, April 2, 1917, *PWW*, 41:524.
86. Woodrow Wilson, Annual Message to Congress on the State of the Union, December 7, 1915, *PWW*, 35:297.
87. Herring, *From Colony to Superpower*, 405.
88. Ibid., 405–406.
89. See Nichols, *Promise and Peril*.
90. Ibid., 407.
91. Cooper, *Woodrow Wilson*, 352.
92. See www.nationalarchives.gov.uk/pathways/firstworldwar/spotlights/blockade.htm.
93. Herring, *From Colony to Superpower*, 407–408.
94. Mazower, *Governing the World*, 124.
95. Cooper, *The Warrior and the Priest*, 315.
96. Ibid., 317.

97. Woodrow Wilson, An Address to a Joint Session of Congress, April 2, 1917, *PWW*, 41:526–27.
98. Ibid., 524, 525.
99. Tumulty, *Woodrow Wilson as I Know Him*, 256.
100. See Thompson, *Reformers and War*, 185–89.
101. See Zelizer, *Arsenal of Democracy*, 28.
102. Ibid., 179–80.
103. Cooper, *The Warrior and the Priest*, 320.
104. "Quits Columbia; Assails Trustees," *The New York Times*, October 9, 1917, 1.
105. Zelizer, *Arsenal of Democracy*, 28, 29.
106. Herring, *From Colony to Superpower*, 419.
107. Gelfand, *The Inquiry*, 41.
108. Shotwell, *At the Paris Peace Conference*, 6–8.
109. See Steel, *Walter Lippmann*, xiii.
110. Grose, *Continuing the Inquiry*, 1.
111. "A Memorandum by Sidney Edward Mezes, David Hunter Miller, and Walter Lippmann," undated, *PWW*, 45:459–74.
112. "From the Diary of Colonel House," January 9, 1918, ibid., 551.
113. Nicolson, *Peacemaking, 1919*, 28.
114. "The Final Draft of the Fourteen Points Address," January 7, 1918, *PWW*, 45:519–31.
115. Kissinger, *Diplomacy*, 19–20.
116. Preston, *Sword of the Spirit, Shield of Faith*, 275.
117. Macmillan, *Peacemakers*, 41.
118. Ikenberry et al., *The Crisis of American Foreign Policy*, 42.
119. Thompson, *Woodrow Wilson*, 176.
120. Widmer, *Ark of the Liberties*, 32.
121. Thompson, *Woodrow Wilson*, 177.
122. Cooper, *The Warrior and the Priest*, 334.
123. Edward J. Renehan Jr., *The Lion's Pride: Theodore Roosevelt and His Family in Peace and War* (New York: Oxford University Press, 1998), 222.
124. Thompson, *Woodrow Wilson*, 178.
125. "Address in the Princess Theater in Cheyenne," September 24, 1919, *PWW*, 24:469.
126. Herring, *From Colony to Superpower*, 418.
127. Zweig, *The World of Yesterday*, 304.
128. Raymond D. Fosdick, Personal Recollections of Woodrow Wilson, January 30, 1956, Henry Allen Moe Papers, 18.
129. Wells, *The Shape of Things to Come*, 82.
130. Keynes, *Economic Consequences of the Peace*, 34–35.
131. Macmillan, *Peacemakers*, 31, 35.
132. Herring, *From Colony to Superpower*, 408.
133. Donald Edward Moggridge, *Maynard Keynes: An Economist's Biography* (London: Routledge, 1995), 328.
134. Keynes, *Economic Consequences of the Peace*, 39–40, 44–45.
135. Drinkwater, *Sir Harold Nicolson and International Relations*, vii.
136. Kennan, *American Diplomacy*, 61.
137. Ikenberry et al., *The Crisis of American Foreign Policy*, 43.
138. Ibid., 30.
139. James Scott Brown, ed., *Official Statements of War Aims and Peace Proposals: December 1916 to November 1918* (Washington, D.C.: Carnegie Endowment for International Peace, 1921), 381.
140. Manela, "Imagining Woodrow Wilson in Asia," 1336. See also Manela, *The Wilsonian Moment*.

141. Cooper, *Woodrow Wilson*, 477.
142. "The League of Nations," *The New Republic*, May 24, 1919, 102.
143. See Thompson, *Woodrow Wilson*, 213.
144. Link, *Wilson the Diplomatist*, 130.
145. Speech by Woodrow Wilson, July 19, 1919, *PWW*, 61:436.
146. Cooper, *Woodrow Wilson*, 509.
147. Macmillan, *Peacemakers*, 13.
148. Charles T. Thompson, *The Peace Conference: Day by Day* (New York: Brentano's, 1920), 190.
149. Ronald J. Pestritto, "The Perils of Progress," *The Claremont Review of Books* 4, no. 3 (Summer 2004).
150. Cooper, *The Warrior and the Priest*, 335–36.
151. Herring, *From Colony to Superpower*, 435.

3. Americans First: Charles Beard

1. Beard, *An Economic Interpretation of the Constitution*, 324.
2. Thomas Bender, "Charles A. Beard," in John A. Garraty and Mark C. Carnes, eds., *American National Biography* (New York: Oxford University Press, 1999), 403.
3. Nore, *Charles A. Beard*, 63.
4. Beard, *The Making of Charles A. Beard*, 22.
5. Nore, *Charles A. Beard*, 46.
6. Kennedy, *Charles A. Beard*, 11.
7. Ibid., 29.
8. Gruber, *Mars and Minerva*, 88.
9. Kennedy, *Charles A. Beard*, 29.
10. Nore, *Charles A. Beard*, 80.
11. Ibid., 73.
12. Ibid.
13. *The New York Times*, January 23, 1917, 2.
14. Nore, *Charles A. Beard*, 74.
15. See Gruber, *Mars and Minerva*, 111; and Charles A. Beard, "Political Science in the Crucible," *The New Republic*, November 17, 1917.
16. Gruber, *Mars and Minerva*, 157.
17. Charles Beard, "A Call Upon Every Citizen," *Harper's Magazine*, October 1918, 655–56.
18. Quoted in Cowley and Williams, *International and Historical Roots of American Higher Education*, 174.
19. Quoted in Gruber, *Mars and Minerva*, 199.
20. See Beale, *Charles A. Beard*, 243.
21. See Nore, *Charles A. Beard*, 81.
22. Allan Nevins, Oral History, 145.
23. *The New York Times*, October 9, 1917, 1.
24. Ibid., October 10, 1917, 10.
25. See Charles A. Beard, "The Supreme Issue," *The New Republic*, January 25, 1919, 343.
26. See Nore, *Charles A. Beard*, 83–84.
27. *The New York Times*, January 25, 1919, 1.
28. Nore, *Charles A. Beard*, 77.
29. Quoted in Kennedy, *Charles A. Beard*, 39.
30. See Woodward, "The Age of Reinterpretation," 2–8. For an insightful discussion of Beard's foreign-policy views, see Craig, "The Not-So-Strange Career of Charles Beard," 253.
31. Quoted in Craig, "Not-So-Strange Career of Charles Beard," 262.

32. Beard, *A Foreign Policy for America*, 102.

33. Blower, "From Isolationism to Neutrality."

34. Nore, *Charles A. Beard*, 1.

35. Kennedy, *Charles A. Beard*, 3.

36. Ibid., 15. On the important relationship between Beard and Powell, see Wilkins, "Frederick York Powell and Charles A. Beard."

37. Fink, *Progressive Intellectuals*, 44.

38. Kennedy, *Charles A. Beard*, 15.

39. See Brands, *What America Owes the World*, 113.

40. Beard, *The Making of Charles A. Beard*, 15.

41. Kennedy, *Charles A. Beard*, 7.

42. Nore, *Charles A. Beard*, 24.

43. Ibid., 24–25.

44. Mark C. Smith, "A Tale of Two Charlies: Political Science, History and Civic Reform," in Addock, Bevir, and Stimson, *Modern Political Science*, 129.

45. Barrow, *More Than a Historian*, 1.

46. Nore, *Charles A. Beard*, 36.

47. See Beale, *Charles A. Beard*, 233–34.

48. Ibid., 79.

49. William Appleman Williams, "Charles Austin Beard: The Intellectual as Tory-Radical," in Williams, *History as a Way of Learning*, 229–42.

50. Garraty and Carnes, *American National Biography*, 402.

51. See Ranke, *Theory and Practice of History*; and Novick, *That Noble Dream*, 26–30.

52. See Beard, "That Noble Dream"; and Eric Goldman's veneration of Beard, "Historians and the Ivory Tower," *Social Frontier*, 2, no. 9 (1936).

53. Garraty and Carnes, *American National Biography*, 404.

54. Beale, *Charles A. Beard*, 139.

55. Beard, *The Making of Charles A. Beard*, 103.

56. Smith, "A Tale of Two Charlies," 130.

57. Nore, *Charles A. Beard*, 133–34; Lippmann, *The Phantom Public*.

58. On America's key role in shaping the economics of the interwar period, see Tooze, *The Deluge*.

59. Herring, *From Colony to Superpower*, 439; "French Population Shows Little Gain," *The New York Times*, February 26, 1922, 30.

60. Westad, *The Global Cold War*, 19.

61. Herring, *From Colony to Superpower*, 451.

62. See Zelizer, *Arsenal of Democracy*, 37.

63. Herring, *From Colony to Superpower*, 442.

64. Nore, *Charles A. Beard*, 96.

65. See Kennedy, *Charles A. Beard*, 47, 49–50, and Beard, *Cross-Currents in Europe Today*.

66. For a discussion of the Beards' *Rise of American Civilization*, see Nore, *Charles A. Beard*, 112–26.

67. Charles A. Beard to Lewis Mumford, May 9, 1927, Papers of Lewis Mumford, folder 347.

68. Herring, *From Colony to Superpower*, 439.

69. Charles A. Beard, "Bigger and Better Armaments," *Harper's Magazine*, January 1929, 133–43.

70. Nore, *Charles A. Beard*, 110.

71. Charles A. Beard and William Beard, *The American Leviathan*, 732–36.

72. Kennedy, *Freedom from Fear*, 39.

73. Badger, *FDR*, 6.

74. See Sobel, *The Great Bull Market*, 73–74, and Kennedy, *Freedom from Fear*, 41.

75. David Burner, *Herbert Hoover: A Public Life* (New York: Knopf, 1979), 298.
76. Steel, *Walter Lippmann*, 287–88.
77. Schwartz, *The Interregnum of Despair*, 6.
78. Badger, *The New Deal*, 11.
79. Ibid.
80. Sowell, *Intellectuals and Society*, 130.
81. Hofstadter, *The American Political Tradition*, 283.
82. See Sowell, *Intellectuals and Society*, 130–34.
83. Kennedy, *Charles A. Beard*, 62.
84. Beard, *America Faces the Future*, 137.
85. See Kennedy, *Charles A. Beard*, 57–60.
86. Badger, *The New Deal*, 6.
87. Rofe, "'Under the Influence of Mahan,'" 732.
88. Roosevelt, *My Boy Franklin*, 15.
89. Cumings, *Dominion from Sea to Sea*, 305.
90. See Franklin D. Roosevelt "Our Foreign Policy: A Democratic View," *Foreign Affairs* 6, 1928, quoted in Zelizer, *Arsenal of Democracy*, 37.
91. Cohen, *The American Revisionists*, 135.
92. Nore, *Charles A. Beard*, 144.
93. Beard, *The Open Door at Home*, 135–54. For a discussion of the book, see Nore, *Charles A. Beard*, 144–47.
94. Nore, *Charles A. Beard*, 144.
95. See Kennedy, *Charles A. Beard*, 66–69.
96. Beard, *The Open Door at Home*, 273–74.
97. Ibid., 318.
98. See Kennedy, *Charles A. Beard*, 72.
99. Ibid., 73–74.
100. Ibid., 74–77, Nore, *Charles A. Beard*, 147.
101. Chang, *The Rape of Nanking*; Fogel, *The Nanjing Massacre in History and Historiography*.
102. Kennedy, *Freedom from Fear*, 502.
103. Casey, *Cautious Crusade*, 23.
104. Herring, *From Colony to Superpower*, 521.
105. See Hull, *Memoirs*, 1:544–45; and Beale, *Charles A. Beard*, 176.
106. Burns, *The Lion and the Fox*, 318.
107. Ibid.
108. Hull, *Memoirs*, 1:545.
109. Kennedy, *Charles A. Beard*, 65.
110. Quoted in Beard, *A Foreign Policy for America*, 113.
111. Brands, *What America Owes the World*, 124–25.
112. Charles A. Beard, "National Politics and the War," *Scribner's Magazine,* February 1935, 65–70.
113. Kennedy, *Charles A. Beard*, 82.
114. Ibid., 84.
115. Charles A. Beard, "War—If, How, and When?" *Events* 2, August 1937, 81–86.
116. Brands, *What America Owes the World*, 126.
117. Charles A. Beard, "A Reply to Mr. Browder," *The New Republic*, February 2, 1938, 357–59.
118. Kennedy, *Charles A. Beard*, 88–89.
119. Howe, *England Expects Every American to Do His Duty*, 86.
120. Charles A. Beard, "We're Blundering into War," *The American Mercury*, April 1939, quoted in Brands, *What America Owes the World*, 127.
121. Beard, "Education Under the Nazis," 437–52.

122. H. L. Mencken to Charles A. Beard, May 20, 1939; Charles A. Beard to H. L. Mencken (May 1939?); Charles A. Beard to H. L. Mencken, August 14, 1940; H. L. Mencken to Charles A. Beard, August 15, 1940, Papers of Charles and Mary Beard, folder 27.
123. Brick, "Talcott Parsons's 'Shift Away from Economics,'" 502.
124. Josephson, *Infidel in the Temple*, 413–14.
125. Beard, *A Foreign Policy for America*, 39–47.
126. Ibid., 68.
127. Ibid., 101–103.
128. Ibid., 104.
129. Ibid., 149.
130. Kennedy, *Charles A. Beard*, 98.
131. See Reinhold Niebuhr, "Review of *A Foreign Policy for America*," *The Nation*, May 25, 1940, 656–58.
132. Nore, *Charles A. Beard*, 182.
133. Mumford, "The Corruption of Liberalism," 618–23. Also see Nore, *Charles A. Beard*, 183.
134. Brands, *What America Owes the World*, 129.
135. Nore, *Charles A. Beard*, 185.
136. http://docs.fdrlibrary.marist.edu/odllpc2.html.
137. Brands, *What America Owes the World*, 137.
138. Kennedy, *Charles A. Beard*, 102. For a full transcript, see "Statement of Charles A. Beard," *To Promote the Defense of the U.S.: Hearings Before the Committee on Foreign Relations, U.S. Senate, on Senate [Bill] 275*, 77th Cong., 1st sess., February 4, 1941, 307–12.
139. Brands, *What America Owes the World*, 138.
140. Haufler, *Codebreaker's Victory*, 127.

4. The Syndicated Oracle: Walter Lippmann

1. Judt, *Thinking the Twentieth Century*, 275.
2. Dildy, *Dunkirk 1940*, 89.
3. Steel, *Walter Lippmann*, 281.
4. Arthur Schlesinger Jr., "Walter Lippmann: The Intellectual v. Politics," in Childs and Reston, *Walter Lippmann and His Times*, 189.
5. Interview with Professor Allan Nevins, WLR, 175.
6. Steel, *Walter Lippmann*, 384.
7. Lippmann, "T&T," June 18, 1940.
8. WLR, 196.
9. Steel, *Walter Lippmann*, 385.
10. WLR, 178.
11. Charles Beard to James T. Farrell, February 1 (year illegible due to fire damage, likely 1948), Papers of James T. Farrell, "Charles Beard."
12. Logevall, "First Among Critics," 351.
13. Adam, *Walter Lippmann*, 17.
14. Steel, *Walter Lippmann*, 6–8.
15. Wright, *Five Public Philosophies of Walter Lippmann*, 12.
16. WLR, 27.
17. Steel, *Walter Lippmann*, 18.
18. WLR, 31.
19. Steel, *Walter Lippmann*, 28.
20. Fink, *Progressive Intellectuals and the Dilemmas of Democratic Commitment*, 11.
21. Walter Lippmann to Lincoln Steffens, May 18, 1910, WLP, box 31.
22. Steel, *Walter Lippmann*, 39.

23. Lippmann, *A Preface to Politics*, 33, 49, 17, 60.
24. Steel, *Walter Lippmann*, xiii.
25. WLR, 53.
26. Steel, *Walter Lippmann*, 64–65.
27. Croly, *The Promise of American Life*, 303.
28. Ibid., 28.
29. WLR, 7.
30. Walter Lippmann to Van Wyck Brooks, February 5, 1914, Papers of Van Wyck Brooks, folder 1662.
31. Steel, *Walter Lippmann*, 62.
32. Ibid., 52.
33. Ibid., 72.
34. Walter Lippmann to Felix Frankfurter, August 2, 1914, WLP, box 10, folder 418.
35. Walter Lippmann, "Force and Ideas," *The New Republic*, November 7, 1914.
36. Walter Lippmann to Graham Wallas, August 5, 1915, *PP*, xxiv.
37. Lippmann, *The Stakes of Diplomacy*, 67, 224.
38. WLR, 89.
39. Steel, *Walter Lippmann*, 102–103.
40. WLR, 89.
41. Walter Lippmann, "The Case for Wilson," *The New Republic*, October 14, 1916.
42. Steel, *Walter Lippmann*, 100.
43. WLR, 90.
44. Walter Lippmann, "The Defense of the Atlantic World," *The New Republic*, February 17, 1917. Mary Beard recorded her appreciation of the article in a warm letter to Lippmann. She wrote that it "is superb. Better than ever before you have proved your leadership. I have been liking the New Republic immensely recently." Mary Beard to Walter Lippmann, February 19, 1917, WLR, box 3, folder 125.
45. WLR, 17.
46. Ikenberry et al., *The Crisis of American Foreign Policy*, 41.
47. Steel, *Walter Lippmann*, 158, 161.
48. Walter Lippmann to Bernard Berenson, September 15, 1919, WLP, box 3, folder 128.
49. Hofstadter, *Anti-intellectualism*, 213.
50. Walter Lippmann to Graham Wallas, November 4, 1920, WLP, box 33, folder 1246.
51. WLR, 19–20.
52. Steel, *Walter Lippmann*, 237–38. Also see Walter Lippmann, "The Kellogg Doctrine: Vested Rights and Nationalism in Latin America," *Foreign Affairs* 4 (1927).
53. Lippmann, *Public Opinion*, xiv.
54. Fink, *Progressive Intellectuals*, 31.
55. Steel, *Walter Lippmann*, 183.
56. Lippmann, *The Phantom Public*, 20.
57. Walter Lippmann, "Insiders and Outsiders," *The New Republic*, November 13, 1915.
58. Lippmann, *The Phantom Public*, 155.
59. Steel, *Walter Lippmann*, 212.
60. Dewey, *The Public and Its Problems*, 365. Dewey, Beard, and Lippmann are expertly discussed in Bender, *New York Intellect*.
61. Walter Lippmann to Charles Beard, September 8, 1925; Charles Beard to Walter Lippmann, September 12, 1925; Walter Lippmann to Charles Beard, September 14, 1925; Charles Beard to Walter Lippmann, September 30, 1925; Charles Beard to Walter Lippmann, October 3, 1925, WLP, box 3, folder 125.
62. Steel, *Walter Lippmann*, 253–54.
63. Ibid., 255–56.
64. Ibid., 271, 280.

65. Mark Carnes, ed., *Invisible Giants: Fifty Americans Who Shaped the Nation but Missed the History Books* (New York: Oxford University Press, 2002), 181.
66. Steel, *Walter Lippmann*, 295–96.
67. Ibid., 300.
68. Lippmann, "T&T," April 6, 1933.
69. Herring, *From Colony to Superpower*, 555.
70. Steel, *Walter Lippmann*, 305–306.
71. Syed, *Walter Lippmann's Philosophy of International Politics*, 9.
72. Steel, *Walter Lippmann*, 325.
73. On the intellectual origins of the New Deal from an insider's perspective, see Tugwell, *The Brains Trust*.
74. Lim, *The Anti-Intellectual Presidency*, 29.
75. Steel, *Walter Lippmann*, 320–21.
76. Lippmann, "T&T," May 17, 1934.
77. Ibid., May 12, 1933.
78. Steel, *Walter Lippmann*, 330.
79. WLR, 172.
80. A powerful recently published account of the conflict is Paul Preston, *The Spanish Holocaust: Inquisition and Extermination in Twentieth Century Spain* (New York: W. W. Norton, 2012).
81. Lippmann, "T&T," December 24, 1936.
82. Steel, *Walter Lippmann*, 339.
83. Charles Beard to Walter Lippmann, June 17, 1937, Papers of Hamilton Fish Armstrong, box 41.
84. Lippmann, "T&T," December 2, 1937.
85. Ibid., October 16, 1937.
86. Steel, *Walter Lippmann*, 370.
87. Walter Lippmann to Harold G. Nicolson, December 6, 1938, PP, 374.
88. Louis Johnson to Walter Lippmann, December 22, 1938, WLP, box 80, folder 1160.
89. Steel, *Walter Lippmann*, 376.
90. Ibid.
91. Walter Lippmann to Philip Kerr, September 9, 1939, PP, 379.
92. David Reynolds, *Britannia Overruled: British Policy and World Power in the Twentieth Century* (New York: Longman, 1991), 142.
93. Walter Lippmann to Ronald C. Hood, November 20, 1939, PP, 384.
94. Steel, *Walter Lippmann*, 381.
95. Zelizer, *Arsenal of Democracy*, 45.
96. Lippmann, "T&T," June 15, 1940.
97. Walter Lippmann to Edmund E. Lincoln, August 6, 1940, PP, 384.
98. Lippmann, "T&T," December 19, 1940.
99. WLR, 195.
100. Zelizer, *Arsenal of Democracy*, 10.
101. Lippmann, "T&T," February 12, 1942. Also see Steel, *Walter Lippmann*, 394–95.
102. Walter Lippmann to John M. Vorys, February 17, 1941, PP, 404.
103. Walter Lippmann to Wendell Willkie, July 30, 1940, ibid., 395.
104. Zelizer, *Arsenal of Democracy*, 19.
105. WLR, 204.
106. Walter Lippmann to Henry Cabot Lodge Jr., July 1, 1943, PP, 442.
107. WLR, 204.
108. Lippmann, *U.S. Foreign Policy*, 9–10.
109. Ibid., 37.
110. Ibid., 39.

111. Ibid., 48.
112. Ibid., 93.
113. Ibid., 109.
114. Ibid., 131.
115. Ibid., 149.
116. WLR, 215.
117. Steel, *Walter Lippmann*, 406.
118. Cary, *The Influence of War on Walter Lippmann*, 161.
119. Nore, *Charles Beard*, 199.
120. WLR, 215.
121. Lippmann, "T&T," December 14, 1943.
122. Lippmann, *U.S. War Aims*, 175.
123. Ibid., 182.
124. Ibid., 191, 195.
125. Ibid., 5–6.
126. Ibid., 65.
127. Ibid., 121–22.
128. Ibid., 105.
129. Ibid., 132.
130. Stalin, *Speeches Delivered at Meetings of Voters*, pamphlet collection, 23.
131. Lippmann, *U.S. War Aims*, 142.
132. Harold L. Ickes to Walter Lippmann, July 14, 1944, WLP, box 79, folder 1116.
133. John Foster Dulles to Walter Lippmann, July 5, 1944, ibid., box 68, folder 667.
134. Steel, *Walter Lippmann*, 410.
135. Walter Lippmann to John L. Balderston, July 27, 1944, *PP*, 452.
136. WLR, 216.
137. Ibid., 217.
138. Walter Lippmann to Ross J. S. Hoffman, March 15, 1945, *PP*, 463.
139. Steel, *Walter Lippmann*, 411.
140. Walter Lippmann to Grenville Clark, September 19, 1944, *PP*, 455–56.
141. Editor's note, ibid., 452.
142. Editor's note and Walter Lippmann to John Foster Dulles, October 25, 1944, ibid., 457.
143. Lippmann, "T&T," October 21, 1944.
144. Miscamble, *From Roosevelt to Truman*, 17.
145. Lippmann, "T&T," December 21, 1944.
146. Herring, *From Colony to Superpower*, 585–86.
147. Lippmann, "T&T," February 15, 1945.
148. Steel, *Walter Lippmann*, 416.
149. Lippmann, "T&T," April 7, 1945.
150. Herring, *From Colony to Superpower*, 538–39.
151. Zelizer, *Arsenal of Democracy*, 58.
152. Steel, *Walter Lippmann*, 419.
153. Ambrosius, *Woodrow Wilson and the American Diplomatic Tradition*, 292.
154. Nore, *Charles A. Beard*, 202.
155. Walter Lippmann to James F. Byrnes, May 10, 1945, *PP*, 465–66.
156. WLR, 263.
157. Walter Lippmann to John Maynard Keynes, March 23, 1945, *PP*, 463.
158. Quoted in Kissinger, *Diplomacy*, 97.
159. Walter Lippmann to George Fielding Eliot, June 14, 1945, *PP*, 468.
160. Steel, *Walter Lippmann*, 420.
161. Walter Lippmann to James F. Byrnes, August 23, 1945, *PP*, 474.
162. George F. Kennan, diary entry, August 28, 1995, *KD*, 646.

5. The Artist: George Kennan

1. Gellman, *Contending with Kennan*, 83.
2. Kennan, *Memoirs, 1925–1950*, 276–77.
3. Thompson, *The Hawk and the Dove*, 52.
4. D'Este, *Patton*, 736.
5. George F. Kennan to Charles E. Bohlen, January 26, 1945, GFKP, box 28.
6. Ibid.
7. Mayers, *George Kennan*, 96.
8. Kennan to Bohlen, January 26, 1945.
9. Congdon, *George Kennan*, 1.
10. Thompson, *The Hawk and the Dove*, 24.
11. Kuklick, *Blind Oracles*, 38.
12. Hixson, *George F. Kennan*, 2.
13. Kennan, *Memoirs, 1925–1950*, 16, 9–10.
14. Ibid., 18.
15. George F. Kennan, May 26, 1929, *KD*, 59.
16. Kennan, *Memoirs, 1925–1950*, 69.
17. Mayers, *George Kennan*, 338.
18. Kennan, *Memoirs: 1925–1950*, 130.
19. Stephanson, *Kennan and the Art of Foreign Policy*, 225; Kennan, *Democracy and the Student Left*, 206.
20. Kennan, diary entry, September 3, 1934, GFKP, box 230.
21. Ibid., May 10, 1935, box 230.
22. See Thompson, *The Hawk and the Dove*, 134.
23. Kennan quoted in Gaddis, *George F. Kennan*, 122–23.
24. Kennan, diary entry, March 21, 1940, GFKP, box 231.
25. "Comments," February 1945, GFKP, box 23.
26. Kennan, *Memoirs, 1925–1950*, 129. Mark Mazower's fascinating and convincing *Hitler's Empire* explains why Nazism failed as an imperial ideology.
27. Kennan, diary entry, March 13, 1940, GFKP, box 230.
28. Ibid., July 3, 1940.
29. Kennan, *Memoirs, 1925–1950*, 133–34.
30. Quoted in Lukacs, *George Kennan*, 50.
31. Kennan, *Memoirs, 1925–1950*, 139.
32. See Taylor, *Stalin's Apologist*, and Engerman, *Modernization from the Other Shore*.
33. Gellman, *Contending with Kennan*, 45.
34. Kennan, *Memoirs, 1925–1950*, 178.
35. On the Enlightenment and "inner life," see Rothschild, *The Inner Life of Empire*.
36. George Kennan to James E. Russell (Teachers College, Columbia University), October 11, 1950, GFKP, box 29.
37. Urban, "From Containment to . . . Self-Containment."
38. Ibid.
39. Tilman, *Thorstein Veblen and His Critics*.
40. Kuklick, *Blind Oracles*, 41.
41. Gellman, *Contending with Kennan*, 69.
42. Kennan, *Memoirs, 1925–1950*, 218.
43. Ibid., 211.
44. Kennan, diary entry, August 1, 1944, GFKP, box 231.
45. Kennan, *Memoirs, 1925–1950*, 211–12.
46. George Kennan to W. Averell Harriman, September 18, 1944, GFKP, box 28.
47. Kennan, *Memoirs, 1925–1950*, 232–33.
48. Ibid., 241–43.

49. Ibid., 243–45.
50. Beisner, *Dean Acheson*, 105.
51. Hamilton, *American Caesars*, 57.
52. Sowell, *Intellectuals and Society*, 134.
53. Thompson, *The Hawk and the Dove*, 47.
54. On Potsdam and the presidential transition, see Miscamble, *From Roosevelt to Truman*.
55. Kennan, *Memoirs, 1925–1950*, 259, 256.
56. Maier, *The Cold War in Europe*, 22.
57. Truman, *Year of Decisions*, 416.
58. Zhukov, *The Memoirs of Marshal Zhukov*, 674–75.
59. Herring, *From Colony to Superpower*, 593.
60. Steel, *Walter Lippmann*, 454.
61. Kuklick, *Blind Oracles*, 42.
62. Gellman, *Contending with Kennan*, 112.
63. Kennan, *Memoirs, 1925–1950*, 267.
64. Kennan, diary entry, December 19 and 23, 1945, GFKP, box 231.
65. Ibid.
66. Truman, *Year of Decisions*, 551–52.
67. Kennan, *Memoirs, 1925–1950*, 292–94. The Long Telegram is reprinted in 1946, 6:696–709, and can be accessed at www.gwu.edu/~nsarchiv/coldwar/documents/episode-1/kennan.htm.
68. Lukacs, *George Kennan*, 74.
69. See, for example, Hixson, *George F. Kennan*.
70. Thompson, *The Hawk and the Dove*, 60.
71. Henry Norweb to George Kennan, March 25, 1946, GFKP, box 28.
72. Walter Lippmann to Dwight D. Eisenhower, June 4, 1946, *PP*, 480.
73. Steel, *Walter Lippmann*, 433.
74. Lukacs, *George Kennan*, 78.
75. Thompson, *The Hawk and the Dove*, 63–64.
76. Speech at Naval War College, "Measures Short of War (Diplomatic)," September 16, 1946, GFKP, box 16. See also Gellman, *Contending with Kennan*, 124–25.
77. See Pedaliu, *Britain, Italy and the Origins of the Cold War*, 60–69.
78. Thompson, *The Hawk and the Dove*, 63.
79. Harry S. Truman, Annual Message to the Congress on the State of the Union, January 6, 1947. *Public Papers of the Presidents of the United States: Harry S. Truman, 1947*, p. 12.
80. Hofstadter, *Anti-intellectualism*, 415.
81. Kennan, *Memoirs, 1925–1950*, 345–46.
82. George Kennan to Dean Acheson, January 31, 1947, with attachment "The Framework of Policy Planning," GFKP, box 1.
83. George Kennan to Dean Acheson, February 13, 1947, ibid.
84. Kennan, *Memoirs, 1925–1950*, 326.
85. Ibid., 320.
86. Steel, *Walter Lippmann*, 438–39.
87. Walter Lippmann, "Cassandra Speaking," *The Washington Post*, April 5, 1947. Also Steel, *Walter Lippmann*, 441.
88. Steel, *Walter Lippmann*, 441–42.
89. See Hogan, *The Marshall Plan*. The full text of the speech can be accessed at www.americanrhetoric.com/speeches/georgecmarshall.html.
90. George Kennan to Hamilton Fish Armstrong, February 4, 1947, and Hamilton Fish Armstrong to George Kennan, March 7, 1947, GFKP, box 28.
91. Thompson, *The Hawk and the Dove*, 77–78.

92. X, "The Sources of Soviet Conduct," *Foreign Affairs*, July 1947, www.foreignaffairs .com/articles/23331/x/the-sources-of-soviet-conduct.
93. Lippmann, *The Cold War*, 7.
94. Ibid., 11, 14–16.
95. Ibid., 36.
96. Kennan, *Memoirs, 1925–1950*, 359–61.
97. Thompson, *The Hawk and the Dove*, 78.
98. See Isaacson, *Henry Kissinger*, 60.
99. Kennan, diary entry, January 28, 1948, GFKP, box 231.
100. Kennan, *Memoirs, 1925–1950*, 400–401.
101. Ibid., 361–62.
102. Carnes, *Invisible Giants*, 184.
103. See Stephanson, *Kennan and the Art of Foreign Policy*, 146.
104. Halper and Clarke, *The Silence of the Rational Center*, 71.
105. On Forrestal's career, see Hoopes and Brinkley, *Driven Patriot*.
106. Beisner, *Dean Acheson*, 88.
107. Halper and Clarke, *The Silence of the Rational Center*, 71.
108. Beisner, *Dean Acheson*, 118.
109. Kuklick, *Blind Oracles*, 42.
110. Acheson, *Present at the Creation*, 147–48.
111. Stephanson, *Kennan and the Art of Foreign Policy*, 143–44.
112. George Kennan to Dean Acheson, January 3, 1949, GFKP, box 1.
113. Kennan, *Memoirs, 1925–1950*, 437.
114. Kennan, diary entries, November 19 and 22, 1949, GFKP, box 231.

6. The Scientist: Paul Nitze

1. Nitze, *From Hiroshima to Glasnost*, 42.
2. On the factors underlying the brutality of the Pacific War, see Dower, *War Without Mercy*.
3. Nitze, *From Hiroshima to Glasnost*, 43.
4. Herken, "The Great Foreign Policy Fight," 69.
5. Nitze's *Tension Between Opposites* explains the connection between theory and practice in foreign policy.
6. Callahan, *Dangerous Capabilities*, 12.
7. Thompson, *The Hawk and the Dove*, 27.
8. Nitze, *From Hiroshima to Glasnost*, xi.
9. Thompson, *The Hawk and the Dove*, 37.
10. Ibid., xiv.
11. Callahan, *Dangerous Capabilities*, 15.
12. Nitze, *From Hiroshima to Glasnost*, xiii.
13. Talbott, *Master of the Game*, 27.
14. Nitze, *From Hiroshima to Glasnost*, xviii.
15. Ibid., xx.
16. Talbott, *Master of the Game*, 27.
17. Nitze, *From Hiroshima to Glasnost*, xxi.
18. Ibid.
19. Kuklick, *Blind Oracles*, 43–44.
20. Thompson, *The Hawk and the Dove*, 40.
21. Herken, "The Great Foreign Policy Fight," 68.
22. Nitze, *From Hiroshima to Glasnost*, 9.

23. Callahan, *Dangerous Capabilities*, 44.
24. See Mazower, *Hitler's Empire*.
25. Nitze, *From Hiroshima to Glasnost*, 84.
26. Thompson, *The Hawk and the Dove*, 72.
27. Interview with Paul Nitze, June 12, 1985, Paul H. Nitze Papers, box 119.
28. Thompson, *The Hawk and the Dove*, 80.
29. Nitze, *From Hiroshima to Glasnost*, 68.
30. Thompson, *The Hawk and the Dove*, 107.
31. Nitze, *From Hiroshima to Glasnost*, 86.
32. Herken, "The Great Foreign Policy Fight," 73.
33. Thompson, *The Hawk and the Dove*, 107–108.
34. Abella, *Soldiers of Reason*, 4.
35. NSC-68, "Terms of Reference." The full text of NSC-68 can be accessed at http://fas.org /irp/offdocs/nsc-hst/nsc-68.htm.
36. Beisner, *Dean Acheson*, 239.
37. NSC-68, part three, "Fundamental Designs of the Kremlin." http://fas.org/irp/off docs/nsc-hst/nsc-68.htm.
38. Nitze, *From Hiroshima to Glasnost*, 96.
39. Beisner, *Dean Acheson*, 238.
40. Kaplan, *The Wizards of Armageddon*, 140–41.
41. Herken, *Counsels of War*, 52–53.
42. Kaplan, *The Wizards of Armageddon*, 140.
43. Interview with Paul Nitze, May 7, 1982, Papers of Paul H. Nitze, box 128.
44. Thompson, *The Hawk and the Dove*, 113.
45. Herring, *From Colony to Superpower*, 640.
46. On the Korean War, see Lowe, *The Origins of the Korean War*; Cumings, *The Korean War*; Halberstam, *The Coldest Winter*; and Stueck, *The Korean War*.
47. Interview with Paul Nitze, March 30, 1982, Papers of Paul H. Nitze, box 118.
48. Kennan, diary entry, June 26, 1950, GFKP, box 232.
49. Ibid., July 3, 1950.
50. Zelizer, *Arsenal of Democracy*, 100.
51. Beisner, *Dean Acheson*, 397–98.
52. Nitze, *From Hiroshima to Glasnost*, 107.
53. Congressional Record 3380 (1951).
54. Duffy and Carpenter, *Douglas MacArthur*, 48.
55. Kennan diary entry, April 15, 1951, GFKP, box 232.
56. Ibid., April 17, 1951.
57. Ibid., August 4, 1951.
58. Beisner, *Dean Acheson*, 120.
59. George Kennan to Dean Acheson, September 1, 1951, GFKP, box 1.
60. Weeks, *Conversations with Walter Lippmann*, 3–4.
61. Interview with Paul Nitze, April 20, 1982, Papers of Paul H. Nitze, box 118.
62. Kuklick, *Blind Oracles*, 51.
63. Jacoby, *The Age of American Unreason*, xii.
64. Troy, *Intellectuals and the American Presidency*, 10.
65. Scher, *The Modern Political Campaign*, 22.
66. Gaddis, *Strategies of Containment*, 122.
67. Ibid., 127–28.
68. Kaplan, *Wizards of Armageddon*, 145.
69. Thompson, *The Hawk and the Dove*, 74.
70. Nitze, *From Hiroshima to Glasnost*, 144–45.
71. Ibid., 147–48.

72. Ibid., 151.
73. George Kennan to Adlai Stevenson, January 26, 1954, GFKP, box 46.
74. Nitze, *From Hiroshima to Glasnost*, 152.
75. Kennan, diary entry, April 21, 1959, GFKP, box 233.
76. Thompson, *The Hawk and the Dove*, 136.
77. Nitze, *From Hiroshima to Glasnost*, 131.
78. Westad, *The Global Cold War*, 25.
79. George Kennan to Paul Nitze, September 5, 1956, GFKP, box 36.
80. Remarks by George Kennan, Princeton Stevenson for President Committee, April 30, 1956, Henry DeWolf Smyth Papers, box 5.
81. George Kennan to Adlai Stevenson, March 28, 1956, GFKP, box 46.
82. Callahan, *Dangerous Capabilities*, 161–62.
83. John Kenneth Galbraith, *A Life in Our Times* (Boston: Houghton Mifflin, 1981), 359.
84. George Kennan to Paul Nitze, February 26, 1960, GFKP, box 34.
85. Callahan, *Dangerous Capabilities*, 168–69.
86. Nitze, *From Hiroshima to Glasnost*, 168.
87. Kuklick, *Blind Oracles*, 66.
88. Kaplan, *Wizards of Armageddon*, 147.
89. Paul Nitze to John Foster Dulles, November 16, 1957, Papers of John Foster Dulles, box 3.
90. Thompson, *The Hawk and the Dove*, 165.
91. Kennan's Reith Lectures can be found at www.bbc.co.uk/radio4/features/the-reith-lectures/transcripts/1948/#y1957.
92. George Kennan to Walter Lippmann, June 14, 1951, GFKP, box 27.
93. Interview with Paul Nitze, June 12, 1985, Papers of Paul Nitze, box 119.
94. Nitze, *From Hiroshima to Glasnost*, 177.
95. Callahan, *Dangerous Capabilities*, 186.
96. Paul H. Nitze, Oral History Interview, JFKL, 1.
97. George Kennan to John F. Kennedy, August 17, 1960, GFKP, box 26.
98. Nitze, *From Hiroshima to Glasnost*, 178.
99. For the full text of Kennedy's speech, see Merrill and Paterson, *Major Problems in American Foreign Relations*, 2:290–91.
100. Nitze, *From Hiroshima to Glasnost*, 178–80.
101. Ibid., 181, 182.
102. Callahan, *Dangerous Capabilities*, 194.
103. Frank Costigliola, "U.S. Foreign Policy from Kennedy to Johnson," in Leffler and Westad, *Cambridge History of the Cold War*, 2:122.
104. For the full text of Eisenhower's speech, see *Public Papers of the Presidents: Dwight D. Eisenhower, 1960–1961*, 1037–1040.
105. For the full text of Kennedy's speech, see *Public Papers of the Presidents: John F. Kennedy, 1961*, 1–3.
106. For a discussion of *The Stages of Economic Growth*, see Milne, *America's Rasputin*, 60–66.
107. Matusow, *The Unraveling of America*, 31.
108. Rostow, *The Diffusion of Power*, 126.
109. Martin, *Adlai Stevenson and the World*, 634.
110. Halberstam, *The Best and the Brightest*, xxi.
111. McCormick and LaFeber, *Behind the Throne*, 210.
112. Daalder and Destler, *In the Shadow of the Oval Office*, 21.
113. Nitze, *From Hiroshima to Glasnost*, 184.
114. Herring, *America's Longest War*, 41.
115. Kahin, *Intervention*, 187.

116. Walt W. Rostow to President Kennedy, April 21, 1961, President's Office File, JFKL, box 193.

117. Maxwell Taylor to Secretary of State Dean Rusk, October 25, 1961, *FRUS*: Vietnam, 1961, 430.

118. "Evaluations and Conclusions," tab C, no date, National Security File (NSF), Countries: Vietnam, Taylor Report, November 3, 1961, JFKL.

119. *The Pentagon Papers*, 2:92.

120. Interview with Paul Nitze, June 12, 1985, Papers of Paul H. Nitze, box 119.

121. Nitze, *From Hiroshima to Glasnost*, 256.

122. Callahan, *Dangerous Capabilities*, 289.

123. Interview with Paul Nitze, June 12, 1985.

124. Interview with Paul Nitze, December 10, 1982, Papers of Paul H. Nitze, box 120.

125. Thompson, *The Hawk and the Dove*, 187.

126. Nitze, *From Hiroshima to Glasnost*, 237.

127. Thompson, *The Hawk and the Dove*, 198.

128. Gaddis, *George Kennan*, 577–78.

129. Nitze, *From Hiroshima to Glasnost*, 261.

130. Interview with Paul Nitze, December 22, 1982, Papers of Paul H. Nitze, box 118.

131. Nitze, *From Hiroshima to Glasnost*, 261.

132. Gaddis, *George Kennan*, 590.

133. Memorandum for the Record, November 25, 1963, LBJL, Meeting Notes File, box 1.

134. Schulzinger, *A Time for War*, 127.

135. Neustadt and May, *Thinking in Time*, 86.

136. Leffler and Westad, *The Cambridge History of the Cold War*, 2:126–27.

137. Packenham, *Liberal America and the Third World*, 91.

138. Ekbladh, "Mr. TVA."

139. Carnes, *Invisible Giants*, 186.

140. Walter Lippmann to Allan Nevins, October 14, 1965, *PP*, 614.

141. Walt Rostow to Dean Rusk, January 4, 1966, Confidential File, box 171, LBJL. On the Lippmann-LBJ falling-out, see Logevall, "First Among Critics."

142. See McMaster, *Dereliction of Duty*, 215, and Westmoreland, *A Soldier Reports*, 115.

143. Kennan, diary entry, February 7, 1965, GFKP, box 5R. See also Thompson, *The Hawk and the Dove*, 203.

144. George Kennan, "Our Push-Pull Dilemma in Vietnam," *The Washington Post*, December 12, 1965, E1.

145. Walter Lippmann to George Kennan, December 16, 1965, GFKP, box 27.

146. Thompson, *The Hawk and the Dove*, 203–204.

147. Ibid., 204–205.

148. Ibid., 205.

149. Gaddis, *George Kennan*, 594.

150. Nitze, *From Hiroshima to Glasnost*, 258.

151. See ibid., 259, and Callahan, *Dangerous Capabilities*, 293.

152. Callahan, *Dangerous Capabilities*, 294–95.

153. Telephone conversation between Robert S. McNamara and Lyndon B. Johnson, February 28, 1966, Presidential Tape Recording Series, tape WH6602.10.

154. Alfred Kazin, "The Trouble He's Seen," *The New York Times*, May 5, 1968, www .nytimes.com/books/97/05/04/reviews/mailer-armies.html.

155. Nitze, *From Hiroshima to Glasnost*, 270.

156. Kennan, *Democracy and the Student Left*, 228–29.

157. Thompson, *The Hawk and the Dove*, 214.

158. Buzzanco, *Masters of War*, 342–45.

159. Interview with Paul Nitze, December 22, 1982, Papers of Paul H. Nitze, box 118.

160. Schulzinger, *A Time for War*, 264–67.
161. Notes of Meeting, March 4, 1968, Tom Johnson Meeting Notes File, box 2, LBJL.
162. Isaacson and Thomas, *The Wise Men*, 487.
163. Ibid., 700.
164. Nitze, *From Hiroshima to Glasnost*, 280.
165. Thompson, *The Hawk and the Dove*, 224.
166. Callahan, *Dangerous Capabilities*, 327.
167. George F. Kennan, diary entry, March 10, 1970, *KD*, 462.

7. Metternich Redux: Henry Kissinger

1. Minutes of Weekly Luncheon, September 12, 1967, Tom Johnson Meeting Notes File, box 2, LBJL.
2. Dallek, *Nixon and Kissinger*, 59.
3. Robert K. Brigham and George C. Herring, "The Pennsylvania Peace Initiative," in Gardner and Gittinger, *The Search for Peace in Vietnam*, 68.
4. Interview with Richard V. Allen, May 28, 2002, Ronald Reagan Oral History Project, *Miller Center for Public Affairs Presidential Oral History Program*, http://web1.miller center.org/poh/transcripts/ohp_2002_0528_allen.pdf.
5. Henry Kissinger to Averell Harriman, August 15, 1968, Papers of W. Averell Harriman, box 481.
6. Averell Harriman to Henry Kissinger, September 8, 1968, ibid.
7. Isaacson, *Kissinger*, 131.
8. Dallek, *Nixon and Kissinger*, 73–74. On the Paris negotiations, see Herbert Y. Schandler, "The Pentagon and Peace Negotiations After March 31," in Gardner and Gittinger, *The Search for Peace in Vietnam*, and Milne, "The 1968 Paris Peace Negotiations."
9. Ambassador Bunker to Dean Rusk, November 2, 1968, Papers of W. Averell Harriman, box 506.
10. Jacoby, *The Age of American Unreason*, 153.
11. Isaacson, *Kissinger*, 133.
12. Dallek, *Nixon and Kissinger*, 81.
13. Isaacson, *Kissinger*, 132.
14. Suri, *Henry Kissinger and the American Century*, 28.
15. Isaacson, *Kissinger*, 23.
16. Ibid., 27.
17. Del Pero, *The Eccentric Realist*, 73.
18. Dallek, *Nixon and Kissinger*, 35.
19. Isaacson, *Kissinger*, 26. Suri's *Henry Kissinger and the American Century* is highly effective in connecting Kissinger's experiences as a Jew in Nazi Germany to the ideas he dispensed while in academia and in government.
20. Isaacson, *Kissinger*, 38.
21. Suri, *Henry Kissinger and the American Century*, 57–58.
22. Dallek, *Nixon and Kissinger*, 37.
23. Isaacson, *Kissinger*, 45.
24. Suri, *Henry Kissinger and the American Century*, 68.
25. Dallek, *Nixon and Kissinger*, 49.
26. Quoted in Isaacson, *Kissinger*, 29.
27. Hanhimäki, *Flawed Architect*, 5.
28. Isaacson, *Kissinger*, 58.
29. Graubard, *Kissinger*, 5.
30. Isaacson, *Kissinger*, 61.
31. Dallek, *Nixon and Kissinger*, 41.

32. Suri, *Henry Kissinger and the American Century*, 246, and Isaacson, *Kissinger*, 697.
33. Suri, *Henry Kissinger and the American Century*, 113.
34. Kuklick, *Blind Oracles*, 184–88.
35. Suri, *Henry Kissinger and the American Century*, 124.
36. Isaacson, *Kissinger*, 76–77. The Ph.D. dissertation was later published as *A World Restored: Metternich, Castlereagh and the Problems of Peace.*
37. Isaacson, *Kissinger*, 75.
38. Kissinger, *A World Restored*, 329.
39. Ibid., 330.
40. Kissinger, *White House Years*, 13–14.
41. Dallek, *Nixon and Kissinger*, 47.
42. Kissinger, "Military Policy and Defense of the 'Gray Areas.'"
43. Study Group Reports, "Nuclear Weapons and Foreign Policy," Council on Foreign Relations, May 4, 1955, Henry DeWolf Smyth Papers, Series II, box 4.
44. Henry Kissinger to Hamilton Fish Armstrong, August 17, 1957, Papers of Hamilton Fish Armstrong, box 39.
45. Hanhimäki, *Flawed Architect*, 11.
46. Isaacson, *Kissinger*, 89.
47. Interview with Paul H. Nitze, April 7, 1982, Papers of Paul H. Nitze, box 118.
48. Paul Nitze, *From Hiroshima to Glasnost*, 298.
49. Dallek, *Nixon and Kissinger*, 48.
50. Hanhimäki, *Flawed Architect*, 9.
51. Isaacson, *Kissinger*, 88.
52. Reinhold Niebuhr, "Limited Warfare," *Christianity and Crisis* 17, November 11, 1957, in Suri, *Henry Kissinger and the American Century*, 156.
53. Isaacson, *Kissinger*, 88, and Suri, *Henry Kissinger and the American Century*, 156–57.
54. Henry A. Kissinger, "The Policymaker and the Intellectual," *The Reporter*, March 5, 1959, GFKP, box 26.
55. Dallek, *Nixon and Kissinger*, 55.
56. Isaacson, *Kissinger*, 111, 113.
57. Schlesinger, *Journals, 1952–2000*, 124.
58. Kissinger, *White House Years*, 39–40.
59. Suri, *Henry Kissinger and the American Century*, 176.
60. Schulzinger, *Henry Kissinger*, 14.
61. Dallek, *Nixon and Kissinger*, 56.
62. See Goldberg, *Barry Goldwater*.
63. Isaacson, *Kissinger*, 117–19.
64. Dallek, *Nixon and Kissinger*, 57.
65. Ibid., 57–59.
66. Isaacson, *Kissinger*, 123.
67. Henry Kissinger to Hans Morgenthau, November 13, 1968, Papers of Hans J. Morgenthau, box 33.
68. Hanhimäki, *Flawed Architect*, 15.
69. Isaacson, *Kissinger*, 137.
70. Kissinger, *White House Years*, 15.
71. Conversation between Henry Kissinger and Walt Rostow, January 13, 1970, Kissinger Telcons, reel 3.
72. Interview with Paul H. Nitze, April 20, 1982, Papers of Paul H. Nitze, box 118.
73. Dallek, *Nixon and Kissinger*, 91.
74. Isaacson, *Kissinger*, 148.
75. Herring, *From Colony to Superpower*, 764.
76. Haig, *Inner Circles*, 201.

77. Isaacson, *Kissinger*, 192.
78. Hanhimäki, *Flawed Architect*, 23.
79. Isaacson, *Kissinger*, 139.
80. Patterson, *Grand Expectations*, 735.
81. Zelizer, *Arsenal of Democracy*, 243.
82. Nixon, "Asia After Viet Nam," 121, 123.
83. Zelizer, *Arsenal of Democracy*, 222.
84. Dominic Sandbrook, "Salesmanship and Substance: The Influence of Domestic Politics and Watergate," in Logevall and Preston, *Nixon on the World*, 88.
85. Suri, *Henry Kissinger and the American Century*, 161.
86. Zelizer, *Arsenal of Democracy*, 240.
87. Kissinger, *White House Years*, 61–62.
88. Kennan, diary entry, May 6, 1966, GFKP, box 236.
89. Gaddis, *George F. Kennan*, 617.
90. Nitze, *From Hiroshima to Glasnost*, 293, 295.
91. Ibid., 299.
92. Callahan, *Dangerous Capabilities*, 331.
93. Dobrynin, *In Confidence*, 199.
94. Isaacson, *Kissinger*, 209.
95. Suri, *Henry Kissinger and the American Century*, 225.
96. Nitze, *From Hiroshima to Glasnost*, 309, 313.
97. Callahan, *Dangerous Capabilities*, 357.
98. Transcript of telephone conversation between President Nixon and Kissinger, May 17, 1972, *FRUS: 1969–1976*, 14:922.
99. Hanhimäki, *Flawed Architect*, 226.
100. Nitze, *From Hiroshima to Glasnost*, 328–29.
101. Gaddis, *George F. Kennan*, 621.
102. Zumwalt, *On Watch*, 490.
103. Callahan, *Dangerous Capabilities*, 359.
104. Interview with Paul H. Nitze, October 31, 1985, Box 119, Papers of Paul H. Nitze.
105. See Clark, *The Chinese Cultural Revolution*, and Spence, *The Search for Modern China*.
106. Gaddis, *George F. Kennan*, 583.
107. Hanhimäki, *Flawed Architect*, 55.
108. Suri, *Henry Kissinger and the American Century*, 183–84.
109. See Griffin, *Ping-Pong Diplomacy*.
110. Kissinger, *White House Years*, 727.
111. Ibid., 728.
112. Dallek, *Nixon and Kissinger*, 292.
113. Memorandum for Henry A. Kissinger, "Memcon of Your Conversations with Chou En-lai," July 29, 1971, National Security Archive Electronic Briefing Book no. 66, document 34, 4, www.gwu.edu/~nsarchiv/NSAEBB/NSAEBB66/ch-34.pdf.
114. Ibid., 22.
115. Ibid., 40.
116. Ibid., 41.
117. Zelizer, *Arsenal of Democracy*, 242.
118. For an evocative account of Nixon's visit, see Macmillan, *Nixon and Mao*.
119. A fine recording of *Nixon in China* is Marin Alsop conducting the Colorado Symphony Orchestra in 2008. Naxos American released this three-CD box set in 2009.
120. See Kissinger, *White House Years*, 1053–1056.
121. Nixon, *RN*, 560.
122. For a detailed account of this historic (and occasionally surreal) conversation, see Tyler, *A Great Wall*, 130–34.

123. Keys, "Henry Kissinger: The Emotional Statesman," 600.
124. Kissinger, *White House Years*, 787.
125. Memorandum from Henry Kissinger to Richard Nixon, "My Asian Trip," February 27, 1973, *FRUS: 1969–1976*, 18:203–204.
126. Kissinger, *On China*, 25.
127. Dallek, *Nixon and Kissinger*, 295.
128. Zelizer, *Arsenal of Democracy*, 243.
129. Dallek, *Nixon and Kissinger*, 370.
130. www.time.com/time/specials/packages/article/0,28804,1861543_1861856_1861867,00 .html.
131. In *Sideshow* the journalist William Shawcross makes a strong case that the American bombing of Cambodia in 1969 and 1970 helped set the stage for the rise of Pol Pot. Since 1994, Yale University has been home to a Cambodian Genocide Program, www.yale.edu/cgp/ (from which my statistics are drawn).
132. www.archives.gov/research/military/vietnam-war/casualty-statistics.html#year.
133. A damning critique of Nixon and Kissinger's failure to achieve "peace with honor" is Berman, *No Peace, No Honor*.
134. Schulzinger, *A Time for Peace*, 75.
135. Kissinger, "The Viet Nam Negotiations," 218–19, 234.
136. Kissinger, *White House Years*, 227–28.
137. Ibid., 110.
138. Henry Kissinger to Hans Morgenthau, November 13, 1968, Papers of Hans J. Morgenthau, box 33.
139. Dallek, *Nixon and Kissinger*, 121–24.
140. Isaacson, *Kissinger*, 177.
141. Hanhimäki, *Flawed Architect*, 62.
142. Conversation between Henry Kissinger and Walt Rostow, November 11, 1970, Kissinger Telcons, reel 6.
143. Dallek, *Nixon and Kissinger*, 444.
144. George F. Kennan, May 10, 1972, *KD*, 473.
145. William Broyles, "The Road to Hill 10: A Veteran's Return to Vietnam," *The Atlantic*, April 1, 1985.
146. Dallek, *Nixon and Kissinger*, 452.
147. Hanhimäki, *Flawed Architect*, xiv.
148. Conversation between Henry Kissinger and Richard Nixon, October 17, 1973, Kissinger Telcons, reel 19.
149. Dallek, *Nixon and Kissinger*, 396.
150. For a firsthand account, see Snepp, *Decent Interval*.
151. Kennan, *The Cloud of Danger*, 96.
152. See Hixson, *The Myth of American Diplomacy*, 222, and Dallek, *Nixon and Kissinger*, 229.
153. Herring, *From Colony to Superpower*, 787.
154. Kissinger, *White House Years*, 654.
155. Schulzinger, *Doctor of Diplomacy*, 132–33.
156. Herring, *From Colony to Superpower*, 787.
157. Schulzinger, *Doctor of Diplomacy*, 134.
158. Hanhimäki, *Flawed Architect*, 104.
159. Stern, *Remembering Pinochet's Exile*, xxi.
160. Dallek, *Nixon and Kissinger*, 514.
161. On this harrowing episode, see Saikia, *Women, War, and the Making of Bangladesh*.
162. Bundy, *A Tangled Web*, 269–70.
163. Dallek, *Nixon and Kissinger*, 341, 343, 346.
164. Nixon, *RN*, 527.

165. Bundy, *A Tangled Web*, 291.
166. For a powerful attack on Nixon and Kissinger's approach to the conflict, see Bass, *The Blood Telegram*.
167. Memorandum of Conversation with Mao Zedong, Zhou Enlai, et al., November 12, 1973, in Burr, *The Kissinger Transcripts*, 182.
168. Callahan, *Dangerous Capabilities*, 363.
169. Kissinger, *Years of Upheaval*, 1152.
170. "Impeachment Politics May Cost Nitze Pentagon Post," *The New York Times*, May 22, 1974.
171. Callahan, *Dangerous Capabilities*, 364: Kissinger, *Years of Upheaval*, 1152.
172. George F. Kennan, August 8, 1974, KD, 484.
173. Conversation between Henry Kissinger and Richard Nixon, October 24, 1973, Kissinger Telcons, reel 19.
174. Dallek, *Nixon and Kissinger*, 610.
175. Isaacson, *Kissinger*, 596.
176. Gaddis, *George F. Kennan*, 622.
177. Zelizer, *Arsenal of Democracy*, 246.
178. Ibid., 259.
179. Conversation between Henry Kissinger and J. William Fulbright, September 22, 1973, Kissinger Telcons, reel 19.
180. Isaacson, *Kissinger*, 666.
181. Kissinger, *Years of Renewal*, 107–108.
182. Kissinger, *Years of Upheaval*, 1212.
183. Isaacson, *Kissinger*, 603.
184. Conversation between Henry Kissinger and George Kennan, September 14, 1973, Kissinger Telcons, reel 18.
185. Brinkley, *Gerald R. Ford*, 108.
186. "Ford vs. Solzhenitsyn," *The New York Times*, July 4, 1975, 22.
187. Zelizer, *Arsenal of Democracy*, 258.
188. Kissinger, *Years of Renewal*, 651.
189. Speech by Henry Kissinger, "The Moral Foundation of Foreign Policy," July 15, 1975, Papers of Daniel Patrick Moynihan, box I, 337.
190. John Lewis Gaddis, "Grand Strategies in the Cold War," in Leffler and Westad, *The Cambridge History of the Cold War*, 2:18. The most important books on the Helsinki process are Thomas, *The Helsinki Effect*, and Sarah B. Snyder, *Human Rights Activism and the End of the Cold War: A Transnational History of the Helsinki Network* (New York: Cambridge University Press, 2011).
191. Isaacson, *Kissinger*, 662.
192. Gaddis, *George F. Kennan*, 624.
193. Isaacson, *Kissinger*, 658, 665.
194. Sandbrook, *Mad as Hell*, 97.
195. Kissinger, *Ending the Vietnam War*, 493.
196. Isaacson, *Kissinger*, 647–48. The full transcript of the interview is available at www.fordlibrarymuseum.gov/library/document/0204/1511947.pdf.
197. Sandbrook, *Mad as Hell*, 97.
198. Zelizer, *Arsenal of Democracy*, 261.
199. Callahan, *Dangerous Capabilities*, 377.
200. Sandbrook, *Mad as Hell*, 191.
201. *Public Papers of the Presidents of the United States: Gerald R. Ford, 1976–1977*, 2409–10.
202. Ibid., 2416–17.
203. "Ford Comeback Fatally Stalled by 2nd Debate, Pollster Says," *Deseret News*, November 9, 1976, 2.

204. Isaacson, *Kissinger*, 704.
205. Dallek, *Nixon and Kissinger*, 617.
206. See www.henryakissinger.com/eulogies/042794.html.

8. The Worldmaker: Paul Wolfowitz

1. On Pipes in particular and Sovietology in general, see Engerman, *Know Your Enemy.*
2. Immerman, *Empire for Liberty*, 203.
3. Paul H. Nitze to Zbigniew Brzezinski, March 26, 1976, Papers of Paul H. Nitze, box 70.
4. Anne Hessing Cahn, *Killing Detente*, 158.
5. Mann, *Rise of the Vulcans*, 74.
6. See Rovner, *Fixing the Facts*, chap. 6.
7. Mann, *Rise of the Vulcans*, 75–76.
8. Immerman, *Empire for Liberty*, 202.
9. Packer, *The Assassins' Gate*, 25; Immerman, *Empire for Liberty*, 198–99.
10. Solomon, *Paul D. Wolfowitz*, 10.
11. Bloom's best-known work, *The Closing of the American Mind*, offers an impassioned defense of the teaching of philosophy through a "canon" and denigrates the woolly, relativist direction of U.S. higher education.
12. Anne Norton notes that "other students regarded the [Telluride] circle as a Straussian cult," in *Leo Strauss and the Politics of American Empire*, 59.
13. Paul Wolfowitz interview with Sam Tanenhaus, *Vanity Fair*, May 9, 2003, www .defense.gov/transcripts/transcript.aspx?transcriptid=2594.
14. Paul Wolfowitz interview with Nathan Gardels, *Los Angeles Times*, April 29, 2002, www.defense.gov/transcripts/transcript.aspx?transcriptid=3435.
15. John Cassidy, "The Next Crusade: Paul Wolfowitz at the World Bank," *The New Yorker*, April 9, 2007, www.newyorker.com/reporting/2007/04/09/070409fa_fact_cassidy.
16. Lane, "Plato, Popper, Strauss and Utopianism," 119.
17. Kim Sorensen, *Discourses on Strauss: Revelation and Reason in Leo Strauss and His Critical Study of Machiavelli* (Notre Dame, IN: University of Notre Dame Press, 2006), 178.
18. Leo Strauss, "Relativism," in Harry V. Jaffa, *Crisis of the Strauss Divided*, 171.
19. Paul Wolfowitz interview with Sam Tanenhaus, *Vanity Fair*, May 9, 2003.
20. For a selection of Albert and Roberta Wohlstetter's writings on nuclear strategy, see Zarate and Sokolski, *Nuclear Heuristics.*
21. Mann, *Rise of the Vulcans*, 30.
22. Paul D. Wolfowitz, "Nuclear Proliferation in the Middle East: The Politics and Economics of Proposals for Nuclear Desalting" (Ph.D. diss., University of Chicago, 1972), 32–33, quoted in Mann, *Rise of the Vulcans*, 30–31.
23. See Cohen, *Israel and the Bomb*, and Hersh, *The Samson Option.*
24. See Mann, *Rise of the Vulcans*, 30–32.
25. Cassidy, "The Next Crusade."
26. Ibid., 12. Also see Paul Wolfowitz, "Statesmanship in a New Century," in Kagan and Kristol, *Present Dangers*, 315; and Milne, *America's Rasputin*, 249–54.
27. Packer, *The Assassins' Gate*, 26.
28. On Carter's presidency, see Smith, *Morality, Reason and Power*; Glad, *An Outsider in the White House*; and Kaufman, *Plans Unraveled.*
29. Zelizer, *Arsenal of Democracy*, 275.
30. Herken, "The Great Foreign Policy Fight," 77.
31. Talbott, *The Master of the Game*, 149.
32. Paul Nitze to Zbigniew Brzezinski, March 26, 1976, Papers of Paul H. Nitze, box 70.
33. Mann, *Rise of the Vulcans*, 81.

34. Solomon, *Paul D. Wolfowitz*, 26.

35. Zelizer, *Arsenal of Democracy*, 283, 286.

36. Westad, *The Global Cold War*, 294.

37. For a recent history of the Iranian revolution and its aftermath, see Buchan, *Days of God*.

38. Hamilton, *American Caesars*, 329–30.

39. Gaddis, *George F. Kennan*, 643.

40. Solomon, *Paul D. Wolfowitz*, 26.

41. Mann, *Rise of the Vulcans*, 98.

42. Immerman, *Empire for Liberty*, 204.

43. Thompson, *The Hawk and the Dove*, 278–79.

44. Ibid., 273.

45. Mann, *Rise of the Vulcans*, 109.

46. Solomon, *Paul D. Wolfowitz*, 46.

47. Frances X. Clines and Warren Weaver, "Briefing," *The New York Times*, March 30, 1982, 12. See also Mann, *Rise of the Vulcans*, 115.

48. Mann, *Rise of the Vulcans*, 116.

49. See Rodgers, *Age of Fracture*, chapter 1, for an insightful discussion of the ideational taproots of Reagan's rhetoric.

50. Gaddis, *George F. Kennan*, 651–53.

51. Speech by Ronald Reagan, March 8, 1983, *Public Papers of the Presidents of the United States: Ronald Reagan, 1983* (Washington, D.C.: Government Printing Office, 1983), 363–64.

52. See Scott, *Deciding to Intervene*, and Garthoff, *The Great Transition*.

53. Greg Schneider and Renae Merle, "Reagan's Defense Buildup Bridged Military Eras," *The Washington Post*, June 9, 2004, www.washingtonpost.com/wp-dyn/articles/A26273 -2004Jun8.html. Also see Mann, *The Rebellion of Ronald Reagan*.

54. FitzGerald, *Way Out There in the Blue*, 39.

55. *Public Papers of the Presidents of the United States: Ronald Reagan, 1982*, 746–48.

56. Cannon, *President Reagan*, 272.

57. Kirkpatrick, "Dictatorships & Double Standards," *Commentary*, November 1, 1979, www.commentarymagazine.com/article/dictatorships-double-standards/.

58. Shultz, *Turmoil and Triumph*, 320.

59. Mann, *Rise of the Vulcans*, 130, 92.

60. Ibid., 132–34.

61. Henry A. Kissinger, "What Next When U.S. Intervenes?," *Los Angeles Times*, March 9, 1986.

62. See LaFeber, *Inevitable Revolutions*.

63. Mann, *Rise of the Vulcans*, 136.

64. Immerman, *Empire for Liberty*, 207.

65. Reagan, *An American Life*, 611.

66. Gaddis, *George F. Kennan*, 668.

67. See Wilson, *The Triumph of Improvisation*.

68. See Adelman, *Reagan at Reykjavic*.

69. Cannon, *President Reagan*, 779–81.

70. Mann, *Rise of the Vulcans*, 158.

71. Herring, *From Colony to Superpower*, 898.

72. Cannon, *President Reagan*, 755.

73. Dobrynin, *In Confidence*, 612.

74. Herring, *From Colony to Superpower*, 898–99.

75. Paul Wolfowitz, "How the West Won," *National Review*, September 6, 1993, 62.

76. Lukacs, *George Kennan*, 181.

77. Gaddis, *George F. Kennan*, 671.

78. For a well-reasoned recently published history of the end of the Cold War, see Wilson, *The Triumph of Improvisation*. Sarotte's *1989* is a nuanced account of a pivotal year.
79. Gaddis, *George F. Kennan*, 671.
80. Cheney, *In My Time*, 162. For a study of the relationship between Cheney and George W. Bush, see Baker, *Days of Fire*.
81. Mann, *Rise of the Vulcans*, 170.
82. Mary McGrory, "Kennan—A Prophet Honored," *The Washington Post*, April 9, 1989, B1.
83. Kennan's testimony can be viewed in its entirety at www.c-spanvideo.org/program /6952-1.
84. George H. W. Bush, "Commencement Address at Texas A&M University," May 12, 1989, http://millercenter.org/president/speeches/detail/3421.
85. Jon Margolis, "Bush Carries Labels That Don't Really Fit," *Chicago Tribune*, March 22, 1988.
86. On the conflict and aftermath, see Freedman and Karsh, *The Gulf Conflict*, and Gordon and Trainor, *The Generals' War*.
87. Immerman, *Empire for Liberty*, 214.
88. Mann, *Rise of the Vulcans*, 184.
89. Ibid., 185.
90. Rumsfeld, *Known and Unknown*. Also see Graham, *By His Own Rules*.
91. Herring, *From Colony to Superpower*, 909.
92. George F. Kennan, December 16, 1990, *KD*, 616.
93. Mann, *Rise of the Vulcans*, 192.
94. Baker, *Politics and Diplomacy*, 194.
95. Robert Gates, "The Gulf War: Oral History," *Frontline*, PBS, January 9, 1996, www .pbs.org/wgbh/pages/frontline/gulf/oral/gates/1.html.
96. Mann, *Rise of the Vulcans*, 192.
97. Ibid., 193.
98. Bush and Scowcroft, *A World Transformed*, 489.
99. Rumsfeld, *Known and Unknown*, 414.
100. John Lewis Gaddis, "Grand Strategies in the Cold War," in Leffler and Westad, *The Cambridge History of the Cold War*, 2:43.
101. Mann, *Rise of the Vulcans*, 198.
102. Immerman, *Empire for Liberty*, 217. For the various drafts of the DPG, see the website of the National Security Archive at George Washington University: www.gwu.edu /~nsarchiv/nukevault/ebb245/index.htm.
103. Patrick Tyler, "U.S. Strategy Plan Calls for Insuring No Rivals Develop," *The New York Times*, March 8, 2008.
104. Packer, *The Assassins' Gate*, 21.
105. Mann, *Rise of the Vulcans*, 203.
106. Chollet and Goldgeier, *America Between the Wars*, 45.
107. Memorandum from Paul Wolfowitz to Secretary of Defense Dick Cheney, May 5, 1992, www.gwu.edu/~nsarchiv/nukevault/ebb245/doc14.pdf.
108. Immerman, *Empire for Liberty*, 218.
109. Paul Wolfowitz, "Shaping the Future: Planning at the Pentagon," in Leffler and Legro, *In Uncertain Times*, 45–46.
110. Thompson, *The Hawk and the Dove*, 311.
111. Gaddis, *George F. Kennan*, 680.
112. Mann, *Rise of the Vulcans*, 219.
113. Preble, *The Power Problem*, 31, 33.
114. Paul Wolfowitz, "Clinton's Bay of Pigs," *The Wall Street Journal*, September 27, 1996, in Chollet and Goldgeiger, *America Between the Wars*, 188.

115. Solomon, *Paul D. Wolfowitz*, 69.
116. See Bowden, *Black Hawk Down.*
117. George F. Kennan, December 9, 1992, *KD*, 630–31.
118. See Dallaire, *Shake Hands with the Devil.*
119. Beinart, *The Icarus Syndrome,* 274–75.
120. Paul Wolfowitz, "The United States and Iraq," in Calabrese, *The Future of Iraq,* 111.
121. Zalmay Khalilzad and Paul Wolfowitz, "Overthrow Him," *The Weekly Standard,* December 1, 1997, 14, in Mann, *Rise of the Vulcans,* 236.
122. https://web.archive.org/web/20130112235337/http://www.newamericancentury.org /statementofprinciples.htm.
123. https://web.archive.org/web/20130112203258/http://www.newamericancentury.org /iraqclintonletter.htm.
124. Mann, *Rise of the Vulcans,* 24.
125. Condoleezza Rice and Philip D. Zelikow, *Germany Reunified and Europe Transformed: A Study in Statecraft.*
126. Velasco, *Neoconservatives in U.S. Foreign Policy,* 156.
127. Mann, *Rise of the Vulcans,* 259.
128. Velasco, *Neoconservatives in U.S. Foreign Policy,* 156.
129. Heilbrunn, *They Knew They Were Right,* 230.
130. Mann, *Rise of the Vulcans,* 256.
131. Ibid., 263.
132. Powell, *My American Journey,* 526.
133. DeYoung, *Soldier,* 301.
134. Rumsfeld, *Known and Unknown,* 292.
135. Immerman, *Empire for Liberty,* 223.
136. Gordon and Trainor, *Cobra II,* 14–15.
137. Bacevich, *The Limits of Power,* 144. For a defense of his service to the Bush administration, see Feith, *War and Decision.*
138. DeYoung, *Soldier,* 305.
139. Mann, *Rise of the Vulcans,* 280.
140. "Bush and Putin: Best of Friends," http://news.bbc.co.uk/2/hi/europe/1392791.stm.
141. "No Defense," *The Weekly Standard,* July 23, 2001, 11. See also Mann, *Rise of the Vulcans,* 280–90.
142. Gordon and Trainor, *Cobra II,* 14.
143. Clarke, *Against All Enemies,* 231–32.
144. Paul Wolfowitz interview with Sam Tanenhaus of *Vanity Fair.*
145. *The 9/11 Commission Report,* 8–9.
146. Ibid., 311.
147. Solomon, *Paul D. Wolfowitz,* 74.
148. Wolfowitz interview with Tanenhaus.
149. http://usatoday30.usatoday.com/news/washington/2003-09-06-poll-iraq_x.htm.
150. www.nytimes.com/2004/05/26/international/middleeast/26FTE_NOTE.html.
151. Clarke, *Against All Enemies,* 30–32.
152. Woodward, *Plan of Attack,* 26.
153. Sam Tanenhaus, "Bush's Brain Trust," *Vanity Fair,* July 2003, 169.
154. Solomon, *Paul D. Wolfowitz,* 78.
155. Woodward, *Bush at War,* 99.
156. Rice, *No Higher Honor,* 189.
157. Mearsheimer and Walt, *The Israel Lobby,* 246.
158. Woodward, *Bush at War,* 99.
159. Rumsfeld, *Known and Unknown,* 359.
160. Solomon, *Paul D. Wolfowitz,* 81.

161. Mann, *Rise of the Vulcans*, 300–301.
162. George F. Kennan, diary entry, November 21, 2001, *KD*, 677.
163. Rashid, *Descent into Chaos*, 80.
164. Transcript of Paul Wolfowitz interview with James Dao and Eric Schmitt of *The New York Times*, January 7, 2002, www.defense.gov/transcripts/transcript.aspx?trans criptid=2039.
165. Mann, *Rise of the Vulcans*, 308.
166. Peter Bergen, "The Battle for Tora Bora," *The New Republic*, December 22, 2009, www .newrepublic.com/article/the-battle-tora-bora.
167. Zakheim, *A Vulcan's Tale*, 263.
168. Mann, *Rise of the Vulcans*, 308–309.
169. Solomon, *Paul D. Wolfowitz*, 82–83.
170. See Joost R. Hiltermann, *A Poisonous Affair: America, Iraq, and the Gassing of Halabja* (New York: Cambridge University Press, 2007).
171. George F. Kennan, diary entry, July 13, 2002, *KD*, 679.
172. Colodny and Schactman, *The Forty Years War*, 388.
173. Solomon, *Paul D. Wolfowitz*, 23.
174. Pillar, *Intelligence and U.S. Foreign Policy*, 46.
175. Paul Wolfowitz, interview with Sam Tanenhaus, *Vanity Fair*, May 9, 2003.
176. Velasco, *Neoconservatives in U.S. Foreign Policy*, 206.
177. Bacevich, *The Limits of Power*, 117.
178. Solomon, *Paul D. Wolfowitz*, 7.
179. Heilbrunn, *They Knew They Were Right*, 24.
180. Bill Keller, "The Sunshine Warrior," *The New York Times*, September 22, 2002, www .nytimes.com/2002/09/22/magazine/the-sunshine-warrior.html?pagewanted=all &src=pm.
181. Zakheim, *A Vulcan's Tale*, 186.
182. Max Boot, "Think Again: Neocons," *Foreign Policy*, January 1, 2004, www.foreign policy.com/articles/2004/01/01/think_again_neocons.
183. Albert Eisele, "George Kennan Speaks Out About Iraq," *The Hill*, September 26, 2002, http://hnn.us/articles/997.html.
184. George F. Kennan, diary entry, September 15, 2002, *KD*, 679.
185. Mark Danner, *Stripping Bare the Body*, 470.
186. See Tony Judt, "Bush's Useful Idiots," *London Review of Books*, September 21, 2006, www.lrb.co.uk/v28/n18/tony-judt/bushs-useful-idiots.
187. Mann, *Rise of the Vulcans*, 337.
188. DeYoung, *Soldier*, 399.
189. Solomon, *Paul D. Wolfowitz*, 40.
190. www.state.gov/documents/organization/63562.pdf.
191. Gaddis, *Surprise, Security and the American Experience*.
192. Traub, *The Freedom Agenda*, 118.
193. Rumsfeld, *Known and Unknown*, 454.
194. DeYoung, *Soldier*, 461.
195. Glain, *State vs. Defense*, 392.
196. Rice, *No Higher Honor*, 210.
197. Glain, *State vs. Defense*, 392.
198. http://costsofwar.org. For an earlier estimate, see Stiglitz and Bilmes, *The Three Trillion Dollar War*.
199. Kahneman, *Thinking, Fast and Slow*, 252, 263–64.
200. Solomon, *Paul D. Wolfowitz*, 122.
201. Gellman, *Angler*, 231.
202. Rice, *No Higher Honor*, 208.

203. Bobbitt, *Terror and Consent*, 147–48.
204. Mann, *Rise of the Vulcans*, 365.
205. "Rumsfeld Blames Iraq Problems on 'Pockets of Dead Enders,'" Associated Press, June 18, 2003, in John Ehrenberg, J. Patrice McSherry, José Ramón Sánchez, and Caroleen Marji Sayej, eds., *The Iraq Papers* (New York: Oxford University Press, 2010), 189.
206. Dodge, *Iraq*.
207. http://costsofwar.org.
208. Solomon, *Paul D. Wolfowitz*, 112.
209. See Bush, *Decision Points*, 270.
210. www.freedomhouse.org/report/freedom-world/2013/iraq#.vijxsyczzzs.
211. www.realclearpolitics.com/articles/2013/03/18/10_years_on_paul_wolfowitz_admits _us_bungled_in_iraq_117492.html.
212. Andrew J. Bacevich, "A Letter to Paul Wolfowitz, Occasioned by the Tenth Anniversary of the Iraq War," *Harper's Magazine*, March 2013, harpers.org/archive/2013/03 /a-letter-to-paul-wolfowitz/.
213. Wolfowitz: "We 'Won' the Iraq War," *The Hill*, August 6, 2014, http://thehill.com/policy /defense/214453-wolfowitz-we-won-the-iraq-war.

9. Barack Obama and the Pragmatic Renewal

1. Remnick, *The Bridge*, 346.
2. http://articles.baltimoresun.com/1991-06-08/news/1991159083_1_persian-gulf-gulf -war-troops-home.
3. A partial transcript of Obama's speech against the war (and full audio) is available at www.npr.org/templates/story.php?storyid=99591469.
4. William James, *Pragmatism*, edited and introduced by Bruce Kuklick (Indianapolis: Hackett, 1981), 29.
5. Kloppenberg, *Reading Obama*, xiii.
6. Maraniss, *Barack Obama*, 165.
7. Ibid., 350.
8. Ibid., 386–87.
9. Remnick, *The Bridge*, 111.
10. Maraniss, *Barack Obama*, 452.
11. Obama, *Dreams from My Father*, 121–22.
12. Maraniss, *Barack Obama*; Remnick, *The Bridge*, 113.
13. Obama, *Dreams from My Father*, 86.
14. Kloppenberg, *Reading Obama*, 56–57.
15. Remnick, *The Bridge*, 398–99.
16. Ibid., p. 400.
17. Ryan Lizza, "The Consequentialist," *The New Yorker*, May 2, 2011, www.newyorker.com /reporting/2011/05/02/110502fa_fact_lizza.
18. Mann, *Obamians*, 87.
19. Indyk, Lieberthal, and O'Hanlon, *Bending History*, 6.
20. "Barack Obama, Neocon," *The Wall Street Journal*, August 3, 2007, A8.
21. Ken Gude, "John McCain Versus Osama bin Laden," *The Guardian*, August 1, 2008, www.guardian.co.uk/commentisfree/2008/aug/01/johnmccain.usforeignpolicy.
22. Lizza, "The Consequentialist."
23. David Brooks, "Obama, Gospel and Verse," *The New York Times*, April 26, 2007, www .nytimes.com/2007/04/26/opinion/26brooks.html.
24. Preston, *Sword of the Spirit, Shield of Faith*, 611.
25. Kloppenberg, *Reading Obama*, 121.

26. Jo Becker and Scott Shane, "Secret 'Kill List' Proves a Test of Obama's Principles and Will," *The New York Times*, May 29, 2012, www.nytimes.com/2012/05/29/world /obamas-leadership-in-war-on-al-qaeda.html?pagewanted=2&hp.

27. Mann, *Obamians*, 92.

28. Lindsay, "George W. Bush," 771.

29. Elisabeth Bumiller, "Palin Will Meet with Kissinger and Foreign Leaders," *The New York Times*, September 21, 2008, www.nytimes.com/2008/09/22/us/politics/22veep.html.

30. "Powell: Support for Obama Doesn't Mean Iraq War Wrong," CNN, www.cnn.com /2008/POLITICS/10/19/powell.transcript/.

31. Gurman, *The Dissent Papers*, 203–204. See also Shapiro, *Containment*.

32. The Princeton Project's website is www.princeton.edu/~ppns/. See also Ikenberry et al., *The Crisis of American Foreign Policy*.

33. Woodward, *Obama's Wars*, 290.

34. Indyk, Lieberthal, and O'Hanlon, *Bending History*, 8.

35. Mann, *Obamians*, 117.

36. Woodward, *Obama's Wars*, 3, 11.

37. See press release, "Special Task Force on Interrogation and Transfer Policies Issues Its Recommendations to the President," www.justice.gov/opa/pr/2009/August/09-ag -835.html, and David Johnston, "U.S. Says Rendition to Continue, but with More Oversight," *The New York Times*, August 24, 2009, www.nytimes.com/2009/08/25/us /politics/25rendition.html.

38. Lindsay, "George W. Bush," 774.

39. Sanger, *Confront and Conceal*, 277.

40. George Packer, "Rights and Wrongs," *The New Yorker*, May 17, 2010, www.newyorker .com/talk/comment/2010/05/17/100517taco_talk_packer.

41. James Taranto, "The bin Laden Raid and the 'Virtues of Boldness,'" *The Wall Street Journal*, May 7, 2011.

42. Mann, *Obamians*, 147.

43. Ibid., 161.

44. Taranto, "The bin Laden Raid."

45. www.politicususa.com/2009/06/18/kissinger-obama-iran.html.

46. www.nobelprize.org.

47. Steven Erlanger and Sheryl Gay Stolberg, "Surprise Nobel for Obama Stirs Praise and Doubts," *The New York Times*, October 9, 2009, www.nytimes.com/2009/10/10/world /10nobel.html.

48. Garance Franke-Ruta, "Reaction: Obama Wins Nobel Peace Prize," *The Washington Post*, October 9, 2009, http://voices.washingtonpost.com/44/2009/10/09/reaction _obama_wins_nobel_peac.html.

49. www.whitehouse.gov/the-press-office/remarks-president-acceptance-nobel-peace -prize.

50. Sanger, *Confront and Conceal*, 16.

51. Mann, *Obamians*, 132–33.

52. Woodward, *Obama's Wars*, 102–103, 332–33.

53. Eric Schmitt and Thom Shanker, "General Calls for More U.S. Troops to Avoid Afghan Failure," *The New York Times*, September 20, 2009, www.nytimes.com/2009/09 /21/world/asia/21afghan.html.

54. Woodward, *Obama's Wars*, 175.

55. www.whitehouse.gov/the-press-office/remarks-president-address-nation-way -forward-afghanistan-and-pakistan.

56. Mann, *Obamians*, 139–40.

57. www.whitehouse.gov/the-press-office/remarks-president-address-nation-way -forward-afghanistan-and-pakistan.

58. Mann, *Obamians*, 223.
59. David E. Sanger, "Pursuing Ambitious Global Goals, but Strategy Is More," *The New York Times*, January 20, 2013, www.nytimes.com/2013/01/21/us/politics/obamas -foreign-policy-goals-appear-more-modest.html?hp&pagewanted=print.
60. Michael Hastings, "The Runaway General," *Rolling Stone*, June 22, 2010, www.rolling stone.com/politics/news/the-runaway-general-20100622.
61. Helene Cooper and David E. Sanger, "Obama Says Afghan Policy Won't Change After Dismissal," *The New York Times*, June 23, 2010, www.nytimes.com/2010/06/24 /us/politics/24mcchrystal.html?pagewanted=all.
62. Anne E. Kornblut, "McChrystal Article Renews Attention to Split with Biden over Afghanistan," *The Washington Post*, June 23, 2010, www.washingtonpost.com/wp-dyn /content/article/2010/06/23/AR2010062301109.html.
63. www.whitehouse.gov/the-press-office/2011/06/22/remarks-president-way-forward -afghanistan.
64. On drone warfare, see Mazzetti, *The Way of the Knife*. The negative, unintended effects of drone attacks are discussed in Ahmed, *The Thistle and the Drone*.
65. Mark Mazzetti, Charlie Savage, and Scott Shane, "How a U.S. Citizen Came to Be in America's Cross Hairs," *The New York Times*, March 9, 2013, www.nytimes.com/2013 /03/10/world/middleeast/anwar-al-awlaki-a-us-citizen-in-americas-cross-hairs.html ?pagewanted=all.
66. Mann, *Obamians*, 199.
67. Sanger, *Confront and Conceal*, 246.
68. Ibid., 245.
69. Ibid., 255–57.
70. "The End of the Perpetual War," *The New York Times*, May 23, 2013, www.nytimes.com /2013/05/24/opinion/obama-vows-to-end-of-the-perpetual-war.html?pagewanted=all. For a full transcript of the speech, see http://articles.washingtonpost.com/2013-05-23 /politics/39467399_1_war-and-peace-cold-war-civil-war.
71. Mark Mazzetti and Declan Walsh, "Pakistan Says U.S. Drone Killed Taliban Leader," *The New York Times*, May 29, 2013, www.nytimes.com/2013/05/30/world/asia/drone -strike-hits-near-pakistani-afghan-border.html?pagewanted=all.
72. Mann, *Obamians*, 303, and Mark Mazzetti and Helene Cooper, "Detective Work on Courier Led to Breakthrough on Bin Laden," *The New York Times*, May 2, 2011, www .nytimes.com/2011/05/02/world/asia/02reconstruct-capture-osama-bin-laden.html.
73. Sanger, *Confront and Conceal*, 94.
74. Mann, *Obamians*, 307.
75. Taranto, "The bin Laden Raid."
76. Sanger, *Confront and Conceal*, 283–86.
77. Mann, *Obamians*, 259–60.
78. Sanger, *Confront and Conceal*, 316.
79. Mann, *Obamians*, 261–62, 263.
80. Sanger, *Confront and Conceal*, 297.
81. Henry Kissinger interview with Channel 4 News, February 1, 2011, www.channel4 .com/news/egypt-the-biggest-change-since-world-war-2.
82. Taranto, "The bin Laden Raid."
83. Mann, *Obamians*, 281, 284.
84. Ibid., 288.
85. Dexter Filkins, "What Should Obama Do About Syria?" *The New Yorker*, May 13, 2013, www.newyorker.com/reporting/2013/05/13/130513fa_fact_filkins.
86. Ethan Bronner and David E. Sanger, "Arab League Endorses No-Fly Zone over Libya," *The New York Times*, March 12, 2011, www.nytimes.com/2011/03/13/world /middleeast/13libya.html?pagewanted=all&_r=0.

87. Sanger, *Confront and Conceal*, 345.
88. Indyk, Lieberthal, and O'Hanlon, *Bending History*, 163.
89. Kori Schake, "The U.S. Sits One Out," *ForeignPolicy.com*, March 18, 2011, http://shadow .foreignpolicy.com/posts/2011/03/18/the_us_sits_one_out.
90. Lizza, "The Consequentialist."
91. Indyk, Lieberthal, and O'Hanlon, *Bending History*, 166.
92. Interview with Mitt Romney, CNN, March 26, 2012, http://transcripts.cnn.com /TRANSCRIPTS/1203/26/sitroom.01.html.
93. Milne, "Pragmatism or What?," 936.
94. "CNN Poll, George W. Bush Only Living ex-President Under 50%," http://politicalticker .blogs.cnn.com/2012/06/07/cnn-poll-george-w-bush-only-living-ex-president -under-50/.
95. Transcript of third presidential debate, October 22, 2012, www.debates.org/index .php?page=october-22-2012-the-third-obama-romney-presidential-debate.
96. David E. Sanger, "Is There a Romney Doctrine?" *The New York Times Sunday Review*, May 12, 2012, www.nytimes.com/2012/05/13/sunday-review/is-there-a-romney -doctrine.html?pagewanted=1.
97. "Sustaining U.S. Global Leadership: Priorities for 21st Century Defense," Department of Defense, January 2012, www.defense.gov/news/Defense_Strategic_Guidance.pdf.
98. Sanger, *Confront and Conceal*, 417–19.
99. Nasr, *The Dispensable Nation*, 12.
100. Sanger, *Confront and Conceal*, 421, 314.
101. "The President's National Security Team: Obama Picks His Soldiers," *The Economist*, January 12, 2013.
102. "The Defense Secretary's Nomination: Hagelian Dialectic," *The Economist*, February 16, 2013.
103. Michelle Nichols, "Syria Death Toll Likely Near 70,000, Says U.N. Human Rights Chief," Reuters, February 12, 2013, www.reuters.com/article/2013/02/12/us-syria-crisis -un-idUSBRE91B19C20130212.
104. Noah Rayman, "Report: More than 146,000 People Killed in Syrian Civil War," *Time*, March 13, 2014, http://time.com/24077/syria-death-toll/.
105. Sanger, *Confront and Conceal*, 351, 361.
106. Mark Mazzetti, Michael R. Gordon, and Mark Landler, "U.S. Is Said to Plan to Arm the Syrian Rebels," *The New York Times*, June 13, 2013, www.nytimes.com/2013/06 /14/world/middleeast/syria-chemical-weapons.html?pagewanted=all.
107. Maggie Haberman, "Bill Clinton Splits with President Obama on Syria," *Politico*, June 12, 2013, www.politico.com/story/2013/06/bill-clinton-splits-with-obama-on -syria-92683.html.
108. "Syria Chemical Attack: What We Know," www.bbc.co.uk/news/world-middle-east -23927399.
109. "America and Syria: To Bomb or Not to Bomb," *The Economist*, September 7, 2013.
110. "Syria's Strange Bedfellows: Paul Wolfowitz's Case for Obama's War," an interview with Eli Lake, *Daily Beast*, September 6, 2013, www.thedailybeast.com/articles/2013 /09/06/syria-s-strange-bedfellows-paul-wolfowitz-s-case-for-obama-s-war.html.
111. Michael R. Gordon and Steven Lee Myers, "Obama Calls Russia Offer on Syria Possible 'Breakthrough,'" *The New York Times*, September 9, 2013, www.nytimes.com/2013/09/10 /world/middleeast/kerry-says-syria-should-hand-over-all-chemical-arms.html?_r=0.
112. *This Week* transcript: President Barack Obama, September 15, 2013. http://abcnews .go.com/ThisWeek/week-transcript-president-barack-obama/story?id/20253577 &singlePage/true.
113. "America, Russia and Syria: Style and Substance," *The Economist*, September 21, 2013.

114. Rand Paul, "How U.S. Interventionists Abetted the Rise of ISIS," *The Wall Street Journal*, August 27, 2014, http://online.wsj.com/articles/rand-paul-how-u-s-interventionists -abetted-the-rise-of-isis-1409178958.

115. "Obama's Remarks on Iran and the Budget Debate in Congress," *The New York Times*, September 27, 2013, www.nytimes.com/2013/09/28/us/politics/obamas-remarks-on -iran-and-the-budget-debate-in-congress.html.

116. Ed O'Keefe, "John Cornyn: Iran Deal Designed to 'Distract Attention' from Health-care," *The Washington Post*, November 23, 2013, www.washingtonpost.com/blogs /post-politics/wp/2013/11/23/john-cornyn-iran-deal-designed-to-distract-attention -from-health-care/.

117. Anne Gearan and Joby Warrick, "Iran, World Powers Reach Historical Nuclear Deal," *The Washington Post*, November 23, 2013.

118. John Reed, "Israel's Benjamin Netanyahu Calls Iran Deal a 'Historic Mistake,'" *Financial Times*, November 24, 2013.

119. Harriet Sherwood, "Israel Condemns Iran Nuclear Deal as Historic Mistake," *The Guardian*, November 24, 2013, www.theguardian.com/world/2013/nov/24/israel -condemns-iran-nuclear-deal-binyamin-netanyahu.

120. "Letter from Senate Republicans to the Leaders of Iran," *The New York Times*, March 9, 2015.

121. "Statement by the President on Cuba Policy Changes," https://www.whitehouse.gov /the-press-office/2014/12/17/statement-president-cuba-policy-changes-0.

122. Karen Tumulty and Anne Gearan, "Cuba Decision Marks a Bet by Obama That Cold War Politics Have Turned a Corner," *The Washington Post*, December 17, 2014.

123. "CNN/ORC Poll: Americans Side with Obama on Cuba," December 23, 2014, http:// edition.cnn.com/2014/12/23/politics/cuba-poll/.

124. "Remarks by the President in Year-End Press Conference," https://www.whitehouse .gov/the-press-office/2014/12/19/remarks-president-year-end-press-conference.

125. www.breitbart.com/big-government/2015/02/21/ambassador-john-bolton-obama- worse-than-neville-chamberlain/.

126. Kenneth Rapoza, "Is China's Ownership of U.S. Debt a National Security Threat?" *Forbes*, January 23, 2013, www.forbes.com/sites/kenrapoza/2013/01/23/is-chinas -ownership-of-u-s-debt-a-national-security-threat/.

127. Westad, *Restlesss Empire*, 447.

128. Sanger, *Confront and Conceal*, xix.

129. Kim Chipman and Nicholas Johnston, "Obama Snubbed by Chinese Premier at Climate Meeting," *Bloomberg*, December 18, 2009, www.bloomberg.com/apps/news?pid =newsarchive&sid=a5uY22AnevM4.

130. Mitt Romney, "How I'll Respond to China's Rising Power," *The Wall Street Journal*, February 16, 2012.

131. Quoted in Floyd Whaley, "Clinton Reaffirms Military Ties with the Philippines," *The New York Times*, November 16, 2011.

132. Mann, *Obamians*, 329.

133. Graham Allison, "Thucydides Trap Has Been Sprung in the Pacific," *Financial Times*, August 21, 2012, www.ft.com/cms/s/0/5d695b5a-ead3-11e1-984b-00144feab49a .html#axzz2XnGeFMfK.

134. Niall Ferguson, "What 'Chimerica' Hath Wrought," *The American Interest*, January–February 2009, www.the-american-interest.com/article.cfm?piece=533.

135. Brad Simpson, "Self-Determination in the Age of Putin," *Foreign Policy*, March 21, 2014, www.foreignpolicy.com/articles/2014/03/21/self_determination_in_the_age_of _putin_crimea_referendum.

136. Zbigniew Brzezinski, "What Is to Be Done? Putin's Aggression in Ukraine Needs a Response," *The Washington Post*, March 3, 2014.

137. Charles Krauthammer, "How to Stop—or Slow Putin," *The Washington Post*, March 14, 2014.

138. Stephen F. Cohen, "Distorting Russia: How the American Media Misrepresent Putin, Sochi and Ukraine," *The Nation*, March 3, 2014, www.thenation.com/article/178344 /distorting-russia.

139. Henry A. Kissinger, "How the Ukraine Crisis Ends," March 5, 2014, *The Washington Post*.

140. "Europe's New Battlefield," *The Economist*, February 22, 2014, 20.

141. Scott Wilson, "Obama Dismisses Russia as 'Regional Power' Acting out of Weakness," *The Washington Post*, March 25 2014.

142. Nasr, *Dispensable Nation*, p. 12.

143. Remnick, "Going the Distance."

144. Jeffrey Goldberg, "Hillary Clinton: Failure to Help Syrian Rebels Led to the Rise of ISIS," *The Atlantic*, August 2014, www.theatlantic.com/international/archive/2014 /08/hillary-clinton-failure-to-help-syrian-rebels-led-to-the-rise-of-isis/375832/.

145. Clinton, *Hard Choices*, 32.

146. www.whitehouse.gov/the-press-office/2014/05/28/remarks-president-united-states -military-academy-commencement-ceremony.

147. Charles Krauthammer, "Emptiness at West Point," *The Washington Post*, May 29, 2014.

Conclusion

1. DiNunzio, *Woodrow Wilson: Essential Writings and Speeches*, 68.

2. Mazower, *Governing the World*, 40. On Cobden, see Anthony Howe, "Free Trade and Global Order," in Bell, *Victorian Visions of Global Order*.

3. Paul Nitze, "Reflections of a Cold Warrior," Paul H. Nitze School of Advanced International Study, 1996, www.youtube.com/watch?v=fkjwmjU_V-U.

4. David Brooks, "Obama, Gospel and Verse," *The New York Times*, April 26, 2007; Niebuhr, *The Irony of American History*, dust jacket.

5. Mahan, *The Interest of America in Sea Power*, 267.

6. Sumida, *Inventing Grand Strategy and Teaching Command*, xv. The preface to Sumida's book, titled "Musical Performance, Zen Enlightenment, and Naval Command," focuses skillfully on the division between art and science in naval strategy. The remainder is a penetrating account of Mahan's body of work.

7. See, for example, Ferling, *Jefferson and Hamilton*.

8. Seager, *Alfred Thayer Mahan*, 394.

9. Alfred Thayer Mahan to Stephen Luce, August 31, 1898, ATMLP, 2:592.

10. Kennedy, *Charles A. Beard*, 71.

11. Beard quoted in Morgenthau, *Scientific Man vs. Power Politics*, 29.

12. Kennedy, *Charles A. Beard*, 71.

13. McDougall, *Promised Land, Crusader State*, 40.

14. Scott Wilson, "Obama Announces Plan to Bring Home 33,000 Surge Troops from Afghanistan," *The Washington Post*, June 22, 2011, www.washingtonpost.com/politics /obama-to-order-home-10000-troops-from-afghanistan-officials-say/2011/06/22 /AGUuRCgH_story.html.

15. Spencer Ackerman, "Rand Paul's Foreign Policy Speech Raises More Questions Than It Answers," *The Guardian*, April 9, 2015, www.theguardian.com/us-news/2015/apr /09/rand-paul-foreign-policy-war-south-carolina-speech.

16. Charles Beard to Maury Maverick, September 8, 1937, quoted in VanDeMark, "Beard on Lippmann."

17. Zubok's *Failed Empire* is particularly effective in tracing the way ideology influenced Stalin's ambitions. Roberts's *Stalin's Wars* lends support to Lippmann's portrayal of Stalin as a pragmatic and rational actor.

18. Quoted in Mistry, *The United States, Italy, and the Origins of the Cold War*, 198.
19. Richard Rhodes, *Dark Sun*, 234.
20. George F. Kennan, Testimony before the U.S. Senate Foreign Relations Committee, April 4, 1989, www.c-span.org/video/?6952-1/future-ussoviet-relations.
21. Menand, *The Metaphysical Club*, 61, 4, 440.
22. Anne-Marie Slaughter, "Does Obama Have a Grand Strategy for His Second Term? If Not, He Could Try One of These," *The Washington Post*, January 18, 2013.
23. Remnick, "Going the Distance."
24. Kissinger, *World Order*, 374.

BIBLIOGRAPHY

Unpublished Papers

Acheson, Dean Gooderham. Papers. Yale University Library.

Alsop, Joseph and Stewart. Papers. Library of Congress.

Armstrong, Hamilton Fish. Papers. Department of Rare Books and Special Collections, Princeton University Archives.

Beard, Charles A. and Mary R. Papers. DePauw University Archives, Greencastle, IN.

Brooks, Van Wyck. Papers. University of Pennsylvania Rare Books and Manuscript Library.

Bundy, William P. Papers. Department of Rare Books and Special Collections, Princeton University Archives.

Clifford, Clark M. Papers. Library of Congress.

Dulles, John Foster. Papers. Department of Rare Books and Special Collections, Princeton University Archives.

Evans, Rowland. Papers. Library of Congress.

Farrell, James T. Papers. University of Pennsylvania Rare Books and Manuscript Library.

Harriman, W. Averell. Papers. Library of Congress.

Kennan, George F. Papers. Department of Rare Books and Special Collections, Princeton University Archives.

Kennedy, John F. President's Office Files. John F. Kennedy Library, Boston.

Kissinger, Henry. Telephone Conversations on World Affairs. Library of Congress.

Lilienthal, David. Papers. Department of Rare Books and Special Collections, Princeton University Archives.

Lippmann, Walter. Diaries. Columbia University Rare Books Library.

———. Oral History. Columbia University Rare Books Library.

———. Papers. Yale University Library.
———. Reminiscences. Columbia University Rare Books Library.
McNamara, Robert S. Papers. Library of Congress.
Moe, Henry Allen., Papers. American Philosophical Society, Philadelphia.
Morgenthau, Hans J. Papers. Library of Congress.
Moynihan, Daniel Patrick. Papers. Library of Congress.
Mumford, Lewis. Papers. University of Pennsylvania Rare Books and Manuscript Library.
National Security Files. Presidential Papers. John F. Kennedy Library, Boston.
Neustadt, Richard. Reminiscences. Columbia University Rare Books Library.
Nevins, Allan. Oral History. Columbia University Rare Books Library.
Nitze, Paul H. Oral History Interview. John F. Kennedy Library, Boston.
———. Oral History Interview. Lyndon Baines Johnson Library, Austin, TX.
———. Papers. Library of Congress.
Oppenheimer, J. Robert. Papers. Library of Congress.
Rockefeller, Nelson A. Oral History. Columbia University Rare Books Library.
Schlesinger, Arthur, Jr. Oral History. Columbia University Rare Books Library.
Smith, George H. E. Papers. Yale University Library.
Smyth, Henry DeWolf. Papers. American Philosophical Society.
Tom Johnson Meeting Notes File. Lyndon Baines Johnson Library, Austin, TX.

Published Papers

Blum, John Morton, ed. *Public Philosopher: Selected Letters of Walter Lippmann.* New York: Ticknor and Fields, 1985.
Brown, James Scott, ed. *Official Statements of War Aims and Peace Proposals: December 1916 to November 1918.* Washington, D.C.: Carnegie Endowment for International Peace, 1921.
Costigliola, Frank, ed. *The Kennan Diaries.* New York: W. W. Norton, 2014.
Ehrenberg, John, J. Patrice McSherry, José Ramón Sánchez, and Caroleen Marji Sayej, eds. *The Iraq Papers.* New York: Oxford University Press, 2010.
Foreign Relations of the United States (FRUS). Washington, D.C.: Government Printing Office, various dates.
Hagedorn, Hermann, ed. *The Works of Theodore Roosevelt: Memorial Edition.* 24 vols. New York: Scribner, 1923–1926.
Lilienthal, David E. *The Journals of David E. Lilienthal.* 7 vols. New York: Harper, 1964.
Link, Arthur S., ed. *The Papers of Woodrow Wilson.* 69 vols. Princeton: Princeton University Press, 1966–1994.
Marder, Albert J., ed. *Fear God and Dread Nought: The Correspondence of Admiral of the Fleet, Lord Fisher of Kilverstone.* 3 vols. London: Jonathan Cape, 1952–1959.
Morison, Elting E., ed. *The Letters of Theodore Roosevelt.* 8 vols. Cambridge, MA: Harvard University Press, 1951–1954.
The 9/11 Commission Report: Final Report on the National Commission on Terrorist Attacks upon the United States. New York: W. W. Norton, 2004.
The Pentagon Papers: The Department of Defense History of United States Decision-Making on Vietnam. Senator Gravel Edition. 4 vols. Boston: Beacon Press, 1971.
Public Papers of the Presidents of the United States (Washington, D.C.: Government Printing Office, various dates).
Seager, Robert, II, and Doris D. Maguire, eds. *Letters and Papers of Alfred Thayer Mahan.* 3 vols. Annapolis, MD: Naval Institute Press, 1975.
Stalin, Josef. *Speeches Delivered at Meetings of Voters of the Stalin Electoral District, Moscow.* Moscow: Foreign Languages Publishing House, 1950.

Secondary Sources: Books

Abella, Alex. *Soldiers of Reason: The RAND Corporation and the Rise of the American Empire.* Boston: Houghton Mifflin, 2008.

Acheson, Dean. *Present at the Creation: My Years in the State Department.* New York: W. W. Norton, 1969.

Adam, Larry L. *Walter Lippmann.* Boston: Twayne Publishers, 1977.

Adams, Brooks. *America's Economic Supremacy.* New York: Harper, 1947.

Adcock, Robert, Mark Bevir, and Shannon C. Stimson, eds. *Modern Political Science: Anglo-American Exchanges Since 1880.* Princeton: Princeton University Press, 2007.

Adelman, Ken. *Reagan at Reykjavic: Forty-Eight Hours That Ended the Cold War.* New York: Harper, 2014.

Ahmed, Akbar. *The Thistle and the Drone: How America's War on Terror Became a Global War on Tribal Islam.* Washington, D.C.: Brookings Institution Press, 2013.

Alterman, Eric. *What Liberal Media? The Truth About Bias and the News.* New York: Basic Books, 2003.

Ambrosius, Lloyd E. *Wilsonian Statecraft: Theory and Practice of Liberal Internationalism During World War I.* Lanham, MD: Rowman and Littlefield, 1991.

——. *Woodrow Wilson and the American Diplomatic Tradition: The Treaty Fight in Perspective.* New York: Cambridge University Press, 1987.

Anderson, Judith Icke. *William Howard Taft: An Intimate History.* New York: W. W. Norton, 1981.

Bacevich, Andrew. *The Limits of Power: The End of American Exceptionalism.* New York: Metropolitan Books, 2008.

Badger, Anthony J. *FDR: The First Hundred Days.* New York: Hill and Wang, 2008.

——. *The New Deal: The Depression Years.* New York: Hill and Wang, 1989.

Baer, George W. *One Hundred Years of Sea Power: The U.S. Navy, 1890–1990.* Stanford: Stanford University Press, 1996.

Baker, James A., III. *Politics and Diplomacy.* New York: Putnam, 1995.

Baker, Peter. *Days of Fire: Bush and Cheney in the White House.* New York: Doubleday, 2013.

Barnes, Fred. *Rebel-in-Chief: Inside the Bold and Controversial Presidency of George W. Bush.* New York: Crown, 2006.

Barrow, Clyde W. *More Than a Historian: The Political and Economic Thought of Charles Beard.* New Brunswick, NJ: Transaction, 2000.

Barzun, Jacques. *The House of Intellect.* New York: Harper, 2002.

Bass, Gary. *The Blood Telegram: Nixon, Kissinger and a Forgotten Genocide.* New York: Knopf, 2013.

Beale, Howard K. *Charles A. Beard: An Appraisal.* Lexington: University of Kentucky Press, 1955.

Beard, Charles A., ed. *America Faces the Future.* Boston: Houghton Mifflin, 1932.

——. *American Foreign Policy in the Making, 1932–1940.* New Haven: Yale University Press, 1946.

——. *Cross-Currents in Europe To-day.* Boston: Marshall Jones, 1922.

——. *The Devil Theory of War: An Inquiry into the Nature of History and the Possibility of Keeping Out of War.* New York: Vanguard Press, 1936.

——. *The Economic Basis of Politics.* New York: Knopf, 1922.

——. *An Economic Interpretation of the Constitution of the United States.* New York: Macmillan, 1913.

——. *Economic Origins of Jeffersonian Democracy.* New York: Macmillan, 1915.

——. *A Foreign Policy for America.* New York: Knopf, 1940.

——. *Giddy Minds and Foreign Quarrels: An Estimate of American Foreign Policy.* New York: Macmillan, 1939.

——. *The Idea of the National Interest: An Analytical Study in American Foreign Policy.* New York: Macmillan, 1934.

——. *The Industrial Revolution.* London: S. Sonnenschein, 1901.

——. *The Navy: Defense or Portent.* New York: Harper, 1932.

——. *The Open Door at Home: A Trial Philosophy of National Interest.* New York: Macmillan, 1934.

——. *President Roosevelt and the Coming of the War: A Study in Appearances and Realities.* New Haven: Yale University Press, 1948.

——. *The Republic: Conversations on Fundamentals.* New York: Viking, 1943.

Beard, Charles A., and Mary R. Beard. *America in Midpassage.* 2 vols. New York: Macmillan, 1939.

——. *The Rise of American Civilization.* 2 vols. New York: Macmillan, 1927.

Beard, Charles A., and William Beard. *The American Leviathan: The Republic in the Machine Age.* New York: Macmillan, 1930.

Beard, Charles A., and Frederick A. Ogg. *A National Government and the World War.* New York: Macmillan, 1919.

Beard, Mary Ritter. *The Making of Charles A. Beard: An Interpretation.* New York: Exposition Press, 1955.

Beinart, Peter. *The Icarus Syndrome: A History of American Hubris.* New York: Harper, 2010.

Beisner, Robert L. *Dean Acheson: A Life in the Cold War.* New York: Oxford University Press, 2006.

Bell, Duncan, ed. *Victorian Visions of Global Order: Empire and International Relations in Nineteenth-Century Political Thought.* New York: Cambridge University Press, 2007.

Benda, Julien. *The Betrayal of the Intellectuals.* Boston: Beacon Press, 1955.

Bender, Thomas. *Intellect and Public Life: Essays on the Social History of Academic Intellectuals in the United States.* Baltimore: Johns Hopkins University Press, 1993.

——. *New York Intellect: A History of Intellectual Life in New York City from 1750 to the Beginnings of Our Own Time.* New York: Knopf, 1987.

Berman, Larry. *No Peace, No Honor: Nixon, Kissinger and Betrayal in Vietnam.* New York: Free Press, 2001.

Bird, Kai, and Martin J. Sherwin. *American Prometheus: The Triumph and Tragedy of J. Robert Oppenheimer.* New York: Knopf, 2005.

Bloom, Allan. *The Closing of the American Mind.* New York: Simon and Schuster, 1987.

Blum, D. Steven. *Walter Lippmann: Cosmopolitanism in the Century of Total War.* Ithaca: Cornell University Press, 1984.

Bobbitt, Philip. *Terror and Consent: The Wars for the Twenty-First Century.* New York: Knopf, 2008.

Bowden, Mark. *Black Hawk Down: A Story of Modern War.* New York: Atlantic Monthly Press, 1999.

Braeman, John. *Albert J. Beveridge: American Nationalist.* Chicago: University of Chicago Press, 1971.

Brands, Hal. *What Good Is Grand Strategy? Power and Purpose in American Statecraft from Harry S. Truman to George W. Bush.* Ithaca: Cornell University Press, 2014.

Brands, H. W. *What America Owes the World: The Struggle for the Soul of Foreign Policy.* New York: Cambridge University Press, 1998.

——. *Woodrow Wilson.* New York: Henry Holt, 2003.

Brinkley, Douglas. *Gerald R. Ford.* New York: Times Books, 2007.

Browne, David S. *Richard Hofstadter: An Intellectual Biography.* Chicago: University of Chicago Press, 2006.

Buchan, James. *Days of God: The Revolution in Iran and Its Consequences.* New York: Simon and Schuster, 2013.

Buell, Raymond Leslie. *Isolated America.* New York: Knopf, 1940.

Burke, Edmund. *Reflections on the Revolution in France*. New York: Oxford University Press, 1999.

Burns, James MacGregor. *The Lion and the Fox*. New York: Harcourt, 1956.

Burr, William, ed. *The Kissinger Transcripts: The Top Secret Talks with Beijing and Moscow*. New York: New Press, 1999.

Burton, David H. *William Howard Taft: Confident Peacemaker*. Philadelphia: St. Joseph's University Press, 2004.

Bush, George H. W., and Brent Scowcroft. *A World Transformed*. New York: Knopf, 1998.

Bush, George W. *Decision Points*. New York: Crown, 2010.

Buzzanco, Robert. *Masters of War: Military Dissent and Politics in the Vietnam Era*. New York: Cambridge University Press, 1996.

Cahn, Anne Hessing. *Killing Detente: The Right Attacks the CIA*. University Park, PA: Penn State University Press, 1998.

Calabrese, John, ed. *The Future of Iraq*. Washington, D.C.: Middle East Institute, 1997.

Calder, Bruce J. *The Impact of Intervention: The Dominican Republic During the United States Occupation of 1916–1924*. Austin: University of Texas Press, 1984.

Callahan, David. *Dangerous Capabilities: Paul Nitze and the Cold War*. New York: Harper, 1990.

Campbell, Kurt M., and Michael E. O'Hanlon, *Hard Power*. New York: Basic Books, 2006.

Cannon, Lou. *President Reagan: The Role of a Lifetime*. New York: Public Affairs, 2000.

Carnes, Mark, ed. *Invisible Giants: Fifty Americans Who Shaped the Nation but Missed the History Books*. New York: Oxford University Press, 2002.

Carr, E. H. *The Twenty Years' Crisis, 1919–1939*. Rev. ed. New York: Palgrave Macmillan, 2001.

Cary, Francine Curro. *The Influence of War on Walter Lippmann*. New York: Arno Press, 1967.

Casey, Steven. *Cautious Crusade: Franklin D. Roosevelt, American Public Opinion, and the War Against Nazi Germany*. New York: Oxford University Press, 2001.

Chace, James. *1912: Wilson, Roosevelt, Taft and Debs—The Election That Changed the Country*. New York: Simon and Schuster, 2004.

Chang, Iris. *The Rape of Nanking: The Forgotten Holocaust of World War II*. New York: Basic Books, 1997.

Cheney, Dick. *In My Time: A Personal and Political Memoir*. New York: Threshold Decisions, 2011.

Childs, Marquis, and James Reston, eds. *Walter Lippmann and His Times*. New York: Harcourt, 1959.

Chollet, Derek, and James Goldgeier. *America Between the Wars: The Misunderstood Years Between the Fall of the Berlin Wall and the Start of the War on Terror*. New York: PublicAffairs, 2008.

Clark, Christopher. *The Sleepwalkers: How Europe Went to War in 1914*. New York: Allen Lane, 2012.

Clark, Paul. *The Chinese Cultural Revolution: A History*. New York: Cambridge University Press, 2008.

Clarke, Richard A. *Against All Enemies: Inside America's War on Terror*. New York: Free Press, 1994.

Clinton, Hillary. *Hard Choices: A Memoir*. New York: Simon and Schuster, 2014.

Cohen, Avner. *Israel and the Bomb*. New York: Columbia University Press, 1998.

Cohen, Warren I. *The American Revisionists: The Lessons of Intervention in World War I*. Chicago: University of Chicago Press, 1967.

Cole, Jonathan R. *The Great American University: Its Rise to Preeminence, Its Indispensable National Role, Why It Must be Protected*. New York: PublicAffairs, 2009.

Coletta, Paolo Enrico. *The Presidency of William Howard Taft*. Lawrence: University of Kansas Press, 1973.

Coll, Steve. *Ghost Wars: The Secret History of the CIA, Afghanistan and bin Laden from the Soviet Invasion to September 10, 2001.* New York: Penguin Press, 2004.

Collini, Stefan. *Absent Minds: Intellectuals in Britain.* New York: Oxford University Press, 2006.

Colodny, Len, and Tom Shachtman. *The Forty Years War: The Rise and the Fall of the Neocons, from Nixon to Obama.* New York: Harper, 2009.

Congdon, Lee. *George Kennan: A Writing Life.* Wilmington, DE: ISI Books, 2008.

Cooper, John, Jr. *Breaking the Heart of the World: Woodrow Wilson and the Fight for the League of Nations.* New York: Cambridge University Press, 2001.

———. *The Warrior and the Priest: Woodrow Wilson and Theodore Roosevelt.* Cambridge, MA: Harvard University Press, 1983.

———. *Woodrow Wilson: A Biography.* New York: Knopf, 2009.

Cowley, W. H., and Don Williams. *International and Historical Roots of American Higher Education.* New York: Garland Publishing, 1991.

Craig, Campbell, and Fredrik Logevall. *America's Cold War: The Politics of Insecurity.* Cambridge, MA: Harvard University Press, 2009.

Croly, Herbert T. *The Promise of American Life.* Rev. ed. New York: Adamant, 2001 [1909].

Cumings, Bruce. *Dominion from Sea to Sea: Pacific Ascendancy and American Power.* New Haven: Yale University Press, 2009.

———. *The Korean War: A History.* New York: Modern Library, 2010.

Daalder, Ivo H., and I. M. Destler. *In the Shadow of the Oval Office: Profiles of National Security Advisers and the Presidents They Served.* New York: Simon and Schuster, 2009.

Dallaire, Romeo. *Shake Hands with the Devil: The Failure of Humanity in Rwanda.* New York: Da Capo Press, 2004.

Dallek, Robert. *Franklin Roosevelt and American Foreign Policy, 1932–1945.* New York: Oxford University Press, 1979.

———. *Nixon and Kissinger: Partners in Power.* New York: Harper, 2007.

Danner, Mark. *Stripping Bare the Body: Politics, Violence, War.* New York: Nation Books, 2004.

Darwin, John. *After Tamerlane: The Global History of Empire Since 1405.* New York: Bloomsbury, 2009.

Del Pero, Mario. *The Eccentric Realist: Henry Kissinger and the Shaping of American Foreign Policy.* Ithaca: Cornell University Press, 2011.

Depuy, R. Ernest, and Trevor N. Depuy. *Military Heritage of America.* New York: McGraw-Hill, 1956.

D'Este, Carlo. *Patton: A Genius for War.* New York: Harper, 1995.

Dewey, John. *The Public and Its Problems.* New York: Henry Holt, 1927.

DeYoung, Karen. *Soldier: The Life of Colin Powell.* New York: Knopf, 2006.

Dildy, Doug. *Dunkirk 1940: Operation Dynamo.* Long Island City, NY: Osprey, 2010.

Dinunzio, Mario R., ed. *Woodrow Wilson: Essential Writings and Speeches of the Scholar President.* New York: NYU Press, 2006.

Dobrynin, Anatoly. *In Confidence: Moscow's Ambassador to America's Six Cold War Presidents (1962–1986).* New York: Times Books, 1995.

Dodge, Toby. *Iraq: From War to a New Authoritarianism.* New York: Routledge, 2013.

Dower, John W. *War Without Mercy: Race and Power in the Pacific War.* New York: Pantheon, 1987.

Doyle, Michael W. *Ways of War and Peace.* New York: W. W. Norton, 1997.

Drinkwater, Derek. *Sir Harold Nicolson and International Relations: The Practitioner as Theorist.* New York: Oxford University Press, 2005.

Duffy, Bernard K., and Ronald H. Carpenter. *Douglas MacArthur: Warrior as Wordsmith.* Westport, CT: Greenwood Press, 1997.

Ekbladh, David. *The Great American Mission: Modernization and the Construction of an American World Order.* Princeton: Princeton University Press, 2009.

Elman, Colin, and Miriam Fendius Elman, eds. *Bridges and Boundaries: Historians, Political Scientists, and the Study of International Relations.* Cambridge, MA: MIT Press, 2001.

Engelbrecht, H. C., and F. C. Hanighen. *Merchants of Death: A Study of the International Armaments Industry.* New York: Dodd, Mead, 1934.

Engerman, David. *Know Your Enemy: The Rise and Fall of America's Soviet Experts.* New York: Oxford University Press, 2009.

———. *Modernization from the Other Shore: American Intellectuals and the Romance of Russian Development.* Cambridge, MA: Harvard University Press, 2004.

Evans, Richard J. *In Defense of History.* New York: W. W. Norton, 1999.

Farber, David. *Taken Hostage: The Iran Hostage Crisis and America's First Encounter with Radical Islam.* Princeton: Princeton University Press, 2006.

Feith, Douglas J. *War and Decision: Inside the Pentagon at the Dawn of the War on Terrorism.* New York: Harper, 2008.

Ferguson, Niall. *Colossus: The Price of America's Empire.* New York: Penguin Press, 2004.

Ferling, John. *Jefferson and Hamilton: The Rivalry That Forged a Nation.* New York: Bloomsbury, 2013.

Fink, Leon. *Progressive Intellectuals and the Dilemmas of Democratic Commitment.* Cambridge, MA: Harvard University Press, 1997.

FitzGerald, Frances. *Way Out There in the Blue: Reagan, Star Wars, and the End of the Cold War.* New York: Simon and Schuster, 2000.

Fogel, Joshua, ed. *The Nanjing Massacre in History and Historiography.* Berkeley: University of California Press, 2000.

Foner, Philip. *The Spanish-Cuban War and the Birth of American Imperialism.* New York: Monthly Review Press, 1972.

Freedman, Lawrence, and Efraim Karsh. *The Gulf Conflict, 1990–1991: Diplomacy and War in the New World Order.* Princeton: Princeton University Press, 1993.

Freeman, Joseph. *An American Testament.* New York: Farrar and Rineheart, 1936.

Freud, Sigmund, and William C. Bullitt. *Thomas Woodrow Wilson: A Psychological Study.* Boston: Houghton Mifflin, 1967.

Friedberg, Aaron L. *A Conquest for Supremacy: China, America, and the Struggle for Mastery in Asia.* New York: W. W. Norton, 2011.

Friedman, Murray. *The Neoconservative Revolution: Jewish Intellectuals and the Shaping of Public Policy.* New York: Cambridge University Press, 2005.

Frum, David. *The Right Man: The Surprise Presidency of George W. Bush.* New York: Random House, 2003.

Fukuyama, Francis. *The End of History and the Last Man.* New York: Free Press, 1992.

Gaddis, John Lewis. *The Cold War: A New History.* New York: Penguin Press, 2005.

———. *George F. Kennan: An American Life.* New York: Penguin Press, 2011.

———. *Strategies of Containment: A Critical Appraisal of American National Security Policy During the Cold War.* New York: Oxford University Press, 1982.

———. *Surprise, Security and the American Experience.* Cambridge, MA: Harvard University Press, 2004.

Gardner, Lloyd C. *Architects of Illusion: Men and Ideas in American Foreign Policy.* Chicago: Quadrangle Books, 1970.

Gardner, Lloyd C., and Ted Gittinger, eds. *The Search for Peace in Vietnam, 1964–1968.* College Station: Texas A&M University Press, 2004.

Garthoff, Raymond. *Détente and Confrontation: American-Soviet Relations from Nixon to Reagan.* Washington, D.C.: Brookings Institution Press, 1985.

———. *The Great Transition: American-Soviet Relations and the End of the Cold War.* Washington, D.C.: Brookings Institution Press, 1994.

Gates, Robert M. *Duty: Memoirs of a Secretary at War*. New York: Knopf, 2014.

Gelfand, Lawrence E. *The Inquiry: American Preparations for Peace, 1917–1919*. New Haven: Yale University Press, 1963.

Gellman, Barton. *Angler: The Shadow Presidency of Dick Cheney*. New York: Penguin Press, 2008.

———. *Contending with Kennan: Toward a Philosophy of American Power*. New York: Praeger, 1984.

George, Alexander L., and Juliette L. George. *Woodrow Wilson and Colonel House: A Personality Study*. New York: John Day, 1956.

Gilman, Nils. *Mandarins of the Future: Modernization Theory in Cold War America*. Baltimore: Johns Hopkins University Press, 2004.

Glad, Betty. *An Outsider in the White House: Jimmy Carter, His Advisors, and the Making of American Foreign Policy*. Ithaca: Cornell University Press, 2009.

Glain, Stephen. *State vs. Defense*. New York: Crown, 2011.

Goldberg, Robert Allan. *Barry Goldwater*. New Haven: Yale University Press, 1995.

Goldstein, Gordon M. *Lessons in Disaster: McGeorge Bundy and the Path to War in Vietnam*. New York: Times Books, 2008.

Goodchild, Peter. *Edward Teller: The Real Dr. Strangelove*. Cambridge, MA: Harvard University Press, 2004.

Goodman, Nelson. *Ways of Worldmaking*. Indianapolis: Hackett Publishing, 1978.

Gordon, Michael, R., and Bernard E. Trainor. *Cobra II: The Inside Story of the Invasion and Occupation of Iraq*. New York: Pantheon, 2006.

———. *The Generals' War: The Inside Story of the Conflict in the Gulf*. Boston: Little, Brown, 1995.

Gould, Lewis L. *Four Hats in the Ring: The 1912 Election and the Birth of Modern American Politics*. Lawrence: University of Kansas Press, 2008.

Graebner, Norman A. *Foundations of American Foreign Policy: A Realist Appraisal from Franklin to McKinley*. Wilmington, DE: Scholarly Resources, 1985.

Graham, Bradley. *By His Own Rules: The Ambitions, Successes and Ultimate Failures of Donald Rumsfeld*. New York: PublicAffairs, 2009.

Graubard, Stephen R. *Kissinger: Portrait of a Mind*. New York: W. W. Norton, 1973.

Gray, John. *Black Mass: Apocalyptic Religion and the Death of Utopia*. New York: Farrar, Straus and Giroux, 2007.

Griffin, Nicholas. *Ping-Pong Diplomacy: The Secret History Behind the Game That Changed the World*. New York: Scribner, 2014.

Grose, Peter. *Continuing the Inquiry: The Council on Foreign Relations from 1921 to 1996*. New York: Council on Foreign Relations, 1996.

Gruber, Carol S. *Mars and Minerva: World War I and the Uses of Higher Learning in America*. Baton Rouge: Louisiana State University Press, 1975.

Guilhot, Nicolas. ed. *The Invention of International Relations Theory: Realism, the Rockefeller Foundation, and the 1954 Conference on Theory*. New York: Columbia University Press, 2011.

Gunnell, John G. *The Descent of Political Theory: The Genealogy of an American Vocation*. Chicago: University of Chicago Press, 1993.

Gurman, Hannah. *The Dissent Papers: The Voices of Diplomats in the Cold War and Beyond*. New York: Columbia University Press, 2012.

Guyatt, Nicholas. *Providence and the Invention of the United States, 1607–1876*. New York: Cambridge University Press, 2007.

Haass, Richard N. *War of Necessity, War of Choice: A Memoir of Two Iraq Wars*. New York: Simon and Schuster, 2009.

Haig, Alexander M., Jr. *Inner Circles: How America Changed the World: A Memoir*. New York: Warner Books, 1992.

Halberstam, David. *The Best and the Brightest*. New York: Random House, 1972.

——. *The Coldest Winter: America and the Korean War*. New York: Hyperion, 2007.

Halper, Stefan, and Jonathan Clarke. *America Alone: The Neoconservatives and the Global Order*. New York: Cambridge University Press, 2004.

——. *The Silence of the Rational Center: Why American Foreign Policy Is Failing*. New York: Basic Books, 2007.

Hamilton, Nigel. *American Caesars: Lives of the Presidents from Franklin D. Roosevelt to George W. Bush*. New Haven: Yale University Press, 2010.

Hanhimäki, Jussi. *Flawed Architect: Henry Kissinger and American Foreign Policy*. New York: Oxford University Press, 2004.

Hannigan, Robert E. *The New World Power: American Foreign Policy, 1898–1917*. Philadelphia: University of Pennsylvania Press, 2002.

Harper, John Lamberton. *American Visions of Europe: Franklin D. Roosevelt, George F. Kennan and Dean G. Acheson*. New York: Cambridge University Press, 1994.

Haufler, Hervie. *Codebreaker's Victory: How the Allied Cryptographers Won World War II*. New York: New American Library, 2003.

Heilbrunn, Jacob. *They Knew They Were Right: The Rise of the Neocons*. New York: Doubleday, 2008.

Herken, Gregg. *Counsels of War*. New York: Knopf, 1985.

Herring, George. *America's Longest War: The United States and Vietnam, 1950–1975*. 2nd ed. New York: Knopf, 1979.

——. *From Colony to Superpower: U.S. Foreign Relations Since 1776*. New York: Oxford University Press, 2008.

Hersh, Seymour. *The Price of Power: Kissinger in the Nixon White House*. New York: Summit Books, 1983.

——. *The Samson Option: Israel's Nuclear Arsenal and American Foreign Policy*. New York: Random House, 1991.

Hirsch, H. N. *The Enigma of Felix Frankfurter*. New York: Basic Books, 1981.

Hixson, Walter. *George F. Kennan: Cold War Iconoclast*. New York: Columbia University Press, 1989.

——. *The Myth of American Diplomacy: National Identity and U.S. Foreign Policy*. New Haven: Yale University Press, 2008.

Hobsbawm, Eric. *On Empire: America, War and Global Supremacy*. New York: Pantheon, 2008.

Hoffman, Elizabeth Cobbs. *American Umpire*. Cambridge, MA: Harvard University Press, 2013.

Hofstadter, Richard. *The American Political Tradition and the Men Who Made It*. New York: Knopf, 1948.

——. *Anti-intellectualism in American Life*. New York: Knopf, 1963.

——. *The Progressive Historians*. New York: Knopf, 1968.

——. *The Progressive Movement, 1900–1915*. Englewood Cliffs, NJ: Prentice Hall, 1963.

Hofstadter, Richard, and Wilson Smith. *Higher Education: A Documentary History*. 2 vols. Chicago: University of Chicago Press, 1961.

Hogan, Michael, ed. *The End of the Cold War: Its Meaning and Implications*. New York: Cambridge University Press, 1992.

Hogan, Michael. *The Marshall Plan: America, Britain, and the Reconstruction of Western Europe, 1947–1952*. New York: Cambridge University Press, 1989.

Hoganson, Kristin L. *Fighting for American Manhood: How Gender Politics Provoked the Spanish-American and Philippine-American Wars*. New Haven: Yale University Press, 1998.

Hollinger, David, and Charles Capper, eds. *The American Intellectual Tradition*. Volume II: *1865 to the Present*. New York: Oxford University Press, 2001.

Hoopes, Townsend, and Douglas Brinkley. *Driven Patriot: The Life and Times of James Forrestal.* Annapolis, MD: Naval Institute Press, 2000.

Howe, Quincy. *England Expects Every American to Do His Duty.* New York: Simon and Schuster, 1937.

Hull, Cordell. *Memoirs.* 2 vols. New York: Macmillan, 1948.

Humes, James C. *Churchill: A Biography.* London: Dorling Kindersley, 2003.

Hunt, Michael. *Ideology and U.S. Foreign Policy.* New Haven: Yale University Press, 1987.

Huntington, Samuel P. *American Politics: The Promise of Harmony.* Cambridge, MA: Harvard University Press, 1981.

———. *The Clash of Civilizations and the Remaking of the World Order.* New York: Simon and Schuster, 1996.

Hyde, Lewis. *Common as Air: Revolution, Art, and Ownership.* New York: Farrar, Straus and Giroux, 2010.

Ignatieff, Michael. *Empire Lite: Nation Building in Bosnia, Kosovo, Afghanistan.* New York: Vintage, 2003.

Ikenberry, G. John. *After Victory: Institutions, Strategic Restraint, and the Rebuilding of Order After Major Wars.* Princeton: Princeton University Press, 2000.

Ikenberry, G. John, Thomas J. Knock, Anne-Marie Slaughter, and Tony Smith. *The Crisis of American Foreign Policy: Wilsonianism in the Twenty-First Century.* Princeton: Princeton University Press, 2009.

Immerman, Richard H. *Empire for Liberty: A History of American Imperialism from Benjamin Franklin to Paul Wolfowitz.* Princeton: Princeton University Press, 2010.

Indyk, Martin, Kenneth G. Lieberthal, and Michael E. O'Hanlon. *Ending History: Barack Obama's Foreign Policy.* Washington, D.C.: Brookings Institution Press, 2012.

Isaacson, Walter. *Kissinger: A Biography.* New York: Simon and Schuster, 1992.

Isaacson, Walter, and Evan Thomas. *The Wise Men.* New York: Simon and Schuster, 1996.

Jacoby, Russell. *The Last Intellectuals: American Culture in the Age of Academe.* New York: Basic Books, 1987.

Jacoby, Susan. *The Age of American Unreason.* New York: Pantheon, 2008.

Jaffa, Harry. *Crisis of the Strauss Divided: Essays on Leo Strauss and Straussianism, East and West.* Lanham, MD: Rowman and Littlefield, 2012.

Jennings, Jeremy, and Anthony Kemp-Welch, eds. *Intellectuals in Politics: From the Dreyfus Affair to Salman Rushdie.* New York: Routledge, 1997.

Jervis, Robert. *Why Intelligence Fails: Lessons from the Iranian Revolution and the Iraq War.* Ithaca: Cornell University Press, 2010.

Johnson, Chalmers. *Nemesis: The Last Days of the American Republic.* New York: Metropolitan Books, 2007.

———. *The Sorrows of Empire: Militarism, Secrecy and the End of the Republic.* New York: Metropolitan Books, 2004.

Jonas, Manfred. *Isolationism in America, 1935–1941.* Ithaca: Cornell University Press, 1966.

Josephson, Matthew. *Infidel in the Temple: A Memoir of the Nineteen-Thirties.* New York: Knopf, 1967.

Judt, Tony. *Postwar: A History of Europe Since 1945.* New York: Penguin Press, 2005.

Judt, Tony, with Timothy Snyder. *Thinking the Twentieth Century.* New York: Penguin Press, 2012.

Kagan, Robert. *Dangerous Nation: America's Place in the World from Its Earliest Days to the Dawn of the Twentieth Century.* New York: Knopf, 2006.

Kagan, Robert, and William Kristol. *Present Dangers: Crisis and Opportunity in American Foreign and Defense Policy.* San Francisco: Encounter Books, 2000.

Kahin, George McT. *Intervention: How America Became Involved in Vietnam.* Garden City, NY: Doubleday, 1987.

Kahneman, Daniel. *Thinking, Fast and Slow.* New York: Farrar, Straus and Giroux, 2011.

Kaplan, Fred. *The Wizards of Armageddon*. New York: Simon and Schuster, 1983.

Karsten, Peter. *The Naval Aristocracy: The Golden Age of Annapolis and the Emergence of Modern American Navalism*. New York: Free Press, 1972.

Kaufman, Scott. *Plans Unraveled: The Foreign Policy of the Carter Administration*. DeKalb: Northern Illinois University Press, 2008.

Kazin, Michael. *A Godly Hero: The Life of William Jennings Bryan*. New York: Knopf, 2006.

Kennan, George F. *American Diplomacy, 1900–1950*. Chicago: University of Chicago Press, 1951.

———. *An American Family: The Kennans*. New York: W. W. Norton, 2000.

———. *The Cloud of Danger: Current Realties of American Foreign Policy*. Boston: Little, Brown, 1972.

———. *Dealing with the Communist World*. New York: Harper, 1964.

———. *Democracy and the Student Left*. Boston: Little, Brown, 1968.

———. *Memoirs, 1925–1950*. Boston: Little, Brown, 1967.

———. *Memoirs, 1950–1963*. Boston: Little, Brown, 1972.

———. *Realities of American Foreign Policy*. Princeton: Princeton University Press, 1954.

———. *Russia and the West Under Lenin and Stalin*. Boston: Little, Brown, 1960.

———. *Sketches from a Life*. New York: Pantheon, 1989.

Kennedy, David M. *Freedom from Fear: The American People in Depression and War, 1932–1945*. New York: Oxford University Press, 1999.

Kennedy, Thomas C. *Charles A. Beard and American Foreign Policy*. Gainesville: University of Florida Press, 1975.

Keynes, John Maynard. *The Economic Consequences of the Peace*. New York: Harcourt, 1920.

———. *The General Theory of Employment, Interest, and Money*. New York: Harcourt, 1936.

Kimball, Warren F. *The Juggler: Franklin Roosevelt as Wartime Statesman*. Princeton: Princeton University Press, 1991.

———. *The Most Unsordid Act: Lend-Lease, 1939–1941*. Baltimore: Johns Hopkins University Press, 1969.

Kissinger, Henry A. *Diplomacy*. New York: Simon and Schuster, 1994.

———. *Ending the Vietnam War: A History of America's Involvement in and Extrication from the Vietnam War*. New York: Simon and Schuster, 2003.

———. *The Necessity for Choice: Prospects of American Foreign Policy*. New York: Harper, 1961.

———. *Nuclear Weapons and Foreign Policy*. New York: Harper, 1957.

———. *On China*. New York: Penguin Press, 2011.

———. *The White House Years*. Boston: Little, Brown, 1979.

———. *World Order*. New York: Penguin Press, 2014.

———. *A World Restored: Metternich, Castlereagh and the Problems of Peace*. Boston: Houghton Mifflin, 1957.

———. *Years of Renewal*. New York: Simon and Schuster, 1999.

———. *Years of Upheaval*. Boston: Little, Brown, 1982.

Kloppenberg, James T. *Reading Obama: Dreams, Hope and the American Political Tradition*. Princeton: Princeton University Press, 2011.

Knock, Thomas. *To End All Wars: Woodrow Wilson and the Quest for a New World Order*. Princeton: Princeton University Press, 1995.

Krabbendam, Hans, and John M. Thompson, eds. *America's Transatlantic Turn: Theodore Roosevelt and the Discovery of Europe*. New York: Palgrave Macmillan, 2012.

Kuklick, Bruce. *Blind Oracles: Intellectuals and War from Kennan to Kissinger*. Princeton: Princeton University Press, 2006.

———. *A Political History of the USA: One Nation Under God*. New York: Palgrave Macmillan, 2009.

LaFeber, Walter. *Inevitable Revolutions: The United States in Central America*. 2nd ed. New York: W. W. Norton, 1993.

Langer, William L. *The Challenge of Isolation: The World Crisis of 1937–1940 and American Foreign Policy*. 2 vols. New York: Harper, 1952.

Lasch, Christopher. *The New Radicalism in America 1889–1963: The Intellectual as a Social Type*. New York: W. W. Norton, 1965.

Lasser, William. *Benjamin V. Cohen, Architect of the New Deal*. New Haven: Yale University Press, 2002.

Layne, Christopher. *The Peace of Illusions: American Grand Strategy from 1940 to the Present*. Ithaca: Cornell University Press, 2006.

Lebow, Richard Ned. *A Cultural Theory of International Relations*. New York: Cambridge University Press, 2009.

———. *The Tragic Vision of Politics: Ethics, Interests, and Orders*. New York: Cambridge University Press, 2003.

Leffler, Melvyn P., and Jeffrey W. Legro. *In Uncertain Times: American Foreign Policy After the Berlin Wall and 9/11*. Ithaca: Cornell University Press, 2011.

Leffler, Melvyn P., and Odd Arne Westad, eds. *The Cambridge History of the Cold War*. Volume II: *Crises and Détente*. New York: Cambridge University Press, 2010.

Leites, Nathan. *The Operational Code of the Politburo*. New York: McGraw-Hill, 1951.

Levin, N. Gordon, Jr. *Woodrow Wilson and World Politics: America's Response to War and Revolution*. New York: Oxford University Press, 1968.

Lieven, Anatol, and John Hulsman. *Ethical Realism: A Vision for America's Role in the World*. New York: Pantheon, 2006.

Lilla, Mark. *The Reckless Mind: Intellectuals in Politics*. New York: New York Review of Books, 2001.

Lim, Elvin T. *The Anti-Intellectual Presidency: The Decline of Presidential Rhetoric from George Washington to George W. Bush*. New York: Oxford University Press, 2008.

Link, Arthur S. *The Higher Realism of Woodrow Wilson*. Nashville, TN: Vanderbilt University Press, 1971.

———. *Wilson the Diplomatist: A Look at His Major Foreign Policies*. Baltimore: Johns Hopkins University Press, 1957.

Lippmann, Walter. *The Cold War*. Boston: Little, Brown, 1947.

———. *Drift and Mastery*. New York: Mitchell Kennerley 1914.

———. *The Good Society*. Boston: Little, Brown, 1937.

———. *The Phantom Public*. New York: Macmillan, 1925.

———. *The Political Scene: An Essay on the Victory of 1918*. New York: Henry Holt, 1919.

———. *A Preface to Morals*. New York: Macmillan, 1929.

———. *A Preface to Politics*. New York: Mitchell Kennerley, 1913.

———. *Public Opinion*. New York: Harcourt, 1922.

———. *The Stakes of Diplomacy*. New York: Henry Holt, 1915.

———. *U.S. Foreign Policy: Shield of the Republic*. Boston: Little, Brown, 1943.

———. *U.S. War Aims*. Boston: Little, Brown, 1944.

Logevall, Fredrik, and Andrew Preston, eds. *Nixon on the World: American Foreign Relations, 1969–1977*. New York: Oxford University Press, 2008.

Lowe, Peter. *The Origins of the Korean War*. New York: Longman, 1986.

Lukacs, John. *George Kennan: A Study of Character*. New Haven: Yale University Press, 2007.

Macmillan, Margaret. *Nixon and Mao: The Week That Changed the World*. New York: Random House, 2007.

———. *Peacemakers: The Paris Conference of 1919 and Its Attempt to End War*. London: John Murray, 2001.

Mahan, Alfred Thayer. *From Sail to Steam: Recollections of Naval Life*. New York: Harper, 1907.

———. *The Gulf and Inland Waters.* New York: Scribner, 1883.

———. *The Influence of Sea Power upon History.* Boston: Little, Brown, 1890.

———. *The Influence of Sea Power upon the French Revolution and Empire.* Boston: Little, Brown, 1892.

———. *The Interest of America in Sea Power, Present and Future.* Boston: Little, Brown, 1918.

———. *Lessons of the War with Spain, and Other Articles.* Boston: Little, Brown, 1899.

Maier, Charles S., ed. *The Cold War in Europe.* New York: Markus Wiener, 1991.

Manela, Erez. *The Wilsonian Moment: Self-Determination and the International Origins of Anticolonial Nationalism.* New York: Oxford University Press, 2007.

Mann, James. *The Obamians: The Struggle Inside the White House to Redefine American Power.* New York: Viking, 2012.

———. *The Rebellion of Ronald Reagan.* New York: Viking, 2009.

———. *Rise of the Vulcans: The History of Bush's War Cabinet.* New York: Viking, 2004.

Maraniss, David. *Barack Obama: The Story.* New York: Simon and Schuster, 2012.

Martin, John Bartlow. *Adlai Stevenson and the World.* New York: Doubleday, 1977.

Matusow, Allen J. *The Unraveling of America.* New York: Harper, 1994.

May, Ernest. *Imperial Democracy: The Emergence of America as a Great Power.* New York: Harper, 1961.

May, Lary, ed. *Recasting America: Culture and Politics in the Age of Cold War.* Chicago: University of Chicago Press, 1988.

Mayers, David. *George Kennan and the Dilemmas of U.S. Foreign Policy.* New York: Oxford University Press, 1988.

Mazower, Mark. *Governing the World: The History of an Idea, 1815 to the Present.* New York: Penguin Press, 2012.

———. *Hitler's Empire: How the Nazis Ruled Europe.* New York: Penguin Press, 2008.

Mazzetti, Mark. *The Way of the Knife: The CIA, a Secret Army, and a War to the Ends of the Earth.* New York: Penguin Press, 2013.

McCormick, Thomas J., and Walter LaFeber. *Behind the Throne: Servants of Power to Imperial Presidents, 1898–1968.* Madison: University of Wisconsin Press, 1993.

McCullough, David. *The Path Between the Seas, 1870–1914.* New York: Simon and Shuster, 1977.

McDougall, Walter. *Promised Land, Crusader State: The American Encounter with the World Since 1776.* Boston: Houghton Mifflin, 1997.

McDowell, George R. *Land Grant Universities and Extension into the 21st Century: Renegotiating or Abandoning a Social Contract.* Ames: Iowa State University Press, 2001.

McMaster, H. R. *Dereliction of Duty: Lyndon Johnson, Robert McNamara, the Joint Chiefs, and the Lies That Led to Vietnam.* New York: Harper, 1997.

Mead, Walter Russell. *Power, Terror, Peace and War: America's Grand Strategy in a World at Risk.* New York: Knopf, 2004.

Mearsheimer, John J., and Stephen M. Walt. *The Israel Lobby and U.S. Foreign Policy.* New York: Farrar, Straus and Giroux, 2007.

Menand, Louis. *The Metaphysical Club.* New York: Farrar, Straus and Giroux, 2001.

Merrill, Dennis, and Thomas Paterson, eds. *Major Problems in American Foreign Relations.* Volume 2: *Since 1914.* Boston: Wadsworth, 2009.

Micklethwait, John, and Adrian Wooldridge. *The Right Nation: Conservative Power in America.* New York: Penguin, 2004.

Miller, Nathan. *Theodore Roosevelt: A Life.* New York: Morrow, 1992.

Milne, David. *America's Rasputin: Walt Rostow and the Vietnam War.* New York: Hill and Wang, 2008.

Miłosz, Czesław. *The Captive Mind.* New York: Knopf, 1953.

Miscamble, Wilson. *From Roosevelt to Truman: Potsdam, Hiroshima, and the Cold War.* New York: Cambridge University Press, 2007.

———. *George F. Kennan and the Making of American Foreign Policy.* Princeton: Princeton University Press, 1992.

Mistry, Kaeten. *The United States, Italy and the Origins of Cold War: Waging Political Warfare, 1945–1950.* Cambridge: Cambridge University Press, 2014.

Morgan, H. Wayne. *America's Road to Empire: The War with Spain and Overseas Expansion.* New York: John Wiley, 1966.

Morgenthau, Hans. *Defense.* New York: Knopf, 1951.

Morgenthau, Hans J. *Scientific Man vs. Power Politics.* Chicago: University of Chicago Press, 1946.

Morris, Edmund. *The Rise of Theodore Roosevelt.* New York: Coward, McCann, 1979.

———. *Theodore Rex.* New York: Random House, 2001.

Morris, Ian. *Why the West Rules—For Now.* New York: Farrar, Straus and Giroux, 2010.

Mylroie, Laurie. *Bush vs. the Beltway: How the CIA and the State Department Tried to Stop the War on Terror.* New York: Harper, 2003.

Nasr, Vali. *The Dispensable Nation: American Foreign Policy in Retreat.* New York: Doubleday, 2013.

Neustadt, Richard, and Ernest R. May. *Thinking in Time: The Uses of History for Decision-Makers.* New York: Free Press, 1986.

Nichols, Christopher McKnight. *Promise and Peril: America at the Dawn of a Global Age.* Cambridge, MA: Harvard University Press, 2011.

Nicolson, Harold. *Diplomacy.* New York: Oxford University Press, 1963 [1939].

———. *Peacemaking, 1919.* Boston: Houghton Mifflin, 1933.

Niebuhr, Reinhold. *The Children of Light and Children of Darkness.* Chicago: University of Chicago Press, 2011.

———. *The Irony of American History.* Chicago: University of Chicago Press, 2008.

Ninkovich, Frank. *The Wilsonian Century: U.S. Foreign Policy Since 1900.* Chicago: University of Chicago Press, 1999.

Nitze, Paul H. *From Hiroshima to Glasnost: At the Center of Decision—A Memoir.* New York: Grove Weidenfeld, 1989.

———. *Tension Between Opposites: Reflections on the Practice and Theory of Politics.* New York: Scribner, 1993.

Nixon, Richard. *RN: The Memoirs of Richard Nixon.* New York: Grosset and Dunlap, 1978.

Nordholt, J. W. Schulte. *Woodrow Wilson: A Life for World Peace.* Berkeley: University of California Press, 1992.

Nore, Ellen. *Charles A. Beard: An Intellectual Biography.* Carbondale: Southern Illinois University Press, 1983.

Norton, Anne. *Leo Strauss and the Politics of American Empire.* New Haven: Yale University Press, 2004.

Novick, Peter. *That Noble Dream: The "Objectivity Question" and the American Historical Profession.* Cambridge: Cambridge University Press, 1988.

Nye, Joseph S., Jr. *The Future of Power.* New York: PublicAffairs, 2011.

———. *The Powers to Lead.* New York: Oxford University Press, 2008.

———. *Soft Power: The Means to Success in World Politics.* New York: PublicAffairs, 2004.

Obama, Barack. *Dreams from My Father: A Story of Race and Inheritance.* New York: Crown, 2004.

Offner, John L. *An Unwanted War: The Diplomacy of the United States and Spain over Cuba, 1895–1898.* Chapel Hill: University of North Carolina Press.

Osgood, Robert Endicott. *Ideals and Self-Interest in America's Foreign Relations: The Great Transformation of the Twentieth Century.* Chicago: University of Chicago Press, 1953.

Otte, T. G. *The Foreign Office Mind: The Making of British Foreign Policy, 1865–1914.* New York: Cambridge University Press, 2011.

Packenham, Robert. *Liberal America and the Third World: Political Development Ideas in Foreign Aid and Social Science.* Princeton: Princeton University Press, 1973.

Packer, George. *The Assassins' Gate: America in Iraq.* New York: Farrar, Straus and Giroux, 2005.

———. *Interesting Times.* New York: Farrar, Straus and Giroux, 2009.

Pangle, Thomas. *The Rebirth of Classical Political Rationalism: Essays and Lectures by Leo Strauss.* Chicago: University of Chicago Press, 1989.

Paret, Peter, ed. *Makers of Modern Strategy: From Machiavelli to the Nuclear Age.* Princeton: Princeton University Press, 1986.

Parrish, Michael E. *Felix Frankfurter and His Times: The War Years.* New York: Free Press, 1982.

Patterson, James T. *Grand Expectations: The United States, 1945–1974.* New York: Oxford University Press, 1996.

Pedaliu, Effie G. H. *Britain, Italy and the Origins of the Cold War.* New York: Palgrave Macmillan, 2003.

Pederson, William D. *The FDR Years.* New York: Facts on File, 2006.

Pillar, Paul R. *Intelligence and U.S. Foreign Policy: Iraq, 9/11, and Misguided Reform.* New York: Columbia University Press, 2011.

Popper, Karl. *The Open Society and Its Enemies.* Princeton: Princeton University Press, 2013.

Posner, Richard A. *Public Intellectuals: A Study of Decline.* Cambridge, MA: Harvard University Press, 2001.

Powell, Colin. *My American Journey.* New York: Random House, 1995.

Preble, Christopher A. *The Power Problem: How American Military Dominance Makes Us Less Safe, Less Prosperous, and Less Free.* Ithaca: Cornell University Press, 2009.

Preston, Andrew. *Sword of the Spirit, Shield of Faith: Religion in American War and Diplomacy.* New York: Knopf, 2012.

———. *The War Council: McGeorge Bundy, the NSC, and the Vietnam War.* Cambridge, MA: Harvard University Press, 2006.

Preston, Paul. *The Spanish Holocaust: Inquisition and Extermination in Twentieth Century Spain.* New York: W. W. Norton, 2012.

Puleston, Captain W. D. *Mahan: The Life and Work of Alfred Thayer Mahan, U.S.N.* New Haven: Yale University Press, 1939.

Quirk, Robert E. *An Affair of Honor: Woodrow Wilson and the Occupation of Vera Cruz.* Lexington: University of Kentucky Press, 1962.

Rabe, Stephen G. *The Most Dangerous Area in the World.* Chapel Hill: University of North Carolina Press, 1999.

Ranke, Leopold von. *The Theory and Practice of History.* Edited and translated by George G. Iggers and Konrad von Moltke. Indianapolis: Bobbs-Merrill, 1973.

Rashid, Ahmed. *Descent into Chaos: The U.S. and the Disaster in Pakistan, Afghanistan, and Central Asia.* New York: Viking, 2008.

Rathmell, Andrew et al. *Developing Iraq's Security Sector: The Coalition Provisional Authority's Experience.* Santa Monica, CA: RAND Corporation, 2005.

Reagan, Ronald. *An American Life: The Autobiography.* New York: Simon and Schuster, 1990.

Remnick, David. *The Bridge: The Life and Rise of Barack Obama.* New York: Knopf, 2010.

Reynolds, David. *Britannia Overruled: British Policy and World Power in the Twentieth Century.* New York: Longman, 1991.

——. *From Munich to Pearl Harbor: Roosevelt's America and the Origins of the Second World War.* Chicago: Ivan R. Dee, 2001.

Rhodes, Richard. *Dark Sun: The Making of the Hydrogen Bomb.* New York: Simon and Schuster, 1995.

Rice, Condoleezza. *No Higher Honor: A Memoir of My Years in Washington.* New York: Simon and Schuster, 2011.

Rice, Condoleezza, and Philip D. Zelikow. *Germany Reunified and Europe Transformed: A Study in Statecraft.* Cambridge, MA: Harvard University Press, 1995.

Roberts, Geoffrey. *Stalin's Wars: From World War to Cold War, 1939–1953.* New Haven: Yale University Press, 2008.

Rodgers, Daniel T. *Age of Fracture.* Cambridge, MA: Harvard University Press, 2011.

Romilly, Jacqueline de. *Thucydides and Athenian Imperialism.* Oxford: Basil Blackwell, 1963.

Roosevelt, Sara Delano. *My Boy Franklin, as Told by Mrs. James Roosevelt . . .* New York: R. Long and R. R. Smith, 1933.

Roosevelt, Theodore. *The Naval War of 1812: Or, The History of the United States Navy During the Last War with Great Britain.* New York: Putnam, 1882.

Rossiter, Clinton, and James Lare, eds. *The Essential Lippmann: A Political Philosophy for Liberal Democracy.* New York: Random House, 1963.

Rostow, Walt W. *The Diffusion of Power: An Essay in Recent History.* New York: Macmillan, 1972.

Rothschild, Emma. *The Inner Life of Empires: An Eighteenth-Century History.* Princeton: Princeton University Press, 2011.

Rovner, Joshua. *Fixing the Facts: National Security and the Politics of Intelligence.* Ithaca: Cornell University Press, 2011.

Rumsfeld, Donald. *Known and Unknown: A Memoir.* New York: Sentinel, 2011.

Safire, William. *Safire's Political Dictionary.* New York: Oxford University Press, 2008.

Saikia, Yasmin. *Women, War, and the Making of Bangladesh.* Durham, NC: Duke University Press, 2011.

Sakharov, Andrei. *Memoirs.* New York: Knopf, 1990.

Sandbrook, Dominic. *Mad as Hell: The Crisis of the 1970s and the Rise of the Populist Right.* New York: Knopf, 2011.

Sanger, David E. *Confront and Conceal: Obama's Secret Wars and Surprising Use of American Power.* New York: Crown, 2012.

Sarotte, Mary. *1989: The Struggle to Create Post–Cold War Europe.* Princeton: Princeton University Press, 2013.

Schelling, Thomas. *Arms and Influence.* New Haven: Yale University Press, 1996.

——. *The Strategy of Conflict.* Cambridge, MA: Harvard University Press, 1960.

Scher, Richard K. *The Modern Political Campaign: Mudslinging, Bombast, and the Vitality of American Politics.* New York: M. E. Sharpe, 1997.

Schlesinger, Arthur M., Jr. *Journals: 1952–2000.* New York: Penguin Press, 2007.

Schulzinger, Robert D. *Henry Kissinger: Doctor of Diplomacy.* New York: Columbia University Press, 1989.

——. *A Time for Peace: The Legacy of the Vietnam War.* New York: Oxford University Press, 2006.

——. *A Time for War: The United States and Vietnam, 1941–1975.* New York: Oxford University Press, 1997.

——. *The Wise Men of Foreign Affairs: The History of the Council on Foreign Relations.* New York: Columbia University Press, 1984.

Schwartz, Jordan A. *The Interregnum of Despair: Hoover, Congress, and the Depression.* Urbana: University of Illinois Press, 1970.

Scott, James M. *Deciding to Intervene: The Reagan Doctrine and American Foreign Policy.* Durham, NC: Duke University Press, 1996.

Seager, Robert, II. *Alfred Thayer Mahan: The Man and His Letters*. Annapolis, MD: Naval Institute Press, 1977.

Seligman, E.R.A. *The Economic Interpretation of History*. New York: Macmillan, 1902.

Sen, Amartya. *The Idea of Justice*. Cambridge, MA: Harvard University Press, 2009.

Shapiro, Ian. *Containment: Rebuilding a Strategy Against Global Terror*. Princeton: Princeton University Press, 2008.

Shawcross, William. *Sideshow: Kissinger, Nixon, and the Destruction of Cambodia*. New York: Simon and Schuster, 1979.

Shenin, Sergei Y. *The United States and the Third World: The Origins of the Postwar Relations and the Point Four Program*. New York: Nova Science Publishers, 1999.

Shotwell, James T. *At the Paris Peace Conference*. New York: Macmillan, 1937.

Shultz, George P. *Turmoil and Triumph: My Years as Secretary of State*. New York: Scribner's, 1993.

Simpson, Christopher, ed. *Universities and Empire: Money and Politics in the Social Sciences During the Cold War*. New York: New Press, 1998.

Smith, Adam. *The Theory of Moral Sentiments*. New York: Penguin Books, 2009 [1759].

Smith, Gaddis. *Morality, Reason and Power: American Diplomacy in the Carter Years*. New York: Hill and Wang, 1986.

Smith, Jean Edward. *FDR*. New York: Random House, 2007.

Smith, Tony. *America's Mission: The United States and the Worldwide Struggle for Democracy in the Twentieth Century*. Princeton: Princeton University Press, 1994.

Snepp, Frank. *Decent Interval: An Inside Account of Saigon's Indecent End*. New York: Random House, 1977.

Snow, C. P. *The Two Cultures*. New York: Cambridge University Press, 2012 [1959].

Sobel, Robert. *The Great Bull Market: Wall Street in the 1920s*. New York: W. W. Norton, 1968.

Solomon, Lewis D. *Paul D. Wolfowitz: Visionary Intellectual, Policymaker, and Strategist*. Westport, CT: Praeger, 2007.

Sowell, Thomas. *Intellectuals and Society*. New York: Basic Books, 2009.

Spence, Jonathan D. *The Search for Modern China*. New York: W. W. Norton, 1999.

Spengler, Oswald. *The Decline of the West*. Abridged ed. New York: Oxford University Press, 1991 [1918].

Steel, Ronald. *Walter Lippmann and the American Century*. Boston: Little, Brown, 1980.

Stephanson, Anders. *Kennan and the Art of Foreign Policy*. Cambridge, MA: Harvard University Press, 1989.

Stern, Steve. *Remembering Pinochet's Exile: On the Eve of London 1998*. Durham, NC: Duke University Press, 2004.

Stiglitz, Joseph, and Linda Bilmes. *The Three Trillion Dollar War: The True Cost of the Iraqi Conflict*. New York: W. W. Norton, 2008.

Stueck, William. *The Korean War: An International History*. Princeton: Princeton University Press, 1995.

Sumida, Jon Tetsuro. *Inventing Grand Strategy and Teaching Command: The Classic Works of Alfred Thayer Mahan Reconsidered*. Baltimore: Johns Hopkins University Press, 1997.

Suri, Jeremi. *Henry Kissinger and the American Century*. Cambridge, MA: Harvard University Press, 2007.

Syed, Anwar Hussein. *Walter Lippmann's Philosophy of International Politics*. Philadelphia: University of Pennsylvania Press, 1963.

Talbott, Strobe. *The Master of the Game: Paul Nitze and the Nuclear Peace*. New York: Knopf, 1988.

Taylor, S. J. *Stalin's Apologist: Walter Duranty: The New York Times's Man in Moscow*. New York: Oxford University Press, 1990.

Tenet, George. *At the Center of the Storm: My Years in the CIA*. New York: Harper, 2007.

Thomas, Daniel C. *The Helsinki Effect: International Norms, Human Rights, and the Demise of Communism*. Princeton: Princeton University Press, 2001.

Thomas, Evan. *The War Lovers: Roosevelt, Lodge, Hearst, and the Rush to Empire, 1898*. Boston: Little, Brown, 2010.

Thompson, John A. *Reformers and War: American Progressive Publicists and the First World War*. New York: Cambridge University Press, 1987.

———. *Woodrow Wilson: A Profile in Power*. London: Longman, 2002.

Thompson, Nicholas. *The Hawk and the Dove: Paul Nitze, George Kennan, and the History of the Cold War*. New York: Henry Holt, 2009.

Thorsen, Niels Aage. *The Political Thought of Woodrow Wilson*. Princeton: Princeton University Press, 1988.

Tilman, Rick. *Thorstein Veblen and His Critics, 1891–1963*. Princeton: Princeton University Press, 1992.

Tooze, Adam. *The Deluge: The Great War, America, and the Remaking of the Global Order, 1916–1931*. New York: Viking, 2014.

Traub, James. *The Freedom Agenda: Why America Must Spread Democracy, Just Not the Way George Bush Did*. New York: Farrar, Straus and Giroux, 2008.

Troy, Tevi. *Intellectuals and the American Presidency: Philosophers, Jesters, or Technicians?* Lanham, MA: Rowman and Littlefield, 2002.

Truman, Harry S. *Year of Decisions*. Garden City, NY: Doubleday, 1955.

Tugwell, Rexford Guy. *The Brains Trust*. New York: Viking, 1968.

Tumulty, Joseph Patrick. *Woodrow Wilson as I Know Him*. Garden City, NY: Doubleday, 1921.

Turk, Richard. *The Ambiguous Relationship: Theodore Roosevelt and Alfred Thayer Mahan*. Westport, CT: Greenwood Press, 1987.

Tyler, Patrick. *A Great Wall: Six Presidents and China: An Investigative History*. New York: PublicAffairs, 2000.

Unger, Nancy C. *Fighting Bob La Follette: The Righteous Reformer*. Chapel Hill: University of North Carolina Press, 2000.

Vaïsse, Justin. *Neoconservatism: The Biography of a Movement*. Cambridge, MA: Harvard University Press, 2010.

Velasco, Jesús. *Neoconservatives in U.S. Foreign Policy Under Ronald Reagan and George W. Bush*. Washington, D.C.: Woodrow Wilson Center Press, 2010.

Waltz, Kenneth N. *Theory of International Politics*. New York: Random House, 1979.

Walworth, Arthur. *Woodrow Wilson*. Boston: Houghton Mifflin, 1958.

Weeks, Edward, ed. *Conversations with Walter Lippmann*. Boston: Little, Brown, 1965.

Weiner, Tim. *Legacy of Ashes: The History of the CIA*. New York: Doubleday, 2007.

Weinstein, Edwin A. *Woodrow Wilson: A Medical and Psychological Biography*. Princeton: Princeton University Press, 1981.

Welles, Sumner. *The Time for Decision*. New York: Harper, 1944.

Wells, H. G. *The Shape of Things to Come*. New York: Macmillan, 1933.

Westad, Odd Arne. *The Global Cold War: Third World Interventions and the Making of Our Times*. New York: Cambridge University Press, 2005.

———. *Restlesss Empire: China and the World Since 1750*. New York: Basic Books, 2012.

Westcott, Allan, ed. *Mahan on Naval Warfare: Selections from the Writings of Rear Admiral Alfred T. Mahan*. Boston: Little, Brown, 1941.

Westmoreland, William. *A Soldier Reports*. New York: Doubleday, 1975.

White, William Allen. *Woodrow Wilson: The Man, His Times, and His Task*. Boston: Houghton Mifflin, 1925.

Widmer, Ted. *The Ark of the Liberties: America and the World*. New York: Hill and Wang, 2008.

Wilford, Hugh. *The Mighty Wurlitzer: How the CIA Played America.* Cambridge, MA: Harvard University Press, 2008.

Williams, William Appleman, ed. *History as a Way of Learning.* New York: Franklin Watts, 1974.

Williams, William Appleman. *The Tragedy of American Diplomacy.* Rev. ed. New York: W. W. Norton, 2009.

Willkie, Wendell. *One World.* New York: Simon and Schuster, 1943.

Wills, Garry. *The Kennedy Imprisonment: A Meditation on Power.* New York: Houghton Mifflin, 2001.

Wilson, James Graham. *The Triumph of Improvisation: Gorbachev's Adaptability, Reagan's Engagement, and the End of the Cold War.* Ithaca: Cornell University Press, 2014.

Wilson, Woodrow, *Congressional Government: A Study in American Politics.* New Brunswick, NJ: Transaction, 2002 [1885].

———. *Constitutional Government in the United States.* New York: Columbia University Press, 1908.

Wimmel, Kenneth. *Theodore Roosevelt and the Great White Fleet: American Sea Power Comes of Age.* Dulles, VA: Brassey's, 1998.

Wohlstetter, Albert. *The Delicate Balance of Terror.* Santa Monica, CA: RAND Corporation, 1958.

Woodward, Bob. *Bush at War.* New York: Simon and Schuster, 2002.

———. *Plan of Attack.* New York: Simon and Schuster, 2004.

———. *State of Denial.* New York: Simon and Schuster, 2006.

———. *Obama's Wars: The Inside Story.* New York: Simon and Schuster, 2010.

Wright, Benjamin F. *Five Public Philosophies of Walter Lippmann.* Austin: University of Texas Press, 1973.

Zakaria, Fareed. *From Wealth to Power: The Unusual Origins of America's World Role.* Princeton: Princeton University Press, 1998.

Zakheim, Dov S. *A Vulcan's Tale: How the Bush Administration Mismanaged the Reconstruction of Afghanistan.* Washington, D.C.: Brookings Institution Press, 2011.

Zarate, Robert, and Henry D. Sokolski, eds. *Nuclear Heuristics: Selected Writings of Albert and Roberta Wohlstetter.* Washington, D.C.: Strategic Studies Institute, 2009.

Zelizer, Julian E. *Arsenal of Democracy: The Politics of National Security—From World War II to the War on Terrorism.* New York: Basic Books, 2010.

Zhukov, Georgii Konstantinovich. *The Memoirs of Marshal Zhukov.* New York: Delacorte Press, 1971.

Zieger, Robert H. *America's Great War: World War I and the American Experience.* Lanham, MD: Rowman and Littlefield, 2000.

Zubok, Vladislav M. *Failed Empire: The Soviet Union in the Cold War from Stalin to Gorbachev.* Chapel Hill: University of North Carolina Press, 2008.

Zubok, Vladislav, and Konstantin Pleshakov. *Inside the Kremlin's Cold War: From Stalin to Khrushchev.* Cambridge, MA: Harvard University Press, 1996.

Zumwalt, Elmo R., Jr. *On Watch: A Memoir.* New York: Quadrangle/New York Times Book Co., 1976.

Zweig, Stefan. *The World of Yesterday.* London: Pushkin Press, 2009.

Secondary Sources: Articles

Anderson, Perry. "American Foreign Policy and Its Thinkers," *New Left Review* 83 (September/October 2013).

Bacevich, Andrew. "Charles Beard, Properly Understood." *The National Interest*, March 22, 1994.

——. "Trigger Man." *The American Conservative*, June 6, 2005.

Beard, Charles A. "The Future of Democracy in the United States." *The Political Quarterly* 8, no. 4 (1937).

——. "Education Under the Nazis." *Foreign Affairs* 14, no. 3 (1936).

——. "The Noble Dream." *American Historical Review* 41, no. 1 (1935).

Bell, Duncan. "Writing the World: Disciplinary History and Beyond." *International Affairs* 85, no. 1 (January 2009).

Blower, Brooke L. "From Isolationism to Neutrality: A New Framework for Understanding American Political Culture, 1919–1941." *Diplomatic History* 38, no. 2 (Spring 2014).

Botts, Joshua. " 'Nothing to Seek and . . . Nothing to Defend': George F. Kennan's Core Values and American Foreign Policy, 1938–1993." *Diplomatic History* 30, no. 5 (November 2006).

Bowden, Mark. "Wolfowitz: The Exit Interviews," *The Atlantic*, July–August 2004.

Brick, Howard. "Talcott Parsons's 'Shift Away from Economics,' 1937–1946." *The Journal of American History* 87, no. 2 (September 2000).

Campbell, John P. "Taft, Roosevelt, and the Arbitration Treaties of 1911." *The Journal of American History* 53, no. 2 (September 1966).

Craig, Campbell. "The Not-So-Strange Career of Charles Beard." *Diplomatic History* 25, no. 2 (Spring 2001).

Crockatt, Richard. "American Liberalism and the Atlantic World, 1916–1917." *Journal of American Studies* 11, no. 1 (April 1977).

Ekbladh, David. "Mr. TVA: Grass Roots Development, David Lilienthal, and the Rise of the Tennessee Valley Authority as a Symbol for U.S. Overseas Development, 1933–1973." *Diplomatic History* 26, no. 3 (Summer 2002).

Gaddis, John Lewis. "Containment: A Reassessment." *Foreign Affairs* 55, no. 4 (July 1977).

Galison, Peter, and Barton Bernstein. "In Any Light: Scientists and the Decision to Build the Superbomb." *Historical Studies in the Physical and Biological Sciences* 19, no. 2 (1989).

Gelb, Leslie H. "Necessity, Choice, and Common Sense." *Foreign Affairs* 88, no. 3 (May/June 2009).

Herken, Gregg. "The Great Foreign Policy Fight." *American Heritage*, April–May 1986.

Immerman, Richard. "Confessions of an Eisenhower Revisionist." *Diplomatic History* 14, no. 3 (Summer 1990).

Isaac, Joel. "The Human Sciences in Cold War America." *The Historical Journal* 20, no. 3 (September 2007).

——. "Tangled Loops: Theory, History, and the Human Sciences in Modern America." *Modern Intellectual History* 6, no. 2 (September 2009).

Kagan, Frederick W. "Back to the Future: NSC 68 and the Right Course for America Today." *SAIS Review* 19 (1999).

Kaplan, Robert D. "Center Stage for the Twenty-First Century: Power Plays in the Indian Ocean." *Foreign Affairs*, March/April 2009.

Karsten, Peter. "The Nature of 'Influence': Roosevelt, Mahan and the Concept of Sea Power." *American Quarterly* 23, no. 4 (October 1971).

Katz, Friedrich. "Pancho Villa and the Attack on Columbus, New Mexico." *The American Historical Review* 83, no. 1 (February 1978).

Keys, Barbara. "Henry Kissinger: The Emotional Statesman." *Diplomatic History* 35, no. 4 (September 2011).

Kirkpatrick, Jeane. "Dictatorships & Double Standards." *Commentary* 68, no. 5 (November 1979).

Kissinger, Henry A. "Military Policy and Defense of the 'Gray Areas.' " *Foreign Affairs* 3, no. 3 (April 1955).

——. "The Viet Nam Negotiations." *Foreign Affairs* 47, no. 2 (January 1969).

Krepon, Michael. "The Mushroom Cloud That Wasn't: Why Inflating Threats Won't Reduce Them." *Foreign Affairs* 88, no. 3 (May/June 2009).

LaFeber, Walter. "A Note on the 'Mercantillistic Imperialism' of Alfred Thayer Mahan." *The Mississippi Valley Historical Review* 48 (March 1962).

Lane, Melissa. "Plato, Popper, Strauss and Utopianism: Open Secrets?" *History of Philosophy Quarterly* 16, no. 2 (April 1999).

Lawson, George. "The Eternal Divide: History and International Relations." *European Journal of International Relations* 18 (2012).

Lindsay, James M. "George W. Bush, Barack Obama and the Future of U.S. Global Leadership." *International Affairs* 87, no. 4 (July 2011).

Lippmann, Walter. "The Kellogg Doctrine: Vested Rights and Nationalism in Latin-America." *Foreign Affairs* 4 (1927).

Lipset, Seymour Martin, and Richard B. Dobson. "The Intellectual as Critic and Rebel: With Special Reference to the United States and the Soviet Union." *Daedalus* 1, no. 3 (Summer 1972).

Logevall, Fredrik. "First Among Critics: Walter Lippmann and the Vietnam War." *The Journal of American–East Asian Relations* 4, no. 4 (Winter 1995).

Lucas, W. S., and Kaeten Mistry. "Illusions of Coherence: George F. Kennan, U.S. Strategy and Political Warfare in the Early Cold War." *Diplomatic History* 33, no. 1 (January 2009).

Mahan, Alfred Thayer. "The Peace Conference and the Moral Aspects of War." *North American Review*, October 1899.

Manela, Erez. "Imagining Woodrow Wilson in Asia: Dreams of East-West Harmony and the Revolt Against Empire in 1919." *The American Historical Review* 111, no. 5 (December 2006).

Milne, David. "The 1968 Paris Peace Negotiations: A Two Level Game?" *Review of International Studies* 37, no. 2 (April 2011).

———. "Pragmatism or What? The Future of U.S. Foreign Policy." *International Affairs* 88, no. 5 (September 2012).

Mueller, Tim B. "The Rockefeller Foundation, the Social Sciences, and the Humanities in the Cold War." *Journal of Cold War Studies* 15, no. 3 (Summer 2013).

Mumford, Lewis. "The Corruption of Liberalism." *The New Republic*, May 18, 1940.

Ninkovitch, Frank. "Beyond Containment." *Reviews in American History* 18, no. 2 (1990).

Nitze, Paul H. "Atoms, Strategy and Policy." *Foreign Affairs* 34, no. 2 (January 1956).

———. "The Role of the Learned Man in Government." *Review of Politics*, 20, no. 3 (July 1958).

Nixon, Richard M. "Asia After Viet Nam." *Foreign Affairs* 46, no. 3 (October 1967).

Preston, Andrew. "Bridging the Gap Between the Sacred and the Secular in the History of American Foreign Relations." *Diplomatic History* 30, no. 5 (November 2006).

Rice, Condoleezza. "Promoting the National Interest." *Foreign Affairs* 79, no. 1 (January–February 2000).

Rofe, J. Simon. "'Under the Influence of Mahan': Theodore and Franklin Roosevelt and Their Understanding of American National Interest." *Diplomacy and Statecraft* 19 (2008).

Rostow, Eugene. "Searching for Kennan's Grand Design." *The Yale Law Journal* 87, no. 7 (June 1978).

Russell, Greg. "Alfred Thayer Mahan and American Geopolitics: The Conservatism and Realism of an Imperialist." *Geopolitics* 11, no. 1 (2006).

Sumida, Jon. "Alfred Thayer Mahan, Geopolitician." *The Journal of Strategic Studies* 22, nos. 2 and 3 (June 1999).

Tarlton, Charles D. "The Styles of American International Thought: Mahan, Bryan and Lippmann." *World Politics* 17, no. 4 (July 1965).

Thompson, John A. "The Overestimation of American Power: Sobering Lessons from the Past." *World Policy Journal* 23, no.2 (Summer 2006).

Urban, George. "From Containment to . . . Self-Containment: A Conversation with George Kennan." *Encounter,* September 1976.

VanDeMark, Brian. "Beard on Lippmann: The Scholar vs. the Critic." *The New England Quarterly* 59, no. 3 (September 1986).

Wilkins, Burleigh Taylor. "Frederick York Powell and Charles A. Beard: A Study in Anglo-American Historiography." *American Quarterly* 11, no. 1 (1959).

Williams, Andrew. "Why Don't the French Do Think Tanks? France Faces Up to the Anglo-Saxon Superpowers, 1918–1921." *Review of International Studies* 34, no. 1, (January 2008).

Wilson, Woodrow. "The Law and the Facts." *American Political Science Review* 9 (1911).

Wolfowitz, Paul D. "Remembering the Future." *The National Interest* 59 (Spring 2000).

Woodward, C. Vann. "The Age of Reinterpretation." *The American Historical Review* 66, no. 1 (October 1960).

X. "The Sources of Soviet Conduct." *Foreign Affairs,* July 1947.

Zelizer, Julian E. "History and Political Science: Together Again?" *The Journal of Policy History* 16, no. 2 (2004).

ACKNOWLEDGMENTS

In British academia, where research "outputs" are counted, weighed, and graded over five-year cycles, spending a decade writing a single book is not a wise course. That I've been able to pursue this project in continuous paid employment owes much to the forbearance of academic colleagues at the University of Nottingham and the University of East Anglia.

At Nottingham, I would like to thank Richard Aldrich and Simon Tormey for their support. In the School of American Studies, I was fortunate to discuss the ideas animating the book with Richard King, a superb intellectual historian. I also benefited from Fredrik Logevall's year at Nottingham as a Visiting Leverhulme Professor, during which we co-taught a seminar on George Kennan and had many fine conversations about writing. (Fred's *Embers of War* is my favorite history book of the past decade.) My friend and colleague Matthew Jones was a superb mentor to me, and I continue to benefit from his deep historical knowledge. I also thank Nottingham for supporting my research with an "early career researcher" award.

At the University of East Anglia, I owe a special debt of gratitude to John Street, not least for hiring me. Like Richard Aldrich at Nottingham, John is as thoughtful and attentive a head of department as one could hope to have. Hussein Kassim has supported my research unfailingly and, with Sara Connolly, hosted some memorable evenings. My sincere thanks also go to Simon Curtis, Heather Savigny, Valentino Cardo, Chris Hanretty, Alex Brown, Adriana Sinclair, Nick Selby, John Turnpenny, John Greenaway, Alan Finlayson, and Lee Marsden. Kaeten Mistry, Richard Crockatt, and David Gill all read multiple chapters, and I'm particularly grateful to all three for their smart and incisive comments.

The book began life at the University of Cambridge, and I would like to express gratitude to colleagues there. I am fortunate to have two good friends—Joel Isaac and Andrew Preston—who also happen to be outstanding scholars of American history. My conversations with both, in Cambridge and elsewhere, greatly enriched the book. John Thompson and I discussed the book on numerous occasions, and his comments on various draft chapters were typically insightful. My thanks also go to Tony Badger, both for agreeing to supervise my Ph.D. in John's absence and for assisting my career in many ways since.

I was fortunate to receive substantial financial support in completing this book. My thanks go to the British Academy, the Arts and Humanities Research Council, the Gilder Lehrman Institute of American History, the Fox International Fellowship program at Yale University, and the American Philosophical Society in Philadelphia. The University of Nottingham and UEA each granted me a semester's sabbatical leave to research the book, for which I am very grateful.

This funding allowed me to conduct research at various archives, where I received first-rate assistance. At Princeton's Seeley Mudd Library, I'd like to thank Dan Linke, Jennifer Cole, and John DeLooper. At the Library of Congress, my thanks go to Jennifer Brathovde. At the American Philosophical Society, I'd like to extend my appreciation to Marty Levitt and Roy Goodman. At the University of Pennsylvania, Nancy Shawcross pointed me in the direction of some archival gems. At Columbia University Archives, Sady Sullivan provided vital assistance.

Other friends and colleagues read draft chapters and offered helpful feedback. With all the usual disclaimers, my sincere thanks go to Richard Immerman, whose comments on the early chapters were immensely helpful. I am also very grateful to Bevan Sewell, John Griffin, and Nick Hermann for reading and commenting. During a stint in Philadelphia in 2009, Bruce Kuklick was generous in offering his perspective on the project. My sister, Eve Hepburn, read the entire manuscript and offered a thoughtful commentary throughout. I'm also grateful to other family and friends including Margo Milne, John Griffin, Nathaniel Millett, Robert Reed, Austin Fido, Dan Crowe, Andrew and Christine Rudalevige, Christopher McKnight Nichols, Samuel Windham, Deirdre Williams, John Kimbell, Hannah Hunter and Jason Chilvers, Martin and Verity Conway, Simon Gerrard, Giles Foden, Tom and Caroline Ablewhite, Sarah Pearsall, Andrew Trask, Christine Carroll, Tim Lynch, and Steve and Debbie Scalet for their companionship and good cheer.

I have taught a module based on this book since 2005, and I'd like to extend my thanks to all my students for the stimulating conversations we've had. In particular, I'd like to record my appreciation for Thomas Tunstall Allcock and Charlie Laderman, now embarking on what I'm sure will be distinguished academic careers. This book would have been very difficult to research and write without having the opportunity to teach it. So I thank Nottingham and UEA for putting the course on their books, and the students who chose it as a final-year option.

I am very grateful to Andrew Wylie for his encouragement, patience, and fine eye for author-editor matchmaking. At the Wylie Agency, my thanks also go to James Pullen and Nina Ellis. Just as he was with *America's Rasputin*, my editor at Farrar, Straus and Giroux, Eric Chinski, has been an outstanding reader and critic. His very smart comments on the manuscript at multiple stages improved the book immensely. I'm very fortunate to be one of his authors. At FSG, I'm also very grateful to Peng Shepherd, Gabriella Doob, Eugenie Cha, Gena Hamshaw, Cynthia Merman, Jim Guida, Noreen McAuliffe, Lyn Rosen, and Scott Auerbach for their assistance on multiple levels.

I owe the greatest debt to my wife, Emma, who offered her love and support, commented insightfully on draft chapters, and shared equally in the running of the home. These past eight years have been particularly special. Our son, Benedict, was born in 2007, and our daughter, Anna, was born in 2009. They have enriched my life in ways I couldn't have imagined. This book is dedicated with much love to Emma, Ben, and Anna.

INDEX

A NOTE ABOUT THE AUTHOR

David Milne is a senior lecturer in modern history at the University of East Anglia. He is the author of *America's Rasputin: Walt Rostow and the Vietnam War* and a senior editor of the two-volume *Oxford Encyclopedia of American Military and Diplomatic History*. Milne has held visiting fellowships at Yale University, the Gilder Lehrman Institute of American History, and the American Philosophical Society. His writing has appeared in the *Los Angeles Times* and *The Nation* in addition to academic journals.